Sixth Edition

DRUGS, BRAIN, AND BEHAVIOR

David M. Grilly Ph.D.
Cleveland State University

John D. Salamone Ph.D.
University of Connecticut

PEARSON

Boston   Columbus   Indianapolis   New York   San Francisco   Upper Saddle River
Amsterdam   Cape Town   Dubai   London   Madrid   Milan   Munich   Paris   Montreal   Toronto
Delhi   Mexico City   São Paulo   Sydney   Hong Kong   Seoul   Singapore   Taipei   Tokyo

Executive Acquisitions Editor: Susan Hartman
Editorial Assistant: Alexandra Mitton
Marketing Manager: Nicole Kunzman
Marketing Assistant: Jessica Warren
Production Manager: Fran Russello
Editorial Production Service: Saraswathi Muralidhar/PreMediaGlobal
Cover Administrator: Jayne Conte
Cover Designer: Suzanne Behnke

Many of the designations by manufacturers and seller to distinguish their products are claimed as trademarks. Where those designations appear in this book, and the publisher was aware of a trademark claim, the designations have been printed in initial caps or all caps.

Cataloging-in-Publication data unavailable at press time.

10 9 8 7 6 5 4 3 2 1—DOH—15 14 13 12 11

ISBN-10:   0-205-75052-4
ISBN-13: 978-0-205-75052-8

To my wife, Debra,
for her patience and support

CONTENTS

PREFACE

It is a very rare person who does not, at some time or another, use a psychoactive drug—that is, a drug that alters psychological processes such as mood, thought, and behavior. In fact, use of some drugs, such as caffeine, nicotine, and alcohol, is so common in our society that we usually do not even think of them as drugs. Although the use of psychoactive drugs has a long history, the actual systematic study of the relationships between drugs and psychological processes—psychopharmacology—is quite new. Therefore, our knowledge about psychoactive drugs is relatively limited. This is rather unfortunate because their use is pervasive in most Western cultures, particularly our own. Drugs are used in a wide variety of social, recreational, and therapeutic settings.

The purpose of this book is to introduce the student to the field of psychopharmacology, with special emphasis on the relationships between drugs, their mechanisms of action in the nervous system, and human behavior. For most students, this book will be their first exposure to this diverse field. The text is written for psychology students who wish to go into some field of research associated with drugs or into clinical areas where the persons they deal with are taking psychoactive medications or using psychoactive drugs recreationally, and perhaps abusing them. It is also written for nursing students, who will be observing patients who are prescribed psychoactive medications; chemistry students, who may be interested in going into pharmacy; biology students, who may enter the field of medicine and eventually prescribe a number of psychoactive medications for their patients; and any other students interested in the fascinating relationships among drugs, the brain, emotions, mental activities, and behavior. It is hoped that the information contained in this book will enable the student to appreciate more fully why people use drugs and what the consequences of that use might be.

Because psychopharmacology involves biological functions, chemical reactions, physics, and psychological processes, ideally students reading this book will already have a basic familiarity with each of these areas. The text is not written for the specialist. Therefore, the usage of esoteric and specialized jargon to describe the effects of drugs and the psychiatric and psychological conditions they induce or alleviate has been minimized. Key pharmacological terms are set in boldface type and defined the first time they appear. Other scientific and clinical terms that could impede the students' understanding of certain principles are italicized and defined. All definitions in this text are from the following sources: *Stedman's Medical Dictionary*, 25th edition; *Dictionary of Psychology*, 2nd edition, by A. S. Reber; *Mosby's Medical, Nursing, and Allied Health Dictionary*; and *Webster's Deluxe Unabridged Dictionary*, 2nd edition. The descriptions and classifications of mental disorders are roughly based on those described in the *Diagnostic and Statistical Manual of Mental Disorders*, 4th edition, textual revisions, published by the American Psychiatric Association in 2000.

I would like to thank the many students I have taught over the years who have provided the inspiration for this book and whose comments and suggestions on the previous editions led to considerable modification in the content of the present edition. I am most indebted to Barb Simon, Jody Pickle, Rachel Wolf, Elizabeth Gnizak, and Lindsay Gervais for their assistance in putting the 2nd, 3rd, 4th, and 5th editions together and making them more readable from the standpoint of the student. Finally, I would like to thank my colleagues who commented on previous editions. They include Mark A. Duva, Pitzer College; John Salamone, University of Connecticut; Lee Bakner, Linfield College; Jeffrey S. Mogil, University of Illinois; Kim Roberts, Sacramento State University; Thomas F. Sawyer (who also suggested supplementing the text with websites and who contributed a number of those included, along with their descriptions), North Central College; Brent C. White, Centre College; Lisa Baker, Western Michigan University; Robert W. Bell, Texas Tech University; John Broida, University of Southern Maine; Mark Masaki, Youngstown State University; Helen M. Murphy, John Carroll University; Gaylord Ellison, University of California, Los Angeles; Dennis Glanzman, Arizona State University; Carol van Hartesveldt, University of Florida, Gainesville; Keith Jacobs, Loyola University, New Orleans; and W. Jeffrey Wilson, Purdue University at Fort Wayne.

This is the 6th edition of this book, first published in 1989. Writing these editions provided me with a great deal of satisfaction as well as a wonderful educational experience, and each edition presented me with a new and different challenge. However, after 35 years as a faculty member at Cleveland State University, I decided to retire and made the decision to turn over the responsibility of updating this book to a younger person who is still actively involved in conducting behavioral research with drugs and who used previous editions of the book in his classes. I recommended John Salamone to the editors of the book, who I believed to be highly qualified to update the book, and I was most grateful that he accepted this responsibility. In addition to updating the book, John and I decided to change the title of the book, *Drugs and Human Behavior*, to *Drugs, Brain, and Behavior*. We did this for two reasons. First, we wanted to make it clear that throughout the book the functions of the brain that are altered by psychotropic drugs are extensively described and discussed. Second, we decided that a lot of the content of the book is related to animal research, which reflects the field as it really is, and John added even more in that regard in the revision. The title *Drugs and Human Behavior* tends to convey the image that there is very little animal research cited in the book, or that there is an exclusively human focus. Much of the book still reflects an emphasis on human behavior, but we believe that the expanded coverage of nonhuman research with psychotropic drugs will appeal to a wider audience.

David M. Grilly
Cleveland State University

It has been more than 50 years since the "psychopharmacology revolution" swept through our society, radically changing mental health practice, and altering the way people view psychiatric disorders. An ever larger percentage of people in the United States are now being treated with psychoactive drugs, including antianxiety agents, antidepressants, antipsychotics, stimulants for the treatment of attention deficit hyperactivity disorder, and a host of other medications. Furthermore, recreational drug taking is a very common phenomenon, and drug dependence and addiction are behavioral disorders that have substantial health consequences, both physical and mental. Of course, despite the explosive development of new drugs, both licit and illicit, over the last several decades, there is nothing new about the phenomenon of people taking drugs for their psychopharmacological properties. People have been drinking, eating, or smoking psychoactive substances for thousands of years. Through the centuries, people have been taking drugs, mostly plant products, either to relax themselves; to blunt the sense of pain; to stimulate perceived energy, instigate action, and enhance performance; or to fundamentally alter sensation or consciousness. In a sense, the explosive growth of drug development over the last few decades has simply added to a tendency that was already present in several millennia of human history. Drug taking in all its social, recreational, and therapeutic contexts is a very important human phenomenon and one that warrants serious scientific investigation. The modern field of psychopharmacology focuses on the behavioral effects of drugs across these different contexts and includes information from several disciplines, including not only psychology but also physiology, neurochemistry, and neuroanatomy, all of which are ultimately necessary for explaining the ability of drugs to alter psychological processes. This book is intended to introduce students to the field of psychopharmacology and provide a scientific basis for understanding the fundamental principles of drug effects on behavior by integrating information from these diverse disciplines.

Because of my lifelong interest in this important area of inquiry, it was a great pleasure for me to accept David Grilly's invitation to become his coauthor and take over revisions of the new edition of his classic text book. I have used earlier editions of this book for several years in my own drugs and behavior class at the University of Connecticut. For me, this book has had the scope, emphasis, and clarity that were perfect for my own class. In making the revisions, I wanted to build upon the strengths of the earlier editions. For that reason, we continue to place emphasis on the use of drug treatments for psychiatric and neurological disorders. In this new edition of the book (*Drugs, Brain, and Behavior*), there are revised chapters or sections focusing on drug treatments for parkinsonism (Chapter 7), schizophrenia (Chapter 8), depression (Chapter 9), and anxiety (Chapter 10). Chapter 11 focuses on treatments for ADHD and Alzheimer's disease. In addition, there are chapters and sections that discuss drug abuse and dependence, both from a general perspective (Chapter 6) and in terms of specific substances and drug categories such as stimulants, sedative–hypnotics, ethanol and its metabolites, opiates, cannabinoids, hallucinogens, and others (Chapters 7 and 10–13). Finally, considerable emphasis was placed upon revising the first five chapters, which discuss basic principles of pharmacology, neurochemistry, neurophysiology, and anatomy that are critical for understanding this field. As a part of this aspect of the revision, many of the figures have been revised, and new figures have been added.

I would like to thank several people who have contributed to this book, and to my own training in the fields of psychopharmacology and neuroscience. First of all, I would like to thank David Grilly for inviting me to participate. It was, and continues to be, a distinct pleasure. I would also like to thank my colleague and research collaborator Merce Correa, who read several revised chapters and whose expertise was critical for revising the sections in Chapter 10 dealing with anxiety and ethanol and its metabolism. Another person who deserves great thanks is my daughter Isabella Salamone, who contributed substantially to the revisions of the internet links and whose artwork adorns some of the figures. I want to thank the many students who gave me helpful feedback by reading the draft chapters and offering comments. Also, I would like to express my gratitude to those colleagues and Pearson reviewers who reviewed material for this book and helped shape the revision process: John S. Conklin, Camosun College; Julie David, Normandale Community College; Chris Jones-Cage, Palo Verde College; Jacqueline Griswold, Holyoke Community College; John Kowalczyk, University of

Minnesota, Duluth; Gina Lindsley, Lesley University; Mark A. Pendergast, University of Kentucky; Victoria Rae Smith, North Hennepin Community College; Manoj Sharma, University of Cinncinnati; and David Yells, Utah Valley State College.

Moreover, I want to acknowledge the many research collaborations and discussions I have had with various colleagues who have contributed greatly to my research, teaching, and thinking in this area (Christa Muller, James Chrobak, Etan Markus, Benjamin Sachs, Debbie Fein, Jerry Richards, Steve Fowler, Martin Sarter, Kent Berridge, and Alex Makriyannis). Finally, I want to take this opportunity to thank those mentors and advisors who have been so critical for shaping my education, my views toward the field, and my own research. These include Marilyn Rigby and Steve Milliser (undergraduate advisors at Rockhurst University), Darryl Neill and Joseph Justice (graduate advisors at Emory University), and my postdoctoral mentors, Susan Iversen and Leslie Iversen (Cambridge University and Merck), Trevor Robbins (Cambridge University), and Michael Zigmond and Edward Stricker (University of Pittsburgh). I deeply appreciate all of those great figures in the field who have helped me so much through the years.

John D. Salamone
University of Connecticut

SUPPLEMENTS

Pearson Education is pleased to offer the following supplements to qualified adopters.

Instructor's Manual and Test Bank (0205246702)

The Instructor's Manual is a wonderful tool for classroom preparation and management. Corresponding to the chapters in the text, each of the manual's 13 chapters contains a brief overview of the chapter with suggestions on how to present the material, sample lecture outlines, classroom activities and discussion topics, ideas for class projects, and recommended outside readings.

The Test Bank contains over 1,300 multiple choice, short answer, and essay questions, each referencing the relevant page in the text.

Pearson MyTest Computerized Test Bank mytest ☑ (0205247075; www.pearsonmytest.com)

The Test Bank comes with Pearson MyTest, a powerful assessment-generation program that helps instructors easily create and print quizzes and exams. You can do this online, allowing flexibility and the ability to efficiently manage assessments at any time. You can easily access existing questions and edit, create, and store questions using the simple drag-and-drop and Wordlike controls. Each question comes with information on its level of difficulty and related page number in the text. For more information, go to **www.pearsonmytest.com**.

PowerPoint Presentation (0205246710)

The PowerPoint Presentation is an exciting interactive tool for use in the classroom. Each chapter pairs key concepts with images from the textbook to reinforce student learning.

MySearchLab (0205699421)

MySearchLab is an engaging online experience that personalizes learning for students. Features include the ability to highlight and add notes to the eText online or download changes straight to the iPad. Chapter quizzes and flashcards offer immediate feedback and report directly to the grade book. A wide range of writing, grammar, and research tools and access to a variety of academic journals, census data, Associated Press news-feeds, and discipline-specific readings help students hone their writing and research skills.

Psychopharmacology in Perspective

The use of drugs that alter brain function and behavior is ubiquitous, with considerable ramifications for individuals and society. For example, seven of the ten leading causes of disability in the United States either involve disorders that drugs are commonly used to treat (major depression, schizophrenia, manic depressive illness, obsessive-compulsive disorder, dementia, and degenerative CNS disorders) or involve alcohol or other drug use disorders (Hyman, 2000). **Psychopharmacology** is the discipline that attempts to systematically study the effects of drugs on behavior, cognitive functioning, and emotions. Drugs that alter behavior, cognitive functioning, or emotions are called **psychoactive** or **psychotropic drugs.** The term *psychopharmacology* is a combination of the terms *psychology* and *pharmacology*, which refer, respectively, to the study of the variables affecting behavior and the study of the effects of drugs on biological systems. Originally the Greek word psyche referred to the soul, but lately it has been used to refer to the mind—an abstract concept commonly used to represent the totality of hypothesized mental processes, which acts to serve as an explanatory device for psychological data. Pharmakos originally meant "scapegoat"; a pharmakos was a person who was sacrificed as a remedy for whatever maladies another person might have been experiencing. For obvious reasons, there were few volunteers for the position, but I suppose that the procedure worked in roughly a third of the cases—about the same success rate one might get nowadays using a placebo. Later on, around 600 B.C., the term came to refer to a medicine, drug, or poison.

Psychoactive drugs are chemicals that induce psychological effects by altering the normal biochemical reactions that take place in the nervous system. A drug's chemical structure, how much of the drug is taken, how long it has been since the drug was taken, and how frequently it is taken are important factors that will be discussed in relation to the drug experience. In addition, three other ingredients in the drug experience should always be kept in mind: the **set** (the psychological makeup and the expectations of the individual taking the drug), the **setting** (the social and physical environment in which the drug is taken), and the individual's unique biochemical makeup, some of which are dependent upon genetic factors. Taken together, all these factors help to explain why there are enormous individual differences in terms of responsiveness to drugs.

Although drugs are chemicals that alter the normal biological functions of the body, they should not be viewed as simply bad or good. Consideration must be given to how much of the drug is taken, what it is taken for, and in what context it is taken. For example, heroin can be a very effective drug in the treatment of pain in terminally ill cancer patients, and methamphetamine can treat the symptoms of attention deficit hyperactivity disorder. However, when injected in unknown quantities for their euphoric properties, these drugs can lead to dependence, economic and social disaster, incarceration, toxic reactions, and death.

A HISTORICAL OVERVIEW OF PSYCHOPHARMACOLOGY

Ancient records indicate that human beings have been using drugs to alter mood and behavior for thousands of years. (For fascinating and more detailed discussion of this topic, see Brecher, 1972; Caldwell, 1978; and Szasz, 1974.) Considering the thousands of plants available that contain psychoactive substances and the likelihood that our ancestors were just as curious and willing to experiment on themselves as some people are today, this information should not come as any surprise. Substances that can induce mystical experiences and hallucinations are found in cannabis and in numerous herbs, mushrooms, and cacti, all of which grow throughout the world.

For example, in order to enhance their ferociousness, early Viking warriors were said to ingest the mushroom *Amanita muscaria*, which is capable of inducing gaiety, exuberance, and berserk behavior—a term derived from the name of their warrior cult, the *Berserkers*. Some Native American Indians have used the peyote cactus, which contains the hallucinogen (hallucination-producing substance) mescaline, in their religious ceremonies for centuries. (Their use of peyote for this purpose was legal until 1990, when a U.S. Supreme Court ruling made it illegal. It was returned to legal status in 1993 when Congress passed the Religious Freedom Restoration Act, but the Act was subsequently ruled unconstitutional by the U.S. Supreme Court in 1997. Several states have since enacted laws similar to the federal act that do allow the use of peyote as a religious sacrament by members of the Native American Church.) Archaeological findings of "mushroom stones" in Guatemala indicate that a sophisticated mushroom cult existed there some 3,500 years ago. Early Spanish chroniclers wrote of their opposition to the Aztecs' ceremonial eating of the diabolical mushroom *teonanacatl* (food of the gods) for purposes of divination, prophecy, and worship. It is likely that these mushrooms contained the hallucinogenic substances psilocybin and psilocin. Cannabis, which we now call marijuana, was first used more than 4,000 years ago, primarily for its medical value in treating a number of different ailments.

Opium poppies, which contain the narcotics morphine and codeine, were probably used by the ancient Sumerians in Mesopotamia almost 7,000 years ago. Substances that effectively suppress manic symptoms can be found in rauwolfia, a plant common to the Himalayas. Substances that elevate mood and reduce fatigue are found in many plants. For centuries South American Indians have chewed the coca leaf, which contains small amounts of the drug cocaine, to alleviate fatigue, elevate mood, and reduce hunger, and archaeological evidence suggests that early humans may have used coca as far back as 3000 B.C.

The use of tea as a pleasurable stimulant began about A.D. 600 in China. An intoxicating beverage made from coffee beans was introduced to the Arabians in the 13th century. Numerous other plants containing caffeine or similar-acting substances have been used by ancient cultures in Mexico, South America, and Africa, among many others. The use of nicotine-containing tobacco by Native Americans goes back at least 2,200 years. In ceremonies during medieval times, witches used various herbs (e.g., mandrake, henbane, and belladonna) containing scopolamine, hyoscyamine, and atropine to induce hallucinations and the sensation of flying. They also may have thrown in a few toads, whose sweat glands contain the hallucinogenic drug bufotenine, one of the few psychoactive drugs of animal origin. Physicians during this and later periods used the same substances as sleep inducers and analgesics, as well as for other purposes.

Except perhaps for caffeine, the most common psychoactive substance used around the world today is alcohol, and it has been available for thousands of years. There is hardly a culture, primitive or advanced, that does not value its peculiar properties. Alcohol is a simple product of fermentation, which occurs when certain yeasts, molds, and bacteria act upon sugar in a variety of fruits and which is easily produced both accidentally and purposefully. The earliest records of purposeful alcohol production were left by the Egyptians more than 5,500 years ago, and there is physical evidence that wine was being produced in present-day Iran 2,000 years before this. Every culture that we are aware of has used a plant or plants with psychoactive properties at one time or another. In their experimentation over the centuries, human beings must have eaten, drunk, smoked, or rubbed on their bodies thousands of substances. They found that some of these substances nourished them, while others made them ill or killed them, relieved their psychological or physical discomforts, or had extraordinary and incomprehensible effects on mood, consciousness, or behavior.

Even nonhuman animals have been observed to seek out substances with mood-altering properties (Siegel, 1989). In the laboratory, rodents and nonhuman primates will self-administer many of the drugs used by humans. Elephants, chimpanzees, baboons, and horses have been noted to prefer water containing a small percentage of alcohol over pure water. Some birds prefer fermented berries over unfermented berries. Goats nibble coffee berries; some species of bees guzzle stupefying nectars of specialized flowers; llamas chew coca leaves (which contain cocaine); and some species of ants maintain "herds" of beetles, apparently for their intoxicating secretions. These observations have led Siegel to propose the intriguing—and controversial—hypothesis that intoxication is a universal "fourth drive," as natural as the innate drives of hunger, thirst, and sex. In fact, research with invertebrates such as *Caenorhabditis elegans* (a worm) and *Drosophila melanogaster* (fruit fly) indicates that they possess many of the proteins that are the sites of action of many drugs of abuse.

PREDECESSORS TO MODERN PHARMACOTHERAPIES

During the 1800s a number of psychoactive drugs were isolated or distilled from plants or developed from nonplant sources. Morphine was isolated from opium in 1805 and was viewed as a most effective treatment for periodic insanity. Cocaine was extracted from the coca leaf in 1857 and was suggested as a potential treatment for depression. Bromine, discovered in 1826, and chloral, discovered in 1832, were used as sedatives and sleep-inducing agents. The anesthetic gases chloroform and nitrous oxide were suggested as potential treatments for insanity. Compounds such as cannabis, hemlock, strychnine, and *Datura stramonium*—used for centuries to treat a variety of disorders—were still viewed as valuable psychiatric tools, although we realize today that they probably did more harm than good. The first phenothiazine (a type of antipsychotic discussed in Chapter 12), methylene blue, was developed in 1883. A few years later, it was reported to have calming effects on manic and hallucinating patients. Despite its apparent effectiveness, it would take another 50 years before the closely related compound chlorpromazine would revolutionize the treatment of the severely mentally disturbed. Drug-induced sleep therapy, where emotionally disturbed patients were kept unconscious for several days, became popular toward the end of the 19th century.

It was during the 1800s that investigations of the formal relationships between drug variables and psychological processes, particularly those involved in mental illness, began. The first of these investigations was probably that conducted by Jacques-Joseph Moreau de Tours, a highly respected physician in France. In the mid-1800s he published a book, for which he is most noted, called *Hashish and Mental Illness*. After taking a hashish-laced concoction (hashish is a concentrated form of marijuana) on numerous occasions and observing others who volunteered to ingest his concoction, he compared the drug-induced symptoms with the mental symptoms that occur spontaneously in psychoses. Moreau was one of the first to emphasize that the person's particular or immediate context greatly influenced both the quality and intensity of the drug experience. He also observed the effects of hashish on some of his patients with mental disorders and suggested that hashish-induced excitement may be beneficial in treating depressed patients. He reported that some depressed individuals, after taking his hashish concoction, chatted, laughed, and acted silly all evening. Unfortunately, however, those effects were transitory, and the patients relapsed. He also found that occasionally manic patients improved after taking hashish.

Moreau also studied the psychoactive effects of opiates, nitrous oxide, and a number of sedative–hypnotic drugs. Unfortunately, his work in this area went largely unrecognized by his contemporaries, but shortly after *Hashish and Mental Illness* was published, a few American psychiatrists who read of his work tried cannabis preparations in the treatment of insanity. Despite the lack of recognition during his time, today some people view Moreau as the first psychopharmacologist.

However, the very first book in modern experimental psychopharmacology, as well as the first book solely devoted to drugs and animal behavior, was published in 1826 by A. P. Charvel, a young medical student (Siegel, 1989). Charvel studied the effects of opium on a variety of animals, including water beetles, crayfish, snails, fish, toads, birds, and various mammals (including himself and other medical students). Like Moreau, Charvel discovered that a drug's effects depend on numerous factors, such as the individual's history, tolerance to the drug, dose, and method of administration. But like the observations of Moreau, Charvel's discoveries were largely ignored by his contemporaries.

During the late 1800s and early 1900s, some of the most famous early psychologists were also some of the first to explore systematically the relationship between various drugs and psychological variables. Early in his career, Sigmund Freud spent 3 years investigating the effects of cocaine on fatigue, depression, strength, and morphine addiction, among other things. In many of these studies, he was the test subject. Until recently, many of the most comprehensive, up-to-date descriptions of cocaine's effects were contained in Freud's 25-page essay "Über Coca" (On Coca), published in 1884. However, a growing number of reports critical of cocaine at that time, as well as Freud's own dismal failure in treating a good friend's morphine addiction with cocaine (the friend turned from morphine to heavy cocaine use), led him to direct his scientific interests into very different areas. However, Freud retained an interest in drugs and behavior throughout his lifetime. Curiously, although Freud was able to give up cocaine, apparently with very little discomfort, he remained a nicotine addict who chain-smoked cigars despite suffering from angina (chest pain) and having had multiple operations for oral cancer (Brecher, 1972). Even the man who discovered the ego-defense mechanism of denial was unable to avoid its consequences.

Ivan Pavlov, best known for his work in the conditioning of reflexes, attempted to treat schizophrenics by using some of his conditioning techniques and inducing long periods of sleep with bromides. However, it is doubtful that he was very successful with this technique, because bromides tend to accumulate in the body and can reach levels that can induce toxic symptoms such as headache, sedation, violent delirium, mental confusion, and gastric distress. In some cases, these symptoms are very similar to those of a psychosis. Pavlov's work in the area of conditioning reflexes led some of his colleagues to use drugs like morphine as potential stimuli for the induction of new reflexes. These researchers probably did not realize just how important the Pavlovian process is in what we now refer to as *drug dependence*. William James, who established the first psychology laboratory in the United States, wrote about some of his fascinating experiences while under the influence of nitrous oxide, sometimes known as "laughing gas" (Leavitt, 1982). He found that consciousness, in which he was very interested, could be profoundly altered by nitrous oxide, although not necessarily for the better. It seems that while he was under the influence of nitrous oxide (the effects last but a few minutes), he was capable of mystic revelations. Unfortunately, though, he could never remember what the revelations were when the effects wore off.

The first half of the 20th century was accompanied by the synthesis or clinical use of a wide variety of new psychoactive substances with potential therapeutic value. Barbiturates were introduced in 1903 and helped sustain interest in sleep therapy for various mental ailments. Amphetamine, first synthesized in the 1800s, came into clinical use in 1927 in the treatment of narcolepsy and mild depressive states. Albert Hofmann first synthesized lysergic acid diethylamide (LSD) in 1938. Five years later, when he accidentally ingested LSD during one of his experiments, he discovered that it was one of the most potent psychoactive substances known to humankind. LSD would be used a few years later as a psychedelic (mind-manifesting) adjunct to psychotherapy and as a means of inducing what many people believed to be a model psychosis.

THE PSYCHOPHARMACOLOGICAL REVOLUTION

Despite the extensive history of drug use and these early investigations, there was no concerted interest in studying drugs and their influence on cognition, emotions, and behavior until the middle of the 20th century. This all changed following the discovery that a drug (chlorpromazine) could dramatically reduce the core symptoms of schizophrenia—a drug that did more than simply sedate schizophrenic patients, but actually was able to improve their thought processes and improve their relationships with others. Previously, many different drugs had been used in the treatment of schizophrenia, a particularly intractable and debilitating disorder; all of these simply put the patients to sleep or made them so drowsy or sedated that they could not do anything. This discovery also provided evidence that certain forms of mental illness could be linked to abnormalities in the biochemistry in the brain, rather than being due to purely environmental conditions (e.g., "bad" parenting), which was a common view at the time. It was this discovery that led to the formation of the formal and distinct discipline known as psychopharmacology.

The story begins with the development of one of the first antihistamines in 1937. Although antihistamines were initially used in the treatment of allergies, their sedative properties, viewed by those taking them for allergic conditions as an undesirable side effect, were suspected as being beneficial in the treatment of other clinical conditions. The antihistamine promethazine was introduced in 1949 as an adjunct to surgery. It was found to reduce surgical shock, to calm patients both before and after major surgery, and to reduce the emotional suffering associated with surgery. A year later it was used by a psychiatrist in the treatment of schizophrenia, primarily for its hypnotic effects. Although promethazine calmed his patients, the psychiatrist apparently saw it as just another sedative. In the same year another psychiatrist noted similar calming effects in schizophrenic patients with a related compound, but the manufacturer was not interested in developing such a drug. However, reports of these effects in surgical patients and schizophrenics eventually led to the evaluation and development of compounds with similar structures with even more specific actions.

One of these compounds, initially called 4560 RP, was found to have some interesting pharmacological properties (Mitchell, 1993). It had minimal antihistaminic action, but it reduced both sympathetic and parasympathetic activity, abolished conditioned reflexes, and had a host of other desirable properties. In clinical trials it abolished preoperative anxiety, reduced surgical stress, and eliminated the postoperative consequences of stress. Here was a drug that could turn off the world and its harrowing stress without inebriating the patient or putting the patient to sleep. The surgeon who attempted these clinical tests closed his report with the suggestion that 4560 RP, now called chlorpromazine, be used in treating psychiatric conditions. The first report on chlorpromazine treatment of psychosis was published in France in 1952. In 1953 chlorpromazine was tried more extensively in psychiatric wards in Paris.

It could be said that at that time chlorpromazine started the pharmacological revolution in psychiatry. Although it did not cure mania and schizophrenia, chlorpromazine did suspend their symptoms with great efficacy and much less toxicity than any previous drug. Chlorpromazine was used immediately in Italy and Switzerland, and shortly thereafter in the United States. Its use spread to England and South America in 1954 and to Australia, Japan, and the Soviet Union in 1955. Its trade name in Europe was Largactil, because of its *large* spectrum of therapeutic *activity*. In the United States it was marketed as Thorazine.

The pharmacological revolution expanded. Between 1952 and 1954, chlorpromazine monopolized drug therapy for all mental diseases. It stirred the ambitions of drug manufacturers and researchers. New drugs were developed, and drugs that had been abandoned were clinically tested again. In India as early as 1931 it was suggested that the rauwolfia plant, which contains reserpine, had some beneficial effects in the treatment of mental disorders, but it was not introduced to the Western world until 1954. Meprobamate, the first of the so-called anxiolytics (anxiety reducers), was first used clinically in 1955 and became as popular for the treatment of neuroses as chlorpromazine was for psychoses. The treatment of depression with the first of the monoamine oxidase inhibitors (iproniazide) became acceptable in 1957, five years after its antidepressant action was noted in tuberculosis patients who were administered the drug for its antituberculosis properties. A drug developed in 1948, with properties that did not generate any enthusiasm on the part of its manufacturer, was again tested clinically in 1957 because of its molecular resemblance to chlorpromazine. Unlike the phenothiazines, however, the drug was relatively ineffective in quieting agitated psychotic patients. Instead, it seemed to have remarkable mood-lifting properties in severely depressed patients. Thus was born the first tricyclic antidepressant, imipramine (Tofranil).

The enthusiasm created by chlorpromazine led to one oversight with respect to a drug that would later take the place of chlorpromazine as one of the most valuable treatments for cyclical mood disorders. As early as 1870, it was suggested that lithium, an alkali metal, had mood-altering effects. It wasn't until 1949, however, that the Australian psychiatrist John Cade discovered, quite fortuitously, that lithium had profound mood-stabilizing effects in manic patients. Despite verification of his findings in studies conducted 1 or 2 years later, the vast majority of psychiatric practitioners remained unimpressed with his findings. Lithium was believed to be too toxic. It also had minimal marketability because it was unpatentable as a natural substance. In addition, chlorpromazine suppressed the symptoms of mania much more quickly than lithium did and had a much lower potential for lethal toxicity. It took almost 10 years for the medical community, at least in the United States, to recognize the true value of lithium and to rectify the oversight.

Lysergic diethylamide also created a considerable amount of excitement in the field of psychopharmacology during the 1950s. LSD and chlorpromazine made an interesting team. Whereas chlorpromazine reduced psychotic symptoms, LSD was viewed as a way of inducing the symptoms of psychosis. In addition, LSD was touted by a number of psychotherapists as a potential therapeutic tool in the treatment of a number of disorders, ranging from alcoholism to anxiety, sexual dysfunction, blocked creativity, and general malaise (Novak, 1998). During the 1950s over a thousand medical articles on LSD's potential therapeutic benefits were published, with many studies claiming success in over two-thirds of the patients. Together, LSD and chlorpromazine instigated a tremendous interest in the biochemistry of the brain and psychoses. Because chlorpromazine could readily block the effects of LSD, it made research and psychotherapy with LSD safer. LSD-induced psychosis became the model with which other potential antipsychotic drugs could be tested, and it became a tool for exploring the etiology (the science of causes or origins of diseases) of schizophrenia.

By the beginning of the 1960s, however, the enthusiasm over LSD in the medical community began to drop off dramatically. As discussed in Chapter 11, the realization that the psychotic state it could induce did not resemble any endogenous psychosis, the indiscriminant self-experimentation with LSD by both medical practitioners and laypersons, its unreliable effects, its association with the counterculture hippie movement of the time, and so on, essentially relegated LSD to playing a relatively minor role in the field of psychopharmacology over the next 4 decades.

Beginning in the early 1950s, a multitude of drugs were developed that revolutionized the treatment of major mental and emotional illnesses. Despite the increase in the number of diagnosed schizophrenic patients due to the growth in the general population, the number of schizophrenic patients hospitalized in the United States has dropped from around 600,000 in 1954 to less than 200,000 today. The goal of the community mental health movement—to deinstitutionalize patients and allow them to function successfully in the community—became a reality. Many patients who were totally refractory to behavioral therapy and psychotherapies became more amenable to these treatments with the use of these drugs. The new pharmacotherapies also encouraged practitioners to become more rigorous in their diagnoses. The drugs stimulated interest in the relationships between brain biochemistry and behavior.

Since the 1950s psychopharmacologists have made great strides in understanding and treating virtually every affliction of the human mind. Many, if not most, mental disorders are now viewed as having a biochemical basis and can often be treated as such. (It should not be inferred from this statement that environmental events such as stress, conflict, and inappropriate parental activities are not important factors in these biochemical disturbances or that psychologically based therapies are inappropriate in treating many forms of mental dysfunctions. We will leave these issues for others to discuss in textbooks more suited for those purposes.)

With new techniques, such as magnetic resonance imaging, computerized axial tomography, and positron emission tomography, researchers are now able to look at the machinery and workings of the living brain. Molecular biologists are even beginning to relate abnormal behavior to specific parts of chromosomes. The specific actions of new drugs like aripiprazole (Abilify), memantine (Namenda), risperidone (Risperdal), fluoxetine (Prozac), and atomoxetine (Strattera) are giving us a better understanding of the relationship between moods and feelings and the action of specific chemicals in the brain. Drugs with greater degrees of specificity and effectiveness have been developed for treating schizophrenia and depression. Symptoms of disorders such as Tourette's syndrome, panic and phobic disorders, and obsessive-compulsive disorder, which were previously treated with ineffective psychoanalytic talk therapy, can now be reduced or eliminated with newly developed drugs. Different methods of delivering older drugs, like morphine, into the body have been developed that have enhanced their effectiveness or reduced their side effects. More information about these drugs, disorders, mechanisms of action, and methods will be presented in subsequent chapters.

Unfortunately, however, psychotherapeutic drugs do not cure mental disorders or suppress their symptoms in all individuals. Sometimes they cause toxic or irreversible side effects. The potential for such side effects brings out a number of ethical questions about the right of a society to control the behavior of individuals with substances that might do them harm. Although drugs allow patients to leave hospitals, the communities to which the patients return are often poorly prepared to provide continuing care. In other cases practitioners rely solely on medications to deal with their patients' problems, without looking into other psychological or socioeconomic interventions that might be available and beneficial for their patients. In spite of the fact that the prognosis for mentally and emotionally ill people is much better now than it was 50 years ago, we as a society must continue searching for drugs with greater specificity and for other interventions that will help us deal with these problems and allow these individuals to lead happier and more productive lives.

RECREATIONAL AND SOCIAL DRUG USE

Many individuals who exhibit the normal range of moods, emotions, cognitive activity, and behavior willingly administer drugs to themselves to alter their emotional experiences, consciousness, or behavior in recreational, social, or religious settings. Such phenomena are of particular interest to psychopharmacologists. Very few individuals in modern cultures do not, at some time or another, use a psychoactive drug for such a purpose. Even caffeine, nicotine, and alcohol, which we often do not even think of as drugs, are psychoactive drugs. In many cases, taking these drugs is explicitly (in advertisements) or implicitly indicated as having positive or beneficial effects. For example, smoking cigarettes and drinking alcohol are often portrayed in fiction as beneficial tools for coping with emotionally stressful situations (Kushnir, 1986). As a whole the mass media reflect the national culture and have conditioned Americans to accept drug use as part of daily life (Gitlin, 1990). (With all the references to drugs—many of them uncritical, to say the least—it is reasonable that questions should be raised about the media's contributions to drug use.)

In 2002, national surveys indicated that approximately two-thirds of Americans over the age of 12 drank alcoholic beverages, with an annual per capita consumption of 21.7 gallons of beer, 2.0 gallons of wine, and 1.3 gallons of spirits (a total of 1.8 gallons of pure ethyl alcohol). According to estimates from the U.S. Department of Agriculture and the Centers for Disease Control and Prevention, in 2002, 23% of adult Americans were cigarette smokers who smoked 430 packs of cigarettes per year; the good news is that these figures were down from 42% smokers who smoked 512 packs per year in the mid-1960s—the peak years for cigarette sales and use in the United States.

The average American adult consumes approximately 100 grams of caffeine a year; most of this amount comes from drinking coffee or tea, but in young adults up to 50% of dietary caffeine may come from soft drinks, and the use of "energy drinks" has been increasing dramatically in recent years (Barone & Roberts, 1996; Miller, 2008).

In addition to these socially accepted drugs—caffeine, nicotine, and alcohol—Americans are heavy consumers of numerous illicit substances. Because of its nature, the extent of illicit drug use in the United States is difficult to estimate, but it is clearly pervasive. Estimates from the office of National Drug Control Policy indicate that, in 2000, Americans spent an estimated $64.8 billion on illicit drugs: $36 billion on cocaine, $11 billion on marijuana, $10 billion on heroin, $5.4 billion on methamphetamine, and $2.4 billion on other illicit drugs, such as black-market amphetamines and barbiturates and illicitly manufactured hallucinogens.

Statistics from the National Survey on Drug Use and Health (formerly known as the National Household Survey on Drug Abuse, a large nationwide survey conducted yearly by the federal government since 1971) indicate that in 2002 about one-half of Americans over the age of 12 had used an illicit drug at least once; 15% had used one or more illicit drugs during the previous year; and 8% were current users of one or more illicit drugs. Marijuana (including hashish) was the most popular illicit drug used, with 40% of the sample having used it at least once and 11% using it in the past year. (Since the 1980s, the National Organization for the Reform of Marijuana Laws [NORML] has consistently estimated that marijuana is in the top 10 of cash crops in the United States. In California, it is estimated to be the number-one cash crop.) However, for those individuals under the age of 18, for whom alcoholic beverages and tobacco would be considered illicit substances, marijuana use ranked third behind alcohol (first) and tobacco (second). Table 1.1 indicates the percentage of use of various illicit

TABLE 1.1   Percentage of Persons Aged 12 or Older Using Illicit Drugs: Lifetime, Past Year, and Past Month (2007)

Drug	Lifetime	Past Year	Past Month
	Time Period		
Any Illicit Drug[1]	46.1	14.4	8.0
Marijuana and Hashish	40.6	10.1	5.8
Cocaine	14.5	2.3	0.8
Crack	3.5	0.6	0.2
Heroin	1.5	0.1	0.1
Hallucinogens	13.8	1.5	0.4
LSD	9.1	0.3	0.1
PCP	2.5	0.1	0.0
Ecstasy	5.0	0.9	0.2
Inhalants	9.1	0.8	0.2
Nonmedical Use of Any Psychotherapeutic[2]	20.3	6.6	2.8
Pain Relievers	13.3	5.0	2.1
OxyContin	1.8	0.6	0.1
Tranquilizers	8.2	2.1	0.7
Stimulants	8.7	1.2	0.4
Methamphetamine	5.3	0.5	0.2
Sedatives	3.4	0.3	0.1
Any Illicit Drug Other Than Marijuana[1]	29.7	8.5	3.7

[1]Illicit drugs include marijuana/hashish, cocaine (including crack), heroin, hallucinogens, inhalants, or prescription-type psychotherapeutics used nonmedically. Illicit drugs other than marijuana include cocaine (including crack), heroin, hallucinogens, inhalants, or prescription-type psychotherapeutics used nonmedically. The estimates for nonmedical use of psychotherapeutics, stimulants, and methamphetamine incorporated in these summary estimates do not include data from the methamphetamine items added in 2005 and 2006. See Section B.4.6 in Appendix B of the *Results from the 2007 National Survey on Drug Use and Health: National Findings*.

[2]Nonmedical Use of Prescription-Type Psychotherapeutics includes the nonmedical use of pain relievers, tranquilizers, stimulants, or sedatives and does not include over-the-counter drugs. Estimates of nonmedical use of psychotherapeutics, stimulants, and methamphetamine in the designated rows include data from methamphetamine items added in 2005 and 2006 and are not comparable with estimates presented in prior NSDUH reports. See Section B.4.6 in Appendix B of the *Results from the 2007 National Survey on Drug Use and Health: National Findings*.

Source: SAMHSA, Office of Applied Studies, National Survey on Drug Use and Health, 2006 and 2007.

drugs by persons aged 12 or older, according to the National Survey on Drug Use and Mental Health.

According to national surveys, the use of recreational and social drugs in the United States rose dramatically from the mid-1960s to around 1980 and was followed by a cyclical pattern of use over the next 2 decades (e.g., see Figure 1.1). For example, following a dramatic rise in the use of marijuana (including hashish) from 1965 to 1980, its use fell substantially and then rose again over the next 2 decades. These data may not be representative of drug use by individuals in all age groups; however, they do serve as a barometer of changes in drug use by the general population over the past 40 years.

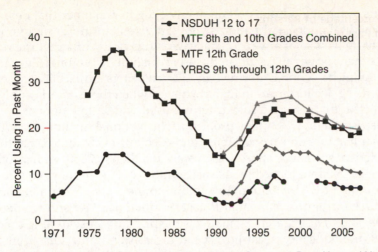

MTF = Monitoring the Future; NSDUH = National Survey on Drug Use and Health; YRBS = Youth Risk Behavior Survey.

FIGURE 1.1   From 2007 National Survey on Drug Use and Health.

Clearly those who engage in recreational or social use of drugs may eventually cause behavioral or physical problems for themselves or others around them. For as long as humankind has been using drugs for such purposes, there have been concerns over drug abuse and attempts to restrict it (Szasz, 1974). As far back as 2000 B.C., an Egyptian priest attempted to proselytize alcohol users, suggesting that they were degraded like the beasts. In the 17th century a prince in England paid money to people to denounce coffee drinkers, and the Russian tsar executed those found to possess tobacco (after torturing them into divulging the names of their suppliers). A similar penalty was levied by the sultan of the Ottoman Empire.

In 1736 the Gin Act of England was passed, making alcohol so expensive that the poor could not use it excessively. Note that whiskey, which only the rich could afford, was not included in this act. In 1792 the first prohibitory laws against opium in China went into effect; the punishment for possession was strangulation. Similar draconian attempts to reduce drug use have been made around the world. The United States passed the Harrison Narcotic Act in 1914 and the Marijuana Tax Act in 1937, among others, which basically outlawed the nonmedical (or untaxed) possession or sale of a number of drugs, including opium, morphine, heroin, and marijuana. In addition, prohibition of alcoholic beverages was in effect in the United States from 1920 to 1933. In 1921 cigarettes were illegal in 14 states.

Unfortunately, however, drug use did not decline in most cases (Brecher, 1972). One of the fundamental reasons restrictions have failed is that it is not clear to many users why they must stop using the drugs, because they feel their drug consumption affects only themselves. Society as a whole might agree that there are certain forms of drug consumption that should be avoided and that can be called drug abuse, but there is no universal agreement as to what these are. The criteria for what constitutes drug abuse are heavily dependent on one's culture and the time period. Generally, the term *drug abuse* refers to the self-administration of any drug in a manner that deviates from the approved medical or societal patterns within a given culture. A more operational definition might be the use of any drug that causes functional or structural damage to the users or to others, or which results in the users' inability to voluntarily control their social or drug-taking behavior. Unfortunately, human beings are excellent at self-deception and rarely recognize instances in their own lives when these criteria apply.

Thus it is clear that psychotropic drugs are used widely in a nonmedical context and that this use is fraught with many problems. The National Institute on Drug Abuse and the National Institute on Alcohol Abuse and Alcoholism estimated that the annual cost to U.S. society of substance abuse was over $500 billion in 2000, with alcohol abuse accounting for $196 billion, tobacco abuse accounting for $157 billion, and abuse of illicit drugs accounting for $161 billion. In addition to the costs of treatment and health care, these figures include costs related to lost productivity, law enforcement, crime, traffic accidents, and fires. Cigarette smoking is the primary cause of lung cancer and a key component of other cancers, cardiovascular disease, and other disorders, and it is the leading cause of mortality in the United States, with approximately 435,000 Americans dying from smoking every year (Mokdad et al., 2004). The Centers for Disease Control and Prevention has estimated that, on average, adult men and women lose 13.2 and 14.5 years of life, respectively, as a result of their smoking cigarettes. About three-fourths of poisoning deaths in 1995 were caused by drugs, with opiates and cocaine accounting for the majority of these deaths (Fingerhut & Cox, 1998). Drug Abuse Warning Network (DAWN) records indicate that there were more than 680,000 drug-related hospital emergency department episodes in the United States in 2002.

Use of other psychotropic drugs, and the rapid development of new ones, can only worsen the situation. The question frequently asked is, What can be done about it? Some people rely on the legislative process, whereby certain drug-taking practices are declared illegal. Unfortunately, though, history reveals that the legislative approach has rarely had much impact on these practices except to make them less safe than they were originally, and it has numerous other repercussions.

Since the passage of the Harrison Narcotic Act in 1914, the United States has engaged in a war on drug abuse. This and subsequent legislation have done little to dampen the desire for or use of drugs (Marshall et al. 1988a). Traditionally, around 70% of the money appropriated for drug control has gone toward interdiction of supply, and only 30% has gone toward manipulating the demand for drugs (Jarvik, 1990). Because of difficulties in smuggling and concealment of drugs, less bulky, more potent drugs became preferred (e.g., heroin instead of morphine or opium), and more hazardous methods of administering drugs came into use (e.g., injecting or smoking instead of oral administration). Drug prices skyrocketed, and drug quality declined. Sellers willing to take high risks for lucrative financial gain began to engage in violence to settle disputes over drug trading, and users began committing crimes to help finance their drug purchases. In response, federal antidrug expenditures continued to grow (e.g., from around $130 million in 1970 to around $18 billion in 2000), with most of this directed toward catching and jailing drug law violators. Collectively, federal, state, and local governments spent around $40 billion per year to reduce illegal drug use and trafficking and to deal with their consequences.

Drug control policies bear primary responsibility for the quadrupling of the national prison population since 1980 and a soaring incarceration rate, the highest among Western democracies. According to retired General Barry McCaffrey, director of the

Office of National Drug Control Policy under the Clinton administration, the nation's war on drugs has propelled the creation of a vast "drug gulag." At the present time, more people are sent to prison in the United States for nonviolent drug offenses than for crimes of violence. Throughout the 1990s, more than 100,000 drug offenders were sent to prison annually. More than 1.5 million prison admissions on drug charges have occurred since 1980. The rate at which drug offenders are incarcerated has increased ninefold. The rate of incarceration has been particularly devastating to the African American community. Research by the Human Rights Watch organization shows that Blacks comprise 63% and Whites 37% of all drug offenders admitted to state prisons, even though federal surveys and other data show clearly that this racial disparity bears scant relation to racial differences in actual drug offending (Human Rights Watch, 2000). There are, for example, five times more White drug users than Black. Relative to population, Black men are admitted to state prisons on drug charges at a rate that is 13.4 times greater than that of White men. In large part because of the extraordinary racial disparities in incarceration for drug offenses, Blacks are incarcerated for all offenses at 8.2 times the rate of Whites. One in every twenty Black men over the age of 18 in the United States is in state or federal prison, compared to one in 180 White men. Meanwhile, prisons are so overcrowded that convicts often have to be released early to make room for new arrivals. Despite these efforts, the illicit drug business has continued to grow.

In recognition of these phenomena, a number of political and academic leaders began to raise a provocative alternative—drug legalization. They argued that the cheapest and cleanest way to reduce drug-related crime and the hazards of drugs of unknown quality and quantity would be to do away with the laws that make drug use a crime. Their assumption was that society would be better off if it did not stand in the way of the drug users and their habit. Less tax money would be needed for interdiction, prosecution, and imprisonment of illicit drug suppliers; in fact, legalization could enhance tax revenues. Users would not be submitted to the hazards of unknown drug quality or quantity or the disastrous consequences of imprisonment. Violent crimes against property and people would be significantly reduced. Urban street gangs and organized crime, now sustained by the illegal drug trade, would be severely weakened.

Critics of this idea (Goldstein & Kalant, 1990; Jarvik, 1990) were quick to point out that it would likely have some potentially disastrous outcomes. They argue it would probably increase the number of new addicts. Some drugs, such as cocaine and phencyclidine (PCP), have properties that are potentially hazardous to users and society no matter how they are used. Other drugs would likely be developed that produce faster and more intense effects, and thus be more addictive, than currently available ones. Finally, even with legalization, there would have to be age restrictions, as with alcohol, for legally obtaining drugs; consequently, there would still be a group of individuals for which a black market would likely exist.

At the present time, there is little impetus at the federal level to move away from the criminalization approaches for dealing with drug abuse. In contrast, state officials and the voting public are moving forward with a number of drug policy reforms, which have been enacted in a wide variety of states (Piper et al., 2003). These actions vary from allowing people to grow and use marijuana for medical purposes, reducing long and costly prison sentences for nonviolent drug offenders, increasing legal access to sterile syringes in order to reduce the spread of HIV, restoring the rights and duties of citizenship to felony drug convictions in their past, diverting certain nonviolent drug possession offenders from prison to treatment, and so on. For example, between 1996 and 2004, 9 states enacted laws legalizing marijuana for people with physician recommendations or prescriptions, and 35 states have passed legislation recognizing marijuana's medicinal value. Voters or legislators of several states have approved or enacted measures mandating that first- and second-time nonviolent drug possession offenders receive drug treatment instead of incarceration. In 2008, Massachusetts voters approved a measure to decriminalize possession of small amounts of marijuana, and state government officials across the United States are openly discussing the issue of marijuana decriminalization.

In virtually all of these cases, the federal government has attempted to block or circumvent these measures. For example, agents of the Drug Enforcement Administration recently conducted raids in California of medical marijuana hospices, and federal law prevents doctors from prescribing marijuana in the several states that allow such prescriptions. The Justice Department even threatened to prosecute physicians for recommending or even discussing the use of marijuana for their patients, until the U.S. Supreme Court ruled that this would be a violation of the free speech rights provided by the U.S. Constitution.

Although we have little empirical evidence for what would happen if all drugs were decriminalized and regulated, much like alcohol presently is in the United States, we do have evidence on what might happen if marijuana were to be decriminalized (Zimmer & Morgan, 1997). The Netherlands' policy regarding marijuana is the least punitive in Europe. Although technically illegal, for over 20 years Dutch citizens over the age of 18 have not been prosecuted for buying and using small amounts of marijuana and hashish in government-regulated coffee shops. In contrast, in the 1990s almost one in five prisoners in U.S. federal prisons was there for marijuana sales or possession, and in some states the incarceration rate was considerably higher. However, surveys of drug use in these two countries in the 1990s indicated that the use of marijuana and most other illegal drugs was similar for most age groups, and lower in young adolescents in the Netherlands than in the United States (Smart & Ogborne, 2000; Zimmer & Morgan, 1997). The prevalence of cannabis use in the Netherlands is also similar to that of other European countries, including those with much harsher prohibition policies. Furthermore, in the 1970s, the penalties for marijuana offenses were reduced in the United States, with some states instituting what amounts to de facto decriminalization, with possession of small amounts of marijuana being a minor misdemeanor punished with a fine. Interestingly, according to national surveys, the lifetime prevalence of marijuana/hashish use in the United States by individuals under the age of 25 decreased dramatically from the late 1970s until the early 1990s.

A number of other countries have been using, or are beginning to experiment with, drug decriminalization approaches. For example, in 1994 the German Supreme Court overturned federal laws banning possession of cannabis (marijuana) in small quantities for personal use. Previously, sale or possession of cannabis in Germany carried a maximum 5-year prison term, with no distinctions made between traffickers and individuals who smoked an occasional joint. Over the past several years, the Swiss government has been trying a number of approaches to deal with heroin abuse (Nadelmann, 1995). In the early 1990s, the Swiss first tried establishing a "Needle Park" in Zurich—an open drug scene where people could use drugs without being arrested—but the scene grew unmanageable, and it was closed down in 1992. A second attempt faced similar problems and was shut down in 1995.

However, the Swiss idea of prescribing heroin to addicts in hopes of reducing both their criminal activity and their risk of spreading AIDS and other diseases took off in 1991, after the International Narcotics Control Board—a United Nations organization that oversees international antidrug treaties—was convinced that the Swiss innovation was experimental, which is permitted under these treaties, rather than a shift in policy (Nadelmann, 1995). Their experiments with heroin prescriptions (which, as discussed in Chapter 10, are variations of the approach used in the United Kingdom for over 3 decades) started in January 1994 with various programs being conducted, although most provide supplemental doses of oral methadone, psychological counseling, and other assistance. Some are located in cities, others in towns. Some provide just one drug, while others offer a choice. Some allow addicts to vary their dose each day, while others work with addicts to establish a stable dosage level. One program is primarily for women. Another program permits addicts to take heroin-injected cigarettes home.

The Swiss experiments are designed to answer a host of questions about how to deal with heroin abuse. For instance, can addicts stabilize their drug use if they are assured of a legal, safe, and stable source of heroin? Can they hold steady jobs? Do they stop using illegal heroin or cut back on the use of other illegal drugs? Do they commit fewer crimes? Are they healthier and less likely to contract HIV? Are they less likely to overdose? In 1994 the Social Welfare Department in Zurich issued some preliminary findings related to some of these questions: (a) heroin prescription is feasible and has produced no black market in diverted heroin; (b) the health of addicts in the programs clearly improved; and (c) heroin per se causes very few, if any, problems when used in a controlled fashion and administered in hygienic conditions. Program administrators also found little support for the widespread belief that addicts' cravings for heroin are insatiable, as addicts offered practically unlimited amounts of heroin soon realized that the maximum doses provided less of a "flash" than lower doses and cut back their dosage levels accordingly. However, it was also concluded that heroin prescription alone cannot solve the problems that led to the heroin addiction in the first place.

Officials in other countries—for instance, the Netherlands, Austria, and Germany—are either conducting or contemplating similar heroin prescription programs. These approaches fit with a strategy many countries have pursued since the mid-1980s, that is, tough police measures against drug dealers and a "harm reduction" approach toward users (Nadelmann, 1995), for example, making sterile syringes more available through needle-exchange programs, selling needles in pharmacies and vending machines, and creating legal "injection rooms," where addicts can inject heroin in a regulated, sanitary environment, epitomize the harm reduction philosophy. Numerous studies have shown that these approaches are effective in reducing the spread of AIDS and drug-risk behaviors without increasing illicit drug injection rates (Durante et al., 1995; Nadelmann, 1995; Paone et al., 1995). In the United States, many states and municipalities have acted to improve access to sterile syringes through syringe-exchange programs and by allowing pharmacies and clinics to dispense needles without prescriptions (Lerner, 2000). However, the possession, distribution, and sale of syringes remains a criminal offense in much of the country, and the federal government—while officially acknowledging the efficacy of such programs—prohibits the use of its funds for syringe-exchange programs.

For a number of years, drug legislation in the Netherlands has been directed primarily toward reducing the risks of drug use for the individual users as well as society in general (National Drug Monitor, 2000). Although harm to society is taken into consideration, a great effort is made to prevent criminal prosecution from being more damaging to the individual drug user than the relevant drug itself. For example, the Dutch distinguish between the market for "soft" drugs (cannabis products, such as hashish and marijuana) and the market for "harder" drugs (e.g., heroin and cocaine). This policy allows for some limited freedom for the retail trade—typically in so-called coffee shops—and the possession of small quantities of cannabis products for individual (not minors') consumption, while at the same time trying to combat the hard-drug trade in every possible way. The point of these innovations is not to coddle drug users but to reduce the human and economic costs of drug use—costs paid not only by users but also by nonusers through increased health-care, justice, and law-enforcement expenditures (Nadelmann, 1995).

One approach in dealing with illicit drug use that has not been particularly fruitful has been to tell exaggerated stories about the potentially harmful effects of particular drugs. For example, in the 1930s authorities indicated that even occasional use of marijuana commonly led to permanent insanity, excessive violence, criminal activities, and sexual depravity (the movie *Reefer Madness* portrays many of these ideas). Such stories are quickly recognized by the potential drug users for their hypocrisy and misrepresentation, and, before long, warnings about any drugs are no longer heeded, no matter what the truth is (Newcomb & Bentler, 1989).

The National Institute on Drug Abuse has estimated that for every dollar spent on drug use prevention, communities can save $4 to $5 in costs for drug abuse treatment and counseling. However, it is likely that truly effective prevention efforts will require numerous (and in many cases, politically difficult) strategies and approaches. Because use of alcohol and tobacco by adolescents has been so strongly associated with the subsequent use of illegal drugs (e.g., marijuana, cocaine, heroin), and because alcohol and tobacco themselves may produce more adverse consequences than many illegal drugs, approaches focusing on the demand for (e.g., price and accessibility) and acceptability of these substances may be the most fruitful approach to decreasing all forms of drug abuse (Goldstein & Kalant, 1990; Jarvik, 1990; Mosher, 1990; Wallack & Corbett, 1990). Nevertheless, each of these approaches, by itself, has a small impact on alcohol and tobacco use. For example, numerous lines of research have indicated that for every 10% increase in the price of cigarettes, there is an approximately 3% to 5% reduction in the demand for cigarettes by adults, and research indicates that youths may be more price sensitive than adults (Chaloupka & Grossman, 1996; Harris & Chan, 1999). There is also recent evidence that states with more extensive tobacco control policies have significantly lower youth smoking rates (Luke et al., 2000). If all of these approaches were combined, it is likely that they would have a much greater impact than they have had in the past. Unfortunately, drug prevention programs targeted at young people, which have attempted to provide correct information on the long-term consequences of drug use, provide general skills useful in resisting drugs, or provide peer models of not using drugs, have produced minimal benefits in altering drug-taking patterns of behavior (Dukes et al., 1997; Ellickson & Bell, 1990; Lynam et al., 1999).

The Food and Drug Administration (FDA) officially determined in 1996 that tobacco was a nicotine delivery system and that tobacco companies intended to provide nicotine to satisfy users' addiction. This intention would have allowed the FDA to regulate cigarettes under the Federal Food, Drug, and Cosmetic Act, which considers a product a drug if the vendor intends it to be one (Kessler et al., 1996). The FDA subsequently issued a number of rules to curb the use of tobacco by youths. Among these were the following: (a) vending-machine sales would be allowed only in adults-only areas; (b) tobacco-product billboard ads would be banned within 1,000 feet of schools and playgrounds; (c) color imagery would be allowed in tobacco ads only in adults-only areas, providing the image couldn't be seen from outside and couldn't be removed easily; (d) tobacco ads wouldn't be placed in publications with a significant youth readership; (e) brand-name tobacco sponsorship of sporting events (or individuals, teams, or cars in sporting events) would be banned; and (f) publicity items such as hats and T-shirts bearing tobacco product names and logos would be banned. In addition, the FDA began discussions with tobacco companies to fund an education campaign regarding the health hazards of tobacco.

In 1997 the tobacco industry essentially conceded the FDA's authority over tobacco products and agreed to a settlement that went well beyond the FDA's rules attempting to reduce youth access to tobacco products and tobacco marketing. For example, the industry accepted even further constraints on tobacco advertising, agreed to replace health warnings on tobacco product packages with more specific, detailed, prominently displayed warnings (e.g., Cigarettes are Addictive, Cigarettes Cause Cancer, Smoking Can Kill You), and agreed to provide funds for tobacco cessation programs and devices for those who want to quit. These concessions by the tobacco industry are quite remarkable considering that over the years there have been numerous attempts to curtail the positive image of tobacco and alcohol use by the mass media and to increase the knowledge of their harmful consequences. However, the hundreds of billions of dollars a year earned by the tobacco and alcohol industries is a tremendous incentive for them to fight most of these proposals with every legal recourse available to them, which until recently they have done fairly successfully.

In March 2000, the U.S. Supreme Court, despite its acknowledgment that "tobacco alone kills more Americans annually than AIDS, alcohol, car accidents, homicides, suicides, illegal drugs and fire combined," ruled that the FDA did not have the power to regulate the manufacture and sale of tobacco products. Concluding that Congress never intended tobacco products to be treated as drugs under the Food, Drug and Cosmetic Act, the Court ruled that the Clinton administration exceeded its authority when it announced new antismoking regulations designed to protect the nation's youth. A primary argument against allowing the FDA to regulate tobacco products was the fact that, as an agency whose primary responsibility is to determine the efficacy and safety of drug products, it would almost automatically require the FDA to ban them from the market entirely as dangerous drugs. However, the ruling did not shield the tobacco industry from huge money judgments in the trial courts, which at this point amounted to $246 billion to settle lawsuits filed by the states, and in all likelihood the industry will continue to adhere to its original concessions to prevent Congress from enacting legislation that might force them to make further concessions.

Despite the often glaring headlines in the media about the increasing incidence of illicit drug use in the United States, national surveys have indicated that illicit drug use is considerably lower now than it was in the late 1970s, the peak years of Americans' illicit drug use. An estimated 21.8 million Americans were current users of illicit drugs in 2009, meaning they used an illicit drug at least once in the prior 30 days (National Survey on Drug Use and Health, 2009). By comparison, the number of current illicit drug users was at its highest level in 1979, when the estimate was 25 million. However, as noted earlier (see Figure 1.1), illicit drug use has been cyclical, so that, for example, after a steady and dramatic decrease in reported use of illicit drugs from the late 1970s to the early 1990s there was an equally dramatic increase in reported use for several years. That trend now appears to have leveled off or been reversed.

The incidence of use of specific illicit drugs other than marijuana is generally too low to register clear trends in surveys, although use of hallucinogens appears to have peaked between 1975 and 1980 and then gradually declined. The most significant change in hallucinogen use has been associated with the use of the mildly hallucinogenic Ecstasy (MDMA), in which the percentage of young adults who used Ecstasy at least once increased from virtually zero in 1970 to less than 2% in 1990 to over 15% in 2009 (National Survey on Drug Use and Health, 2009). Estimates of heroin incidence have been subject to wide variability and usually have not shown any clear trend, although there was an increase in the number of first-time users of heroin in the late 1990s. Most of these young initiates took heroin by way of smoking, sniffing, or snorting rather than by injection because of the increased availability of higher grades of heroin, which allowed these routes of administration to produce desirable effects at a low cost. Use of cocaine rose rapidly in the 1970s, reaching a peak in 1979. It then remained relatively stable until 1985, at which point use declined, from 5.8 million users in 1985 to 2.0 million users in 2002. On the other hand, the proportion of frequent users has remained basically unchanged between 500,000 and 700,000 since 1985, and the number of emergency room episodes related to cocaine use increased dramatically from 1985 to 1989, most likely as a consequence of cocaine being marketed and administered in a form called **crack** (Dawn Survey, 2002).

Alcohol is the most commonly used illegal drug for individuals under the age of 21, and its use by high school students also declined from the late 1970s to the present, although with some cyclical variations along the way (Monitoring the Future Survey, 2010). Use of cigarettes (technically an illicit substance for individuals under the age of 18) by high school students also reached its peak in the late 1970s and declined until the early 1990s, when adolescent use began to increase, primarily among Whites. However, this trend appears to have reversed again.

The general trend toward increased use of illicit drugs by youths from the early to late 1990s appears to be coupled with their decreased perception of the negative consequences of drug use (Monitoring the Future Survey, 2003). Recent data indicate that use of marijuana and Ecstasy is in the rise (Monitoring the Future Survey, 2010). Unfortunately, these perceptions are inconsistent with the increase in the number of drug-related emergency department episodes reported across the nation in the 1990s (Dawn Survey, 2002). Whether these trends will continue remains to be seen. (The statistics in this section are provided by surveys that are notorious for their methodological inadequacies, but likely reflect trends in drug use in the United States over the past 50 years.)

The approach to drug abuse taken in this book is an educational one. In order to understand and treat drug abuse, people need to be educated as to what drugs are and what the effects of drugs actually are. People should know under which circumstances drugs may be beneficial and under which they may be detrimental. The information given must have validity and must not be hypocritical. A person sipping on a martini cannot give a very convincing argument against marijuana use. Unfortunately, as just discussed, information alone will not necessarily stop, or even decrease, drug use. But it is hoped that individuals reading this book will adopt safer drug-taking practices, at the very least.

Summary and Overview

In summary, drug use is important to understand for three main reasons, two of which have been reviewed earlier. Recreational use and abuse of drugs are persistent phenomena that need to be understood. In addition, the use of drugs as treatments for psychiatric disorders has become extremely common, and this fact requires considerable emphasis in any serious book on psychopharmacology. The third reason also is critically important, and is directly related to the other two. Drugs are tools for unlocking the mysteries of the brain. Drugs have specific effects that allow them to interact with neural mechanisms, usually by altering the process of chemical transmission. Research with drugs has yielded tremendous benefits in terms of our understanding of the neural basis of normal and pathological behavior. By investigating both the neurochemical and behavioral effects of drugs, researchers have come to understand how particular neurotransmitter systems participate in the regulation of psychological processes. In that sense, the Psychopharmacology Revolution is critically intertwined with the Neuroscience Revolution, which has done much to change our perspective on the relation between brain and behavior over the last few decades. This book places emphasis on all three points, and is intended to provide the reader with an integrated view of the modern field of psychopharmacology.

Websites for Further Information

This National Clearinghouse for Alcohol and Drug Information website provides information on drug abuse prevention, treatment, education, research, survey databases, resources, and so on:

http://www.health.org

The Substance Abuse and Mental Health Services Administration website provides information from the National Household Survey on Drug Abuse:

http://www.samhsa.gov/index.aspx

Information from the Monitoring the Future Survey, which is an ongoing survey of the incidence of drug use, behaviors, attitudes, and values of American secondary school students, college students, and young adults:

http://monitoringthefuture.org

Information on D.A.R.E.—Drug Abuse Resistance Education:

http://www.dare-america.com/home/default.asp (proponent site for D.A.R.E.)

http://drcnet.org/DARE/index.html (site critical of D.A.R.E.)

Websites devoted to the topic of harm reduction as an approach to dealing with drug use and abuse:

http://www.lindesmith.org/homepage. cfm

http://www.harmreduction.org

General information sites on federal government drug policies:

http://www.druglibrary.org
http://www.whitehousedrugpolicy.gov

These are a sampling of the many websites that have sprung up that are critical of U.S. drug control policy, or provide libraries of information about recreational drugs:

http://www.november.org/index.html
http://www.ibiblio.org/warstop/ warstop.html
http://www.drugsense.org/cms/
http://stopthedrugwar.org/index.shtml
http://www.csdp.org
http://www.erowid.org/

Drug Classification and Behavioral Assessment

Classifying drugs is no easy task, because in many cases no sharp distinctions can be made among them. Drugs with almost identical molecular structures may induce entirely different effects, while other drugs whose molecular structures are quite different may induce almost identical effects (Barden & Mason, 1977; Weissman & Milne, 1979). Some drugs may have one effect at one dose and an entirely different effect at another. A drug may have multiple psychological effects in a certain dose range, and depending on the population taking it (or the persons prescribing it), some of these effects may be viewed as desirable in one person and undesirable in another. For example, certain marijuana-like substances may effectively reduce nausea in cancer patients undergoing chemotherapy but may lead to an undesirable clouding of consciousness. In other groups of individuals, these "side effects" are the effects desired. Therefore, it is not surprising that different textbooks may classify drugs in a number of different ways.

DRUG CLASSIFICATIONS BASED UPON BEHAVIORAL OR THERAPEUTIC ACTIONS

Despite some inherent problems with any classification system, it is common in psychopharmacology to describe a drug as belonging to a particular class or type based upon the psychological effect produced or the desired therapeutic action. There is no universal agreement on how to classify drugs, but Table 2.1 has an example of such a system, with some individual drugs listed. There are some advantages to using such a classification system. For instance, if a new drug is discovered, and it is said to have a profile of an "**anxiolytic**" (i.e., antianxiety agent) or a "minor **stimulant,**" this does convey some

TABLE 2.1   Drug Categories Related to Psychopharmacology
Major stimulants—amphetamine
Minor stimulants—caffeine
Antipsychotics—Thorazine
Antidepressants—Prozac
Anxiolytic—Valium
Sedative–hypnotics—alcohol
Opiates—morphine
Hallucinogens—LSD

meaning about the effects of the new drug. At the very least, it indicates that the new drug shares a profile of effects with other drugs that already belong to that class. Drugs that are classed as "major psychomotor stimulants" share a set of properties, including actions such as enhancing attention and increasing various types of motor activities. Drugs that are classed as **"antipsychotic"** blunt the florid symptoms of schizophrenia (e.g., hallucinations and delusions), and also are useful for treating mania. Nevertheless, there are limitations to this type of system. Many drugs that are classed as sedative–hypnotics induce stimulant-like effects or behavioral disinhibition at low doses (e.g., ethyl alcohol). In clinical practice, **"antidepressants"** are sometimes used to treat anxiety, while "anxiolytics" can be used to treat depression. Furthermore, in each therapeutic category, there are drugs that are labeled as "atypical" because they show an unusual preclinical or clinical profile; clozapine is considered an atypical antipsychotic, and buspirone is classed as an atypical anxiolytic. Finally, there are some drugs that defy categorization because they exert actions that cross several categories, but do not fit easily into any one category. For example, delta-9-tetrahydrocannabinol has some of the properties of a sedative–hypnotic, a stimulant, and a mild hallucinogen, but does not fit squarely into any of these classes. MDMA (Ecstasy) has some properties of stimulants and hallucinogens, but some researchers have argued that it should not be put in either category, and instead would merit membership in a newer category (entactogen). Given both the utility and the vagaries of such a classification system, it is perhaps best to recognize the usefulness of classifying drugs as belonging to particular categories based upon behavioral and therapeutic effects, while at the same time recognizing that the limitations of such categorization warrants considerable flexibility.

This discussion of classifying the behavioral and therapeutic effects of drugs raises the question of how such effects are measured. In the language of experimental design, control or drug treatments at various doses reflect levels of the independent variable (i.e., the variable being manipulated or controlled), while the response to that drug is a dependent variable (the variable being measured). Several fields, including clinical psychology, psychiatry, neurology, and experimental psychology and behavioral neuroscience, have contributed to the modern science of measuring drug effects in psychopharmacology. In humans, the therapeutic effects of drugs often are assessed by rating scales that attempt to measure the symptoms of a particular disorder; these scales were typically developed for diagnostic purposes but also are used for measuring the effects of drugs. For example, the Hamilton Depression Rating Scale or the Beck Depression Inventory can be used to assess the effects of antidepressant drugs, while

TABLE 2.2   An Example of Behavioral Tests in Animals That Are Used to Assess the Effects of Drugs

Behavioral Test	Drug Type	Drug Effect
Open Field Locomotion	Stimulants	Increase locomotor activity
Operant response rate	Stimulants	Increase rate on schedules of reinforcement generating low rates
Rotarod	Sedative–hypnotics	Induce ataxia or incoordination
Elevated plus maze	Anxiolytics	Increase entry to or time spent in open arms
Radial arm Maze; Morris Water maze	Cognitive enhancers	Enhance spatial working memory. Or reverse effect of a drug or lesion that impairs memory

the Hamilton Anxiety Scale is used to measure the anxiolytic effects of drugs. Similarly, the Brief Psychiatric Rating Scale and the Positive and Negative Syndrome Scale are used to measure the therapeutic effects of antipsychotic drugs. In addition to these clinical assessments, it should be recognized that much of psychopharmacology is experimental or preclinical in nature. Thus, there are a wide variety of animal tests that also are used to assess the effects of drugs (Table 2.2). These tests can be used to determine if a drug has a particular set of properties (e.g., the characteristics of a stimulant-locomotor activity), or if the drug has a likelihood of showing a particular side effect (e.g., ataxia or incoordination-rotarod). In addition, animal models are typically used in the process of drug development. For example, a test such as the elevated plus maze is one of the standard preclinical tests in rodents for assessing potential anxiolytic effects of a drug (Figure 2.1). Moreover, drugs often are assessed for abuse liability by tests of self-administration (operant conditioning experiments are performed to determine if a drug can act as a reinforcer for an operant response such as lever pressing).

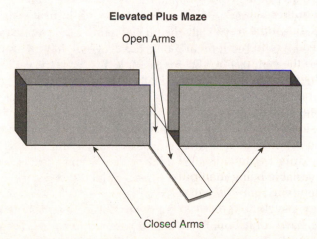

Elevated Plus Maze

Open Arms

Closed Arms

FIGURE 2.1 The elevated plus maze, which is a preclinical test of potential anxiolytic (i.e., antianxiety) effects in rodents. Rodents normally avoid open spaces, such as the open arms, and prefer to be in the closed arms, which have solid walls and are shaded. Thus, increases in the number of entries into or time spent in the open arms, as opposed to the closed arms, can be used to predict anxiolytic effects in humans. Several common anxiolytic drugs, such as Valium or Xanax, produce this effect.

DRUG CLASSIFICATION BASED UPON BASIC NEUROCHEMICAL ACTIONS

In addition to classifying drugs based upon their psychological effects, one can describe drugs in terms of their direct neurochemical actions. The ability of a drug to induce a behavioral effect is dependent upon its ability to alter the process of chemical transmission in the nervous system. As discussed in subsequent chapters, there are five basic stages of neurotransmission (synthesis, storage, release, postsynaptic action, and inactivation). In addition, there are numerous neurotransmitters and neuromodulators (e.g., signaling molecules such as gamma-aminobutyric acid (GABA), glutamate, dopamine, norepinephrine, serotonin, adenosine, and many more). Thus, the action of a drug can be described as the intersection of the transmission process being affected and the neurotransmitter/neuromodulator being affected. For example, a drug can be said to increase dopamine synthesis or block serotonin storage. Moreover, when combined with a general behavioral/therapeutic classification system like that described earlier, one can get a clearer picture of the overall effect of the drug than either system alone would yield. Some major psychomotor stimulants (e.g., amphetamine) act to stimulate the release of dopamine and norepinephrine. Virtually all antipsychotic drugs currently used block dopamine receptors, while the minor stimulant caffeine antagonizes adenosine receptors. The use of neuropharmacological actions to define the specific effects of a drug will be a common feature of the rest of this book.

DRUG NAMES AND MEDICAL USES OF DRUGS

A single drug has several official names (Nies, 2001). Initially, when a pharmaceutical company discovers or synthesizes a promising new drug, it is given a **code name,** generally consisting of two or more letters and a series of numbers (e.g., SCH 23390). Its **chemical name** provides a complete description of a particular molecule according to specific rules of organic chemistry. The **generic name** of the compound indicates its legal, official, or nonproprietary name, which is typically the official name cited in research reports on the drug. Once it has been approved for marketing, the drug will have a **brand** or **proprietary name,** given to it by its manufacturer. So, for example, Prozac is the well-recognized brand name for the generic fluoxetine, which originally was given the code name Lilly 110140, which appeared in the early research publications describing its characteristics. It's pretty obvious why its chemical name, 3-(p-trifluoromethylphenoxy)-N-methyl-3-phenylpropyline, isn't used very often. After 20 years, when the patent on a compound runs out, anybody can market it, so it may then have several other brand names. Drugs used for medical purposes often are also used for recreational purposes. When a drug is marketed illicitly or used recreationally, it may have a variety of "street" names. (For example, see the websites for street-drug slang terms at the end of this chapter.)

Because there may be a number of proprietary (brand) names for a single drug and because these may differ from country to country, the nonproprietary (generic) name for drugs will be used throughout this text. However, because most students reading this text are more likely to recognize various drugs by their brand names, along with their generic names, they will be referred to by their most common or initially used brand names the first time they are mentioned. Use of street names for drugs has generally been avoided because there are so many—as soon as one becomes popular, another is generated to take its place. For example, there are well over 100 different street names for heroin.

One of the most frequently used reference books that describes psychotropic drugs according to their medical uses is the *Physicians' Desk Reference* (PDR). Product descriptions in the PDR include lengthy explanations of the drugs' chemical structure, how they work, conditions for which they have been approved for use (but not necessarily those they may actually be used for), dosage, and administration. There are also warnings about possible adverse reactions or drug interactions, and indications as to whether a drug can be used in children, pregnant women, or nursing mothers. What it doesn't provide are drug prices and comparison information on which of several drugs in the same category may be most appropriate for a particular type of condition or set of symptoms.

The fact that a drug may have many uses is of particular concern to those in the area of drug therapeutics. When a drug has been shown to be reasonably safe and effective for some specific symptoms, it is approved for medical use by the Food and Drug Administration (FDA) and officially labeled (Kessler & Feiden, 1995). This labeling includes the information that appears both on the container of the drug and on the package insert. The FDA is legally responsible for ensuring that all statements made by the drug manufacturer in labeling the drug are backed by substantial evidence. The FDA has final approval over what the manufacturer may recommend the drug for and what it may say in its advertisements and marketing publications. The FDA also determines whether the drug must be obtained by prescription—generally the case with any new drug—or can be obtained over the counter without a prescription—which generally occurs after the drug has been used long enough and by enough people to determine that it has an acceptably low incidence of adverse reactions or significant side effects.

However, the FDA does not have any authority over the practice of medicine. There is no federal law prohibiting physicians from prescribing an approved drug for anything they choose, although some states place restrictions on what certain drugs can be prescribed for. As a result, many drugs that have been approved for specific symptoms or disorders are commonly prescribed for entirely different purposes (or unlabeled uses) than those stated by the manufacturer (Pugh & Pugh, 1987). For example, drugs approved for use in the treatment of cardiovascular disease (propranolol), high blood pressure (clonidine), nausea associated with cancer chemotherapy (metoclopramide), and depression and bed-wetting (imipramine) can also be found being prescribed for stage fright, morphine withdrawal, tardive dyskinesia (a side effect of antipsychotic drugs), and chronic pain, respectively. However, because a new approved use of a drug by the FDA can enhance its marketability, pharmaceutical companies will sometimes undergo the clinical trials to obtain approval for that use—oftentimes with a new proprietary name. So, for example, fluoxetine, which originally was approved for use as an antidepressant (as Prozac), has been approved for the use in premenstrual dysphoric disorder (as Serafem); bupropion, which originally was approved for use as an antidepressant (as Wellbutrin), has been approved for use in the treatment of tobacco addiction (as Zyban); and naltrexone, which was originally approved for use in the treatment of opiate addiction (as Trexan), has been approved for use in the treatment of alcoholism (as ReVia).

SCHEDULE-CONTROLLED DRUGS

One final classification system is provided by the U.S. government. Ever since the passage of the Harrison Narcotic Act of 1914, the federal government has classified psychoactive drugs for legal purposes. The most recent of such drug classification schemes came out of the Controlled Substances Act of 1970, which was designed by the government to improve the administration and regulation of manufacturing, distributing, and dispensing of potentially dangerous drugs. The present branch of the government responsible for this task is the Drug Enforcement Administration (DEA).

The drugs that come under the jurisdiction of the Controlled Substances Act are divided into five schedules and are referred to as **controlled substances**. Schedule I drugs are those that have no currently accepted medical use in treatment in the United States, are presumed to have a high potential for abuse, and lack accepted safety for use under medical supervision; such drugs can be used only for experimental research purposes. Schedule II drugs are those that have some currently accepted medical uses in the United States but have a high abuse potential. Schedule III, IV, and V drugs are those with current medical uses and successively lower abuse potentials than those of Schedules I and II. As one might expect, the penalties for nonprescription possession or sale of schedule-controlled drugs increase dramatically as one goes from Schedule V to Schedule I.

Table 2.3 provides some examples of different controlled substances according to schedule. Note that, in several cases, drugs are placed under different schedules, not so much because of differences in their mechanisms of action, but because of differences in pharmacokinetics. For example, the narcotic drugs heroin and morphine have the same action in the brain; they differ only in terms of their ability to penetrate the blood–brain barrier. The barbiturates secobarbital and phenobarbital both exert basically the same action in the brain, but again differ in how rapidly they penetrate the blood–brain barrier. Dronabinol (also known as delta-9-tetrahydrocannabinol) is the major psychoactive compound in marijuana; in its oral form, it is a Schedule III drug, but in its smokeable form (i.e., marijuana), it is a Schedule I drug. In its prescription formulation, gamma hydroxybutyrate (Xyrem) is a Schedule III drug used in the treatment of narcolepsy; in its nonprescription formulation (sometimes referred to as *GHB*), which is sometimes used as a *date rape* drug commonly combined with alcohol, it is a Schedule I drug. Placement in these schedules may also be dependent on what a drug is combined with (e.g., codeine with aspirin as opposed to codeine with Actifed) or the concentration of the drug (mg/ml); for example, opium-containing compounds can be placed in Schedules II–V depending on the concentration of opium in them.

The fact that small alterations in a drug molecule can produce minimal changes in its effects at one time led to considerable problems for the DEA, which is responsible for controlling illegal drugs. By slightly altering the structure of an already illegal drug, "underground chemists" attempted to produce new compounds—often referred to as **designer drugs**—with the same properties as the illegal drug. Until the new chemical structure was specifically designated by the DEA as illegal, its manufacture, sale, and use were legal. Most designer drugs have been analogues (i.e., drugs with similar structures) of amphetamine, fentanyl (a very potent synthetic narcotic), meperidine (a synthetic narcotic), or phencyclidine. Although these designer drugs gained the attention of the mass media, it appears that their production and use has declined significantly over the past several years. This decline has been attributed to reports of lethal and toxic reactions to some of these compounds (see the discussion of MPTP in Chapters 7 and 12), prosecution of the few individuals with the biochemical expertise and equipment necessary to develop them, and the passing of the Controlled Substance

TABLE 2.3   **Examples of Controlled Substances According to Schedule**

Schedule I
Bufotenine
Dimethyltryptamine
Heroin
Lysergic acid diethylamide—LSD
Marijuana
Mescaline
Psilocybin

Schedule II
Cocaine
Dextroamphetamine (Dexedrine)
Meperidine (Demerol)
Methadone (Dolophine)
Methylphenidate (Ritalin)
Morphine
Secobarbital (Seconal)

Schedule III
Buprenorphine (Buprenex, Subutex, Suboxone)
Dronabinol (Marinol)
Gamma hydroxybutyrate (Xyrem)
Phendimetrazine
Some codeine-containing compounds

Schedule IV
Alprazolam (Xanax)
Chloral hydrate
Chlordiazepoxide (Librium)
Diazepam (Valium)
Phenobarbital
Propoxyphene (Darvon)
Sibutramine (Meridia)

Schedule V
Some codeine-containing compounds
Some opium-containing compounds

Note: Common brand name is in parentheses.

Analogues Enforcement Act in 1986, which essentially treats any analogue of a controlled substance intended for human consumption as a Schedule I controlled substance (Frank Sapienza, DEA agent, 1988, personal communication).

Laypersons and the mass media often refer to drugs as *hard* or *soft*, although it is never clear what characteristics of drugs are being referred to when these terms are used. One might expect that the hard-drug category would correspond to Schedule I and II drugs, and soft drugs would correspond to legal drugs or Schedule IV and V drugs. However, if hard drugs are those with high abuse potential, or those that are relatively toxic to the body, or those that are likely to produce notable behavioral or emotional disturbances, as discussed in later chapters, alcohol and nicotine certainly fit this description. On the other hand, marijuana, a Schedule I drug, is often viewed as one of the soft drugs. Thus, describing drugs as hard or soft really does not provide one with any useful information about them. It should be made clear that all psychotropic drugs can be safe or harmful, depending on the circumstances in which they are used, how frequently they are used, or how much is used.

Websites for Further Information

The DEA's home page (focuses on controlled substances and federal drug enforcement):

> http://www.usdoj.gov/dea

The National Institute for Drug Abuse classification of abused drugs:

> http://www.nida.nih.gov/DrugPages/
> DrugsofAbuse.html

Listing and general information about FDA-approved drugs:

> http://www.fda.gov/cder/ob/default.htm
> http://www.fda.gov/cder/index.html

Dictionaries of street-drug slang terms:

> http://www.drugs.indiana.edu/
> drug-slang.aspx

Basic Principles
of Pharmacology

The psychological effects of a drug at any particular time depend on many factors, including the individual's set and setting, the particular way the drug changes activities in the central nervous system (CNS), the route of administration of the drug, the amount of drug administered, the frequency with which it is administered, and so on. There are several basic pharmacological principles that are involved in the action of psychotropic drugs. The next few chapters will briefly describe these principles and define many terms that will be used in subsequent chapters.

How does one define the word *drug*? This might appear to be a simple task, but in fact there is no commonly accepted definition of the word *drug*. The term originally referred to any substance used in chemistry or medical practice. Gradually, the term was restricted to any agent used in medicine or any ingredient in medicines. Today many people use the term as a synonym for a narcotic agent or an illicit substance. What is a drug then? In general, it is a chemical that affects one or more biological processes. However, not all chemicals that affect biological processes are considered drugs. Substances that are commonly used for nutritional purposes, such as salt, water, proteins, fats, carbohydrates, vitamins, and minerals, are not generally considered drugs, because they are necessary for carrying out the normal biological functions of the body. However, certain vitamins and minerals that might be found in our diet, if isolated and used in certain quantities, might also be thought of as drugs.

Recently, a related issue has come up regarding the status of "dietary supplements," which have developed into a multibillion dollar industry. Unlike food additives and drugs that are subjected to strict premarket tests for safety and effectiveness, because of the 1994 Dietary Supplement Health and Education Act, products labeled "dietary supplement" may enter the market untested, and the Food and Drug Administration (FDA) cannot restrict the use of such supplements unless substantial harm has been proven (Chang, 2000). One of the most popular of these "supplements" is St. John's wort, which has become phenomenally successful as an herbal antidepressant. Not only is there documented evidence for its effectiveness in the treatment of mild to moderate cases of depression, but there is also considerable evidence for its interacting with a variety of medications in adverse ways (Ernst, 1999). These properties indicate that, pharmacologically, one or more ingredients in St. John's wort would be considered a drug, but until there is legislation to change its status, the FDA cannot regulate it as a drug.

What about nicotine? Is it a drug? For decades, virtually all of the individuals working in the field of pharmacology and related disciplines have viewed nicotine as a drug, and for those trying to quit cigarettes, it seemed obvious that nicotine is an addictive drug. But in the mid-1990s, governmental hearings were held to determine whether scientific evidence supported these assumptions. The reason: If the FDA could prove that tobacco companies intended for cigarettes to provide nicotine to satisfy an addiction, the FDA would have the right to regulate cigarettes under the Federal Food, Drug, and Cosmetic Act, which considers a product to be a drug if the vendor intends it to be one (Kessler et al., 1996). However, as indicated in Chapter 1, in spite of the general acknowledgment by virtually everyone that the tobacco companies knew nicotine was addictive and that they manipulated the nicotine levels in cigarettes to enhance the tobacco users' "enjoyment," the U.S. Supreme Court eventually ruled against allowing the FDA to regulate tobacco products. This decision was made on the basis of political and legal considerations and not on the basis of pharmacological principles. A similar issue revolves around alcohol (ethanol). The manufacturers of alcoholic beverages (and perhaps their consumers) would prefer not to view alcohol as a drug. It certainly contains calories, but I doubt that it is consumed by humans for its nutritional value. Thus, ethanol should be considered a drug in that it affects the normal biological activities of the body.

Chemicals originating or produced within an organism that are used to carry out the normal biological functions in the body are not usually thought of as drugs. Such chemicals are referred to as *endogenous* substances, as opposed to drugs that are *exogenous* substances. However, biochemists and neuroscientists have isolated a variety of substances found to be important in the functions of the body, have extracted or synthesized them, and have administered them in purified form to reverse neurological deficits. The use of L-DOPA, a precursor of the neurotransmitter dopamine, for the treatment of Parkinson's disease is one example, and it is viewed as a drug. From a pharmacological perspective, it seems most appropriate to define a **drug** as a *nonfood, nonmechanical substance (usually a chemical substance) that exerts an effect upon a living system*.

BASIC CHEMICAL PRINCIPLES RELATED TO PSYCHOPHARMACOLOGY

In order to understand how drugs interact with living systems, it is important to review some of the basic chemical properties of living things. By far, the largest chemical constituent of animals is water. Water has such important chemical properties that it can be

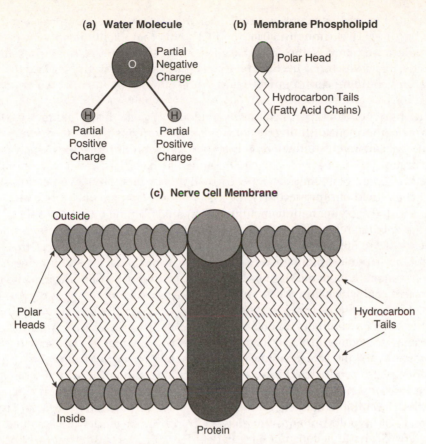

(a) Water Molecule

Partial Negative Charge

Partial Positive Charge

Partial Positive Charge

(b) Membrane Phospholipid

Polar Head

Hydrocarbon Tails (Fatty Acid Chains)

(c) Nerve Cell Membrane

Outside

Polar Heads

Hydrocarbon Tails

Inside

Protein

FIGURE 3.1   Water, phospholipds and membranes. **(a)** Chemical structure of the water molecule, showing the partial positive and negative charges that make water a polar substance. **(b)** Schematic drawing of a membrane phospholipid, showing the polar head and the hydrocarbon tails. **(c)** Schematic drawing of a nerve cell membrane, showing the phospholipid bilayer and a membrane-bound protein.

the subject of considerable focus; in a biochemistry class, one could spend several lectures just talking about water. The chemical structure of water leads to many of the chemical characteristics that are evident in living systems. In three dimensions, the water molecule (H_2O; see Figure 3.1) takes on a kind of V-shape, and there is an uneven distribution of charge: Though electrically neutral overall, the oxygen end of the molecule has a partial negative charge, while the two hydrogen ends have partial positive charges. Because of this, we say that the water molecule is polar. The polarity of the water molecule yields several interesting and important characteristics. Water molecules are attracted to each other very powerfully. The partial positive charge of the oxygen end of one molecule is attracted to the partial negative charge of the hydrogen end of another by a type of bond known as a hydrogen bond. This bonding results in the fluid characteristics of water; water tends to form beads or drops, in which the complex strings of water molecules are bound together with mutual attraction. In addition, water is an excellent solvent for other substances that are polar or ionic (i.e., charged molecules). Table salt, for example, readily dissolves in water. When immersed in water, the NaCl crystals dissociate into Na^+ and Cl^- ions that easily dissolve in the water medium. Because many of the salts that dissolve in sea water also are present in our body fluids, it is noteworthy to consider that life first evolved in the sea and that terrestrial creatures could be said to carry the sea inside of us, in the form of water and many dissolved ions.

In terms of how an organic chemist would view the chemistry of life, we could say that a large component of living systems is in the aqueous phase (i.e., water based). Substances that are readily attracted to water (i.e., hydrophilic molecules), such as ions or other polar molecules, dissolve easily in the aqueous phase. However, hydrophilic molecules are also lipophobic; they are repelled by lipids or fats. Thus, we need to consider the other chemical phase present in living systems—the organic phase. In chemistry, the term organic does not mean the same thing as organic farming or food products. Rather, this term refers to the chemistry of carbon-based substances. In living systems, the major constituents of the organic phase are hydrocarbons, which are substances that contain carbon and hydrogen bound together covalently. Fats or lipids have a high degree of hydrocarbon content. For example, cholesterol is made up mostly of hydrogen and carbon, and fatty acid chains are strings of hydrocarbons. As is evident to anyone who has ever made chicken soup, the aqueous and organic phases do not mix well. If you put chicken into boiling water, eventually something floats to the top—it is lipid from the chicken that has separated out, which does not dissolve readily in water. If you were to add table salt to the chicken soup, where would the Na^+ and Cl^- ions go? Most would dissolve in the aqueous phase (water) and few would dissolve in the fat. However, the opposite would be true of any flavorant molecules in the chicken that had a high hydrocarbon content; these are lipid-soluble and would be dissolved in the fatty (organic) layer. The immiscibility of organic and aqueous phases also should be evident to anyone who has ever had a frozen fuel line in his or her car. Petroleum products, such as gasoline, have a very high hydrocarbon content (octane is an eight-chain hydrocarbon) and do not mix well with water (which can then freeze when it is cold, blocking the fuel line).

Other than cholesterol and triglycerides (fats with three fatty acid chains), some very important fats that we need to consider for understanding drug distribution and drug action are membrane phospholipids. Phospholipids are a type of diglyceride; they have a polar head and two fatty acid hydrocarbon tails (Figure 3.1). Thus, the polar head, which has ionic charges and polar components, is attracted to water, while the hydrocarbon tails are repelled by water, and attracted to each other as well as other hydrocarbon chains. These characteristics lead to important features of the chemical composition of cell membranes, including nerve cell membranes. As shown in Figure 3.1, nerve cell membranes are composed of a phospholipid bilayer (as are the membranes of other cells). The polar heads point inward and outward toward the largely aqueous environments inside and outside of the cell, while the fatty acid tails from each layer point toward the center of the membrane. Of course, there are other substances in the membrane too. There are proteins that serve various functions (as receptors, channels, enzymes, and transporters) that will be discussed in subsequent chapters, because they are important substrates for drug action. Nevertheless, the phospholipid bilayer itself gives cell membranes an important characteristic that exerts a powerful influence over brain chemistry and drug distribution: This lipid bilayer provides a barrier to the movement of any polar and charged substances.

Putting all this together helps us understand the process of drug distribution in living organisms. Our bodies are made up of various compartments (e.g., organs, systems), with varying degrees of water, lipid, and other substances. We have blood, lymph, cerebrospinal fluid, and other fluids that are mostly water. On the other hand, we also have deposits of lipid in various places in our bodies (e.g., depot fat from adipose tissue). Any drug that is highly lipid-soluble would easily be stored in adipose tissue, and if it is not metabolized, it could stay there for a considerable time. Furthermore, the barriers between different compartments are cells, and as we saw earlier, the cell membrane, which is made up mostly of a lipid bilayer, would present a barrier to the diffusion of any substance that is too water-soluble (i.e., lipophobic), and is not transported across the membrane by proteins. Thus, the stomach and intestines are lined with cells, and if a pill is introduced into the body, this would represent the first barrier to entry into systemic circulation. There are additional barriers provided by the entry into the circulatory system, and the metabolic enzymes in the liver. Finally, most drugs studied in psychopharmacology must pass into the brain. An additional and very significant barrier is present here—it is known as the blood–brain barrier (BBB). The BBB is made up of tight junctions between the endothelial cells that compose the outer lining of the blood vessels (see discussion later). This barrier can provide a significant resistance to the entry of drugs and other substances into the brain, and subtle alterations in the chemical structure of drugs can yield substantial differences in passage across the brain–blood barrier. For example, scopolamine and atropine are anticholinergic drugs (i.e., they block a type of acetylcholine receptor known as the muscarinic receptor) and readily penetrate into the brain to produce therapeutic effects (antiparkinsonian effects) or other actions (hallucinations at high doses). However, there are two close structural analogs of these drugs, known as methylscopolamine and methylatropine, respectively, which have an additional positive charge that renders them much more water-soluble and much less likely to penetrate into the brain. Of course, if a therapeutic target is in the brain, such a drug would not be useful. Nevertheless, such compounds are extremely useful for studying the peripheral effects of drugs, and also for providing an important experimental control. If one wanted to determine which effects of scopolamine were brain-related and which were peripheral in origin, one could compare the effects of scopolamine with those of methylscopolamine.

Interesting examples of the role of water versus lipid solubility in drug distribution are provided by two very common drugs—ethyl alcohol (ethanol) and Δ-9 THC, which is an active ingredient in marijuana. Ethanol is an example of a substance that is relatively soluble in both water and lipid. One end of the molecule is a hydrocarbon, while the other end has oxygen and hydrogen, and interacts easily with water. If you have ever made a tequila sunrise, you know that ethanol dissolves in water; orange juice is mostly water, and the alcohol in the tequila dissolves readily in the aqueous mixture. However, you may also see evidence that ethanol dissolves in organic solvents the next time you go to a gas station. In the United States, much of the gasoline is sold in a mixture that includes up to 10% ethanol. In your body, these properties mean that ethanol easily passes from the stomach into widespread circulation, easily dissolves in the blood, and easily passes into the brain. Also, ethanol is metabolized by enzymes at a rate of about 1 ounce/hr, and the metabolites (the breakdown products acetaldehyde and acetate) are also water-soluble and are removed in the urine. These properties of ethanol can be contrasted with those of Δ-9 THC, which is mostly hydrocarbon and is therefore highly lipid-soluble. THC is rapidly absorbed when smoked and easily passes through the BBB. However, unlike ethanol, THC is not rapidly metabolized, and is not very water-soluble, so it deposits itself in adipose tissue for a very long time, perhaps several weeks. There are many other examples of the importance of water versus lipid solubility for drug distribution and action. For example, the differences in onset, intensity, and duration of the three analgesics morphine, meperidine (Demerol), and fentanyl (Sublimaze) are largely due to differences in their lipid solubility (van den Hoogen & Colpaert, 1987); that is, morphine's lower lipid solubility results in a slower onset of analgesia and less intensity, but a longer duration of action than fentanyl.

To summarize, in order for a drug to exert any effects on an organism, it must get to its sites of action in the nervous system. Getting the drug to these sites typically requires passage through many barriers and involves traveling through many tissues. Along the way, the drug may interact with other chemicals in the body that prevent it from getting there at all. In many cases, the effects of a particular drug on an organism depend heavily on the rate of accumulation and the concentration of the drug at its sites of action and the duration of contact at those sites. These are a function not only of the amount of drug administered but also of its **pharmacokinetics.** This term refers to the dynamic processes involved in the movement of drugs within biological systems with respect to the drug's absorption, distribution, binding or localization in tissues, metabolic alterations, and excretion from the body (see Wilkinson [2001] for a complete discussion of this area). In contrast, **pharmacodynamics** refers to the biochemical and physiological effects of drugs and their mechanisms of action (Ross & Kenakin, 2001). Chapters 4 and 5 will have a thorough discussion of the pharmacodynamics of drug action, but several sections of this chapter are intended to discuss pharmacokinetics. Obviously, the chemical composition of the drug is an important factor related to pharmacokinetics, but other factors, including route of administration, metabolism, passage through the BBB, transport and physiological processes related to excretion, also are very important (see the following pages).

ROUTES OF ADMINISTRATION

The most common route of drug administration is through the mouth (**per os** or PO) so that the drug is absorbed in various parts of the gastrointestinal (GI) tract. Rectal administration (through the rectal mucosa) may serve as an alternative *enteral* (within the intestine) route for drugs destroyed in the stomach or small intestine. The PO route is generally the safest, cheapest, and most convenient way of administering drugs. However, several factors can influence the absorption of drugs from the GI tract, which can greatly alter the rate of drug accumulation, its concentration, and its duration at the site(s) of action. Most drugs are thought to penetrate the GI mucosa by a process of passive diffusion, which in turn is limited mostly by their lipid solubility. Many drugs are weak bases (alkaloids) or weak acids, and this alkalinity or acidity often results in their being *ionized* (a state in which an atom or a molecule has a net electrical charge). Because proteins embedded in these membranes have a mixture of positive and negative charges that tend to repel charged particles, such ionization reduces their solubility in cellular membranes. Therefore, to facilitate their absorption, such drugs are commonly administered in the form of a *salt*, a compound formed by ionic bond between a negative ion (*anion*) and a positive ion (*cation*). However, because the components of a salt dissociate in a solution, the drug may exist as both the nonionized and ionized species. Because the nonionized form is more lipid-soluble than the ionized form, the proportion of nonionized to ionized drug molecules present in a given area is important for drug absorption.

The pH of the local area determines the ratio of ionized to nonionized drug in that area. The pH value represents the negative log of the hydrogen ion concentration. Solutions with a pH of 7.0 are neutral; those with a pH of less than 7.0 are acid; and those with a pH of greater than 7.0 are basic. Weak acids, like aspirin, are less ionized in an acid medium and are therefore more lipid-soluble through the stomach, with a pH of less than 3.0. Alkaloids like heroin, morphine, and cocaine are poorly absorbed from the stomach. On the other hand, further down the GI tract, in the small intestine, where the contents are nearly neutral or slightly alkaline, the environment favors the absorption of weak bases. However, local pH is only one factor influencing drug absorption. This explains why the greater surface area of the small intestine, combined with a longer duration of drug contact, favors drug absorption there. This is the reason why people get intoxicated faster with carbonated alcoholic drinks; the carbonation forces the alcohol quickly out of the stomach and into the small intestine, where it is absorbed more rapidly.

In contrast to the slower absorption after oral administration, the introduction of a drug directly into the blood, most commonly done through **intravenous (IV) injection,** results in rapid onset of drug action and relatively intense effects. For example, the time it takes a drug to circulate between the vein of the forearm and the brain is less than 15 seconds. An amount of drug (e.g., heroin) that may exert minimal effects when administered PO may be extremely toxic when administered intravenously. Although fine adjustments in drug dosage are possible with the IV route (important in general anesthesia), if overdosage does occur, little can be done about it, unless a specific antagonist for the drug is readily available. Drugs injected intravenously must also be in solution or microsuspension and must have an aqueous vehicle. For example, injecting illicit drugs such as heroin or cocaine that are diluted with talc, which does not dissolve in water, may eventually clog the capillaries in organs with high blood flow—for instance, the lungs, kidneys, and brain—and cause organ failure. Repeated injections can lead to clot formation, vessel irritation, or vessel collapse. Finally, there is a high incidence of allergic reaction, pronounced cardiovascular action, and side effects with this route.

In addition to the PO and IV routes, there are several alternative ways of determining and controlling the intensity and duration of drug action. Because of the relatively good blood supply surrounding muscles, **intramuscular (IM) injection** generally results in a more rapid absorption than does the PO route. Drugs dissolved in an aqueous vehicle are more rapidly absorbed through the IM route than when dissolved or suspended in oil. Because the lining of the inside of the lungs provides a large surface area in proximity to many blood vessels, **drug inhalation** leads to rapid onset of drug action and intense effects. This route eliminates drug loss through first-pass metabolism by the liver (discussed shortly). However, irritants or oils can cause pneumonia, and long-term consequences, such as cancer associated with cigarette smoking, often occur with this route.

The injection of a drug underneath the skin into the tissue between the skin and muscle (i.e., into the body fat) is referred to as **subcutaneous (SC) drug injection.**

Because of the relatively poor blood supply in fatty tissue, this method can be used with nonirritating substances to produce fairly slow and even absorption. The rate of absorption can be controlled through the form of the drug. For instance, it can be in aqueous solution, promoting fast absorption; in suspension, promoting somewhat slower absorption; or in solid form, such as a pellet, allowing for very slow absorption.

Sublingual or **buccal administration** (through the oral mucosa under the tongue or between the cheek and gum) may be used with drugs that are destroyed in the stomach or intestines, such as nitroglycerin and nicotine. Other, but rarely used, routes of administration are **intra-arterial administration** (generally very hazardous because the drug is so concentrated); bone marrow administration (e.g., used in an infant, or when the veins are collapsed); rubbing drugs over a large surface area of the skin (although normal skin is an effective barrier to drug absorption); application of drugs to the mucous membranes of the nose (**intranasal administration**), vagina, or urethra; and administration through the eye. Although rarely used in humans, injection of drugs into the abdominal cavity (peritoneum), called **intraperitoneal injection,** is commonly used with small animals such as mice and rats. Absorption by this route is somewhat faster and more uniform than with oral administration, and the drug is not affected by enzymes in the stomach or intestines. The routes of administration listed earlier all involve systemic administration (i.e., allowing for general distribution in the body), but there are other routes of administration that deliver drugs directly into the nervous system. **Intrathecal administration,** or injection of the drug into the subdural spaces of the spinal cord (e.g., spinal anesthesia), and **intracerebroventricular injection,** or injection into the ventricular spaces of the brain, may be used to bypass the BBB and directly administer the drug into nervous system tissue. In addition, **intracranial administration** involves direct infusion of a drug into a discrete brain area. This is often done in animal research to localize the brain area responsible for a drug effect, and sometimes is done in human research as well.

The increasing awareness that drug-release patterns (continuous vs. pulsatile) significantly affect therapeutic responses has led to research aimed at creating new drug delivery systems (Langer, 1990). Several experimental approaches have been developed that facilitate a drug's ability to cross the BBB—for example, by rendering it more lipid-soluble or coupling it to a molecule that has a specific transport mechanism. Controlled-release systems that are even better than older *sustained-release* or *slow-release* preparations in maintaining drug plasma levels in the desired therapeutic range have been developed. In addition, drugs can be administered as *pro-drugs*; in this case, the active compound is covalently bound to another chemical structure and is relatively inert when combined with the other substituent, but after administration the active compound is then gradually liberated by spontaneous or enzymatic chemical reactions (Müller, 2009).

Although the skin is often considered a barrier to all agents, including drugs, several transdermal delivery systems have been developed to allow clinically relevant doses of drugs to penetrate the skin—for example, scopolamine-containing patches to prevent nausea associated with motion sickness and nicotine-containing patches to alleviate nicotine withdrawal. Transdermal drug delivery is a useful alternative to conventional routes of administration because it avoids degradation in the GI tract and first-pass metabolism (discussed shortly), allows steady or time varying controlled delivery, and improves patient compliance. However, very few drugs, particularly charged or large molecules such as peptides, can be administered transdermally due to the low permeability of the skin. Chemical and physical means to promote transdermal transport have been explored to expand the range of drugs that can be delivered in this fashion.

IMPORTANCE OF THE BLOOD–BRAIN BARRIER IN PSYCHOPHARMACOLOGY

Considering the fact that the brain comprises only about 2% of the body's entire mass but receives approximately 20% of the blood flow from the heart, we would expect a relatively large amount of a drug to enter the brain. However, the brain has evolved a way of preventing most nonnutritive substances from entering it and affecting nervous tissue. As discussed earlier, the BBB limits entry of substances into the brain and is a vital source of stability, as well as a defense. For example, after a meal, blood concentrations of numerous chemicals can rise sharply and could be very disruptive of brain functions if it were not for the BBB, which protects the brain against such fluctuations. The rate of entry of potentially abusable drugs into the brain, which can affect their rate of receptor occupancy, plays a significant role in their abuse/dependence liability; the faster the drug penetrates the BBB, the greater the likelihood of its being abused and producing dependence (Hatsukami & Fischman, 1996).

The BBB is actually a feature of the physical structure of the capillaries supplying blood to brain tissue. It is the peculiar characteristics of the capillary *endothelial cells* that constitute the primary barrier to drugs and other chemicals that are potentially toxic to the brain. Unlike the endothelial cells of the capillaries elsewhere in the body, the endothelial cells lining the vascular wall of brain capillaries are tightly linked with junctional complexes that eliminate gaps or spaces between cells and prevent any free diffusion of blood-borne substances into the brain extracellular space (Drewes, 1999). Also, ordinary endothelial cells lining the capillaries in the body have apertures, like small pores, through which drug molecules can pass. Brain capillaries have very few of these apertures. In addition, each brain capillary is typically in contact with long processes (extensions) of several glial (non-neural) cells known as *astrocytes*. There is a lipid sheath made up of extensions of "glial feet" from nearby astrocytes that surrounds the brain capillaries.

Endothelial cells selectively transport nutrients into the brain by way of several carrier-mediated or active transport systems. *Active transport systems* are systems in which ions or molecules are transported by proteins that expend energy in order to pump the substance across a membrane. Apparently, these active transport systems have evolved in such a way that nutritive but nonlipid-soluble substances, such as glucose, vitamins, and minerals, can get into the brain. There are also *carrier-mediated transport system* that can transport substances across biological membranes. In order for a drug (administered by any route other than directly into the brain) to have access to CNS neurons, it must be (a) lipid-soluble to some degree or (b) compatible with one of the several carrier-mediated or active transport systems developed in the capillary and astrocyte cells (Pardridge, 1999).

The BBB is not completely impermeable to chemicals that do not possess the characteristics just described. The capillaries atop the brain stem where the vomiting center is located are permeable to chemicals because the neurons there must monitor the blood for deadly poisons, detection of which induces vomiting. Also, the BBB may temporarily break down as a result of injury (e.g., a blow to the head or a stroke) or illness (e.g., meningitis), thus allowing chemicals to penetrate it. Such penetrability could be beneficial or detrimental to the person, depending on whether a specific chemical is wanted in the brain or not.

DOSE–RESPONSE RELATIONSHIPS

From the previous discussion, we learned that a drug's actions depend on the amount of drug available, which, in turn, is dependent on the dose of drug given (Ross & Kenakin, 2001). Other than the chemical structure and basic neurochemical effect of the drug itself, the dose administered is the single most important variable to consider when considering the effect of a drug. The usual way of discussing a drug's effects is in terms of the **dose–response function,** which expresses the relationship between the dose administered and the response observed. Dose–response functions are determined by taking groups of individual subjects (humans or animals), which represent a certain population that one is interested in, administering different doses of the drug being studied, waiting for a sufficient length of time for the drug to act, and assessing the degree of effect or the number of individuals displaying a specified effect of the drug.

For purposes of comparison, one group or condition involves the administration of a substance without any physiological effects, called a **placebo,** instead of the drug, because many individuals display physical or psychological symptoms if they expect to receive a drug (Rudorfer, 1993). In animals, a control condition generally consists of a **vehicle** solution, which most commonly is the solution that the drug itself is dissolved in (e.g., saline, or some other solution that is optimal for dissolving the drug). In some cases—for instance, with humans who may be knowledgeable about some of the characteristics of a drug they are reportedly taking—it is advisable to administer an **active placebo.** This is a substance that mimics some of the noticeable physiological characteristics of the drug being evaluated but without the effects on the brain that the researcher is interested in. For example, if the researcher wanted to evaluate the clinical *efficacy* of a potential antidepressant drug with sedative properties, he or she could compare its efficacy with that of an antihistamine that also has sedative effects but has no efficacy in reducing depression. As a final control measure, a **double-blind procedure** is used, whereby neither the subject nor the person administering the preparation knows whether it is a drug or a placebo.

Though proper experimental drug protocols require the use of a control condition such as the placebo, in clinical trials in which a drug is being evaluated for its effectiveness in relieving the symptoms of a particular disorder, the use of a placebo may be unethical or impractical. For example, if a drug is being evaluated for its antidepressant properties, it may be unethical to give depressed patients a placebo when there are drugs currently in use that have a 50% to 60% effectiveness rate. If these patients do not show symptom remission and they attempt or commit suicide or feel even more hopeless than they did before the treatment, the researchers might be held morally, if not legally, responsible. Fortunately, there is little, if any, evidence that the use of placebo control groups in psychiatric drug research is associated with an increased risk of harm (Leber, 2000). It is also understandable why some patients are reluctant to participate in such a trial when they know they might be part of a control group that receives an inactive substance. Thus, it may be necessary for those who are placed in a control group to receive a substance that has a medically accepted level of effectiveness. The effectiveness of the experimental drug would then be compared with that of the control drug. Unfortunately, this procedure makes it more difficult to establish the experimental drug's true level of effectiveness, because it is often easier to obtain results indicating that there is no difference between two treatments when they are in fact different, than it is to demonstrate that they are different. (See Leber [2000] and Miller [2000] for a more complete discussion of this issue.)

In considering the overall information to be gained from an analysis of dose–response relationships, we must introduce two important concepts, efficacy and potency. **Efficacy** refers to the magnitude of the effect of a drug at the system or organism level; typically, it is expressed in terms of the maximal effect produced by the drug. Perhaps the most commonly used example is the therapeutic efficacy of a drug, which refers specifically to the magnitude of the therapeutic effect, but the term efficacy can also be used to describe effects of drugs that are not necessarily therapeutic. Efficacy can vary greatly from drug to drug. Also, one should be cautious when using this term at different levels of analysis. Sometimes the term is also used to describe the basic effect of a neurotransmitter or drug at the receptor level. Such a usage can be confusing, because some drugs have efficacy at the systems or behavioral level (because they induce an effect), but not as a result of binding to a receptor. For that reason it is probably best to use a term such as *intrinsic biological activity* or *signal transduction* when defining the effects at the cellular level that occur directly as a result of receptor binding, and use the term *efficacy* to describe the magnitude of any effect seen at the systems or organism level. (Chapter 5 will discuss receptor binding, intrinsic activity and signal transduction in detail.)

The **potency** of a drug refers specifically to the dose at which the effect occurs. The concept of potency gets at the question of *how much drug* is needed to produce an effect; a drug that is highly potent produces effects at very low doses, while a drug that is not very potent must be administered at relatively high doses to produce an effect. LSD can produce hallucinations at microgram doses, which makes it a very potent drug. Drugs within a given class often vary greatly in terms of their potency, even if they have similar efficacy. The dopamine antagonist haloperidol can yield an antipsychotic effect at doses as low as 5 mg, while other antipsychotics such as chlorpromazine and clozapine require several hundred milligrams. Potency is usually defined by the **ED50** (effective dose 50), that is, the dose that produces an effect that is 50% of the maximal effect. Potency is inversely related to the ED50; a drug with a lower ED50 value is more potent than a drug with a high ED50. As we shall see later, information about potency and efficacy can be determined from an analysis of dose–response curves.

In the language of experimental design, the dose of a drug is an independent variable (the variable being manipulated or controlled), while the response is a dependent variable (the variable being measured). How are responses measured in psychopharmacology? In some cases, they are expressed directly in terms of the units that are appropriate for the behavioral measure being used (see Chapter 2). In other words, the response can be expressed in locomotor counts, or operant response rate, or a score on a rating scale for depression or anxiety. However, responses also can be expressed in terms of the percentage of subjects that show a particular effect. This is common in clinical research, in which there is a specific target endpoint, and criteria are established to determine if a drug produced a particular effect in an individual or not. In this sense, one can state that a drug produced a therapeutic effect in 60–70% of the people being tested, which may be an improvement over the 30–50% of people who improve under the control condition. In either case, whether we are talking about direct measurement or percentage of subjects, responses are expressed on the *y*-axis of a dose–response curve, which is the convention for dependent variables. The dose of the drug is therefore expressed on the *x*-axis of the dose–response curve.

Although there are several types of dose–response relationships that can be observed (discussed later), an example of a typical dose–response curve is shown in Figure 3.2. The shape of this function is said to be sigmoidal (S-shaped) or hyperbolic in nature. Generally speaking, as dose gets higher, response gets higher, up to a point. There is a linear portion of the dose–response curve, but then, as higher doses are reached, the effect begins to reach an asymptote as maximal levels of the response are seen. Measures of efficacy and potency can be extracted from the dose–response curve. As seen in Figure 3.2, the efficacy of the drug effect is shown in *y*-axis units. In contrast, a measure of potency such as the ED50 is expressed in *x*-axis units (i.e., dose units). Also, an examination of the dose–response function on this graph is useful for reinforcing what was said earlier about the ED50 and potency. If a drug is highly potent, it has a low ED50 value, because the effect is produced at relatively low doses, while a less potent drug has a high ED50 value because a higher dose is required to produce effects.

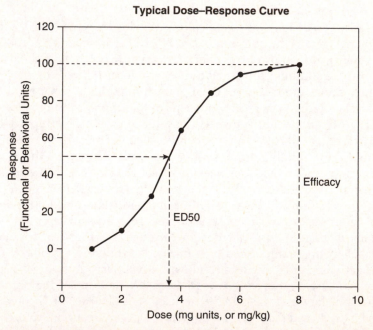

FIGURE 3.2 Idealized dose–response curve showing how efficacy and potency (as measured by the ED50) are determined. Typically, these parameters of the dose–response function are empirically determined by curve-fitting programs.

The dose–response function can be used to illustrate differences in potency and efficacy across drugs. Figure 3.3 depicts the dose–response functions for three analgesic drugs. The differences depicted reflect clear differences in efficacy and potency. Note that the doses of heroin needed to achieve analgesia are smaller than the doses of morphine needed to induce equivalent degrees of analgesia, which, in turn, are smaller than the doses of aspirin needed. Based upon these observations, heroin is considered to be the most potent of the three drugs in inducing analgesia. Moreover, heroin and morphine are depicted as being comparable in efficacy, while aspirin has a lower efficacy. Thus, aspirin is the drug that has both the lowest potency and the lowest efficacy in this example.

Let us look at some additional typical dose–response functions, shown in Figure 3.4, and discuss their various attributes. In this case, three different effects (desired effect, side effect, and lethal effect) for the same drug are depicted. First, note that there are

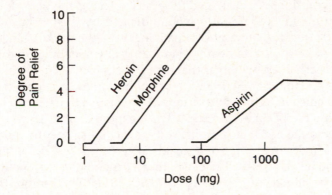

FIGURE 3.3 Dose–response relationships for aspirin, morphine, and heroin with respect to their relative potencies in reducing moderately severe pain, with 0 indicating no pain relief and 10 indicating complete absence of pain.

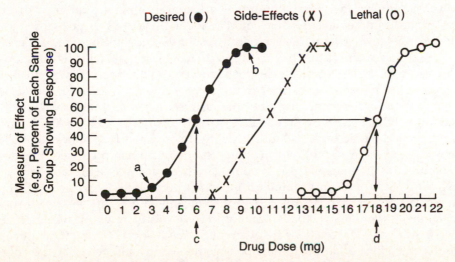

FIGURE 3.4 Stylized dose–response functions depicting (*a*) the threshold dose, (*b*) maximal (desired) response, (*c*) the ED50 of the drug, and (*d*) the LD50 of the drug.

some doses that do not induce any noticeable effects. The arrow at point *a* indicates the threshold dose (or minimally effective dose), which is the dose just large enough to produce a detectable change in the response. The arrow at point *b* indicates the maximum (or maximal) response, which is the greatest degree of a given response that can be achieved with that drug. The maximal response is not necessarily produced by the largest effective dose of a drug, because at higher doses some agents (e.g., nicotine) antagonize the response brought about at lower doses, and some agents (e.g., amphetamine) induce effects that may compete with, interfere with, or suppress the behavior noted at lower doses. The arrow at point *c* depicts the ED50. At this point it should be mentioned that because drugs are often used in different therapeutic contexts, a drug may have several ED50s. For instance, a barbiturate may have one ED50 for its anti-anxiety effects, another for its sleep-inducing effects, and yet another for its anesthetic actions. Moreover, all drugs can have lethal consequences, and clearly there is a relationship between the dose of a drug and its lethality. Just as the ED50 for a drug can be specified, so can the **LD50** (lethal dose 50, indicated by the arrow at point *d* in the figure). The LD50 is the dose that causes death in 50% of the population; essentially, it is the ED50 when the response is death. Therapeutically speaking, one hopes that the LD50 for a drug is considerably larger than its ED50. In fact, a drug's relative margin of safety, called the **therapeutic index** (not to be confused with a drug's therapeutic window), is often specified in terms of the drug's LD50 relative to its ED50. It is determined by simply dividing the LD50 by the ED50. For the hypothetical drug in Figure 3.4, the ED50 is 6 units and the LD50 is 18 units, so the drug's therapeutic index is 3. A drug with a therapeutic index of around 100—that is, where the LD50 is 100 times larger than the ED50—is generally considered safe, whereas a drug with a therapeutic index under 10 is generally considered quite hazardous. Unfortunately, though, the therapeutic index is a rough measure of a drug's potential hazards, because many drugs have side effects, some of which may be very disabling, which can occur at doses much lower than the LD50. Also, one drug may have a considerably higher therapeutic index than another drug, but may have certain properties that increase the likelihood of the individual self-administering lethal amounts. For example, a person taking a drug that induces euphoria or mental confusion could accidentally take too large a dose.

Figure 3.5 shows several idealized dose–response functions for some of the effects of the drug *d*-amphetamine that have occurred in laboratory rats. This figure shows the complex nature of the various dose–response curves and illustrates how some of them appear to deviate markedly from the typical curves shown earlier. In Figure 3.5(a), we can see that as the dose of amphetamine administered increases, the percentage of time that the rats exhibit stereotypy (a repetitive, ritualistic, or compulsive set of behaviors, such as moving the head back and forth repetitively or gnawing at nonexistent objects) also increases. In Figure 3.5(b), which expresses the relationship between the dose of amphetamine and the generalized locomotor activity of rats, we see that activity tends to increase with increases in amphetamine dose up to a point. With larger doses of amphetamine, activity appears to be less and less apparent, and with a sufficiently large dose of amphetamine, activity may actually occur at lower levels than with no drug at all (depicted as 0 mg/kg). Such functions are often called *biphasic* or *curvilinear*. In Figure 3.5(c), we see that the effect of amphetamine on schedule-controlled behavior (i.e., operant responses whose rate of occurrence is determined by the schedule of reinforcement) is quite complex. The effect depends on the dose of amphetamine and the normal rate of

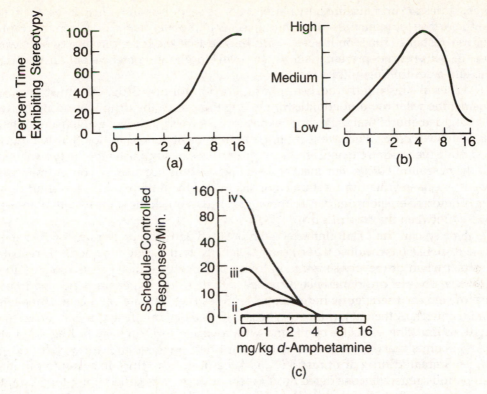

FIGURE 3.5 Various relationships between the dose of *d*-amphetamine and its behavioral effects in rats.

response without the drug (Seiden & Dykstra, 1977). That is, responses that occur at a fairly high rate to begin with become relatively less frequent with increasingly larger doses of amphetamine, whereas responses that occur somewhat infrequently become relatively more frequent with low-to-moderate doses of amphetamine, and then decrease with high doses of amphetamine (this is known as *rate dependency*, and is a classic feature of the behavioral effects of many stimulants; see the chapter on psychomotor stimulants, Chapter 7). In Figure 3.5(c), condition *i* might occur if there were no reinforcement provided; condition *ii* might occur if responses were only reinforced if the animal spaced its responses with some minimum interval (e.g., 10 seconds) between them; condition *iii* might occur if responses were reinforced after variable periods of time had elapsed; and condition *iv* might occur if responses were reinforced after a specified number of responses had occurred. In each of these cases, the direction of amphetamine's effect at each dose—that is, whether there is a relative increase or decrease in the response frequency—depends on the normal rate of responding that occurs without the drug.

As was the case with amphetamine that was described in Figure 3.5(b), a number of drugs in psychopharmacology can have biphasic effects. For example, a sedative–hypnotic drug such as ethanol can show a biphasic effect on measures such as locomotor activity. Ethanol can stimulate locomotion at relatively low doses, but as higher doses are administered, less locomotion is seen. At still higher doses, there can be little or no locomotion, because the subject is immobile, ataxic, or asleep. If a biphasic dose–response function is seen, it can be said that there are actually two different dose–response curves present, each with its own efficacy and potency (i.e., an ascending limb and a descending limb).

When discussing the dose–response function for any drug, one must take into consideration the route of administration, the time since the drug was administered, and the number and spacing of drug exposures. As we saw earlier, a given amount of a drug can have very different effects, in terms of intensity and duration, when administered orally versus intravenously. Once a drug has been administered, the type of effect and the magnitude of a given effect will vary across time because the concentration of a drug is rarely sufficient to exert much of an effect if the time period is too short or too long. Thus time–response curves are often graphed in much the same way that dose–response functions are graphed.

Finally, if a drug is administered on more than one occasion, a number of changes in the response (sometimes called *neuroadaptations*) to the drug may occur. If repeated administration of the drug results in lower potency or efficacy, it is referred to as **tolerance.** Thus, if drug tolerance develops, a higher dose is generally needed to produce the effect. However, under some conditions, the opposite can occur. If repeated administration of the drug leads to increases in potency or efficacy, it is referred to as **sensitization.** This effect can be found with a variety of drugs, including amphetamine, cocaine, marijuana, antipsychotics, antidepressants, and antianxiety drugs. Because repeated drug administration is a feature of the chronic administration of therapeutic drugs, and also is a critical aspect of drug abuse, these long-term adaptations to drug effects are an important topic in psychopharmacology and will be discussed in subsequent chapters. Moreover, it should be recognized that tolerance and sensitization are influenced by psychological factors; for example, there are examples in the literature of environmentally specific tolerance and sensitization, which indicate that conditioning mechanisms also are involved. One of the motor responses to antipsychotic drugs (the catalepsy response) shows environmentally specific sensitization (Amtage & Schimdt, 2009).

DRUG METABOLISM AND EXCRETION

Once a drug has been introduced into the body, it generally undergoes several chemical changes before it is eliminated from the body. The term **metabolism** (also known as **biotransformation**) refers to any process resulting in any chemical change in the drug in the body. This chemical change may result in the drug molecule becoming more active, less active, or unchanged in terms of its activity at its binding sites, so metabolism does not mean inactivation. When complex chemical compounds are metabolized, or broken down, into simpler ones, the term *catabolism* is sometimes used; the reverse process is *anabolism*. It should be noted that drugs may be affected by all three types of metabolization. For example, codeine is transformed into the inactive codeine glucuronide, the more active molecule morphine, and the equally active compound norcodeine. The duration of action, or the drug's qualitative effects, may depend on which of these types of transformations is most rapid. Because the termination of a drug's action also is dependent to some extent on its being excreted from the body, metabolization of the drug into a more water-soluble compound generally must take place.

Many types of metabolic processes affect drugs in the body, and many drugs go through several metabolic changes before they are eliminated from the body. The major metabolic processes are *cleavage* reactions (the splitting of the molecule into two or more simpler molecules), *oxidation* (combining the molecule with oxygen or increasing the electropositive charge of the molecule through the loss of hydrogen or of one or more electrons), *conjugation* (the combining of the molecule with glucuronic or sulfuric acid), and *reduction* (the opposite of oxidation, in which the molecule becomes more negatively charged by gaining one or more electrons). Nearly all tissues of the body are capable of carrying out some type of drug metabolic activity. The most active tissues are generally those involved in the excretion of drugs, particularly the liver, kidneys, lungs, and GI tract. Within the cells of these tissues, the different subcellular parts carry out different metabolic activities.

It should be pointed out that some drugs are excreted intact, with only minimal metabolic transformation. This appears to be the case with the active ingredients of *Amanita muscaria,* a mushroom that is toxic and lethal in large enough quantities, but hallucinogenic in smaller quantities, which are passed into the urine and excreted. Siberian tribespeople, for whom the mushroom is quite a treat, take advantage of this fact by recycling the drug. (The recycling process they use and how they discovered it will be left to your imagination!)

As stated earlier, psychotropic drugs are generally lipid-soluble. Before there is any significant elimination of them from the body, they must become more water-soluble, because the excretion of drugs and their metabolites by way of the kidneys into the urine is, by far, the most important in terms of volume. Also, with the exception of the removal of volatile substances through the lungs, other excreta, like feces and perspiration, are aqueous in nature.

Drugs administered orally must initially pass through portions of the GI tract, where various enzymes may metabolize them. After the drug molecules cross the membranes of the cells in the GI tract, they move into a blood circulation system that goes directly to the liver before getting into the blood that supplies the body and brain. Thus, the molecules can be further metabolized in the liver—that is, the hepatic system. This phenomenon is known as **first-pass metabolism,** and it is for this reason that plasma or brain concentrations of drugs administered orally are generally lower than those of drugs administered through other routes. For example, blood ethanol levels are approximately 60% lower following oral administration than following intravenous administration if ethanol is given after a meal, and approximately 20% lower if given after overnight fasting (DiPadova et al., 1987). For most drugs, first-pass metabolism is primarily hepatic, although for some drugs, notably ethanol, it occurs predominantly at an upper GI site (Frezza et al., 1990).

By far, the organ most responsible for metabolizing drugs is the liver. Within the membranes of the primary liver cells exists a large complex of *enzymes.* (Enzymes are proteins secreted by cells that act as a catalyst to induce chemical changes in other substances, but which themselves are unchanged in the process.) These particular liver enzymes—technically the *hepatic microsomal enzyme system*—have apparently been developed through millions of years of evolution in order to deal with toxic substances that animals may be exposed to in their food and other environmental pollutants

(Guengerich, 1993). Because the actions of these enzymes are nonspecific in nature—that is, they may act on many different types of substances—they also metabolize drugs. Many drug-metabolizing enzymes comprise a large family of proteins called *cytochrome P450 enzymes* (a name derived from one of their physical properties displayed during one of their chemical reactions). Although found in high concentrations in the liver, the enzymes of this large family are found in virtually every type of cell in the body.

As blood passes through the liver, drugs diffuse into the liver cells and are acted on by P450 proteins and other drug-metabolizing enzymes. The metabolites (or, in some cases, the unchanged drugs) then diffuse back into the plasma or are secreted into the bile. Metabolites that are in the plasma and are sufficiently water-soluble are excreted primarily in the urine. If they are not sufficiently water-soluble, they may undergo further metabolization in the liver. Metabolites in the bile are delivered into the intestines. If they are water-soluble, they are excreted in the feces. However, if they are still lipid-soluble, they may be reabsorbed from the intestines to undergo further metabolization.

In most cases, the rate of drug metabolization is proportional to the plasma concentration of the drug (in log units), a relationship that is referred to as **first-order kinetics.** Some drugs exhibit **zero-order kinetics;** that is, they are metabolized at a fairly constant rate regardless of the amount taken—for example, ethanol (the alcohol we drink; Ritchie, 1985) and certain antidepressants taken in very large doses (Jarvis, 1991). The rate of metabolism is also dependent upon the concentration of P450 enzymes in the liver. This level can be elevated—in some cases several times over—with continuous exposure to certain drugs, which activate the genes regulating the synthesis of P450 proteins, although the process generally takes several days or weeks. This is an important factor in many cases of drug tolerance, in which the effects of a given amount of a drug are decreased because of previous exposure to the drug. For example, long-term exposure to alcohol can induce a 30% elevation in the amount of some P450 enzymes of the liver, and barbiturates can elevate the levels of certain drug-metabolizing enzymes up to five times that of the normal level. Because all psychotropic medications (except lithium) are metabolized by these enzymes, their plasma levels can be considerably reduced due to this factor (Shoaf & Linnoila, 1991).

In fact, chronic use of most drugs that depress brain functions (e.g., sedatives) tends to induce higher levels of the P450 enzymes. Such effects are not restricted to sedative-type drugs. Tobacco smoking, for example, can enhance the metabolism and elimination from the body of many psychotropics (e.g., antipsychotics, antidepressants, and caffeine) because of its ability to enhance the hepatic microsomal enzyme system (Shoaf & Linnoila, 1991).

Drugs can also inhibit the metabolization of other drugs through various mechanisms. Some drugs, including estrogens (female hormones) in oral contraceptives, have been suggested to reduce the level of enzymes (Wilkinson, 2001). Other drugs, including Antabuse, a drug used in the treatment of alcoholism, may combine with the active sites of the enzyme complex and prevent them from being available for metabolizing other drugs. Alcohol normally undergoes several metabolic changes. It first changes into acetaldehyde, which is fairly toxic. Normally, acetaldehyde is metabolized into nontoxic acetic acid. However, Antabuse competes for the enzyme that changes acetaldehyde into acetic acid. Thus, if the person who is taking Antabuse drinks alcohol, acetaldehyde levels build up and cause the person to become nauseated and to throw up. Supposedly the alcoholics' knowledge of these consequences prevents them from drinking alcohol. Finally, one drug may inhibit the metabolization of another because the two drugs share a common metabolic pathway. For example, higher-than-normal brain levels of barbiturates and other sedative–hypnotics may occur if accompanied by alcohol intake because the enzymes are busy metabolizing the alcohol (Hoyumpa & Schenker, 1982). Because the biotransformation of most psychotropics involves the same type of P450 enzymes, this phenomenon is responsible for the increased blood levels and potentially serious drug interactions that occur with a wide variety of antipsychotics, antidepressants, and anxiolytics that are often combined in the treatment of mental illness (Lin et al., 1996).

Not only can a drug influence the rate of metabolizing other drugs, but also the presence of one drug may alter the types of metabolites formed from another drug. A notable example occurs when the liver enzymes, in the presence of alcohol, convert cocaine into cocaethylene, a metabolite that appears to be synergistic with cocaine in terms of its reward properties as well as its toxicity (Farre et al., 1993).

Because there are vast differences in the ways in which different species metabolize drugs, it is very difficult to predict the response of humans to drugs on the basis of the response of other animals. For example, only around 50 of the approximately 750 varieties of P450 enzymes identified so far in mammals and other animal species are believed to exist in humans (Lewis, 2000). In humans it is now recognized that there are marked between- and within-race variations in the level of drug-metabolizing enzymes and the rates of metabolizing drugs, and perhaps as much as 50% of this variation is due to genetics (Reed & Hanna, 1986). Indeed, one of the more striking observations of recent studies is that an individual's response to a particular drug is partly a consequence of the number of active P450 enzymes in that individual's body, with, in some cases, a 50-fold range in enzyme activity (Guengerich, 1993). In a few people—perhaps up to 10% of the population—particular enzymes may be effectively missing. This is a likely factor in why there is often a lack of correlation between the dosages of drugs used in the treatment of mental illness and their therapeutic response, why there are differences in the side effects experienced, and why ethnic and racial groups often differ in terms of their response (Jeste et al., 1996; Matsuda et al., 1996; Risby, 1996).

P450 enzymes can activate (e.g., codeine to morphine via the CYP2D6 enzyme) or deactivate (e.g., nicotine to cotinine via the CYP2A6 enzyme) drugs of abuse; thus, pharmacogenetic variations in the patterns of metabolism among individuals can also modulate the risk of drug dependence (Sellers & Tyndale, 2000). For example, individuals with gene mutations that result in little or no activity of the CYP2D6 enzyme may have less risk of dependence on oral opiates (e.g., codeine, oxycodone, and hydrocodone) because of lower levels of metabolites (e.g., morphine, oxymorphone, and hydromorphone) with greater psychoactivity, and individuals with genetically deficient CYP2A6 nicotine metabolism may smoke fewer cigarettes and be able to quit more easily because they achieve toxic levels of nicotine quite readily.

Age may also be a factor in drug metabolization, because older people tend to lose their ability to produce many of these enzymes, making them particularly susceptible to the toxic effects of drugs. In the developing fetus and in newborn infants, in which drugs are metabolized chiefly in the liver, the activity and concentration of many metabolizing enzymes is less than in adults, prolonging and exaggerating drug effects (Ramirez, 1989). Children do not have a full complement of these enzymes until they are a year or two old.

Other important factors in drug metabolization are nutrition and disease (Hoyumpa & Schenker, 1982). For example, in animals, blood alcohol concentration has been found to be lowered and alcohol clearance from the body accelerated with high-carbohydrate (e.g., simple sugar) diets, whereas alcohol concentration is increased and clearance is reduced with low-carbohydrate diets (Rao et al., 1986). In the initial stages of starvation, drug metabolization may be enhanced, whereas in later stages it will be reduced. Severe liver diseases, such as cirrhosis, obstructive jaundice, and hepatitis, can significantly reduce the ability of the organism to metabolize drugs. The ability of skid-row alcoholics to get drunk on as little as a half pint of wine—what some people might refer to as *reverse tolerance*—is probably due to both nutritional deficiencies and disease (Wilson et al., 1986).

Very little work has been done on human sex differences in metabolizing drugs. Although some studies have concluded that gender differences are not very significant for most drugs (Dawkins & Potter, 1991), other studies have indicated that there may be notable differences in the ways in which men and women metabolize some drugs. One study indicated that because women exhibit lower gastric first-pass metabolism of alcohol, the blood levels of alcohol in women were significantly higher than in men who had been given the same amount of alcohol (relative to their body weights; Frezza et al., 1990). Other studies have indicated that premenopausal women tend to metabolize some antianxiety, antidepressant, and antipsychotic drugs more slowly than men do (Kando et al., 1995). Therefore, premenopausal women are prone to accumulate higher, and potentially more dangerous, levels of these drugs with repeated administrations. In contrast, induction of certain drug-metabolizing enzymes occurs during pregnancy in the second and third trimesters, which may necessitate an increase in drug dosage during this period with a return to its previous level after the baby's birth (Wilkinson, 2001). Although some gender differences in metabolism may result from hormonal differences, suggesting that they may not occur when comparing postmenopausal women with men of comparable age, the fact that there are gender differences in body composition, weight, and ratio of fat to total body water that may affect pharmacokinetic processes other than metabolism makes such a suggestion very tentative.

The liver excretes drugs into the bile by a secretory process. Highly water-soluble metabolites are not reabsorbed and are removed from the body by way of the feces. However, renal (kidney) excretion of drugs—primarily their metabolites—is the primary way in which they are removed from the body. Excretion of drugs by way of sweat, tears, and saliva is quantitatively unimportant. Excretion of drugs in breast milk may also occur, but this is important not because of the amounts eliminated but because the excreted drugs may be potential sources of unwanted pharmacological effects in nursing infants. For example, the breast milk of women who smoke smells like cigarettes, and the breast-fed babies of these women may learn to like the taste of tobacco this way and may be more likely to smoke when they grow up (Mennella & Beauchamp, 1998).

Because of their lipid-solubility, psychotropic drugs are always excreted slowly in their active forms. To a great extent, the metabolites' rate of excretion depends on their lipid-solubility, on whether they are actively secreted (as opposed to passively diffused) into the urine by the kidney cells, and on their pH and that of the urine. For example, an increase in the urinary pH (i.e., a decrease in acidity) enhances the excretion of a weak organic acid, like aspirin, but reduces the rate of excretion of a weak base, like morphine. Therefore, the rate of excretion of certain acidic drugs can be enhanced by alkalinization of the urine—for example, with bicarbonate of soda (Alka-Seltzer)—while the excretion of alkaline drugs can be enhanced by acidification—for example, with vitamin C. This process is called *ion-trapping*. It should be noted that urine is usually acid, although it may not be if a person's drinking water is highly alkaline.

Like metabolism, renal function and, therefore, one's ability to excrete drugs, varies considerably with age. Fetal excretion of most drugs, via the placenta and fetal urine, is delayed. Excretion through urine increases to maximal levels in humans between the ages of 5 and 10. Renal functioning then declines somewhat, tends to stabilize between the ages of 10 and 40, and then begins to decline thereafter. Thus the plasma half-life of most drugs progressively increases from childhood to old age (Geller, 1991).

IMPLICATIONS OF PHARMACOKINETICS IN THE FETUS AND NEONATE

One can make an argument that adults who take drugs are doing so by choice and that they are responsible for whatever consequences a drug may have on their body. Unfortunately, the developing fetus or newborn of a woman who takes psychotropic drugs does not have that choice. As many as 80% of all pregnant women take prescribed drugs, and up to 35% take psychotropic drugs, none of which have been proved safe for use during pregnancy (Kerns, 1986). In one large-scale survey, approximately 11% of the urine samples of women presenting for delivery in California hospitals in 1992 tested positive for at least one drug (e.g., alcohol, nicotine, cannabinoids, benzodiazepines, opiates, cocaine; Vega et al., 1993). This estimate of drug use by pregnant women is only for very recent use, because the detection period for most of these drugs is less than 2 weeks.

The tissue through which most psychotropic drugs can easily pass, and which expectant parents should be fully aware of, is the *placenta*. This tissue is specialized to allow transport of oxygen, nutrients, and waste between the woman and the fetus, but it is no different from other cell membranes in its general permeability to drugs. In fact, drugs can cross the placenta, nearly always through passive diffusion, even more easily than they can penetrate the BBB in the adult brain. Therefore, any psychoactive drug can pass through the placenta and accumulate in the developing fetus in significant quantities. Passive diffusion through the placenta is dependent upon characteristics of the drug (e.g., molecular size, lipid-solubility, and so on), drug concentration, and duration of exposure.

In a fetus, a greater proportion of blood flow is distributed to its brain than is the case in adults. Combined with the less-developed BBB of the fetus and fewer plasma proteins for drug binding, this greater flow leads to more rapid and complete drug exposure of the fetal brain. Furthermore, with a lower level of hepatic metabolizing enzymes, and slower drug excretion, the fetus and newborn are much more susceptible to the potential toxic effects of drugs than adults are (Guyon, 1989; Kerns, 1986). This lesson was most agonizingly learned more than 30 years ago when a large number of women who had been taking a mild sedative called thalidomide during their pregnancy gave birth to infants with missing or malformed limbs.

The risks to the fetus include **teratogenic effects** (abnormal development), long-term behavioral effects, and direct toxic effects. Teratogenic effects may be apparent immediately and result in spontaneous abortion, malformation, or altered fetal growth, or they may be delayed and not measurable or manifested for years after birth. The majority of drugs of abuse, including alcohol, nicotine, marijuana, cocaine, and opiates, have been found to impair fetal growth, resulting in lower birth weights and shorter gestational periods (Kaye et al., 1989; Zuckerman et al., 1989). Low birth weight, coupled with exposure to socially disadvantaged environments, has been found to be associated with long-lasting and clinically significant attention problems in children (Breslau & Chilcoat, 2000; Johnson & Breslau, 2000).

In addition to obvious physical abnormalities, psychotropic drugs can disturb nerve cell proliferation, differentiation, and neurotransmitter concentrations that result in disruptions in psychomotor activity, behavioral development, and performance. In fact, numerous studies with rodents indicate that a variety of drugs that reduce neuronal excitability can kill neurons during fetal development by inducing neuronal apoptosis, that is, programmed cell death in which neurons act on an internally generated signal and commit suicide (Olney et al., 2004). These include drugs that: (a) inhibit voltage-gated sodium channels (e.g., several anticonvulsant agents [phenytoin, valproate]), (b) enhance activity of inhibitory $GABA_A$ receptors (e.g., benzodiazepines, barbiturates, ethanol, anesthetics), or (c) inhibit excitatory NMDA receptors (e.g., ketamine, ethanol). (See Chapters 4 and 5 for descriptions of these types of channels and receptors.) In humans, alcohol, opiates, and some anticonvulsants are well-established behavioral teratogens, producing disturbances of arousal and motor coordination, specific learning disabilities, and mental retardation.

Whether subtle or transient, behavioral effects may still cause problems. Subtle ones may be evidenced only if the infant is exposed to certain environments, such as an impoverished one. Transient ones, like neonatal withdrawal symptoms when drug exposure ceases at birth, can disrupt early mother–infant interactions and bonding, which can lead to long-term consequences for the child's psychological development. Unfortunately, some emotional or mental disorders require that the pregnant female be maintained on medication in order to protect the fetus. For example, an actively psychotic, manic, or severely depressed female may engage in activities that would endanger the fetus. An epileptic fit, with the likelihood of experiencing seizures, has a significant potential for fetal damage. Fortunately, most studies indicate that the majority of psychotropic drugs used to treat these disorders have minimal teratogenic potential (Hawkins, 1989). Problems with medications that have some teratogenic potential (e.g., lithium and anticonvulsants) can be minimized by reducing dosage or eliminating drug treatment during the first trimester or by taking other precautions. (See Elia et al., [1987] and Hawkins [1989] for a more complete description of potential teratogenic effects of specific psychotherapeutic drugs.)

PHARMACOGENETIC AND ETHNIC FACTORS IN DRUG ACTION

The present chapter has been discussing some of the general principles in pharmacology, but of course, there is substantial individual variability in the response to drugs. Some variability is an inherent part of any biological or psychological characteristic, and drug responses in psychopharmacology are no exception. Due to a growing body of evidence that variable drug responsiveness is caused by polymorphisms (variations) within multiple genes—protein products of which are involved in critical metabolic and/or physiologic pathways relevant for drug action—the disciplines of *pharmacogenetics* and pharmacodynamics have evolved. Those in the discipline of **pharmacogenetics** attempt to discover differential effects of a drug in different patients, depending on the presence of inherited variations in genes, with the goal of providing more patient/disease-specific health care. Those in the discipline of **pharmacogenomics** attempt to discover differential effects of compounds, either in vivo or in vitro, on gene expression among all the genes that are expressed in humans, with the goal of finding the "best" drug candidate from a given series of compounds under evaluation (Lindpaintner, 2003). However, the two terms—*pharmacogenetics* and *pharmacogenomics*—are often used interchangeably. For most drugs, variations in patient response have, until recently, been considered a result of pharmacokinetic factors rather than pharmacodynamic differences. However, it now appears that pharmacodynamic variability in humans is substantial and may be more pronounced than pharmacokinetic variability. For example, polymorphisms in the gene that encodes for a type of receptor protein in the brain (adenosine A_{2A} receptors) are associated with the induction of anxiety by caffeine in humans (Alsene et al., 2003). There also is evidence that variability in genetic factors related to both pharmacokinetics and pharmacodynamics can be related to variability in the response to antidepressants (Keers & Aitchison, 2011) and marijuana (Onaivi, 2009), as well as the metabolism of ethyl alcohol (Yin & Peng, 2007) and drug treatment of alcoholism (Ray et al., 2010). This research has led to the hope that, within a few years, prospective genotyping will lead to patients being prescribed drugs that are both safer and more effective ("the right drug for the right patient," or personalized medicine).

This discussion of genetics also leads one to consider that a person's ethnic heritage also can be a source of variability in drug action (Urban, 2010). Response to drugs can vary across various population groups (e.g., European, African American, Latino, Native American, Asian), and for that reason, it is important that experiments should have subjects that reflect this variability. For example, in studying the antidepressant effects of the drug *citalopram*, Garriock et al. (2010) had a participant group that included non-Hispanics Caucasians, Hispanic Caucasians, and African Americans, and the subject stratification was corrected using over 100 ancestry-informative genetic markers. This subject composition enabled the authors to analyze the data in terms of both ethnic and specific genetic factors. Another example is in the treatment of high blood pressure. The rate of high blood pressure in African Americans is considerably higher than that seen in Caucasians and some Hispanic populations, and research has shown that some drugs may be more effective in the African American population than others; when given as a monotherapy (i.e., on their own), diuretics and calcium channel blockers appear to be relatively more effective in lowering blood pressure in African Americans than other drugs such as beta blockers (drugs that block receptors for norepinephrine and epinephrine), angiotensin-converting enzyme inhibitors, and angiotensin II receptor blockers (Ferdinand & Saunders 2006). A well-known example for the role of ethnicity as a mediator of pharmacogenetic variability is in the response of some populations to ethyl alcohol. For example, some East Asian populations (especially Japanese) are highly sensitive to the effects of ethyl alcohol because they have a polymorphism in the gene that encodes for an enzyme known as aldehyde dehydrogenase, which breaks down a metabolite of alcohol (Chen et al., 2009). People with this genetic variation show enhanced responses to some of the aversive effects of ethyl alcohol (e.g., flushed face, cardiovascular changes, anxiety), which depending upon the degree of genetic variation can protect against the development of alcoholism.

Of course, humans are not the only organism in which genetic characteristics exert a powerful influence on drug effects. Because of the characterization of the mouse genome, there has been an enormous growth in studies involving genetically modified mice. This line of research includes studies that characterize the basic effect of a knockout or knockdown of a particular protein by genetic manipulations (Cagniard et al., 2006; Cannon et al., 2005), as well as experiments that are designed to determine how genetic manipulations affect drug action (Giardino et al., 2011; Hnasko et al., 2007; Phillips et al., 2008).

Websites for Further Information

Medical dictionaries that define most psychopharmacological terms:

http://my.webmd.com/webmd_today/home/default.htm

http://www.pharma-lexicon.com/medicaldictionary.php

http://www.ats-group.net/medical/dictionary-glossary-pharmacology.html

Excitability and Chemical Signaling in Nerve Cells

All thoughts, emotions, and behaviors come about because of biochemical and electrochemical processes that take place in specialized cells in the nervous system called *neurons*. Drugs that affect these psychological variables do so because they alter these biochemical and electrochemical processes. Therefore, in order for a student to appreciate how psychotropic drugs work and what their short- and long-term consequences are, he or she should be familiar with these basic processes. The purpose of this chapter is to describe the biochemical and electrochemical activities that take place in the nervous system and how they are related to psychotropic drug action.

The nervous system is divided into the *central nervous system* (CNS; composed of the brain and the spinal cord) and the *peripheral nervous system*, or PNS (made up of all neurons outside the brain and spinal cord). Neurons are also mixed in with numerous other nonneuronal cellular elements called *glial cells* (i.e., *astrocytes*, which ensheath synaptic connections between neurons and are required for synapse formation and maintenance, and *oligodendrocytes*, which wrap layers of myelin membrane around axons to insulate them for impulse conduction [Fields & Stevens-Graham, 2002], which serve important metabolic and supportive functions. It has been estimated that the human nervous system contains approximately 85 billion neurons (Williams & Herrup, 1988). To illustrate how enormous this number is, if you were to lose 100,000 neurons a day for 70 years, you would still have around 82 billion left. (Although several recent findings have invalidated the long-standing position that CNS neurons do not regenerate in the adult mammalian brain, the importance of long-term, regular cellular self-renewal in the CNS is still uncertain [Gage, 2000].) So, just in terms of sheer numbers, the CNS is a very complex system—far more sophisticated and complex than any computer ever built, utilizing from 20% (in adults) to 60% (in infants) of the resting energy consumption in humans (Laughlin & Sejnowski, 2003).

Neurons act to *transduce* information about their physical and chemical environment, which means that they convert one form of energy into another form of energy or one type of signal into another type of signal. In addition, neurons *transmit* information, typically by generating electrical changes in one part of the cell, conducting these electrical changes to distant parts of the cell, and then releasing chemical signals on to neighboring neurons. Thus, neurons are electrically active; they generate electrical impulses (i.e., voltage changes, flows of electrical current in and out of the cell) in response to changes in their environment and propagate those electrical signals. Moreover, they are chemically active—they release signaling molecules known as **neurotransmitters** that then become a part of the chemical environment of the next cells in the circuit. Common neurotransmitters include glutamate (GLU), GABA, dopamine (DA), norepinephrine (NE), and serotonin (5-HT), as well as a host of others that will be discussed in later chapters.

THE NEURON

Figure 4.1 depicts a stylized neuron and parts of other neurons that interact with it. Note that each neuron in this figure has numerous excitatory (E) and inhibitory (I) inputs or synapses, which regulate the frequency of action potentials (discussed in the next section) produced by them. The large arrows indicate the most common direction of information flow. The main body of the neuron is called its *soma*, parts of which serve integrative functions in the communication of information. Extensions from the soma are termed *dendrites* and *axons*. Normally, there are many dendrites extending from the soma, which serve as receivers of information from other neurons, and one axon, which serves as the pathway over which signals pass from the soma to other neurons. Thus, in a sense, information typically flows from dendrite to soma to axon. Dendrites tend to be relatively short, but axons can be quite long. For instance, a spinal motor neuron may have an axon several feet long, although they too may be quite short in CNS neurons. The enlarged region where the axon emerges from the soma is called the *axon hillock*. A short distance from their origin, many axons have a coating called the *myelin sheath*, which is analogous to the insulation on a wire. Gaps in the myelin sheath, where the axon comes into direct contact with the extracellular fluid, are called the *nodes of Ranvier*. The presence of these gaps allows for an increase in the rate of conduction down the axon. Near its end, the axon branches, and at the tip of each branch is an enlargement called a *terminal* (some terminals are actually at the tip of the axon, while in some neurons terminals are strung along the axons like beads; in the latter case, the terminals are also known as *varicosities*). Chemicals found within the axon terminal can be released into an exceedingly small gap between the neurons, called a *synaptic cleft*, allowing the neuron to affect the excitability of adjacent neurons. The point of functional connection between neurons is called a *synapse*, and it consists of the presynaptic membrane of the axon terminal, the synaptic cleft, and the postsynaptic membrane of the "target" neuron (Dustin & Colman, 2002).

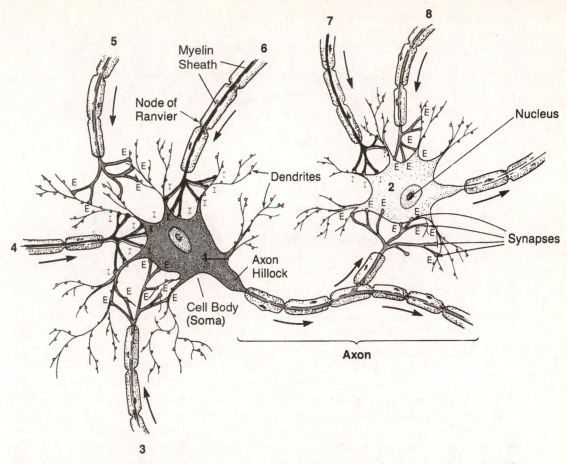

FIGURE 4.1 Schematic of the major parts of two CNS interneurons (1 and 2), depicting the relationship between them and the axons and terminals of other neurons (3-8). *Source:* Adapted from Carlson (1988).

ELECTRICAL EXCITABILITY OF NEURONS: THE RESTING MEMBRANE POTENTIAL

As discussed earlier, neurons are electrically active. Under baseline conditions, each neuron is said to be *polarized;* that is, they have a voltage difference between the inside and the outside of the cell that is known as the **resting membrane potential.** In this sense, the neuron is analogous to a tiny biological battery with positive poles outside the cell and negative poles inside the cell (Figure 4.2). A typical flashlight battery has a voltage difference of about 1.5 volts (V) between the top and the bottom, while a car battery usually has a 12 V difference between the two poles. In neurons, the voltage difference between the inside and outside of the membrane is approximately 70 mV (70 thousandths of a volt). Because the inside of the cell membrane is negative relative to the outside of the cell membrane, it is conventional to refer to this voltage as –70 mV. (The resting potential of individual neurons varies between –60 and –90 mV, but

Resting Membrane Potential

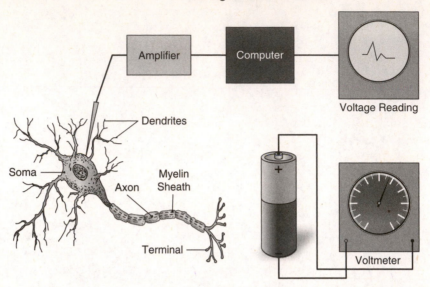

FIGURE 4.2   A neuronal membrane has a voltage difference between the inside and the outside surfaces. In some ways, this is analogous to a battery, which has a voltage difference between the top and bottom poles.

–70 mV will be used here as a ballpark figure for purposes of discussion.) To someone who has some familiarity with electronics, it is even more accurate to say that each neuronal membrane acts like a capacitor, because it stores a charge, and then at some point, it discharges. As we shall see later, this electrical potential or charge (or electromotive force) is largely powered by sodium ions (Na^+).

What generates the resting membrane potential? We will consider several important factors, such as (a) the electrical characteristics of ions, (b) the physical forces that drive the movements of ions, and (c) the characteristics of the nerve cell membrane, including both the lipid and protein components. There are several ions we must consider, including sodium (designated as Na^+, where the Na is the abbreviation for the sodium atom and the symbol + stands for the positive charge the atom possesses), potassium (K^+), and chloride (Cl^-). There also are large negatively charged groups on protein molecules, which tend to be present in higher concentrations inside the membrane. Another ion, a calcium ion with two positive charges (Ca^{++}), is also involved, and it plays a vital role in a wide variety of actions within the nervous system, including but not limited to neurotransmitter release. Any positive ion is called a *cation,* while a negative ion is called an *anion.* In addition, there are two main physical forces that we need to consider, which drive the movement of ions and other molecules. Movement along a *concentration gradient* (i.e., diffusion) refers to the fact that molecules move from an area of high concentration to an area of low concentration. Another important force is movement along an *electrical gradient.* This refers to the fact that ions can be driven by electrical forces because like charges repel and opposite charges attract.

In addition to the ions and physical forces that must be considered, we should also discuss the characteristics of the neuronal membrane, and the conditions present when the resting membrane potential is in place. As reviewed in Chapter 3, the nerve cell membrane consists of a phospholipid bilayer with imbedded proteins. The lipid portion of the bilayer (i.e., the fatty acid chains, which are hydrocarbon) acts as a barrier to the movement of ions or polar substances. The protein components can include *enzymes*, *receptors*, *channels*, and *transporters*. As discussed in the remaining chapters of this book, each of these protein components can serve as a substrate for drug action, but for the purposes of the present discussion, we should emphasize how each of these contributes to the resting membrane potential and nerve cell excitability (Figure 4.3). Enzymes are biological catalysts that promote biochemical reactions, including neurotransmitter synthesis and metabolism. Receptor proteins bind to neurotransmitters, essentially acting as the initial detection device for the presence of the transmitter. Channels are proteins that act as gates that can be opened or closed. When opened, channels allow for the passage of ions through the membrane. Channels are defined in terms of what ions they let through, so for example, there are cation channels, anion channels, Na^+ channels, K^+ channels, Cl^- channels, and Ca^{++} channels. They also are defined in terms of their gating mechanism (i.e., the factor that opens or closes them).

Membrane Proteins and the Movement of Ions

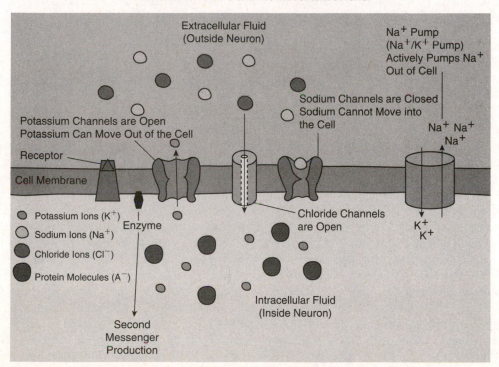

FIGURE 4.3 This figure demonstrates some of the general features of the nerve cell membrane, including various proteins (channels, receptors, enzymes, and a transport protein" "the sodium pump). In addition, various ions are shown, and some of the conditions that lead to the resting membrane potential are depicted.

Thus, there are chemically gated channels, which are linked to receptors, and voltage-gated channels, which are opened or closed based upon the voltage conditions of the local portion of the membrane. Finally, there are transport proteins, which act as pumps that move substances across the membrane. For example, there are transporters for various transmitters, including DA, NE, 5-HT and GABA, which serve to remove transmitter molecules from the synaptic cleft as a means of inactivation. Furthermore, there is a very important transporter known as the Na^+/K^+ pump (also known as the sodium pump, or the Na^+/K^+ dependent ATPase), which is critical for establishing the resting membrane potential (Payne et al., 2003). This transporter pumps Na^+ ions inside the cell, and K^+ outside (approximately three Na^+ ions per two K^+ ions). In doing so, it utilizes a significant fraction of all the energy spent by the brain and represents a substantial energy input into the system that establishes the *resting* potential. Thus, in some sense the term resting is not really appropriate, because the cell is actually expending approximately one quarter of its total energy maintaining this state (Lennie, 2003).

Given these factors, how is the resting membrane potential generated? If this were a neurophysiology book, we would have to go into considerable detail to explain how a specific resting membrane potential is generated (e.g., why is it −72 mV in a particular cell, at a particular moment?). Because this is a drugs and behavior book, it will be sufficient to discuss why the inside is negative relative to the outside, and what significance that has for neuron excitability, chemical signaling, and drug action. In order to understand the fundamental electronegativity of the inside of the cell, we must consider three important conditions that are present. Under baseline or "resting" conditions:

- Cl^- and K^+ channels are mostly open
- Na^+ channels are virtually all closed
- Na^+/K^+ pump actively transports some K^+ into the cell but transports more Na^+ out of the cell

These conditions lead to the generation of the resting membrane potential. It is negative on the inside because positively charged Na^+ ions are pumped out, and these ions are not allowed back in because the Na^+ channels are closed. Thus, we say that under resting or baseline conditions, the membrane is *impermeable* to sodium ions. This establishes the condition that the inside of the membrane is relatively negative, and the outside is relatively positive. The exact voltage difference achieved is then determined by the response of K^+ and Cl^- ions to these voltage conditions; that is, these ions can move back and forth across the membrane because their channels are open, and they move in such a way as to approach the equilibrium (or balance point) between the concentration and electrical gradient forces that are acting upon them. These conditions represent how the sodium-powered "battery" or "capacitor" is established, but what makes it discharge? With more Na^+ ions on the outside, the two forces that impinge upon the movement of ions are aligned, and have the potential to act upon Na^+ in the same direction (move it toward the inside). If the membrane were to suddenly become permeable to Na^+, the sodium ions would rush into the cell driven by both the concentration gradient force (there is more Na^+ on the outside, so it moves in) and the electrical gradient force (it is negative on the inside, and the positive Na^+ ions are attracted inside). Thus, the resting or baseline condition represents an electrically unstable state, because anything that increases permeability to Na^+ would discharge this capacitor; that is, it would allow a sodium current to flow through the membrane, driven by the electrical and chemical gradient forces, and make the inside of the membrane more positive in the process. In some ways, this situation is analogous to a town that uses a water tower. Energy is used to pump water against a physical force (gravity) and store it in an elevated position. The potential energy inherent in this system can be discharged if any valve that is hooked up to the system and is lower than the water in the tower is opened. So, when we open our faucets, a current of water is driven through them by gravity. In the case of the neuron, the pump in question is the Na^+/K^+ pump, and this transporter pumps against physical forces—in this instance, not gravity, but the chemical and electrical gradient forces. The current of Na^+ ions flows through when a "valve" is opened; in a neural membrane, any channel that allows Na^+ to pass through will, when opened, allow an inward Na^+ current to flow. This is how neurons change from the polarized resting or baseline state to become excited or *depolarized*.

ELECTRICAL EXCITABILITY OF NEURONS: EXCITATION, INHIBITION, AND THE ACTION POTENTIAL

As described earlier, the electrical conditions across the membrane can be recorded by electrodes, and when this is done, a variety of voltage or current changes can be measured. For the present discussion, we will consider three different types of electrical phenomena that are commonly recorded from nerve cells (Figure 4.4). These are excitatory postsynaptic potentials (**EPSPs**), inhibitory postsynaptic potentials (**IPSPs**), and **action**

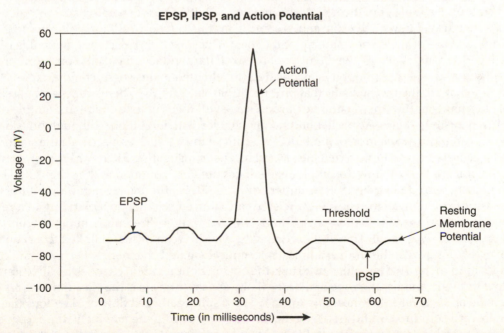

FIGURE 4.4 Electrical recordings of individual neurons can yield several types of voltage changes, including EPSPs, IPSPs, and action potentials. Action potentials are instigated when the level of excitation crosses the threshold.

potentials (also known as *spikes,* or neuronal *firing*). The term *potential* here refers to a voltage change, and the term *postsynaptic* refers to the convention that these are generally recorded from the postsynaptic membrane. The EPSP is a small transient change in the positive direction (i.e., the voltage moves in the positive direction, then returns to baseline). The IPSP is a small change in the negative direction (i.e., the cell becomes more negative, or *hyperpolarized*). The action potential is a rapid and dramatic movement in the positive direction, followed by a rapid restoration of the resting potential. We say that EPSPs and IPSPs are propagated in a graded and decremental fashion. They originate at one point (a synapse or group of synapses) and move outward in all directions across the surface of the membrane. They are said to be graded because they can vary in size, depending upon the magnitude of the stimulus (usually a transmitter under physiological conditions). Thus, EPSPs and IPSPs convey information about the magnitude of the chemical signal that a neuron is receiving. Also, EPSPs and IPSPs are said to be decremental because they diminish in size as they travel out from the original point of stimulation. EPSPs and IPSPs are analogous to the ripples that occur when we throw a stone into a pond. A little pebble creates a small wave, while a larger stone creates a bigger wave, but in either case, the waves get smaller as they move over the surface of the pond away from the point at which the rock went in. In contrast to EPSPs and IPSPs, action potentials are not graded or decremental. When the level of excitation is great enough to cross the *threshold,* an action potential is triggered, and action potentials are considered to be "all-or-none"; they either occur or don't, and when they occur, they typically maintain their size as they travel along the axonal membrane. Because they do not generally convey information based upon their size, action potentials encode information in terms of their frequency (how many are fired per unit time) and overall pattern (e.g., bursts or single firings) of activity. Once generated, action potentials then travel down the axon, and in some cases this can be a very long distance (e.g., from the base of the spine to the tip of the toes). The speed of the action potential is related to two main factors: the diameter of the axon (larger diameter axons conduct more rapidly) and whether or not it is myelinated (myelinated axons conduct more rapidly).

What are the mechanisms that produce EPSPs and IPSPs? There are several possible mechanisms, but for illustrative purposes, we will focus on one common example of a mechanism that leads to excitation, and one that leads to inhibition. Although physiologists can induce excitation or inhibition by artificial means such as electrical stimulation or injection of current into a cell, the natural means of instigating EPSPs or IPSPs is from neurotransmitters. The two examples we will use are very common in the brain: GLU is the most common excitatory transmitter, while GABA is the most common inhibitory transmitter. One way in which GLU release can induce excitation is by binding to a receptor known as the N-methyl D-aspartate (NMDA) receptor (receptor subtypes will be discussed in Chapter 5). The NMDA receptor is a GLU receptor that is linked to a cation channel (Figure 4.5; this is an example of a chemically gated channel). When GLU molecules bind to the binding site, it instigates the opening of the cation channel; positive ions flow through, and because one of the ions that can pass through is the $Na+$ ion, this represents an increase in permeability to Na^+. The resulting inward flow of $Na+$ ions (i.e., an inward sodium current) results in the inside of the membrane moving in the positive direction, which is recorded as an EPSP. One way in which GABA can induce inhibition is by binding to a receptor subtype known as the $GABA_A$ receptor. The $GABA_A$ receptor is linked to a Cl^- channel (Figure 4.5), and therefore when GABA molecules bind to the

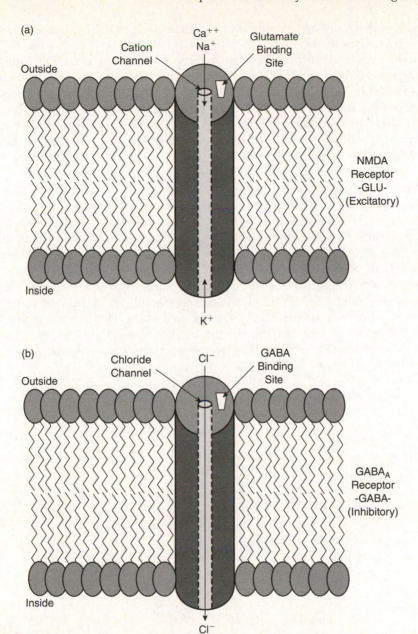

FIGURE 4.5 Examples of mechanisms that can generate an EPSP and an IPSP. **TOP:** This is an NMDA receptor, which is a type of glutamate (GLU) receptor. This receptor contains an outer group of receptor proteins, which has the glutamate binding site, and an inner channel protein. When glutamate binds to its binding site, it leads to an opening of the cation (positive ion) channel, which allows Na$^+$ ions to enter the cell and leads to an EPSP. **BOTTOM:** This is a GABA$_A$ receptor, which is a type of glutamate receptor. This receptor also contains an outer group of receptor proteins that has the GABA binding site, and an inner channel protein. When glutamate binds to its binding site, it leads to an opening of the Cl$^-$ channel, which increases the flow of Cl$^-$ ions into the cell and leads to an IPSP.

binding site, it instigates an opening of this chemically gated Cl^- channel. As a result, there is an inward flow of Cl^- ions (i.e., an inward chloride current), which moves the voltage in the negative direction, a change that can be recorded as an IPSP (inhibition or hyperpolarization). What makes GLU excitatory and GABA inhibitory? Is it something about the molecule itself? In fact, it is the mechanism that the receptor is linked to that makes one transmitter excitatory and another inhibitory. GLU is excitatory because the receptor is linked to a cation channel, and Na^+ permeability is increased when the channel is opened. In contrast, the $GABA_A$ receptor is linked to a Cl^- channel, so the binding of the GABA to the receptor opens a Cl^- channel. It is the different channels being opened that leads to either excitation or inhibition in each of these cases.

Action potentials are generated by a different mechanism than EPSPs and IPSPs. Under physiological conditions, action potentials are most frequently generated at the initial portion of the axon (the *axon hillock*). The best way to think of how an action potential is generated is to consider that it has two parts—an ascending limb and a descending limb. The *ascending limb* (i.e., when the voltage shoots up in the positive direction) is instigated because of the opening of voltage-gated Na^+ channels. An initial voltage change triggers the opening of these channels, which leads Na^+ ions to go into the neuron (an *influx* of Na^+), which leads the membrane to become more positive on the inside, which is a further voltage change, and so on. This cascade of events leads to a large influx of Na^+, leading the membrane potential on the inside to shoot up in the positive direction (Figure 4.6). Meanwhile, the membrane depolarization induces

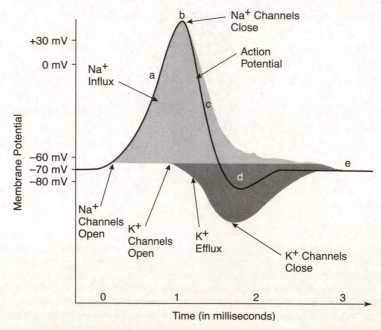

FIGURE 4.6 The action potential depicted here is the result of the rapid exchange of sodium (Na^+) and potassium (K^+) ions across the neuron cell membrane. (See text for explanation of the dynamics occurring at points a–e.)

the opening of voltage-gated K^+ channels. Because the inside of the membrane is now positive, K^+ is repelled and rapidly leaves the cell (called *efflux*), which then drives the membrane potential back toward its resting potential (point c in the figure), that is, the *descending limb* of the action potential, which then closes the voltage-gated K^+ channels. However, the K^+ ions flow so rapidly outside the cell that there is an overshoot of K^+ ions, and the electrical potential becomes even more negative than the normal resting potential (point d in Figure 4.6). This event is referred to as *hyperpolarization*. Finally, the –70 mV resting potential is restored as K^+ diffuses away and the sodium–potassium pump works to pump Na^+ ions out of and K^+ ions back into the cell (point e in Figure 4.6). Thus, the electrical changes that underlie the action potential are caused by a wave of Na^+ moving into the cell, which shoots the voltage inside the membrane in the positive direction, followed by a wave of K^+ moving out, which drives the voltage in the negative direction. In an unmyelinated axon, these two waves of ion currents flow along the length of the axon to reach the terminals. Myelinated axons have a conduction velocity that is much faster, because the action potential disappears under the myelin sheath, but then rapidly reconstitutes at the next gap, appearing to "jump" from one node of Ranvier to another (this is known as *saltatory conduction*, which comes from the Latin *saltare*, which, like the Spanish verb *saltar*, means "to jump").

The excitability of a neuron—that is, its ability to initiate an action potential as a result of an outside stimulus—is dependent upon the degree of polarization when stimulation is applied. If the cell is hyperpolarized (the resting potential moves further from the threshold), it is less excitable; if it is slightly depolarized (between –70 and –60 mV), it is more excitable. For example, in a brain area known as the caudate/putamen or neostriatum, which is the region depleted of DA in Parkinson's disease patients, an important cell type known as the *medium* spiny neuron transitions back and forth between a depolarized "up state," from which it is more easily excited, to a hyperpolarized "down state," during which it is very difficult to generate action potentials (Shen et al., 2005). The excitability of a neuron is also dependent upon whether an action potential has already occurred. Immediately following the action potential, there is a *refractory period* of a millisecond or two, during which no new action potential is generated. During the last part of the refractory period, an action potential can be triggered, but only if the stimulus is much stronger than normal. The cell is also less excitable during phase d, a form of hyperpolarization.

INTEGRATION, COMPUTATION, AND CHEMICAL SIGNALING IN NEURONS

In some ways, physiology is the science that views living systems as operating according to mechanical and physical principles, and therefore it can be useful to make analogies between the functions of various cells, tissues, or organs and those of a particular machine. Several centuries ago, the English physician Harvey likened the function of a heart to that of a well-known machine—a pump. In the present day, we often say that the brain acts like a computer. But, how does the neural circuitry of the brain perform computations? This would seem to be a critical question if one is trying to understand how drugs affect that neural circuitry, thereby altering the computations generated.

Neuroscientists are trying to answer this difficult question, but it is evident that the computational power of the brain is based upon the computational operations performed by the individual neurons in the brain and the interactions between these networks of neurons that constantly communicate with each other. In this context, we can say that each neuron is a chemically sensitive device that integrates its chemical inputs over time and space and then converts this integrated signal into a frequency and pattern of action potentials.

Although action potentials can be generated by various mechanisms, probably the most common mode of communication under physiological conditions involves signals passing from the somatodendritic region to the axon, and ultimately to the terminals. Chemical signals from an array of synaptic inputs are detected by receptors in the somatodendritic region, and electrical changes such as EPSPs and IPSPs are generated locally. Because they are graded (i.e., EPSP and IPSP magnitude is related to the degree of chemical input), these initial electrical signals already convey information about the external chemical environment of that particular neuron. These graded signals are then propagated over the surface of the membrane, though they decrease in size as they travel. Ultimately, these electrical signals are integrated (i.e., summed). There are two types of summation. With temporal summation, EPSPs or IPSPs that occur in rapid succession are integrated. In the case of spatial summation, EPSPs or IPSPs that take place simultaneously at different places on the somatodendritic region are integrated. Integration of EPSPs moves the membrane potential toward the threshold (i.e., it reflects an increased excitability), while integration of IPSPs essentially subtracts from this, moving the membrane potential in the more negative direction. If the integrated EPSP and IPSP activity, which is summed over time, and across different places on the neuron, reaches the threshold at the axon hillock (the initial portion of the axon), an action potential is triggered. Over time, the integrated electrical signals processed by the axon hillock are therefore translated into a code that consists of the particular frequency and pattern of action potential firing that is generated.

As stated earlier, action potentials travel along the axon, and ultimately reach the terminals, where they stimulate release of neurotransmitter. Although there are multiple mechanisms of neurotransmitter release, the most common involves a process that couples the excitation of the action potential to the release (or "secretion") of the transmitter (this has sometimes been called excitation-secretion coupling). When the action potential reaches the terminal, it opens voltage-gated Ca^{++} channels. The influx of Ca^{++} ions into the terminal acts as a trigger for the release of transmitter (Ghosh & Greenberg, 1995; Kasai, 1999; Rettig & Neher, 2002). This calcium-dependent process involves the release of neurotransmitter molecules that are stored in membranous *vesicles* in the terminal. The influx of Ca^{++} ions into the terminal promotes the fusion of the vesicular membrane with the outer membrane of the cell, and the contents of the vesicle are then dumped into the synaptic cleft. These neurotransmitter molecules diffuse across the cleft and act upon the postsynaptic membrane, essentially becoming a part of the chemical environment of that next neuron, instigating EPSPs or IPSPs on that cell depending upon which transmitter is released, and which receptors detect it. Neurotransmitter release will be discussed more in Chapter 5.

In summary, information is processed by neurons in a series of steps, and different codes or "languages" are used at these different stages. At the level of the somatodendritic region, the signals used to encode features of the chemical environment are the graded and summed EPSPs and IPSPs. Then, this signal is translated into a frequency and pattern of action potentials. In turn, the signal conveyed by the action potentials is translated into the magnitude and temporal pattern of neurotransmitter release. The neurotransmitter being released then becomes a part of the chemical environment of the next neuron, which generates new signals in that cell that are integrated and summed with all the other signals being received. Finally, the processes described earlier are repeated over and over throughout the circuitry of the nervous system, and the net computational power of the brain results from the interaction between the multitude of circuits distributed across different brain areas, and the billions of neurons that contribute to each circuit.

How do drugs fit into this picture? Some drugs act on the basic electrophysiological properties of nerve cells. One example is phenytoin (Dilantin), a drug commonly used in the treatment of epilepsy, which has a variety of neuronal membrane-stabilizing properties (Pincus & Kiss, 1986). These properties decrease the Na^+ flow during the resting and action potentials, thus reducing the cell's excitability, and decrease the outward flow of K^+ during the action potential, thus increasing the duration of the refractory period. Another example is *tetrodotoxin* (TTX), which is a naturally occurring substance that comes from the pufferfish. The pufferfish is eaten as a sushi or sashimi delicacy called *fogu* in Japan, but if improperly prepared, it can be lethal. TTX blocks Na^+ channels, and thus inhibits the generation of action potentials. TTX is a very useful tool in physiology and neurochemistry research, because it can be used to demonstrate if a particular effect or condition depends upon action potentials. Interestingly, it also could be a useful tool for creating "zombies"; although even low doses of TTX can easily be lethal, ethnobotanist Wade Davis has suggested that very low doses of TTX have been used in Haiti to create "zombies" that have the temporary appearance of being dead, as part of a voodoo ritual (Davis [1985]; though this idea also has been challenged, see Hines [2008]). Ethanol and general anesthetics—including volatile solvents found in glue, industrial solvents, aerosol sprays (such as toluene, acetone, benzene, hexane, and ether)—have been shown to indirectly perturb lipid bilayers of neuronal membranes and inhibit the opening of voltage-gated ion channels that play a role in axonal conduction. However, these actions occur only at very high doses that are probably not relevant in explaining their psychopharmacological effects (Franks & Lieb, 1994). **Local anesthetics** (drugs that block sensation from a specific part of the body) act by blocking voltage-gated sodium channels in neuronal membranes (Ragsdale et al., 1994). One of cocaine's clinical uses is that of a local anesthetic, which in the PNS is the result of its ability to occupy sodium channels, preventing the influx of Na^+ and thereby preventing the triggering and conduction of an action potential (VanDyke & Byck, 1982). This action prevents any sensory information from reaching the CNS.

In addition to these examples, most drugs studied in psychopharmacology act by altering the processes involved in chemical neurotransmission in the brain. As reviewed in detail in Chapter 5, there are five basic processes that underlie chemical neurotransmission: synthesis, storage, release, postsynaptic action, and inactivation. Drugs can alter these processes in many ways—by increasing or decreasing synthesis, by blocking storage, by enhancing or reducing release, by stimulating or blocking receptors, or by inhibiting the process of inactivation.

ADDITIONAL FEATURES OF CHEMICAL NEUROTRANSMISSION

When presenting material as an instructor, one is faced with a challenge—how to simplify the material enough to make it comprehensible, while at the same time preserving much of the complex reality of the processes being discussed. Given the vast complexities of the brain, its neural circuitry and chemistry, this is a daunting task. In this section, we will take the basic model of nerve excitability and chemical transmission presented earlier and add some additional information that makes the narrative more complex, but closer to the reality of the living brain into which drugs are introduced.

First of all, the description presented earlier represents the core features of nerve excitability and chemical transmission, but more details need to be mentioned. Dendrites not only receive information but also transmit it; in many neurons, there is *dendritic release* of transmitters as well as release from terminals. Dendritic release of trophic signaling chemicals such as brain-derived neurotrophic factor can modulate synaptic plasticity and neural network construction (Kuczewski et al., 2009), while dendritic release of classical transmitters such as DA can provide a mechanism for inhibition of neighboring cells or self-inhibition (Falkenburger et al., 2001). How does a neuron inhibit itself? Such an action serves as a negative-feedback mechanism and is typically provided by the presence of autoreceptors. *Autoreceptors* (i.e., "self" receptors) are activated by the same neurotransmitter that is used by a particular neuron (Carlsson, 1987). Thus, if a DA receptor is on a DA neuron, it is referred to as an autoreceptor. Some neurons have autoreceptors located on their cell bodies or dendrites. These appear to play a role in the modulation of the physiological activity of these neurons, such as their rate of firing. For instance, when these neurons become active, their dendrites, as well as their axon terminals, can release transmitters. These transmitters then stimulate autoreceptors located on these same dendrites, which decrease neural firing by hyperpolarizing the neuronal membrane and preventing these neurons from becoming too active. Autoreceptors may also be localized on the terminals of some neurons; thus, they are members of a class of receptors referred to as *presynaptic receptors* (Figure 4.7). Stimulation of presynaptic autoreceptors generally reduces the rate of both transmitter biosynthesis and action potential–induced transmitter release, although these two functions may be mediated via different autoreceptor subtypes. The presence or absence of autoreceptors on neurons may be an important factor in their differential sensitivity to certain types of drugs and to the development of drug tolerance with chronic drug exposure. Moreover, drug-induced modifications in autoreceptors may also be responsible for the delayed therapeutic effects shown to numerous drugs (e.g., antidepressants and antipsychotics) that require chronic exposure in order to be effective.

In addition to autoreceptors, there are presynaptic *heteroreceptors* that can act to modulate transmitter release (Engelman & MacDermott, 2004). If a DA terminal contained a release-modulating receptor for another transmitter (e.g., ACh), this receptor would be known as a heteroreceptor (Figure 4.7). For example, some types of heteroreceptors may inhibit Ca^{++} flow into the axon terminal, thus reducing transmitter release, whereas others may facilitate Ca^{++} flow into the axon terminal or prolong depolarization when an action potential arrives, thus enhancing transmitter release. Heteroreceptor activation can enhance spontaneous neurotransmitter release but inhibit evoked neurotransmitter release, or vice versa. In some cases,

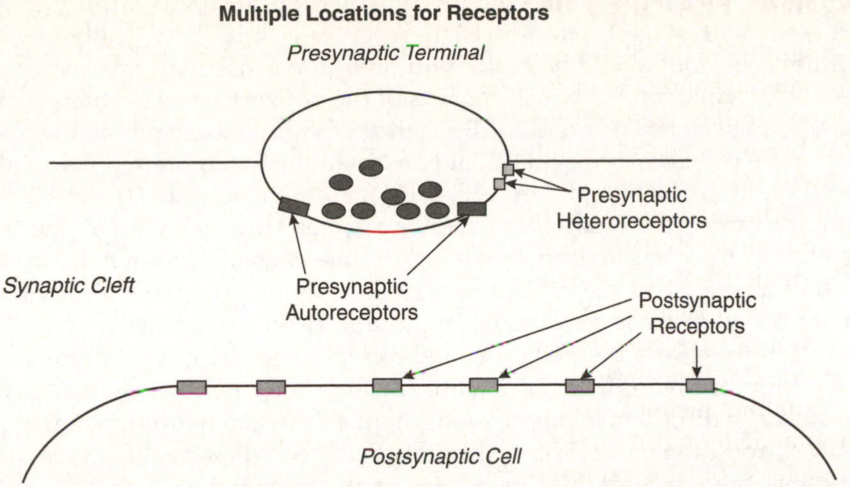

Multiple Locations for Receptors

Presynaptic Terminal

Presynaptic
Heteroreceptors

Synaptic Cleft

Presynaptic
Autoreceptors

Postsynaptic
Receptors

Postsynaptic Cell

FIGURE 4.7   In addition to postsynaptic receptors, there are presynaptic receptors that modulate neurotransmitter release. Presynaptic autoreceptors located on terminals detect the same transmitter that the neuron uses, and typically inhibit release from that terminal. Presynaptic heteroreceptors detect a transmitter that is not the one used by that terminal, and can act to increase or decrease release.

stimulation of heteroreceptors can induce biphasic effects, depending on the agonist concentration. For example, low agonist concentrations that activate few receptors and slightly depolarize the presynaptic membrane can enhance evoked release by bringing the membrane potential closer to threshold, whereas higher agonist concentrations that activate many receptors might depolarize the membrane to the point that the action potential amplitude is depressed, which would tend to decrease neurotransmitter release. Obviously, the presence of autoreceptors and heteroreceptors in the synapse makes the overall interactions between the release of various transmitters very complex.

Up to this point, we have largely described neurotransmission as involving a communication system between neuronal membranes that are very close together, that is, across the synaptic cleft. However, there is accumulating evidence that chemical transmission can occur among neurons that are relatively far apart—a form of intercellular communication called *volume transmission* or *nonsynaptic neurotransmission*, in which transmitters released from some neurons diffuse in a three-dimensional fashion within the extracellular fluid of the brain and interact with receptors that are located relatively long distances away (Agnati et al., 1995). This type of distal communication in the brain is analogous to that in the peripheral endocrine system, in which the signal (neurotransmitter or hormone), once released by the source cell, diffuses in the neighboring extracellular fluid, enters a specialized fluid compartment (CSF and blood, respectively) in which it is moved by convection forces, and finally diffuses into the extracellular fluid around the target cell and acts on receptors there. This phenomenon explains a long-standing puzzle as to why so often there is no obvious spatial correspondence between the sites of transmitter storage and sites of receptor concentration in the brain. It also accounts for the differential affinities of receptors for some transmitters. For example, with volume transmission, receptor affinity is typically high, whereas with synaptic transmission, receptor affinity is typically low, because high-affinity receptors would be easily saturated in a synapse. It has been suggested that there is a "wired brain," which consists of the network of fast synapses mediated by transmitters such as GLU and GABA, but that volume transmission is a spatially and temporally diffuse process that is laid on top of the wired brain (Fuxe et al., 2010). Many of the monoamine (e.g., DA, NE, 5-HT), amino acid (GLU, GABA), and neuropeptide transmitters discussed in Chapter 5 appear to work via volume transmission, as well as by synaptic transmission. Volume transmission may be involved in slowly fluctuating psychological processes such as mood, stress, motivation, and sleep, as opposed to those that require rapid and precise synaptic activity, in which there is a need for clearly defined onset and offset of signals of short duration (i.e., visual perception or fine movements). Thus, disorders of mood and other psychiatric disorders may be disorders involving nonsynaptic diffusion neurotransmission (Bach-y-Rita, 1994), and drugs, like Prozac, that are effective in their treatment may work because of their ability to alter this type of neurotransmission.

Synaptic neurotransmission is typically depicted as a one-way street in synapses formed between two neurons—a presynaptic neuron that releases neurotransmitters which then activate receptors on a postsynaptic neuron to alter its excitability. However, there is considerable evidence that at some synapses, following activation of receptors on the postsynaptic neuron, the postsynaptic neuron releases chemicals that diffuse backward to act on receptors on the presynaptic neuron, and their activation causes an alteration in presynaptic transmitter release when the neuron fires on subsequent occasions (Alger, 2002). That is, these chemicals serve as *retrograde messengers* that allow the postsynaptic cell to convey feedback to the presynaptic cell that something has happened, for example, that its message has been received. Retrograde messengers appear to be membrane-permeable, diffusible chemicals that do not require vesicles for storage or release, and they may be released from undifferentiated regions, that is, nonsynaptic areas, of neurons. Candidates for retrograde messengers include some of the classical neurotransmitters (e.g., DA, GABA, GLU), the simple gases such as nitric oxide and carbon monoxide, and arachidonic acid (a fatty acid common to cell membranes) and its derivatives. Retrograde messengers have been speculated to be involved in long-term potentiation (LTP), which refers to long-lasting change in a neuron's excitability and is a widely studied model of the synaptic basis of learning and memory in the mammalian brain (Maffei et al., 2003). The induction of LTP is triggered by the postsynaptic entry of Ca^{++} through the channel associated with a specialized receptor (the NMDA receptor, which was mentioned earlier), whereas its maintenance is mediated, at least in part, by presynaptic mechanisms. To explain how postsynaptic events can lead to an increase in transmitter release, it has been hypothesized that there are retrograde messengers that carry information from the postsynaptic side of the synapse to recently active presynaptic terminals. Presumably, this signal allows for the connection between the two neurons to be strengthened. Although retrograde messengers often are considered in the context of long-term synaptic plasticity, they have also been ascribed numerous roles on the short-term regulation of synaptic transmission (Alger, 2002). For example, a class of neurotransmitters called endocannabinoids (endogenous cannabinoids, which are derivatives of arachidonic acid) has recently emerged as one of the most widely accepted classes of retrograde messengers in the brain. The major active ingredient in marijuana, Δ-9-THC, is believed to work on the presynaptic receptors normally activated by endocannabinoids, which in most cases inhibits the release of a variety of neurotransmitters from presynaptic neurons.

Websites for Further Information

Sites providing general information on neuroscience or synaptic transmission:

> http://apu.sfn.org
> http://www.mind.ilstu.edu/flash/
> synapse_1.swf
> http://www.rnceus.com/meth/
> introneurotrans.html

Sites offering brain anatomy information and tutorials:

> http://www.pbs.org/wnet/brain/3d
> http://www.med.harvard.edu/AANLIB/
> home.html

> http://www.gwc.maricopa.edu/class/
> bio201/brain/1neuro.htm
> http://www.brainmuseum.org

Read more about TTX and Haitian "zombies"

> http://neurophilosophy.wordpress.com/
> 2006/05/24/voodoo-zombies-
> the-puffer-fish/

Synaptic Transmission, Drugs, and Chemical Neuroanatomy

There are literally hundreds of neuroactive chemicals found in and among the billions of cells making up the brain. Some of them appear to exert actions of very short duration (e.g., a few milliseconds), whereas others appear to exert actions of relatively long duration (e.g., several seconds or minutes). Some travel very short distances from the cells in which they originate, and others travel relatively long distances. Some exert an action by themselves, whereas others appear to exert an action only in the presence of other endogenous chemicals. Specific neuroactive ligands (a *ligand* is a substance that binds to a receptor) are highly localized in some areas of the brain, whereas others are distributed widely throughout the nervous system.

The nervous system itself has a variety of highly interrelated subsystems, all of which allow us to engage in extremely complex psychological activities, such as thinking, planning, learning, speaking, experiencing emotions, preparing the body for action, and so on. By interacting with the natural neuroactive signaling molecules in various areas of the brain, drugs can shift normal psychological activities carried out by the brain into abnormal ones and, in some cases, can serve to normalize abnormal psychological activities. In either case, drugs are acting to alter brain function. The purpose of this chapter is to familiarize you with some of the more important ligands found in the nervous system, to review briefly some of the major subsystems of the nervous system, and to discuss how psychoactive drugs affect chemical signaling and why they induce the effects they do.

NEUROTRANSMITTERS AND CHEMICAL SIGNALING IN THE NERVOUS SYSTEM

Neurotransmitters are commonly viewed as chemicals that are located in specific regions of neurons, are released under specific stimulation, act on a specific set of receptors, and induce some type of postsynaptic action such as a change in membrane potentials or metabolic activity. The list of neurotransmitters is ever growing (see Table 5.1), and it now includes both "classical transmitters" such as glutamate (GLU), gamma-aminobutyric acid (GABA), acetylcholine (ACh), dopamine (DA), norepinephrine (NE), and serotonin (5-HT), as well as more recently characterized substances such as anandamide (AN; an endogenous cannabinoid) and adenosine. Researchers and instructors sometimes struggle with the definition of a *neurotransmitter*, and how this term is distinct from related terms such as *neurohormone* and *neuromodulator*. The term *neurohormone* refers to substances that are synthesized and released from neurons, but act as hormones; these substances include hormones such as corticotrophin releasing factor, which is released from hypothalamic neurons and acts on the anterior pituitary gland, and also includes oxytocin and vasopressin, which are synthesized in the hypothalamus and released into systemic circulation in the posterior pituitary. The term *neuromodulator* has been defined in several different ways. In some instances, it is used as a general term to include any substance that alters neurotransmission in some way. Defined in this manner, neurotransmission is a specific subclass of neuromodulation. However, neuromodulation is sometimes used to describe the condition in which a substance modifies neural transmission but is not itself the means of transmission (i.e., it does not show any direct shifts in membrane potential or conductance when tested for actions on its own). When defined in this way, there appears to be a clear distinction between neurotransmitters and neuromodulators. To add to the confusion, the same substance can meet the definition of a *neurohormone*, *neuromodulator*, and *neurotransmitter* (e.g., DA), and most substances that are neurotransmitters also act as neuromodulators. Perhaps the best way to view these terms is to make a distinction between the different types of signaling processes (e.g., neurotransmission vs. neuromodulation), but also to recognize that the same substance can modify neural transmission in multiple ways. Table 5.1 contains a list of neurotransmitters that is a useful working list for this book, and Figure 5.1 shows the chemical structures of some of these transmitters. A more detailed listing of neurotransmitters and description of the processes involved in chemical neurotransmission can be obtained by additional reading (e.g., Iversen et al., 2009).

TABLE 5.1   List of Receptor Subtypes for Several Neurotransmitters

DA: D_1 family (D_1,D_5), D_2 family (D_2,D_3,D_4)

Adrenergic (NE, EPI): α_{1-2} β_{-3}
ACh: nicotinic, muscarinic (M_1, M_2, M_3, M_4, M_5)
5-HT: 5-HT_{1-7}
GLU, ASP: NMDA, AMPA, KAINATE, metabotropic
GABA: $GABA_A$, $GABA_B$
Cannabinoid: CB_1, CB_2
Adenosine: A_1, A_{2A}, A_{2B}, A_3
Opiate: mu, delta, kappa

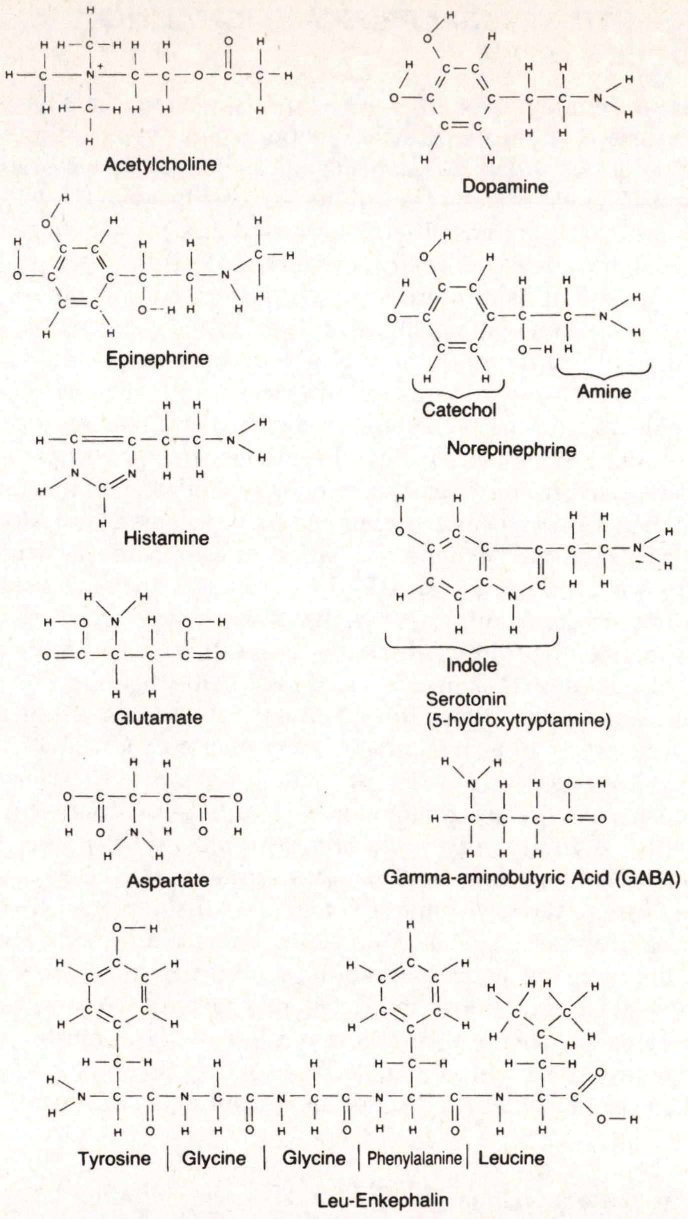

Acetylcholine

Dopamine

Epinephrine

Catechol   Amine

Norepinephrine

Histamine

Indole

Serotonin (5-hydroxytryptamine)

Glutamate

Aspartate

Gamma-aminobutyric Acid (GABA)

Tyrosine | Glycine | Glycine | Phenylalanine | Leucine

Leu-Enkephalin

FIGURE 5.1 Molecular structures of some of the key chemicals found in the mammalian nervous system that are believed to serve either a neurotransmitter or a neuromodulatory role. The symbols stand for atoms: C, carbon; H, hydrogen; O, oxygen; and N, nitrogen. A single bond between atoms is indicated by —, and a double bond by ═.

Another issue to be discussed is whether or not a neuron uses only one transmitter or multiple ones. For a time, there was a rule named Dale's Law or Dale's Principle, named after Henry Dale, the famous British neurochemist. According to Dale's original formation (the principle was recast and named in association with Dale by another seminal figure in this field, John Eccles), a given neuron uses the same neurotransmitter at all its synapses. Thus, a given neuron can be identified in terms of which transmitter it uses (i.e., a dopaminergic neuron, a GABAergic neuron, or a cholinergic neuron). This observation was first formulated based upon early studies of classical transmitters, but it sometimes has been misinterpreted to mean that one neuron uses only one transmitter. We now know that a given neuron can co-localize multiple transmitters (Bartfai et al., 1988; Jonas et al., 1998; Kennedy, 2000), often a combination of a classical transmitter and a neuropeptide (a peptide is a small string of amino acids). More recently, it has been suggested that DA neurons projecting to the forebrain also use GLU at some synapses (Chuhma et al., 2009; Lapish et al., 2007). Yet, regardless of these phenomena of co-localization and co-release, it is not true that any given neuron can have any combination of transmitters. Thus, despite some exceptions, we can identify the distinction between a DA neuron and neurons that use NE, ACh, 5-HT; such a distinction is useful for describing the chemical neuroanatomy of various transmitter projection systems, as is done at the end of this chapter.

The first group of neurotransmitters to be discussed will be the *monoamines* (MA), which includes the *catecholamines* DA, NE, and epinephrine (EPI), as well as the *indolamine* 5-HT. Monoamines are grouped together because the neurons that utilize monoamines share biochemical features (metabolic pathways, protein expression), and this also means that some drugs act broadly on all monoamines. The catecholamines DA, NE, and EPI are structurally related to each other (i.e., they contain the catechol functional group, as shown in Figure 5.1). They also share common synthesis and enzymatic breakdown pathways (the same starting material, tyrosine, and many of the same enzymes; see next sections); catecholamine neurons are closely related to each other in terms of many features of their neurochemistry. If one could consider all the catecholamine neurons as "siblings" because they are closely related in terms of their gene expression and biochemistry, then one should consider 5-HT neurons as their "cousin." 5-HT is labeled as an indolamine because of its structure (Figure 5.1), but it is considered a monoamine because of its close similarity to the catecholamines. The synthetic pathway for 5-HT resembles that of catecholamines, and one of the metabolizing enzymes (monoamine oxidase or *MAO*) is involved in the breakdown of all the monoamines. Monoamines are involved in many functions that will be discussed in this book, and drugs belonging to many drug classes, including stimulants, antiparkinsonian agents, antipsychotics, antidepressants, and hallucinogens, act on one or more monoamines (Iversen et al., 2009).

A number of neurotransmitters that are not monoamines also need to be discussed because of their relevance for psychopharmacology. ACh was the first neurotransmitter discovered and characterized (Taylor, 1985). Originally named *vagusstoff* (a German word meaning "stuff from the vagus nerve"), ACh was shown to be released by electrical stimulation of the vagus nerve, because the fluid surrounding the stimulated nerve terminals was shown to slow the heart rate (these experiments won Otto Loewi the Nobel Prize, which he shared with Henry Dale). ACh is involved in motor control (Collins et al., 2010a), sleep, emotional and cognitive processes, and many drugs that are used to treat parkinsonism and Alzheimer's disease act on ACh. Histamine (H) is a neurotransmitter that promotes secretion in many tissues (lungs, stomach, etc.). For this reason, drugs that block H receptors (known as antihistamines) are used to treat colds and allergies, as well as stomach ulcers. In addition, H is involved in regulating sleep and wakefulness. For that reason, antihistamines can produce drowsiness, which is useful for sleep-promoting formulations, but is an unwanted side effect in some allergy medicines.

Amino acids are important compounds for metabolism and are the basic building blocks for proteins and peptides, but some amino acids also act as neurotransmitters (Iversen et al., 2009). GLU and aspartate (ASP) are known as *excitatory amino acids*, because of their ability to induce excitation (excitatory postsynaptic potentials or EPSPs) in neurons (see Chapter 4 for a discussion of GLU-mediated EPSPs). GLU is probably the most common excitatory transmitter in the nervous system, and glutamatergic pathways form much of the basic excitatory wiring of the neural circuitry of the brain. Excitatory amino acids are very important for neural plasticity (i.e., the changeability that underlies the modification of synapses), and the plastic changes in synaptic function that are regulated by GLU are thought to be critical for aspects of learning and memory. Long-term potentiation (LTP) is a widely studied model of synaptic plasticity, and considerable evidence indicates that GLU is involved in LTP (O'Neill et al., 2004). In addition, overstimulation of excitatory amino acid receptors can cause brain damage (i.e., *excitotoxicity*), which is considered to be a factor in the secondary brain damage induced by cerebral strokes or hypoxia, because when GLU neurons die, they dump their GLU into the extracellular space. This finding has been useful, not only because it sheds light on the mechanisms underlying brain damage, but also because drugs that mimic this effect can be used as tools in lesion experiments (Olney, 1990). Moreover, drugs that block excitatory amino acid transmission can act as *neuroprotective agents* (substances that reduce loss of neurons under various conditions). In addition, drugs that block N-Methyl-D-aspartic acid (NMDA) receptors (a subtype of excitatory amino acid receptor) can produce hallucinogenic effects, can alter sensory functions, and can sometimes induce psychotic side effects. Phencyclidine and ketamine are two examples of drugs with this type of action. Glycine (GLY) is another amino acid that functions as a neurotransmitter. It is inhibitory because of its actions on some receptors, but it also can act as an excitatory neuromodulator at a specific binding site on NMDA excitatory amino acid receptors. GLU, ASP, and GLY are all called alpha amino acids; they are in the group of amino acids that normally are the building block units for peptides and proteins. However, another important neurotransmitter, GABA, is an amino acid, but it is not the type of amino acid that is used to build proteins. GABA is the most common inhibitory neurotransmitter in the brain (although it can be excitatory early in development), and was used in Chapter 4 as an example of a substance that induces inhibitory postsynaptic potentials (IPSPs; see also Greengard, 2001). Many important drugs in psychopharmacology, including sedative–hypnotics, anticonvulsants, and antianxiety agents such as Valium and similar compounds, act to modify GABAergic transmission. The $GABA_A$ subtype of receptor turns out to be a very heterogenous type of receptor made up of five subunits that can combine in a wide variety of configurations. Research with genetically manipulated mice suggests that the particular combination of subunits determines whether the receptor has anticonvulsant, anxiolytic, sedative, or hypnotic effects (Rudolph et al., 2001).

Several additional neurotransmitters/neuromodulators are important to consider because they are substrates of action for many psychoactive drugs. AN is an example of an *endogenous cannabinoid*; it is a fatty acid derivative that acts as a neural signaling molecule. The well-known recreational drug Δ-9 THC, the active ingredient in marijuana, acts to mimic the effects of AN on its receptors. In addition to being important because of the widespread use of marijuana, cannabinoid pharmacology has become widely studied because of the possible medicinal uses of drugs that stimulate cannabinoid transmission, and also because blockers of cannabinoid receptors may be useful as appetite suppressants (Le Foll et al., 2009; Salamone et al., 2007; Sink et al., 2008). Adenosine is a purine neurotransmitter/neuromodulator that is a very ubiquitous substance. It is synthesized from cell energy pathways that use AMP-ADP-ATP (adenosine triphosphate or ATP is the basic energy currency of the cell; AMP is adenosine monophosphate, ADP is adenosine diphosphate) and is present with a widespread distribution throughout the body and brain. Although it is typically described as a neurotransmitter, adenosine is not stored in vesicles, nor is it released in a calcium-dependent process (Masino et al., 2009). Nevertheless, there are adenosine receptors in the brain, and there are several well-known drugs that act as adenosine antagonists. The minor stimulants caffeine, theophylline, and theobromine are all adenosine antagonists (Ferré 2008, 2010), and novel adenosine antagonists that are selective in their actions (e.g., istradefylline and preladenant) are being developed as potential treatments for parkinsonism and depression (Pinna et al., 2010; Salamone 2010a).

A number of neurotransmitters are peptides, that is, small strings of amino acids. One important group of peptide neurotransmitters is the *endogenous opiates*. Morphine and codeine are two active ingredients from the opium poppy (heroin is a semisynthetic derivative of morphine), and the psychoactive effects of the opium plant and its active ingredients have been known for many years (e.g., analgesia, euphoria, and dependence). During the last few decades, endogenous peptides (endorphins, enkephalins, and dynorphins) have been identified and characterized. Naturally occurring and synthetic opiates, as well as opiate antagonists, are so important for psychopharmacology that an entire chapter of this book (Chapter 12) is devoted to them. In addition to the opiate peptides, there are other peptides that should be mentioned. Substance P, oxytocin, vasopressin, and cholecystokinin are all peptides that are used as neurotransmitters. Substance P is an important transmitter of information related to pain in the spinal cord, and also is a central transmitter involved in motor control and other functions. Oxytocin, vasopressin, and cholecystokinin are all peptides that are used as hormones in the periphery, but also are central neurotransmitters. This list of peptides is only partial; there are many additional neuroactive peptides that have been identified (e.g., neuropeptide Y, vasoactive intestinal peptide, neurotensin, and galanin; see Iversen et al., 2009).

For the rest of this chapter, we will discuss the processes involved in neurotransmission in more detail, and will also discuss several psychoactive drugs in terms of their basic neurochemical effects. As described earlier, this book will organize the steps involved in chemical neurotransmission by dividing it into five stages: synthesis, storage, release, postsynaptic action, and inactivation (see Figure 5.2).

Synthesis   Neurotransmitters are made from a starting material known as a *precursor*.

Storage   Transmitters are stored in membranous *vesicles*, most concentrated in terminals.

Release   Release is usually stimulated by an influx of *calcium* (CA^{++} ions) into terminal.

Postsynaptic Action   Transmitter binds to *receptors*, and as a result of binding stimulates intrinsic biological activity.

Inactivation   *Enzymes* break down (i.e., *metabolize*) transmitter, or *transporters* take transmitter back into the terminal.

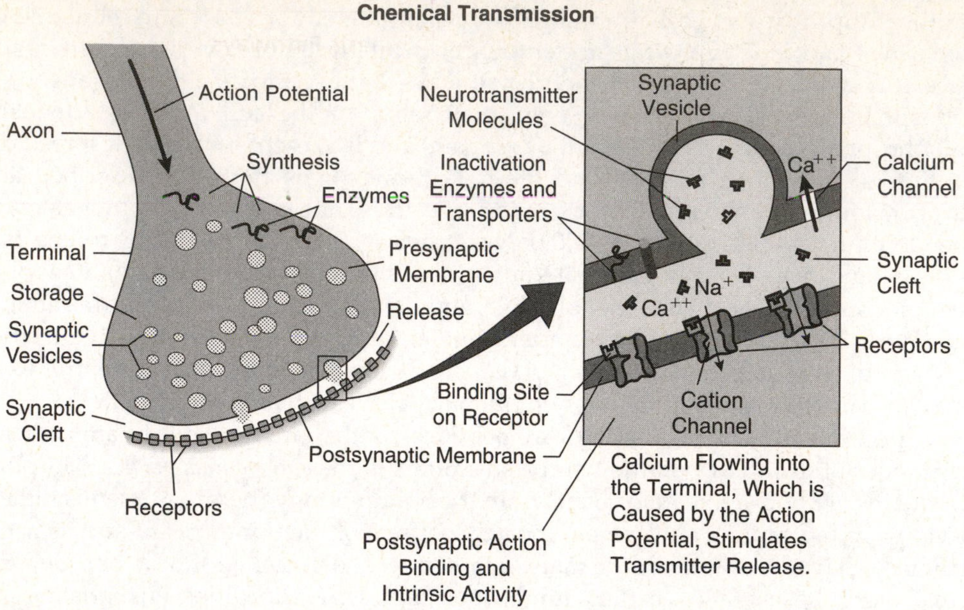

Chemical Transmission

FIGURE 5.2 Five major steps in chemical neurotransmission (synthesis, storage, release, postsynaptic activation, and inactivation).

Given this organizational scheme, the effect of any drug on neurotransmission can be defined in terms of an action on some neurotransmitter or group of transmitters, in combination with the stages of neurotransmission being affected. Drugs can facilitate or inhibit synthesis, block storage, stimulate or inhibit release, stimulate or block receptors, or inhibit enzymatic breakdown or uptake. Thus, a drug can be said to block the inactivation of 5-HT by blocking uptake (e.g., the antidepressant Prozac), block monoamine storage (the antipsychotic reserpine) or stimulate release of DA and NE (e.g., the stimulant amphetamine). Over the next several sections, these stages of neurotransmission will be discussed, and several drugs will be characterized in terms of their specific actions.

SYNTHESIS OF NEUROTRANSMITTERS

Neurotransmitter molecules are synthesized from a starting material known as a "precursor." Precursors are either very common metabolites or common nutrients, or both. One or more enzymatic reactions convert the precursor into the neurotransmitter, depending upon the particular transmitter in question. In addition, neurotransmitter synthesis is a very common site of drug action. Figure 5.3 depicts the synthesis pathways for the catecholamines, 5-HT, ACh, and GABA, to provide a few examples (see Iversen et al., 2009, for more reading about neurotransmitter synthesis).

The starting material for catecholamine synthesis is the amino acid *tyrosine*, which is either obtained in the diet or converted from another amino acid, phenylalanine. Tyrosine is acted upon by the first enzyme in the sequence, tyrosine hydroxylase (TH), and converted into L-DOPA. TH is a very important enzyme; it is the rate-limiting (i.e., slowest) enzyme in the sequence, and it undergoes a negative feedback effect

```
┌─────────────────────────────────────────────────────────────────────┐
│              Examples of Neurotransmitter Synthesis Pathways          │
│                                                                       │
│  Catecholamines:                                                      │
│                                                                       │
│  Tyrosine → L-DOPA → DA → NE → EPI                                     │
│          TH                                                           │
│  Tyrosine: amino acid precursor                                       │
│  TH: tyrosine hydroxylase- first enzyme in sequence; rate limiting step│
│  L-DOPA: also administered as a drug that stimulates synthesis        │
│                                                                       │
│  Serotonin:                                                           │
│                                                                       │
│  Tryptophan → 5-HTP → 5-HT                                             │
│              TrpH                                                     │
│  Tryptophan: precursor amino acid                                     │
│  TrpH: tryptophan hydroxylase, first enzyme in sequence;              │
│  rate limiting step                                                   │
│  5-HTP: can be given as a drug to stimulate synthesis                 │
│                                                                       │
│  Acetylcholine:                                                       │
│                                                                       │
│  AcetylCoA + Choline → ACh                                            │
│                    CAT                                                │
│  AcetylCoA: ubiquitous metabolite, involved in energy metabolism Choline: a very common metabo-│
│  lite, component of phospholipids CAT: choline acetyltransferase, enyzme that forms ACh│
│                                                                       │
│  GABA (gamma amino butyric acid):                                     │
│                                                                       │
│  Glu → GABA                                                           │
│     GAD                                                               │
│  GABA is formed from Glutamate                                        │
│  GAD: glutamic acid decarboxylase, enzyme that forms GABA in neurons  │
│                                                                       │
│  Peptides:                                                            │
│                                                                       │
│  peptide neurotransmitters are cleaved from larger precursor peptides │
│  or proteins                                                          │
│  (e.g. prodynorphin → dynorphin)                                      │
└─────────────────────────────────────────────────────────────────────┘
```

FIGURE 5.3 Synthesis pathways for some neurotransmitters. Each arrow depicts an enzymatic reaction, but only one enzyme is named in each sequence.

known as end-product inhibition (i.e., it is inhibited by the catecholamines). Also, immunohistochemical stains for TH are used as a marker of catecholamine neurons. L-DOPA is a precursor molecule that is converted into DA by the next enzyme in the sequence (L-aromatic amino acid decarboxylase). In DA neurons, this is as far as the synthetic pathway is expressed, and DA serves as the neurotransmitter (Arvid Carlsson won the Nobel Prize for discovering that DA was a neurotransmitter in the brain). However, in NE neurons, an additional enzyme is expressed (dopamine β-hydroxylase), and DA is converted into NE. Finally, in EPI neurons, the last enzyme in the sequence (phenylethanolamine N-methyltransferase) converts NE into EPI. So, in EPI neurons, both DA and NE are precursors, not neurotransmitters. This synthetic pathway is also used by the adrenal gland to make catecholamine hormones (NE is also known as noradrenalin, and EPI is also known as adrenalin; sometimes, these alternate names are more common when referring to these substances as hormones). Several drugs can affect catecholamine synthesis. TH can be inhibited by *α-methyl tyrosine*, which is used in basic and clinical research to reduce catecholamine synthesis. Another interesting approach to the pharmacological modulation of catecholamine synthesis is the drug *α-methyl dopa* (Aldomet). This drug enters catecholamine synthesis at the same stage as L-DOPA, and during the rest of the sequence of enzymatic reactions, it is converted into a series of "false transmitters" that are stored and released, but do not have a postsynaptic action. For many years, this drug was the leading treatment for high blood pressure. Perhaps the most well-known drug that is used to alter catecholamine synthesis is L-DOPA. When given exogenously to patients with Parkinson's disease, L-DOPA increases the synthesis of catecholamines, having the biggest effects on DA synthesis. L-DOPA is used to restore DA levels in parkinsonian patients, because this disease results from a severe degeneration of DA neurons that innervate a brain area known as the striatum (see section on Chemical Neuroanatomy).

Synthesis of 5-HT begins with the amino acid precursor tryptophan, which is converted into *5-HTP* (5-hydroxytryptophan) by the action of the enzyme *tryptophan hydroxylase* (TrpH). Like TH, TrpH is the rate-limiting (i.e., slowest) enzyme in 5-HT synthesis, and it also undergoes end-product inhibition. 5-HTP is the precursor molecule that is converted into the neurotransmitter 5-HT by the next enzyme in the sequence (L-aromatic amino acid decarboxylase). It should be very clear that 5-HT synthesis is quite similar to catecholamine synthesis. Both pathways begin with an amino acid precursor, which then undergoes the same chemical reaction (an enzyme-mediated hydroxylase reaction). Then, the next enzyme in the sequence is actually shared by the catecholamines and 5-HT (L-aromatic amino acid decarboxylase). The biosynthesis of 5-HT is therefore analogous to the synthesis of DA. An example of a drug that inhibits 5-HT synthesis is the TrpH inhibitor *p-chlorophenylalanine*, which is a useful research tool for studying processes that depend upon 5-HT synthesis. Also, just like exogenous L-DOPA can be given as a drug to boost catecholamine synthesis, 5-HTP can be given to increase 5-HT synthesis. 5-HTP is available as a "dietary supplement" in health food stores and over the Internet, and people use this compound to self-medicate for problems ranging from insomnia and obesity to anxiety and depression.

Acetylcholine (ACh) is synthesized from two very common precursor substances. *Choline* is a ubiquitous substance distributed widely either as free choline or as a component of a common phospholipid known as phosphatidyl choline or *lecithin*. AcetylCoA (or acetylcoenzyme A) is the other precursor of ACh. The coenzyme A portion of the molecule is a common substance with a wide distribution in all cells. This compound acts as an acetyl group donor (hence the term *acetylCoA* when they are bound together) for many biochemical reactions, including some involved in the oxidative metabolism of carbohydrates and fatty acids. Every cell in the body has choline and acetylCoA, but only cholinergic neurons have the enzyme choline acetyltransferase (CAT), which puts them together to form ACh. Staining for CAT serves as an anatomical marker of ACh neurons.

As shown in Figure 5.3, GABA is synthesized from GLU by the action of the enzyme glutamic acid decarboxylase (GAD). In addition, we should briefly mention the synthesis of some other neurotransmitters. Though there are many sources of GLU, it appears that the primary neural source of GLU that is used as a neurotransmitter is from glutamine. H is synthesized from the amino acid histidine, and AN is synthesized from the fatty acid arachidonic acid. The immediate source of peptides that are used as neurotransmitters is not the individual amino acids themselves, but instead the active peptide sequence that is cleaved from larger precursor proteins or peptides (e.g., a peptide known as prodynorphin is cleaved to from the dynorphins).

One important question to consider in relation to neurotransmitter synthesis is the effect of "precursor loading" (i.e., taking an exogenous supply of precursor as a drug or dietary supplement). Does this have an effect on neurotransmitter synthesis? Well, it depends upon the precursor. L-DOPA and 5-HTP clearly act to elevate synthesis of catecholamines and 5-HT, respectively, but that is because these substances bypass the rate-limiting step in the enzymatic pathway. In other words, as we discussed earlier, TH and TrpH are relatively slow enzymes. Thus, administration of L-DOPA or 5-HTP is a convenient way to bypass these initial metabolic roadblocks, and for that reason these substances can exert a powerful influence on transmitter synthesis. However, what about tyrosine or tryptophan? This is a much more complex question. Precisely because TH and TrpH are relatively slow enzymes, they can be easily saturated in a person with normal nutrition; if an enzyme is saturated, giving more of the precursor would not further stimulate the rate of synthesis. Administration of lecithin to provide a source of choline also has been used as a strategy for boosting ACh synthesis in order to treat Alzheimer's disease or achieve some other cognitive benefits. Nevertheless, the clinical studies on the effects of lecithin in Alzheimer's patients yielded decidedly mixed results (Parnetti et al., 2007), in contrast to the use of L-DOPA, which is the gold standard of treatment for Parkinson's disease.

This discussion of precursor loading brings up the role of diet. It makes sense that dietary manipulations can alter the chemical composition of the brain and thus modify brain function and affect mood and behavior (Wurtman, 1982). For example, loading up on protein-rich foods might be expected to enhance the brain's production of 5-HT, which is believed to promote relaxation and hasten the onset of sleep (Radulovacki, 1982). It has been suggested that people who have trouble sleeping should drink warm milk, which contains high levels of tryptophan, before bedtime. Unfortunately, however, it is not that simple. Numerous biochemical processes must follow in sequence if the consumption of a meal rich in a particular nutrient is to increase the synthesis of a neurotransmitter in the brain (Wurtman, 1982). For example, in the case of tryptophan, you might think that a high-protein meal would make you drowsy because of the role of 5-HT in sleep. However, high-protein foods contain several amino acids, not just tryptophan, and they all compete for the same transporter molecules in the blood–brain barrier. Because tryptophan occurs in food in relatively small quantities, it does not have much of a chance of getting into the brain if all one eats is protein. If one eats food with carbohydrates (e.g., sweets, bread, pasta, and potatoes), which stimulate the production of insulin, all the other amino acids can get drawn out of the blood while having little effect on tryptophan blood levels. Thus, if one consumes carbohydrates a few hours before or after a protein-containing meal, brain concentrations of tryptophan and 5-HT synthesis may increase (Fernstrom & Fernstrom, 1995). In fact, many of the behavioral effects that have been attributed to eating carbohydrates may be due to the ability of carbohydrates to enhance the influx of tryptophan into the brain (Spring et al., 1987). In general, single meals, depending on their protein content, can rapidly influence uptake of the aromatic amino acids (tryptophan, tyrosine, and phenylalanine) into the brain and, as a result, directly modify their conversion to neurotransmitters and influence brain function. On the other hand, the acidic amino acids GLU and ASP, which are neurotransmitters themselves, do not have ready access to the brain from the circulation. As a result, the ingestion of proteins, which are naturally rich in GLU and ASP, has no effect on the level of the acidic amino acids in the brain. Furthermore, despite claims that the food additives monosodium glutamate and aspartame (an artificial sweetener containing ASP) may raise the level of acidic amino acids in the brain and modify its functions or even cause neuronal damage, a substantial body of published evidence clearly indicates that the brain is not affected by ingestion of aspartame and is affected by GLU only when it is administered alone in extremely large doses (Fernstrom, 1994).

Because various nutrients in food interact in such complicated ways, most of which are not well understood, it is very difficult to predict in advance what increased consumption of a particular nutrient will do with respect to mood and behavior. In most studies showing links between diet and behavior in human beings, the effects have been subtle, in comparison with a multitude of other factors influencing mood and behavior. Nevertheless, it does seem clear that poor nutrition can result in substantial alterations in neurotransmitter synthesis. In fact, some experiments deliberately deplete neurotransmitters by providing a diet that is free of precursors of catecholamines (tyrosine and phenylalanine) or 5-HT (tryptophan). These methods have been used to study the role of monoamine synthesis in depression (see Altman et al., 2010), and will be discussed in the chapter on antidepressant drugs (Chapter 9).

STORAGE OF NEUROTRANSMITTERS

Once synthesized, most transmitters are stored in *vesicles* (known as storage vesicles or synaptic vesicles; Figure 5.2). Vesicle membranes are composed of materials that are similar to those typically found in neuronal membranes—a phospholipid bilayer and transmembrane proteins. Vesicles can vary in size, shape, and appearance. Inside, synaptic vesicles are hollow and fluid-filled, and this interior of the vesicle provides the storage area for the neurotransmitter molecules. There are three major functions of storing neurotransmitter molecules inside vesicles. Firstly, storage in a vesicle provides a form of protection to the neurotransmitter. The interior of the cell contains enzymes that can metabolize (i.e., break down) the transmitter, and thus vesicular storage provides a safe haven for the pool of neurotransmitter that has been synthesized. Secondly, storage of the neurotransmitter in vesicles results in a situation such that the neuron generally has more neurotransmitter than it actually needs, which means that a ready supply of transmitter is always available. If a neuron had to synthesize new transmitter molecules every time it was excited, the process of neurotransmission would be much slower. Some of these vesicles represent a long-term storage pool of neurotransmitter molecules, and researchers have hypothesized that there could be several distinct pools of neurotransmitter stored in vesicles, which vary in terms of the temporal dynamics of their storage. Finally, there is a subset of vesicles that maintains a pool of neurotransmitter in a kind of pre-release state. These vesicles are in close association with release sites on the terminal membrane and represent a readily releasable pool of transmitter molecules.

Inhibition of vesicular storage provides a locus for the action of some drugs. Two antipsychotic drugs, *reserpine* and *tetrabenazine*, block vesicular storage in monoamine terminals by inhibiting the vesicular transporter that pumps the transmitter into the vesicle. Because the monoamine molecules that fail to be stored are vulnerable to enzymatic breakdown, inhibition of monoamine storage leads to a depletion of DA, NE, EPI, and 5-HT. The antipsychotic effects of these manipulations are likely to be due to a depletion of DA, but the decrease in NE and EPI also means that these drugs have been used to treat high blood pressure. Moreover, reserpine has been shown to produce symptoms of depression in people, and therefore, it is used in some animal models of depression (Chapter 9 has a discussion of the potential role of monoamines in depression).

RELEASE OF NEUROTRANSMITTERS

The most common mode of release of neurotransmitter release is a calcium-dependent process. As described earlier, when an action potential arrives at the terminal, it opens voltage-gated calcium channels, which allows calcium ions (Ca^{++}) to enter the axonal cytoplasm and promote the fusion of vesicles with the presynaptic membrane (Ghosh & Greenberg, 1995; Rettig & Neher, 2002). Those vesicles held in the prerelease state as described earlier fuse with the terminal membrane, whereas longer-term storage vesicles are held in reserve some distance away. The contents of the fused vesicles, including the transmitter(s), enzymes, and other proteins, are then discharged into the cleft (Figure 5.2). All of this takes place very quickly—that is, approximately 1 ms for the Ca^{++} spike and 0.3 to 2 ms for synaptic vesicle exocytosis (Kasai, 1999). There are also intracellular presynaptic storage sites for Ca^{++}, which under some conditions can be released to facilitate neurotransmitter release and modulate neuronal transmission at synapses (Tsuzuki et al., 2004). Calcium-dependent release is also said to be quantal in nature (i.e., it consists of basic units of neurotransmission). Upon the arrival of an action potential at axon terminals, a package of neurotransmitter molecules, called a *quantal package* or *quantum*, is released from vesicles; thus a quantum of neurotransmission (the basic unit) is the content of one vesicle. The size of these quanta (in terms of the number of neurotransmitter molecules) is not fixed, and can vary as a function of several factors (see Markov et al., 2008). Also, the probability of the release of transmitters from axons when an action potential arrives varies considerably, depending on the type of synapse (Levy & Baxter, 2002). At some synapses, release occurs virtually 100% of the time, whereas in others, it is common to observe release of a quantal package around 25% of the time. In addition to calcium-dependent neurotransmitter release, there is considerable evidence of calcium-independent release. Calcium-independent release can occur because the uptake transport proteins, which we normally think of as being solely a mechanism of inactivation of the transmitter from the synaptic cleft, can also reverse directions and transport neurotransmitter molecules from the inside to the outside of the membrane (Richerson & Wu, 2003).

There are many drugs that can modulate release of neurotransmitters (Iversen et al., 2009). Several well-known stimulant drugs act to enhance release of some transmitters. The amphetamine family of major psychomotor stimulants, including *d-amphetamine, l-amphetamine,* and *methamphetamine*, can increase monoamine release. *Methylphenidate* (Ritalin), which is commonly used as a treatment for attention-deficit hyperactivity disorder, stimulates release of catecholamines.*Para-chloroamphetamine* stimulates release of 5-HT. In addition, blockade of calcium ion channels can reduce neurotransmitter release.

POSTSYNAPTIC ACTIONS OF NEUROTRANSMITTERS

The next step in the neurotransmission process, postsynaptic action, is a vitally important one because it represents the actual reception of the chemical signal, and also because it is a common locus for the action of many drugs. There are two aspects of the postsynaptic action of neurotransmitters:

1. binding—a neurotransmitter binds to receptor protein; neurotransmitter has affinity for receptor.
2. intrinsic biological activity—as a result of binding, the neurotransmitter instigates a biological change in postsynaptic cell; these changes are collectively referred to as *intrinsic activity* or *signal transduction mechanisms*.

Affinity refers to the tendency of a ligand to bind to a receptor. A *ligand* is the term used for any substance, including a transmitter or drug, which binds to a receptor. In a few paragraphs, we will talk about drugs that bind to receptors, but for now, we will emphasize neurotransmitters (which are sometimes called *endogenous ligands*) and their binding characteristics. Affinity is not a property of a ligand, nor is it a property of a receptor; rather, it is a property of the relation between a particular ligand and a particular receptor. For example, DA has a high affinity for DA receptors, a low affinity for other catecholamine receptors, and essentially no affinity for other receptors. Affinity is not an all-or-none phenomenon. As we will see when we discuss drugs binding to receptors, if one were to take a particular receptor, one could easily find a host of substances that show varying degrees of affinity for that receptor. Affinity can be defined by the following chemical equilibrium equation:

$$L + R \rightleftharpoons LR$$

Even for someone with a bad case of chemophobia (a fear of chemistry, which can happen in a course like this—ha ha!), the equation is relatively easy to understand. L + R refers to the ligand and the receptor being in the unbound state, whereas LR refers to the bound state (i.e., the *ligand/receptor complex*). The reaction is reversible, as signified by the arrows going in both directions; so the separate ligand and receptor can become associated (bound together), but also can dissociate (become unbound). Also, this equation can capture the variation in affinity across different ligands. For the case in which a ligand has a high affinity for a receptor, the tendency to form the bound ligand/receptor complex is relatively high compared to the tendency to exist as separate (unbound) ligand and receptor, whereas a ligand with lower affinity would have a lower tendency to exist in the bound state and a higher tendency to exist in the unbound state.

How does one empirically determine binding affinity in an experiment? Neurochemists measure affinity (i.e., a receptor-binding assay) with procedures in which tissue samples containing the receptor proteins are exposed to varying concentrations of the ligand, and specific binding of the ligand across different concentrations is depicted. Figure 5.4 is an example of a typical binding curve, which follows the

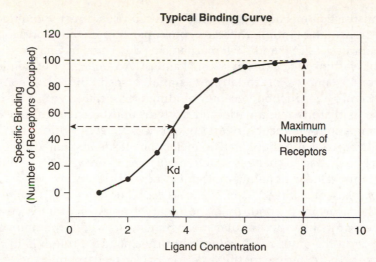

FIGURE 5.4 A typical binding curve. As concentration of the ligand increases, specific binding is increased until it reaches asymptotic levels and saturates the receptors. Kd and IC50 are two measures of binding affinity.

shape of a rectangular hyperbola. In this graph, the x-axis represents the concentration of the ligand added to the tissue, whereas the y-axis is the degree of specific binding (binding to the receptor, as opposed to other sites). The asymptote of the binding curve represents the total number of receptors in the tissue, whereas the dissociation constant or Kd is the concentration of ligand that occupies 50% of the receptors. The Kd value (in concentration units) is one of the two most common measure of affinity (the other being the IC50 or inhibitory concentration 50, which is used if you are inhibiting the binding of another substance with your ligand in the binding procedure). In either case, a measure such as Kd or IC50 is inversely related to affinity. If the Kd or IC50 value is low, it means the substance has a high affinity for that receptor, because receptors are being occupied at relatively low concentrations. In that sense, the Kd or IC50 values are kind of analogous to the ED50, which, as we saw in Chapter 3, is a measure of potency. The important difference, though, is this: Any drug that has an effect of some sort can be characterized in terms of its potency, whereas binding affinity is something much more specific; it refers only to the tendency to bind to receptors at this specific stage of neurotransmission, which not all drugs do. With drugs that act on receptors, sometimes affinity and potency are related, because a drug with a very high affinity often can exert actions at low doses. But this is not always the case, because potency of a drug can be influenced by a number of factors that do not directly affect affinity, such as penetration into the target tissue, duration of action, and metabolism (which are features of a whole organism, but not a tissue preparation like that used to measure receptor binding in vitro).

As described at the beginning of this section, neurotransmitters do more than just bind; as a result of binding, they instigate some *intrinsic activity* or *signal transduction* effect in the postsynaptic cell as well. There are two major classes of signal transduction: ionotropic and metabotropic (Figure 5.5). *Ionotropic* refers to the type of signal transduction mechanism in which a receptor is directly coupled to an ion channel, the transmitter binding to the receptor opens the channel, and ionic currents flow. The examples of EPSP and IPSP mechanisms described in Chapter 4, in which a GLU receptor was linked to a cation channel and a GABA receptor was linked to a Cl^- channel, were examples of ionotropic signal transduction. In contrast, with *metabotropic* signal transduction, receptor binding is associated with a cascade of biochemical events that involve a variety of proteins and biochemical reactions. Most commonly, metabotropic receptors are linked to *g-proteins*, which then instigate a variety of other enzymatic changes. The metabolic effects instigated by activation of g-proteins typically lead to changes in activity of various enzymes, and ultimately the regulation of intracellular signaling molecules known as *second messengers* (e.g., *cyclic-adenosine monophosphate* or *c-AMP, inositol phosphate 3* or *IP3, Ca^{++} ions*). As shown in Figure 5.5, the structure of ionotropic and metabotropic receptors is very different. Ionotropic receptors have an annular arrangement, in which the neurotransmitter binding site is on the outer ring proteins, but the channel protein is in the middle, spanning from the exterior to the interior of the cell membrane. In contrast, metabotropic g-protein coupled receptors have seven parts of the proteins that cross back and forth across the membrane, an outer binding site that binds the neurotransmitter, and an inner part that interacts with the g-protein. Different g-proteins perform distinct functions. For example, one called Gs stimulates the enzyme that synthesizes c-AMP, whereas another one called Gi inibits this enzyme, thereby reducing c-AMP synthesis. Regulation of c-AMP is very important, because it activates an enzyme that phosphorylates various proteins, which can change the activity of an enzyme or regulate the opening of a channel. (Paul Greengard won the Nobel Prize for his pioneering work on the role of phosphorylation in the brain.) A third g-protein is called Gq, which stimulates formation of a second messenger known as IP_3 that in turn increases Ca^{++} ion concentration inside the cell (the Ca^{++} in this case is released from storage sites inside the neuron).

There are several important differences between ionotropic and metabotropic signal transduction. Ionotropic signal transduction is very specific, because a particular ion channel is targeted, whereas metabotropic signal transduction results in a cascade of metabolic events that can affect a wide array of proteins with diverse functions in the neuron. Also, ionotropic signaling is very fast (e.g., millisecond time scale), although metabotropic communication can be much more temporally diffuse. Metabotropic signals can span all the way from the millisecond range, to the second range, and into the range of several minutes (Lapish et al., 2007). Lavin et al. (2005) reported that metabotropic changes in neuron excitability induced by DA lasted for at least 45 minutes. In view of the fact that metabotropic signal transduction pathways also influence gene expression, which in turn can produce even longer lasting changes in neuronal function, it is clear that metabotropic signals exert a long-term influence over neural activity. Of course, although this time scale may seem to be slow on a neurophysiological timescale, it is well suited for modifying the neural regulation of behavioral activities such as learning, stress, emotion, and motivation, which play out over long time periods. Thus, the combination of ionotropic and metabotropic signaling enables chemical communication between neurons to take place over a variety of different timescales, which is very adaptive in view of the varied conditions that organisms must respond to.

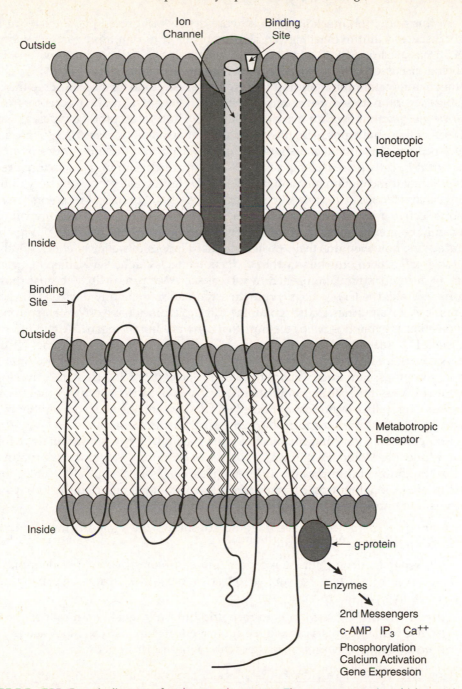

FIGURE 5.5   TOP: Generic diagram of an ionotropic receptor. The receptor protein, which contains the binding site for the transmitter, is directly linked to an ion channel. BOTTOM: Generic diagram of a metabotropic receptor. The receptor protein has an outer binding site, and an inner site that interacts with g-proteins that in turn instigate a variety of different metabolic effects in the cell, typically involving production of second messengers.

At this point, it is important to add more detail about receptors. We have already briefly discussed the idea that a given neurotransmitter has multiple receptor subtypes. Table 5.1 has a list of general classes of receptor subtypes for some of the neurotransmitters being discussed in this book (for more reading, see Iversen et al., 2009). We should emphasize a few important points related to these receptors. First of all, some transmitters share receptor classes. For example, NE and EPI share a family of receptors known as *adrenergic* receptors. Within this class, there are α and β receptor subtypes, as well as subtypes of these subtypes. Also, the excitatory amino acids GLU and ASP share a family of receptors. Additionally, it should be emphasized that the different receptor subtypes within a group are distinct proteins, with different binding characteristics and distinct signal transduction mechanisms. D_1 and D_2 family receptors have very different binding characteristics; so while some drugs bind to both families of receptors (i.e., they are nonselective in this sense), others are selective for one or the other receptor subtypes. This can have great clinical significance. For example, most antipsychotic drugs block DA receptors; however, it is the D_2 blockade that renders this clinical effect, not the D_1 antagonism. Furthermore, the signal transduction effects can be very different, even opposite. D_1 receptor stimulation generally increases c-AMP production (because those receptors are linked to Gs), while D_2 receptor stimulation generally decreases or has no effect on c-AMP synthesis. Although all the catecholamines have only metabotropic receptors, other transmitters have receptors that can vary in this regard. With 5-HT receptors, the $5-HT_3$ receptor is ionotropic, whereas the others are metabotropic. Nicotinic ACh receptors are ionotropic, whereas muscarinic ACh receptors are metabotropic. The $GABA_A$ receptor is ionotropic (but not the $GABA_B$ receptor), and excitatory amino acid receptor subtypes also have examples of both forms of intrinsic activity (one receptor subtype is even called "metabotropic"). All this means that one neurotransmitter can exert a multitude of physiological effects on the postsynaptic neuron.

Receptors are a very important site for drug action. Drugs can stimulate or inhibit receptor function. Moreover, they can act on the same binding site as the neurotransmitter, or act on different sites. First of all, let us consider classes of drugs that affect postsynaptic mechanisms by binding to the same site as the transmitter. In this group, there are drugs that mimic neurotransmitters:

Agonist   drug binds to receptor, and stimulates the same intrinsic activity as neurotransmitter.

Full Agonist   drug binds to receptor, and stimulates maximal or near-maximal levels of intrinsic activity (similar to transmitter); these drugs essentially mimic the action of the neurotransmitter itself.

Partial Agonist   drug binds to receptor, but only weakly stimulates intrinsic activity; partial agonists can induce agonist effects but also can block activity produced by drugs or neurotransmitter with higher intrinsic activity.

However, there also are drugs that block or oppose neurotransmission:

Competitive Antagonist   binds to receptor, has no intrinsic activity, and blocks activity produced by the neurotransmitter.

Inverse Agonist   binds to receptor, but stimulates intrinsic activity opposite of neurotransmitter; for example, if the neurotransmitter inhibits c-AMP production, the inverse agonist would actually increase it.

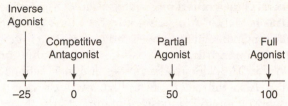

FIGURE 5.6 Hypothetical graph depicting the effects of several classes of drugs that all bind to the same binding site as the neurotransmitter (agonists, competitive antagonists, inverse agonists) in terms of their differential effects on signal transduction (intrinsic activity). The values assigned for partial agonists and inverse agonists are meant to be representative estimates.

Figure 5.6 is a scheme for summarizing the actions of agonists, competitive antagonists and inverse agonists, in terms of their signal transduction (i.e., intrinsic activity) effects.

Finally, there are drugs that affect postsynaptic mechanisms by acting at other sites on the receptor complex:

Noncompetitive Antagonist   acts on some other part of receptor/signal transduction mechanism and reduces activity of transmitter.

Positive or Negative Allosteric Modulator   binds to a different site on the receptor and modulates receptor function and signal transduction (e.g., *benzodiazepines* such as Valium facilitate the inhibitory actions of GABA; they are *positive allosteric modulators* of $GABA_A$ receptors).

Having discussed these general classes of action, let us mention some individual drugs that belong to each category. There are several examples of drugs that are full agonists at their respective receptors, including *bromocriptine* (DA D_2 family agonist and antiparkinsonian agent), *Δ 9-THC* (cannabinoid agonist, mimics effect of AN at CB_1 receptors), *morphine* (μ opiate receptor agonist, analgesic, drug of abuse), and *nicotine* (nicotinic ACh agonist, active ingredient in cigarette smoke). A good example of a partial agonist is *varenicline* (*Chantix*), which is a nicotinic ACh receptor partial agonist that is used for smoking cessation treatment. Several drugs that are important for psychopharmacology act as competitive antagonists. Many DA antagonists, such as *haloperidol, chlorpromazine,* and *clozapine,* are used as antipsychotic drugs. Drugs that antagonize B adrenergic receptors are used to treat high blood pressure (they often are called beta blockers). *Scopolamine* and *atropine* are examples of drugs that block muscarinic ACh receptors; they have antiparkinsonian effects, but they also interfere with cognitive processes and can induce hallucinations at high doses. There also are examples of inverse agonists; the drug *rimonabant*, which binds to cannabinoid CB_1 receptors, not only is able to compete with the endogenous ligand AN or the drug THC, but also produces signal transduction effects that are opposite to those produced by AN. Examples of noncompetitive antagonists include *picrotoxin*, which is a noncompetitive antagonist of $GABA_A$ receptors (it is a naturally occurring drug from the plant *Cocculus indicus*), and *phencyclidine* or *PCP*, which is a noncompetitive antagonist of NMDA receptors. In both cases, these drugs do not bind to the binding site for the transmitter, but rather bind to the channel protein and interfere with its function. Finally, as stated earlier, the antianxiety agents that belong to the family known as benzodiazepines (e.g., *Valium, Librium,* and *Xanax*) act as positive allosteric modulators of the GABA$_A$ receptor. They bind to a site on the receptor that is not the binding site for GABA (in fact, they bind at a site that is generally called the benzodiazepine binding site), and they increase GABA transmission by increasing the affinity of the receptor for GABA. Benzodiazepines and their actions are discussed in detail in Chapter 10, which deals with sedatives and anxiolytic drugs.

At this point, it is worthwhile to emphasize the importance of this terminology as a tool for communicating in psychopharmacology. Although it has become common in psychopharmacology or physiological psychology textbooks to refer to any drug that stimulates transmission in any way as an agonist, this is not technically precise and can be misleading. For example, by this definition, a drug that acted as an antagonist of autoreceptors, and thus stimulated neurotransmitter release, could be considered an agonist. But, it is confusing to say that an antagonist is really an agonist, because its net effect is to stimulate neurotransmission. Such a drug should be referred to as an autoreceptor antagonist to avoid this confusion. Is L-DOPA a DA agonist? No, because it does not bind to DA receptors. As discussed earlier, L-DOPA is properly referred to as a precursor of DA. Is Valium a GABA agonist? No; technically, it is an agonist at the benzodiazepine site; with reference to GABA, it is referred to as a positive allosteric modulator, but not an agonist. Sometimes, one sees the term *indirect* agonist used, and although it does convey some meaning, it is technically an oxymoron because, by definition, an agonist binds to the receptor and therefore cannot be indirect.

There are important drug interactions that can occur between drugs that act on receptor binding and signal transduction processes on the same receptor. For example, drugs that act as agonists and antagonists of the same receptor can directly interact, and some characteristics of this interaction can be displayed by examination of the resulting dose-response curves. Figure 5.7 shows how the dose–response curve of an agonist can be altered by co-administration of either a competitive antagonist or a noncompetitive antagonist of the same receptor. If one compares the dose–response curve for the agonist (solid line) with the dose–response curve of the agonist in the presence of a single dose of the competitive antagonist (dotted line), one sees that the competitive antagonist produces a parallel shift to the right in the dose–response curve for an agonist of the same receptor. In other words, in the presence of the competitive antagonist, higher doses of the agonist are required to produce the same effect, but the maximum response is still the same. This pattern occurs because the agonist and the competitive agonist literally compete for the same binding site. In contrast, a different pattern of effects is produced when the agonist is administered in combination with a noncompetitive antagonist (dashed line). In this case, the noncompetitive antagonist not only shifts the agonist dose–response curve, but also decreases the maximal response produced by the agonist. This pattern occurs because the noncompetitive antagonist is not competing for the same binding site as the agonist, and therefore, giving a higher dose of the agonist cannot overcome the effect of the noncompetitive antagonist by displacing it off the receptor.

Interactions between drugs that act on different neurotransmitters also can occur, and in some cases, this is due to the fact that receptors for different neurotransmitters can converge onto the same signal transduction pathway in the same neuron. For example, there is considerable evidence that drugs acting on DA D$_2$ receptors can interact

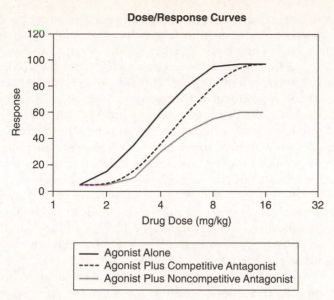

FIGURE 5.7   Graphs depicting the effects of a competitive and a noncompetitive antagonist on the agonist dose–response curve.

with drugs that act on adenosine A_{2A} receptors. DA D_2 antagonists produce a host of behavioral effects that can be reversed by co-administration of adenosine A_{2A} antagonists, including suppression of locomotion (Collins et al., 2010b), reductions in lever pressing (Nunes et al., 2010), and induction of an oral tremor that resembles parkinsonian tremor (Correa et al., 2004). Moreover, evidence indicates that this behavioral interaction is marked by changes in a gene product known as *c-Fos*, which is used as measure of neural activation and signal transduction (Betz et al., 2009; Farrar et al., 2010). Of course, it also is true that drugs acting on different transmitters can interact because of the effects they produce on different parts of the neural circuitry mediating a behavioral effect (Betz et al., 2009), or even on different brain areas.

INACTIVATION OF NEUROTRANSMITTERS

The last stage of neurotransmission is inactivation. In a sense, this stage works against the other stages, by reducing levels of the neurotransmitter in the synaptic cleft. The interaction of synthesis, storage, and release versus inactivation essentially maintains the limits of *synaptic homeostasis*; that is, the balance in neurotransmission is such that neurotransmitter levels are maintained within limits, going neither too high nor too low. This balance is important to maintain normal physiological processes in the nervous system. Inactivation processes may be related to pathologies in neurotransmission that result in neurological or psychiatric problems, but also serve as a substrate of action for many psychoactive drugs. As shown in Figure 5.2, there are two major means of inactivation: enzymatic breakdown and uptake by transport proteins.

With enzymatic breakdown, an enzyme metabolizes the neurotransmitter molecular into an intersubstance that is generally known as a *metabolite* of the neurotransmitter. There are several examples of enzymes that break down neurotransmitters. For example, MAO is an enzyme that breaks down all the monoamines (DA, NE, EPI, and 5-HT). Catecholamine o-methyl transferase (COMT) breaks down the catecholamines DA, NE, and EPI. The breakdown products of neurotransmitter are referred to as *metabolites*. Metabolites of neurotransmitters are frequently studied in order to get a glimpse into drug action and also to provide a marker of neurotransmitter activity or turnover. In studies of depression, for example, it is common to measure monoamine metabolite levels in the cerebrospinal fluid in order to understand how changes in neurochemistry could be associated with depressive symptoms (see Chapter 9 on antidepressants). Although there are several compounds that are metabolites of monoamine neurotransmitters, we will mention a few here as examples. Commonly studied DA metabolites include DOPAC (3,4-dihydroxy phenylalanine) and HVA (homovanillic acid), while MHPG (3-methoxy-4-hydroxyphenylglycol) is the NE metabolite that is most commonly used as a marker of brain metabolism of NE (Iversen et al., 2009). The primary metabolite of 5-HT is called 5-HIAA (5-hydroxyindoleacetic acid). ACh is metabolized by the enzyme acetylcholinesterase, which breaks down the ACh molecule into acetic acid and choline. In turn, the choline molecules are then taken back up into the ACh terminal by a protein transporter and recycled to make new ACh molecules. Thus, choline is both a precursor and a metabolite of ACh.

Neurotransmitter metabolism is also a process that is a major target of drug action in psychopharmacology. Any drug that inhibits enzymatic breakdown of a transmitter increases synaptic levels of that neurotransmitter, because it is blocking a major means of inactivation. *Phenylzine* (*Nardil*) is an MAO inhibitor that is used as an antidepressant; Nardil is relatively nonselective for the different forms of MAO. There are two forms (isozymes) of MAO, known as MAO-A and MAO-B, and selective inhibitors of these isozymes also are clinically important. *Moclobemide* (*Moclobamine*) is an MAO-A blocker that is used as an antidepressant, whereas *deprenyl* (*Selegiline*) is an MAO-B inhibitor that is given as a treatment for Parkinson's disease. In addition, there are several compounds that inhibit acetylcholinesterase (these drugs also are called *anticholinesterases*). Several anticholinesterases are used to treat Alzheimer's disease, including *tacrine* (*Cognex*) and *galantamine* (*Reminyl*). These drugs are administered as a treatment for Alzheimer's disease because Alzheimer's is a neurodegenerative disease, and although several brain systems deteriorate, one of the ACh projections in the brain that is involved in cognitive processes (the basal forebrain system, see next section) is severely impaired in Alzheimer's patients. For this reason, administration of an anticholinesterase is intended to preserve ACh molecules in the brain by blocking their enzymatic breakdown. Peripherally acting anticholinesterases are used to treat neuromuscular disorders such as myasthenia gravis. In addition to these clinical uses, it should also be emphasized that, at high doses, irreversible anticholinesterases are highly toxic, even lethal. For example, some *insecticides* are anticholinesterases (e.g., the organophosphate compound Malathion). In addition, some *nerve gasses* such as *Tabun* and *Sarin* are lethal because of their anticholinesterase activity. Although there are many ways in which cholinergic overstimulation could kill an organism, it seems that overstimulation of central muscarinic receptors has the most lethal effect; for that reason, treatment with a muscarinic antagonist such as scopolamine or atropine can serve as a temporary antidote to the lethal effects of these nerve gasses.

In addition to enzymatic breakdown, neurotransmitters can also be inactivated by protein transporters that remove the neurotransmitter molecules from the synaptic cleft, often back into the presynaptic terminal where it is either recycled or broken down by enzymes. This process, known as *high affinity uptake* (and sometimes reuptake), is the major means of inactivation for some transmitters (such as monoamines). There are uptake proteins for the inactivation of DA, NE, EPI, and 5-HT; these uptake proteins for the different monoamines are similar in structure, but not identical, and for that reason, there are some drugs that act to block all of them in a nonspecific way, but others act in more specific ways. Several stimulants inhibit uptake of one or more monoamines. *Amphetamines* such as d-amphetamine, l-amphetamine, or methamphetamine all act to block uptake of monoamines, as does cocaine. The stimulant *methylphenidate* (*Ritalin*) blocks catecholamine uptake. In addition, several widely used antidepressants block uptake of monoamines. *Fluoxetine* (*Prozac*) selectively blocks 5-HT uptake, while *bupropion* (*Wellbutrin*) and *nomifensine* (*Merital*) inhibit catecholamine uptake. The use of monoamine uptake inhibitors as antidepressants will be discussed in Chapter 9, which deals with drug treatment of depression. In addition to the monoamine transporters, there are uptake proteins that inactivate a wide variety of neurotransmitters, including GABA, GLU, and adenosine.

CHEMICAL NEUROANATOMY AND NEUROTRANSMITTER DISTRIBUTION

There are several things that need to be considered when trying to understand the psychological effect of a drug. As stated earlier, one needs to know which aspect of the neurotransmission process (synthesis, storage, release, postsynaptic action, or inactivation) is being affected. In addition, one needs to know which particular transmitter or group of transmitters is being affected. But this, on its own, is not enough. In order to understand how drugs can have behavioral effects, we have to consider *where* the neurotransmitter is in the nervous system, and what functions that neural system or circuit performs. For that reason, a fundamental part of psychopharmacology is the discussion of the anatomical distribution of various neurotransmitter systems; sometimes, this area of inquiry is known as *chemical neuroanatomy*. A discussion of chemical neuroanatomy is critical because it integrates the field of psychopharmacology with related fields such as physiological psychology/behavioral neuroscience; it helps to explain the behavioral actions of drugs in neuroscientific terms and also aids in understanding how drugs can produce multiple effects, including both therapeutic and side effects, or desirable and undesirable effects.

Peripheral Nervous System

The *peripheral nervous system* (PNS) is composed of all nervous tissues outside of the spinal cord and the brain. The PNS can be differentiated into *nerves* (bundles of axons outside the central nervous system [CNS]), which serve sensory functions (e.g., allowing light, sound, and chemicals from the environment to impact on the CNS) or motor functions (such as allowing the CNS to induce changes in bodily functions), as well as *ganglia* (a *ganglion* is a grouping of neuron cell bodies outside the CNS) that represent collections of nerve cell bodies. *Motor neurons* form connections with voluntary or striated muscles, and in this case, the point of functional connection is not called a synapse but, rather, a neuromuscular junction. The neurotransmitter for the neuromuscular junction is ACh, and the muscle fibers have nicotinic ACh receptors on them. For this reason, the nicotinic antagonist curare can be lethal; it blocks the neuromuscular junction and therefore inhibits the action of the diaphragm, which leads to suppression of breathing and death. Curare is a naturally occurring substance that comes from the Chondrodendron tomentosum plant that grows in South America, which was discovered because extracts of this plant were used by indigenous people to coat the tips of arrows or blow darts (adding a lethal effect to an already dangerous weapon).

The *autonomic nervous system* controls smooth and cardiac muscle activity and several glands, including the adrenal glands, salivary glands, and sweat glands. Virtually all of these organs are innervated (connected to nerves) by two opposing systems within the autonomic nervous system. One is called the *parasympathetic nervous system*, which is responsible for controlling vegetative, restorative, and energy-saving processes. It is particularly active during digestion. The other is called the *sympathetic nervous system*, which is responsible for preparing the body for dealing with situations requiring fighting or fleeing, or at times when the organism is frightened (the *fight-flight-fright* system). It is particularly active in response to emotional stimuli and stressors. Table 5.2 indicates the major activities carried out by the sympathetic and parasympathetic nerve fibers comprising the autonomic nervous system.

The axons from both the parasympathetic and sympathetic systems that originate from neurons in the spinal cord and brain are referred to as *preganglionic fibers,* and they release the neurotransmitter ACh. The cell bodies of target neurons for these fibers are

TABLE 5.2   Effect of Activity of Autonomic Nerve Fibers

Organ	Sympathetic	Parasympathetic
Adrenal medulla	Secretion of epinephrine and norepinephrine	
Bladder	Inhibition of contraction	Contraction
Blood vessels		
Abdomen	Constriction	
Muscles	Dilation	Constriction
Skin	Constriction or dilation	Dilation
Heart	Faster rate of contraction	Slower rate of contraction
Intestines	Decreased activity	Increased activity (motility of smooth muscle
Lacrimal glands	Secretion of tears	
Liver	Release of glucose	
Lungs	Dilation of bronchi	Constriction of bronchi
Penis	Ejaculation	Erection
Pupil of eye	Dilation	Constriction
Salivary glands	Dry mouth	Secretion of thin enzyme-rich saliva
Sweat glands	Secretion of sweat	
Vagina	Orgasm	Secretion of lubricating fluid

clustered together in ganglia. The receptors on the target neurons are those I referred to a little earlier as nicotinic receptors. The axons that originate from these ganglionic cells and connect with, or innervate, the organs are referred to as *postganglionic fibers*. The point of functional connection between the terminals of the postganglionic axons and the target tissue (typically a gland or smooth muscle) is known as a *neuroeffector junction*. The neurotransmitter at the neuroeffector junction in the sympathetic system release NE, which depending upon the tissue can stimulate alpha or beta adrenergic receptors on the membranes of the target organ cells. In contrast, the neurotransmitter at the neuroeffector junction in the parasympathetic system is ACh, which activates muscarinic receptors in the target organ cells. Because NE activates receptors in the sympathetic division of the autonomic nervous system, and ACh activates receptors in the parasympathetic division of the autonomic nervous system, this differential chemical coding means that drugs acting on NE and ACH can have very distinct effects on autonomic functions. Drugs that stimulate sympathetic activity by facilitating NE transmission are often referred to as **sympathomimetics,** and those whose actions mimic parasympathetic activity are referred to as **parasympathomimetics.** Thus, stimulants, cold medicines, and some diet pills that stimulate NE transmission by stimulating release or blocking uptake produce autonomic effects that reflect increases in sympathetic activity (sympathomimetic effects such as increased heart rate or blood pressure or dilation of the bronchioles in the lungs). By contrast, drugs that stimulate ACh transmission, such as muscarinic agonists or anticholinesterases (collectively known as cholinomimetics), stimulate parasympathetic activity. This results in an effect known as SLUD (salivation, lacrimation, urination, defecation). SLUD effects can be produced as a side effect of a cholinomimetic targeting the brain. In addition, any drug that blocks muscarinic receptors can produce effects such as dry mouth and constipation, which result from the blockade of parasympathetic activity.

Central Nervous System: General Overview of Brain Anatomy

The *central nervous system,* or CNS, comprises the brain and spinal cord. Based upon embryonic development, the brain is divided into three distinct areas called the forebrain, the midbrain, and the hindbrain (Figure 5.8). Most of the outer surface of the forebrain is called the *cerebral cortex,* shown in Figure 5.8 (bottom), and it is composed of several densely packed layers of neuron cell bodies. Certain parts of the cortex are called *sensory projection areas* because these are areas of the cortex where the information from the senses is processed. The *temporal lobes* contain the primary receiving area for auditory information and visual recognition. The *parietal lobes* are the primary receiving area for bodily sensations and are involved in spatial perception. The *occipital lobes* are the primary receiving area for visual information. The cortex in the *frontal lobes* allows us to ascribe meaning to the incoming stimuli initially processed in the sensory projection areas. It is essential for higher order thought processing, such as synthetic reasoning and abstract thought, and it allows us to organize events from independent places and times and to make plans. The *prefrontal cortex,* which is most highly developed in humans and is heavily innervated with dopaminergic inputs, is important for planning and organization of behavior (Richmond et al., 2003). The lateral prefrontal cortex is a primary site for working memory, which is the type involved with remembering a phone number for a short period or remembering a sequence of actions or

Major Divisions of Brain

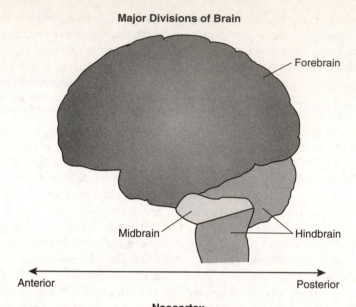

Neocortex

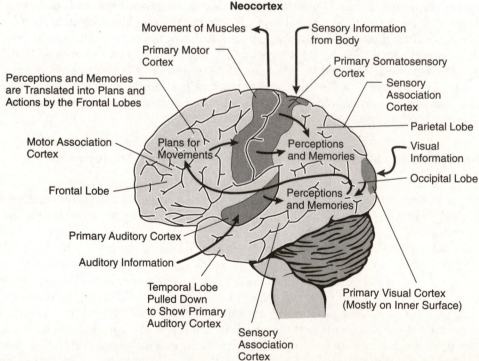

FIGURE 5.8   TOP: Schematic diagram of the human brain showing the forebrain, midbrain, and hindbrain. BOTTOM: Diagram of the various parts of the neocortex, which is most of the outer surface of the human brain.

tasks, and the medial prefrontal cortex (including the anterior cingulate cortex, a part of the limbic system described later) appears to be important for judging the value of rewards and assessing the value of an action for obtaining a predicted outcome. The posterior part of the frontal lobe, called the primary motor cortex, acts in combination with other motor areas to control movement. In patients with hereditary depressive disorders, parts of the cingulate cortex have been shown in magnetic resonance imaging and postmortem histopathological studies to have reduced gray matter volume and reduced glial cell numbers. Humans with damage in the anterior cingulate cortex exhibit a blunted emotional affect to pain and other emotionally charged events and appear quite apathetic (Richmond et al., 2003). Finally, although the cerebral hemispheres are viewed as specializing in processing different kinds of information—for example, language in the left and visual-spatial in the right—they are connected by some 200 million nerve axons collectively referred to as the *corpus callosum*, which allows them to communicate with one another.

Figure 5.9 shows a schematic drawing of several parts of the brain, with particular emphasis on structures that are points of origin and termination for the major neurotransmitter systems that will be discussed here. The hindbrain includes the medulla, the cerebellum, and the pons. The *medulla* controls vital reflex functions such as respiration, heartbeat, and blood pressure, which tend to be decreased by opiates and sedative–hypnotic drugs and increased by psychostimulants. The *pons* connects higher

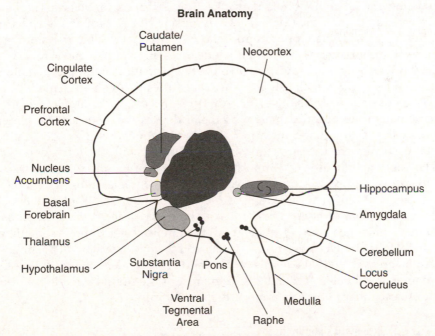

Brain Anatomy

FIGURE 5.9 Schematic drawing of the human brain; cutaway view depicts various cortical and subcortical structures that are labeled for various neurotransmitter systems in Figures 5.10 and 5.11.

brain centers with the cerebellum and also has several important sensory and motor functions; in addition, it contains the *locus coeruleus* ("blue spot" in Latin), from which much of the NE innervation of the brain comes. The *cerebellum* has traditionally been viewed primarily as an important part of the motor system that controls automatic skeletal motor activities and coordinates balance and the body's movements (Carlson, 2004). However, recent studies in humans indicate that this structure is also involved in aspects of learning, emotion, and motivation (Annoni et al., 2003; Holstege et al., 2003; Sell et al., 1999). The midbrain contains nuclei (groups of neuron cell bodies in the CNS) that are involved in auditory and visual processing. It is also important for the perception of pain, a function that is consistent with the high concentrations of enkephalins found there. The midbrain also contains DA neurons that originate in the *substantia nigra* ("black substance" in Latin) and *ventral tegmental area*, and 5-HT neurons from the *raphe* nuclei. One major division of the forebrain is the *diencephalon*, which contains the thalamus and the hypothalamus. The *thalamus* is the great "relay" station in the brain, in that it relays incoming sensory information to the appropriate areas of the neocortex, as well as relaying information from higher regions of the brain to lower ones. The *hypothalamus* contains several discrete nuclei that are involved in various aspects of motivation, including regulation of feeding, drinking, and sexual behavior, as well as autonomic and neuroendocrine regulation. The *limbic system* is a conglomeration of diverse structures in the cerebral hemispheres (most are part of the *telencephalon*, the other major division of the forebrain) where a large number of circuits relating to different functions come together. It is thought to play a key role in the cognitive arousal of emotion and the formation of memory (McGinty & Szymusiak, 1988). Limbic system structures include the septal area, the hippocampus, and the amygdala. Some parts of the limbic system are critically important for certain kinds of learning and memory formation. For example, the *hippocampus* is heavily involved in the formation of long-term memories of facts, events, and spatial relationships. Others are critically involved in mood, emotionality, and emotional expressions—for example, the *amygdala* and *cingulate gyrus*. Neuroimaging studies of individuals with major depressive disorders have identified abnormalities of resting blood flow and glucose metabolism in the amygdala and in prefrontal cortical areas that are extensively connected with the amygdala (Drevets, 1999). The basal ganglia are very important for aspects of motor control, sensorimotor integration, response organization, motivation, instrumental learning, and habit formation (Graybiel et al., 1994). Basal ganglia structures include the *caudate/putamen*, which is also known as the *neostriatum* or *striatum*, and the *nucleus accumbens*, which is a striatal area that sometimes is also grouped with the limbic system, and is sometimes considered an interface between the limbic system and the motor system in the brain. Other basal ganglia areas include the *globus pallidus* and *ventral pallidum*, which link the caudate/putamen and nucleus accumbens to the rest of the brain by having output neurons that project either to the thalamus or to the midbrain.

Central Nervous System: Some Neurotransmitter Projection Systems in the Brain

Figures 5.10 and 5.11 show some of the major neurotransmitter projection systems that are particularly relevant for understanding psychopharmacology. These systems are described in terms of the point of origin (where the cell bodies or somata are) and the

Brain Anatomy: DA

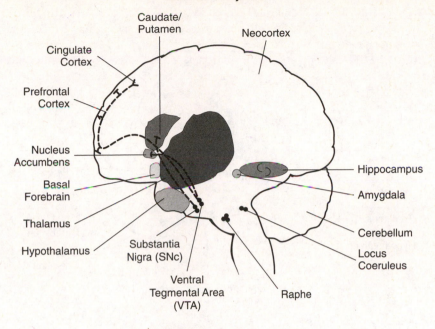

Brain Anatomy: ACh

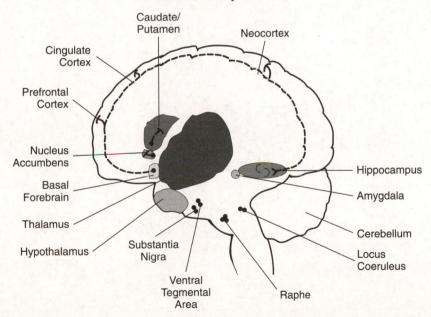

FIGURE 5.10   TOP: Schematic diagram of the human brain showing three major DA pathways in the brain. BOTTOM: Diagram showing two major ACh pathways in the brain.

Brain Anatomy: NE

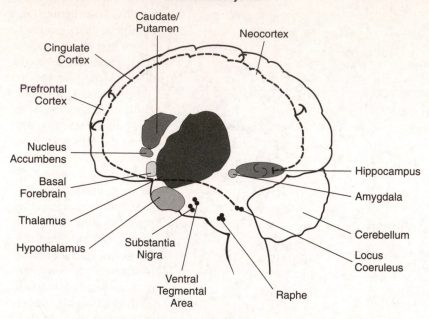

Brain Anatomy: Serotonin (5-HT)

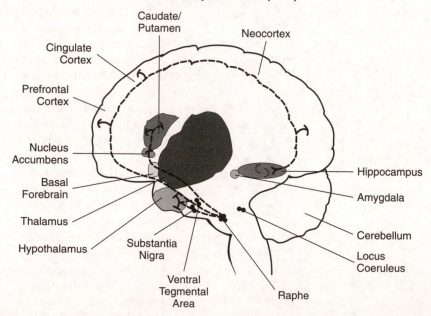

FIGURE 5.11   TOP: Schematic diagram of the human brain showing the dorsal noradrenergic bundle system, which provides a widespread innervation of the forebrain. BOTTOM: Diagram showing the raphe system, which provides a diffuse 5-HT innervation of the forebrain.

point of termination (where the system projects to and where the terminals are). Figure 5.10 (top) shows three of the major projection systems for DA. The **nigrostriatal** DA system originates in a part of the substantia nigra known as substantia nigra pars compact, and projects to the caudate/putamen. This is the DA system that shows the greatest degeneration in patients with Parkinson's disease, and it also mediates the parkinsonian side effects of antipsychotic drugs that act as DA antagonists. Moreover, the stereotyped behaviors induced by high doses of psychomotor stimulants such as amphetamines are dependent upon an increase in DA transmission in the caudate/putamen (Iversen et al., 2009). The **mesolimbic** DA system originates in the ventral tegmental area and projects to the nucleus accumbens, and to the adjacent areas such as the olfactory tubercle. This system is involved in stimulant-induced locomotor activity, behavioral activation, aspects of motivation, depression, drug use, and instrumental learning (Salamone, 2010b). Finally, the **mesocortical** DA system originates in the ventral tegmental area and projects to neocortex, with a heavy innervation of prefrontal and anterior cingulate cortex. This system is thought to be involved in schizophrenia, as well as aspects of learning, planning, organization, and decision making. A fourth DA system known as the tuberoinfundibular system is not shown. Figure 5.10 also shows some of the projection systems for ACh (bottom). Two major ACh systems are shown, one consisting of local interneurons, and another consisting of long projection neurons. The **intrinsic striatal system** has neurons that originate and terminate within the caudate/putamen and nucleus accumbens. This system is thought to be the anatomical locus of the DA/ACh interaction that is seen in Parkinson's disease and the parkinsonian side effects of antipsychotic drugs. Parkinson's disease not only involves DA, but also involves many other transmitters, including ACh and others. Pharmacological studies have shown that drug-induced parkinsonism can be produced by cholinomimetic drugs (Collins et al., 2010a), and that muscarinic antagonists can be used as antiparkinsonian drugs (Betz et al., 2007). The other major ACh system shown in Figure 5.10 is called the **basal forebrain system.** This system originates in the septal area, basal nucleus of Meynert, and adjacent areas, and terminates in a wide area of the brain, including all of neocortex and hippocampus. This is the ACh system that degenerates in patients with Alzheimer's disease and is the target for administration of anticholinesterases such as tacrine to Alzheimer's patients.

Figure 5.11 shows some of the NE and 5-HT projection systems that are highly relevant for understanding psychopharmacology. The two major NE systems that project to the forebrain are sometimes called the ventral noradrenergic bundle and the dorsal noradrenergic bundle (remember that NE is also called noradrenalin). The ventral bundle system originates from a diffuse collection of NE cell bodies in the midbrain/pons and projects to the hypothalamus. The dorsal bundle system (Figure 5.11 top) originates at a discrete nucleus in the dorsal pons known as the locus coeruleus, and has a very wide projection area, that includes parts of hypothalamus, thalamus, limbic system, and neocortex. This system is involved in arousal, stress, attention, and learning, and is thought to be one of the targets for the attention-promoting effects of stimulants, as well as the therapeutic effects of some antidepressants. Finally, the last system shown is the raphe system, which provides the major serotonergic innervation of the forebrain (Figure 5.11 bottom). The median raphe and dorsal raphe nuclei are in the midbrain and pons, and the neurons that originate here terminate in the hypothalamus and thalamus, basal ganglia and limbic system, and also the neocortex. The 5-HT innervation of the hypothalamus is hypothesized to be an important substrate for the action of some appetite suppressant drugs, such as *fenfluramine*. Also, serotonergic antidepressants (such as Prozac) are thought to act on prefrontal or limbic 5-HT terminals.

Websites for Further Information

Sites offering brain anatomy information and tutorials:

http://www.pbs.org/wnet/brain/3d

http://www.med.harvard.edu/AANLIB/home.html

http://www.gwc.maricopa.edu/class/bio201/brain/1neuro.htm

http://www.brainmuseum.org/index.html

Some basics on the organization of the autonomic nervous system:

http://faculty.washington.edu/chudler/auto.html

Additional information about curare:

http://www.rain-tree.com/curare.htm

Images of neurotransmitter release:

http://www.youtube.com/watch?v=Ntenaz7Sf4k

Tolerance, Sensitization, Dependence, and Addiction

Now that this book has reviewed some of the basic principles of drug action and the processes involved with neurophysiology, neurotransmission, and brain function, some phenomena that can have a profound influence on drug action, drug taking, and drug abuse should be discussed. These include drug tolerance and sensitization, as well as drug dependence and addiction. These phenomena are important theoretically because they provide additional information about the physiological and behavioral factors that affect drug action. Furthermore, they are critical to discuss because recreational drug taking is an important and persistent aspect of human behavior (as reviewed in Chapter 1), and the fact that some people engage in a pattern of drug taking that can be detrimental to themselves and others has important implications for physical health, mental health, and society at large.

TOLERANCE AND SENSITIZATION

Drug tolerance (hereafter referred to as **tolerance**) occurs when there is a reduction in the potency or efficacy of a drug with repeated administration. This implies that increasingly larger doses of the drug are required to induce the same behavioral effect, although in some cases, tolerance can be so dramatic that no amount of drug is capable of inducing its original effects. Tolerance due to drug exposure is different from so-called genetic or dispositional tolerance, whereby an individual may not be affected by the drug as much as other individuals are because of genetic or dispositional factors. For example, evidence suggests that some individuals predisposed to alcoholism exhibit fewer signs of alcohol intoxication an hour or two after consuming a moderate dose of alcohol than those not predisposed to alcoholism, even if they have had little exposure to alcohol before. This characteristic would allow such persons to consume alcohol at more frequent intervals than normal, which may be a factor in their becoming an alcoholic.

Although tolerance generally requires several drug exposures before it is evidenced, there is a special case of tolerance in which a noticeable decrease in the organism's sensitivity to the drug occurs over a very short period of time—on the order of a few hours. This is referred to as **tachyphylaxis** or **acute tolerance**. In this form of tolerance, the same amount of drug administered on two separate occasions a couple of hours apart may induce greater effects with the first dose than with the second dose. Tachyphylaxis is also evident when the behavioral or physiological effects of a given dose of a drug dissipate at a faster rate than the rate at which the drug is eliminated from the brain (through metabolism or excretion). For example, a person may experience much greater effects of alcohol as the alcohol is accumulating in the brain than an hour or so later when it is being eliminated from the brain, despite the fact that at both points in time the brain has the same concentration of alcohol in it. **Cross-tolerance** refers to the phenomenon in which the development of tolerance to one type of drug results in decreased sensitivity to the effects of another type of drug. For example, a heavy drinker who has developed tolerance to alcohol's sleep-inducing properties may not even get sleepy when given a dose of a barbiturate that normally induces sleep in other individuals.

Tolerance can have substantial effects on drug-taking behaviors. First, most psychoactive drugs we take in our culture are not especially harmful in and of themselves when taken in reasonable quantities with sufficient time between administrations. However, once tolerance to a drug's effects develops, larger and more frequent doses that do become toxic are often administered. Second, tolerance to the effects of drugs does not develop uniformly; that is, some effects may show profound tolerance, whereas others may show little or no tolerance. This is a distinct problem with alcohol and many sedative–hypnotic drugs, where the beneficial or recreational effects of the drugs may show considerable tolerance, but little tolerance develops to the lethal effects of these drugs (O'Brien, 2001). In effect, with this type of tolerance, the therapeutic index for these drugs gets smaller and smaller. With other drugs, tolerance to the desirable effects of a drug may occur while the person actually becomes more sensitive to the side effects of the drug. For example, the ability of amphetamine to induce euphoria decreases with regular use, but the ability for amphetamine to induce psychotic-like effects may actually increase with regular use of large doses. Finally, tolerance is of concern because many of the mechanisms resulting in tolerance contribute to a person's compulsion to take a drug with loss of control over drug intake—that is, drug addiction (Koob, 1996).

Drug **sensitization** is essentially the opposite of drug tolerance (for that reason, it is sometimes called reverse tolerance). With sensitization, there is an increase in potency or efficacy with repeated administration. This means that the drug produces greater effects at the same dose with repeated administration, and that the same effect can be produced by lower doses. Sensitization has been reported to occur with a number of the behavioral effects of drugs. For example, dopamine (DA) antagonists induce a behavioral effect known as catalepsy (an immobile posture), and this effect shows sensitization (Amtage & Schmidt, 2009). In addition, sensitization has been shown with the locomotor effects of stimulants such as amphetamines (Kalivas & Stewart, 1991; Vezina,

2004), cocaine (Bachtell et al., 2008), and nicotine (Vezina et al., 2007), as well as other drugs such as morphine (Sanchis-Segura et al., 2009) and ethanol (Correa et al., 2004). Over the last 20 years, an enormous research effort has focused upon the ability of various drugs of abuse to induce sensitization. Several researchers have suggested that sensitization of drug responses could be a critical aspect of drug seeking, drug taking, and related processes (Robinson & Berridge, 2001, 2003; Schmidt & Pierce, 2010; Vanderschuren & Pierce, 2010; Vezina 2004). Although much of the literature on drug sensitization is related to drug abuse, this subject also is relevant for understanding many types of therapeutic drugs. For example, as discussed in later chapters, neuroadaptations that result in sensitization are important for characterizing the effects of antidepressant drugs that block enzymatic breakdown or inhibit uptake of monoamines (such as serotonin-selective uptake inhibitors).

TOLERANCE AND SENSITIZATION MECHANISMS

Generally speaking, there are three types of drug tolerance and sensitization: **pharmacokinetic, pharmacodynamic,** and **context-specific** (also called behavioral, learned, or conditioned). Pharmacokinetic and pharmacodynamic forms of tolerance are produced by exposure to high concentrations of a drug, generally with a certain minimum amount of exposure time required, and are not affected by environmental or behavioral manipulations of the organism. Context-specific tolerance is due to behavioral and environmental manipulations that involve learning and memory. What follows is a description of the various processes that are involved in these forms of drug tolerance and sensitization.

Pharmacokinetic and Pharmacodynamic Mechanisms

The most prominent mechanism behind pharmacokinetic tolerance has already been discussed in Chapter 3. It involves the ability of the liver to synthesize more drug-metabolizing enzymes than normal when exposed to a drug (O'Brien, 2001). Generally, this process requires several exposures to the drug for some length of time. Once this repeated exposure has taken place, the liver can metabolize the drug at a faster rate than it could previously, thereby decreasing its duration of action. However, the peak intensity of the drug's action may not be reduced very much through this mechanism if it is administered through a route other than oral, because the drug must first pass through the liver before it can be metabolized. This mechanism is also responsible for some cross-tolerance between drugs, because the actions of the drug-metabolizing enzymes are not specific to one particular drug. (This form of tolerance is sometimes referred to as *metabolic*, or dispositional, tolerance by other authors. However, at the beginning of this chapter, I used the term *dispositional tolerance* to refer to a type of genetically based tolerance that is unrelated to previous drug exposures. Therefore, if you run across this term in other sources, look at the context in which it is used to determine what the author means by it.)

Tolerance to a drug may also develop because the drug's pharmacodynamic properties lead to a depletion of neurotransmitters critical to the drug's effects. That is, some drugs (such as amphetamine and cocaine) act by augmenting a specific type of neurotransmitter activity because they enhance the transmitters' release or inhibit their reuptake and increase the transmitters' access to receptors. However, the drug's actions may lead to a depletion of the transmitters (Gold & Dackis, 1984), either because the transmitters are used faster than they can be replenished or because the actual synthesis of the transmitters is decreased (perhaps because of excessive activity at autoreceptors). Therefore, with fewer transmitter molecules available, a larger drug dose must be administered. If this cycle continues long enough, this form of tolerance can lead to the drug becoming completely ineffective, regardless of the dose administered. A drug's ability to deplete neurotransmitters can also be a factor in some forms of cross-tolerance. For example, one drug may act by enhancing the transmitters' release, and another may act by reducing the transmitters' reuptake. With either drug, depletion of the transmitters will reduce the effects of the drug. Finally, depletion of neurotransmitters can lead to the person experiencing symptoms that are the opposite of those he or she experienced with the drug; that is, where the drug initially induces its effects by amplifying a neurotransmitter's activity on its target neurons (e.g., drugs such as amphetamine enhance the release of monoamines from neurons), absence of the drug results in a reduction in the neurotransmitter's activity on its target neurons (Gold & Dackis, 1984).

There appear to be several mechanisms for tolerance involving cellular adaptations related to **homeostasis** (the processes that maintain a state of equilibrium in the body with respect to various functions and to the chemical compositions of the fluids and tissues; Koob, 1996). One of the more common homeostatic adaptations (sometimes called *neuroadaptations*) observed involve drug-induced alterations in the receptors in neuronal membranes. The alterations may reflect either qualitative changes in the neurotransmitters' receptor configuration or changes in the actual number of receptors, which, in turn, affect the transmitters' binding or signal transduction effects. In most cases, continuous exposure to drugs that mimic or amplify the action of neurotransmitters at their receptors tends to decrease receptor activity through processes referred to as *down-regulation* or *receptor subsensitivity*. **Down-regulation** can occur due to reductions in receptor number, reductions in the affinity of the receptor for its ligands, or reductions in signal transduction activity (Iversen et al., 2009). Reductions in receptor number can occur because the receptors dissociate from the neuronal membrane and become sequestered inside the cytoplasm of the neuron, thus making them inaccessible for activation by agonists, or it can occur because the receptors are degraded but are not replaced by synthesis of new protein at a fast-enough rate. In the former case, the down-regulation may be short-lived, as the receptors can subsequently be recycled to the neuronal membrane and become available for activation again. In the latter case, the down-regulation may persist for some length of time, because the neuron would need to synthesize new receptors to replace the degraded receptors. There also can be a decrease in the receptors' ability to elicit cellular changes upon agonist binding but no change in receptor number. This can occur, for example, with metabotropic receptors that become uncoupled from their g-protein unit that is essentially for activating intracellular units (e.g., second messengers). In contrast, repeated exposure to drugs that act as antagonists or dampen the action of neurotransmitters at receptors tends to increase receptor activity, as if there were more receptors, which may involve **up-regulation** or **supersensitivity** of receptors—that is, processes that are just the reverse of down-regulation.

According to this model of tolerance, with fewer receptors with which the drug molecules or transmitter can interact, higher doses of the agonist must be administered so that the original effect can be induced. This dosage increase, of course, may decrease the receptor population further, so that successively higher doses of the agonist are needed to activate the increasingly smaller population of receptors. With drug antagonists, the reverse process may occur; that is, with a greater population of receptors, higher doses of the antagonist are needed to block them. This model of drug tolerance has great appeal because it explains cross-tolerance between different classes of drugs and because it makes a direct connection between tolerance and physical dependence. Figure 6.1 graphically displays in a step-by-step fashion these theoretical processes for both drug antagonists, seen in Figure 6.1(a), and agonists, in Figure 6.1(b).

If, for example, the actions of drug A are due to its ability to block the postsynaptic receptors for neurotransmitter B, and this blockade is maintained for several hours, the population of postsynaptic receptors may increase. With more receptors available for activation by neurotransmitter B, a greater dose of drug A will be needed in order to block a sufficient number of receptors to bring about the original drug effects; that is, tolerance occurs. Now if the actions of drug C are due to its ability to block the release of neurotransmitter B, and drug C is substituted for drug A, drug C's effects will also be decreased. Conversely, if drug A is not given, there will be more than the normal population of receptors for neurotransmitter B to activate, and effects directly opposite of those induced by the drug—that is, withdrawal effects—will occur.

For how long must exposure to a drug occur for the receptor population to change? Studies with a variety of drugs suggest that several hours of continuous exposure to high drug concentrations may be sufficient to induce significant alterations in many hormone and neurotransmitter receptors (Nathanson, 1987). This time period may be linked to the approximate "lifetime" for a receptor. For example, the receptor for the hormone insulin has been estimated to have a half-life of between 7 and 12 hours in different cell types, which is shortened by exposure of the cell to the insulin ligand; that is, receptor down-regulation occurs (Rosen, 1987). Other receptors may have considerably longer half-lives. For example, adrenergic receptors have been shown to have half-lives greater than 20 hours (Mahan et al., 1987). Nevertheless, agonist exposure markedly shortens their half-life. Thus, we can speculate that the lifetime of a receptor is reduced when extensively activated, and increased when activation is prevented. Furthermore, the number of receptors gradually returns to normal values, after the drug is removed, on a time course that depends on many factors. For example, when some muscarinic receptors are down-regulated with exposure to cholinergic agonists, it appears that they must first be newly synthesized from proteins and then slowly converted to physiologically functional forms before normal cholinergic activity returns (Nathanson, 1987).

Several mechanisms also have been proposed for drug sensitization, and in some cases, the proposed mechanisms are essentially opposite to those proposed for tolerance. As noted earlier, much of the research in this area has focused upon drugs of abuse, and the effects of these drugs on nucleus accumbens (a terminal area for the mesolimbic DA system that is part of the striatal complex) have received particular emphasis. There is evidence that intracellular proteins associated with second-messenger systems show adaptive up-regulation following chronic stimulant administration (Self & Nestler, 1995). Enhanced levels of gene transcription factors such as delta FosB in orbitofrontal cortex have been implicated in sensitization (Winstanley et al., 2009). Li et al. (2004) reported that behavioral sensitization to cocaine was related to increases in dendritic

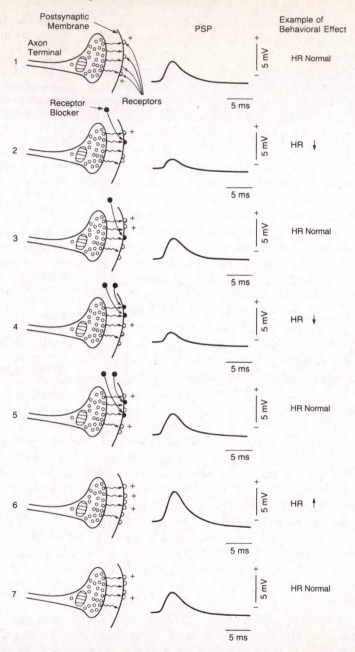

FIGURE 6.1(a)   Model for drug tolerance involving alterations in neurotransmitter (NT) receptor population on postsynaptic membrane, how these might affect the magnitude (in mV) of an excitatory postsynaptic potential (PSP), and how the behavioral effect or effector organ activity, for example, heart rate (HR), may be altered. (1) Normal NT release (with action potential), receptor activation (receptors activated indicated by +), PSP, and HR. (2) Drug antagonist blocks receptors, decreases PSP, and lowers HR. (3) Receptor population increases, so despite drug blockade of other receptors, normal PSP is created, and HR is normal. (4) Drug dose is increased so that more receptors are occupied and blocked; PSP is reduced and HR decreases. (5) Receptor population increases further; PSP and HR return to normal. (6) Drug not given; with greater number of receptors available, NT has increased probability of activating more of them, which results in greater PSP than normal and an exaggerated behavioral effect (i.e., HR elevation). (7) With no further drug exposure, receptor population, PSP, and effector organ activity eventually return to normal.

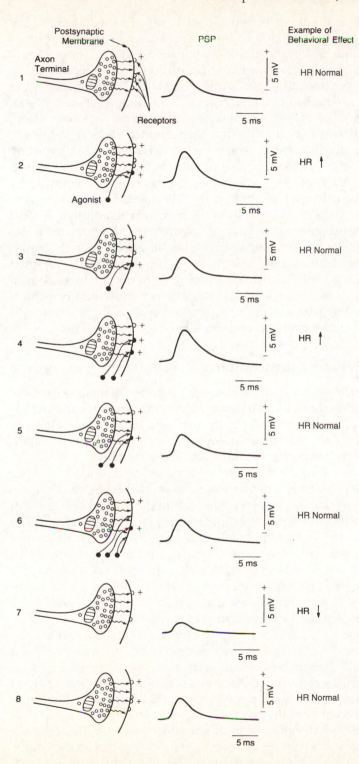

FIGURE 6.1(b)   The same model for drug tolerance depicted in Figure 6.1(a), except the drug is an agonist. (1) Normal NT release, receptor activation, PSP, and HR. (2) Drug agonist activates additional receptors, increases PSP, and increases HR. (3) Receptor population decreases, so despite subsequent exposure to the original concentration of the drug, normal PSP is created, and HR is normal. (4) Drug dose is increased so that more receptors are occupied and activated; PSP is enhanced and HR increases.
(5) Receptor population decreases further, so that despite the presence of the drug molecules, the PSP and HR are maintained at normal levels. (6) Receptor population is at minimal levels, so that even though the concentration of the drug may be increased with larger doses, no further amplification of the PSP is possible, and HR stays at normal levels. (7) Drug is eliminated from the body; with smaller numbers of receptors now available, NT has decreased probability of activating those that remain, which results in smaller PSP than normal and reduced behavioral activity (i.e., HR declines).
(8) with no further drug exposure, receptor population, PSP, and effector organ activity eventually return to normal.

spines in the core subregion nucleus accumbens as well as in the medial prefrontal cortex. Considerable evidence indicates that behavioral sensitization to cocaine is related to plastic changes in neurotransmission at α-amino-3-hydroxy-5-methylisoxazole-4 propionic acid (AMPA) receptors, which are a type of excitatory amino acid receptors, in the nucleus accumbens (Wolf & Ferrario, 2010; McCutcheon et al., 2011). These changes in AMPA transmission appear to depend upon many factors, including whether exposure is contingent or noncontingent (i.e., dependent upon an instrumental response or not), and the duration of the withdrawal period. It also has been reported that sensitization to stimulants such as amphetamine or cocaine, which elevate extracellular DA by acting presynaptically to stimulate release or block uptake or both, produce behavioral sensitization because of increased levels of DA in the nucleus accumbens. As reviewed by Vezina and Leyton (2009), the enhanced ability of drugs like amphetamine to increase extracellular levels of DA in nucleus accumbens is the neuroadaptation that is most frequently associated with the expression of behavioral sensitization. However, there also are conditions under which behavioral or neurochemical sensitization does not occur in response to repeated stimulant administration. For example, Bradberry (2007) reported that behavioral and neurochemical sensitization often does not occur in studies of humans and nonhuman primates. Several factors in addition to basic neurochemical characteristics of stimulant administration, including the presence or absence of conditioning cues, could be important determinants of the occurrence of sensitization.

Context-Specific Tolerance and Sensitization

Over the last several decades, there has been increasing recognition that many forms of drug tolerance and sensitization come about because of learning processes and behavioral adaptations that may occur in the presence of the drug and that are highly task- or situation-specific. Such effects are called **context-specific** tolerance or sensitization (these also are called **environment-specific** tolerance and sensitization).

Several mechanisms through which this form of tolerance can develop have been proposed. The term *context-specific* or *behavioral tolerance* is applied when an organism that is exposed to a drug in one context displays tolerance to the drug in that context, but then loses the tolerance when it is exposed to the same drug in another context. The most common processes involved in this form of tolerance are *habituation, Pavlovian conditioning,* and *instrumental conditioning.* Habituation is perhaps the most fundamental of these. When an organism is first exposed to a novel stimulus, the stimulus often induces a reaction. A *stimulus* is any event—external or internal—that is capable of activating receptors in one of the senses. A *response* is any measurable reaction in an organism, such as skeletal, smooth, and cardiac muscle contractions; glandular secretions and excretions; neurotransmitter release; EEG pattern changes; or emotional reactions. When the stimulus is presented repeatedly to an organism without variation, there generally is a decrease in the magnitude of the reaction to the stimulus, a phenomenon referred to as habituation. (As noted later in this chapter, habituation is sometimes used in the field of drug abuse as a synonym for psychological dependence, or the process of forming a drug habit, which is very different from the process being described here.)

By definition, psychoactive drugs have both stimulus- and response-eliciting properties. When a psychotropic drug is first administered to an organism, it introduces the organism to a new stimulus complex, and, much like a novel sound or visual stimulus, it may interrupt or alter the organism's ongoing behavior. However, after repeated exposures to the drug-induced stimulus complex with no further consequences, the organism's behavior is going to be less and less affected. This is habituation; it is also a form of tolerance (Kesner & Cook, 1983). Evidence that the decreased sensitivity to the drug is due to habituation, and not to pharmacodynamic mechanisms, is provided when the organism is subsequently given the drug in a different environment and the drug again induces a reaction (Baker & Tiffany, 1985).

It has been proposed that Pavlovian conditioning is another process through which behavioral tolerance develops (Stewart & Eikelboom, 1987). As is widely discussed in the psychology literature, the Russian physiologist Ivan Pavlov conditioned dogs to salivate to tones or lights when these stimuli were paired with food. This process may be a factor in developing tolerance, and it can have a profound impact with respect to the induction of psychological dependence on drugs. In some cases, it can induce conditioned reactions that appear to be similar to the abstinence symptoms associated with physical dependence. Because of its potential role in the areas of tolerance and dependence, this process will be explored in some detail. Pavlovian conditioning begins when an organism is exposed to a stimulus that automatically (i.e., innately) elicits one or more reactions in the organism. The stimulus is called an *unconditioned stimulus* (US), and the responses it elicits are called *unconditioned responses* (URs). Examples of these stimulus–response cause-and-effect relationships, called reflexes, are the withdrawal of your hand (UR) from a hot stove (US), the elicitation of tears (UR) by onion fumes (US), sneezing (UR) elicited by pepper in the nose (US), bronchial constriction (UR) elicited by pollen (US), and increased heart rate, blood pressure, and sweating and fright (URs) elicited by a loud, unexpected sound (US). Because psychoactive drugs induce a number of automatic reactions, they also constitute unconditioned stimuli. Thus, we can say that administration of morphine (US) elicits, among other reactions, constriction of the pupils, drying up of secretions, constipation, respiratory depression, analgesia, and euphoria, as URs. As another example, nicotine (US) elicits increased heart rate and blood pressure and altered cortical arousal (URs).

When a stimulus that generally does not produce much of a reaction by itself occurs prior to a US so that it reliably signals or predicts the occurrence of the US, conditioning may take place. We recognize that conditioning has occurred when the signal stimulus begins to elicit its own responses, which in many (but not all) cases resemble the URs elicited by the US. Because the new responses' occurrences are conditional upon the stimulus being paired with the US, they are termed *conditioned responses* (CRs), and the stimulus now eliciting them is termed a *conditioned stimulus* (CS).

In most cases, CRs elicited by a CS prepare the organism for dealing with the impending US (Holland, 1984; Hollis, 1984; Lennartz & Weinberger, 1992). For example, if food is put in the mouth, it is a US for salivation (UR). Because one sees the food before it enters the mouth, the sight of food is a signal for food entering the mouth. Thus, the sight of food becomes a CS that elicits salivation, which serves a function—in this case, to enhance the digestion and chewability of the food. Some CRs are very general preparatory responses—for example, "get-ready-for-something-important-to-happen" responses such as fear, increased heart rate, blood pressure, and respiration—whereas others are very specific—for example, the "get-ready-to-get-hit-in-the-eye" response of an eye blink. Depending on a number of factors too complicated to discuss here (many of which we simply don't understand), some CRs may appear to be similar to the URs provoked by USs, whereas other CRs appear to be very different from the URs—even opposite in their direction.

In the same fashion, signals for impending drug actions come to elicit CRs that prepare the body for the impending drug actions. Unfortunately, as we shall see, some of these CRs may, in the long run, actually be maladaptive for the person—for example, creating a conditioned incentive motivational state that leads the person to take the drug more and more frequently and in larger and larger amounts. It appears that a wide variety of external stimuli (i.e., the smell of a "joint" or the sight of a syringe), as well as internal stimuli (those of an emotional state such as depression or anxiety, for example), can take on the properties of a CS. The number of pairings of a CS with a US that are required for conditioning to take place are dependent on many factors, but to some extent, the species' particular characteristics play a role. For example, rats can associate a novel taste with nausea after only one exposure, even if there is a gap of several hours between experiencing the novel taste and receiving the nausea-inducing stimulus. Chickens, on the other hand, do not appear to associate these events, even after many pairings. Birds can associate novel visual stimuli with sickness after only a few pairings, whereas rats do not appear to do so even after many pairings of these events. I mention these esoteric little facts because, in a similar fashion, humans may vary in their tendency to associate certain events with the drug effects they experience. Therefore, humans may vary in their tendency to experience conditioned reactions that play a role in their becoming psychologically dependent on the drug.

How can Pavlovian CRs play a role in many types of tolerance phenomena? In most of the studies that have dealt with this question, animals were exposed to a drug like morphine or alcohol (US) on several occasions in a specific environmental context (CS; Siegel et al., 2000). Some of these animals were then given a behavioral test following exposure to the drug in this same (CS) environmental context, while other animals were given the same drug dose but were tested in a different context (no CS). Usually, the animals tested in the no-CS context exhibited larger drug effects than the animals tested in the CS context. One explanation is that, in the CS environment, a CR was elicited that was opposite to the drug-induced effects (URs); thus it was termed a *compensatory CR*. The net outcome was that the effectiveness of the drug (US) appeared to be reduced. However, in the no-CS context, there would be no compensatory CR to counteract the drug-induced UR. The interesting implication of these studies is that if the organism is exposed to the CS, but without the drug being given, a compensatory CR should occur. Such a reaction would appear withdrawal-like. However, in the few cases in which attempts have been made to directly observe compensatory-type CRs under laboratory conditions (i.e., when the organism is exposed to the CS without the drug [US] being present), the CRs appear weak and extinguish rapidly, if they occur at all (Sobrero & Bouton, 1989; Tiffany et al., 1983). Because the withdrawal symptoms associated with chronic use of many drugs are often quite severe and persist for several days, it is likely that other mechanisms, which may act synergistically with compensatory CRs, are involved in their production. In any case, compensatory CRs may be a factor in drug tolerance and drug dependence. As will be discussed later on, other types of CRs may also be involved in producing drug dependence.

A third behavioral mechanism that can be related to drug tolerance and sensitization, as well as other aspects of behavioral pharmacology, is *instrumental conditioning* (or Pavlovian/instrumental interactions). Whereas Pavlovian conditioning occurs without the organism necessarily doing anything—that is, the process occurs by the simple pairing of two different types of stimuli—instrumental conditioning begins with responses that are originally emitted without any apparent stimulus needed to produce them. The form and frequency of their subsequent occurrence are then altered depending upon the consequences of those responses. (The term *instrumental* is used to indicate that the behavior is instrumental or necessary for the conditioning process to occur. Common examples of instrumental behaviors are those involved in driving a car, hitting a golf ball, lighting a cigarette, snorting cocaine, and writing a letter.) These consequences are generally referred to as reinforcers and punishers. Stimuli that follow behavior and subsequently increase the probability of occurrence of that behavior in similar settings are termed *reinforcers. Positive reinforcement* occurs when a response is emitted, then a stimulus is presented, and response probability increases. In contrast, negative *reinforcement* occurs when a response occurs, then a stimulus is removed, and response probability increases. Stimuli that follow behavior and decrease the probability of occurrence of that behavior in similar settings are called *punishers.* Reinforcers can be either primary or secondary. Primary reinforcers are stimuli that are reinforcing in and of themselves (e.g., food, sex, and water). Secondary (also called *conditioned*) reinforcers are stimuli that signal access to or are associated with the increased probability of obtaining primary reinforcers (i.e., getting money increases one's chances of obtaining food, sex, and water). Drugs can act as primary reinforcers, and drug-seeking behavior is an instrumental behavior (this is evident in humans, and also in self-administration studies in animals). Environmental context cues in the presence of which the drugs are taken may become secondary reinforcers. Therefore, instrumental conditioning plays a role in drug dependence, and also in the development of tolerance and sensitization to drugs. Organisms can learn how to compensate for drug-induced effects on reinforced behavior with repeated experience, which can lead to tolerance, or to identify the drug-associated stimuli that predict the drug-induced behavioral effect, which could enhance the effect of the drug and lead to sensitization. Tolerance due to the development of instrumental compensatory responses that counteract a drug's effects has been demonstrated to occur with a variety of psychotropic drugs, including amphetamine, cocaine, morphine, alcohol, and barbiturates. Interestingly, the compensatory responses need not be overtly behavioral; they can also be cognitive. For example, it has been shown that tolerance to some of alcohol's behaviorally disruptive properties is facilitated even in persons who merely mentally rehearsed performing a task while under the influence of alcohol (Sdao-Jarvie & Vogel-Sprott, 1986).

Environment-specific sensitization has been shown to depend upon conditioning factors such as exposure to behavioral testing. DA antagonists produce an effect called catalepsy, which is the maintenance of an immobile posture for long periods of time (this is sometimes used as a behavioral screen for DA antagonism, and is an effect produced by most antipsychotic drugs). Evidence indicates that the catalepsy induced by DA antagonists can show environmentally specific tolerance, and that one of the critical factors in this case is the experience of prior catalepsy testing on the drug (Amtage & Schmidt, 2009), which appears to depend upon Pavlovian conditioning mechanisms. Another example of learning factors related to sensitization is with subjective reports of the effects of marijuana, which has the reputation of not inducing much of an effect the first time a person tries it, but with more exposure to the drug, the person begins to experience more of an effect from the same amount. Similar statements have been made by cocaine users.

It has been suggested that low doses of these drugs do not induce particularly noticeable effects in the user, but that with continued usage, the person learns to recognize the effects that have been labeled by users as pleasurable. It is also possible, through Pavlovian conditioning, that CRs, which are like the URs produced by the drug, summate with the drug-induced effects to induce a larger overall subjective effect.

Clearly there are many mechanisms through which drug tolerance and sensitization occurs. No single mechanism can account for all the phenomena associated with tolerance—particularly the fact that some drug effects dissipate with successive drug exposures,whereas others remain unchanged or increase in magnitude. We have discussed tolerance in two main frameworks: learning factors and neurochemical factors. Yet, from a reductionistic perspective, both neuropharmacological and learned forms of tolerance or sensitization may come about because of the same physiological mechanisms. Learning models simply emphasize the stimulus context, the task requirements, and the behavioral effects of drugs as factors in tolerance development. Pharmacological models emphasize the drug concentration and time between drug exposures as the primary factors in tolerance development.

DEPENDENCE, ABUSE, AND ADDICTION

A related set of terms is used to describe behavioral patterns of excessive or chronic drug taking that can result in deleterious effects; these terms include **drug abuse, drug dependence,** and **drug addiction.** The term *drug abuse* generally emphasizes that drug-taking behavior can result in adverse consequences (Newcomb & Bentler, 1989). *Drug dependence* is a term that has been defined in different ways; it can refer to the real or perceived need of the drug for normal physiological or psychological function, and the deleterious consequences of drug withdrawal. However, drug dependence can also be used as a synonym for drug addiction. According to a World Health Organization (WHO) definition, addiction is a state of periodic or chronic intoxication detrimental to the individual or society, produced by the repeated consumption of a drug; its characteristics were described as an overpowering desire or need (or compulsion) to continue taking the drug, because of either psychological or physical dependence on the effects of the drug, and a tendency to increase the dose or frequency of use. The *Diagnostic and Statistical Manual of Mental Disorders-IV (DSM-IV)*, which is produced by the American Psychiatric Association, uses the term **drug dependence** instead of addiction, and it defines drug dependence as a persistent use of alcohol or other drugs despite problems associated with the use of that substance. In addition, the *DSM-IV-TR* (a revised edition of the manual) establishes the following criteria for diagnosis of drug dependence (any three of which can lead to the diagnosis of a substance dependence:

1. tolerance, as defined by either of the following:
   a. a need for markedly increased amounts of the substance to achieve intoxication or desired effect
   b. markedly diminished effect with continued use of the same amount of the substance
2. withdrawal, as manifested by either of the following:
   a. the characteristic withdrawal syndrome for the substance (refer to Criteria A and B of the criteria sets for withdrawal from the specific substances)
   b. the same (or a closely related) substance is taken to relieve or avoid withdrawal symptoms

3. the substance is often taken in larger amounts or over a longer period than was intended
4. there is a persistent desire or unsuccessful efforts to cut down or control substance use
5. a great deal of time is spent in activities necessary to obtain the substance (e.g., visiting multiple doctors or driving long distances), use the substance (e.g., chain-smoking), or recover from its effects
6. important social, occupational, or recreational activities are given up or reduced because of substance use
7. the substance use is continued despite knowledge of having a persistent or recurrent physical or psychological problem that is likely to have been caused or exacerbated by the substance (e.g., current cocaine use despite recognition of cocaine-induced depression, or continued drinking despite recognition that an ulcer was made worse by alcohol consumption)

It should be noted that prior to the 20th century, the term *addiction* meant simply a strong inclination toward certain kinds of conduct, with little or no stigma associated with it. Often it referred to a habit—good or bad, but more often good, such as an addiction to reading. However, as the term came to be more and more associated with drugs, the term became stigmatic. Furthermore, it often became synonymous with physiological dependence, in spite of the WHO definition indicating that either psychological dependence or physical dependence (or both) may be involved. For these reasons, many experts today often avoid using the term *addiction* with respect to drugs. However, because the term has become so ingrained in our language, it will continue to be used. When, on occasion, it is used in the remainder of this book, it will be used in the sense of the WHO definition. In this context, whenever the term **addict** is used in this text, it will refer to someone who has a strong compulsion to use a particular substance.

There are two basic forms of drug dependence: psychological dependence and physical (or physiological) dependence. Neither of these is particularly easy to define, and it is sometimes difficult to distinguish between the two, not only because the symptoms associated with them can be confused, but also because the two often occur together. **Psychological dependence** refers to a strong compulsion or desire (or *craving*) to experience the effects of a drug because it produces pleasure or reduces emotional discomfort. Generally, it leads to regular or continuous administration of the drug, so that taking the drug becomes habitual. Because of these characteristics, some authors in the area of drug abuse refer to psychological dependence as habituation. However, because this term can be confused with the phenomenon of habituation described earlier in this chapter, I do not view it as an appropriate term. In a sense, psychological dependence is the counterpart to context-specific tolerance because the affective states underlying it are heavily influenced by the context the person is in and because it is primarily the result of learning and memory processes. Similarly, physiological dependence is the counterpart to pharmacodynamic tolerance because some of the mechanisms behind the latter are the likely causes of the manifestations of physiological dependence. Psychological dependence comes about because drug-taking behavior is regularly followed by the reinforcing effects of a drug. Human beings self-administer nonprescribed drugs for a variety of purposes, for example, to enhance mood or some aspect of performance, to cope with adverse or stressful situations, to socialize, to conform, or to expand experiential awareness (Cooper, 1994; Simons et al., 2000). Some of these motives (e.g., social motives) appear to have little or no association with excessive drug use or drug-related problems, whereas others (e.g., enhancement and coping motives) have been shown to be predictive of excessive use and problems.

Physical (or physiological) dependence is said to occur when a state, termed an **abstinence syndrome,** characterized by physical disturbances develops when the administration of a drug is suspended after prolonged use or its actions are terminated by the administration of a specific antagonist. In almost all cases, the effects of withdrawal are the opposite of the direct effects induced by the drug (O'Brien, 2001). Thus, for example, withdrawal from barbiturates, which normally exert a calming, sleep-inducing, anticonvulsant action, is characterized by anxiety, inability to sleep, and convulsions (which can be lethal). Withdrawal from opiates (which cause constipation, dry nasal passages, sleep, reductions in sex drive, and reduction in pain, among many other effects) is characterized by diarrhea, runny nose, inability to sleep, spontaneous ejaculations (men) or orgasms (women), and hypersensitivity to pain.

The duration and intensity of an abstinence syndrome are also highly correlated with the duration and intensity of a drug's direct effects (Figure 6.2). For example, a drug with a short plasma half-life (say, 4 hours) will likely induce a relatively intense but short-lasting behavioral effect. If given infrequently, cessation of its use will not likely result in abstinence symptoms. However, if taken frequently so that the CNS (central nervous system) is continuously exposed to the drug, its withdrawal will likely result in a relatively intense abstinence syndrome that dissipates fairly quickly (i.e., over a few days). Conversely, a drug with a long plasma half-life (say, 24 hours) will likely induce relatively weak but long-lasting behavioral effects. If taken frequently enough so that the CNS is continuously exposed to the drug, its withdrawal is likely to result in a relatively weak abstinence syndrome that dissipates slowly (i.e., over a few weeks). Also, as one might expect, the more frequently a drug is administered and the greater the dose, the more extensive the abstinence syndrome will be (Okamoto et al., 1986).

In Figure 6.2, we see that in case A, with a short-acting drug administered at spaced intervals, there is likely to be no pharmacodynamic tolerance and no withdrawal. In case B, in which a short-acting drug is administered at a constant dosage and at closely spaced intervals, there is likely to be pharmacodynamic tolerance and a mild, but short-lasting, abstinence syndrome. In case C, in which the short-acting drug is administered at closely spaced intervals and the dose is increased (indicated by X), there is likely to be a relatively more intense and longer-lasting abstinence syndrome than in case B. In case D, with a longer-lasting drug administered at spaced intervals, pharmacodynamic tolerance will not be readily apparent, and the abstinence syndrome (if evident at all) will be mild. In case E, in which the longer-lasting drug is administered at more closely spaced intervals, pharmacodynamic tolerance and the abstinence syndrome will be somewhat more apparent than in case D. Furthermore, although the abstinence syndrome in case E may be less severe than in case C, it is likely to be more protracted.

In most cases, abstinence symptoms are not typically displayed unless the individual has consumed the drug for several days or weeks at high dosage levels that would normally induce tolerance to the drug's effects. However, with sufficiently high dosages, signs of abstinence may occur within a relatively short span of time—that is, following high drug concentrations for 12 hours or so. For example, behavioral studies have shown that a single dose of morphine, if large enough to maintain morphine concentrations in the rat

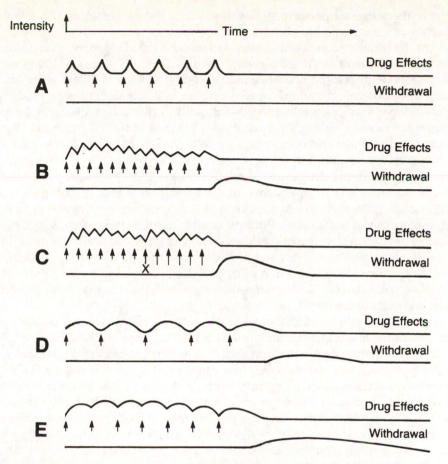

FIGURE 6.2   Relationships between the intensity of a drug's effects and the intensity of the abstinence syndrome when the drug is no longer administered. The arrows indicate when the drug is administered.

for approximately 12 hours, can increase the perceived intensity of mild shock (indicative of a withdrawal-like increase in pain perception) 24 to 72 hours later (Grilly & Gowans, 1986). On a more personal level, if you have ever had an alcohol hangover (which may very likely constitute a mini-withdrawal syndrome), it is probably because you drank sufficient amounts of alcohol to maintain significant brain concentrations of alcohol for at least 12 hours. If you drink enough alcohol to become legally intoxicated in most states—0.10% blood alcohol content—it takes approximately 7 hours to eliminate it from your body. (A 0.10% blood alcohol content means that in every 1,000 ml of blood there is 1 ml of pure ethanol.) Therefore, if you experience a hangover after a night of drinking, it is likely that you were well over the legal limit by the time you finished drinking.

If a person becomes physically dependent on a drug, a second form of psychological dependence can develop. That is, once physical dependence exists and the person becomes familiar with the symptoms of abstinence, the person may develop a craving for the drug that is based on the person's fear or anxiety of experiencing the abstinence syndrome. Therefore, the person seeks out and administers the drug to alleviate the fear or anxiety.

Although tolerance and physical dependence often accompany each other, they are not necessarily related. At least some degree of drug tolerance inevitably precedes physical dependence, but physical dependence does not always follow when tolerance to a drug develops. In other words, if someone is physically dependent on a drug, that person will have developed tolerance to many of its effects. However, if a person has developed tolerance to a drug's effects, it does not mean that the person is physically dependent on the drug. This is most likely due to the fact there are many mechanisms for inducing tolerance, and only some of them may also result in physical dependence.

Some psychotropic drugs have a relatively strong potential for producing both physical and psychological dependence; others appear capable of inducing one without the other; and still others do not appear to induce either to any significant degree. I would hesitate to say that any psychotropic drug is incapable of inducing either or only one kind of dependence; it is just that there is no clear evidence one way or another in some cases. However, the argument has been made that just about any psychotropic drug, if the organism is exposed to it in large enough doses and for a long enough period of time, will provoke abstinence symptoms when the drug is rapidly eliminated from the body (Hollister, 1987).

Classes of drugs for which there is clear evidence of a moderate to strong potential for both physical and psychological dependence would include all drugs with sedative–hypnotic properties. Among them are alcohol, barbiturates, nonbarbiturate sedative–hypnotics, antianxiety drugs (sometimes called "minor tranquilizers"), and the narcotics, such as heroin, morphine, codeine, and methadone. Drugs that have a high potential for inducing psychological dependence, but for which physical dependence is unclear, would include the psychostimulants, such as cocaine, amphetamines, and related compounds (of course, this depends upon the definition of dependence; lack of energy or motivation induced by stimulant withdrawal could constitute a basis for physical dependence). Marijuana is considered to have a moderate potential for inducing psychological dependence and may induce mild symptoms of physical dependence. Psychological dependence on hallucinogens such as LSD, mescaline, and psilocybin is rare, and physical dependence associated with their use has not been documented.

Some drugs have minimal potential for inducing psychological dependence, but, if taken for a period of time, will induce physical dependence and provoke withdrawal symptoms if the person ceases taking them. (Nasal spray, although not a psychotropic drug, is capable of having this effect.) Certain narcotics with mixed agonist–antagonist properties are in this category. Finally, drugs used in the treatment of major mental and emotional disturbances, such as lithium, antidepressants, and antipsychotics, have minimal potential for inducing psychological dependence or signs of abstinence. In fact, many patients would prefer to stop taking these types of drugs because of the unpleasant side effects associated with them.

As stated earlier, even drugs that traditionally were not thought of as being capable of inducing physical dependence (cocaine, for instance) will, if given in large enough quantities and for a long enough period of time, upon cessation of drug administration induce physiological and psychological disturbances opposite to the drug-induced effects. Perhaps these symptoms were not recognized as withdrawal because they do not resemble, quantitatively or qualitatively, the symptoms associated with the sedative–hypnotics and the narcotics. This issue will be dealt with more fully when these drugs are discussed in later chapters. (Several years ago, when I pointed out the possibility of physical dependence with all psychotropic drugs, a student suggested that if this were true, giving LSD chronically in large amounts to schizophrenics might result in their becoming rational and nondelusional upon withdrawal. I quickly pointed out that although it was an intriguing hypothesis, there are exceptions to every generalization.)

Neurobiological Approaches to Drug Dependence and Addiction

For ethical reasons, most of the research on the basic causes of and potential treatments for drug addictions is conducted with nonhumans. However, how does one go about determining whether a drug has abuse potential in nonhumans? A common laboratory technique used to assess the dependence liability of a drug, removed from social, cultural, or expectancy factors, involves determining whether or not nonhumans (e.g., monkeys or rats) will engage in *self-administration* of the drug. Typically, the procedure entails a small catheter (tube) being permanently implanted in a laboratory animal (although with alcohol, it can simply involve oral intake). The catheter is typically placed intravenously (though it can be connected to a cannula directly into the brain) and is connected to a pump outside the animal. The animal can activate the pump, and thus self-administer a dose of the drug, by performing some learned instrumental response, like pressing a lever. The dependence liability of the drug is determined by how frequently the animal responds when the drug is injected versus when an inert substance is injected. Animals will readily perform the response in order to administer most drugs that are abused by humans. For example, morphine, heroin, cocaine, and amphetamine, drugs that can induce a strong psychological dependence in humans, are very readily self-administered by rats and monkeys with this procedure, but caffeine, which is not readily abused by humans, is not reliably self-administered by animals (Woods, 1978). This technique is not an infallible approach to determining the potential dependence liability of a drug, because some drugs used by humans are not self-administered by nonhumans—for example, LSD. Although drug self-administration studies with nonhumans most commonly employ the IV (intravenous) route of administration, other routes of administration have been used to demonstrate drug self-administration in nonhumans. Even the oral route can be used, although it is a bit more difficult to establish drug-reinforced response due primarily to the aversive taste of many drugs and the delayed onset of CNS effects (Macenski & Meisch, 1994). Nevertheless, there have been several studies using orally administered ethanol as a reinforcer (e.g., Samson & Chappel, 2004; Samson & Czachowski, 2003).

The self-administration procedure can also be used to determine what factors might contribute to addiction and what manipulations might be useful in its treatment. After an animal has learned the response that produces drug injections, it can be exposed to extinction conditions; that is, once the response no longer produces drug injections, the animal eventually stops making the response. Then the animal's environment can be manipulated to determine what reinstates the response, that is, induces relapse. For example, in animals trained to self-administer cocaine and that then underwent extinction, several different kinds of stimuli are capable of reinstating drug seeking (called **priming** or **reinstatement**), for example, electrical stimulation of the hippocampus, exposure to a variety of stressors, cues previously predictive of drug availability, and re-exposure to the previously self-administered drug (Everitt & Wolf, 2002; Stewart & Vezina, 1988; Vorel et al., 2001). These manipulations provide information on what might trigger drug craving in humans as well as what types of treatments might be useful in reducing drug craving and relapse.

The self-administration model has been modified to incorporate the observation that some, but not all, rats after extensive experience with cocaine self-administration exhibit the classic signs of addiction in humans (Deroche-Gamonet et al., 2004; Vanderschuren & Everitt, 2004). For human addicts, these signs include: (1) continued drug seeking even when the drug is unlikely to be available; (2) unusually strong desire for the drug; and (3) continued drug use even in the face of adverse consequences. Interestingly, only 17% of rats displayed all three characteristics, approximately the same percentage of humans that move from "recreational" use of cocaine to addiction. That is, in comparison to the rest of the animals, a subpopulation of rats continued to make the response that led to cocaine administration even when a cue was provided to them that cocaine was no longer available, made many more responses to obtain a single injection of cocaine, and continued to work for cocaine even when their responses produced an electric shock or when a cue was presented that had previously been paired with shock. Rats that displayed this addiction-like pattern of behavior also exhibited another classic effect: they showed a high propensity to relapse even after a long period of abstinence, that is, following extinction training, their responses were more easily reinstated when given a priming injection of cocaine or exposed to a drug-associated cue. Similarly, Cantin et al. (2010) reported that only a small percentage of rats tested in self-administration procedures (about 15% under the best conditions) showed a strong preference for cocaine reinforcement relative to sucrose, which matches well with the human epidemiology of cocaine addiction. The next step will be to determine what differentiates these groups of rats that differ in terms of their drug preference or usage pattern—for example, genes, environmental history, and cocaine-induced changes in the brain—to assist us in illuminating the factors that lead to addiction in humans.

Other procedures for measuring drug abuse liability in animals include place preference and intracranial self-stimulation. Conditioned place preference involves the conditioning of a drug effect to a particular place (e.g., portion of a test chamber), which leads an animal to prefer that place in the future. Typically, animals are placed in a chamber that has distinct stimulus characteristics when they are exposed to the drug in question. Then, during a retention test, they are allowed to choose the portion of the test apparatus that was paired with the drug as opposed to the section of the apparatus that was not paired with the drug. Conditioned place preference is said to occur when the animal prefers the area that was previously paired with the drug. In contrast, place aversion occurs when the animal prefers the chamber that was not paired with the drug. Several drugs that have abuse potential in humans have been shown to induce place preference, including cocaine, amphetamine, ethanol, morphine, heroin, and others (Carr & White 1983; Cunningham et al., 2006; McBride et al., 1999; Sellings et al., 2006). Another test that is sometimes used to assess drug abuse liability in animals is intracranial self-stimulation (sometimes called brain stimulation reward). Several decades ago, Olds and Milner (1954) discovered that lever pressing in rats could be reinforced by a brief presentation of electrical stimulation of the brain. In some experiments, alterations in brain-stimulation reward thresholds (i.e., the threshold of the current needed to maintain the reinforced behavior) have been used to assess the effects of drugs such as amphetamines, cocaine, ethanol and opiates, which lower the threshold (e.g., Esposito et al., 1980; Fish et al., 2010; Hayes & Gardner, 2004).

There are many theoretical approaches that are used to describe the process of how drugs can have reinforcing properties, and how drug use can ultimately lead to dependence or addiction. These include behavioral as well as neurobiological approaches. For many years, the dominant neurobiological hypothesis in the field of addiction research has been the DA hypothesis of reward (see Wise, 2008, for a discussion of the history of the DA hypothesis of reward). According to this hypothesis, DA transmission, especially in the nucleus accumbens (a target of the mesolimbic DA system reviewed in the previous chapter), mediates the primary reinforcing effects of virtually all stimuli, including natural stimuli such as food, water, and sex, as well as abstract rewards in humans, such as winning money, success in fictitious competition, and financial reward. Typically, DA is said to mediate "reward" processes, and the term *reward* is generally used to convey a sense of pleasure, such as that experienced during sex, falling in love, consumption of chocolate, or listening to music (e.g., Acevedo et al., 2011; Elliott et al., 2003; Nestler, 1996; Salimpoor et al., 2011). Furthermore, it is sometimes stated that this so-called natural reward system can be "hijacked" by drugs of abuse (Kauer & Malenka, 2007). What is the evidence that is generally cited to support the DA hypothesis of reward? Most drugs of abuse have been shown to elevate extracellular DA in nucleus accumbens, and virtually all abuse-prone drugs, including widely disparate pharmacologically acting drugs like morphine, cocaine, alcohol, and marijuana, have been found to enhance brain stimulation reward or lower brain reward thresholds in these circuits (e.g., Fish et al., 2010; Gardner & Lowinson, 1991; Wise, 1998). Furthermore, interference with DA transmission in nucleus accumbens is hypothesized to block the primary reinforcing effects of natural rewards, such as food (producing effects that resemble extinction, or withdrawal of reward), as well as drugs of abuse; this has been studied with procedures involving instrumental behaviors such as positively reinforced lever pressing, as well as conditioned place preference.

The main function of a scientific hypothesis is to stimulate research, and the DA hypothesis of reward has indeed instigated a considerable amount of research over the last few decades. Nevertheless, much of that research can lead one to conclude that it is oversimplified to consider nucleus accumbens DA as a mediator of primary "reward" or primary motivation for natural stimuli such as food, water, and sex. In fact, there are several conceptual limitations and numerous empirical difficulties with the traditional DA hypothesis of "reward" (Baldo & Kelley, 2007; Salamone et al., 1997, Salamone et al., 2007, 2009a), not the least of which is related to the use of the term *reward* itself (Cannon & Bseikri, 2004; Salamone, 2006). Investigators rarely define what they mean by *reward* when they are using the term to describe a psychological process (it can be synonymous with reinforcement, or can refer to primary motivation, appetite, or pleasure), and it is difficult to know what the term actually means in any particular case. Also, it is ironic that the processes most directly linked to the use of the term *reward* (i.e., primary motivation, subjective pleasure) are actually the ones that are the most troublesome in terms of demonstrating the involvement of mesolimbic DA (Salamone et al., 2007, 2009a). In studies of food-reinforced behavior, low doses of DA antagonists and depletions of nucleus accumbens DA have been shown to produce effects that do not closely resemble motivational manipulations such as extinction (Salamone et al., 1997), prefeeding to reduce food motivation (Aberman & Salamone, 1999; Salamone et al., 1991), or appetite-suppressant drugs (Sink et al., 2008). Nucleus accumbens DA depletions or antagonism does not substantially impair appetite for food, or produce a general disruption of primary food motivation (Bakshi & Kelley 1991; Baldo et al., 2002; Koob et al., 1978; Salamone et al., 1993; Ungerstedt, 1971), and interference with accumbens DA transmission also does not impair appetitive taste reactivity for sucrose (an animal test that is used to assess hedonic reactions to food; Berridge, 2007; Berridge & Kringlebach, 2008). Moreover, the involvement of DA systems in instrumental behavior and learning is not limited to situations involving appetitive motivation. There is considerable evidence that mesolimbic DA also is involved in aspects of aversive learning and aversive motivation (Delgado et al., 2008, 2011; Faure et al., 2008; Pezze & Feldon, 2004; Salamone, 1994; Salamone et al., 1997).

Although imaging studies often are used to support the idea that nucleus accumbens mediates pleasure (e.g., Acevedo et al., 2011; Salimpoor et al., 2011; Sarchiapone et al., 2006), this is only part of the story, because imaging research also has demonstrated that the nucleus accumbens responds to stress, aversion, and hyperarousal/irritability (Jensen et al., 2003; Levita et al., 2009; Liberzon et al., 1999; Pavic, 2003; Phan et al., 2004; Pruessner et al., 2004). Physiological and neurochemical studies in animals clearly indicate that DA neuron activity is not simply tied to the delivery of primary reinforcers or pleasurable stimuli. Instead, accumbens DA release and VTA (ventral tegmental area) neuron firing can be increased by a number of different aversive conditions (Anstrom & Woodward, 2005; Brischoux et al., 2009; Broom & Yamamoto, 2005; Marinelli et al., 2005; McCullough & Salamone, 1992; McCullough et al., 1993; Zink et al., 2003). Administration of DA antagonists not only interferes with drug-induced place preference, but also blocks place aversion induced by drugs (Acquas et al., 1989). These observations have led to a substantial revision of concepts related to the behavioral functions of mesolimbic DA, and it has been suggested that this field is undergoing a "paradigm shift" (Salamone et al., 2007; see Kuhn, 1962, for a discussion of paradigm shifts in science). Thus, it clearly is problematic to continue to label DA as a "pleasure chemical," because this system participates in several complex functions related to aspects of instrumental behavior, including learning about reinforcers and punishers, incentive motivation, behavioral activation and exertion of effort, and Pavlovian/instrumental interactions (Berridge, 2007; Everitt & Robbins, 2005; Kelley et al., 2005; Mingote et al., 2005; Redgrave et al., 2008; Robbins & Everitt, 2007; Roitman et al., 2004; Salamone et al., 2005; Salamone, 2010b; Salamone et al., 2007; Schultz & Dickinson, 2000; Wise, 2008; Yin et al., 2009; Ghods-Sharifi & Floresco, 2010, Venugopalan et al., 2011).

Concepts about the role of DA in drug-induced euphoria, dependence, and addiction also have undergone considerable revision in the last few years. Benzodiazepines (a class of drugs with sedative and anxiolytic properties, which also have considerable dependence liability) have been shown to reduce rather than increase DA levels in the nucleus accumbens (Motzo et al., 1997), whereas anxiogenic benzodiazepines actually increase DA release (McCullough & Salamone, 1992). Recent studies with intracranial self-stimulation thresholds, which for years were thought to be a measure of hedonia in animals, indicate that DAergic modulation of self-stimulation thresholds does not affect reward value per se, but instead alters the tendency to pay response costs (Hernandez et al., 2010). Several studies in humans have reported that DA antagonists did not blunt the subjective euphoria produced by drugs of abuse in humans (Brauer & De Wit, 1997; Gawin, 1986; Haney et al., 2001; Nann-Vernotica et al., 2001; Wachtel et al., 2002).

Consistent with these evolving concepts, there is an ongoing theoretical restructuring in the field, and several additional hypotheses are being offered to explain drug dependence and addiction. Drug reinforcement appears to involve a distributed network that spans multiple brain regions beyond just mesolimbic DA (Ikemoto, 2010). Glutamate (GLU), the major excitatory amino acid neurotransmitter in the brain, plays a critical role in this drug reinforcement circuitry, as glutamatergic inputs to the VTA and nucleus accumbens, arising from the prefrontal cortex, hippocampus, and amygdala, have all been implicated in addiction (White, 2002). For example, GLU appears to play a critical role in drug craving; acamprosate, a drug that blocks the ability of GLU to stimulate electrical activity in the cortex of rats, has been shown to decrease the craving for alcohol in alcoholic patients (Dahchour & De Witte, 2000). On the other hand, drugs that mimic GLU action at one of its receptors have been shown to reinstate previously extinguished cocaine-seeking behavior in rats (see how drug seeking in animals is demonstrated later in the chapter), which suggests that the rats were craving cocaine (Cornish et al., 1999). Also, the degree of cocaine craving in human cocaine abusers watching films displaying cocaine-associated stimuli has been shown to parallel the intensity of neural activity in the frontal cortex and the amygdala (Grant et al., 1996), areas that release GLU in the nucleus accumbens. Thus, it appears that brain structures that mediate learning and memory functions and that greatly depend on GLU seem to play a role in the cravings elicited by conditioned stimuli.

The **incentive sensitization** hypothesis (e.g., Peciña et al., 2003; Robinson & Berridge, 2001, 2003) posits that DA systems modulate the process of incentive motivation and the establishment of conditioned incentives, and that DA release results in rewards being more "wanted" without them necessarily being more "liked." According to this view, addiction results from the sensitization of the incentive properties of stimuli via mechanisms that depend upon mesolimbic DA, and ultimately leads to excessive "wanting" to consume drugs. It also has been suggested that **sign-tracking** (the phenomenon in which some animals approach and engage a CS that predicts a reinforcer) is related to the neural plasticity that leads to the development of addiction (Flagel et al., 2008). Over the last few years, there has been a growing interest in the "dark side" of addiction; drug withdrawal can trigger negative emotional states, a process known as hedonic **"allostasis"** (Koob & LeMoal, 2005, 2008), which serves to provide motivation for the negative reinforcement of drug-taking behavior (i.e., that taking the drug can alleviate an aversive motivational state, and removal of this state serves as a negative reinforcer). Finally, an emerging concept in the field that is gaining considerable support is that drug addiction is a maladaptive and compulsive **incentive habit,** which, through chronic exposure to the drug, eventually subverts the basal ganglia mechanisms involved in instrumental and Pavlovian control over behavior (Belin et al., 2009; Everitt & Robbins, 2005). According to this approach, repeated exposure to addictive drugs recruits basal ganglia circuits that lead to a shift from action–outcome processes (i.e., response–reinforcement) to stimulus–response mechanisms that gain control over drug seeking, allowing this pattern of seeking to become established as an incentive habit that is relatively independent of instrumental reinforcement. One of the compelling aspects of this view is that it provides an explanation for several features of drug dependence and addiction, including the compulsive pattern of drug taking, the persistence of drug consumption despite negative consequences, the apparent loss of control over drug-related behavior, and the striking influence that drug-related cues have over behavior (Pierce & Vanderschuren, 2010). Furthermore, it allows one to conceive of the process of drug addiction as involving a competition between prefrontal cortex circuits that are important for executive control of behavior and flexible decision making versus basal ganglia mechanisms involved in the execution of habits (Kalivas, 2008).

Various Factors in Dependence

A multitude of sociological, psychological, and genetic factors have been suggested to be involved in the abuse of drugs (see Shadel et al., 2000; and National Institute on Drug Abuse monographs edited by Harris, 1980, 1981; and Thompson & Johanson, 1981; for extensive reviews of this topic). Genetic influences appear to be nearly universally important in determining sensitivity to drugs, and several hundred reports have appeared documenting genetic differences in sensitivity or toxic responses to almost all drugs subject to abuse. Family, twin, and adoption studies have provided overwhelming evidence that variation in the liability to substance abuse is influenced by differences in individual genetic makeup (Vanyukov et al., 2003). Twin studies suggest that genetic factors may account for up to 79% of the variation in the liability to any illicit drug abuse or dependence in both males and females, and may account for 73% (males) and 61% (females) in liability for alcoholism. Heritability estimates for tobacco initiation have ranged from 32% to 70% in females and from 31% to 40% in males. Genetic factors have consistently accounted for 60% to 71% in variation smoking persistence. Liability for use and abuse of various categories of drugs, alcohol, and tobacco has been shown to share a considerable proportion of genes, which suggests that some common genetic background predisposes individuals to exhibiting a variety of pathological characteristics involving drug use—the particular type or types being generated by environmental factors that are not yet clearly delineated.

Variations in genes controlling both pharmacodynamic (e.g., differences in dopamine D_2-like receptors) and pharmacokinetic (e.g., differences in enzymes that metabolize ethanol, opiates, and nicotine) processes have been implicated in the predisposition to develop substance abuse disorders (Kreek et al., 2004). For example, as discussed in Chapter 10 on sedative–hypnotics, ethanol, which often induces pleasant sensations in most individuals, is metabolized into acetaldehyde (the first metabolite) and then acetate (the second metabolite). Variations in the particular form (allele) of the genes that produce the enzymes that convert ethanol into acetaldehyde or subsequently convert acetaldehyde into its inactive metabolite can contribute to the propensity to become alcoholic; for example, those individuals who rapidly convert ethanol into acetaldehyde or those who poorly metabolize acetaldehyde are much less likely to become alcoholics. These are examples of genetic variations that contribute to a specific type of substance dependence. Variations in the genes regulating the enzymes monoamine oxidase (MAO), which metabolically inactivates the neurotransmitters DA, NE (norepinephrine), and 5-HT (serotonin), and catechol-O-methyltransferase (COMT), which inactivates the catecholamines DA and NE, have been implicated in vulnerability in the development of dependence to a variety of drugs (Boettiger et al., 2007), with the specific drug being dependent on the person's environment (e.g., access to specific drugs). Similarly, variations in the genes regulating DA, 5-HT, and opiate receptors have been tied to substance dependence liability.

However, this area of research is still in its infancy, and there are several problems that need to be overcome before we can determine whether there is a definitive linkage between specific alleles and drug addiction. One is the lack of replicability across studies utilizing different samples of individuals and different methodologies to determine linkage. The second stems from the fact that substance dependence disorders are commonly comorbid with personality characteristics and psychiatric disorders, which themselves have been linked to many of these same genetic variations. For example, antisocial personality, conduct disorder, and sensation-seeking characteristics, as well as mood and anxiety disorders and schizophrenia are all associated with a high level of substance dependence (Kendler et al., 2003; Zuckerman, 1979). Thus, it is difficult to disentangle the alleles that are specific to substance dependence from those that contribute to characteristics that might make persons vulnerable to substance dependence. Finally, it also is true that there is not a simple relation between particular genes and propensity for drug dependence. There are many genes that have some association with dependence, but usually any particular gene does not have a very strong predictive relationship. If indeed there are dozens of genes related to drug dependence liability in people (as many researchers think there are), it will require painstaking work and elaborate statistical analyses to determine how groups of gene polymorphisms may contribute, in combination with environmental factors, to the tendency to engage in a pattern of drug dependence or addiction.

Sociological factors in drug involvement have been discussed at length (Harris, 1980, 1981). With respect to extensive illicit drug use, the strongest and most direct factor is the user's selling of drugs, which in turn is strongly related to factors such as drug availability, significant others' labeling of the person as deviant, peer influence, early childhood deviance, poor school adjustment, and weak family influence (Clayton & Voss, 1981). For example, when one's family influence (defined in terms of family control, closeness to mother, and communication with parents) is weak, there is a higher likelihood during the early teens that the person will (1) exhibit signs of early deviance (i.e., be involved in unconventional or deviant activities); (2) be strongly influenced by peers who are delinquent, steal, engage in gang fights, drink alcohol, smoke marijuana, or use other drugs; and (3) exhibit poor school adjustment (i.e., dislike school and get low grades). Early deviance will also tend to increase the degree of peer influence and decrease the person's school adjustment. These factors then increase the person's likelihood of becoming labeled as a troublemaker, increasing the person's drug availability. These then make the person more likely to sell and use illicit drugs.

Although race or ethnic group might be expected to be a factor in the incidence of drug abuse, the findings are not consistent with the impressions that many people in the United States have about drug-use rates. One of the more interesting findings from population-based epidemiologic studies conducted over the past three decades is that African American youths, in spite of the fact that they are more likely to be economically disadvantaged, have reported the lowest prevalence of lifetime use of all types of psychotropic drugs in comparison with Whites and Hispanics. Except for higher use of cocaine by Hispanics, it has been White youths who have reported the highest prevalence of use of psychotropic drugs (Johnston et al., 2003). Perhaps not coincidentally, Whites were least likely to perceive risks for substance abuse (Ma & Shive, 2000). (African Americans, however, may have greater secondary problems arising out of substance abuse than Whites—for example, liver damage, cancer, pulmonary disease, malnutrition, hypertension, and birth defects.) Compared with adolescents of other American ethnic and racial groups, Native American adolescents are likely to use tobacco products, alcohol, and other drugs more frequently, and earlier, and with more serious health, social, and economic consequences (Schinke et al., 2000).

Exposure to licit substances, such as alcohol and tobacco, is also a major factor in abuse of both licit and illicit substances. In fact, numerous studies have demonstrated that there has been a reasonably consistent sequence of stages of drug involvement in North American and similar cultures over the last 30 years or so (Blaze-Temple & Lo, 1992; Fleming et al., 1989; Kandel, 1975). Generally, the sequence begins with the use of more socially accepted substances like tobacco and beer, and is followed by an increased likelihood of using hard liquor and marijuana; for example, in one study, less than 2% of middle school students reported trying marijuana without trying cigarettes first (Fleming et al., 1989). This stage then leads to an increased likelihood of using other illicit drugs such as cocaine, heroin, and LSD. (Note the use of the words "increased likelihood of using." These words should not be construed as meaning "a likelihood of using.") In other words, it is very rare in American culture for a person to start using hard liquor or marijuana without first using tobacco or beer, or other illicit drugs without first using marijuana or hard liquor.

The developmental processes of substance use are complex. Some abstainers progress to drug use, others remain abstinent, and still others shift from a pattern of use to nonuse (Coombs et al., 1986). Thus, escalation into more extensive patterns of drug use is not inevitable, nor is it always a gradual, progressive occurrence. Why some individuals undergo a transition from periodic recreational or circumstantial drug use to the compulsive patterns of drug-seeking and drug-taking behavior, as well as the propensity to relapse, has been the focus of a great deal of research. One factor that is widely accepted is that drugs, either because of their particular pharmacokinetic properties or because of the means of administration, that most rapidly enter the brain are potentially the most likely going to be abused and lead to addiction (Gossop et al., 1992; Hatsukami & Fischman, 1996; Samaha et al., 2004).

A number of hypotheses for predisposing factors in chronic drug use have emphasized personality characteristics, such as sensation- or novelty-seeking traits, extroversion and introversion, antisocial personality characteristics, anxiety, and other social motives. The most consistent finding is that many substance abusers exhibit a history of antisocial behavior (e.g., nonconformity, acting out, and impulsivity) and a high level of depression or low self-esteem (Kendler et al., 2003; Marlatt et al., 1988). Another consistent observation is that high sensation seekers are much more likely to abuse all types of psychotropic drugs than low sensation seekers (Zuckerman, 1979).

There is considerable epidemiological and clinical evidence of high comorbidity (i.e., two or more disorders are observed in the same person) between drug dependence and psychiatric disorders, particularly major depression, generalized anxiety disorder, and phobias (Kendler et al., 2003). These findings have led to the hypothesis that for many abusers their drug use is a form of self-medication (Khantzian & Treece, 1985; Markou et al., 1998). However, in many cases it is not clear whether these individuals' painful affective (mood or feeling) states existed prior to their drug abuse or came about as a consequence of their abuse. In support of this hypothesis, many (but not all) studies have shown that antidepressant drug treatment can significantly enhance the patients' mood as well as reduce their use of opiates, psychostimulants, alcohol, and nicotine (Cornelius et al., 2000; Markou et al., 1998). Further support for this hypothesis comes from family and twin studies (see Chapter 9) that indicate that there are genetic links between depression and a variety of substance abuse disorders.

In addition to preexisting motivational variables associated with drug depend-ence, once drug taking begins, a number of physiological and conditioning factors enter into the process (Marlatt et al., 1988). If drug taking is shortly followed by the reinforc-ing effects of the drug, instrumental conditioning is involved and leads to drug seeking and further drug taking. Because drugs serve as unconditioned stimuli, the person's negative mood state or the environmental context in which one takes drugs can come to serve as conditioned stimuli for *conditioned drive states*, that is, drug craving (Childress et al., 1994; O'Brien et al., 1993). Following extensive drug use, re-exposure to even small amounts of the drug, or drugs with similar effects, can induce craving in humans (Bossert & Shaham, 2004). As discussed earlier in this chapter, CRs that are compensa-tory to the drug-induced effects (i.e., are opposite to the drug effects) may also occur. Thus, exposure to these environmental cues will potentially lead to drive states and withdrawal-like effects, which will further increase the desire to engage in drug-taking behavior (Stewart & Eikelboom, 1987). Furthermore, if the drug is capable of inducing pharmacodynamic physical dependence, it can create a physiological drive state most conducive to continuing drug-taking behavior. Once this condition has been created, secondary psychological dependence may be an additional motive for drug taking.

Perhaps a few examples will enhance your appreciation of the potency of these conditioning factors in drug dependence. It has long been recognized that individuals who self-administer drugs are more likely to abuse them than are passive recipients of drugs. For example, doctors who administer narcotics to themselves show a much higher incidence of narcotic abuse than do their patients, to whom narcotics are admin-istered (Leavitt, 1982). Because there are many reasons why this result might occur (e.g., doctors have easy access to pharmaceutical-grade narcotics), we cannot say for sure that it is the act of self-administering the drug that is the primary factor in this differential abuse rate.

Studies with rats have shown that they are more likely to exhibit signs of with-drawal following a few days of alcohol exposure if they have previously been adminis-tered alcohol chronically and have undergone withdrawal. That is, rats that have not previously experienced withdrawal will not exhibit withdrawal signs following only a few days exposure to alcohol (Leavitt, 1982). In humans undergoing narcotic detoxica-tion, the severity of withdrawal symptoms has often been shown to be more closely re-lated to the patient's anxiety and degree of expected distress than to the amount of narcotic used or the length of narcotic use (Phillips et al., 1986).

In clinical studies with drug abusers, stimuli that are predictive of drug availabil-ity increase self-reports of craving and the motivation to consume drugs and have been shown to increase drug seeking and self-administration of drugs (O'Brien et al., 1992). A *conditioned withdrawal* phenomenon has been established in the laboratory with pa-tient volunteers maintained on a methadone regimen by pairing naloxone, a drug (US) that induces withdrawal (UR) in opiate addicts, with a novel stimulus (CS). Upon in-jecting a placebo instead of naloxone (the injection procedure is the CS), the resulting CRs resembled the withdrawal URs. Similar behavioral withdrawal and subjective craving responses (a CR similar to, but not identical to, the withdrawal-type CR) have been shown to occur in abstinent narcotic users watching videotapes of themselves or others administering drugs or seeing other drug-related stimuli (Childress et al., 1986a, 1986b). Furthermore, this cue reactivity in opiate-addicted subjects has been shown to persist as long as 12 months after intensive inpatient treatment (Franken et al., 1999).

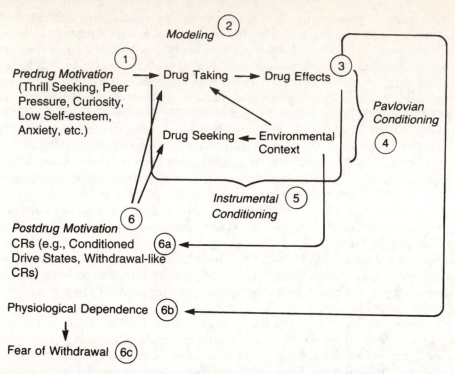

FIGURE 6.3 Summary of the basic steps and factors involved in the drug-dependence process.

These are just a few examples indicating the power of conditioning processes, both instrumental and Pavlovian, in the development of drug dependence. Figure 6.3 summarizes the involvement of these processes in drug-taking behavior in terms of the following steps:

1. Predisposing factors motivate the individual to try a drug.
2. With drug availability, drug-taking behavior is initially modeled after drug-taking behavior in parents, peers, and so forth.
3. The individual experiences primary reinforcing and physiological effects of the drug.
4. Pairing of the environmental context with drug effects constitutes a Pavlovian conditioning trial.
5. Drug-taking behavior is followed by primary (or secondary) reinforcing effects of the drug in the environmental context, which constitutes instrumental conditioning.
6. Postdrug motivational states induced through Pavlovian processes (6a), or because continued exposure to drug effects results in physiological dependence (6b) and fear of undergoing withdrawal (6c), lead to further drug seeking and drug taking.

Note that genetic predispositions may interact or be involved in most, if not all, of the steps.

The statement that drugs may be habit-forming is no longer just a metaphor, but is a statement supported by considerable empirical research that indicates that dependence-producing drugs alter the basic neuronal processes that many believe underlie learning, that is, long-term potentiation (LTP) and long-term depression (LTD; Gerdeman et al., 2003). Needless to say, these long-lasting changes in synaptic efficacy (increases and decreases, respectively) involve a complicated orchestration of events (many of which remain to be determined) that is far beyond the scope of this book. However, all drugs of abuse alter one or more of the neurotransmitter systems believed to be involved in these processes, which can contribute to the behavioral phenomenon of casual drug use progressing toward compulsive drug use and addiction.

A number of lessons can be gained from all of this. First of all, there are many predisposing factors leading to initial drug use. Second, once drug taking begins, there are many additional factors that can lead to the maintenance of drug-taking behavior. Third, conditioned withdrawal-type effects can often be confused with pharmacodynamic withdrawal effects. Fourth, although there has long been a concern that physical dependence is a factor in the maintenance of drug-taking behavior, it is a relatively minor aspect in the maintenance of an addict's habit. Therefore, methods that simply focus on the control of physiological withdrawal are not going to work in the long run (Schuster & Johanson, 1981).

GENERAL FACTORS IN TREATMENT FOR DRUG DEPENDENCY

The first step in the treatment for drug dependency involves recognizing that a person's drug use is a problem. This recognition is not always easy to make. Once dependence processes begin with drug use, they almost always lead to numerous detrimental consequences for the user, the user's significant others, and, potentially, society in general. (Some specific consequences of drug dependency will be discussed more fully in subsequent chapters.) One would think that these consequences would be recognized by the users, or their friends and family, and would be sufficient reason to get the users to stop or at least seek help. However, two psychological processes generally prevent these things from happening: *denial* and *enabling*.

One of the symptoms of alcoholism and other chemical dependencies is *denial*, a defense mechanism that prevents users from consciously recognizing that they have a problem. Others may see the problem, but the users cannot. Perhaps, at some level, the users know their drug use is a problem, but they make excuses, minimize the magnitude of the problem, and blame others for their unpleasant feelings instead of blaming their relationship with mood-altering chemicals.

On the other hand, many of us do well-meaning things for our drug-dependent friends that actually encourage their drug use. Doing such things is called *enabling*, because it enables drug use to continue. We allow them to keep denying their problem whenever we do anything to help them escape the harmful consequences of their drug use. We do it out of love or concern, but it only makes things worse. We enable when we lie or make excuses for them to friends or employers, lend them money after they have spent their own on drugs, deny that they have a compulsive disorder, drink or take other drugs along with them, stop talking about their drug use because they become angry when we do so, or join them in blaming others for their own bad feelings. In short, any action we take to rescue them from the harmful consequences of their drug use is enabling. It sounds irrational, but when we take away their discomfort, we take away the only thing that might help them see that they are in trouble.

Therefore, the two essential keys to any effective treatment for drug abuse and dependence are these: (1) The person must recognize or be convinced that his or her drug use is a problem; and (2) he or she must have the incentive to change. These statements do not mean that these two conditions must be met before treatment can begin. In most cases, even voluntary patients submit themselves to treatment initially only because of strong social pressure or external coercion; their primary goal is to convince everyone (including themselves) that they do not have a problem (Cummings, 1979).

In fact, treatment outcome studies strongly suggest that coercion may be fundamental to addiction treatment and the achievement of favorable outcomes from therapeutic interventions (Miller & Flaherty, 2000). Often, drug abusers must feel, face, or experience the "consequences" of their drug use before the denial of their problem can be penetrated and motivation for treatment can develop. Typically, coercion involves giving the drug abuser the choice between an opportunity to comply with treatment and an opportunity to receive the "alternative consequences," which could include such things as loss or receipt of employment or benefits, incarceration or probation (if he or she has engaged in drug-related criminal activity), if compliance with treatment is not met. Several lines of evidence suggest that coercion can be a therapeutic step in initiating treatment interventions and facilitating long-term recovery from abuse and dependence. If applied therapeutically, coercion can result in improved psychosocial status for patients; can reduce costs from criminal, health, and employment consequences; and can reduce illegal drug use or the criminal activity engendered by their drug use. Research indicates that coercion may be effective in the majority of individuals with drug abuse disorders.

Any treatment program for addiction will probably have to deal with the predisposing psychological and sociological factors that originally led to drug taking. (This can be a very difficult task when dealing with a person who has a poor self-image, has labeled himself or herself as a drug user, has a history of deviance, comes from a broken home, or has few education-related skills.) Strategies that empirical research has suggested may be helpful are discussed in Chapter 10 with respect to the treatment of alcoholism (the area in which the bulk of research on treatment effectiveness has been conducted). Most of these strategies are applicable to the treatment of other types of drug abuse and dependence.

To deal with cue-dependent cravings that may lead to relapse, a treatment program might include permanently removing the addict from drug-associated environmental stimuli. However, because this approach would rarely be feasible for most people, a more practical approach would be to expose the addict to the original drug-taking environment without allowing him or her to experience the rewarding effects of the drug so that the conditioned craving can be extinguished (O'Brien et al., 1993). Such a program could involve therapy sessions in which patients listen to audiotapes and watch videos of drug deals, handle drug paraphernalia, and look at or handle anything else that triggers their craving for the drug. It has been suggested that the extinction procedure should resemble actual drug-taking conditions as closely as possible, even to the extent of providing the real possibility of consuming the drug one is dependent on, in order to elicit conditioned reactions that can then be adequately extinguished (Corty et al., 1988). (Unfortunately, Pavlov demonstrated many years ago that even with extensive extinction training, the spontaneous recovery of CRs can occur with the simple passage of time.) Because cue reactivity (i.e., the intensity of the CR) has been suggested to be greater in drug-dependent persons when they are in a negative mood, and such individuals commonly report negative mood states as the most frequent initiator of relapse, exposure to negative emotional cues has sometimes been added to cue exposure therapy (Bradizza et al., 1999). However, there is no clear evidence that negative mood (using procedures that can temporarily induce such moods) alters cue reactivity in drug-dependent persons (Jansma et al., 2000; Robbins et al., 2000).

As will be discussed in subsequent chapters, a number of drugs have been or are being used as adjuncts to the treatment of drug abuse/dependence. Some drugs may be helpful because they reduce the negative affective states that may be a motivational factor underlying the person's drug taking (e.g., antidepressants). Drug substitutes—drugs with similar pharmacological properties as the drug(s) of abuse but with less toxic effects—may also be employed, either for detoxification during withdrawal (e.g., benzodiazepines for alcohol withdrawal) or for maintenance purposes. In the latter instance, the drug may simultaneously reduce the craving for the original drug(s) as well as reduce its rewarding properties because of cross-tolerance (i.e., methadone for heroin addiction). Other drugs may serve as pure drug antagonists, which simply block the rewarding effects of the abused drug (e.g., naltrexone for heroin and alcohol addiction). Alternatively, drugs may be used that result in aversive bodily reactions whenever the addict takes the drug of abuse (e.g., disulfiram in the treatment of alcoholism).

The ideal drug for this type of treatment would have the following characteristics (in order of importance): (1) possesses significantly less toxicity and/or side effects than the drug of abuse; (2) inhibits craving for the abused drug; (3) provides an unsurmountable blockade of the effects of the abused drug; (4) blocks the effects of all drugs of abuse; (5) is long lasting; and (6) is orally effective. Obviously, the first characteristic is extremely important; a treatment that is more toxic than the drug you're trying to get the person to stop abusing is counterproductive. A drug with the second characteristic would be very valuable because it would eliminate much of the motivation to use the drug of abuse in the first place. Characteristic 3 is important because you want to prevent the rewarding effects of the abused drug as well as prevent the person from attempting to override the blockade with very high doses of the drug that may be toxic. Characteristic 4 is important because in many cases abusers of one drug also abuse other drugs or if prevented from using one drug will substitute another type of abused drug. Finally, drugs that are long lasting and are orally effective are preferable for the sake of convenience and cost of treatment and for keeping the drug abuser in the treatment program.

It has been suggested that drugs with antagonist properties at NMDA (N-Methyl-D-aspartic acid) receptors (a major receptor for GLU) may fit many of these characteristics. Because several lines of evidence suggest that NMDA receptors mediate the common adaptive processes that are involved in the development, maintenance, and expression of addiction to a wide variety of drugs, it has been proposed that NMDA antagonists may have multiple functions in treating addictions. These include the attenuation of withdrawal, the normalization of the mood changes following initiation of abstinence, and an attenuation of CRs arising from drug-related stimuli (Bisaga & Popik, 2000). A variety of compounds with NMDA antagonistic actions (e.g., dextromethorphan, amantadine, memantine, ibogaine, acamprosate, and lamotrigine) have been or are being tested in drug-dependent persons, but none has yet produced more than modest benefits, and some of these may exert potentially adverse reactions that would severely limit their use.

Numerous therapeutic interventions have been attempted in order to deal with drug addiction. All of them appear to work some of the time with some individuals. Often the efficacy of a technique depends on what stage of change the drug abuser is in: "precontemplation" (the person does not perceive that he or she has a problem or needs help and is not considering a change); "contemplation" (the person perceives that he or she may have a problem and partially wants to change and partially does not); "preparation" (the person finally recognizes a change is needed); "action" (the person chooses a strategy for change and pursues it); and "maintenance" (the person attempts to maintain the gains he or she has made and keep from relapsing; Prochaska et al., 1992; Velicer et al., 1995).

No single technique works for the majority of individuals, perhaps because their efficacy is contingent upon the patient's voluntary participation in the treatment. Furthermore, even when treatment appears successful, relapse is common. However, the likelihood of relapse is reduced when the drug user (1) is under compulsory supervision or experiences a consistent aversive reaction related to drinking or other drug use (e.g., use of disulfiram or suffering from a painful ulcer); (2) finds a substitute dependency to compete with drug use (e.g., meditation, compulsive gambling, overeating, running); or (3) obtains new social supports (e.g., a grateful employer or new significant other, belonging to a support group; Vaillant, 1988). Relapse prevention may be enhanced by teaching addicts how to (1) anticipate, identify, and manage high-risk situations that may lead to relapse; (2) cope effectively if (or, more likely, when) relapse occurs to minimize its negative consequences and maximize learning from the experience; and (3) reduce global health risks and replace lifestyle imbalance with balance and moderation (Brownell et al., 1986; Dimeff & Marlatt, 1995).

The bottom line is—based on the criteria of reduction in substance use, improvement in personal health and social function, and reduction in public health and safety risks—treatment for drug abuse has been shown to be effective, especially when compared to alternatives such as no treatment or incarceration (Miller & Flaherty, 2000). For example, in one extensive study conducted in California, in which treatment effectiveness was assessed in randomly selected drug abusers who participated in four types of treatment programs (residential, residential "social model," outpatient, and outpatient methadone), it was determined that, on the average, for every dollar of treatment costs, the state saved at least seven dollars in other medical and social costs (Gerstein et al., 1994).

STATE-DEPENDENT LEARNING

The phenomenon to be described in this section is normally discussed in the context of how drugs may influence learning and memory. However, because it can have a profound influence on the maintenance of drug-taking behavior, it seems appropriate to discuss it here in the context of drug dependence. Approximately 35 years ago, some studies were performed in which animals learned tasks under one set of drug conditions and then were tested for their retention of the behavior under another set of drug conditions. The results indicated that the animals did not perform the tasks during the test as well as they would have if the retention test had been conducted under the same drug conditions as those present during the learning phase. This was found to be the case whether a drug was present during the acquisition phase and a nondrug condition was present during the retention phase, or vice versa. In other words, if learning was accomplished under nondrug conditions, retention was best under nondrug conditions; and if learning was accomplished under a drug, retention was best when the drug was present. The phenomenon was noted to occur with a wide variety of drugs and tasks, and it was found to occur in humans (Horton & Mills, 1984). It became known as **state-dependent learning** (also known as **drug-dissociative learning** or **drug-state learning**). In essence, it can be defined as learning under one set of drug (or nondrug) conditions that does not completely transfer to another set of drug conditions.

The usual explanation for the phenomenon is that certain cues—in this case, drug-related cues (perhaps internally produced)—present during the acquisition of information or behaviors become associated with the information or behaviors. Therefore, in order to successfully retrieve that information or perform that behavior during retention, those cues must be present. The more the context cues change between learning and retention, the greater the difficulty in exhibiting the information or behavior.

It should not be difficult now to see how state-dependent learning can become a factor in the continuation of drug-taking behavior. That is, if a person is exposed to a drug on a number of occasions, he (or she) is bound to acquire some new strategies or skills for dealing with the world. If the person then tries to perform those skills at a later time without the drug, he (or she) may experience difficulty in doing so and feel that he (or she) must be under the influence of the drug in order to perform appropriately. This experience starts a vicious cycle in which the more the person engages in the behavior under the drug's influence, the more likely he (or she) will be to feel the need to administer the drug in order to perform the behavior. For example, there are many anecdotal reports of alcoholic writers who have discovered that they are no longer able to write when sober, in spite of the fact that we generally expect people to think and write better without alcohol (particularly large doses). Thus, in order to maintain their success as writers, they continue to expose themselves to a chemical that will eventually lead to a great deal of psychological, neurological, and physiological damage.

State-dependent learning may also play a role in limiting the potential benefits of psychotherapy in a patient who is also taking psychotropic medications. That is, patients may develop new coping strategies during therapy that may be lost or diminished when the patients' drug state changes or they go off their medication. A patient may feel that the therapy was a failure or may become dependent on the medication. Therapists should be aware of this possibility.

Websites for Further Information

The National Institute for Drug Abuse criteria for substance-dependence diagnosis:

http://www.nida.nih.gov/Drugpages

Site providing news on substance-abuse issues:

http://www.drugfree.org

Web of Addictions (information on a multitude of aspects of drugs, their use and abuse):

http://www.well.com/user/woa

Psychomotor Stimulants and Antiparkinsonian Drugs

In this chapter, we will discuss the category of drugs known as **psychomotor stimulants.** This term is used because, at low to moderate doses, these drugs produce motor stimulation, reduce fatigue, increase resistance to sleep, increase vigilance and alertness, and, depending upon the individual or the context, induce a heightened mood (at its extreme, it is described as euphoria) or anxiety. These properties also result in enhanced performance on a variety of tasks, although the dose–response functions typically are inverted U-shaped. That is, there are a range of doses in which enhancement occurs, but as the dose increases beyond this range, performance returns to nondrug levels or worsens. Generally, signs of increased sympathetic nervous system activity, such as increased heart rate and blood pressure, are evidenced.

Other frequently used terms for these drugs are *behavioral stimulants* and *CNS* (central nervous system) *stimulants;* however, these terms do not do justice to the actual common properties of these drugs. Although some behaviors may increase in some individuals with these drugs, other behaviors may dramatically decrease, depending on the dose, the frequency of the behavior typically observed without the drug, and the individual (Grilly, 1977; Tecce & Cole, 1974; Wender et al., 1981). Likewise, whereas some neurons become more excitable and increase their rate of firing upon psychostimulant administration, other neurons dramatically reduce their rate of firing, and energy utilization may increase in some areas of the CNS whereas it decreases in others. Actually, none of the terms mentioned adequately describes the effects of these drugs if the drugs are used in large amounts acutely or moderate amounts chronically. Some of these effects will be dealt with shortly.

Within this category are several structurally different types of drugs (see Figure 7.1 for their basic molecular structures). By far, the most commonly used psychostimulant is

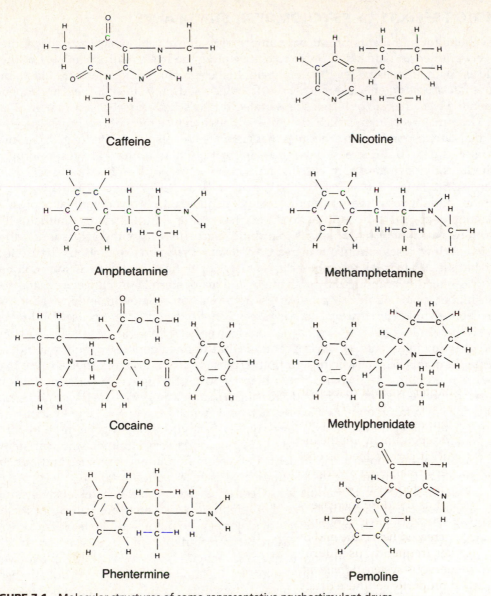

FIGURE 7.1   Molecular structures of some representative psychostimulant drugs.

caffeine. Nicotine is another popular drug with psychostimulant properties. Sometimes, nicotine is grouped together with caffeine and related substances (other *methylxanthines* such as theophylline and theobromine) into a group called *minor stimulants*. The amphetamines, methylphenidate (Ritalin), pemoline (Cylert), cocaine, and several dopamine (DA) agonists such as apomorphine often are grouped together as *major stimulants*. In addition to reviewing minor and major stimulants, this chapter also includes a discussion of drugs that are used to treat Parkinson's disease, some of which are also considered to be stimulants.

MOTOR EFFECTS OF PSYCHOMOTOR STIMULANTS

Psychomotor stimulants produce a number of motor effects, which have been intensively studied in animals in order to characterize the basic neurochemistry of these effects. With animals responding on operant lever-pressing schedules, stimulants produce *rate-dependent* effects on responses. In other words, the effect of the drug depends upon the baseline rate of response generated by the schedule (see also Chapters 2 and 3). Thus, major stimulants such as amphetamines enhance rates of lever pressing when animals are responding on schedules that generate low response rates (e.g., fixed interval schedules), but decrease lever-pressing rates when animals are responding on schedules that generate high baseline rates of response (such as fixed ratio schedules; Dews, 1958; Sanger & Blackman, 1974; Wenger & Dews, 1976). Minor stimulants such as caffeine and theophylline also produce rate-dependent effects on operant lever pressing (Randall et al., 2011). In addition to these effects on operant behavior, stimulants also produce a variety of motor effects that differ markedly across the spectrum of doses tested. At low doses, stimulants increase *locomotor activity* and exploration. These effects can be assessed in small locomotor cages or large open fields. Increases in locomotor activity can readily be induced by both minor and major stimulants. However, as the dose gets higher, major stimulants produce less in the way of locomotion, and instead induce a response known as *stereotypy* (see Figure 3.5). *Stereotypy* refers to focused and repetitive (and seemingly purposeless) behaviors such as head bobbing, nose poking, licking, and gnawing in rodents, which can continue for extended periods of time in stimulant-treated animals. The classic description of these motor stimulant effects came from Lyon and Robbins (1975), who stated that, as dose gets higher, major stimulants increase response frequency within decreasing response categories. At lower doses, animals engage in locomotion and exploration, and switch from one activity to another. In contrast, at higher doses, they do fewer types of activities, and engage more in perseveration (i.e., repetition of the same response over and over). Stimulant-induced stereotypies are not only observed in rodents but also in nonhuman primates and humans (an effect that is sometimes called "punding"; Fasano & Petrovic (2010).

The neurobiology of stimulant-induced motor effects has been extensively studied. Considerable evidence indicates that forebrain DA systems are critical for the expression of the motor stimulant effects of major psychomotor stimulants. Seminal work in this area was performed by Susan Iversen and her colleagues at Cambridge University in the United Kingdom (Creese & Iversen, 1975; Kelly et al. 1975), who were able to show a "double-dissociation" effect for the motor stimulant effects of amphetamines (i.e., two distinct brain areas mediate two different behaviors, and the effects of selective lesions can dissociate these effects). In this study, the lesions were produced by local injections of the neurotoxic agent 6-hydroxydopamine, which enters into the terminals of catecholamine neurons and then depletes DA by killing the entire cell or destroying the terminals. Depletion of DA in the nucleus accumbens suppressed the locomotor stimulant effects of low doses of amphetamine, but did not suppress the stereotypy seen with high doses. In contrast, depletion of DA in the neostriatum (caudate/putamen) reduced the stereotypy induced by high doses of amphetamine, but not the locomotion induced by low doses. Interestingly, although caudate/putamen DA depletions reduced amphetamine-induced stereotypy, they actually enhanced apomorphine-induced stereotypy within a few days after the DA depletion. This effect occurred because depletion of DA by destruction of DA terminals removes the substrate of action for amphetamine (which stimulates release and blocks uptake of DA, and therefore needs DA terminals), but also results in postsynaptic receptor supersensitivity (i.e., an increase in receptor number). Because apomorphine is a DA agonist that binds directly to the DA receptors, the DA depletion actually enhanced the stereotypy induced by apomorphine. Another behavioral manifestation of receptor supersensitivity seen after DA depletions was observed in experiments involving the *rotation model*. With this model (typically done in rats), a unilateral (i.e., one-sided) DA depletion is produced (Figure 7.2), and administration of stimulants causes an asymmetrical locomotion known as rotation or circling (Ungerstedt, 1971). However, the direction of the rotation is opposite, depending upon whether the stimulant drug acts presynaptically (such as amphetamine) or is an agonist that binds to postsynaptic DA receptors (such as apomorphine). The effect of DA depletions on one side of the brain is to make that side less sensitive to the effects of amphetamine (because the DA depletion destroys terminals, which provide the basis of action for amphetamine), and to make that same side more sensitive to the effects of a DA agonist such as apomorphine (because of receptor supersensitivity; Figure 7.2). The rotation model has been used to assess antiparkinsonian drugs for many years (see a discussion of antiparkinsonian agents, later in this chapter), but it also has its limitations (Castañeda et al., 2005).

CAFFEINE

Caffeine is the most widely used behaviorally active drug in the world (Barone & Roberts, 1996). Coffee, tea, energy drinks, and many sodas all contain this minor psychostimulant (Table 7.1). It is one of several substances referred to as methylxanthines. The typical adult in the United States consumes about 200 mg to 300 mg of caffeine a day, with coffee and tea consumption accounting for the majority of total caffeine intake (Barone & Roberts, 1996). Some energy drinks contain very high doses of caffeine (up to 500 mg). Based on typical patterns of use throughout the day and a plasma half-life of approximately 5 hours, peak caffeine plasma levels typically occur in the early evening (Lorist & Tops, 2003). However, owing to variability in absorption, metabolization, and excretion, as well as the fact that numerous metabolites of caffeine are formed that are also psychoactive (e.g., theophylline, theobromine, and paraxanthine), it is difficult to determine the overall time course and impact of caffeine on an individual.

Although caffeine has a variety of pharmacodynamic properties, there is general agreement that, at doses comparable to those of typical human exposure, most of its effects are related to its ability to act as a nonselective antagonist of adenosine receptors. Adenosine is found throughout the body and acts as a neuromodulator that affects neuronal excitability, and actions on the A_1 subtype of receptor, and inhibits presynaptic neuronal release of a variety of neurotransmitters—for example, ACh (acetylcholine), NE (norepinephrine), DA, GABA (gamma-aminobutyric acid), and 5-HT (serotonin; Iversen et al., 2009). Thus caffeine's ability to block these receptors enhances the release of these neurotransmitters in the brain and increases circulating catecholamines. In addition to the A_1 receptor subtype, the other adenosine receptor commonly found in the brain is the A_{2A} receptor. Striatal areas such as caudate/putamen and nucleus

Amphetamine-Induced Rotation

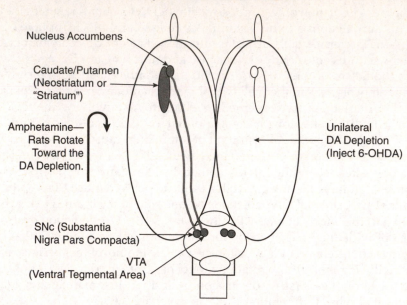

Nucleus Accumbens

Caudate/Putamen
(Neostriatum or
"Striatum")

Amphetamine—
Rats Rotate
Toward the
DA Depletion.

Unilateral
DA Depletion
(Inject 6-OHDA)

SNc (Substantia
Nigra Pars Compacta)

VTA
(Ventral Tegmental Area)

Apomorphine-Induced Rotation

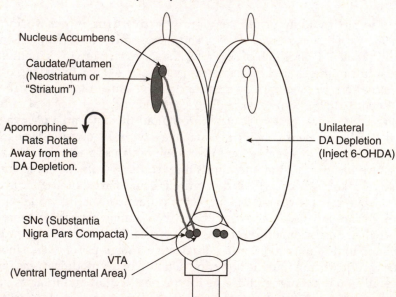

Nucleus Accumbens

Caudate/Putamen
(Neostriatum or
"Striatum")

Apomorphine—
Rats Rotate
Away from the
DA Depletion.

Unilateral
DA Depletion
(Inject 6-OHDA)

SNc (Substantia
Nigra Pars Compacta)

VTA
(Ventral Tegmental Area)

FIGURE 7.2 Rotation in rodents resulting from unilateral DA depletion and drug administration. These figures are a schematic of a overhead view of a rat brain, showing a unilateral DA depletion on the right side. Note that amphetamine (top) and apomorphine (bottom) produce rotation in opposite directions.

TABLE 7.1 Caffeine in Beverages and Foods

	Caffeine (milligrams)
Coffee (5-ounce cup)	
Brewed, drip method	60–180
Brewed, percolator	40–170
Instant	30–120
Decaffeinated	2–5
Tea (5-ounce cup)	
Brewed	20–110
Instant	25–50
Cocoa (5-ounce cup)	2–20
Chocolate milk (8 ounces)	2–7
Chocolate (1 ounce)	1–35
Soft drinks (12 ounces; in which caffeine is listed as an ingredient)	30–60
Energy drinks (1 can, volumes vary)	80–400

Source: "The Latest Caffeine Scorecard" by C. Lecos, 1984, *Consumer's Research, 67,* 35–36
Reissig et al., (2009).

accumbens, which are rich in DA, also have a high concentration of adenosine A_{2A} receptors (Ferré et al., 2004). In these striatal areas, there is a functional interaction between DA D_2 and adenosine A_{2A} receptors, which are co-localized on the same neurons (Ferré et al., 2008; Fuxe et al., 2003). Caffeine stimulates locomotor activity (Ferré et al., 2008) and produces rate-dependent effects on operant lever pressing (Randall et al., 2011). Caffeine, as well as selective adenosine A_{2A} receptor antagonists such as istradefylline and MSX-3, also can reverse many of the behavioral effects of DA D_2 antagonists, including the suppression of operant lever pressing (Nunes et al., 2010; Salamone et al., 2009a, 2009b) and locomotion (Collins et al., 2010a). Thus, caffeine and other methylxanthenes act to antagonize receptors, but in doing so, their effects interact with dopaminergic mechanisms that also are involved in psychomotor stimulant effects. Moreover, the ability of adenosine antagonists to increase rates of operant responding appears to depend upon blockade of adenosine A_{2A} receptors (Randall et al., 2011). Because of these interactions with DA systems, adenosine A_{2A} antagonists are being developed as potential antiparkinsonian drugs (Salamone, 2010a; see the section "Parkinson's Disease").

What makes caffeine or coffee so popular is still unclear. In intravenous (IV) drug self-administration experiments with animals, caffeine has been shown to have reinforcing effects in some cases but not in others. Likewise, with humans, the reinforcing effects of caffeine have been variable, and in some individuals, caffeine has been found to induce dysphoric effects. Most evidence suggests that caffeine is rated as having the most desirable and pleasant reactions in heavy coffee drinkers, particularly after they have not had any coffee for several hours. Coffee abstainers are more likely to report unpleasant and undesirable reactions to caffeine. This finding suggests that many of the reinforcing effects of caffeine stem from its ability to terminate caffeine withdrawal (Griffiths et al., 1986; Rogers et al., 2003; Tinley et al., 2003). However, research indicates that the average caffeine intake of coffee consumers does not predict the occurrence of withdrawal (Hughes et al., 1993). On the other hand, when coffee consumers are tested over a series of days without knowing whether they are consuming caffeinated or de-caffeinated coffee, they are more likely to self-administer caffeinated than decaffeinated coffee (Hughes et al., 1993).

The effects of caffeine vary considerably among individuals in terms of wakeful-ness, psychomotor coordination, mood alterations, and autonomic nervous system re-sponse (Lorist & Tops, 2003). Two cups of coffee, which contains approximately 150 mg of caffeine (unless it is decaffeinated), has the mood-elevating and fatigue-relieving properties of threshold doses of amphetamine (approximately 2 to 5 mg). However, larger doses generally do not have more of a mood-elevating effect, and 7 to 10 cups of coffee may cause insomnia, restlessness, mild sensory disturbances, or muscle tense-ness (collectively called "caffeinism"), or may precipitate anxiety or panic attacks in susceptible individuals (Charney et al., 1985). Caffeine typically raises blood pressure slightly in both men and women, but apparently via different mechanisms (Hartley et al., 2004). Similarly, heart rate changes are variable and, with some caffeine doses, may actually decrease. Increases in galvanic skin conductance level and reactivity are generally noted (Davidson & Smith, 1991). Thus, the evidence suggests that caffeine may not increase all indexes of arousal or change them in the same way in all persons (Zahn & Rapoport, 1987).

Persons who consume low to moderate doses of caffeine (30 to 450 mg) typically display dose-dependent improvements in indices of arousal, daytime alertness, vigi-lance, and some aspects of psychomotor performance and cognitive functions, such as reaction time, sustained attention, and information processing, and they experience predominantly positive subjective effects on mood, characterized by increased well-be-ing, energy, and concentration (Graham et al., 1994; Patat et al., 2000; Zwyghuizen-Doorenbos et al., 1990). These beneficial effects are particularly evidenced when the individuals are tested under conditions of caffeine deprivation or total abstinence in regular caffeine users or following partial or total sleep deprivation. As little as 32 mg of caffeine has been shown to significantly improve auditory vigilance and visual reaction time (Lieberman et al., 1987). Caffeine can produce an increased capacity for both mus-cular work and sustained intellectual effort (Sawyer et al., 1982), but it can also disrupt arithmetic skills and task performance when delicate muscular coordination and accu-rate timing are required (Rall, 1985). The effects of caffeine on endurance (and probably other aspects of performance) are biphasic; that is, lower doses (3–6 mg/kg) enhance performance and higher doses produce no benefits or decrease performance (Lorist & Tops, 2003).

Several studies on efficiency of information processing in humans have shown that the effects of caffeine are dependent upon dose, task demands, the subject's sex, and the subject's typical level of arousal (Anderson & Revelle, 1983; Erikson et al., 1985). Some studies have concluded that extroverts (or high impulsives) tend to show dose-dependent improvements in performance, whereas introverts (or low impulsives) show improvements with lower doses and decrements with higher doses (Eysenck, 1967; Gupta & Gupta, 1990). Others have shown either no change or decrements in informa-tion processing, depending on the sex of the subject and the task demands (Erikson et al., 1985). (The dose ranges of caffeine used in these studies were equivalent to zero to four cups of regular coffee.) Thus, other than the conclusion that the behavioral effects of caffeine are quite subtle, there does not appear to be a consensus as to whether caf-feine improves information-processing efficiency in general (Lorist & Tops, 2003). Its most pronounced effects are likely to be observed in situations of lowered arousal or fatigue, or in tasks placing high demands on controlled processing or conditions with explicit attentional demands. It may all depend on whether the individual is a heavy consumer of coffee in the first place.

It is a common belief that caffeine can counteract the effects of sedative–hypnotic type drugs, but the empirical evidence for this belief is equivocal. The equivalent of two or three cups of coffee (250 mg caffeine) has been shown to significantly reduce next-day benzodiazepine-induced drowsiness (Johnson et al., 1990). Caffeine has also been shown to reduce the detrimental effects of alcohol on various types of complex reaction time. However, in terms of the subjective feelings of drunkenness and for most tasks—such as manual dexterity, balance, numerical reasoning, and verbal fluency—the deleterious effects of alcohol intoxication are not reduced by caffeine (Azcona et al., 1995; Fudin & Nicastro, 1988). Thus, an intoxicated driver, after consuming a few cups of coffee, might feel more alert, but he or she will still be impaired in terms of the motor coordination and decision making required for properly driving a motor vehicle.

Caffeine also exhibits some interesting interactions with another drug with which it is commonly used, that is, nicotine. In such case, the evidence suggests that caffeine can enhance the reinforcing and subjective stimulant qualities of nicotine in humans (Jones & Griffiths, 2003). On the other hand, cigarette smokers, who generally consume more coffee than nonsmokers, metabolize caffeine at an accelerated rate. Upon smoking cessation, consumption of caffeinated substances can increase caffeine plasma levels on average more than 200%—an effect that may persist for as long as 6 months (Benowitz et al., 1989). This in turn could increase the person's "jitteriness" and be a contributing factor in tobacco withdrawal symptoms (Swanson et al., 1994). These drug interactions, plus the possibility that the consumption of caffeine-containing beverages can serve as a conditioned stimulus triggering tobacco craving, suggest that (as abhorrent as it may seem to caffeine/tobacco users) the effectiveness of programs to treat nicotine addiction might be improved by eliminating the use of caffeine prior to treatment.

Tolerance develops to many of the effects of caffeine, most likely due to up-regulation of adenosine receptors in the brain (Graham et al., 1994). Withdrawal symptoms are uncommon, except following heavy use (around 500 mg per day; Sawyer et al., 1982). Headaches are the most common symptom. They may be due to a rebound effect from caffeine's normal vasoconstrictive properties. Caffeine withdrawal symptoms may also include increased fatigue, sleepiness, and laziness, and decreased vigor and alertness. A neonatal withdrawal syndrome, consisting of irritability, jitteriness, and vomiting, may occur in infants born to mothers who consume large amounts of caffeine during pregnancy. However, the dependence liability of caffeine is very low, and classical clinical indicators of dependence, such as difficulty in stopping the use of caffeine and use despite harm, have not been documented (Hughes et al., 1992).

In the last few years, there has been an explosion in the sales and consumption of "energy drinks" (Reissig et al., 2009). These drinks can have a very high caffeine content. For example, although a 12-ounce (333 ml) can of Coca Cola contains around 34 mg, an energy drink called "Wired X 344" has 344 mg of caffeine, plus additional caffeine-containing substances such as guarana extract (www.wiredenergydrink.com), and "Fixx Extreme" has 400 mg of caffeine (www.getyourfixx.com). Consumption of high doses of caffeine spurred on by growing consumption of energy drinks has led to increasing reports of caffeine intoxication (Reissig et al., 2009). In addition, the combined use of energy drinks with alcohol (e.g., often combined with vodka) is becoming prevalent. Currently, the federal government does not regulate energy drinks in the same way that it regulates other soft drinks, but this could change in the future.

NICOTINE

Every year thousands of young people take up smoking tobacco. Over time their use changes from sporadic, occasional use to more continuous, daily use. On the other hand, thousands of people who have smoked for years try to stop; in most cases these attempts fail because the process is so aversive. In fact, several years ago, the surgeon general of the United States issued a report that stated that the pharmacologic and behavioral processes that determine tobacco addiction are similar to those that determine addiction to drugs such as heroin and cocaine. Most people—smokers and nonsmokers—recognize that there are costs for smoking. Although cheap in comparison to most other drug habits, smoking is not inexpensive. However, this expense is a drop in the bucket compared to the potential health costs of lung cancer, emphysema, cardiovascular dysfunction, and other diseases associated with cigarette smoking. The problems are compounded by the fact that cigarette smoking is prominent among most abusers of other drugs; for example, more than 90% of alcoholic inpatients are smokers (Bien & Burge, 1990). Smoking exacerbates their health risks and complicates their treatment. (For example, it is not clear whether treatment for alcohol, cocaine, or heroin dependence would be facilitated or worsened by concomitant cessation of smoking.) Considerable evidence indicates that the main active ingredient in cigarette smoke is nicotine, which acts as a nicotinic ACh agonist. Thus, a cigarette essentially acts as a vehicle for the self-administration of nicotine.

Questions as to why people start smoking in the first place and what makes stopping smoking so difficult for the majority of heavy smokers have been addressed by researchers for years. So far, only pieces of the puzzle exist. A large majority of adult smokers in the United States report that they began smoking when they were adolescents (Eissenberg & Balster, 2000). A wide variety of studies have indicated that there are numerous predictors of adolescent tobacco use. These include being male and White, holding positive attitudes toward smoking, having concerns over body weight, having parents who smoke or have permissive attitudes toward smoking, perceiving that smoking has positive benefits, having low expectations for school achievement, having easy access to tobacco, and having a number of smoking friends (Mayhew et al., 2000). Adolescents who take up smoking tend to exhibit lower self-esteem, perceive themselves as having less internal control over their lives, and have higher levels of trait anxiety than those who do not take up smoking (Penny & Robinson, 1986). About one-third to one-half of those who experiment with cigarettes become regular users. Although there has been a reduction in the prevalence of smoking among many segments of the U.S. population—particularly among adults and Black adolescents—and a decline in per capita consumption, there has been minimal progress in reducing smoking by adolescents, especially Whites and males (Giovino et al., 1995).

Once smoking begins, genetic factors probably play a role in developing nicotine dependency. It has long been recognized that nicotine dependency is strongly associated with alcohol dependency, which, as we have noted earlier, has an established linkage to genes. Studies have also noted that nicotine-dependent persons, at some point in their lives, are more than twice as likely as nondependent nicotine users (or nonusers) to have suffered from major depression, which has also been viewed as involving a genetic predisposition (Glassman et al., 1990). In one study, teenagers with a depressive disorder had odds of nicotine dependence that were 2.3 times those of teenagers without a depressive disorder (Fergusson et al., 1996). In addition, persons with histories of major depression or any anxiety disorder tend to report more severe nicotine withdrawal symptoms than persons with neither of these disorders (Breslau et al., 1992). However, another study suggests that the causal link between cigarette use and the development of depressive symptoms may be opposite of what has been previously presumed. In that study, depression was not found to be an antecedent to heavy cigarette use among teens (Goodman & Capitman, 2000). On the other hand, teen smokers who were not depressed at baseline were about four times as likely to develop highly depressed symptoms during a year's time.

Despite a multitude of studies on tobacco use, it is still not clear what is so reinforcing about the practice. For the majority of individuals, the initial smoking experiences are more likely to be unpleasant than pleasant (Eissenberg & Balster, 2000). Apparently, the psychosocial rewards, such as peer acceptance and role-model identification, are sufficiently strong to maintain smoking behavior until the individuals learn to monitor the amount of smoke and the unpleasant side effects subside. Nicotine has been long presumed to be the most important, but not the only, reinforcing factor behind smoking tobacco (Henningfield & Goldberg, 1988). If it were the only factor, then chewing nicotine gum would induce effects similar to smoking tobacco, which it does not do, and the treatment for smoking using nicotine gum would be much more effective than it is (Pickworth et al., 1986). In fact, most tobacco smokers cannot describe any attractive effect except what they might describe as the "taste" of tobacco smoke in their mouth, lungs, and nasal passages (Schelling, 1992). One important factor in maintaining the use of tobacco is its ability to reduce negative affective states—transient aversive emotional states such as sadness, boredom, and anxiety, which may occur as a function of endogenous characteristics of the individual (e.g., depression), environmental stressors, and, of course, nicotine withdrawal (Brandon, 1994). Finally, smoking may be reinforcing because it gives one something to do with one's hands, it may affect one's public image (although lately the image of a smoker has become considerably more negative), or it may be associated with other social reinforcers, such as acceptance by one's peers.

On the other hand, there are several lines of evidence that indicate that nicotine is the principal reinforcer for smoking behavior. First, human tobacco users who were administered low doses of nicotine (0.01 mg/kg) intravenously reported enhancement of mood and drug liking, although higher doses (0.04 mg/kg) produced aversive effects (Lundahl et al., 2000). Both effects can be blocked with nicotinic receptor blockade. Second, nicotine administered to animals increases extracellular and synaptic concentrations of DA in the nucleus accumbens (Mihailescu & Drucker-Colin, 2000), which, as discussed previously, is a phenomenon observed with many drugs of abuse and is potentially associated with primary reward. However, this phenomenon may have more to do with the development of motivational or incentive states (drug craving) than the drug enjoyment. Third, animals have been shown to self-administer nicotine via both oral and IV routes of administration (Donny et al., 1999; Maehler et al., 2000). However, self-administration of nicotine in animals is often not as robust as it is with most other drugs of abuse, and its efficacy as a reinforcer may depend on administration under certain environmental conditions. For example, in one study, monkeys self-administered nicotine at a relatively high rate if a discrete signal came on just as the nicotine infusions were delivered, but their rate of administering nicotine dropped sharply when the signal did not occur (Goldberg et al., 1981). Perhaps this relationship explains why nicotine by way of smoking is the most popular route of administration; that is, with this route, discrete stimuli (smoke upon exhalation) always accompany the nicotine just before it reaches the brain (Schelling, 1992).

Working on the hypothesis that chronic smokers maximize the reinforcing effects of nicotine by titrating their intake, several studies have attempted to determine whether or not cigarette smokers can effectively regulate the amount of nicotine in their blood when given high- and low-nicotine cigarettes to smoke (Henningfield & Goldberg, 1988). Most agree that though some regulation of nicotine plasma levels is often achieved—by increasing the number of low-nicotine cigarettes or reducing the number of high-nicotine cigarettes consumed—it is nowhere near perfect. In two of the studies that varied nicotine and tar content independently, the number of cigarettes smoked was inversely related to nicotine content, not tar content. Finally, studies in which the subjects were preloaded with nicotine (in gum or in capsules) found a decrease in cigarettes consumed, whereas when a nicotine antagonist was administered, cigarette smoking increased.

In some individuals, nicotine has a mild psychostimulant effect, particularly with respect to enhanced vigilance (Jaffe, 1990). In fact, socially relevant doses of nicotine may be comparable to socially relevant doses of caffeine in facilitating choice reaction time, motor tracking, and short-term memory retrieval, as well as antagonizing some of the debilitating effects of alcohol (Kerr et al., 1991). In most cases nicotine shifts EEG patterns toward those often associated with increased psychological arousal—that is, higher-frequency, lower-amplitude waves—and are most pronounced when the individual is relaxed with eyes closed (Pickworth et al., 1986). On the other hand, smokers often report that a cigarette calms them down and reduces tension (Schelling, 1992)—perhaps because it relieves their craving for a cigarette or stops withdrawal.

The effects of nicotine on performance are typically subtle and variable. Various lines of evidence suggest that nicotine can enhance task performance, memory, cognition, and learning in some individuals, in some situations, some of the time (Gentry et al., 2000; Heishman, 1998; Heishman et al., 1994; Sherwood, 1993; Waters & Sutton, 2000). The problem in determining the who, where, and when is that there are so many potential factors involved: (1) whether the person being tested is a tobacco user or not (most studies are done with users); (2) the degree of nicotine dependence and deprivation level at the time of testing; (3) the route of administration (smoking, injection, nasal spray, nicotine gum, or nicotine patch), which influences the onset and duration of effects; (4) the dose (dose–response functions of performance-enhancing drugs are typically inverted U-shaped); (5) the predrug psychological state of the person; (6) the type of task used; and so forth. Furthermore, nicotine can affect mood, cognition, or arousal, all of which can interact in complicated ways; for example, cognition could be enhanced directly by nicotine, or it could be enhanced because nicotine improves the person's mood.

It is clear that nicotine and smoking can reverse deprivation-induced deficits in certain abilities in abstinent smokers. Studies conducted with nondeprived smokers and nonsmokers have shown that nicotine may enhance finger-tapping rate and motor responding in tests of focused attention. Additionally, nicotine has been shown to enhance sustained attention and recognition memory in both nondeprived smokers and nonsmokers. In simulated driving tests, nondeprived smokers have been shown to exhibit decreased braking time and improved tracking after smoking. Enhanced performance most typically occurs in relatively simple tasks requiring sustained attention or fast reaction times. In more complex tasks, such as understanding articles or solving problems, nicotine may actually be detrimental to performance. At the present time, no studies have reported true enhancement of sensory abilities, selective attention, learning, and other cognitive (e.g., problem solving, reasoning) abilities.

Presumably, these psychological effects occur because of nicotine's ability to stimulate nicotinic ACh receptors (nAChRs). Which of the particular nAChRs are most important is not clear, because they are found throughout the nervous system. In the peripheral nervous system (PNS), activation of nAChRs produces sympathomimetic effects, primarily because the nAChRs found in the adrenal gland trigger the release of adrenaline (epinephrine) from the adrenal gland into the bloodstream. Adrenaline, in turn, is transported to adrenergic receptors in the heart and blood vessels, leading to increases in heart rate and elevated blood pressure (through constriction of blood vessels). Although adrenaline may potentially affect CNS function, it is unlikely to have much effect because it does not cross the blood–brain barrier (BBB) very well. (Because there are nAChRs on postganglionic parasympathetic neurons, activation of nAChRs would also be expected to enhance parasympathetic activity, but the sympathetic effects predominate over the parasympathetic effects.) Despite these multiple PNS effects, they are probably not of major importance in reinforcing smoking because they can be blocked without appreciably altering the psychological effects of nicotine in humans.

There are also numerous nAChRs in the CNS. Research indicates that nicotine enhances both inhibitory and excitatory transmission in the CNS by acting on nAChRs located on presynaptic nerve endings, which increase intracellular Ca^{++} levels and enhance release of a variety of transmitters—for example, glutamate (GLU), ACh, NE, GABA, and DA (Mihailescu & Drucker-Colin, 2000). Which (if any) of these actions is relevant to the effects of nicotine in humans is unknown. The importance of cholinergic systems on working memory (discussed in Chapter 11) suggests that nicotine may facilitate some aspects of this type of memory (Levin & Simon, 1998).

In addition to the nicotine in tobacco, research suggests that an unidentified ingredient in tobacco smoke reduces levels of monoamine oxidase (MAO) B (the enzyme that breaks down DA) in smokers (Fowler et al., 1996). Thus, these two factors may synergistically lead to higher DA levels, enhancing the reward and the high associated with smoking tobacco. These actions may also explain the prevalence of, and increase in, smoking in, patients treated with antipsychotics, which are DA receptor blockers (McEvoy et al., 1995). It is also possible that the light-headed feeling that one gets by depriving the brain of oxygen—because of the carbon monoxide in smoke—is perceived as pleasurable.

Following chronic tobacco exposure, nicotine may also be reinforcing because it immediately stops withdrawal symptoms, indicative of the physical dependence on nicotine that many believe exists. The onset of withdrawal symptoms may occur within hours of the last cigarette. In addition to a craving for tobacco, these symptoms may consist of decreased heart rate, reduced EEG, irritability, increased hunger, sleep disturbances, gastrointestinal disturbances, drowsiness, headache, and impairment of concentration, judgment, and psychomotor performance (Hughes et al., 1987; Sommese & Patterson, 1995).

Some of these withdrawal symptoms may be mediated by changes in nAChRs that may occur with chronic nicotine exposure (Buisson & Bertrand, 2002; Mihailescu & Drucker-Colin, 2000). In general, long-term nicotine exposure induces functional up-regulation of nAChRs—opposite to what one might normally expect from agonist–receptor interactions (i.e., receptor down-regulation). However, the nAChR is a bit unusual in that after an agonist binds to it and activates it, the nAChR quickly desensitizes. Low levels of nicotine may cause significant nAChR desensitization, and over the long term, the nAChRs may enter a long-lasting inactive state, which then triggers a homeostatic up-regulation of the nAChRs. Thus, aspects of nicotine tolerance could be explained by nAChRs undergoing desensitization and inactivation, and withdrawal could be explained by their slow recovery to functional states from various levels of desensitization and inactivation. Also, the increased number of nAChRs could account for why the first smoke of the day in chronic smokers is particularly enjoyable. However, different models that can account for the acute and chronic effects of nicotine on nAChRs have been developed (Buisson & Bertrand, 2002), and more research is needed to determine which of these is most likely to be responsible for nicotine's psychological effects and its propensity to induce addiction.

Furthermore, observations that none of these abstinence symptoms may occur, that they may be delayed for several days, or that they may wax and wane over a period of months suggest that many of these symptoms may be more psychological than pharmacodynamic in origin (Henningfield & Goldberg, 1988). In other words, if the symptoms were purely physiological in origin, they would be strongly and inversely related to how much the person had been smoking recently and how long it had been since the person's last cigarette. If this were the case, all heavy smokers (those smoking at least 20 cigarettes a day) would undergo withdrawal every morning, because nicotine plasma levels are essentially zero at this time; yet, some do not start smoking until the afternoon. Others may forgo smoking altogether for proscribed periods of time without undue discomfort—for example, Orthodox Jews on the Sabbath.

Conversely, if abstinence symptoms were psychological in origin, they would be directly related to the type of environment, social setting, and mood states that regularly have accompanied cigarette smoking, as well as the person's expectations and attitudes about cigarette withdrawal. The fact that these vary considerably within and among individuals more easily accounts for the variability in the degree of discomfort and the times when it occurs. For example, one study found that smokers in a treatment program who believed they were getting nicotine gum, but actually were receiving a placebo, reported fewer withdrawal symptoms and smoked fewer cigarettes during the first week of quitting smoking than those smokers who thought they were getting a placebo (Gottlieb et al., 1987). Also, there was no relationship between the actual nicotine content of the gum and reported withdrawal symptoms or eventual relapse rates. Unfortunately, as stressed in Chapter 6, once the underlying conditioning factors take place and the expectations develop, their presence may be felt for the rest of the person's life.

In summary, despite the inconsistencies in the evidence, there is a very strong case that nicotine is addictive (Stolerman & Jarvis, 1995). Patterns of use by most smokers are consistent with compulsive use. Although a majority of chronic smokers report the desire to quit, the likelihood of success in a cessation attempt is low, relapse is a common occurrence, and nicotine replacement enhances outcomes in smoking cessation. There is evidence of both tolerance development to nicotine's effects and abstinence symptoms upon cessation. Nicotine has both positive (enhancement of mood or performance) and negative (relief of abstinence symptoms) reinforcing properties. Nonhumans will self-administer nicotine, albeit under more limited conditions than with a number of other addictive drugs. Finally, nicotine shares some discriminative properties with cocaine and amphetamine, and many of its biochemical actions are shared by a variety of other addictive drugs.

Although smoking tobacco is the most common route of nicotine administration, smokeless tobacco (snuff, chewing tobacco) is used by a substantial percentage of adolescents, primarily males, although its use has declined considerably over the past decade, for example, in twelfth graders from approximately 30% in 1990 to 17% in 2003 (Monitoring the Future Survey, 2003). The perception by most users is that smokeless tobacco is safer and more socially acceptable than cigarette smoking, and that smokeless tobacco enhances athletic performance. Although the health risks of smokeless tobacco use are indeed much lower than those associated with tobacco smoking (Vigneswaran et al., 1995), smokeless tobacco is not harmless. Its use has been associated with oral and pharyngeal cancer, numerous dental and gum problems, and cardiovascular abnormalities related to elevated blood pressure and heart rate. Also, smokeless tobacco does not appear to facilitate performance, because differences between users and nonusers of smokeless tobacco have not been observed with respect to neuromuscular reactivity or perceptual-motor task performance (Edwards & Glover, 1986; Edwards et al., 1987).

Many people "mature out" of their drug habits because their drug use ceases to match a change in their lifestyle—for example, marriage, job, or parenthood. Hardly anybody matures out of cigarettes. Smokers quit, but not through loss of interest—quitting requires determination (Schelling, 1992). The most promising aids to quitting are medicines that contain nicotine, such as chewing gum (Nicorette) or nicotine-containing skin patches (ProStep, Habitrol, Nicoderm), which release a constant, small amount of nicotine into the bloodstream and presumably lessen the craving for cigarettes. After a few weeks, patients can chew less gum or receive smaller patches that release less nicotine until they are weaned off the substance. When used in conjunction with appropriate nonpharmacologic interventions, these nicotine-replacement therapies roughly double the rate of quitting smoking, in comparison to placebo treatments (Watts et al., 2002). For example, in over a dozen studies, nicotine patches produced 6-month abstinence rates of 22% to 42%, compared to 5% to 28% rates with placebo patches. These nicotine-replacement systems reduce most, but not all, nicotine withdrawal symptoms, including craving for cigarettes, negative moods, hypoarousal, and increased appetite. In addition, the satisfaction and good taste of cigarettes appear to be decreased in subjects using nicotine-replacement therapies (Levin et al., 1994). The evidence for their efficacy and safety has been deemed sufficient for both types of nicotine-replacement systems to be approved as nonprescription drugs.

A nicotine nasal spray and inhaler have also been approved by the Food and Drug Administration (FDA) as prescription smoking cessation medications. Several studies evaluating these forms of nicotine replacement therapy have indicated that their efficacy is comparable to that of nicotine patches and gum (Watts et al., 2002). However, a substantial percentage of users experience unpleasant side effects (e.g., mouth and throat irritation with the inhaler and moderate to severe nasal irritation with the nasal spray). Thus, these medications are unlikely to offer any benefits beyond those provided by patches and gum.

Which nicotine-replacement therapy may be most appropriate is mostly dependent on individual preferences. The nicotine patch may be the more effective treatment because it is easier to use and comply with than gum and induces fewer side effects than the inhaler and nasal spray. It should be emphasized that while using these aids, smoking tobacco should be avoided, because of nicotine's potential cardiovascular toxicity at high doses.

Sustained-release bupropion (Zyban), a drug originally approved for use as an antidepressant (marketed as Wellbutrin and discussed in Chapter 9), has also been approved for use as a smoking cessation aid in the pharmacologic treatment of tobacco dependence. Limited information suggests that sustained-release bupropion may result in higher tobacco abstinence rates than with the nicotine patch and that sustained-release bupropion used concurrently with the patch may be slightly more efficacious than either treatment alone (Watts et al., 2002). Interestingly, the efficacy of sustained-release bupropion does not appear to be dependent on the smoker having a former history of major depression.

AMPHETAMINES AND RELATED DRUGS

In contrast to caffeine and nicotine, amphetamines and structurally related drugs exert more intense and distinct emotional and cognitive effects, which may account for their popular recreational use and abuse potential. Amphetamine was initially synthesized in the late 1800s, but medical uses for it were not developed until the late 1920s. Although it is quite effective when administered orally, it was initially marketed in the form of inhalers for use in asthma treatment. It quickly gained popularity because of its potent CNS effects. Shortly thereafter, amphetamine (marketed as Benzedrine in the United States) was discovered to be made up of two isomers, *l*- and *d*-amphetamine. The latter was found to be considerably more potent and was marketed as Dexedrine. A minor modification in the amphetamine molecule yielded the slightly more potent methamphetamine (Desoxyn, Methedrine). With the recognition of the potential psychopathological toxicity and dependence associated with the amphetamines, other compounds with very similar molecular structures were synthesized, including methylphenidate (Ritalin), pipradol (Meratran), phenmetrazine (Preludin), and phentermine (Ionamin). These amphetamine-related substances exert basically the same qualitative effects as the amphetamines do. (Some of these drugs are no longer on the market, or the brand names they are marketed under have changed.)

Methcathinone is the newest of the potent amphetamine-related psychostimulants to be introduced into the United States, and it appears to be as addictive as crack cocaine and methamphetamine (Emerson & Cisek, 1993; Glennon et al., 1995). It is a derivative of a naturally occurring stimulant drug, cathinone, which is found in the khat plant native to Africa and the southern Arabian peninsula. Methcathinone was originally synthesized in Germany in 1928 and used in the Soviet Union as an antidepressant drug in the 1930s and 1940s. In the mid-1950s, an American pharmaceutical company conducted preliminary studies on its potential medical uses. After determining that methcathinone had substantial side effects, with effects essentially identical to those of amphetamine (its molecular structure is virtually identical to that of metham-phetamine), the company abandoned its research. In the 1980s, methcathinone reap-peared on the illicit market after a student working at the company stole samples and documentation on the manufacturing process. In 1990, associates of the student began manufacturing the drug (a relatively simple process) in clandestine laboratories and selling it—a practice that rapidly spread to several states. It was subsequently relegated to Controlled Substance Schedule I status by the Drug Enforcement Administration in 1993. However, the use of methcathinone in the United States at the present time ap-pears very limited, most likely due to the fact that its effects are so similar to cocaine and methamphetamine, and the illicit manufacturing and distribution systems for the latter drugs have already been so well established that there is no market for this drug.

Minor changes in the chemical structure of the basic amphetamine molecule can significantly alter the particular spectrum of its pharmacological and biochemical activ-ities (Biel, 1970). Some changes may abolish both psychostimulant and appetite sup-pressant (anorexic) effects. Some other changes may decrease only the anorexic effects, and others may decrease only the psychostimulant effects. Other changes profoundly enhance the MAO-inhibiting properties of the compound; for example, the ampheta-mine-like antidepressant tranylcypromine (Parnate) is about 5,000 times more potent than amphetamine in terms of MAO inhibition. Other modifications result in some psy-chotomimetic compounds, such as DOM (dimethoxymethylamphetamine), that pro-duce effects similar to those of mescaline but possess considerably higher potency. Many of these compounds will be dealt with in later chapters.

Behavioral Effects of Amphetamines

The specific behavioral effects of amphetamine and related compounds depend to a great extent on the task requirements, the normal frequency of the behavior, the dose, and individual characteristics. Although psychostimulants are commonly believed to have effects in hyperactive children that are different from those observed in normal children or adults, empirical evidence indicates that, other than the magnitude of ob-served effects, amphetamines produce qualitatively similar effects in all three groups (Rapoport et al., 1980).

In terms of quality of performance on various tasks, the most striking beneficial effects are noted when the person is fatigued (Lombardo, 1986). However, even in non-fatigued individuals, low to moderate doses of amphetamines tend to facilitate per-formance of tasks dependent on sustained attention (i.e., detecting infrequently occurring objects on radar screens) or those requiring quickness and strength (such as blocking and tackling in football, swimming, and track events; Grilly & Loveland, 2001). High doses generally interfere with performance of these types of tasks. In tasks requiring smooth, accurate motions, low doses induce variable effects in individuals, in some cases enhancing, but in most cases interfering with, performance. In moderate to high doses, performance is hindered. Perhaps these task–drug interactions are the reason football players (at least linemen and linebackers) may be more prone to use these substances, whereas golfers and tennis players invariably avoid them. Amphetamines and related compounds may also enhance performance on tasks in-volving strength and endurance due to their sympathomimetic effects. These include increased blood pressure and heart rate, constriction of the blood vessels to the viscera and intestinal relaxation, increased body temperature and muscle tension, and bronchial dilation.

Although amphetamine-related drugs often increase many kinds of activities, some kinds of behaviors, particularly those that occur frequently to begin with, are actually reduced by these drugs. Part of the reason for these differential effects is that not all behaviors can be increased simultaneously because one type of activity may compete with another (Grilly, 1977). Thus, for example, undifferentiated motor activity (hyperactivity) observed in many children with attention deficit disorder may be reduced with psychostimulants because they enhance on-task activity.

Adult humans typically report enhanced mood and increases in subjective indices of alertness, energy, vigor, and arousal after exposure to acute doses of *d*-amphetamine up to about 0.5 mg/kg (Grilly & Loveland, 2001). Interestingly, in the few studies that have used objective measures of activity, results have indicated that general motor activity of adult humans is either unaffected or decreased at these doses (quite unlike what is typically observed in adult rodents, which display clear increases in spontaneous motor activity). These effects are similar to those observed in children with attention deficit hyperactivity disorder, although to a much lesser degree because the baseline activity of adults is much lower than that of hyperactive children. However, these doses do tend to increase indices of sociability and talkativeness in humans when observed under contrived social situations. On the other hand, a sizeable minority of adults do experience a paradoxical drowsiness with amphetamine, at least for the first hour or so after administration (Tecce & Cole, 1974). Somewhere in the 0.7 mg/kg dose range, humans experience dysphoria, social withdrawal, and depression (Griffith et al., 1970). Exposure to higher doses can precipitate a psychosis with symptoms very similar to paranoid schizophrenia (Jonsson & Gunne, 1970; Lyon et al., 1986). Behavior often becomes very stereotyped and repetitive. Simple movements such as continuous chewing, rubbing of the tongue on the inside of the lips, and teeth grinding occur. The individual may engage in a repetitious thought or meaningless acts for hours. Often users seem fascinated or preoccupied with their own thought processes and with philosophical concerns on a grand scale. The person may get very suspicious of others and become antisocial, and in some cases may become very prone to violence. Similar actions have been described with the other amphetamine-like substances—for example, methylphenidate.

Very similar behavioral effects have been noted to occur in all mammals, although in each case the specific type of stereotypic reaction is dependent on the species. Rats typically bob their heads back and forth and display gnawing behaviors. Monkeys have been observed to exhibit continuous grooming-like movements of body and limbs without actually grooming, and chimpanzees have been observed to rock and sway back and forth. Because of the similarities between the behavioral effects of high doses of amphetamines in humans and nonhumans, and because the human reactions are so similar to paranoid schizophrenia, the effects in nonhumans induced by higher doses of amphetamine are commonly viewed as a way of producing a model animal "psychosis" (Ellison, 1993).

With chronic use, tolerance to the reinforcing effects of amphetamine may be marked, leading to administration of very high drug doses (Hyman, 1996). In contrast, one of the curious aspects of amphetamine-induced motor and psychosis-mimicking effects in animals is that repeated exposure to amphetamine appears to sensitize, rather than reduce, the organism's susceptibility to them. This phenomenon can occur even if the exposures are several days apart (Kilbey & Ellinwood, 1977). Exposure to similar-acting drugs, such as cocaine, and severe stress also appear to sensitize the organism to the psychosis-mimicking effects (Antelman et al., 1980; Fitzgerald et al., 1996; MacLennan & Maier, 1983). These findings have led to the speculation that humans who have been exposed to stress or drugs of this nature may also be predisposed to developing the psychotic reactions to amphetamine or cocaine. The behavioral sensitization observed in rodents administered high doses of amphetamine and cocaine has also been proposed to indicate sensitization of the mesocorticolimbic system that increases incentive salience. The same process may be the cause of humans developing a compulsive motivation or excessive "wanting" to take these drugs without them necessarily being more "liked" (Robinson & Berridge, 2003).

Other explanations for the sensitization effects with these drugs have been proposed. One possibility is that the prolonged depletion of catecholamines following heavy use (see "Dependence on Amphetamines") induces increased receptor sensitivity or receptor up-regulation. Sensitization may also be the result of neuronal damage. Some studies indicate that stress-induced sensitization appears to be mediated by stress-induced secretion of stress-related hormones, called glucocorticoids, that promote increases in extracellular DA concentrations in the nucleus accumbens when psychostimulants like amphetamine and cocaine are administered (Rougé-Pont et al., 1995). Furthermore, excessive exposure to both glucocorticoids and amphetamine has been shown to exert neurotoxic effects in the brains of several species (Ellison, 1993; Sapolsky, 1996), which, at least with amphetamine, have been linked to its ability to sensitize the animal-type psychosis (Ellison, 1993).

Limited evidence also suggests that amphetamine-induced sensitization can occur in humans. In three studies by Strakowski, Sax, and colleagues, sensitization to a 0.25 mg/kg oral dose of *d*-amphetamine was observed in amphetamine-naïve volunteers. In these studies the participants were exposed to *d*-amphetamine on two or three separate occasions 48 hours apart. In two of these studies (Strakowski et al., 1996; Strakowski & Sax, 1998), they found greater subjective effects during the second or third drug exposure than the first, suggestive of sensitization. In one of these studies both sensitization and tolerance were observed (Strakowski et al., 2001). Specifically, subjective measures of vigor and euphoria were higher after the third dose of *d*-amphetamine than the first, that is, apparent sensitization. In contrast, the first dose of *d*-amphetamine produced the greater response in subjective ratings of drug liking than the third dose, that is, apparent tolerance. Interestingly, these effects were found primarily in the women subjects and not in the men; this suggests that women may be more at risk to develop stimulant dependence than men. (However, other factors, e.g., higher levels of sensation-seeking, antisocial personality characteristics, and frequency of drug use in males, may account for stimulant abuse and dependence typically being more common in men than women.) Because drug exposures were always conducted with the same contextual cues present, some of these effects could have been due to Pavlovian conditioning; that is, conditioned responses combined with unconditioned responses to the drug could have altered the net effect observed across the treatment sessions.

In another study, in which 0.3 mg/kg amphetamine was administered intravenously to amphetamine-naïve humans on two separate occasions 7 to 35 days apart, neither tolerance nor sensitization in the second drug-exposure test was observed either on DA release in the brain or on the subjective effects of the drug (Kegeles et al., 1999). One study observed acute exacerbation of a paranoid psychotic state by methamphetamine in 16 of 21 patients who had been treated for chronic methamphetamine psychosis (Sato et al., 1983). Four of these patients relapsed following a single methamphetamine exposure to an amount less than that initially used, and one relapsed without evidence of methamphetamine use. A positive prophylactic effect of small doses of the antipsychotic haloperidol on the acute exacerbation in eight of the patients suggested that dopaminergic supersensitivity may have been a mechanism for the paranoid psychotic state.

Clinical Uses of Amphetamines

Following its use in the treatment of asthma, one of amphetamine's first clinical uses for its CNS effects was in the treatment of *narcolepsy,* a rare but serious disorder in which the person falls asleep repeatedly during the day, often without warning. Shortly thereafter, amphetamine was found to significantly reduce many of the symptoms of children whose cognitive functioning was impaired by the inability to concentrate and who were overly active (a disorder now called *attention deficit hyperactivity disorder; see* Chapter 11). Currently, these are the only two disorders for which most experts agree amphetamines may be legitimately prescribed, although there are a number of other uses for them—most notably in the treatment of obesity (Holmes, 1995).

Over the past 70 years, amphetamines have been used for a variety of purposes. During World War II, most of the armed forces on both sides of the war issued amphetamines to their men to counteract fatigue, elevate mood, and heighten endurance (Brecher, 1972). Whether this practice hurt or helped their cause in the long run is debatable, for as we shall see, escalating the dose of amphetamine is a tempting probability in such times of stress. It can lead to a psychotic state involving a severe case of perceptual and cognitive disorganization. Some historians have suggested that, at the end of the war, Adolf Hitler's increasingly bizarre behavior may have been due to his use of amphetamines, along with a variety of other stimulants. As stated by one historian:

> No one who has read about his behavior during this time or about his pronouncements at the situation conferences on 23, 25 and 27 April 1945, then still being recorded, can fail to recognize what it was that made him conjure up in all good faith such patently harebrained schemes. The rapid alternation of depression and euphoria, exhaustion and artificially induced buoyancy clearly reflect Hitler's dependence on the stimulants prescribed by Morell. (Maser, 1971, pp. 228–229)

After the war, amphetamines were routinely prescribed for weight control and mood depression, now recognized as inappropriate because amphetamine can lead to a person becoming even more depressed and suicidal. To blunt the nervousness and sleep-disrupting properties of amphetamine, individuals often combined it with a sedative–hypnotic, or tranquilizer, which in some cases produced other deleterious side effects.

Pharmacokinetics and Pharmacodynamics of Amphetamines

Amphetamines are relatively high in lipid-solubility and are very well absorbed when taken orally or inhaled as a vapor. IV administration results in brain penetration within seconds. Although most amphetamines are not sufficiently volatile to vaporize when smoked, a form of methamphetamine hydrochloride (called "ice" because of its transparent, sheetlike crystals) has been developed so that it can be inhaled through smoking. Inhalation allows it to produce a rapid onset of effect, similar to smoking cocaine, but as with other amphetamines, its effects last much longer—on the order of several hours (Cho, 1993).

Although the amphetamines and related compounds bear a strong molecular resemblance to the catecholamines (NE and DA), little of their activities appear to be due to a direct agonist action at catecholamine receptors. Instead, they have neuropharmacological properties that enhance the level of catecholamines in the synaptic cleft, which then increases catecholamine receptor activation. Amphetamine also increases extracellular levels of 5-HT, but this action appears to play a minimal role in most of its behavioral effects.

Amphetamines and related drugs increase extracellular concentrations of the monoamines through two primary mechanisms, both of which involve the protein transporters that normally terminate the action of monoamines via reuptake: (1) they bind to these transporters and inhibit monoamine reuptake into neurons; and (2) they promote reverse transport of monoamines, that is, they induce the release of monoamines from neurons through these transporters. Amphetamine and its derivatives differ primarily in terms of their potency in these two processes, as well as their potency for affecting the three monoamine transporters (Wall et al., 1995). Methamphetamine and dextroamphetamine are roughly equipotent in promoting release and inhibiting reuptake and are more potent in affecting the DA and NE transporters than the 5-HT transporter. Methylphenidate (Ritalin, discussed Chapter 11) is very weak in promoting release and works primarily by inhibiting reuptake; it also has greater potency in affecting the DA and NE transporters than the 5-HT transporter. Methylenedioxymethamphetamine (MDMA, Ecstasy, a mildly hallucinogenic amphetamine discussed in Chapter 13) promotes release and inhibits reuptake but is more potent in affecting the 5-HT transporter than the DA and NE transporters. These compounds also differ to some degree in other pharmacodynamic properties. Amphetamine also has a mild, temporary, inhibitory action on the enzyme MAO (which, you may recall, normally metabolizes the monoamines intraneuronally into inactive molecules) and redistributes monoamines from the synaptic vesicles to the cytoplasm, so there are more monoamines to be released (Biel, 1970; Sulzer et al., 1995).

Although amphetamine and related psychostimulants (and cocaine) enhance monoamine activity throughout the nervous system, which then results in a variety of effects on mood and behavior, most studies have indicated that the primary reward properties of these drugs are due to their ability to enhance dopaminergic activity in a part of the limbic system called the nucleus accumbens. Amphetamine and many of its analogs nonselectively elevate extracellular levels of DA, NE, and 5-HT, but their reinforcing properties and abuse potential are best correlated with their ability to increase extracellular levels of DA, because the rewarding effects of these agents are attenuated by selective DA antagonists and not by selective NE or 5-HT antagonists (Wise, 1998). Also, neither the selective NE uptake inhibitors nor 5-HT uptake inhibitors, which are effective antidepressants, induces primary reward effects (e.g., euphoria) in normal humans, and their mood-elevating effects in depressed individuals take several days or weeks of exposure to develop.

The actions just described occur with acute drug exposure. However, with chronic drug exposure, a multitude of changes have been documented to take place in the brain. With sufficiently high dosages of amphetamine, catecholamines can be depleted as a result of neurotoxic processes (discussed shortly), increased metabolization by extraneuronal catechol-O-methyltransferase (COMT), or decreased synthesis resulting from excessive catecholamine autoreceptor activation (Paulson et al., 1991; Robinson & Becker, 1986). These changes could account for some tolerance phenomena and mood depression following amphetamine exposure and withdrawal. Alterations in catecholamine receptors (e.g., down-regulation of catecholamine autoreceptors and postsynaptic receptors) can occur with chronic amphetamine exposure, with the former accounting for some sensitization to amphetamine (due to loss of the inhibitory control over catecholaminergic neuron activity) and the latter accounting for some tolerance phenomena.

Interestingly, some of these neuroadaptations may depend on whether amphetamine is self-administered by the organism or is passively administered to the organism. For example, rats that had been allowed to self-administer methamphetamine for 5 weeks and were then withdrawn from methamphetamine for 24 hours showed marked decreases in somatodendritic DA D_2 autoreceptor levels in midbrain regions, with a corresponding down-regulation of DA D_1 receptors in the nucleus accumbens. These changes were not observed in rats that passively received the same amounts of methamphetamine with the same temporal pattern of exposure (Stefanski et al., 1999). A subsequent study using the same procedure revealed that there were no differences among the groups of rats in terms of densities of DA uptake sites and DA D_1 and D_2 receptors in different brain regions, 7 and 30 days following withdrawal from chronic methamphetamine self-administration (Stefanski et al., 2002). These results suggest that the organism's motivational state or expectancy of drug effects present when the drug is administered can play a critical role in amphetamine-induced neuroadaptations.

Although most of the evidence for these changes has come from research with nonhumans exposed to much higher dosages than humans would likely administer, reduced levels of DA and tyrosine hydroxylase (the initial enzyme necessary for catecholamine synthesis; see Chapter 5), and fewer DA reuptake sites have been found in the striatum (nucleus accumbens, caudate, putamen) of deceased chronic methamphetamine users (Wilson et al., 1996). Lower concentrations of g-proteins (major components of catecholamine receptor activation) have also been found in the nucleus accumbens of deceased methamphetamine users (McLeman et al., 2000).

Dependence on Amphetamines

In the early 1970s, more than 30 amphetamine-containing preparations were on the market. Some government sources estimated that there were enough doses of amphetamine and related compounds being marketed in the United States to supply every man, woman, and child several times daily. Furthermore, there were plenty of unscrupulous and ignorant physicians around willing to prescribe them. In addition to amphetamine's medically prescribed uses, it was being used by truck drivers who were doing long hauls without adequate rest, students who were cramming for exams, and "speed freaks" who were injecting it just to get high. With all of its use and potential misuse, something had to give. Beginning in the mid-1970s, the use of amphetamines gradually decreased, for many reasons. First, the government began to exert legal pressures on pharmaceutical companies to decrease their production. Second, the number of legitimate medical uses was drastically reduced. Third, the general population and physicians became more educated about the potential hazards and misuse. Fourth, compounds with less abuse potential and more specific actions with respect to major mood depression were developed—for example, antidepressants. Finally, cocaine, which users were led to believe was much less harmful than amphetamine, came on the scene to replace it as a drug for recreational use.

Unfortunately, in the 1990s, there was a resurgence in the illicit use of amphetamine, in this case, methamphetamine, with the expected consequences of earlier amphetamine epidemics—an increase in violence, criminal behavior, deaths, psychotic behavior, and extreme addiction (Kleiman & Satel, 1996). Making the situation worse is the fact that the quality (i.e., purity) of methamphetamine has improved drastically over the past several years due to refinements in the manufacturing process and marketing factors—apparently so much is available that dealers aren't cutting (diluting) the drug as much as they used to.

Despite the dysphoric effects of high doses or chronic use, the dependence liability of amphetamine and similar-acting drugs is considered to be among the highest of all drugs (Jaffe, 1990). Although physical dependence may be a factor, unequivocal evidence for abstinence symptoms associated with these drugs is lacking. There is no question that when individuals stop taking amphetamines after a few days of moderate to heavy amphetamine exposure, they generally "crash"; that is, they experience exhaustion, depression, lethargy, and hunger. These are all symptoms opposite to the direct effects of the drug. However, rather than being signs of an abstinence syndrome, these symptoms may be due to lack of decent sleep, low blood sugar, or depletion of DA or NE, among other things. One can speculate that because of the enhanced activity at catecholamine receptors, there may also be a short-lived decrease in the sensitivity of postsynaptic catecholamine receptors, an effect that would be consistent with a true abstinence syndrome. (However, note that this speculation contrasts with the possibility for up-regulation of receptors following catecholamine depletion.) Even if the postdrug symptoms associated with chronic psychostimulant use are due to a true abstinence syndrome, they clearly are qualitatively and quantitatively very different from those symptoms associated with sedative–hypnotics and narcotics. Furthermore, it is questionable whether these symptoms are a major factor in the maintenance of drug-taking behavior with this class of drugs.

On the other hand, the psychological dependence associated with amphetamines and related drugs can be overwhelming. The euphoria, feelings of well-being, and enhanced self-confidence in both physical and mental abilities serve as powerful primary reinforcers—even more powerful than food in a hungry animal (Aigner & Balster, 1978). Even animals find their effects very reinforcing. Self-administration studies with nonhumans have indicated that, if given free access to amphetamines or cocaine, they are highly likely to administer larger and larger amounts—in many cases to the point of administering lethal doses (which induce convulsions; Aigner & Balster, 1978; Brady & Griffiths, 1977). This phenomenon rarely occurs with narcotics like heroin, where animals typically stabilize at a fairly constant daily dosage somewhat below lethal levels. Thus, it appears that these drugs have very strong primary reinforcing properties, and it is these properties that potentially lead to the heavy psychological dependence on them.

As with all psychotropic drugs, there is considerable individual variability in vulnerability to dependence on amphetamines. Some users go for months or years before becoming daily users, whereas others report such an intense positive response with the first dose that addiction occurs almost immediately. Some of the factors leading to this variability are likely to be genetic (e.g., differential reactivity to novel stimulation), whereas others may be environmental (e.g., the result of differential exposure to stressful events during some critical period of life; Piazza et al., 1989).

Effects of Chronic Amphetamine Exposure

Even in animals that do not administer lethal amounts, continued exposure to amphetamines and related drugs eventually leads to problems associated with malnutrition, nonhealing ulcers, high blood pressure, and brain damage resulting from restricted blood flow to the brain. Repeated administration of high doses of amphetamines has also been found to induce irreversible neuronal damage in animals (Wagner et al., 1985). This includes long-lasting depletion of central monoamine concentrations, a decrease in the number of monoamine uptake sites, a decrease in monoamine synthesis, and nerve terminal degeneration. These effects can also occur in humans. A study using high-resolution magnetic resonance imaging (MRI) and other techniques found severe gray-matter deficits in the cingulate, limbic, and paralimbic cortices and smaller hippocampal volumes of methamphetamine abusers than control subjects. Furthermore, the hippocampal deficits in the subjects were correlated with the degree to which they exhibited impaired memory performance (Thompson et al., 2004).

It has been speculated that these effects are due to amphetamine's ability to enhance the release of DA, NE, and 5-HT from synaptic vesicles into the cytoplasm as well as inhibit MAO activity, which leads to the nonenzymatic oxidation of these monoamines into neurotoxins that trigger terminal degeneration (Cubells et al., 1994; Sonsalla et al., 1989). Consistent with this view are studies that have demonstrated that the neurotoxic actions of methamphetamine can be attenuated by pretreatment with vitamin C (an antioxidant) and α-methyl-p-tyrosine (a catecholamine synthesis inhibitor), and can be exacerbated by pretreatment with reserpine (a drug that enhances cytoplasmic pools of monoamines). Positron emission tomography (PET) scan studies indicating that humans with a history of abusing methamphetamine or methcathinone (a similar acting drug discussed earlier) have reduced DA transporter density in the basal ganglia suggest that these neurotoxic effects may also occur with doses used by humans (McCann et al., 1998), although these results may be a cause or effect of their drug use, among other factors. Many of these neurotoxic effects may be reversible, as evidenced by the finding of considerable recovery of DA function in monkeys several weeks after acute, high-dosage amphetamine- and methamphetamine-induced neurotoxicity (Melega et al., 1997).

COCAINE

South American Indians have been using cocaine for centuries to increase their endurance and to reduce their fatigue and hunger. The early European explorers of South America, who essentially enslaved the natives, soon found the natives' fondness of the coca leaf to be useful as an incentive for performing hard labor. Eventually, the coca leaf was introduced in Europe with little fanfare. In the mid-1800s cocaine was isolated from coca extracts, but its general use did not begin until the late 1800s. Sir Arthur Conan Doyle's famous fictional detective, Sherlock Holmes, was reported to have injected cocaine (circa 1888) occasionally between cases. He said he found it "transcendentally stimulating and clarifying to the mind" (Grilly, 1980).

Perhaps the earliest leading proponent of cocaine's clinical use was a young physician by the name of Sigmund Freud (Brecher, 1972). Between 1884 and 1887 Freud performed the functions of a psychopharmacologist by testing the various mood- and behavior-altering properties of cocaine, primarily on himself and a few friends. Freud initially believed that cocaine had many beneficial characteristics; for example, to enhance mood, alleviate depression, reduce the effects of fatigue, and enhance sexual potency. He felt it could be a potential treatment for morphine and alcohol addiction, numerous psychological disorders (such as hysteria and hypochondria), and a variety of physical debilities (e.g., diseases involving tissue degeneration, asthma, and digestive problems). Finally, he suggested that its local anesthetic properties might be of value.

Although Freud initially believed that cocaine was a wonder drug through which he could establish his medical reputation (as well as provide himself with recreation), he eventually became disillusioned with the drug (Jones, 1953). One reason may have been that his own work indicated that there was tremendous individual variability in the reaction to cocaine. He also attempted to wean a good friend off of his dependence on morphine, using cocaine as a substitute. Although the friend was successfully weaned from his morphine habit, he quickly developed a very strong cocaine dependence. After observing the effects of both kinds of dependence, Freud was perhaps the first to recognize that dependence on cocaine can have far more deleterious effects than morphine dependence. As will be discussed in Chapter 12, chronic morphine use has relatively benign effects on the person, whereas chronic cocaine use induces a psychotic state, extreme loss of appetite leading to nutritional deficiencies, impaired interpersonal relations, and a variety of other pathological effects.

Freud has long been recognized as a high achiever who wanted to become famous—something that was unattainable as long as he was associated with a drug with such a poor reputation. In recognizing his error in judgment regarding cocaine's therapeutic promise, Freud turned away from pursuing physical, organic approaches to the treatment of mental illness—perhaps leading him toward an approach emphasizing unconscious forces in its cause. However, his work with cocaine may have led to its use by an eye surgeon, Karl Koller, as a local anesthetic in the eye. It was the first drug physicians had for this purpose. Cocaine was later used as therapy for asthma and colic. Although Freud's work with cocaine ceased, he continued to use cocaine regularly until at least 1895, and probably quite a bit longer (but encouraged the widely held view that he stopped using the drug in 1887). Many have speculated that his cocaine use not only was a factor in his prodigious writings, but also may have played a causal role in the early development of his psychoanalytic theories by facilitating his capacity for introspection and self-analysis (Fuller, 1992).

Behavioral Effects of Cocaine

Because of the similarities of the neurochemical effects of cocaine and those induced by amphetamine, it is not surprising that their mood-altering and behavioral effects are also quite similar. With few exceptions, the effects noted earlier for amphetamine also apply to cocaine. These effects include euphoria, enhanced arousal and vigilance, reversal of fatigue-induced deficits in performance, and increases in blood pressure and heart rate. Furthermore, like amphetamine, euphorigenic doses of cocaine have been shown to decrease cerebral metabolism of glucose in most regions of the human and monkey brains (London et al., 1990; Lyons et al., 1996). However, self-administering cocaine induces a pattern of glucose utilization that is significantly different from that induced by receiving equivalent amounts of cocaine noncontingently (Porrino et al., 2002).

Although users of cocaine and amphetamine will often assert that the effects of the two drugs are different, most studies have found that, when users of cocaine and amphetamine are administered these drugs intravenously, they are unable to distinguish between them, except for the duration of the drug effect (Van Dyke & Byck, 1982). The time course for amphetamine is approximately 2 to 3 hours, whereas cocaine's effects dissipate in about 30 minutes. In studies with animals, the behavioral effects of cocaine and amphetamine are quite similar in a variety of procedures. Also, after chronic exposure to either substance, those effects exhibiting tolerance to one will sometimes confer tolerance to the other (Fischman et al., 1985; Wood & Emmett-Oglesby, 1986). Similarly, when enhanced sensitivity is observed with one, sometimes it will also be evidenced with the other (Kilbey & Ellinwood, 1977; Short & Shuster, 1976). On the other hand, neither is cross-tolerant with opiates like morphine (Short & Shuster, 1976; Jaffe, 1990).

High doses of cocaine induce the same psychopathological effects noted earlier with respect to amphetamine: suicidal thoughts, irritability, anxiety, rebound depression, and paranoid ideation. (Robert Louis Stevenson gives us a glimpse of this behavior in his book, *The Strange Case of Dr. Jekyll and Mr. Hyde,* which he wrote in six days and nights under the influence of cocaine [Siegel, 1989]. Presumably, the drug that Dr. Jekyll took that turned him into the demonic murderer Mr. Hyde was modeled after cocaine.) The most common of the perceptual changes and pseudohallucinations induced by cocaine are tactile disturbances, in which there is a sensation of bugs running over the skin (referred to as *formication*), and visual disturbances (termed *snow lights*; Jaffe, 1990).

There are some differences between cocaine and amphetamine in addition to those mentioned earlier. Although the potency of cocaine is about 60% that of amphetamine when the two drugs are administered intravenously, cocaine is considerably less potent when they are administered orally (Jaffe, 1990). Oral cocaine, because of its alkaloid nature and the effects of gastrointestinal (GI) secretions, is not well absorbed, whereas amphetamine is readily absorbed from the GI tract. There is also a difference between them when taken intranasally; cocaine has local anesthetic properties, whereas amphetamine does not. This local anesthetic action also appears to make it difficult for cocaine users to distinguish cocaine from other local anesthetics with minimal CNS actions, such as procaine (Novocain; Van Dyke & Byck, 1982). Perhaps some of the subjective differences between amphetamine and cocaine are due to reputation, expectation, and setting, all of which are potent factors in many so-called drug-induced effects.

Pharmacokinetics and Pharmacodynamics of Cocaine

Despite the South American Indians' long-term use of cocaine, there are no reports of them suffering from any unpleasant side effects or toxicity. On the other hand, in the 1980s in the United States, we began to experience an epidemic of use and abuse of, and extreme dependence on, cocaine. Why is there such a difference in these two cultures' reactions to cocaine? Basically the difference lies in the way in which the drug is administered. The South American Indians generally chew the coca leaf, which contains very small amounts of cocaine. Because cocaine in the coca plant is an alkaloid that is slowly absorbed from the GI tract, very little cocaine accumulates in the brain. North American users administer a highly concentrated form of cocaine intranasally, intravenously, or, most recently, through inhalation—all of which result in a rapid and high concentration of the drug in the brain (Volkow et al., 2000).

South American Indians have traditionally administered cocaine in its untransformed alkaloid form by chewing the leaves with an alkaloid substance so that absorption through the oral mucous membranes is enhanced. Apparently, there are very few cases in which this practice results in acute overdosage, psychosis, neglect of one's responsibility, or extensive focus on cocaine use. But later, though, some young South Americans in urban areas have begun to mix the cocaine paste, which is extracted from the leaves for subsequent synthesis into cocaine hydrochloride, with tobacco and smoke it. In these individuals, the same patterns of pathological states, neglect of work, and preoccupation with cocaine use seen in North American users are evidenced (Jaffe, 1990).

In North America and other developed countries, cocaine hydrochloride is commonly self-administered by sniffing it (referred to as "snorting") so that it is absorbed through the nasal membranes. This leads to a somewhat faster onset of action and higher brain concentrations than when it is ingested orally (Van Dyke & Byck, 1982). The local vasoconstrictive properties of cocaine result in slower absorption and longer effects when the drug is snorted as opposed to smoked. Cocaine's vasoconstrictive properties in the nose also lead to tissue degeneration (e.g., a perforated septum) because of ischemia (localized tissue anemia). Although much higher brain concentrations of cocaine can be achieved when administered intravenously, this mode of administration is uncommon in the vast majority of users, perhaps because users recognize the hazards associated with this route of administration. On the other hand, smoking of cocaine became popular in the 1980s because it allows high concentrations of cocaine to accumulate in the brain in a fashion very similar to IV administration, but avoids the hazards of injections—particularly the development of AIDS. Also, because users generally have had experience with smoking marijuana, they do not have to learn a new drug administration procedure.

Because cocaine hydrochloride is volatilized at temperatures that degrade it, in order for it to be effective when smoked, it must be reconverted chemically to its alkaloid (base) state. This practice is generally called **free-basing,** and in its crystalline form the compound is commonly referred to as **crack.** In this mode it is easily volatilized in active form at relatively low temperatures. Due to the efficiency with which cocaine gets into the brain via smoking, crack requires low doses (approximately 25–50 mg) to be effective, which makes it relatively inexpensive—a moderate day's use can be financed for $10 to $20—while producing a rapid-onset, intense high, which makes it extremely addictive (Foltin et al., 2003). Unfortunately, the toxic and lethal effects of cocaine, as well as the profound dependency, are just as readily induced by smoking the drug as with IV administration. Because of incomplete absorption, the potency of smoked cocaine is somewhat lower than IV cocaine, but several of the positive subjective effects of cocaine (e.g., "stimulated," "high," "liking") may actually be greater when it is smoked than when it is administered intravenously, even when the cocaine plasma levels are similar (Foltin & Fischmann, 1991).

The dependence liability of cocaine with either of these modes of administration may actually be greater than that of amphetamine, because the subjective "crash" following smoking or IV administration of cocaine is much more noticeable than with amphetamine (American Society for Pharmacology, 1987). This outcome is probably related to cocaine's very short duration of action. Once in the body, cocaine is widely distributed throughout the body and is rapidly metabolized. Minimal amounts of cocaine are excreted in an unmetabolized form. Although cocaine's plasma half-life is around 30 to 90 minutes, several metabolites can be detected by way of urinalysis for up to 2 to 5 days after a cocaine binge, with the major metabolite (benzoylecgonine) being detectable in the urine of heavy users for up to 10 days following a binge (O'Brien, 2001).

Use of alcohol along with cocaine, a common occurrence in users, results in increased plasma concentrations of cocaine and the formation of a psychoactive metabolite, cocaethylene, both of which enhance and prolong the subjective euphoria and cardiovascular effects of cocaine (McCance et al., 1995). These phenomena potentially play a role in the toxicity and abuse associated with this drug combination. Cocaethylene and cocaine both dramatically increase the extracellular levels of DA in the primate brain (Iyer et al., 1995), although in humans, cocaethylene appears to have a somewhat longer elimination half-life and somewhat lower potency than cocaine in its subjective and cardiovascular effects (Perez-Reyes et al., 1994).

Although cocaine has local anesthetic properties because of its ability to block neural conduction, its CNS effects are mediated primarily by its potent ability to inhibit the reuptake of the monoamines, that is, DA, NE, and 5-HT, from the synaptic cleft (Moore et al., 1977). Unlike amphetamine, cocaine is very weak in promoting monoamine release through the uptake transporters (Wall et al., 1995). It has now been fairly well established that the reinforcing properties of cocaine are predominantly due to its DA-reuptake–inhibiting properties (Volkow et al., 2000), which with acute exposure to cocaine results in large increases in extracellular levels of DA. There is, however, debate over the primary region of the brain that is responsible for the rewarding actions of cocaine—with some evidence favoring the nucleus accumbens and other evidence favoring the medial prefrontal cortex (Wise, 1998). Both of these areas are primary terminal areas for dopaminergic input originating in the ventral tegmental area of the midbrain.

The neurochemical effects of cocaine are similar to those of methylphenidate, amphetamine, and some antidepressants, although in many cases there are subtle, but potentially important, differences. Methylphenidate, for example, binds to the same uptake sites in the brain as cocaine, but cocaine's clearance from the brain is significantly faster, which promotes its more frequent self-administration (Volkow et al., 1995). Although some antidepressants, such as tricyclics and 5-HT uptake blockers (to be discussed in Chapter 9), share cocaine's monoamine-reuptake–inhibiting properties, they do not elevate mood until after several days of exposure, nor do they elevate mood in nondepressed individuals. Some of these differences may be due to these drugs having considerably weaker effects at the DA-uptake–binding site than cocaine; for instance, it would account for their lacking reinforcing effects in humans and animals. 5-HT uptake blockers have virtually no effect on DA transporters, and in order to achieve blood levels of the tricyclic imipramine that would induce DA-uptake blockade comparable to that of cocaine, the imipramine blood levels would be in the range of human lethality (Ritz et al., 1987).

Cocaine Dependence

Although most reports prior to 1980 indicated that cocaine had relatively benign effects on most individuals, the majority of reports in the 1980s and 1990s indicated considerable concern over cocaine's dependence liability and toxicity. These reports indicated that, particularly when administered intravenously or through smoking, cocaine can induce a very strong psychological dependence (Gawin, 1993). For example, cocaine addicts report that virtually all thoughts are focused on cocaine during binges (which can last up to several days); nourishment, sleep, money, loved ones, responsibility, and survival lose all significance. It is estimated that 5–6% of cocaine users in the United States become cocaine dependent in the first year of use and that 15–16% of cocaine users develop cocaine dependence within 10 years of first cocaine use (Wagner & Anthony, 2002). The risk of addiction is significantly higher for smoking cocaine or IV use than intranasal use (Hatsukami & Fischman, 1996).

For many years, there was some question whether tolerance occurred with cocaine use. There is now considerable evidence that tolerance does develop to many of the physiological and subjective rewarding effects of cocaine, and in some cases it develops very rapidly (Fischman et al., 1985; Mendelson et al., 1998; Wood & Emmett-Oglesby, 1986). Some acute tolerance to cocaine's effects may be due to the activation of negative-feedback systems, that is, autoreceptor activation, which reduces monoamine neurotransmitter release, whereas long-term tolerance with chronic cocaine exposure may be related to the depletion of monoamines and/or down-regulation of monoamine receptors (with implications for dependence, which will be discussed shortly; Volkow et al., 1990). Evidence suggests that cocaine exposure modifies subsequent responsiveness to the drug through a complicated intracellular cascade—culminating in gene expression—via what is called the transcription factor CREB (adenosine 3', 5'-monophosphate response element binding protein) in the nucleus accumbens. It has been suggested that overexpression of CREB in this region decreases the rewarding effects of cocaine and makes low doses of the drug aversive (Carlezon et al., 1998), which may be the result of a diminished release of DA in the nucleus accumbens. In cases in which cocaine disrupts task performance, lowers reinforcement availability, or increases exposure to aversive stimuli (punishment), the learning of compensatory behaviors (e.g., instrumental conditioning) has long been viewed as a mechanism for tolerance development.

It has also been recognized that, as is the case with amphetamine, exposure to cocaine can induce sensitization to many of cocaine's effects in animals, most notably its locomotor and stereotypy-inducing effects (Stripling & Ellinwood, 1977). A similar phenomenon has been observed in humans, in which sensitization to the psychosis-mimicking properties of cocaine appears to occur in a substantial percentage of heavy cocaine users (Bartlett et al., 1997; Brady et al., 1991; Satel et al., 1991). Thus, with repeated use of cocaine in humans, the rewarding effects often diminish and are overshadowed by unpleasant side effects such as anxiety, irritability, and delusional paranoia. Interestingly, despite these effects, the individuals continue to use cocaine.

Whether tolerance or sensitization occurs with chronic cocaine use appears to depend on complex interactions among dose, the behavior involved, the pattern of use, and the species, as well as other as yet unknown factors (Grabowski & Dworkin, 1985). For example, in animals exposed continuously to cocaine for several days (i.e., by way of a small pump implanted under the skin), tolerance to the behavioral effects may occur. In contrast, in animals exposed intermittently to the same total daily amount of cocaine for the same number of days (i.e., one subcutaneous injection per day), sensitization to the behavioral effects may occur (King et al., 1994; Martin-Iverson & Burger, 1995). Along with these behavior phenomena, a puzzling array of alterations in DA receptors, as well as other receptors (e.g., opioidergic, glutamatergic) that regulate dopaminergic functions, have been reported to occur with different cocaine administration regimens (Fitzgerald et al., 1996; Maisonneuve & Kreek, 1994; Unterwald et al., 1994a, 1994b). Perhaps this should not be surprising, because the neurons affected by cocaine, which has potent but short-duration actions, are literally getting mixed messages—at certain points during the day there is dopaminergic overactivity, and at other points there is dopaminergic underactivity.

The relevance of these findings to humans is unclear, as human cocaine abusers commonly combine these patterns by binging (administering cocaine every 10 to 30 minutes for several hours or even days) and then abstaining for one or more days before binging again. It is this pattern of use that often leads to the development of symptoms of paranoid psychosis in the user (Gawin, 1993). In humans, panic attacks and seizures may also develop with chronic cocaine use. However, in human laboratory research, in which the doses of cocaine are much lower and the length of exposure is much shorter than those typically reported by street abusers, acute tolerance to the subjective and cardiovascular effects is commonly observed (Ambre, 1993; Foltin & Fischman, 1991; Foltin et al., 1995). Similarly, when low doses of cocaine are used to maintain self-administration in rats, tolerance to its reinforcing effects has been shown to develop with chronic exposure to cocaine, whether cocaine was given contingently (i.e., self-administered by the rats) or noncontingently (i.e., infused by the experimenter; Emmett-Oglesby et al., 1993).

In most instances, research with animals indicates that cocaine-induced sensitization is context-specific and typically involves intermittent high dose exposure (either experimenter administered or self-administered), that is, conditions under which the organism can develop an expectancy of drug effects. However, with sufficiently high doses of cocaine, a context-independent sensitization effect can also occur (Post et al., 1987). Sensitization also is long-lasting; that is, it can be evidenced weeks or months after the last cocaine exposure. These phenomena suggest that sensitization (as is the case with many other drugs of abuse that dramatically increase dopaminergic activity in the brain) is due to associative processes (e.g., Pavlovian conditioning) and neuroadaptations in the CNS, perhaps coupled with cocaine-induced brain damage. These in turn may lead to excessive craving for cocaine as well as the reduced ability to consciously recognize the negative consequences of its use to the cocaine user. One popular hypothesis is that repeated use of cocaine sensitizes the person to the "wanting" or "desire" for cocaine, even though it may induce tolerance to the "liking" or "pleasure" induced by cocaine (Robinson & Berridge, 2003).

Thus, many investigators are pursuing the mechanisms through which these processes occur. For example, research has assessed the changes in functional activity (the rate of glucose utilization) in various areas of the brain receiving dopaminergic inputs, which take place with successive exposures to cocaine. In monkeys trained to self-administer cocaine intravenously, it was determined that during the first few days of cocaine exposure there was decreased glucose utilization in ventral subcortical regions, a limbic area that mediates motivational and affective functions; this effect was observed only in very restricted portions of dorsal subcortical regions encompassing the shell of the nucleus accumbens. However, with chronic cocaine self-administration, the effects of cocaine intensified and spread dorsally to include most domains involved in cognitive, sensory, and motor processes (Porrino et al., 2004). Other research with mice has indicated that repeated exposure to cocaine may contribute to persistent neuroadaptations in the brain by altering the expression of genes mediated by the DA D_1 and D_3 receptors, which have been shown to be involved in the rewarding and lo-comotion-enhancing effects of psychostimulants (Zhang et al., 2004). The alterations in gene expression, and the resulting changes in the brain that take time to develop, could account for why cocaine seeking induced by exposure to cocaine-associated cues in the rat relapse model progressively increases and then gradually subsides after withdrawal. This progressive increase has been associated with increases in levels of brain-derived nerve growth factor (a growth factor involved in synaptic plasticity and in cellular events thought to underlie learning and memory processes such as long-term potentiation) within the mesolimbic DA system (Grimm et al., 2003; Lu et al., 2004).

Several lines of evidence also suggest that cocaine-induced orbitofrontal cortex (OFC) damage can contribute to compulsive drug seeking and drug taking in cocaine users (Volkow & Fowler, 2000). Damage to the OFC results in impulsivity and persever-ation, and neuropsychological studies indicate that cocaine users exhibit deficits in ex-ecutive cognitive functions ascribed to this area, including decision making and response inhibition (Bolla et al., 2003). Studies with rats suggest that neuronal damage in the OFC may modulate the propensity for cocaine seeking in a subregion-specific manner (Fuchs et al., 2004). The rats were initially reinforced to lever press for IV infu-sions of cocaine; then their lever pressing was extinguished when cocaine infusions were no longer delivered upon lever pressing. The investigators determined that le-sions in some areas of the rats' OFC augmented cocaine-primed reinstatement of lever pressing in a perseverative manner. In contrast, lesions in other areas of the OFC atten-uated cocaine-primed reinstatement.

Evidence also suggests that repetitive administration of subconvulsive doses of cocaine can decrease the organism's seizure threshold (Kaminski et al., 2003), a phe-nomenon known as pharmacological *kindling,* which may be due to its pharmacological properties that produce its local anesthetic actions. Local anesthetics such as lidocaine (a local anesthetic with minimal euphoric properties), when administered repetitively in high doses, produce an alteration in the threshold for seizures such that previously subconvulsive doses become capable of eliciting major motor seizures. (This phenome-non appears to be similar to that of electrophysiological kindling, in which repeated electrical stimulation below the convulsive threshold eventually provokes full-blown seizures.) However, studies with animals have shown that, in contrast to seizures kin-dled by lidocaine, which are generally well tolerated for weeks or months of repetitions, cocaine-induced seizures are extremely lethal. The hypothesis that links electrical kin-dling in the limbic system (leading to seizures) to sensitivity to cocaine's effects was a factor in the use of anticonvulsant drugs in the treatment of cocaine dependence (dis-cussed shortly). It has also been suggested that the anticonvulsant effects of neuroactive steroids may be useful in reducing cocaine-induced seizures, particularly in light of the fact that this class of compounds may have therapeutic potential in reducing tolerance and withdrawal associated with cocaine use (Kaminski et al., 2003).

As I indicated earlier, withdrawal-like effects do occur after extensive cocaine use. Furthermore, anecdotal reports from cocaine-dependent persons suggest that with-drawal involves several phases, with mixtures of different dependence-inducing processes being implicated (Gawin, 1993). During the first few hours after a binge (which generally ceases only when all the cocaine is gone), the user feels depressed and agitated, lacks appetite, and experiences high cocaine craving. In the next several hours or days, the user experiences extreme hunger, although cocaine craving is absent. In some individuals there is also a strong abhorrence for cocaine during this time period, and the need for sleep is overwhelming. During the next several days, the user's sleep patterns and mood return to normal, and there is little cocaine craving. However, subsequently the user experiences anxiety, a lack of energy, an inability to enjoy normal activities, and high cocaine craving that is exacerbated by environmental cues previously associated with cocaine use. After several weeks, the user's mood and pleasure response return to normal, and he or she experiences only episodic cocaine craving, which again is most common in the presence of specific environments. If the person begins taking cocaine again at any point, he or she generally returns to the first phase.

In contrast to this phasic model of cocaine withdrawal, other studies conducted with cocaine-dependent persons undergoing abstinence in both outpatient and inpatient settings over 3- or 4-week periods have reported mild symptoms of cocaine craving, anxiety, depression, physical discomfort, and drug withdrawal, which decreased in a linear fashion over the course of the studies (Coffey et al., 2000; Satel et al., 1991a; Weddington et al., 1990). Thus, it is unclear under what conditions, if any, the phasic model of cocaine withdrawal is applicable to the majority of cocaine-dependent persons.

Differential time-related changes in brain glucose metabolism in frontal cortex regions and other regions have been observed in cocaine abusers undergoing cocaine withdrawal: increases in activity occurring within 1 week, normal levels occurring at 2 to 4 weeks, and subsequent decreases persisting for 3 to 4 months after detoxification (Volkow et al., 1991, 1993). Furthermore, the greatest cocaine craving occurred during the period in which the glucose metabolism activity was highest.

In addition, there is abundant evidence that pharmacologically induced biochemical disruptions, particularly central DA neuronal systems, play a role in the cocaine-induced abstinence syndrome. One model proposes that chronic cocaine exposure leads to a depletion of intraneuronal DA (Dackis & Gold, 1985; Maisonneuve et al., 1995). That is, it is assumed that acute exposure to cocaine inhibits DA reuptake and abruptly elevates extraneuronal DA levels. This increase is followed by a rapid return to normal DA levels, due presumably to the activation of a negative-feedback system, such as DA autoreceptor activation, which in turn leads the user to administer more cocaine. With continued cocaine exposure there is a depletion of intraneuronal DA stores, either because of reduced synthesis via autoreceptor activity or because of enhanced catabolization via COMT (extraneuronally) or MAO (intraneuronally). In addition, studies utilizing PET scan techniques indicate that chronic cocaine exposure can decrease postsynaptic DA receptor availability (i.e., down-regulation), presumably due to the excessive and chronic DA exposure (Volkow et al., 1991, 1993). Chronic self-administration of cocaine in monkeys has also been found to increase (up-regulate) DA transporters in several areas of the brain, including the nucleus accumbens, which would lead to enhanced reuptake of extracellular DA (Letchworth et al., 2001). All of these processes would result in decreased dopaminergic activity with chronic cocaine use and contribute to cocaine dependence.

Whether or not the discomfort following extensive cocaine use is due to an actual physiological abstinence syndrome, it probably plays a minimal role in motivating drug-seeking in users. In most cases withdrawal symptoms are maximal 1–2 days after cessation of drug use, whereas the susceptibility to relapse may continue to grow for weeks or months (Robinson & Berridge, 2003). However, the intensity and persistence of cocaine craving following cocaine exposure are major factors behind its abuse and relapse, with higher levels of cocaine craving being reported by cocaine-dependent persons when they are experiencing negative mood states (Robbins et al., 2000). Cocaine craving and other types of Pavlovian conditioned responses have been shown to be triggered by environmental stimuli or by internal mood states associated with the drug experience (Ehrman et al., 1992; Jaffe et al., 1989). Cue-induced craving in humans has been found to be associated with increases in activity (based on cerebral blood flow) in areas of the limbic system (amygdala and anterior cingulate cortex) and decreases in the basal ganglia (Childress et al., 1999). Interestingly, both pleasant (e.g., "high," "aroused") and unpleasant (e.g., "craving," "withdrawal," "negative mood") conditioned responses can be elicited in cocaine-dependent persons (Robbins et al., 2000). Cocaine craving can also be initiated in cocaine abusers by the administration of small doses of cocaine or similar-acting drugs, a phenomenon called *priming* (Spealman et al., 1999). Research with animals indicates that these priming effects can be mimicked by activation of the ventral tegmental area dopaminergic system (Stewart, 1984).

Any aspect of a drug that may increase its likelihood of being used on subsequent occasions may be a factor in its being a positive reinforcer and being abused (Stolerman & Jarvis, 1995). Cocaine has a reputation of enhancing a person's subjective self-worth, competence, and performance, and we would expect this to be a factor in the maintenance of cocaine drug use. Cocaine has been shown to enhance the performance of sleep-deprived individuals, but evidence that cocaine can enhance the learning or performance of nonfatigued individuals is weak (Johnson et al., 1998). Animal studies have shown that low doses of cocaine can enhance certain aspects of performance, such as accuracy and reaction time, in some tasks—even when the animals are not fatigued (Grilly et al., 1989; Grilly & Grogan, 1990).

Adverse Consequences of Cocaine Use

Many of the problems attributed to cocaine, such as lower productivity, financial losses, family disruptions, legal difficulties, and so on, are indirectly related to its use. These problems come about because of the user's preoccupation with the drug or the U.S. legal system's views on its possession and use. However, unlike opiates, where most of the problems with their use are due to these factors rather than to direct effects on the body, cocaine also has several potential direct adverse consequences. As noted previously, the adverse effects of heavy amphetamine use—for example, psychosis, profound irritability, misperception, paranoid thought, impaired interpersonal relations, and eating and sleeping disturbances—have also been well-documented to occur with heavy cocaine use (Post & Contel, 1983). Cocaine has also been shown to precipitate panic attacks, which may subsequently recur without further cocaine use (Aronson & Craig, 1986).

Cocaine can produce a variety of neurological problems, including seizures, headaches, and transient symptoms such as sensory loss on one side of the body, visual impairment, and tremor (Rowbotham & Lowenstein, 1990). Other than seizure activity, which is dose related, there does not appear to be a correlation between these neurological problems and the dose, route of administration, or prior cocaine use patterns. Although neurocognitive impairments may precede cocaine use (and may be a factor in its initial use), there is considerable support for the conclusion that subgroups of cocaine-abusing patients may demonstrate sustained and persistent neurocognitive deficits that are consequences of their cocaine use (Bolla et al., 2003; Volkow & Fowler, 2000).

Whereas news reports in the 1980s, such as those discussing the deaths of well-known athletes like Maryland basketball player Len Bias and Cleveland Browns football player Don Rogers, tended to emphasize cocaine's potential lethality, it is not clear how many deaths are directly due to cocaine overdoses. Statistics regarding fatalities attributable to cocaine use are not particularly reliable, but it does appear that only about one-quarter of the deaths are actually due directly to the recreational use of cocaine. The majority of cocaine-associated deaths can be attributed to suicide induced by or facilitated by cocaine; accidental overdoses (e.g., the person swallowed cocaine for smuggling purposes or to elude detection when arrested); homicides; death from natural causes; or the combining of cocaine with other drugs (primarily opiates; Finkle & McCloskey, 1977; Lichtenfeld et al., 1984). For most individuals, the lethal dose of cocaine—approximately 1 to 2 grams in an hour—would be quite expensive. Cocaine use may cause sudden death because of cerebral hemorrhaging (bleeding within the brain; Lichtenfeld et al., 1984), convulsion induction (Ellinwood et al., 1977), lethal cardiac arrhythmias (Chakko & Myerberg, 1995), or acute myocardial infarction (sudden insufficiency of blood to the heart muscles)—even in individuals with no preexisting arterial dysfunctions (Isner & Chokshi, 1991). The mechanism behind sudden deaths is still obscure, but evidence suggests that even low doses of cocaine can lead to inflammation of the muscular walls of the heart in certain individuals. Also, contrary to what is commonly believed, intranasal cocaine can lead to sudden death (Finkle & McCloskey, 1977).

As noted in Chapter 3, most psychoactive substances are likely to be teratogenic. Considering cocaine's lipid solubility, there is no reason to believe that cocaine is an exception. Although only a small fraction of babies exposed to cocaine in the womb develop medical problems, since 1985, a number of studies, with both humans and nonhumans, have documented the potential teratogenic effects of cocaine (Slutsker, 1992). In humans, cocaine abuse has been associated with an increased stillbirth rate and premature delivery. Physically, cocaine-exposed neonates exhibit lower average birth weights, body lengths, and head circumferences. There is also evidence that such infants exhibit retarded brain growth and skull defects. Behaviorally, these infants exhibit more jitteriness and irritability and appear less attentive than infants not exposed to cocaine. After birth, there is evidence that cocaine-exposed neonates are more prone to sudden unexplained infant death syndrome. Many of these effects are likely to be the result of impaired fetal oxygenation caused by cocaine's tendency to constrict blood vessels. Cocaine also produces a number of biochemical disruptions that may be responsible for many of its observed neurobehavioral effects. For example, recent studies with animals suggest that in utero exposure to cocaine can produce dysfunction of DA D_1 receptor signaling and induce abnormal dendritic growth patterns of some cerebral cortical neurons (Jones et al., 2000).

Unfortunately, the true extent of the severity and incidence of the harmful effects of prenatal cocaine exposure in humans is simply not known, because of a number of methodological problems in the studies addressing this issue. Among many problems, for example, the women in these studies (1) are more likely to be poor and undereducated (factors that, for a variety of reasons, can be detrimental to pre- and postnatal development); (2) may differ considerably in the amount, frequency, and time of cocaine use; (3) commonly use other drugs, such as alcohol (by itself a potent teratogen), nicotine, marijuana, and heroin, that may also compromise prenatal development; (4) may under- or overreport their drug use; and (5) may practice other poor health behaviors, such as inadequate nutrition and pre- and postnatal care (Gonzalez & Campbell, 1994; Griffith et al., 1994).

Recent analyses of a large number of studies suggest that the effects of prenatal cocaine exposure on language and cognitive functioning of children are more subtle than previously assumed (e.g., an average decrease of 3.26 IQ points; Lester et al., 1998). However, these effects can have profound consequences for the success of these children in school and for the cost of special education services. For example, a downward shift in the IQ distribution of 3.26 IQ points would result in a 1.5-fold increase in the number of children typically requiring early intervention and special education services (often defined by a child exhibiting IQ scores less than 70, or in some cases less than 78). If the estimates of 375,000 cocaine-exposed children being born each year are correct, the additional number of children necessitating special education services would range from around 1,700 to 38,000, and the additional monetary costs would range from $4 million to $80 million per year. Because the mothers' cocaine use often occurs in the context of poverty and other known risks to children, including tobacco, alcohol, and other drug use, these children's prenatal exposure to cocaine compounds their problems. A longitudinal, prospective study assessing long-term cognitive effects of prenatal cocaine exposure in preschool children detected even smaller full-scale IQ deficits (approximately 2 IQ points) along with small but significant deficits on several subscales (Singer et al., 2004). A notable finding from this study was that those cocaine-exposed children who were raised in homes with more stimulating environments and caregivers with better vocabulary scores attained full-scale and performance IQ scores that were essentially the same as those of the noncocaine-exposed children in the study. This suggests that exposure to a better home environment can significantly ameliorate cognitive deficits associated with prenatal cocaine exposure.

TREATMENT OF COCAINE AND AMPHETAMINE ABUSE

The important factor in drug dependence is the dynamics among the individual's environment, genetic predispositions, behavior, and drug exposure—not the drug. The key to treatment is getting compulsive drug users to acknowledge that they are out of control and should do whatever they need to, to get well; thus, social, behavioral, and cognitive treatments for psychostimulant abuse are often the same as those described earlier for alcohol abuse. Furthermore, a large number of psychostimulant abusers also meet the diagnostic criteria for alcohol dependence (Gossop et al., 2000; Higgins et al., 1994a). Because most of the recent research on treatment for psychostimulant dependence has focused on cocaine, I will focus my comments on this drug, but with few exceptions, they can be applied equally to amphetamines as well.

Getting the cocaine addict to quit taking cocaine is not the major problem in treatment; it is preventing relapse—often triggered by intense cravings for cocaine—that appears most difficult. Rehabilitation by way of self-help groups, behavioral modification procedures (e.g., vouchers given for cocaine-free urine samples), involvement of significant others in the treatment, helping the patient learn to cope with everyday problems and stress, and extinction of cue-triggered cravings result in significant improvement in the majority of cocaine abusers (Flynn et al., 2003; Gossop et al., 2000; Higgins et al., 1994b, 1994c; O'Brien et al., 1993; Simpson et al., 1999; Weiss et al., 2003). These improvements consist of not only reductions in the use of cocaine and other psychostimulants (on the order of 70% to 80% reductions in amounts used), but also sizeable reductions in other drug use (alcohol, opiates, benzodiazepines), acquisitive crimes and selling drugs, drug injecting and sharing of needles, and physical and psychological health problems.

Unfortunately, even after extensive psychological and social treatment for their dependence, for example, long-term treatment ($\geq$90 days) in 24-hour residential programs, a substantial percentage of cocaine-dependent persons (15–30% depending on treatment modality and level of the patients' psychosocial problems at intake) revert to cocaine use or reenter within a year following treatment (Simpson et al., 1999). Thus, adjunctive treatments, typically involving pharmacotherapy, have been actively sought to facilitate the therapeutic process. In contrast to sedative–hypnotic or narcotic dependence, there are some differences in the chemical interventions potentially used in the treatment of dependence on cocaine and other psychostimulants. In the case of the psychostimulants, physical withdrawal is neither life-threatening nor exceedingly uncomfortable (Satel et al., 1991a; Weddington et al., 1990); thus, drugs to facilitate detoxification are unnecessary. With respect to cocaine dependence, the primary strategies have involved (1) preventing cocaine's entry into the brain; (2) blocking cocaine's access to its binding/activity sites; (3) eliminating cocaine's reinforcing actions by blocking DA receptors in the brain; (4) replacing cocaine with a drug with similar but less destructive properties; (5) reducing glutamatergic input into limbic areas that presumably trigger craving; and (6) reducing comorbid conditions that may contribute to relapse.

During the past decade, vaccines have been developed that induce drug-specific antibodies in the bloodstream that bind to the drug of abuse and prevent its entry into the brain. These could potentially offer long-term protection against drug use as well as drug overdose and neurotoxicity with minimal treatment compliance (Kantak, 2003). The majority of work in this area has been with drug-specific antibodies for cocaine and nicotine, and clinical trials with vaccines for these drugs are presently being conducted to determine their efficacy and safety. However, there are several drawbacks that need to be considered with this approach. These include a lack of protection against structurally dissimilar drugs that the drug user could use to produce the same effects as the original drug of abuse, a lack of an effect on drug craving that predisposes addicts to relapse, and tremendous individual variability in antibody formation. Also, forced or coerced vaccination involves serious legal and ethical issues. Thus, vaccination against cocaine abuse is likely to work best with individuals who are highly motivated to quit using drugs altogether and as part of a comprehensive treatment program. A related strategy would be to develop a way of preventing the drug from crossing the BBB. Unfortunately, cocaine, as is the case with virtually all drugs of abuse, crosses the BBB via passive diffusion; all that is required is sufficient lipid solubility, and the drug can diffuse out of the bloodstream across the BBB and into the brain.

Because the DA transporter plays a role in the reinforcing effects of cocaine, drugs that prevent cocaine from binding to DA transporters, thus preventing its effects, have been developed and tested for efficacy in the treatment of cocaine dependence. Several classes of DA uptake inhibitors, with an emphasis on those that enhance potency and selectivity at transporters for DA relative to those for 5-HT or NE, have been explored (Dutta et al., 2003). Unfortunately, none of the compounds developed has sufficient specificity as a cocaine antagonist (at the level of the DA transporter) to be useful as a deterrent to relapse to cocaine use or as a detoxifying agent in treating cocaine overdose. For example, mazindol, which inhibits the binding of cocaine to DA transporters and does not appear to be addictive or to produce euphoria, has not been found to be more effective than placebos in treating cocaine dependence (Mendelson & Mello, 1996).

Another way that has been proposed for reducing or eliminating the reinforcing effects of cocaine and other stimulants would be to block DA receptors. However, as noted in Chapter 6, several studies in humans have reported that DA antagonists did not blunt the subjective euphoria or drug taking produced by stimulant drugs in humans (Brauer & De Wit, 1997; Gawin, 1986; Haney et al., 2001; Nann-Vernotica et al., 2001; Wachtel et al., 2002). Furthermore, as will be discussed in Chapter 8, DA antagonists induce a number of undesirable side effects that make them unlikely to be acceptable to most cocaine addicts for treatment. Not surprisingly, studies assessing their efficacy in the treatment of cocaine dependence have found them to be ineffective or to worsen cocaine treatment outcome (Grabowski et al., 2004; Kampman et al., 2003).

The opposite approach, that is, the use of DA receptor agonists that could serve as a cocaine substitute with more benign qualities, has been attempted. The basic premise of this approach is that following extensive cocaine or amphetamine use, the individual experiences intense drug craving and symptoms such as depression, fatigue, irritability, anorexia, and sleep disturbances due to decreased DA concentrations in the brain. Thus, pharmacological treatment that enhances DA receptor activity could theoretically reduce these symptoms and relapse. Several drugs with known or suspected dopaminergic augmenting properties that do not have euphoric or abuse properties have been evaluated for efficacy in cocaine-dependence treatment, for example, amantadine (Symmetrel), bromocriptine (Parlodel), and pergolide (Permax). However, in a review of these studies, it was concluded that, in terms of efficacy (positive urine sample for cocaine metabolites) and acceptability by the subjects (retention in treatment), the evidence does not support the clinical use of these drugs in the treatment of cocaine dependence (Soares et al., 2003). Placebo-controlled studies have also failed to find benefits of treatment with the DA precursors tyrosine or L-DOPA (for L-dihydroxyphenylalanine; Chadwick et al., 1990; Wolfsohn et al., 1993). Bupropion (Wellbutrin), an antidepressant that weakly facilitates dopaminergic function, has also not been found to be more effective than placebos in treating cocaine dependence (Mendelson & Mello, 1996).

A related strategy has been to use long-acting indirect DA agonists that induce subjective effects similar to cocaine, for example, d-amphetamine and methylphenidate, to reduce cocaine craving and use. A few studies have found some benefits for this approach. For example, in a placebo-controlled clinical trial of d-amphetamine replacement therapy in cocaine-dependent injecting drug users, it was determined that although retention in treatment was equivalent for the d-amphetamine and placebo groups, the outcomes favored the treatment group with no improvements observed in the placebo control group. The proportion of cocaine-positive urine samples decreased 40% in the treatment group compared to no change in the placebo group, and there was significantly reduced self-reported cocaine use, criminal activity, cravings and severity of cocaine dependence in the treatment group compared with no improvements found in the placebo group (Shearer et al., 2003). Similar benefits have been found utilizing sustained release d-amphetamine in cocaine-dependent persons (Grabowski et al., 2001) or sustained release d-amphetamine plus methadone in persons who were dependent on both cocaine and heroin (Grabowski et al., 2004). Studies utilizing methylphenidate in the treatment of cocaine dependence have also reported some favorable results (Dutta et al., 2003; Somoza et al., 2004). Theoretically, these drugs could work as adjuncts to reducing cocaine dependence because they do possess many of the qualities that are required for drug substitution to be effective. Taken orally they enter the brain slowly, they exhibit a long duration of action, they produce some of the subjective effects of cocaine that should reduce cocaine craving, and at lower dosages they exhibit minimal side effects. The basic problem with this strategy is that both *d*-amphetamine and methylphenidate have moderate to strong potential for abuse and dependence themselves; thus there is considerable concern that cocaine-dependent individuals would simply shift their addiction to these drugs.

Several lines of research with animals have indicated that glutamatergic mechanisms underlie several clinical aspects of cocaine dependence, including euphoria, withdrawal, craving, and hedonic dysfunction. Thus, medications with actions on the receptors for GLU have been explored for efficacy in reducing cocaine craving (Dackis & O'Brien, 2003). Because cue-induced cocaine craving is associated with increased metabolic activity in GLU-rich brain regions, and cocaine-paired cues release GLU in the nucleus accumbens in animal studies, several investigators have suggested that antagonists at GLU receptors might be effective in dampening cue-induced cocaine craving, a common factor in relapse. For example, memantine (Namenda), a noncompetitive NMDA (N-Methyl-D-aspartic acid) receptor antagonist, has been evaluated for its effects on cocaine self-administration, subjective effects, and psychomotor performance in frequent cocaine smokers. Participants were maintained on memantine or placebo for several days prior to smoking cocaine base. Memantine maintenance had no influence on cocaine's psychomotor performance effects; however, it was associated with significant increases in several measures of the subjective reinforcing effects of cocaine (Collins et al., 1998). On the other hand, preliminary research with modafinil (Provigil), a GLU-enhancing agent presently used in the treatment of narcolepsy, has shown some promise in the treatment of cocaine-addicted individuals. One of the primary problems with manipulations of the glutamatergic systems is that these are vital to so many normal neuronal functions, and it may not be possible to affect one system that may be involved in craving without disturbing others that are critical to other processes. Too much GLU activity can contribute to neurotoxicity and too little can interfere with processes such as learning and memory. A similar strategy has been attempted with isradipine, a calcium channel antagonist that inhibits cocaine-mediated increases in mesolimbic DA, which might reduce cocaine's abuse liability (Johnson et al., 2004). However, tests with cocaine-dependent volunteers found that although isradipine lacked any stimulant or abuse liability effects or the propensity to elicit craving, it did not antagonize any of cocaine's stimulant-related effects associated with its abuse liability.

Another potential anticraving drug is the hallucinogen ibogaine (Endabuse; see Chapter 13), which has been proposed to possess broad-spectrum antiaddiction properties that may be useful in the treatment of dependence on many types of drugs (Mash et al., 1998). In animal studies, ibogaine has been shown to reduce a number of cocaine- and amphetamine-induced effects, including self-administration and locomotion effects—in some cases, for several days following ibogaine exposure—although these effects and their persistence may depend upon the dose, dose pattern, and species and sex of the animals (Popik et al., 1995). Multiple mechanisms of action have been proposed to account for ibogaine's effects, but two prominent actions that are likely to be relevant are its ability to block NMDA receptor–activated ion channels and its ability to block 5-HT reuptake sites and elevate extracellular 5-HT levels. Numerous lines of evidence suggest that these types of actions can interrupt drug-seeking behavior in animals. Clinical trials are presently being conducted in a number of centers around the world to test the safety and efficacy of ibogaine as a treatment for addiction. However, due to its notoriety and potential side effects, it is highly unlikely that ibogaine will ever be developed for use as an approved legal medication in the United States; thus, more recent work has focused on developing safer and more efficacious structural derivatives of ibogaine, for example, 18-Methoxycoronaridine, for treatment of addiction (Maisonneuve & Glick, 2003).

It is not uncommon to observe comorbidity between cocaine dependence and psychiatric disorders as well as abuse or dependence on other drugs. Although the order in which these disorders develop is often unclear, it is clear that comorbidity exacerbates the problems of the user as well as contributes to the likelihood of relapse into cocaine use. Because symptoms of depression commonly precede cocaine use and may be a factor in its initial use—and almost always follow chronic heavy use—the efficacy of antidepressants in the treatment of cocaine abuse has been investigated in numerous studies. A meta-analysis of these studies found that decrease in positive urine samples for cocaine metabolites was the main efficacy outcome, with no significant results obtained regardless of the type of antidepressant; however, desipramine, a tricyclic antidepressant with primarily NE reuptake-inhibiting properties, tended to have the greatest efficacy (Lima et al., 2003). The only significant outcome from a study utilizing the selective 5-HT reuptake inhibitor fluoxetine was that the higher the dose of fluoxetine, the more likely the subjects were to drop out of the study. The authors of this meta-analysis concluded that antidepressants do not provide much benefit in the majority of cocaine addicts.

Several double-blind, controlled clinical trials have also been conducted to determine the efficacy of antidepressant treatment in cocaine-dependent individuals diagnosed with a current unipolar depressive disorder. A meta-analysis of these studies determined that those studies showing moderately large effects in reducing depression demonstrated favorable effects of medication on measures of quantity of substance use, but rates of sustained abstinence were low (Nunes & Levin, 2004). The authors concluded that antidepressant medication exerts a modest beneficial effect for patients with combined depression and substance-use disorders, but that it is not a sufficient standalone treatment.

Mood stabilizers (drugs used in the treatment of bipolar affective disorders), such as lithium and carbamazepine, have been shown in most studies to be no more effective than placebos in providing benefits to cocaine addicts (Mendelson & Mello, 1996). Phenytoin and gabapentin, which are anticonvulsants primarily used in the treatment of epilepsy but are sometimes used in the treatment of bipolar disorder, have been shown to significantly lower cocaine use in cocaine-using subjects, as well as to reduce craving intensity (Crosby et al., 1996; Raby & Coomaraswamy, 2004). The efficacy of lamotrigine, an anticonvulsant that is commonly used in the treatment of epilepsy and bipolar disorders, has been investigated in patients diagnosed with bipolar disorder and cocaine dependence. Although lamotragine treatment was associated with statistically significant improvements in the subjects' mood and reductions in their drug cravings, there was no significant effect on their cocaine use (Brown et al., 2003). Thus, more research utilizing this class of drug for the treatment of cocaine dependence is warranted.

Concurrent use of other drugs can contribute to continued cocaine use in dependent individuals. For cocaine addicts concurrently dependent on opiates, treatment with the mixed opioid agonist/antagonist buprenorphine has been examined in several studies (Compton et al., 1995). However, clinical evidence of buprenorphine's effectiveness in treating cocaine abuse has not been clearly demonstrated. The dose of buprenorphine used may be a critical factor in the attenuation of cocaine effects, with higher doses being more effective than lower doses (Stine & Kosten, 1994).

Because cocaine addicts commonly use and abuse alcohol, the use of disulfiram (described in Chapter 10 for the treatment of alcoholism) for the treatment of cocaine dependence has been suggested. The basic premise of this approach is that by eliminating alcohol usage, the tendency for alcohol to prime cocaine craving would be removed, and there should be a reduction in alcohol-induced impaired judgment that can contribute to increased cocaine usage. To test this hypothesis, a randomized placebo-controlled trial exploring the efficacy of disulfiram combined with cognitive behavior therapy (CBT) or interpersonal therapy (IPT) in cocaine-dependent outpatients was conducted (Carroll et al., 2004). The results indicated that subjects taking disulfiram exhibited significantly greater reductions in their cocaine intake than the placebo group. It was also found that CBT was superior to IPT in reducing cocaine intake, but that the combination of disulfiram and CBT did not offer significant improvement in cocaine abstinence when compared with one of the treatments alone. Patients who were not alcohol dependent actually did better in terms of abstinence from cocaine than those who were alcohol dependent, apparently because those who were alcohol dependent tended to stop the disulfiram and went on to abuse alcohol and cocaine at greater rates than those who were not alcohol dependent. Interestingly, disulfiram appeared to exert a direct effect on cocaine usage as opposed to reducing alcohol craving in individuals with both cocaine and alcohol dependence, which suggests that it might also be useful in nonalcohol-using cocaine addicts (although these are very rare).

Thus far, all studies of medications used to help prevent relapse to cocaine dependence have revealed modest benefits at best. One of the basic problems with drugs used in the treatment for dependence on cocaine, or any other drug, is their lack of long-term effects. That is, even with the longest acting drugs, the effects last only a few days. Thus, if the addict stops taking them, perhaps with the desire to reexperience the effects of cocaine, their efficacy is lost. This may have been a factor in a study finding that fluoxetine was not effective in reducing cocaine use in cocaine-dependent subjects (Grabowski et al., 1995). The main outcome in the study was that fluoxetine treatment dose-dependently increased the dropout rate of the subjects over the 12-week study phase. One interpretation of this result is that the subjects (most of whom apparently continued to use cocaine) found the effects of cocaine unfulfilling and dropped out of the study so that they could reexperience the pleasurable effects of the drug.

Many of the approaches described earlier may also be employed in the treatment of dependence on other psychostimulants with properties similar to cocaine, but the same problems described are likely going to apply to these as well.

MODAFINIL

Narcolepsy is a disabling neurological disorder characterized by excessive daytime sleepiness, which is similar to the feeling experienced by normal people when they are sleep deprived. Individuals with this disorder often experience uncontrollable "sleep attacks" in which there is a sudden episode of muscle weakness. In severe episodes, the person may become temporarily paralyzed and fall down. Attacks generally last a few seconds, but they may last for several minutes. The individual is usually awake at the start of the attack and may remain conscious and alert throughout the episode. However, in longer attacks, the individual may fall into rapid eye movement (REM) sleep and experience vivid hallucinations (auditory, visual, and tactile). After the episode, the individual typically regains full muscle strength, although in some cases the paralysis may continue for a short time after awakening.

As a lifelong disorder, narcolepsy requires long-term management of symptoms, which may involve nonpharmacological interventions such as lifestyle changes, and often requires drug treatment (Fry, 1998). For years, the psychostimulants such as the amphetamines, pemoline, and methylphenidate have been used in the treatment of narcolepsy to increase wakefulness, vigilance, and performance. However, these stimulants are associated with dependence liability, sympathomimetic side effects, limitations in efficacy, and negative effects on nighttime sleep. Modafinil (Provigil), a new wake-promoting agent, has been approved by the FDA for the treatment of narcolepsy. Several double-blind, placebo-controlled trials have shown modafinil to be effective in reducing daytime sleepiness in patients with narcolepsy (U.S. Modafinil, 2000). Patients receiving modafinil report significant improvement in all subjective and objective measures of sleepiness. Modafinil appears to be well tolerated, with headache being the only adverse event typically reported, although the incidence may not be significantly greater than with placebo. Nighttime sleep does not appear to be adversely affected with modafinil treatment compared with placebo treatment. Its efficacy has been maintained for many weeks, with no evidence of tolerance development. During treatment discontinuation, patients who had been receiving modafinil experienced a return of their symptoms to baseline levels, but they did not experience symptoms associated with amphetamine withdrawal syndrome.

In a double-blind evaluation of the abuse potential of modafinil, the effects of modafinil were compared with methylphenidate in male volunteers with a history of polysubstance abuse that included the stimulant cocaine (Jasinski, 2000). The subjects discriminated both modafinil and methylphenidate from placebo and liked the effects of both drugs. However, modafinil differed from methylphenidate in its lack of a significant response on a scale commonly used to assess amphetamine-like effects of drugs. The profile of physiological effects for modafinil also differed from methylphenidate in that modafinil showed greater inhibition of observed and reported sleep, less facilitation of orthostatic tachycardia, and less reduction of caloric intake. These findings were consistent with previous data suggesting that modafinil is not an amphetamine-like agent. The data indicate that modafinil has an excellent safety profile.

Based on its efficacy in promoting wakefulness in narcoleptic patients, its relatively benign side effect profile and apparently low abuse liability, a number of investigators have explored modafinil's potential efficacy in a variety of other types of individuals and conditions. It has been found to effectively reduce many of the symptoms of attention deficit hyperactivity disorder in both adults and children (Rugino & Samsock, 2003; Turner et al., 2004). It reduces the sleepiness associated with a variety of psychiatric drugs, for example, antipsychotics and anticonvulsants (Berigan, 2004; Makela et al., 2003). It has been shown to increase wakefulness and enhance a variety of cognitive functions in both normal adults (Walsh et al., 2004; Wesensten et al., 2002) and children (Ivanenko et al., 2003) and patients with symptoms of mental disorders, for example, depression, schizophrenia, and chronic fatigue syndrome (DeBattista et al., 2004; Turkington et al., 2004; Turner et al., 2003, 2004).

However, despite these positive findings, several questions remain. Does modafinil cause unexpected toxic effects or exhibit greater abuse potential with extended use by a wider variety and number of individuals? Does modafinil have advantages over caffeine (which is more readily available and less expensive) in terms of improving performance and alertness in these same types of conditions? At least for normal, healthy adults, the answer to the second question appears to be "no." In a double-blind, placebo-controlled trial comparing modafinil with caffeine in sleep-deprived normal, healthy adults, it was determined that like caffeine, modafinil maintained performance and alertness during the early morning hours when the combined effects of sleep loss and the low points in the circadian rhythm for performance and alertness were most evident. Furthermore, there was no significant difference in their performance- and alertness-enhancing effects (Wesensten et al., 2002).

DRUG TREATMENT OF PARKINSON'S DISEASE

Parkinson's disease (PD) is a **neurodegenerative disorder** that afflicts approximately 1% of the population over 60 years old. In 90% of the cases, the symptoms develop after the age of 55 (the actor and PD patient advocate Michael J. Fox is an example of someone who developed PD at a relatively young age). The main symptoms are difficulty in initiating voluntary movements (*akinesia*), slowness of movement (*bradykinesia*), *resting tremor* (shaking movements in a body part that is not currently at rest), muscular *rigidity* (resistance to passive movement), and *postural instability*. A significant number of cases eventually develop an accompanying dementia (cognitive impairment). Furthermore, many patients with PD develop motivational symptoms such as anergia, apathy, or fatigue (Friedman et al., 2007), which is a self-reported lack of "energy" or motivation (e.g., patients say things like "my battery runs down").

Parkinson's disease belongs to a family of disorders generally known as *parkinsonism*. The classic disorder that most people generally think of when they hear of PD is technically referred to as *idiopathic Parkinson's disease* (idiopathic means "of unknown origin"). It has been well established that most of the core motor symptoms of idiopathic Parkinson's disease are due to the destruction of nigrostriatal DA neurons providing input to the caudate/putamen (or neostriatum; Hornykiewicz, 1973). The symptoms generally appear when approximately 80–90% of these neurons have been lost (Dakof & Mendelsohn, 1986). In most patients, the DA depletion is greatest in the putamen (which receives input from sensory and motor areas of neocortex), and a little less in the caudate; furthermore, there are smaller but significant depletions of DA in nucleus accumbens. As well as having a severe depletion of DA, most patients with PD have other types of neural pathologies (e.g., Lewy bodies, which are microscopic protein deposits, and depletions in other transmitters). In addition to idiopathic Parkinson's disease, there are other forms of parkinsonism. *Post-encephalitic* parkinsonism occurred in people who survived the encephalitis pandemic of 1918–1919 (this was popularized in the book by Oliver Sachs, and the resulting movie, *Awakenings*).

Pugilistic parkinsonism results from head injuries suffered as a result of boxing (though it is not absolutely certain, it is likely that boxing contributed to the disorder suffered by Mohammed Ali). *MPTP* parkinsonism results from people taking a toxic substance known as MPTP (1-Methyl-4-phenyl-1,2,3,6-tetrahydropyridine, which can be made during the synthesis of a designer drug; this substance is converted into the neurotoxic agent MPP^+ in the brain). Moreover, many people suffer from *drug-induced parkinsonism*. The most common source of this condition is the administration of DA antagonists to patients with psychoses (see Chapter 8). In addition, patients who receive anti-cholinesterase treatment for Alzheimer's disease also can develop drug-induced parkinsonism. It is worth emphasizing that in drug-induced parkinsonism, there is not a neural degeneration, but, rather, a pharmacological effect that impairs synaptic function and results in symptoms that resemble PD.

The causes underlying the neuropathologies seen in PD are unclear. For most people with PD, there is not a high degree of heritability for the disorder (Duvoisin, 1986; Plomin et al., 1994). However, this is not to say that there is no contribution of genetics. For example, there are familial cases of PD that have been identified in Italian and Greek extended families (Polymeropoulos et al., 1996), and mutations in six genes (SNCA, LRRK2, PRKN, DJ1, PINK1, and ATP13A2) have been identified as causes for familial parkinsonism (Bekris et al. 2010). Furthermore, polymorphisms of three genes (MAPT, LRRK2, and SNCA) have been identified as susceptibility factors for PD. Currently, researchers think that idiopathic Parkinson's disease in most cases is caused by a combination of genetic and environmental factors, history of infectious disease and head injury, and maturational processes (Wu et al. 2011); several studies are attempting to find biomarkers that could be used to predict the onset of parkinsonian symptoms (Schwarzschild et al., 2008; Wu et al. 2011). The discovery that MPTP consumption is capable of inducing both CNS lesions and symptoms that are almost indistinguishable from PD (Kopin & Markey, 1988) has focused attention on environmental pollutants with similar structures, such as industrial chemicals. Other environmental contributors can include insecticides (Lewin, 1985).

Almost immediately after the discovery of the association between DA deficiency and PD, attention turned to the use of L-DOPA as a treatment for the disorder (Hornykiewicz, 1973). As discussed in Chapter 5, L-DOPA is the immediate precursor of DA and, once it enters the brain, it is enzymatically converted into DA (administering DA itself is not of value because it cannot pass through the BBB, and is easily taken up by terminals or metabolized by enzymes). In approximately 80% of the patients, this treatment induces dramatic reductions in all motor symptoms of the disorder, though it does not treat the symptoms of dementia in some patients (Quinn, 1995).

L-DOPA was clearly the miracle drug of the 1960s and 1970s, and is still the gold standard of treatments for PD. Unfortunately, though, as its use became more and more widespread, more and more problems with its use emerged. Although the majority of patients respond well to L-DOPA initially, after about 3 to 5 years on L-DOPA therapy, the drug begins to lose its effectiveness. Sometimes, the responses of patients fluctuate abruptly between symptom control and no control; this pattern is often referred to as the *on–off phenomenon* because the control is switched on and off like a light. In addition, patients often develop distressing and incapacitating problems with chronic L-DOPA therapy, including abnormal involuntary movements known as dyskinesias (Salamone, 2010c). L-DOPA-treated patients may also exhibit psychiatric symptoms, such as hallucinations, paranoia, and mania, that are sometimes referred to as L-DOPA-induced psychosis (Quinn, 1995). A number of these symptoms (e.g., psychosis, abnormal movements) can be reduced with the atypical antipsychotic clozapine, which unlike conventional antipsychotics does not induce parkinsonian-like motor disturbances (Pfeiffer & Wagner, 1994). In any event, some clinicians have suggested that individuals who can function adequately in their occupations and social interactions should not be treated with L-DOPA until their condition begins to deteriorate (Quinn, 1995). Until this time, other drugs (discussed shortly) may be given so that the beneficial effects of L-DOPA may be saved until they are truly necessary.

L-DOPA's optimal effect comes from keeping concentrations of the drug within a therapeutic window that becomes increasingly narrow with time; thus, pharmacokinetic factors are critical for its efficacy (LeWitt, 1992). The most commonly used formulation of L-DOPA is Sinemet, a combination of L-DOPA and carbidopa, which prevents the peripheral conversion of L-DOPA to DA. This formulation produces more reliable brain concentrations, but even with multiple daily doses, plasma concentrations may increase too fast, producing motor disturbances and adverse psychic effects, or fall off too quickly, allowing the disease symptoms to appear suddenly. This problem has been reduced considerably by putting Sinemet in an erodible matrix (called Sinemet CR) that retards gastric tablet dissolution and allows plasma level concentrations to be maintained longer and more smoothly.

Because of the various problems associated with L-DOPA therapy, a number of investigators have explored the use of DA receptor agonists in the treatment of PD. Although this class of drugs has historically been used as adjuncts to L-DOPA, a growing body of evidence suggests that it may be preferable to use such drugs as first-line therapy for patients with early PD prior to L-DOPA to delay or reduce the risk of development of motor complications associated with L-DOPA (Lebrun-Frenay & Borg, 2002). Bromocriptine (Parlodel) and pergolide (Permax) have been used for the treatment of PD for many years, and two new DA receptor agonists, ropinirole (Requip) and pramipexole (Mirapex), have been approved by the FDA for use in PD. Bromocriptine and pergolide are agonists at both D_1 and D_2 family receptors. They appear to be equivalent to L-DOPA in therapeutic efficacy and may manage the on–off phenomenon more smoothly than L-DOPA and induce less dyskinesia (Standaert & Young, 2001). However, because they may cause profound hypertension, as well as nausea and fatigue, with initial administration, their dosages need to begin low with gradual increases over a period of weeks to months. They may also induce visual and auditory hallucinations, which is a potential problem with all DA-enhancing drugs. Ropinirole and pramipexole are long-acting selective D_2 family receptor agonists that induce less nausea, gastrointestinal problems, and fatigue than bromocriptine and pergolide and can reach therapeutic levels much more quickly (Standaert & Young, 2001). Studies employing ropinirole as monotherapy or with supplementation with L-DOPA have found it to be comparable to bromocriptine or L-DOPA as an initial therapy in newly diagnosed PD patients with a reduced or delayed risk of developing motor dyskinesias (Matheson & Spencer, 2000; Rascol et al., 2000). It has also been found to be effective in the management of more advanced parkinsonian patients who were experiencing motor complications after long-term L-DOPA treatment. Ropinirole may also be used to augment L-DOPA treatment, as it allows for a reduction in L-DOPA dosage with enhanced clinical benefit for parkinsonian patients with motor fluctuations. However, adverse effects, such as hallucinations, somnolence, and peripheral edema, may be more common with ropinirole. Pramipexole may have similar benefits in early PD patients, either as monotherapy or with L-DOPA added if necessary. In a 4-year randomized controlled trial comparing pramipexole with L-DOPA as initial treatment for PD, treatment with pramipexole resulted in lower incidences of dyskinesias and wearing off compared with L-DOPA, whereas treatment with L-DOPA resulted in lower incidences of freezing, somnolence, and edema and provided for better symptomatic control (Parkinson Study Group, 2004). Both options resulted in similar effects on the patients' quality of life. Thus, L-DOPA, ropinirole, and pramipexole all appear to be reasonable options as initial therapy for PD, but they are associated with different efficacy and adverse-effect profiles.

Over the past several years, a great deal of interest has been generated by selegiline (also called L-deprenyl and marketed as Eldepryl) in the treatment of PD in terms of not only reducing the disabling symptoms but perhaps altering the course of its development. Selegiline is a selective, irreversible inhibitor of MAO-B, which is an enzyme that inactivates DA. Inhibition of MAO-B should lead to a diminished metabolism of DA in the nigrostriatal system and significantly increase its concentration (Knoll, 1995). Selegiline also inhibits the reuptake of catecholamines and has other actions that facilitate catecholamine activity in the brain. However, it does not interact with tyramine to produce sympathomimetic effects, such as the hypertensive crises common to other MAOIs (MAO inhibitors). Selegiline has been shown to significantly postpone the need for L-DOPA and allows a significant saving in the patient's subsequent L-DOPA dosage (Myllyla et al., 1995). Randomized, placebo-controlled, double-blind, 5-year trials evaluating the possible advantages of combining selegiline and L-DOPA in the early treatment of PD have indicated that patients treated with the combination of selegiline and L-DOPA developed markedly less severe parkinsonism and required lower doses of L-DOPA during the 5-year study periods than patients treated with levodopa and placebo (Larsen et al., 1999; Przuntek et al., 1999).

Although one study has reported that selegiline augmentation of L-DOPA–carbidopa therapy may actually increase the mortality rate in PD patients, a meta-analysis of a number of studies employing MAO type B inhibitors in early PD indicated that there was no significant difference in mortality between patients treated with these drugs relative to nonexposed patients (Ives et al., 2004). It was also determined that compared with placebo subjects, these drugs significantly reduced patients' disability, their need for L-DOPA, and the incidence of motor fluctuations, without substantial side effects. It supported findings that early use of selegiline delays the need for L-DOPA and that when selegiline is given concomitantly with L-DOPA, lower dosages of L-DOPA are needed.

Unfortunately, as the neurodegeneration progresses, it reaches the point at which no drugs exert beneficial effects, or they exert side effects that cannot be tolerated. Thus, research has focused on ways of lessening the progression of PD using two primary strategies: inhibition of MAO-B with selegiline and the use of general antioxidant drugs, such as vitamin E (LeWitt, 1994). The reasoning behind this approach comes from the previously mentioned hypothesis concerning environmental toxins in the degeneration process, which might well be speeded up by the oxidation enzyme MAO or the presence of harmful oxidative molecules. For example, selegiline has been shown to protect nigrostriatal dopaminergic neurons against several selective neurotoxins, including MPTP (Knoll, 1995). Unfortunately, studies comparing the effectiveness of

L-DOPA–carbidopa treatment alone or combined with selegiline in patients with early, mild PD have failed to find neuroprotective effects of selegiline (Brannan & Yahr, 1995; Lees, 1995). Studies have also failed to show evidence of neuroprotection with vitamin E treatment (LeWitt, 1994).

Recently, the potential therapeutic use of COMT inhibitors in PD has been explored with some success (Kaakkola, 2000). As described in Chapter 5, COMT is another enzyme that can break down DA and other catecholamines. Although peripheral metabolism of L-DOPA can be blocked by carbidopa, it may still be metabolically inactivated by COMT. Thus, inhibiting the COMT activity should improve the bioavailability and decrease the elimination of L-DOPA and improve its efficacy. Entacapone (Comtan) and tolcapone are new potent, selective, and reversible COMT inhibitors that have been shown to enhance and extend the therapeutic effect of L-DOPA in patients with advanced and fluctuating PD. Clinical studies show that they increase the daily *on* time by an average of 1 to 3 hours, improve the activities of daily living, and allow daily L-DOPA dosage to be decreased. Correspondingly, they significantly reduce the daily *off* time. These COMT inhibitors may also be combined with other antiparkinsonian drugs, such as DA agonists, selegiline, and anticholinergics, without adverse interactions. The main adverse effects of the COMT inhibitors are related to their dopaminergic and gastrointestinal effects. Enhancement of dopaminergic activity may cause an initial worsening of L-DOPA–induced adverse effects, such as dyskinesia, nausea, vomiting, orthostatic hypotension, sleep disorders, and hallucinations, which may be avoided through L-DOPA dose adjustment. Diarrhea occurs in a minority of patients treated with tolcapone and entacapone, with a lower incidence occurring with entacapone. Unfortunately, tolcapone has been associated with acute, fatal hepatitis and potentially fatal neurological reactions such as malignant syndrome, and degeneration of skeletal muscle, which has led to the suspension of its marketing authorization in the European community and Canada. In many other countries, the use of tolcapone is restricted to patients who are not responding satisfactorily to other therapies, and regular monitoring of liver enzymes is required. Nevertheless, on the basis of entacapone's efficacy when combined with L-DOPA carbidopa, the combination of these three drugs (Stalevo) has been approved for use in PD.

In addition to the various dopaminergic approaches to the treatment of PD, there are several non-dopaminergic approaches. Some of these non-dopaminergic approaches represent attempts to control the deleterious side effects of L-DOPA, such as the dyskinesias (Salamone, 2010c). In addition, some of these alternative strategies are based upon research showing that DA interacts with other transmitters in the basal ganglia circuitry. Although we tend to view the depletion of DA as the immediate cause of parkinsonian symptoms, it is nevertheless true that reductions in DA transmission initiate a host of other biochemical changes that reverberate through the circuitry of the basal ganglia. For example, there is considerable evidence that caudate/putamen DA and ACh interact in the control of movement (Betz et al., 2009; Salamone et al., 2001). The first drug treatments ever used for the treatment of PD were in fact muscarinic antagonists (a natural preparation of scopolamine, known as hyoscine, was used for several years), and currently several muscarinic antagonists, including scopolamine, atropine, biperiden (Akeniton), orphenadrine (Norflex), trihexyphenidyl (Artane or Benzhexol), and benztropine (Cogentin) have been used (Katzenschlager, 2003; Quinn,

1995). Cogentin and Artane also are frequently used to treat the parkinsonism induced by antipsychotic drugs. There is some evidence from animal studies that blockade of the M4 subtype of muscarinic receptors may be particularly useful for suppressing the parkinsonian symptoms induced by DA antagonists (Betz et al., 2007, 2009; Salamone et al., 2001).

Another non-dopaminergic strategy for the treatment of drug-induced or idiopathic parkinsonism is adenosine A_{2A} antagonists. As discussed earlier, the caudate/putamen has a high concentration of adenosine A_{2A} receptors (Ferré et al., 2004), and biochemical studies have shown that there is a functional interaction between DA D_2 and adenosine A_{2A} receptors, which are co-localized on the same striatal neurons (Ferré et al., 2008; Fuxe et al., 2003). A_{2A} and D_2 receptors are capable of forming heteromeric complexes (a complex formed from two receptors linking together, which influences their function), and also converge onto the same c-AMP-related signal transduction pathways (Ferré et al., 2004, 2008; Fuxe et al., 2003). In animal models, adenosine A_{2A} receptor antagonists, such as istradefylline, KF 17837, SCH 58261, ANR 94, and MSX-3, have been shown to reverse attenuate the motor effects of DA D_2 antagonists, including the suppression of locomotion (Collins et al. 2010a; Correa et al., 2004; Ishiwari et al., 2007), and the induction of tremor (Betz et al., 2009; Correa et al., 2004; Salamone et al., 2008a, 2008b; Simola et al., 2004; Pinna et al., 2010). So far, istradefylline and preladenant are the drugs that have made it furthest through clinical trials (LeWitt et al., 2008; Salamone, 2010a). Adenosine A_{2A} antagonists may be useful for treating the parkinsonian side effects of antipsychotic drugs (Correa et al., 2004; Salamone et al., 2008a, 2008b).

For reasons unknown, epidemiological studies have repeatedly shown that PD occurs less frequently among chronic cigarette smokers than among nonsmokers (Yong & Perry, 1986); these results suggest that there may be a compound in tobacco smoke that somehow protects the individual. Animal studies have indicated that nicotine and other nicotinic receptor agonists can have neuroprotective actions in neurodegenerative processes (Mihailescu & Drucker-Colin, 2000). In addition, there is an unidentified ingredient in tobacco smoke that reduces the levels of MAO-B (the enzyme that breaks down DA) in the brains of smokers (Fowler et al., 1996). Theoretically, this should allow higher levels of DA to accumulate in the brain and, in turn, potentially compensate for the diminished dopaminergic functioning that leads to the symptoms of parkinsonism. On the other hand, this phenomenon may simply be due to the fact that smokers die sooner than nonsmokers, so that they don't live long enough to develop the neurological and behavioral manifestations of PD (Riggs, 1992). Coffee drinking may also be a protective factor in developing PD. Although early studies suggesting such a phenomenon were equivocal in their results, a 30-year prospective study has found a dramatic inverse relationship between coffee and caffeine exposure and the development of PD in Japanese American men (Ross et al., 2000). In fact, nondrinkers of coffee had a risk of PD more than five times that of men who consumed the equivalent of seven or more cups of coffee a day—an effect that was independent of the individuals' tobacco smoking, which was also associated with lower risk for developing the disease. What the mechanism behind this phenomenon might be and whether this relationship is causal are still undetermined. However, it is possible that the adenosine antagonism provided by caffeine is a factor.

Websites for Further Information

Information on recent research on Parkinson's disease:

> http://www.parkinson.org

Cocaine Anonymous website:

> http://www.ca.org

A site covering many aspects of cocaine, along with a number of links:

> http://www.erowid.org/chemicals/
> cocaine/cocaine.shtml

Information on the influence of interdiction efforts on price for cocaine:

> http://books.nap.edu/books/
> 0309064775/html/29.html

Information on many aspects of amphetamines:

> http://www.erowid.org/chemicals/am-
> phetamines

Antipsychotic Drugs and Neurochemical Hypotheses of Schizophrenia

Schizophrenia is one of the most common major mental disorders for which drug treatment is almost a necessity for functioning in daily life. This form of *psychosis* (a general term used to reflect a severe disorganization in personality, thought, emotion, and behavior) afflicts approximately 1% of individuals at some point in their lives, and approximately 1 out of 200 individuals in the United States is currently being treated for this disorder with one or more drugs. Schizophrenia is most commonly evidenced in young adulthood. The symptoms may occur suddenly, generally following severe environmental stress (often termed reactive schizophrenia), or they may develop gradually over a period of time (often termed process schizophrenia). Symptoms include distorted thinking (evidenced in delusions and in speech patterns wandering and failing to lead to their apparent goals), perceptual distortions and hallucinations (mostly auditory), flattened affect or inappropriate expression of emotion, withdrawal of the individual's interest from other people and the outside world, and altered motor behavior (ranging from complete immobilization to frantic, purposeless, or ritualistic activity), among many others.

SYMPTOMS OF SCHIZOPHRENIA

The core symptoms of schizophrenia have traditionally been grouped into two clusters: (1) positive symptoms, which include hallucinations, delusions, and bizarre thoughts; and (2) negative symptoms, which include lack of motivation, blunted affect, inability to experience pleasure, and apathy. However, there is a growing recognition that schizophrenia is also characterized by broad cognitive impairments, which is a major factor in why schizophrenic patients typically have significantly lower than normal IQ scores. These consist of deficits in verbal memory performance (verbal learning and recall), vigilance, verbal fluency, visuomotor skills, and executive functioning (cognitive flexibility, maintenance of a cognitive set, and working memory). Although delusions and hallucinations have traditionally been the primary focus in the development of therapeutic drugs for this disorder, the cognitive impairments together with motivational impairments appear to be the symptoms most associated with the profound long-term disability typically found in the disease (Hyman & Fenton, 2003). Finally, there may be accompanying mood symptoms, particularly depressive symptoms, which may lead to a diagnosis of schizoaffective disorder. These symptoms could be of sufficient severity that if the patient did not have schizophrenia, a diagnosis of major depression or bipolar disorder would be determined in a substantial percentage of the patients. These dimensions appear to involve different brain circuitries and underlying brain mechanisms, and their pattern of response to treatment differs.

People have been using drugs for thousands of years to counteract abnormal mental and emotional states. Unfortunately, though, until about 50 years ago, there was no drug (or any other treatment, for that matter) that specifically reduced the symptoms of schizophrenia without severely stupefying the individual and without inducing a strong physical dependence. This all changed with the discovery of the selective effects of chlorpromazine and reserpine, drugs that are capable of blunting the hallucinations, delusions, and other florid positive symptoms of schizophrenia.

Unfortunately, these statistics do not mean that a cure for schizophrenia has been found, that fewer people are developing the disorder, that there are fewer people being admitted to hospitals for the disorder, or that these drugs are a panacea with few side effects or social consequences. The fact is that although these drugs reduce the core symptoms of schizophrenia in three out of four individuals, there is no known cure for the vast majority of them. Furthermore, most patients exhibiting a favorable response to drug treatment will relapse, and only around 10% of schizophrenic patients become fully functional in daily living, although this figure may change now that second- and third-generation antipsychotics have replaced the earlier (conventional) drugs in the treatment of schizophrenia (Harvey et al., 2004; Robinson et al., 1999, 2002). Proportionally, there is the same number of individuals developing the disorder now as in the past, and the number of admissions to hospitals with the diagnosis of schizophrenia is far higher now than it was 50 years ago. In addition, regardless of the drugs used, the side effects associated with their use range from those that involve relatively minor discomfort to those with socially disabling qualities to those that may be lethal.

Most experts believe that there are many causes of the symptoms of schizophrenia (perhaps the plural, schizophrenias, would be more appropriate in this context)—many of these having some common biochemical denominator. It is likely that the symptoms are the result of a complex interaction between environmental factors and genetic susceptibility (Tsuang, 2000), and several candidate genes have been identified (Meyer-Lindenberg, 2010). In addition to life stress, parental and societal factors, chemicals in the environment, and nutritional factors, among other things, may be involved. Many researchers conceive of schizophrenia as a neurodevelopmental disorder, which involves a combination of environmental and genetic factors interacting with the trajectory of normal brain development (Owen et al., 2011; Weinberger, 1987). As indicated in earlier chapters, abuse of various drugs also has been suggested to be an important correlate of schizophrenia-like psychoses.

DISCOVERY AND CHARACTERIZATION OF ANTIPSYCHOTIC DRUGS

Prior to the 1950s, the major nondrug "therapies" for schizophrenia consisted of isolation, restraint, electroshock treatment, and surgery (prefrontal lobotomy). In 1954, there were approximately 600,000 hospitalized patients diagnosed as schizophrenics. Today, with the use of antipsychotic drugs, there are fewer than one-third that number currently in hospitals. In some sense, the discovery of antipsychotic drugs, in combination with the increasing use and development of anxiolytic and antidepressant drugs, initiated a wave known as the "psychopharmacology revolution." With the continued development of drug treatments for various psychiatric disorders, this wave has continued for more than five decades.

Antipsychotics (also termed *neuroleptics* and *major tranquilizers*) are unrelated chemically and pharmacologically to previously known sedative–hypnotics and anxiolytics, for example, barbiturates and benzodiazepines (sometimes referred to as *minor tranquilizers*). The first antipsychotic drugs discovered were chlorpromazine and reserpine. Reserpine is a naturally occurring substance that is extracted from the plant *Rauwolfia serpentina*. Chlorpromazine (Thorazine) was originally developed as an antihistamine. Early research in the mid-1950s demonstrated that these drugs blunted the symptoms of schizophrenia, particularly the positive symptoms such as hallucinations and delusions (Delay & Deniker, 1956; Freed, 1955). As soon as the efficacy of chlorpromazine in reducing many of the core features of schizophrenia was established, pharmaceutical companies began to develop their own versions of this "miracle" drug (e.g., haloperidol (Haldol), fluphenazine (Prolixin), pimozide (Orap), and many others). In some cases the strategy was to develop derivatives of the chlorpromazine molecule and in others it was to analyze and develop compounds that exhibited many of its neurochemical or behavioral properties in animals. Janssen et al. (1965) conducted exhaustive research on the basic behavioral effects of the early antipsychotic drugs, in the attempt to identify a behavioral profile that could promote the development of novel antipsychotics. They observed that antipsychotic drugs produced a reversible inhibition of movement, suppressing spontaneous activity, as well as stimulant-induced locomotion and stereotypy. Moreover, antipsychotic drugs impaired active avoidance behavior (in which rats had to avoid an aversive stimulus that was signaled by presentation of a cue) and induced a response known as catalepsy (a posture, such as hanging with the forepaws on a horizontal bar, that is maintained for an extended period of time). Although some other types of drugs could produce some of these effects, antipsychotics produced the entire pattern in a very reliable manner.

In the immediate aftermath of these discoveries, a host of antipsychotics (now called "first-generation" drugs) were developed. These drugs revolutionized the treatment of schizophrenia, and also stimulated tremendous interest in what mechanism of action could result in such an effect. During this seminal period of psychopharmacology research (i.e., 1960s–1970s), several other developments were occurring in parallel.

As discussed in Chapter 7, researchers discovered that Parkinson's disease was caused by a depletion of dopamine (DA) in the caudate/putamen and also that this neurological disorder could be treated by the DA precursor L-DOPA. Furthermore, biochemists developed receptor binding methods, which could allow for direct measurement of the ability of drugs to bind to receptors, as well as newer assays for the measurement of neurotransmitters. Using a combination of behavioral, pharmacological, and biochemical methods, researchers were able to piece together the puzzle and determine that reserpine acted by depleting DA, whereas the vast majority of antipsychotics acted as DA antagonists. Consistent with this idea, Seeman et al. (1976) demonstrated that there was a strong correlation between antipsychotic potency in humans and the affinity of these drugs to bind to DA receptors. Thus, in a relatively short period of time (a little over 20 years), researchers had gone from identifying the first antipsychotic drugs, to developing a host of others, to characterizing the basic neurochemical mechanism of action of these drugs. In addition, this first generation of research helped to clarify some clinical issues related to the side effects of antipsychotics. It was clear from the initial clinical use of these compounds that they could produce motor side effects, such as parkinsonism, tardive dyskinesia, and related effects (see a discussion of the motor side effects, in a later section). This observation made sense, in view of the evidence emerging at the time that DA systems were involved in motor control and that Parkinson's disease was produced by a degeneration of DA neurons. Moreover, as stated earlier, Janssen et al. (1965) were able to identify antipsychotic drugs because of their motor effects. Essentially, these researchers had not developed an animal model of schizophrenia, but had instead developed an animal model of a major side effect of antipsychotics—namely, drug-induced parkinsonism. Identifying drugs based upon their ability to produce these motor effects was useful, because this strategy facilitated the ability to screen a large number of compounds for potential antipsychotic activity. However, it also insured that many of the drugs that were initially developed produced the same motor side effects. This status continued until the development of "atypical" antipsychotics (discussed later). The next sections will provide a brief summary of the current use of typical and atypical antipsychotics for the treatment of schizophrenia.

Conventional (Typical, First-Generation) Antipsychotics

Although antipsychotics often have sedative-like qualities, and benzodiazepines may reduce schizophrenic symptoms in some patients (perhaps by reducing the impact of stressors that may mediate relapse), these drugs differ in several dimensions. First, the bulk of the evidence indicates that the antipsychotics are clearly superior in reducing the core symptoms of schizophrenia (Baldessarini & Tarazi, 2001; Stimmel, 1996). Second, in contrast to sedative–hypnotics, which generally decrease muscle tension, increase the convulsive threshold (which means the potential for seizure activity decreases), and have a moderate degree of abuse potential, antipsychotics tend to increase muscle tone and tension, lower the convulsive threshold, and have no potential for abuse. Antipsychotics also have a wide assortment of potential side effects that are not found with sedative–hypnotics—most notably motor disturbances, anticholinergic effects, and allergic reactions. Unlike many sedative–hypnotics, antipsychotics do not produce anesthesia, although they may be used as preanesthetics to reduce patients' apprehension over pending surgery and to reduce the dose of anesthetic required. By themselves, their

TABLE 8.1   Relative Incidence of Common Side Effects to Conventional and Atypical Antipsychotics

Antipsychotic	Dose Range	Motor EPS	Sedative Activity	Anti-ACH Effects	Hypotension	Weight Gain
Conventional						
Chlorpromazine (Thorazine)	300–800	Mod	High	High	High	High
Fluphenazine (Prolixin)	2–20	High	Low	Low–Mod	Low	Low
Thioridazine (Mellaril)	200–600	Low	Mod–High	High	Mod–High	High
Trifluoperazine (Stelazine)	6–20	High	Low	Low–Mod	Low	?
Thiothixene (Navane)	6–30	Mod–High	Low	Low–Mod	Low–Mod	?
Haloperidol (Haldol)	6–20	High	Low	Very low	Low	Low
Molindone (Moban)	50–225	Low–Mod	Low–Mod	Low	Very low	Absent
Atypical						
Aripiprazole (Abilify)	10–30	Absent	Absent	Absent	Low	Low
Clozapine (Clozaril)	200–650	Absent	Mod–High	Mod–High	Mod–High	High
Risperidone (Risperdal)	2–10	Very low	Mod	Very low	Mod	Mod
Olanzapine (Zyprexa)	7.5–20	Very low	Mod	Low–Mod	Mod	High
Quetiapine (Seroquel)	150–800	Very low	Mod	Mod	Mod	Mod
Ziprasidone (Geodon)	40–160	Very low	Low	Low	Mod	Absent

Sources: Based on Argo et al. (2004), Baldessarini & Tarazi (2001), Gerlach & Peacock (1995), Jibson & Tandon (1996), and Schwartz et al. (2004).

Notes: In parentheses under each generic name is its most common proprietary name. *Dose range* refers to the normal daily clinical oral dosage; *EPS* refers to extrapyramidal symptoms, which is sometimes used as a label for the motor side effects of antipsychotic drugs; and *anti-ACH effects* refers to anticholinergic effects. For the conventional antipsychotics, there is a strong positive correlation between the midrange dose for each drug and the drug's tendency to induce sedation, anti-ACH effects, and orthostatic hypotension. On the other hand, there is a strong negative correlation between the midrange dose for each drug and the drug's tendency to induce motor side effects.

lethal toxicity is very low, but a lethal synergism may occur when they are combined with other sedative-type drugs. Although not particularly effective as antidepressants, antipsychotics may be beneficial as adjunctive treatments in some cases of depression.

Dozens of antipsychotics, comprising a wide variety of basic molecular groups, have been approved for clinical use in the United States. Representative drugs in these groups are shown in Table 8.1, along with their clinically effective doses (for schizophrenia) and some of the more common side effects (to be discussed shortly). For years following the discovery of their efficacy in the treatment of schizophrenia, it was common to refer to antipsychotics according to the chemical class to which they belonged—for example, chlorpromazine and fluphenazine were classified as "phenothiazines," haloperidol was a "butyrophenone," thiothixene was a "thioxanthene," and so forth. However, the therapeutic efficacy of an antipsychotic drug appears to be unrelated to what drug class it belongs to; that is, not all phenothiazines are effective antipsychotics and not all effective antipsychotics are phenothiazines.

As discussed earlier, the first group of antipsychotics developed exhibited a similar spectrum of side effects, although they differed considerably in terms of potency and the incidence and degree of inducing these side effects. For example, haloperidol is more likely to produce motor side effects than chlorpromazine or thioridazine. Most of these differences are due to the fact that the high potency compounds were more selective in binding primarily to D_2-like receptors and blocking them, whereas the low potency compounds were much less selective—binding not only to D_2-like receptors but also to various other receptor proteins, for example, receptors for ACh (acetylcholine), NE (norepinephrine), and H (histamine; Gerlach & Peacock, 1995). Their affinity for cholinergic receptors probably accounts for their lower incidence of early onset motor side effects, because these stem from disturbances in the basal ganglia, where dopaminergic and cholinergic inputs in this area of the brain tend to induce opposing actions. Thus the compounds that were more effective in blocking DA receptors than ACh receptors were more prone to disturb the balance between the dopaminergic and cholinergic inputs into this region of the brain.

Because of the equivalence in efficacy of the first-generation antipsychotics and their similar spectrum of side effects, investigators exploring phenomena associated with antipsychotic treatment (such as relapse rates, dropout rates, incidence of tardive dyskinesia as a function of years of treatment, and so forth) often lumped patients together within or across studies by converting the dosage of different medications into **chlorpromazine equivalents.** For example, in terms of potency, 2 mg of haloperidol is equivalent to 100 mg of chlorpromazine; thus, a patient receiving 7 mg/day of haloperidol would be calculated as receiving 350 chlorpromazine equivalents. Thus they are commonly referred to as *conventional* or *typical* antipsychotics.

Numerous clinical trials with antipsychotic drugs have established their effectiveness in all subtypes of schizophrenia, at all stages of the illness, and at all ages (Baldessarini & Tarazi, 2001). Rarely does a patient treated with adequate doses of these drugs fail to show some degree of improvement, varying from complete remission of the psychosis to minimal symptomatic change. Treatment with conventional antipsychotics results in approximately 70% of the patients diagnosed with schizophrenia showing great improvement in their symptomatology, and approximately 20% showing minimal improvement. There is also considerable evidence to support the view that the earlier schizophrenia is detected and treated with antipsychotics, the more favorable the clinical outcome (Tsuang et al., 2000).

Analysis of the psychotic symptoms most affected by conventional antipsychotics indicates a specificity in their activity. Agitated, belligerent, impulsive behavior in patients is markedly reduced, whereas withdrawn or autistic patients sometimes become more responsive and communicative and less seclusive. Generally over a period of days, positive psychotic symptoms of hallucinations, delusions, and disorganized or incoherent thinking tend to disappear, and there are improvements in sleep, self-care, and appetite (Baldessarini & Tarazi, 2001). Improvement in insight, judgment, memory, and orientation are also likely in cases of acute psychosis, whereas in chronic schizophrenics, changes in these are variable and often unsatisfactory (Baldessarini & Tarazi, 2001). On the other hand, negative symptoms and nonspecific schizophrenic symptoms such as anxiety, tension, and guilt may remain relatively unaffected by antipsychotics. Indeed, in mild cases of schizophrenia these symptoms may be aggravated.

General improvement with conventional antipsychotic treatment approximates a learning curve, in that there is a rapid change in the first few weeks of treatment, a slowing of improvement in the sixth to twelfth weeks, and a very slow change thereafter. There is no evidence that treatment with high-potency drugs given in large doses (e.g., 100 mg or more of haloperidol) induces benefits more rapidly when given at the beginning of treatment than smaller doses of these drugs (Baldessarini & Tarazi, 2001).

However, there are some indications that the high-potency conventional antipsychotics like haloperidol most rapidly control the manic patient. The rate of change for specific symptoms may vary; for example, hyperactive and manic symptoms may disappear after only a few doses of an antipsychotic, whereas delusions or hallucinations may persist with lessened affect after weeks of daily drug exposure. The abnormal thought and poor interpersonal relations of catatonic patients may improve weeks before the pathologic motor pattern is altered.

There is uneven development of tolerance to the effects of conventional antipsychotics (Baldessarini & Tarazi, 2001). Their ability to suppress psychotic symptoms is fairly stable, although symptoms can worsen or improve over time. In fact, once the symptoms subside, most authorities suggest that lower antipsychotic doses should be given unless the patient has a clear history of symptom worsening when the medication dose is decreased. Tolerance does tend to occur to a certain degree with respect to many of the side effects of these drugs, including sedative effects, hypotension, and anticholinergic effects.

Antipsychotic drugs do not possess any potential for inducing psychological dependence, primarily because of the numerous side effects associated with this class of drugs. However, they may induce mild abstinence symptoms after abrupt cessation of high doses; in some cases, there may be signs of malaise, gastrointestinal dysfunction, nausea and vomiting, and tremulousness. A transient worsening of psychotic symptoms may occur. Also, motor disturbances similar to those associated with tardive dyskinesia (discussed shortly) may occur, but then rapidly dissipate. Because most of these drugs have relatively long plasma half-lives or have active metabolites, plasma levels of active drug decline slowly, so these symptoms are generally not very severe or noticeable.

After a patient is stabilized with conventional antipsychotic medication, the question of what to do next remains, particularly in light of the potential side effects (some of which may be irreversible) associated with chronic drug exposure. One possibility is to simply stop the medication. However, a review of 66 studies including over 4,000 patients indicated that, during a mean follow-up period of 10 months, slightly more than half of the patients relapsed (i.e., exhibited symptom recurrence or worsening) when withdrawn from conventional antipsychotic drug therapy, in contrast to only 16% who were maintained on the drugs (Gilbert et al., 1995). As one might expect, the rate of relapse was positively correlated with the length of the follow-up period. Thus, there was both good news and bad news. That is, some patients relapsed even if maintained on conventional antipsychotics, whereas other patients did not relapse when taken off these drugs and did not require continued drug exposure. Fortunately, patients who relapse when taken off conventional antipsychotics completely generally respond fairly quickly once drug treatment is reinstated.

Studies assessing psychosocial factors in the relapse of patients maintained on antipsychotic medications have suggested that interpersonal variables relating to stress and coping may mediate relapse. Schizophrenic patients who live with family members who express high levels of criticism, hostility, or marked emotional over-involvement in their interactions with these patients have a risk of relapse that is two to three times higher than the relapse risk found in patients who live with family members who do not show these characteristics (Butzlaff & Hooley, 1998). Approaches that provide relatives with education about the illness, improve patterns of communication within the family, and facilitate the development of more effective problem-solving skills have been shown to dramatically reduce the risk of relapse in schizophrenic patients (Hooley, 2004). Having social network members with whom patients can discuss problems in a helpful manner may also reduce relapse (Faraone et al., 1986). Patients with good social adjustment who develop symptoms abruptly in response to stress and who usually respond rapidly to conventional antipsychotics probably should not be maintained on them, because they may never develop the symptoms again. Furthermore, chronic hospitalized schizophrenics who respond only minimally to conventional antipsychotics should definitely not be maintained on them, because the risk of tardive dyskinesia outweighs the benefits of these drugs.

In summary, there is general agreement that the conventional antipsychotics are quite effective in reducing the positive symptoms of schizophrenia. However, their efficacy in alleviating the negative symptoms is modest at best, and there is little improvement in general cognitive functioning (Meltzer, 2004). The absence of symptom relief or differential responsiveness to conventional antipsychotics may be due to differences in the neurochemical or neuropathological disturbances within the schizophrenic population, but pharmacokinetic factors also may be involved (Verghese et al., 1991). This hypothesis is consistent with studies on institutionalized patients that have demonstrated that nonresponders to conventional antipsychotics may exhibit drug blood levels far lower (often two to seven times lower) than responders when given the same doses of antipsychotics. Several studies have suggested that, in comparison with poor responders, good responders are more likely to have better social adjustment and less schizoid developmental history, are older at first hospitalization or onset of symptoms, and exhibit a rapid onset of symptoms (Bowers et al., 1987). It is also clear that a history of chronic hospitalization predicts poor response (Volavka & Cooper, 1987). Another factor in nonresponse may relate to the difficulties in diagnosing schizophrenia; that is, some patients diagnosed with this disorder may actually be misdiagnosed unipolar or bipolar patients (discussed in Chapter 9) and may be more appropriately treated with lithium or antidepressants (Glazer et al., 1987).

Conventional antipsychotics induce a variety of side effects, the degree and incidence depending on the particular drug. All conventional antipsychotics have the tendency to induce a variety of motor side effects. Some of these may occur early (1–5 days of exposure) in treatment (e.g., muscle spasms), after 1–4 weeks of treatment (e.g., parkinsonian-like symptoms), or after several months or years of treatment (e.g., tardive dyskinesia; Baldessarini & Tarazi, 2001). These factors contribute to the fact that although these drugs initially result in symptom remission in the majority of schizophrenic patients, there is considerable drop-off in efficacy with chronic treatment. For example, in one sample, 87% of antipsychotic-naive, first-episode patients, most of whom were treated with conventional antipsychotics (some treatment refractory patients were treated with clozapine), exhibited symptom remission for at least 6 weeks during their first year of illness. However, after 5 years, just under 50% of the patients achieved symptom remission, approximately one quarter had adequate social functioning for two years or more, and only 8% of the patients had a job. In addition, 80% of those patients who had an initial remission relapsed, and of these patients, 80% of them had a second relapse (Robinson et al., 2004).

In some cases, these outcomes may be attributed to discontinuation of the medication by the patients due to side effects, particularly those exhibiting motor side effects, and poor premorbid cognitive functioning (Robinson et al., 2002). Other physical side effects including weight gain, anticholinergic effects, and sexual problems are important factors related to patient noncompliance. Other contributing factors include lack of insight; grandiosity or delusions; comorbid substance abuse; use of dosages outside the medications' particular therapeutic window; and inadequate social support, clinical supervision, or psychoeducation. Limited economic resources, inadequate benefits or medical coverage, and problems with transportation may also be major issues for many patients.

Unfortunately, compliance with treatment is often difficult to monitor. In one study in which schizophrenic patients were unaware of a monitoring device that was used to determine the number of bottle openings as well as the date and time of each of the openings, it was found that medication compliance rates were 63% for the first month and ranged from 56% to 45% over the next 5 months and that there was a significant inverse relationship between compliance during the first month and rehospitalization rates (Diaz et al., 2001). It was also determined that the patients' physicians were correct less than half of the time in their predictions concerning compliance.

Atypical (Second-Generation) Antipsychotics

One of the compounds developed as an antipsychotic in the early 1960s was clozapine (Marsellis et al., 2000). Although it displayed some novel antipsychotic properties, it was not actively investigated for its efficacy in the treatment of schizophrenia—apparently because it didn't induce motor side effects. One of the common notions among clinicians at the time was that the ability to induce parkinsonian side effects was a critical factor in antipsychotic drug efficacy. In the 1970s, further research with clozapine established its efficacy in the treatment of schizophrenia, and in some patients it appeared to be more effective than conventional antipsychotics. Unfortunately, one major drawback to clozapine was its greater potential to induce severe agranulocytosis—that is, to suppress white blood cell formation—than conventional antipsychotics. Although agranulocytosis occurs only in 1% to 2% of patients per year of treatment with clozapine, there is a considerable risk of mortality when it does occur. Thus clinicians in most countries, particularly in the United States, were reluctant to use the drug on their patients, and the drug's manufacturer was not encouraged to market it.

By the 1980s, there were considerable concerns over the incidence of tardive dyskinesia induced by the conventional antipsychotics. It was at this time that enthusiasm for clozapine gained considerable momentum, because it did not induce either parkinsonism or tardive dyskinesia (Safferman et al., 1991). This feature established the first criterion of "atypicality." In the 1990s, after the problems with induction of agranulocytosis were dealt with by employing routine blood tests, clozapine (Clozaril) was approved for use in the treatment of schizophrenia. (Unfortunately, this monitoring system—the Clozaril Patient Management System—costs several thousand dollars a year to implement. This expense, of course, is still a major drawback for many patients, whose economic status makes the cost prohibitive.) Further studies at this time also indicated that it had significantly greater efficacy in reducing the negative symptoms of schizophrenia than mainstream antipsychotics, another potential criterion for atypicality. Also, it was found to produce significant clinical benefits in approximately one-third of *treatment refractory patients,* that is, schizophrenic patients who did not exhibit significant symptom reduction following treatment with at least two different conventional antipsychotics for at least 6 weeks at dosages equivalent to 1,000 mg/day of chlorpromazine. In such patients, symptom improvement was observed to continue for as much as a year after clozapine treatment began (Ames et al., 1996). Yet despite these advantages, the fact that clozapine could induce agranulocytosis led researchers to try to develop new atypical antipsychotics. Research assessing compounds that were similar to clozapine's unique pharmacodynamic properties eventually led to the development of several other antipsychotics with its atypical features, most notably a low incidence of motor side effects at clinically effective dosages.

These findings subsequently led to the search for other compounds with the pharmacodynamic properties of clozapine in an attempt to develop antipsychotics with its atypical features without inducing agranulocytosis. Risperidone (Risperdal) was the first to come close to meeting these criteria, and other atypical antipsychotics soon followed, including olanzapine (Zyprexa), ziprasidone (Geodon), and quetiapine (Seroquel; see Table 8.1). These drugs have rapidly become first-line, mainstream treatments for schizophrenia. Although risperidone can induce dose-dependent motor side effects, it is viewed as atypical because the incidence of motor side effects in patients receiving no more than 6 mg of risperidone daily—a dosage that is sufficiently effective in the majority of patients—has been shown to be no higher than in patients receiving placebo. At daily dosages of 10 mg or more, motor side effects may be observed. Controlled studies in several countries also indicated that risperidone was effective in the treatment of both positive and negative symptoms of schizophrenia. One meta-analysis of these studies indicated that the odds were that over 40% more patients treated with risperidone would show significant reductions in negative symptoms than patients treated with conventional antipsychotics (or 7 out of 10 risperidone-treated patients versus 5 out of 10 patients treated with conventional antipsychotics; Carman et al., 1995). Within a few years several other atypical antipsychotics were approved by the Food and Drug Administration (FDA) for the treatment of schizophrenia, including olanzapine (Zyprexa), quetiapine (Seroquel), and ziprasidone (Geodon), which can also be first-line therapies for schizophrenia. Each of these drugs is well tolerated and has a clinical profile very similar to risperidone, but they differ somewhat in side-effect profile and activity against negative symptoms (Jibson & Tandon, 1996). Agranulocytosis is rare with all of them. Their efficacy in treatment refractory patients remains to be established. Although the newer atypical antipsychotics don't necessarily induce fewer motor side effects than low potency conventional antipsychotics (Leucht et al., 2003), they do have a number of other favorable qualities.

In summary, compared with conventional antipsychotics, the atypical antipsychotics are equally effective in reducing the positive symptoms of schizophrenia, and as a group exhibit advantages in terms of fewer motor side effects, greater reductions in negative symptoms, more enhancement of cognitive functions, less dysphoria, and greater compliance with treatment (Jibson & Tandon, 1998). Although there may be subtle differences in their efficacy, the primary differences among the atypical antipsychotics to date are related to their side effects. Clozapine remains the most effective drug for those individuals identified as treatment refractory, and some but not all studies support its greater efficacy in reducing the negative symptoms of the disorder (Meltzer, 2004). A study has also demonstrated that clozapine therapy is significantly better than olanzapine in preventing suicidal behaviors (e.g., suicide attempts) in patients with schizophrenia and schizoaffective disorder at high risk for suicide (Meltzer et al., 2003). This is a particularly important aspect of treatment, because approximately 50% of patients diagnosed with schizophrenia or schizoaffective disorder attempt suicide, and approximately 10% die of suicide. However, its tendency to induce agranulocytosis and the expense of the required blood monitoring system limit its use to selected patients.

In addition to inducing minimal motor side effects, and in some instances being moderately better in reducing negative symptoms than conventional antipsychotics, recent research has also revealed another advantage of the atypical antipsychotics over conventional antipsychotics—clinically significant improvement in basic aspects of cognitive functioning, such as verbal learning, problem solving, attention, verbal fluency, and spatial working memory (Bilder et al., 2002; Harvey et al., 2004). There also is some improvement in motor speed and fine motor performance. Similar improvements in cognitive functioning have been demonstrated with risperidone and olanzapine in elderly, chronic schizophrenics who had been treated for an average of 30 years with conventional antipsychotics (Harvey et al., 2003). Cognitive function, as well as positive, negative, and depressive symptoms, has also been found to improve in stable outpatients with schizophrenia when the patients are switched from conventional antipsychotics to an atypical antipsychotic, and in some cases from one atypical antipsychotic to other, because of suboptimal efficacy or poor tolerability (Harvey et al., 2004; Weiden et al., 2003). These improvements in cognition should result in more compliance with treatment as well as success in employment, adjustment in the community, and improved social skills (Meltzer, 2004).

Of the other atypicals, the most extensive research has been conducted with risperidone; thus, unexpected consequences of chronic risperidone exposure are least likely to develop (e.g., one promising atypical antipsychotic had to be withdrawn from the market shortly after it was approved for use because of induction of lethal cardiac problems). Risperidone is also the first atypical antipsychotic approved by the FDA (in 2004) for use in a long-acting injectable formulation (Love & Conley, 2004). Prior to this, for those patients requiring maintenance therapy who did not take their medications reliably, only conventional antipsychotics like fluphenazine decanoate or haloperidol decanoate were available for injection in a depot form to provide a very long duration of action (perhaps as long as 6 weeks with a single injection). Both risperidone and olanzapine have been shown to produce clinically relevant enhancements of cognitive functioning, but double-blind comparisons among other atypical antipsychotics may reveal little differences. To date, the limited information on aripiprazole has indicated it may induce a lower incidence of the common side effects associated with atypical antipsychotics (Argo et al., 2004; Bowles & Levin, 2003), but double-blind studies comparing aripiprazole with the other atypicals are necessary before any definitive statement on this can be made.

Despite differences in their pharmacodynamic properties, all conventional and second-generation atypical antipsychotics prevent DA from binding to D_2-like receptors and acting as antagonists or inverse agonists at these receptors (more on this later). The first antipsychotic without this property to be developed and approved for the treatment for schizophrenia was aripiprazole (Abilify). It is a partial agonist at these receptors, which means that it induces actions between that of a full agonist (such as DA) and an antagonist (Argo et al., 2004). Thus under hyperdopaminergic conditions, which presumably underlie the positive symptoms of schizophrenia, aripiprazole reduces the impact of DA on D_2 receptors, because its intrinsic activity at these receptors is less than that of endogenous DA. However, under conditions of DA insufficiency, which may underlie the negative symptoms of schizophrenia, aripiprazole results in some D_2 receptor activation.

Aripiprazole also has a high affinity for a variety of receptors that could contribute to its atypical features, several of which are also evidenced with second-generation atypical antipsychotics (Argo et al., 2004). For example, similar to other atypical antipsychotics, it is also an antagonist at serotonin $5\text{-}HT_{2A}$ receptors. Blockade of these receptors, which research indicates can increase dopaminergic transmission in the prefrontal cortex, is one potential mechanism through which atypical antipsychotics may alleviate negative symptoms associated with schizophrenia. This action may also offer some protection from the motor side effects associated with extensive D_2 receptor blockade in other areas of the brain. Aripiprazole is also a partial agonist at $5\text{-}HT_{1A}$ receptors (a property shared with the anxiolytic drug buspirone), which are predominantly autoreceptors in the somatodendritic regions of serotonergic neurons. Agonist activity at these receptors may also contribute to the low incidence of motor side effects with aripiprazole because these receptors exert inhibitory actions on serotonergic neurons, which modulate dopaminergic transmission in the basal ganglia. However, all these actions have been observed only in nonhumans; whether they are pertinent to humans, particularly those exhibiting the symptoms of schizophrenia, remains to be determined.

To summarize, the primary distinguishing feature of atypical antipsychotics is the low incidence of early onset motor side effects and low risk of inducing tardive dyskinesia (the differences will be discussed later)—at least at doses that are effective in reducing the core symptoms of schizophrenia. Other features that some regard as atypical include (1) the ability to effectively reduce the symptoms of schizophrenia in patients who do not respond to conventional antipsychotics; (2) a greater efficacy than the conventional antipsychotics in reducing the negative symptoms of schizophrenia; (3) absence of hyperprolactinemia (excessive prolactin blood levels); and (4) greater efficacy in reducing the cognitive impairments commonly observed in schizophrenic patients (Meltzer, 2004; Remington & Kapur, 2000). Because of the great interest in identifying novel atypical antipsychotics, several behavioral tests in animals have been developed for assessing the difference between typical and atypical antipsychotics (e.g., Betz et al., 2005, 2009; Ishiwari et al., 2005; Trevitt et al., 1997, 1998, 1999).

Neurochemical Effects of Antipsychotic Drugs

Attempts to determine what particular pharmacodynamic properties of antipsychotic drugs contribute to their efficacy have been complicated for many reasons: the variety of symptoms observed in schizophrenic patients (i.e., positive symptoms, negative symptoms, and disturbances in cognition); the likelihood that the symptoms involve different neurotransmitter systems in various areas of the brain; the heterogeneity in the causes of these disturbances; and the wide variety of pharmacodynamic properties evidenced in the drugs that are effective in reducing the symptoms. The bulk of the evidence has suggested that many of the beneficial effects, as well as side effects, induced by most antipsychotic drugs are due to their ability to reduce DA transmission. Reserpine and tetrabenazine deplete DA by blocking vesicular storage, but most antipsychotic drugs act by acting as antagonists of DA D_2 family receptors (D_2, D_3, and

D_4 subtypes). In addition, there is evidence that some antipsychotics not only block the access of DA to these receptors but may also act as inverse agonists (Akam & Strange, 2004). That is, they act in a fashion opposite to DA at these receptors and stimulate cyclic AMP (adenosine monophosphate) accumulation in neurons. So far, the one exception to this is aripiprazole, which acts as a partial agonist at D_2 family receptors. Although aripiprazole acts as a partial agonist at D_3 receptors, it is not clear how this action is related to the antipsychotic effect induced by this drug (Tadori et al., 2008). For example, as discussed earlier in Chapter 5, partial agonists can act as antagonists in the presence of an agonist, or high levels of the neurotransmitter. Thus, it is possible that this drug acts as a DA agonist in some DA terminal areas where baseline release is low, but actually acts as an antagonist in other DA terminal regions at which baseline release is high. Another complication is that the types of effects exerted by antipsychotics appear to depend on which of several dopaminergic systems in the brain is affected (Figure 5.10). The DA innervation of the caudate/putamen (from the nigrostriatal pathway) is likely to result in some of the motor side effects, such as parkinsonism, that are induced by typical antipsychotic drugs. However, the anatomical locus of the therapeutic effects of antipsychotics remains uncertain. Although it is often suggested that targets of the mesolimbic or mesocortical DA systems, such as nucleus accumbens and prefrontal or anterior cingulate cortex, are the most likely site of action, this has not been clearly demonstrated.

One of the key questions is which neuropharmacological actions contribute to the differences between the conventional and the atypical antipsychotics. Several hypotheses have been proposed. A number of studies have shown that clozapine and olanzapine bind to muscarinic receptors (Arnt & Skarsfeldt, 1998; Miller & Hiley, 1974; Richelson & Souder, 2000; Schotte et al., 1996; Snyder et al., 1974). The serotonergic effects of atypical antipsychotics also have been emphasized as possibly being related to the unique clinical characteristics of atypical antipsychotics (e.g., Argo et al., 2004; Meltzer, 1989, 2004). Risperidone has little in the way of antimuscarinic activity, but does have a high affinity for 5-HT_{2A} receptors (Schotte et al., 1996). Quetiapine also has a substantial affinity for 5-HT_{2A} receptors compared to DA receptors (Arnt & Skarsfeldt, 1998; Richelson & Souder, 2000). Roth et al. (1995) suggested that the $5\text{-HT}_{2A}/D_2$ binding ratio could be used to distinguish between typical and atypical antipsychotics. Betz et al. (2005) proposed a model to explain the differences between typical and atypical antipsychotics based upon their actions on multiple receptors. With this model, it is suggested that antipsychotic drugs have the potential for both proparkinsonian actions (i.e., the ability to induce parkinsonism) and antiparkinsonian effects and that these effects can interact and compete with each other. According to this model, the proparkinsonian effects predominate with typical antipsychotics (like haloperidol and pimozide), and there are few, if any, intrinsic antiparkinsonian properties (because these drugs are highly potent antagonists of DA receptors), so the net effect with these drugs is an induction of parkinsonian symptoms. At the other end of this continuum is clozapine, which acts as a DA receptor antagonist but nevertheless has its potential proparkinsonian actions masked by strong intrinsic antiparkinsonian actions that are probably due to a combination of 5-HT and muscarinic antagonism or inverse agonism. Thus, clozapine produces little in the way of parkinsonian effects, and in fact the intrinsic antiparkinsonian effects of clozapine are so strong that this drug can yield a net tremorolytic action in human patients that is clinically significant. Various other antipsychotics, such as quetiapine, olanzapine, risperidone, thioridazine, and fluphenazine, are spread along this continuum, with some being more clozapine-like and others more haloperidol-like. This model is consistent with the conclusion of Caroff et al. (2011), who suggested that the distinction between typical and atypical antipsychotics is not a dichotomy, but rather a situation in which these drugs vary along a continuum.

Another potential factor that may differentiate the conventional from the atypical antipsychotics is their relative rate of dissociating from D_2-like receptors after binding (Kapur & Seeman, 2001). An agent's receptor affinity is determined by the rate at which it binds to receptors and the rate at which it dissociates from the receptors. In the case of most antipsychotics, their D_2-like receptor binding rates are virtually identical, whereas their D_2-like dissociation rates vary nearly a thousand-fold. Because some of the atypical antipsychotics (e.g., clozapine and quetiapine) dissociate from D_2-like receptors more rapidly than conventional antipsychotics, they may allow the receptors to be more responsive to endogenous changes in DA levels, and thus be less likely to give rise to side effects such as EPS and prolactin elevation. However, several atypical antipsychotics (e.g., risperidone, olanzapine, and ziprasidone) dissociate very slowly from D_2-like receptors, so it is unlikely that the fast dissociation hypothesis is valid as a general mechanism of atypicality (Meltzer, 2004).

Because selective antagonists at D_1-like receptors have so far failed to exhibit antipsychotic actions (Karlsson et al., 1995), the actions of presently used antipsychotics at D_1-like receptors have generally not been regarded as a major factor in the reductions in schizophrenia symptoms. However, recent research indicates that the relative affinities of antipsychotics for the D_1-like and D_2-like receptors may be a factor in differences in efficacy, particularly in distinguishing clozapine from conventional as well as other atypical antipsychotics. Using positron emission tomography (PET) scan technology to investigate D_1 and D_2 receptor occupancy in schizophrenic patients treated with the atypical antipsychotics clozapine, olanzapine, quetiapine, or risperidone, it was determined that the occupancy of clozapine at these two types of receptors was fairly similar (Tauscher et al., 2004). The other three atypical antipsychotics exhibited significantly lower occupancy of D_1 receptors relative to their occupancy of D_2 receptors, which could account for clozapine's unique effectiveness in patients who are refractory to treatment with conventional and other atypical antipsychotics. Because D_1-like and D_2-like receptors have opposing actions on adenylate cyclase activity, it has been proposed that these receptors are linked to maintain levels of the secondary messenger cyclic AMP within narrow limits, despite large fluctuations in extracellular DA levels. Thus, a balanced blockade of these two types of receptors might allow antipsychotic effects to be achieved below the threshold for inducing motor side effects. The low affinity of clozapine for D_1-like and D_2-like receptors would allow for endogenous DA to compete for and activate these receptors sufficiently so that compensatory up-regulation of these receptors does not occur, thus preventing late-onset motor disturbances, such as tardive dyskinesia, from occurring. However, one problem with this hypothesis is that, if this were true, nonselective DA antagonists such as fluphenazine should be atypical antipsychotics, but they are not. Clearly, more research is needed in this area.

Because the dissociative anesthetics phencyclidine and ketamine induce symptoms indistinguishable from those of schizophrenia, an imbalance between glutamatergic (low) and dopaminergic (high) activities has been proposed as a causal factor in schizophrenic symptoms. At present, it is not clear whether the efficacy of clozapine and other atypical antipsychotics in reducing both the positive and negative symptoms of schizophrenia is related to their actions on glutamatergic systems. Phencyclidine and ketamine act as noncompetitive antagonists at N-Methyl-D-aspartic acid (NMDA) receptors, and this could be related to their ability to produce psychotic symptoms, which would provide support for the idea of glutamatergic involvement in schizophrenia.

One of the long-standing puzzles regarding all antipsychotics is why many of the core symptoms of schizophrenia gradually subside over several days to weeks of chronic treatment. One explanation lies in their actions on DA autoreceptors, which also happen to belong to the D_2-like class of receptors (Iversen et al., 2009). Normally, the agonist activity of DA at these receptors inhibits the activity of dopaminergic neurons, that is, decreasing their firing rate and inhibiting DA synthesis and release. Thus, when DA autoreceptors at the dopaminergic cell bodies and axon terminals are blocked by antipsychotics, the immediate consequences are an increase in dopaminergic cell activity (i.e., firing) and an increase in DA synthesis and release. The result is that although fewer postsynaptic D_2-like receptors are available for activation by DA, there are more DA molecules available to activate them. Thus the net dopaminergic input to postsynaptic neurons may not change much. With chronic antipsychotic exposure, many of these effects are reversed; that is, dopaminergic cell activity decreases, and DA synthesis and release are reduced. The decreased release of DA with chronic antipsychotic exposure may be attributed to enhanced DA autoreceptor sensitivity at DA nerve terminals.

Chronic exposure to antipsychotics may also produce cessation of firing activity in a majority of midbrain DA cells due to sustained depolarization of the cells' membrane potential as a consequence of prolonged excitation—a phenomenon called *depolarization block* (Grace et al., 1997). It has been proposed that depolarization block of mesolimbic and nigrostriatal DA neurons may contribute, respectively, to the therapeutic effect and EPS associated with conventional antipsychotics (e.g., haloperidol), whereas the selective inactivation of mesolimbic DA neurons may reflect the reduced propensity for extrapyramidal syndromes associated with atypical antipsychotics (e.g., clozapine). This argument is supported by findings that repeated treatment with both conventional and atypical antipsychotics produces depolarization block of midbrain DA neurons. However, although both conventional and atypical antipsychotics inactivate mesolimbic DA neurons, only the conventional inactivate nigrostriatal DA neurons. Behavioral evidence of differential depolarization block has also been demonstrated with haloperidol and clozapine, suggesting that the neural substrates mediating mesolimbic and nigrostriatal activities are functionally independent and differentially sensitive to conventional and atypical antipsychotics (Boye & Rompre, 2000). In vivo research with rats has suggested that the decreased excitability of dopaminergic neurons with chronic antipsychotic treatment may be due to an increase in voltage-regulated K^+ channels resulting from the up-regulation of the genes responsible for the synthesis of these channels (Hahn et al., 2003). These channels play a vital role in spontaneous action potentials and the sensitivity of neurons to synaptic inputs; thus an increase in these channels would tend to dampen DA neuron activity.

Several other receptor systems have been suggested to be involved in both the beneficial and side effects of antipsychotics. For example, several atypical antipsychotics, for example, aripiprazole, are also agonists at $5-HT_{1A}$ receptors (Argo et al., 2004; Ichikawa et al., 2002). Activation of these receptors, which are primarily somatodendritic autoreceptors that exert inhibitory actions on serotonergic neurons, may increase dopaminergic transmission in the basal ganglia, which may help in reducing motor side effects, and in the cortex, which could improve cognition. Chronic treatment with partial agonists at 5-HT$_{1A}$ receptors, for example, buspirone, also exerts antidepressant and anxiolytic actions. Atypical antipsychotics, but not conventional antipsychotics, have also been found to increase cortical acetylcholine release without an effect in the nucleus accumbens and other subcortical regions (Ichikawa et al., 2002). The selective ability of atypical antipsychotics to enhance DA and acetylcholine in the prefrontal cortex may be responsible for the enhancement of cognitive processes with these drugs, because both of these neurotransmitters have been shown to be involved in memory and learning (Meltzer, 2004). Obviously, much research remains to be done to determine the mechanisms that account for the beneficial and side effects of antipsychotics in general and the differences between conventional and atypical antipsychotics.

Augmentation of Antipsychotic Drug Treatment

It is not unusual for schizophrenic patients to receive adjunctive medications along with conventional and atypical antipsychotic drugs (Advokat et al., 2004). In many cases, these are used to counter the side effects of these drugs (described in the next section). However, specific symptoms that are still refractory to antipsychotic drugs may also be treated with anticonvulsants/mood stabilizers, antidepressants, and anxiolytics. Based on the evidence cited earlier in this chapter indicating that a glutamatergic transmission deficiency at NMDA receptors may play a role in the symptoms of schizophrenia, a number of studies have found that dietary supplements of glycine may augment the effectiveness of conventional antipsychotic drugs (Heresco-Levy et al., 1996). Administration of glutamate itself cannot be done because it is too toxic. However, glycine, which is necessary for glutamate-induced NMDA receptor activation and can be viewed as a coagonist at these receptors, can be given in sufficient quantities to raise glycine levels in the brain and potentiate NMDA receptor-mediated neurotransmission without any apparent toxicity. Across these studies, a 15–30% improvement in negative symptoms was observed, with no corresponding worsening of positive symptoms. High-dose glycine has also been found to be therapeutically beneficial when added to treatment with the atypical antipsychotics olanzapine and risperidone. Significant improvements were found in negative, positive, and cognitive symptoms. The negative symptoms improvement remained significant even following statistical corrections for changes in other symptom clusters and motor side effects (Heresco-Levy et al., 2004). These studies suggest that supplementation with glycine or other glycinergic agents may be effective in the treatment of this disease.

There is limited evidence that suggests that schizophrenic symptoms may be the result of altered neuronal membrane structure that is dependent on blood plasma levels of certain essential polyunsaturated fatty acids and their metabolites. A small number of studies have indicated that the use of omega-3 polyunsaturated fatty acids may improve the symptoms of both medicated and unmedicated schizophrenic patients, but larger, well-designed studies are needed before any strong conclusions on the efficacy of this type of supplementation can be made (Joy et al., 2003). Dehydroepiandrosterone (DHEA), which is an important circulating neurosteroid with several vital neurophysiological functions, has also been explored as an adjunctive treatment for schizophrenia. One study found that schizophrenic patients administered DHEA or placebo along with regular antipsychotic treatments showed significant improvements in negative symptoms, as well as depressive and anxiety symptoms in those patients administered DHEA (Strous et al., 2003). Again, further studies of this type of adjunctive treatment are needed before making any strong conclusions regarding its efficacy.

Antipsychotic Side Effects

As noted earlier, the primary differences among the drugs in this class are differential tendencies to induce the numerous side effects (see Table 8.1) associated with their use. Perhaps the most noticeable and common of these side effects are the movement abnormalities (Caroff et al., 2011; Tarsy, 1983). The four major groups of motor side effects induced by antipsychotic drugs are *parkinsonism, tardive dyskinesia, acute dystonia,* and *akathisia.* Parkinsonism is characterized by a cluster of symptoms similar to those seen in Parkinson's disease patients (bradykinesia, akinesia, rigidity, and tremor) and is the most common of the drug-induced motor side effects of antipsychotic drugs. Tardive dyskinesia symptoms include late-onset involuntary movements such as orofacial tics. Acute dystonia and akathisia are less common; dystonia is characterized by spasms or contractions of antagonistic muscle groups (which results in twisting and repetitive movements), whereas akathisia is a form of motor restlessness.

Signs of motor disturbances usually begin within a few days of initiating conventional antipsychotic medication and are almost always noticed within 3 months of treatment. As noted earlier, the absence of motor side effects is a key characteristic of the atypical antipsychotics. Clozapine has minimal propensity for inducing motor side effects, even with high dosages, and risperidone induces motor side effects only at dosages somewhat higher than those necessary to control the core symptoms of schizophrenia. Acute dystonic reactions tend to dissipate quickly, pseudoparkinsonism symptoms may persist or decrease over several weeks, and tardive dyskinesia symptoms may begin to appear after several months (Baldessarini & Tarazi, 2001). With the exception of the late-onset motor disturbances (tardive dyskinesia), most motor side effects can usually be controlled by lowering the dosage of antipsychotic or adding antiparkinsonism agents. These are generally drugs with anticholinergic (i.e., muscarinic antagonist) properties (e.g., Artane and Cogentin). The fact that drugs with anticholinergic properties are effective in reducing both pseudoparkinsonism and parkinsonism has suggested to some researchers that these symptoms are due to an ACh/DA interaction similar to that shown in idiopathic Parkinson's disease (see Chapter 7).

Just about all of the side effects noted in the preceding section go away if antipsychotic medications are reduced in dosage or are eliminated. However, one potential and considerably troublesome side effect that in some cases may not disappear is *tardive dyskinesia* (Baldessarini & Tarazi, 2001). It is a movement disorder consisting of frequent, repetitive, involuntary movements of the lips, tongue, jaw, face, and sometimes trunk or limbs. The symptoms usually occur after prolonged antipsychotic treatment, and once established, they may persist for months or years following antipsychotic treatment. The symptoms decrease or disappear altogether with sedation or sleep and increase under emotional stress or during activities requiring repetition of motor activities or attention to fine motor tasks. Attempts to consciously control the symptoms may increase the movements. Curiously, however, changes within individual patients suggest that it is not unusual for the symptoms of tardive dyskinesia to exhibit spontaneous remissions over time.

The onset of tardive dyskinesia symptoms is typically subtle, and because the drugs that cause most of the symptoms also mask their manifestation, the symptoms may not become apparent until drug treatment ceases or the drug dosage is reduced. Furthermore, the symptoms of tardive dyskinesia often resemble abnormal movements sometimes observed in unmedicated schizophrenic patients (Fenton, 2000). The incidence of symptoms increases most obviously with the duration of antipsychotic drug exposure and with increasing age (Jeste, 2000).

The estimated annual risks of tardive dyskinesia with conventional antipsychotics generally range between 4% and 8% per year of treatment in young and middle-aged patients (Glazer, 2000a). Symptoms of tardive dyskinesia may be five to six times more prevalent in elderly patients than in younger patients (Jeste, 2000), although the true incidence of antipsychotic-induced symptoms is difficult to determine because the prevalence of spontaneous dyskinesias in unmedicated patients also tends to increase as a function of age (Fenton, 2000). All the conventional antipsychotics have been shown to induce tardive dyskinesia to approximately the same degree (Glazer, 2000a). The evidence is fairly clear that the incidence of tardive dyskinesia is virtually absent with chronic clozapine treatment and considerably lower with the other atypical antipsychotics (at low, clinically effective doses), and patients with tardive dyskinesia who are switched from typical to atypical antipsychotic drugs often display dramatic decreases in their symptoms over time (Glazer, 2000b). Research so far indicates that the incidence of tardive dyskinesia is quite rare in aripiprazole-treated patients (Argo et al., 2004). These findings are consistent with evidence that the ability to induce early EPS is associated with the induction of tardive dyskinesia. Higher antipsychotic dosage, female gender, poor response to antipsychotic treatment at the first psychotic episode, and evidence of neurologic soft signs of basal ganglia dysfunction prior to drug exposure have also been linked to tardive dyskinesia induction (Chakos et al., 1996; Latimer, 1995; Schultz et al., 1995). One study found that patients at a very high risk for developing tardive dyskinesia or worsening of symptoms (e.g., middle-aged and older adults with borderline tardive dyskinesia) were twice as likely to develop definitive tardive dyskinesia when treated with conventional antipsychotics than with the atypical antipsychotics risperidone, quetiapine, or olanzapine, despite the fact that the patients treated with the latter drugs were significantly older and exhibited more severe EPS at baseline (Dolder & Jeste, 2003).

Age is also a factor in recovery from tardive dyskinesia symptoms. With young patients, discontinuation of antipsychotic medication generally increases the symptoms, but there may be steady improvement over a period of months or years, provided the antipsychotics are withheld. Most research shows that mild cases in the young are most easily reversible, with current remission rates of 50% to 90% being reported. With older patients, there is poor prognosis for recovery.

A variety of biochemical pathologies are likely involved in tardive dyskinesia. This side effect is believed to be due predominantly to prolonged DA receptor blockade, leading to supersensitive DA receptors and causing a relative dominance of DA over acetylcholine activity (just the opposite of pseudoparkinsonism; Glazer, 2000c). Decreased activity in GABAergic striatonigral neurons and noradrenergic hyperactivity have also been suggested to be factors in the pathophysiology of tardive dyskinesia. The ability of antipsychotics to induce excessive levels of iron in the basal ganglia (Gold & Lenox, 1995) or to induce free radical damage to the basal ganglia neurons (Cadet & Kahler, 1994) has also been proposed as a mechanism behind tardive dyskinesia.

Early drug treatments for the disorder consisted of either trying to reduce DA activity or enhancing cholinergic activity. Unfortunately, the former tactic (e.g., increasing the dose of antipsychotic) leads only to temporary relief and potential worsening of the condition later on. The latter tactic has been shown to exert temporary or negligible benefits or to induce other side effects. A number of other miscellaneous drugs, including lithium, pyridoxine, niacinamide, manganese, estrogen, baclofen, fusaric acid, tryptophan, barbiturates, morphine, naloxone, enkephalins, hydergine, amantadine, and methylphenidate (in other words, just about everything), have been tried and found to be of limited, negligible, or questionable clinical value in the treatment of tardive dyskinesia (Volavka et al., 1986). Some studies conducted in the early 1990s indicated that the antioxidant vitamin E, which is a safe and highly potent scavenger of free radicals, produced significant attenuation of tardive dyskinesia symptoms, but later studies found that it produced little or no benefit, perhaps because the use of one antioxidant alone may be insufficient (Lohr et al., 2003). Thus other antioxidants, for example, melatonin, or a combination of antioxidants may be worthy of research for efficacy.

It is clear that until a satisfactory treatment for tardive dyskinesia is found, the prevention and early diagnosis of these potentially socially disruptive symptoms must be emphasized (Simpson, 2000). Effective prevention lies in cautious use of antipsychotics. The smallest doses that sustain improvement should be used, and patients who can maintain gains without drugs should be afforded such an opportunity. Avoidance of conventional antipsychotics or switching the patient to an atypical antipsychotic, such as risperidone, aripiprazole, olanzapine, or quetiapine, would also be an appropriate strategy. Although clozapine has the most evidence in favor of its reducing the symptoms of tardive dyskinesia over time, all of the newer atypical antipsychotics should be assessed for efficacy before switching to clozapine, because of its risk for inducing agranulocytosis. It is indeed unfortunate that a person exhibiting, and being treated for, one set of socially disruptive behaviors may someday exhibit another set of socially disturbing behaviors—or in severe cases, even more incapacitating or life-threatening symptoms—for which there is no treatment.

Neuroendocrine side effects (weight gain, breast enlargement and tenderness, and decreased sex drive) may also occur. In females, hyperprolactinemia (abnormally high blood levels of prolactin) can result in irregular ovulation, milk accumulation in breasts, decreased vaginal secretions, and light, irregular, short, or no periods. Although nearly every antipsychotic drug has been reported to cause weight gain, several of the atypical antipsychotics have been noted to promote rapid weight gain and the development of prediabetes, diabetes, elevated blood cholesterol levels, and other cardiovascular risk factors (Allison et al., 1999; Schwartz et al., 2004). Mean weight gains of around 2 kg per month have been observed in adult patients treated with clozapine, olanzapine, and quetiapine; risperidone induces more moderate weight gains in adults but has been reported to cause substantial weight gain in children and adolescents. Thus it is highly recommended that patients be screened for personal and family history of obesity, diabetes, problematic cholesterol levels, hypertension, and other predictors of cardiovascular disease before being treated with these drugs. A decrease in calorie intake and increase in exercise would also be advisable—for both physical and mental benefit.

One rare, but potentially fatal, side effect of antipsychotics that has become widely recognized is the so-called *neuroleptic malignant syndrome* (Caroff & Mann,

1993). Core features of this syndrome, which lasts 7 to 10 days in uncomplicated cases, are severe muscle rigidity, instability of the autonomic nervous system (e.g., elevated blood pressure and tachycardia), high fever, and mental status changes (e.g., stupor). Early reports indicated that the syndrome was lethal in approximately 20% to 30% of patients developing this side effect, but later reports suggested that lethality has decreased to almost zero, perhaps because of earlier diagnosis, rapid drug discontinuation, and institution of intensive care, or use of DA-augmenting drugs (e.g., amantadine, L-DOPA, and bromocriptine; Caroff & Mann, 1993). Except for aripiprazole, all antipsychotics, including clozapine (Tsai et al., 1995), have been shown to induce this syndrome, and the potency of the drug is not a proven risk in this development. Upon recovery from the symptoms of this syndrome, a majority of patients can be safely returned to antipsychotic medication, although a significant risk of their recurrence does exist.

Although less disturbing than the motor side effects induced by antipsychotics, the side effects associated with muscarinic ACh receptor blockade (such as blurred vision, dry mouth, nasal congestion, constipation, and difficulty urinating) can be unpleasant. The lower potency compounds also have a higher incidence of orthostatic hypotension and allergic reactions than the high-potency compounds. Examples of such reactions are photosensitivity, dermatitis (skin rash), pigmentary changes (yellow skin and eyes), and agranulocytosis (decrease in white blood cells). The lower potency compounds may also be more prone to induce epileptic seizure activity (Baldessarini & Tarazi, 2001).

There is an absence of motor side effects with clozapine and aripiprazole and a low incidence of motor side effects with other atypical antipsychotics at clinically effective dosages (Argo et al., 2004; Remington & Kapur, 2000). Atypical antipsychotics do have a number of other side effects, which they share with several other conventional antipsychotics. The atypical antipsychotics can produce orthostatic hypotension (associated with α-adrenergic receptor blockade) and sedation or drowsiness (associated with α-adrenergic or histaminic blockade). All but aripiprazole and risperidone may induce unwanted anticholinergic effects (associated with muscarinic receptor blockade), such as dry mouth, blurred vision, constipation, sedation, and confusion. (Oddly, one of clozapine's more common side effects is hypersalivation—a paradoxical reaction, because it generally has potent anticholinergic actions, which typically would produce a dry mouth.) These side effects can be particularly troublesome for the elderly. Orthostatic hypotension can result in patients' falling down and severely hurting themselves, and the anticholinergic side effects may increase confusion in cognitively impaired elderly patients.

The incidence of grand mal seizures and drug-induced EEG abnormalities is reportedly higher for clozapine than for any other antipsychotic, particularly at higher dosages (Baldessarini & Frankenburg, 1991). Curiously, however, evidence suggests that treatment-refractory patients who develop gross EEG abnormalities when treated with clozapine may actually have a more favorable outcome for clinical improvement than patients who do not develop such abnormalities (Risby et al., 1995). Because most of these EEG abnormalities are not predictive of developing epileptic seizures, these results do not support the routine administration of prophylactic anticonvulsant medications to clozapine-treated patients who develop abnormal EEGs in the absence of seizure activity.

NEUROCHEMICAL AND NEUROPATHOLOGICAL HYPOTHESES OF SCHIZOPHRENIA

Perhaps the most familiar hypothesis for the neurochemical pathologies that may underlie schizophrenia is the DA hypothesis. Basically, the *dopamine hypothesis* states that there is an overactive or hypersensitive DA system or systems (Figure 5.10) in many forms of schizophrenia (Seeman, 1987). Several lines of evidence support the hypotheses that excessive DA transmission (due to increases in DA release or in numbers or sensitivity of receptors) could promote the symptoms of schizophrenia. The first clue that DA may be involved in schizophrenia came from the observation that drugs that specifically reduced many of the core symptoms of schizophrenia (antipsychotics) also induced motor disturbances (as reviewed earlier). These motor side effects were indistinguishable from those of Parkinson's disease, which, by the late 1960s, was known to be associated with DA deficiency and controllable with the DA precursor L-DOPA. Furthermore, it was observed that when L-DOPA was used to control the motor side effects of antipsychotics, it only made the psychosis worse. Within a few years, numerous other observations fell in line with the hypothesis. First, it was noted that substances that decreased DA levels tended to decrease the symptoms of schizophrenia (Carlsson, 1978). For example, reserpine (a drug used in the 1950s to control psychotic symptoms) prevents the binding of monoamines to the synaptic vesicles, allowing them to be metabolized by the enzyme MAO (monoamine oxidase), and reduces the amount of DA that can be released from the axon. Synthesis of DA from its initial precursor tyrosine can be reduced with the drug alpha-methyl-p-tyrosine (AMPT). Both of these compounds are capable of reducing the symptoms of schizophrenia; however, because neither of these compounds exerts specific enough effects (e.g., reserpine reduces the levels of all the monoamines, and AMPT reduces the levels of all catecholamines), they are not used clinically.

Second, research indicated that substances that inhibited DA release or blocked its access to DA receptors were all effective in the treatment of schizophrenia. With respect to the traditionally used antipsychotic drugs, there was a high correlation between their clinical potency (determined on the basis of the average daily dose of the drug needed to reduce symptoms) and their potency in inhibiting the stimulated release of DA from brain slices (Seeman & Lee, 1975). It was also determined that there was a high correlation between their clinical potency and their relative ability to bind to D_2 receptors (Seeman, 1987). Third, substances that are agonists at DA postsynaptic receptors (such as apomorphine), that increase DA levels (such as L-DOPA, MAO inhibitors, and phencyclidine [PCP]), that increase DA release (such as amphetamine and methylphenidate), or that block DA reuptake (such as cocaine) have been noted to worsen or produce schizophrenic symptoms (Lieberman et al., 1987; Moskovitz et al., 1978). Interestingly, although high doses of apomorphine may trigger psychotic symptoms, low doses of it may actually reduce schizophrenic symptoms (Tammiga et al., 1978). This contradictory effect has been attributed to its having a greater affinity for autoreceptors for DA than for postsynaptic DA receptors. Because autoreceptors play an inhibitory role in regulating DA synthesis and release, their activation would decrease the amount of DA normally released from the terminal. However, the reduced DA release is more than compensated for when higher doses of apomorphine are given, because the drug directly activates postsynaptic DA receptors.

Finally, a number of studies using radioactive ligands for DA receptors have reported elevated levels of D_2-like receptors, particularly the D_2 subtype, in the basal ganglia of deceased schizophrenics as well as living schizophrenic patients (utilizing PET scan techniques; Gjedde et al., 1995; Murray et al., 1995; Seeman et al., 1995; Kegeles et al., 2010). However, other studies have not found increased D_2-like receptors in schizophrenics (Sedvall & Farde, 1995; Sedvall et al., 1995; Montcrieff, 2009; Howes and Kapur, 2009). Several methodological problems contribute to the confusion. For example, some studies utilized patients treated with DA antagonists (antipsychotics), which tend to result in up-regulation of DA receptors. As mentioned earlier, the D_2-like receptors constitute a family of receptor subtypes (D_2, D_3, and D_4), and the degree of receptor selectivity of the radioactive ligands used to label these receptors differs from one study to another. Furthermore, for some DA receptors no selective ligands are yet available, so indirect methods—based on questionable assumptions—have been used to determine DA receptor binding. Finally, many studies of this nature utilize small numbers of patients; with a disorder that is so heterogeneous in its etiology, it's not surprising that the outcomes of these studies have been equally heterogeneous. Studies utilizing PET scan techniques have also reported intriguing results suggesting that the area of the brain of schizophrenic patients that is particularly sensitive to DA agonists—the cingulate gyrus—is also one of the areas in which there is heightened activity when schizophrenic patients are actively hallucinating (Dolan et al., 1995; Silbersweig et al., 1995).

In summary, there is considerable evidence that DA is critically involved in schizophrenia. Yet, it is arguable that there is still not a conclusive and unequivocal demonstration that enhanced DA transmission is the primary cause of schizophrenia. One way of putting this together is to state that there are **two forms of the DA hypothesis of schizophrenia**—a *strong form* and a *weak form*. According to the strong form, enhanced DA transmission directly mediates the symptoms of schizophrenia. As reviewed earlier, the evidence for this form of the hypothesis remains mixed. However, one can offer a weaker form of the hypothesis, which is that DA is a modulator of the processes involved in schizophrenia. Quite frankly, the pharmacological and neurochemical evidence for this is overwhelming. An analogy can be made between regulation of the processes involved in schizophrenia and those involved in blood pressure regulation. β-adrenergic receptor blockers exert a powerful effect on blood pressure and are very useful clinically to treat hypertension. Why? Because NE synapses are a vital control point in the regulation of blood pressure. Nevertheless, it is not the case that everyone with high blood pressure suffers from too much NE or EPI (epinephrine) transmission. Indeed, there are several possible causes of high blood pressure. Similarly, one can argue that DA transmission may not be the cause of schizophrenic symptoms in every individual. Nevertheless, DA synapses appear to function as a critical control point over the cognitive/executive/information processing functions that are impaired in schizophrenia. Thus, DA antagonism acts to lessen symptoms in most people, and augmentation of DA transmission can induce psychotic symptoms, but it may still not be true that there are consistent increases in DA transmission that are broadly evident across all people with schizophrenia.

Despite several lines of evidence supporting the involvement of DA in schizophrenia, a number of unresolved questions remain to be answered. For example, why does it take several days, or in some cases weeks or months, of continuous exposure to DA-receptor blockers (antipsychotics) before maximum relief from the core symptoms is evidenced? Why are most antipsychotic drugs more effective in reducing the positive symptoms of schizophrenia than the negative symptoms, and why do others appear to reduce both types of symptoms? And why are the latter drugs able to control the symptoms of schizophrenia although at the same time producing minimal disturbances of DA systems that commonly underlie many of the motor side effects associated with the former drugs? Grace (1991) has provided a model that integrates a number of apparently conflicting observations regarding the role of DA in this disorder. Highly simplified, this model proposes that in schizophrenics a prolonged decrease in prefrontal cortical activity (e.g., due to cortical atrophy) reduces the tonic (i.e., sustained) release of DA in subcortical areas. Over time this reduction elicits homeostatic compensations in DA responsivity (e.g., DA receptor up-regulation) in these subcortical areas. These, in turn, increase overall DA responsivity in these subcortical areas and cause enhanced phasic (i.e., transient) DA release—presumably elicited by behaviorally relevant stimuli—to provoke abnormally large responses. It was further assumed that the tonic decrease in DA activity underlies the negative symptoms of the disorder, whereas the phasic increase in DA activity underlies the positive symptoms. This model explains why conventional antipsychotics, which are potent D_2 receptor blockers, are more effective in reducing positive symptoms than negative symptoms and why the atypical antipsychotic clozapine, which decreases phasic DA release but increases tonic DA levels, reduces both types of symptoms. It also explains why amphetamine induces only positive symptoms, because it enhances both tonic and phasic DA release, whereas PCP induces both types of symptoms because it inhibits reuptake of phasically released DA while inhibiting DA released tonically via its action at NMDA ion channels. Although this model is intriguing and handles a lot of diverse phenomena associated with schizophrenia and its treatment, further verification of its various assumptions is needed. It must also be recognized that some cases or symptoms of schizophrenia may be totally unrelated to disturbances in dopaminergic functions.

   In addition to the DA hypothesis, several other hypotheses for schizophrenia have been proposed to explain the underlying neural pathologies. Several lines of evidence have suggested that schizophrenic symptoms may be due to reduced glutamatergic transmission at NMDA receptors, causing an imbalance between glutamatergic and dopaminergic systems in structures of the basal ganglia and limbic system. For example, NMDA channel blockers, such as PCP and ketamine, induce both positive and negative symptoms of schizophrenia with large doses in nonschizophrenic persons and exacerbate the symptoms of chronic schizophrenics with smaller doses (Sawa & Snyder, 2002). On the other hand, treatment with glycine, a potentiator of NMDA-mediated transmission, has been shown to significantly improve the negative symptoms of schizophrenic patients under medication with typical antipsychotics (Javitt et al., 1994). Other lines of research suggest that there is a selective loss of glutamatergic neurons in the brains of deceased schizophrenics (Squires et al., 1993), and increases in NMDA-associated binding sites have been reported in the brains of deceased schizophrenics, possibly due to postsynaptic compensation for impaired glutamatergic neurotransmission (Ishimaru et al., 1994).

   Numerous other abnormalities, which have more to do with structural defects than biochemical defects, have been suggested to be involved with schizophrenia. Imaging techniques for studying living brain structure and functions have improved our understanding of this mental disorder; these include computerized axial tomography (CT) scan, magnetic resonance imaging (MRI), and methods for measuring blood flow, metabolism, and receptor mapping (such as PET scan). These techniques have revealed that schizophrenic patients as a group show excessive brain volume loss, exhibited as excessive ventricular enlargement and excessive expansion of the fluid space around the brain (Goodman & Pardee, 2000). Functional imaging studies show that schizophrenics display a phenomenon known as hypofrontality (i.e., decreases in baseline and task-stimulated prefrontal cortex activity; see Kanahara et al., 2009; Weinberger & Berman, 1988). Changes in the cellular architecture and circuitry in the prefrontal cortex (Volk & Lewis, 2010) also have been reported. Limbic system structures such as amygdala and hippocampus also are involved schizophrenia. For example, hippocampal pyramidal cells show alterations in their orientation and organization that are suggestive of poor cell migration or other developmental anomalies (Conrad & Scheibel, 1987). There also is evidence that the thalamus of schizophrenic patients is smaller and has significantly fewer neurons than normal (Andreasen et al., 1994; Young et al., 2000). This is a plausible site for a schizophrenic abnormality, because the thalamus serves as the major way station that receives input from the reticular activating system, limbic structures involved in emotion and memory, such as the amygdala and hippocampus, and cortical association areas. The thalamus seems to act as the filter or gate for reaching all cortical areas, so that if the filter is defective, the brain might be overloaded with information—or starved of it—and the result would be problems in understanding subtle social cues, monitoring one's own "inner speech," and interpreting information from the outside world. Other studies have found decreases in metabolism in the basal ganglia that are reversed with antipsychotics (Buchsbaum et al., 1987).

Interpreting these findings is difficult because most biological abnormalities currently identified are not exhibited in all cases, and only present themselves as group differences. Furthermore, many of these abnormalities are found in unaffected individuals; for example, excessive brain volume loss can be found in the unaffected twin in monozygotic twin pairs discordant in exhibiting symptoms of schizophrenia (Goodman & Pardee, 2000). Some investigators question whether these effects precede—that is, cause—the disorder or are consequences of the different lifestyle or treatment often applied to the individuals.

There are many other problems with this area of research. Some of these are due to the nature of the illness itself. The diagnosis of schizophrenia is hardly cut and dried. Symptoms vary among and within individuals over time. Occasionally, the syndrome appears suddenly; more commonly the symptoms have a gradual onset. Often studies fail to employ the same diagnostic criteria to all patients included in them and fail to differentiate between long-hospitalized patients and recently admitted patients. For example, if one is trying to determine the efficacy of a particular therapeutic intervention and includes chronic, "burned-out" schizophrenics, failures may be due to the fact that some schizophrenics cannot improve because their illness is so chronic.

Related to this issue is the likelihood that schizophrenia is not a single disorder but is actually a set of symptoms with varying etiology. Therefore, with a heterogeneous sample of individuals, particularly a small sample, it is highly unlikely that any therapeutic intervention, which may benefit only a few individuals in the sample, will result in significant differences between treated and untreated groups. It may be, for example, that there are individuals displaying the symptoms of schizophrenia who respond to megavitamin therapy, but in a large group of schizophrenics, they may not be detected.

Other problems in this line of research stem from not using a double-blind procedure (where neither the patient nor the treatment provider knows what treatment condition the patient is in) or from beginning the treatment assessment before a reasonable *washout period*, in which the patients stop taking all medication, has occurred. The fact is that the overall psychological functioning of many patients (such as nonresponsive chronic schizophrenics and patients whose symptoms remit regardless of whether antipsychotics are administered) actually improves when antipsychotic medications stop. Without a washout period, these patients' improvement would be attributed erroneously to the treatment.

CURRENT PHARMACOTHERAPY FOR SCHIZOPHRENIA

The atypical antipsychotics have rapidly replaced the conventional antipsychotics as first-line agents for treating schizophrenia. They exhibit a clear advantage in their lower incidence of inducing EPS and tardive dyskinesia, and they may also be less likely to induce a neuroleptic malignant syndrome and hyperprolactinemia. In several clinical trials in patients with non–treatment-resistant schizophrenia, the atypical antipsychotics have been shown to be equivalent to conventional antipsychotics in reducing the positive symptoms of schizophrenia, and in most cases they are significantly better in reducing the negative symptoms and improving basic cognitive functions. They also have been found to be superior to haloperidol in improving some global measures of quality of life (Hamilton et al., 1998; Revicki et al., 1999). Head-to-head efficacy comparisons of atypical antipsychotics in non–treatment-resistant schizophrenia have been inconclusive. Whereas some studies have indicated that risperidone and olanzapine may be more effective than conventional antipsychotics in the treatment of treatment-resistant patients, clozapine remains the standard agent for these cases. However, it carries a risk of agranulocytosis and requires that the patients' white blood cell counts be monitored. For treatment-refractory patients who are still nonresponsive or only partially responsive to clozapine, a recent randomized, double-blind, placebo-controlled trial has indicated that augmentation with risperidone may induce significant reductions in their overall symptoms and positive and negative symptoms, without producing additional weight gain, agranulocytosis, or seizures (Josiassen et al., 2005). Some studies also indicate that atypical antipsychotics may exert better therapeutic effects on depression symptoms, hostility, and suicidality than conventional antipsychotics.

The profiles of adverse effects of clozapine and the newer atypical antipsychotics differ, with all but aripiprazole and risperidone producing anticholinergic effects; clozapine producing more fatigue, hypersalivation, nausea, and orthostatic dizziness; and the newer atypical drugs, with the exception of aripiprazole, producing dose-dependent motor side effects. One area in which atypical antipsychotics differ considerably is with respect to promoting weight gain and conditions associated with weight gain (e.g., the development of type 2 diabetes, elevated cholesterol levels, increased blood pressure, and cardiovascular problems). Clozapine and olanzapine promote the most weight gain, quetiapane and risperidone promote moderate weight gain, and aripiprazole and ziprasidone are weight gain neutral. Because weight gain may result in patients' discontinuing their medication and increasing their likelihood of relapse and the conditions associated with weight gain are potentially life-threatening, choosing the appropriate drug based on the individual patient's premorbid characteristics is essential to long-term treatment.

Atypical agents are substantially more expensive than their conventional counterparts, but when one factors in outpatient and inpatient medical costs with the medication costs, the total medical costs are generally equivalent or lower for the atypical antipsychotics (Hamilton et al., 1998; Revicki, 1999; Revicki et al., 1999). For example, higher medication and outpatient costs for clozapine are offset by lower hospital costs for patients, because these patients relapse less frequently and spend less time in the hospital.

Over the last few years, there has been a growing emphasis on the residual cognitive deficits in patients that are medicated with antipsychotic drugs (Alexander et al., 2009; Floresco et al., 2009; Barch, 2010). Sponsored by an NIMH (National Institute of Mental Health) initiative, there has been a tremendous interest in developing treatments for the working memory and other cognitive deficits that have proven to be so elusive (see CNTRICS website, at the end of the chapter). Some research has targeted cholinergic systems for pharmacological intervention (Sarter et al., 2011), whereas other studies have focused on the potential use of DA D_1 agonists (Roberts et al., 2010). Further research in this area will be critical for developing treatments for these cognitive impairments, which are highly resistant to the currently available treatments.

Websites for Further Information

Information on schizophrenia and antipsychotic drugs:

http://www.schizophrenia.com

Information on CNTRICS (Cognitive Neuroscience Treatment Research to Improve Cognitive Symptoms in Schizophrenia):

http://www.cntrics.ucdavis.edu

Antidepressants and Mood Stabilizers

The primary symptoms of schizophrenia are most notable in the cognitive and perceptual domains; distortions in mood and emotions are secondary and variable. However, with the affective disorders—commonly referred to as depression, mania, and manic depression—mood and emotional disturbances are the primary symptoms, and these may be accompanied by distortions in thought patterns. (Unfortunately, these distinctions may not be particularly clear and can lead to variability in clinical diagnoses.)

The clinical (*DSM-IV*) criteria for what is commonly referred to as *clinical depression*, or more technically *major depressive disorder* (MDD), stipulate at least five symptoms from a list that includes depressed mood; diminished interest; disturbances in concentration; poor self-esteem or guilt; disturbances in sleep, energy, and appetite; jitteriness; psychomotor slowing; and thoughts of death or suicide. The symptoms must have been present most of the time for a 2-month period, and they must have a deleterious impact on the individual's life, such as an impaired capacity to work. The milder mood disorder, *dysthymic disorder*, requires the presence of only two symptoms from this list, but the duration of the condition must be at least 2 years, and it must result in substantial impairment. Studies indicate that as many as 17% of the population experience at least one severe depressive episode at some point in their lives. Because depression is a primary factor in tens of thousands of suicides every year, it is a major public health concern requiring intervention. The lifetime suicide risks for men and women diagnosed with major depression have been estimated to be 7% and 1%, respectively (although approximately twice as many women as men are diagnosed with depression); there is an 80% greater suicide risk for untreated sufferers than their treated counterparts (Blair-West et al., 1999). Depression is also the fourth leading cause of major disability in 1990, and by 2020, it has been estimated that it will be the second major cause of disability, with the economic burden associated with this disorder being second only to coronary artery disease (Murray & Lopez, 1997).

A large body of clinical research has demonstrated that motivational symptoms such as tiredness, listlessness, fatigue, and low energy are a critical aspect of depression (Salamone et al., 2006, 2010; Stahl 2002; Swindle et al., 2001; Tylee et al., 1999; Willner, 1983; Yurgelun-Todd et al. 2007). This cluster of symptoms is related to the activational component of motivation (the willingness to engage in activities), and has been referred to as "psychomotor slowing," "psychomotor retardation," or "anergia." Fatigue also is a widely reported problem in many depressed patients. It should be stressed that the term *fatigue* in this context does not refer to muscle fatigue or peripheral metabolic fatigue, per se. Instead, it reflects a concept known as "central fatigue" (Chaudhuri & Behan, 2004), which is a subjective lack of physical and/or mental energy that is not related to sadness or weakness, but is thought to be related to brain mechanisms (Lapierre & Hum, 2007). Although anhedonia is often emphasized as a cardinal symptom of depression, it has been argued that many people with major depression have fundamental deficits in reward seeking, exertion of effort, and effort-related decision making that do not simply depend upon any problems that they may have with experiencing pleasure (Treadway & Zald, 2011). Depressed patients with anergia are more common than patients with anxiety-related symptoms (Tylee et al., 1999). Lack of energy is the depressive symptom that is most strongly correlated with lack of the social function shown by depressed patients, and is closely related to various work-related factors such as days in bed, days of lost work, and low work productivity (Stahl, 2002; Swindle et al., 1998; Tylee et al., 1999). In addition, baseline fatigue and disinterest in activities are some of the best predictors of lack of response to antidepressant drug treatment, as well as overall treatment outcome. In spite of this clinical research demonstrating the importance of anergia as a feature of depression, these symptoms are often less targeted for elimination compared to other symptoms of depression (Stahl, 2002).

For most individuals with symptoms of depression, the contrast with normal mood is in one direction; thus, the diagnosis is typically referred to as *unipolar disorder*. In about one-fifth of persons with symptoms of depression, there may be periods in which there is an extreme shift in mood toward mania; in these cases the condition is called *manic depression* or *bipolar disorder*. (Although manic episodes are not always accompanied by depressive episodes, such cases are extremely rare.) During these manic episodes, the person may exhibit extreme elation, display unusually high activity levels, and be irrationally optimistic and overconfident. However, this mood is brittle—that is, easily and dramatically changed by the specific circumstances—and the person can become irritable if frustrated. The thought patterns during mania are often disturbed, with one thought rapidly following another (referred to as "flight of ideas"). Bipolar disorders can be further differentiated as bipolar I (in which manic episodes are sufficiently severe to cause marked impairment in occupational functioning or in usual social activities or relationships with others, or to necessitate hospitalization to prevent harm to self or others, or there are psychotic features) or bipolar II (in which only hypomanic episodes occur, i.e., the manic symptoms are not sufficiently severe enough to cause those characteristics described for bipolar I manic episodes). Some persons with the bipolar disorder may shift back and forth between the two extremes of depression and mania, whereas others may exhibit long periods of relatively normal functioning between episodes. Because depressive episodes are generally more common in these individuals, it is often difficult to determine whether a unipolar disorder or bipolar disorder is present. However, the distinction is important because the types of drugs that are most effective in the two disorders are quite different. Giving a bipolar patient medication appropriate for the unipolar depressive disorder may precipitate a manic episode, whereas giving a unipolar depressed patient medication appropriate for the bipolar patient may not be beneficial and may prolong unnecessary discomfort. Although mania is much less common, the destructive behaviors accompanying it also require intervention. In many of these cases, drugs are a primary form of intervention, either alone or in combination with other forms of psychotherapy.

The treatment of depression is made difficult by the fact that it is both a normal mood state, which a person encounters during periods of loss and which is generally transitory, and an emotional disorder. Depression can also result from a pattern of drug abuse that the person may be reluctant to change. Symptoms of depression as a disorder may remit spontaneously or may come and go over time. Because fear and anxiety may accompany depression, the person may be physically active but may not be able to concentrate on any one task for very long. Only under extreme conditions, a depressed person may severely distort reality and exhibit unusual beliefs or behaviors. Therefore, it is hard to determine whether intervention is necessary or would even be beneficial.

Individuals suffering from depression often also experience somatic problems. Physical complaints of loss of appetite and weight, insomnia, early morning awakenings, aches and pains, and so forth may also be present. For example, in one study of patients with major depression, more than two-thirds reported physical symptoms, such as headaches, backaches, and gastrointestinal difficulties (Simon et al., 1999). Unfortunately, it is these physical aspects of the disorder that depressed individuals tend to complain about to their physicians, who in turn may focus on treatments that may ordinarily be used in reducing these symptoms without realizing that they are dealing with a person suffering from depression.

PHARMACOTHERAPY FOR DEPRESSION

The two major classes of drugs currently used in the United States for the treatment of depression are the monoamine oxidase inhibitors (MAOIs) and the monoamine uptake blockers. Within the latter category, there are compounds with various pharmacological profiles, including "tricyclic" antidepressants (which act broadly as inhibitors of monoamine uptake), selective monoamine uptake inhibitors (which include the selective inhibitors of serotonin [5-HT] or catecholamine uptake), and dual action compounds that selectively inhibit both 5-HT and NE (norepinephrine) uptake. Sometimes the 5-HT uptake inhibitors are known as SSRIs (selective serotonin reuptake inhibitors; sometimes uptake is referred to as *reuptake*). MAOIs and tricyclic antidepressants were introduced in the 1950s, and the first of the selective monoamine reuptake inhibitors—the SSRI Prozac—was approved for use in the late 1980s. The research literature suggests that, as a group, antidepressants are effective in 50% to 60% of patients with unipolar depression and that placebo treatment is effective in 20% to 30%, with higher placebo rates for patients with mild depression (Quitkin et al., 2000; Thase, 1999). However, only around one-third of patients diagnosed with unipolar depression reach full remission of their symptoms with antidepressant drug treatment, with another one-third exhibiting partial response, which is typically defined as a 50% improvement in depressive symptoms.

No single antidepressant drug has been shown to be effective in relieving the symptoms of unipolar depression in more than two out of every three patients (Davis et al., 1993; Frank et al., 1993; Mulrow et al., 2000). However, drugs with very different pharmacological properties, although appearing comparable in terms of inducing global changes in depression, may differ considerably in terms of their ability to reduce specific symptoms (e.g., depersonalization; depressed mood; early, middle, and late insomnia) commonly assessed in global depression inventories (i.e., the Hamilton Rating Scale for Depression, or HAM-D; Leon et al., 1993). Because there is tremendous variation in the pharmacodynamics of different antidepressants, and because depression may be caused by a variety of mechanisms, it has been argued that with sufficient patience and trials with different types of antidepressants (alone or combined with other drug therapy or psychotherapy) the overall treatment efficacy rate may be higher than 70% (McGrath et al., 1993; Thase, 1999). Unfortunately, about one out of every four patients will relapse, even when maintained on an antidepressant medication; again, shifting to another type of antidepressant will sometimes produce symptom remission in many of these patients.

Placebo efficacy rates vary considerably depending on a variety of factors—for example, approximately 40% efficacy in married or mildly depressed patients versus approximately 20% in single or more severely depressed patients (Wilcox et al., 1992). About half of these responders will relapse with placebo maintenance. There is some evidence that the difference in efficacy between active medications and placebo may increase after 6 weeks of treatment, but because of ethical and economic reasons, many studies of this nature do not go much beyond a 3- or 4-week evaluation period (Prien, 1988). In any case, one must consider the possibility that some patients who improve with these medications do so because of a true drug effect, whereas others do so because of nonspecific (placebo) factors. Evidence suggests that a true drug response is more likely to be delayed and more persistent than a nonspecific response and that those patients who relapse with continued antidepressant therapy are more likely to display placebo-response patterns (early onset and/or fluctuating course; Harrison et al., 1988; Quitkin et al., 2000). Although it is often argued that antidepressant drugs usually take several weeks to produce their therapeutic effects, a part of this may come from the fact that it is more difficult to distinguish antidepressant effects from placebo effects within the first few weeks. For example, in a series of studies by Martin Katz and his colleagues (reviewed in Derivan, 1995), it was found that tricyclic antidepressants do act in responders within the first week of treatment, with responders distinguishable from nonresponders in terms of improving affect and cognitive functioning (such as thinking and concentration). However, in general, it is not until the second week of treatment that active treatment effects begin to separate reliably from placebo treatment effects (Montgomery, 1995).

First-Generation Monoamine Oxidase Inhibitors

Monoamine oxidase (MAO) is an enzyme found in cells throughout the body. It is localized predominantly on the outer membrane of subcellular particles called mitochondria. It comes in two forms, designated Type A and Type B, depending on the substances that they act on. MAO is responsible for the intraneuronal metabolic inactivation (through deamination) of 5-HT, DA (dopamine), and NE. The **monoamine oxidase inhibitor (MAOI)** antidepressants comprise a group of heterogeneous drugs that share the ability to block this action of MAO. The first MAOI (iproniazid) was originally used in the treatment of tuberculosis and was only accidentally found to have mood-elevating properties. However, its toxicity eventually led to its withdrawal from the market, a fate common to many of these types of drugs. The three MAOIs presently used clinically as antidepressants in the United States are tranylcypromine (Parnate), phenelzine (Nardil), and isocarboxazid (Marplan).

As one might expect, the efficacy of MAOIs in treating depression appears to be related to the normal level of MAO activity in the patient; that is, depressed patients with low MAO activity to begin with are less responsive to MAOIs than patients with higher MAO activity (Georgotas et al., 1987). Although enhancement of monoamine activity is presumed to be the primary neurochemical factor in their antidepressant properties, MAOIs have numerous other biochemical actions that may be involved in their effects (e.g., increases in GABA [gamma-aminobutyric acid] levels; Parent et al., 2000). Furthermore, as is the case with other antidepressants, the MAO-inhibiting actions occur rapidly and precede symptom remission by as much as 2 or more weeks.

Although the antidepressant properties of the first MAOI were noted at about the same time as those of the first tricyclic antidepressants (discussed later), the therapeutic use of MAOIs has been very limited, primarily because MAOIs can induce more toxic reactions when combined with certain drugs or foods. MAOIs can interact unpredictably with many adrenergic-related chemicals to induce a *hypertensive crisis*—a serious toxic effect that can lead to headaches, fever, intracranial bleeding, and, in some cases, death. This can occur when MAOIs are combined with tricyclics, psychostimulants, and L-DOPA (L-dihydroxyphenylalanine). For these reasons, the combination of MAOIs and other antidepressants is sometimes contraindicated. Moreover, for reasons as yet unclear, postural hypotension (which can cause dizziness) is commonly observed when MAOIs are used by themselves.

MAOIs also interact in a similar fashion with foods containing the sympathomimetic amine, tyramine. Examples of such foods are cheese, yeast products, chocolate, some wines, milk, beer, pickled herring, chicken liver, and large amounts of coffee, among many others. This problem comes about because the MAO inhibition allows these biologically active amines, which hepatic MAO would normally metabolize, to release catecholamines from axon terminals and produce sympathomimetic effects, which include a marked rise in blood pressure and other cardiovascular changes. MAOIs also interfere with various enzymes to prolong and intensify the effects of nonadrenergic-related drugs (such as sedative–hypnotics, general anesthetics, narcotics, and anticholinergics), and they interfere with the metabolism of various naturally occurring substances. Because of these interactions, individuals being treated with MAOIs (and their families) are normally given a list of drugs and foods to avoid. However, because MAOIs induce long-lasting effects on MAO, it may take up to 2 weeks after discontinuing their use for the body to restore monoamine metabolism to normal (Parent et al., 2000). Thus a period of several days to 2 weeks is recommended before switching a patient from an MAOI to another class of antidepressant (Baldessarini, 2001).

In spite of the long delay in therapeutic response, a number of toxic reactions to overdoses of MAOIs (independent of their interactions with other drugs or foods) can occur within hours (Baldessarini, 2001). These may include agitation, hallucinations, high fever, convulsions, and hypotension or hypertension. Treatment of these symptoms is difficult because of the numerous interactions between MAOIs and other drugs that normally might be useful in dealing with these symptoms. The long duration of MAO inhibition requires that the patient be monitored for several days after a toxic reaction. Several side effects have been noted with doses of MAOIs lower than those inducing acute toxicity—for example, cellular damage to liver cells, tremors, insomnia, agitation, hypomania, hallucinations, dizziness, and anticholinergic-like effects. It is obvious from the list of potential toxic effects of the MAOIs that they are greater and more serious than those of most other psychotherapeutic drugs. Thus, not surprisingly, their use is often reserved for patients who are not responsive to other drugs and refuse electroconvulsive therapy (ECT).

Depressed patients who are most likely to respond preferentially to MAOIs are those diagnosed with what is sometimes referred to as *atypical depression* in the clinical literature (Quitkin et al., 1993). Such patients commonly have a reactive mood and exhibit one or more atypical features of overeating (often with a particular craving for sweets), oversleeping, leaden paralysis, and rejection sensitivity. Atypical depressed patients may also exhibit a reversal of the usual diurnal variation; that is, rather than feeling better in the morning, with mood declining somewhat as the day goes on, they are more likely to feel worse in the morning. Depending on the diagnostic criteria used, patients with atypical depression may account for 10% to 40% of outpatient cases of depression (Zisook et al., 1993). Another form of atypical depression that appears to respond well to phenelzine is termed *hysteroid dysphoria* (Kayser et al., 1985). Patients with this disorder (usually women) are characterized by immaturity, self-centeredness, attention-getting behavior, manipulativeness, and, quite often, vague seductiveness. They experience depressions that are often precipitated by rejection, especially the loss of a romantic attachment. Their depressed episodes are characterized by a tendency to oversleep or spend more than normal amounts of time in bed, to overeat or crave sweets, and a labile mood that temporarily improves when attention or praise is given.

MAOIs have also been shown in many studies to be as effective as tricyclics in elderly depressed patients (Volz et al., 1994) and may be used as an alternative treatment in elderly patients who cannot tolerate some of the side effects of tricyclics. Like the tricyclics, the MAOIs may exert considerable improvement in the moods and eating behavior of bulimics, although their use in a condition whose primary symptoms involve uncontrollable eating behavior may not be advisable (because of the dietary constraints already mentioned; Walsh et al., 1984). MAOIs may also exert a favorable response in people with certain neurotic illnesses with depressive features and in people who suffer from acute anxiety, phobias, and panic attacks (in which the person may experience light-headedness, dizziness, "rubbery" legs, choking, difficulty in breathing, a racing or palpitating heart, tingling sensations, and extreme fright; Buigues & Vallejo, 1987). Disabling obsessive thoughts that are characteristic of the obsessive–compulsive disorder may also respond to MAOIs, whether major symptoms of depression are present or not. As is the case with the tricyclic and SSRI antidepressants, there is little potential for tolerance development or psychological dependence with the MAOIs. Abstinence symptoms associated with MAOI cessation have not been identified.

Reversible Inhibitors of Monoamine Oxidase A

The first-generation MAOIs just described are all effective in the treatment of depression and a variety of other disorders, but they possess three pharmacological properties that minimize their usefulness. First, these MAOIs interact with exogenous amines (e.g., tyramine in food and pressor amine drugs), producing a potentially toxic reaction. Second, they bind irreversibly to MAO enzymes, so that after their use, up to 2 weeks are needed for these enzymes to be resynthesized by the body, which may delay initiating treatment with other drugs for depression or other medical problems the patient might have. Third, in addition to allowing for a buildup of NE and 5-HT, which appears to be crucial for their antidepressant effects, they also allow DA levels to build up, a result that does not appear to be relevant for their antidepressant properties but which may exacerbate or produce schizophrenic or manic symptoms in predisposed individuals. To counter these problems, a number of reversible inhibitors of MAO-A (RIMAs) have been developed (Lavian et al., 1993). Two of the RIMAs showing considerable clinical potential for use are moclobemide and brofaromine. These drugs inhibit only the MAO-A enzyme, which is selective in metabolizing NE and 5-HT but not DA, and being reversibly bound to MAO, their duration of MAO inhibition is short. Also, these drugs may be displaced from their binding site in the intestine by ingested, indirectly acting sympathomimetic amines such as tyramine, which allows the MAO to inactivate these amines, thus avoiding the initiation of an extreme hypertensive reaction (Mayersohn & Guentert, 1995). By themselves, they appear to exert minimal hypotensive effects, including orthostatic hypotension.

In clinical comparisons with other antidepressants, including tricyclics, SSRIs, and the first-generation MAOIs, the efficacy of RIMAs has been comparable in the treatment of depression. Also, as is the case with most of the antidepressants, some depressed patients who are refractory to one type of antidepressant may show dramatic improvements in mood with RIMAs (Reynaert et al., 1995; Volz et al., 1994). Their efficacy has been demonstrated in the treatment of psychotic (i.e., very severe, with delusional thought disturbance) and nonpsychotic depression, exogenous and endogenous depression (both unipolar and bipolar), retarded and agitated depression, and in depression that accompanies dementia (e.g., Alzheimer's type; Priest et al., 1995). Moclobemide and brofaromine lack significant effects on psychomotor performance and cognitive function, and lack anticholinergic effects, which make them particularly useful in elderly patients.

Unfortunately, despite their use worldwide, it is not likely that the RIMAs will be available in the United States in the foreseeable future because there appears to be insufficient financial incentive to support the additional research required for Food and Drug Administration (FDA) approval (Lotufo-Neto et al., 1999). There is simply too much competition from existing approved antidepressants, particularly SSRIs, which have a more extensive track record of safety, especially in overdose. Although head-to-head comparisons indicate that RIMAs may have slightly better antidepressant efficacy than SSRIs and induce fewer complaints of sexual dysfunction, they may induce more insomnia.

First-Generation Monoamine Uptake Inhibitors: Tricyclic Antidepressants

Tricyclics are so named because they consist of three-ringed molecules. Although this structural characteristic is not critical to the effect of the drug (i.e., there are drugs with three rings that are not antidepressants, and there are antidepressants that do not have three rings), the use of this name has persisted. The most common clinically used tricyclic compounds in the United States are imipramine (Tofranil) and a primary metabolite desipramine (Norpramin), amitriptyline and a primary metabolite nortriptyline (Pamelor), doxepin (Sinequan), amoxapine, trimipramine (Surmontil), and protriptyline (Vivactil). These drugs all block reuptake of NE and 5-HT, but they differ considerably in terms of their potency and selectivity in these actions (Baldessarini, 2001). For example, amitriptyline, doxepin, imipramine, and trimipramine tend to inhibit both NE and 5-HT reuptake; desipramine, maprotiline, nortriptyline, and protriptyline exhibit the most selectivity in blocking NE reuptake; and amoxapine tends to block both NE and DA reuptake. These drugs also exhibit wide differences with respect to blocking histamine H_1, muscarinic, 5-HT$_2$, and DA D_2 receptors. Regardless of these differences, they all are equally effective in relieving depression, and they all take several days or weeks to alter the symptoms of depression (Davis et al., 1993; Frank et al., 1993).

Tricyclics appear to be most effective in severe cases of unipolar unremitting depression. Although it has generally been believed that they are more effective in treating endogenous depression (where there is no evidence of obvious precipitating events) characterized by regression and inactivity than exogenous depression (where there are clearly precipitating events, such as loss of a loved one), research has not supported the endogenous versus exogenous dichotomy. The reason that studies have not found tricyclics to be of much benefit in exogenous depression and mild depression may be that there is a high placebo-response rate or a high spontaneous remission rate in these cases, coupled with the slow onset of action by the drugs (Brown, 1988). Tricyclics are not recommended for use in bipolar depression because they may trigger a transition from depression to manic excitement and because this disorder is quite responsive to lithium, which generally induces fewer side effects. As discussed in other chapters of this book, psychological disturbances that do not have a clear link to depression may also show favorable response to tricyclics.

Tricyclic antidepressants can be extremely toxic, and they have relatively low therapeutic indexes—unfortunate characteristics for drugs used in the treatment of a disorder that can lead to suicide. In fact, when they were the most commonly prescribed antidepressants, tricyclics accounted for a quarter of all fatal overdoses in the United States, with 70% of tricyclic deaths never reaching the hospital (Jarvis, 1991). Therefore, a prudent approach to the treatment of depressed patients would be to give them no more than a 2-week supply of these medications. As is the case with many antidepressants, tricyclics have the potential to induce epilepsy-like seizures (Tollefson, 1991). Because of their potent anticholinergic (specifically antimuscarinic) action, tachycardia, blurred vision, dry mouth, constipation, and urinary retention are common—adverse effects that probably account for why the dropout rate in clinical trials is significantly higher with tricyclics than with antidepressants (Mulrow et al., 2000). Therapeutic doses of these drugs have significant effects on the cardiovascular system, such as orthostatic hypotension (a drop in blood pressure upon standing up). In addition, an increased tendency for arrhythmia (irregularity in the heartbeat) to develop with these drugs has resulted in a number of unexpected deaths. With long-term exposure, the risk of heart attacks has been found to be over two times higher in users of tricyclic antidepressants than in users of SSRIs (Cohen et al., 2000). Therefore, great caution must be observed in their use in patients with cardiac problems. Weakness and fatigue may also occur infrequently. Although significant motor disturbances are rare, a fine tremor may occur, particularly in elderly patients. The relatively infrequent side effects of jaundice, agranulocytosis, rashes, weight gain, and orgasmic impotence have also been reported to occur with tricyclics.

Because high doses of these drugs can induce CNS (central nervous system) toxic reactions, there is a biphasic relationship between drug plasma levels and efficacy. That is, there is a therapeutic window, and below or above a particular plasma level the drug is not effective in elevating mood (Tollefson, 1991). Unfortunately, when idealized dosages are administered to different individuals, resulting steady-state plasma concentrations may vary tenfold or more (DeVane et al., 1991). These characteristics contribute to difficulties in establishing optimal dosage regimens for individual patients.

Tolerance development to the antidepressant properties of tricyclics appears to be rare, but there is some indication that tolerance may develop to the sedative and anticholinergic side effects and orthostatic hypotension. Tricyclics do not induce psychological dependence, as they are void of primary reinforcing properties and have numerous side effects. As you might expect, nonhumans also will not self-administer these drugs. Unlike the psychostimulants, there is no evidence that abrupt cessation of tricyclics induces depression. However, reduction of tricyclic medication should be gradual because an abstinence syndrome (sleep disturbance, nightmares, nausea, headache, and hypercholinergic-type effects) may occur if medication is stopped abruptly (Baldessarini, 2001).

Selective Serotonin Reuptake Inhibitors

As discussed shortly, the tricyclic antidepressants were the first-line agents used in the treatment of depression for many years and have been the prototype drugs against which all newcomers have been compared. Although the evidence is clear that they are effective in the treatment of depression, they have a wide variety of potential side effects and a low therapeutic index, which is due to the fact that these drugs act on a wide variety of neurotransmitter receptors and uptake transporters. Because of these problems, along with the growing consensus that 5-HT was a vital component to normal mood, researchers set out to develop drugs that would have a high affinity for the 5-HT uptake site and a low affinity for other neurotransmitter uptake sites and receptors, and thus potentially produce an effective antidepressant without the side effects of the tricyclics. As a result of trial and error research, the **selective serotonin reuptake inhibitors,** or **SSRIs,** were born. The first of these to be approved for clinical use in the United States in 1987 was fluoxetine (Prozac), and it rapidly became one of the most widely prescribed of all antidepressants (Barondes, 1994). Members of this class of drugs available for prescription now include sertraline (Zoloft), paroxetine (Paxil), citalopram (Celexa), escitalopram (Lexapro), and fluvoxamine (Luvox).

Since their introduction in the late 1980s, SSRIs have become the first-line drugs in the treatment of depression. Their popularity derives not from their exhibiting greater efficacy in reducing the core symptoms of depression, which is comparable to that of the tricyclics and MAOIs and may actually be lower than the efficacy of tricyclics in severe cases of depression (Anderson, 2000). It derives instead from their less objectionable side effects and much lower toxicity. That is, they don't have anticholinergic side effects such as dry mouth and abnormal heart rhythms, and they don't increase the risk of heart attacks (myocardial infarctions) as do the tricyclics (Cohen et al., 2000). This makes them more effective in the treatment of some patients—for example, the elderly. Furthermore, they are much less toxic than tricyclics in large doses and therefore pose less danger as a potential instrument for suicide. Also, they do not produce the toxic interaction with a number of foods that many of the MAOIs are capable of. SSRIs are generally better tolerated in combination with most medicines (notable exceptions are lithium and MAOIs) or alcohol (Goodnick, 1991a), although they do inhibit the action of a wide variety of P450 enzymes that are responsible for metabolizing most drugs (Kent, 2000). Thus, the plasma concentrations and actions of drugs such as caffeine, beta-blockers, antipsychotics, nonsteroidal anti-inflammatory analgesics, benzodiazepines, opiates, other SSRIs, and tricyclics, among many others, may be increased when taken with these drugs.

Due to fewer side effects, there is greater patient acceptance of SSRIs and compliance with treatment, which often determines treatment outcome. However, SSRIs do have a wide range of side effects—most notably nausea, headaches, nervousness, insomnia, and sexual dysfunction (i.e., impotence, inability to achieve orgasm)—which some patients are unable to tolerate. Overall, the safety factor is overwhelmingly in favor of the SSRIs over the older tricyclics and MAOIs. However, as with all antidepressants, they are not effective in all patients, even at maximal dosages and with sufficiently long exposure, and some patients may find the side effects intolerable.

One potentially life-threatening complication with SSRIs is their ability to induce a *serotonin syndrome* (Lane & Baldwin, 1997). More often this syndrome occurs when an SSRI is used concurrently with another substance that also increases extracellular levels of 5-HT (e.g., other antidepressants, St. John's wort). The symptoms include disorientation and confusion, behavioral agitation and restlessness, fever, shivering, profuse perspiration, diarrhea, coordination impairment, and involuntary muscle contraction, and they may go undetected because they are sometimes similar to symptoms induced by the SSRI. The difference between this syndrome and the occurrence of adverse effects caused by SSRIs alone is the clustering of the signs and symptoms, their severity, and their duration.

SSRIs belong to different chemical families, and the only common property they share is their capacity to inhibit the uptake of 5-HT; thus, it is indisputable that they exert their therapeutic effect primarily via 5-HT systems (Blier & de Montigny, 1994). However, with over a dozen receptors for 5-HT to act on—many with distinct distributions—the relationship between their neurochemical properties and their therapeutic effects is not clear. It is clear that the immediate actions of these drugs are only the beginning of a series of molecular changes in the brain that eventually lead to symptom relief, because the action of 5-HT reuptake inhibition by these drugs is almost immediate, whereas it generally takes 1 to 2 weeks—in some cases up to a month—of drug exposure for symptom relief to be clearly distinguishable from that which is achieved with a placebo, regardless of the disorder (Barondes, 1994).

Most of the SSRIs have relatively long elimination half-lives, for example, 14 to 26 hours for paroxetine, sertraline, and fluvoxamine, so that they may be administered as a single daily dose (DeVane, 1994). Delayed release preparations (e.g., Paxil CR, Prozac Weekly) have been developed so that even less-frequent dosing is required. The extended half-life of fluoxetine of 4 to 6 days—and of its active metabolite, norfluoxetine, of 4 to 16 days—requires an extended period of time to establish steady-state plasma levels and a prolonged washout period when dosing is discontinued. These drugs are all cleared from the body mostly through hepatic metabolism, and all except paroxetine and fluvoxamine are metabolized into pharmacologically active metabolites. Like the tricyclics, SSRIs display a broad variability in steady-state plasma levels, but due to their greater safety/toxicity profile, the variability in clearance is of lesser importance than with the tricyclics. Unfortunately, no usable relationship between SSRI plasma concentration levels and therapeutic effects has been found, and widely varying concentrations appear to have little relationship to adverse effects.

As discussed in Chapter 10, SSRI antidepressants have been found to be beneficial in a wide variety of anxiety-related disorders with no clear connection with depression. For example, they have been found to be the most effective drug treatment for obsessive–compulsive disorder. They have been prescribed for a number of other symptoms, many of which aren't even considered indicative of a mental disorder (Barondes, 1994). These include excessive sensitivity to criticism, fear of rejection, lack of self-esteem, a deficiency in the ability to experience pleasure, premature ejaculation, premenstrual dysphoric disorder, eating disorders, obesity, borderline personality disorders, self-injurious behavior in the developmentally disabled, alcoholism, and cocaine abuse. However, it should be noted that adequate documentation of the efficacy of these drugs in these symptoms (disorders), in comparison to placebo, is lacking.

None of the SSRIs have been associated with abuse or dependence. Abstinence symptoms of physiological and psychological discomfort (e.g., dizziness, gastrointestinal symptoms, and anxiety/dysphoria) can occur following abrupt discontinuation of chronic SSRI treatment, with the symptoms being more prominent with SSRIs with shorter plasma half-lives (Michelson et al., 2000). Documented evidence for tolerance development to their antidepressant properties is also lacking, but tolerance often occurs to the early onset side effects of these drugs. In general, to prevent or lessen the magnitude of these effects, initial dosages start low and are gradually increased.

Shortly after fluoxetine came on the market and was recognized to be a novel, atypical antidepressant, numerous anecdotal reports came out suggesting that it might induce suicidal thoughts or actions in a small portion of patients. However, because these patients typically exhibit characteristics, such as depression, for which suicidal ideation is not uncommon, it was difficult to assess the degree to which fluoxetine was responsible. Large-scale studies subsequently determined, whether causal or not, that the incidence of violent suicidal preoccupation with fluoxetine treatment was rare—less than 5% of patients treated—and did not appear to be significantly different from that which occurs with other antidepressants (Beasley et al., 1991; Fava & Rosenbaum, 1991). In fact, as one might expect from an antidepressant, reduction in suicidal ideation was much more likely to occur. For example, a study investigating the relationship between fluoxetine use and suicidal behavior in patients with anxiety disorders and/or depression showed that patients using fluoxetine had a significantly lower probability of making suicide attempts or gestures during the follow-up period than patients not using fluoxetine, although patients with more suicide risk factors at intake were more likely to be prescribed fluoxetine than those without these risk factors (Warshaw & Keller, 1996).

There have been concerns over whether SSRIs in particular, and antidepressants in general, may induce suicidal ideation and behaviors resurfaced—initially due to reports that at least some SSRIs were associated with increases in suicidal thinking and behavior in pediatric patients. However, further scrutiny of the research suggested that antidepressants, in general, may increase the risk of suicidal behavior in both adult and pediatric patients in the first month after starting antidepressant drug treatment, especially during the first one to nine days (Jick et al., 2004). (There have been a number of speculations, none with any empirical support, about what might cause suicidal cognitions or behaviors early in antidepressant treatment. These include activation of idiosyncratic side effects that make the individual even more uncomfortable, overstimulation of 5-HT autoreceptors that leads to even further decreases in serotonergic neuron activity and increases in the individual's hostile or aggressive impulses, lifting of mood to the point that the individual gains sufficient energy to actually carry out his or her preexisting suicidal impulses, among others [Couzin, 2004].)

As a result of these types of reports, despite acknowledging a lack of evidence for a causal linkage, in 2004 the FDA ordered drug companies to label all antidepressant medications distributed in the United States with strongly worded warnings that the medications "increase the risk of suicidal thinking and behavior (suicidality) in children and adolescents with major depressive disorder (MDD) or other psychiatric disorders." The FDA has also recommended that adults with major depression or comorbid depression being treated with antidepressants should be observed similarly for clinical worsening and suicidality, especially during the initial few months of a course of drug therapy, or at times of dose changes, either increases or decreases.

Additional Drug Treatments for Depression

Based on the premise that depression may be due to a dysfunction in either 5-HT or NE, or both, drugs that selectively inhibit the reuptake of both of these monoamines have been developed. Venlafaxine (Effexor) was the first of these. Its efficacy and side-effect profile appears to be very similar to those of the SSRI fluoxetine. However, because of its lesser potency in inhibiting NE reuptake than 5-HT reuptake at lower doses, venlafaxine may have greater efficacy in the treatment of clinical depression than SSRIs at the higher ends of the effective dosage ranges (Horst & Preskorn, 1998; Rudolph & Feiger, 1999).

Speculation that venlafaxine may have an earlier onset of action than previously available antidepressants, due to its ability to rapidly down-regulate beta receptors in rat brains, has not been proven in humans (Ellingrod & Perry, 1994). Nor have some clinical trials comparing venlafaxine to other antidepressants, such as imipramine or trazodone, shown significant advantages for venlafaxine in terms of efficacy or onset of effect (Morton et al., 1995). However, two studies using very high doses of venlafaxine (375 mg/day, which can produce an abnormally high incidence of side effects such as nausea, dizziness, somnolence, sweating, and sexual dysfunction) found a significant difference from placebo in decreased depression symptoms in 4 to 7 days (Mendlewicz, 1995).

Duloxetine (Cymbalta) is another dual 5-HT/NE inhibitor that has been approved by the FDA for the treatment of depression. Several controlled studies have indicated that it exhibits a high degree of efficacy, tolerability, and safety for the treatment of MDD. In particular, relatively rapid therapeutic onset and high remission rates have been noted. Duloxetine also appears to have significant benefit in the treatment of the painful physical symptoms associated with depression (Schatzberg, 2003). A clinical trial evaluating duloxetine for the long-term treatment of major depression indicated that it was effective, safe, and well tolerated over a 1-year period. It was also observed that symptom remission continued to increase over the 1-year treatment period; that is, estimated probabilities of remission increased from 51% at week 6 to 76% and 82% at weeks 28 and 52, respectively (Raskin et al., 2003). A double-blind comparison between duloxetine and the SSRI paroxetine found that duloxetine therapy was more efficacious for emotional and physical symptoms of depression, although it did exhibit an SSRI-like profile of side effects (Goldstein et al., 2004). Other clinical trials have indicated that duloxetine can provide rapid relief of anxiety symptoms associated with depression and that the mean improvement with duloxetine may be significantly greater than with the SSRIs paroxetine and fluoxetine (Dunner et al., 2003).

Bupropion (Wellbutrin) has antidepressant efficacy comparable to the tricyclics, but it differs from previous antidepressants because its most potent influence is on inhibiting DA reuptake, with a weaker influence on NE reuptake and no effect on 5-HT reuptake (Horst & Preskorn, 1998). These actions may account for its exerting mild stimulant effects (Goodnick, 1991b). In addition, double-blind, placebo-controlled studies have demonstrated that a majority of patients who were intolerant to or resistant to tricyclics responded favorably when treated with bupropion (Preskorn, 1991). Evidence suggests that this bupropion may be relatively effective at treating motivational symptoms such as anergia and fatigue in people with major depression (Demyttenaere et al. 2005; Pae et al. 2007; Papakostas et al. 2006; Rampello et al., 1991; Stahl, 2002). Bupropion possesses no MAO-inhibition effects and minimal anticholinergic or antihistaminic actions, which result in its producing a low incidence of side effects, sedation, orthostatic hypotension, and adverse cardiac effects. Also, its tendency to induce hypomanic or manic episodes in unipolar depressives appears low, although it may trigger manic episodes in bipolar patients. In contrast to the SSRIs, for which sexual side effects are common, bupropion appears to induce an unusually low incidence of sexual side effects and may actually improve sexual desire in some individuals (Segraves, 1998). The major problem with bupropion is its tendency to induce seizures and other forms of CNS toxicity—for example, delirium and psychosis—at high dosages (Preskorn, 1991). It may also induce mild dryness of the mouth, headache, nausea, constipation, and tremor.

Two relatively new drugs with unique neurochemical properties that may provide benefits beyond those typically provided by earlier antidepressants are mirtazapine (Remeron) and reboxetine (Edronax; Kent, 2000). Mirtazapine potently blocks central α-2-adrenergic presynaptic receptors (autoreceptors and heteroreceptors), as well as 5-HT_2 and 5-HT_3 receptors, while exhibiting minimal affinity for other receptors or uptake transporters. Presumably, NE release is enhanced by the autoreceptor blockade, and 5-HT release is enhanced by the blockade of the heteroreceptors on serotonergic neurons, as well as 5-HT_3 receptors that presynaptically influence 5-HT release. The most common side effects of mirtazapine are sleepiness (more likely with low doses), dizziness, weight gain (due to enhanced appetite), dry mouth, and constipation. Numerous studies have indicated that mirtazapine is comparable in efficacy to various tricyclic antidepressants (Kent, 2000). Comparative studies of mirtazapine versus SSRIs have all reported statistically significant and clinically relevant differences in favor of mirtazapine—for example, faster onset of efficacy and rapid anxiolytic effects (Thompson, 1999; Wheatley et al., 1998). In one study with depressed patients who discontinued SSRI treatment because they experienced sexual dysfunction, all patients displayed significant improvement in depressive symptoms without experiencing sexual dysfunction (Koutouvidis et al, 1999).

Reboxetine is a selective NE uptake inhibitor. Because of its low affinity for other uptake transporters and receptors, it induces fewer anticholinergic side effects than the tricyclics and less nausea and sexual dysfunction than the SSRIs (Montgomery, 1999). Several clinical trials have indicated its efficacy to be comparable to tricyclics and SSRIs in the treatment of moderate depression and to be more effective than SSRIs in the treatment of hospitalized depressed patients and those with severe depression (Massana et al., 1999; Moller, 2000). Enhancement of social functioning of depressed patients also appears to be greater with reboxetine than with SSRIs (Dubini et al., 1997a, 1997b). However, despite its apparent efficacy and its use in several European countries for several years, it has failed to meet FDA standards required for its approval for use in the United States.

Some benzodiazepines, such as alprazolam (Xanax), may be used as antidepressants. Alprazolam has a potent GABA-enhancing effect similar to other benzodiazepines, but unlike other drugs in this class, it has antidepressant efficacy comparable to older tricyclics, with a faster onset of action, primarily in the domain of insomnia relief. However, tolerance may develop to its antidepressant properties after a few weeks. Like the benzodiazepines, it has a low incidence of anticholinergic side effects, low cardiotoxicity, and minimal potential for lethality with overdose. However, drowsiness and lethargy are common, but generally well tolerated, side effects. Because of alprazolam's relatively short plasma half-life and its tendency to induce physical dependence with chronic use, dosages should be gradually tapered over several weeks when treatment with alprazolam is discontinued (Rickels et al., 1990). The nonbenzodiazepine anxiolytic buspirone (BuSpar) has been shown to be effective in relieving symptoms of depression (Charney et al., 1990). Although buspirone's efficacy is more moderate than other drugs discussed in this section, its low toxicity and side effects, lack of dependence liability, and minimal interactions with other drugs (e.g., alcohol) make it an attractive alternative to these other drugs.

The use of herbal medicines as alternative treatments for a variety of disorders has grown tremendously over the last several years. One herbal medicine that has become popular for treatment of depression is St. John's wort (*Hypericum perforatum*). It has been used in Europe as a folk remedy for depression for some time, and a number of clinical trials using extracts of this plant have suggested that it is effective in the treatment of mild to moderate cases of depression. The primary active constituent in hypericum is believed to be hypericin. Some studies have indicated that it has some properties of other antidepressants, but as yet its mechanisms of action are unclear. Comparisons between hypericum extracts and the SSRI fluoxetine have suggested that there is comparable efficacy in the treatment of mild to moderate depression, with hypericum being superior to fluoxetine in overall incidence of side effects (Schrader, 2000; Volz & Laux, 2000). However, a double-blind study assessing hypericum's efficacy in the treatment of moderately severe MDD found that it was not significantly different from placebo (Hypericum Depression Trial Study Group, 2002). Although St. John's wort is reasonably safe, it can induce some potentially severe adverse reactions when combined with other drugs (Fugh-Berman, 2000). It is also fairly inexpensive compared with pharmaceutical antidepressants. However, because the FDA does not regulate it as a drug in the United States, preparations of St. John's wort may be variable in terms of quantity and quality.

Psychomotor Stimulants

Drugs like amphetamine and cocaine have several properties, particularly their fast onset of action, that would appear to make them ideal antidepressants. Although some clinically depressed patients do experience feelings of calmness, well-being, or euphoria when given these drugs, a majority of such patients experience mixed mood effects, or experience dysphoric feelings of tension and increased sadness (Post et al., 1974). Thus, their effects cannot be described as simply antidepressant. Furthermore, as was noted in Chapter 7, their euphoric effects in normal individuals show tolerance, and their chronic use can worsen or induce depression when drug exposure ceases. In fact, the rebound following cocaine use (e.g., the "crash") involves such a severe depression that it can be life-threatening by causing, or at least precipitating, suicidal behavior. Thus, these types of drugs are an outmoded and contraindicated treatment for severe depression (however, see next section).

Drug Combinations in the Treatment of Depression

There is a very good chance that a major depression can be effectively treated in most people with one of the drugs that are currently available. However, there are still a small number of patients who are treatment-resistant. There may be a complete lack of response to medication, a tendency to relapse after an initial response, or an inability to tolerate the drug's side effects. If drugs from the major classes—tricyclics, MAOIs, and SSRIs—and the newer alternative antidepressants have been tried in adequate doses for at least 6 weeks each and the patient still has not responded, or if the side effects cannot be tolerated, it may be fruitful to try some combinations of drugs and/or psychotherapy.

For example, in one study, just under half of the patients with chronic forms of major depression displayed a clinically beneficial response to short-term treatment with either an antidepressant or a cognitive behavioral analysis system of psychotherapy, whereas the combination of the two treatments was effective in 73% of the patients (Keller et al., 2000). A number of drug combinations have also been tried with success (Fava, 2000). Numerous studies have shown that *augmentation* of antidepressants with lithium can produce robust improvements in a number of depressed patients who have not previously responded to single-drug therapy with tricyclics, MAOIs, or SSRIs. However, this strategy seems to have lost favor recently among psychiatrists, perhaps due to the potential toxicity associated with lithium, particularly when combined with SSRIs, and the need to carefully monitor lithium plasma concentrations. Thyroid hormone (T3) augmentation of tricyclic therapy has also been used successfully in patients who are refractory to tricyclics, but there is little information on the use of this approach with SSRIs. There are published studies showing that augmentation with psychostimulants (methylphenidate, pemoline, dextroamphetamine) may enhance the efficacy of a variety of antidepressants—often with a rapid onset of action—but concerns over the potential for abuse of these drugs, particularly in patients with a history of substance abuse, limit this approach. The practice of combining antidepressants with different pharmacological profiles—for example, bupropion or buspirone with SSRIs—appears to be growing in popularity, but there are insufficient quality studies for determining the efficacy of this approach. Augmentation of antidepressants with atypical antipsychotics may also be useful. For example, an open-label study has indicated that augmentation with the atypical antipsychotic ziprasidone was beneficial in patients with MDD who failed to achieve a clinical response with SSRIs alone (Papakostas et al., 2004).

NEUROBIOLOGICAL HYPOTHESES OF AFFECTIVE DISORDERS

In view of the pharmacological studies reviewed earlier, and the basic research related to the neural basis of emotions in general and depressive symptoms in particular, there have been a number of neurobiological hypotheses that have attempted to explain the pathologies that are thought to underlie major depression. This section will review several of these hypotheses.

Genetic Factors

Genetics plays a prominent role in many cases of affective disorder, with the strongest genetic influence being involved in bipolar disorders (Kolata, 1986; Plomin et al., 1994). For many years, it has commonly been assumed that genes interact with an individual's environment to produce mood disorders, particularly depression (diathesis-stress theories); that is, depression occurs in genetically susceptible individuals who are exposed to stressful events. A longitudinal study of a large cohort of individuals who have undergone a variety of assessments over more than 2 decades has provided impressive empirical support for this view (Caspi et al., 2003). This research indicated that individuals who had one or two copies of one form of the 5-HT transporter gene, called the "short allele," exhibited significantly more depressive symptoms, depression, and suicidality when exposed to stressful life events (e.g., romantic disasters, bereavements, illnesses, and job crises) than individuals who had two copies of the other form, called the "long allele." For example, it was found that among those individuals who had experienced severe maltreatment as children, 63% of the double short allele individuals had a major depressive episode in adulthood, in contrast to 30% in the double long allele individuals, whose incidence of depression was unrelated to whether or not they were maltreated as children. As discussed later, 5-HT appears to play a pivotal role in mood, and many antidepressants exert actions on the 5-HT transporter, which presumably mediate their efficacy in the treatment of depression. Other candidate genes include ones related to cortisol secretion, which is relevant for the stress response (Velders et al., 2011), and brain-derived neurotrophic factor (Tsai et al., 2010), which is important for synaptic plasticity. Nevertheless, the heritability of depression appears to be lower than that for schizophrenia, and it is reasonable to consider that multiple genes probably contribute to depression in a complex way, in combination with other factors such as environmental stressors (Belmaker & Agam, 2008).

The Monoamine Hypothesis of Mood Disorders

The first of the hypotheses suggesting a relationship between specific neurotransmitters and mood disorders was coined the *catecholamine hypothesis of affective disorders* (McNeal & Cimbolic, 1986). This hypothesis proposed that depression may be related to a deficiency of NE and/or DA (primarily NE) at functionally important CNS receptors and that mania may be related to the opposite set of conditions. However, as will soon become evident, studies indicated that deficits in serotonergic functioning may also be involved in mood disturbances, so the hypothesis has been modified and is often referred to as the *monoamine hypothesis of depression* (Hirschfeld, 2000). One of the first pieces of evidence for the hypothesis came from the observation that the drug reserpine not only reduced mania in humans but also precipitated a severe depression in some individuals treated with this drug. These phenomena correlate with the finding that reserpine depletes the brain of monoamines by preventing their uptake and storage in synaptic vesicles. Outside of the protection of the vesicles, the catecholamines are accessible to MAO, which is present intraneuronally; MAO then metabolizes the monoamines into inactive molecules. Conversely, it was discovered that some drugs that had mood-elevating properties were also capable of inhibiting the action of MAO (thus they are called MAO inhibitors). Theoretically, this inhibiting action should allow catecholamines to accumulate in neuronal tissues and make more neurotransmitters available for release in the process of neurotransmission. Furthermore, MAOIs were found to block the effects of reserpine; that is, even though reserpine prevents the monoamines from binding to vesicles, without MAO activity there would still be a pool of monoamines in the terminal available for release during an action potential.

The role of catecholamines in affect is consistent with a great deal of research indicating that the catecholamines are highly involved in motivation, emotion, and stress. As noted earlier, one of the primary features of depressed individuals is their inability to experience normal life activities as pleasurable and their lack of motivational drive (behavioral activation). Moreover, deficits in reward seeking and effort-related processes occur in depressed people in a manner that does not depend upon reductions in the experience of pleasure (Treadway & Zald, 2011). Although the precise biological basis of these energy-related symptoms of depression is unknown, several lines of evidence implicate central DA systems (Salamone et al., 2006; Stahl, 2002; Willner, 1983). Several years ago, Korf and van Praag (1971) observed that the DA metabolite homovanillic acid (HVA) was reduced in cerebrospinal fluid (CSF) of endogenously depressed patients with psychomotor retardation, but not in other types of patients. Depressed patients with agitation sometimes have normal or even elevated CSF levels of HVA, although this metabolite typically is reduced in depressed patients with a high degree of anergia (Willner, 1983). Moreover, it has been reported that there is an association between parkinsonism and depression with psychomotor slowing (Brown & Gershon, 1993) and that the antiparkinsonian drugs L-DOPA and bromocriptine have mixed antidepressant characteristics as far as other symptoms of depression are concerned, but can actually ameliorate anergia (Brown & Gershon, 1993). Moreover, among antidepressant drugs, their efficacy at reversing psychomotor slowing in depressed patients is related to the inhibition of DA uptake produced by these agents (Rampello et al., 1991). Stahl (2002) hypothesized that antidepressants with potent actions on DA uptake, such as bupropion, should have a greater initial effect on anergia and fatigue than drugs such as fluoxetine, which acts more potently on 5-HT uptake. In parallel with these developments in the clinical literature, a substantial body of animal research in behavioral neuroscience has demonstrated that DA systems, particularly in nucleus accumbens, are involved in activational (i.e., energetic) aspects of motivation (Salamone & Correa, 2002). Nucleus accumbens DA does not mediate the emotional component of primary reinforcers (as discussed in Chapter 6) but is an important component of the neural circuitry that is involved in behavioral activation and that enables organisms to overcome work-related response costs (Salamone & Correa, 2002; Salamone et al., 2010).

In terms of NE systems, it is also true that the NE innervation of the forebrain (see Chapter 5) is thought to be involved in emotion and stress in various ways. Itoi and Sugimoto (2010) suggest that the ventral noradrenergic bundle, which provides a major NE innervation of the hypothalamus, could be involved in regulating neuroendocrine functions related to stress and depression. Moreover, considerable evidence implicates that dorsal noradrenergic bundle, which originates from cell bodies in the locus coeruleus, is very responsive to stress (Leonard, 2001).

The actions and effects of the psychomotor stimulants amphetamine and cocaine do appear to fit in with the catecholamine hypothesis. As noted in Chapter 7, it has long been recognized that these drugs elevate mood and can induce mania and that these effects correlate with their ability to temporarily increase the levels of catecholamines in the synapse (by increasing the amounts released or blocking their reuptake after release). However, prolonged use of these drugs depletes catecholamines (probably because they are used faster than they are synthesized). This depletion correlates with the depression and lethargy that often occur when the person stops taking these drugs. In a study of methamphetamine abusers, positron emission tomography methods demonstrated that reductions in DA transporter density were associated with psychomotor slowing in the abstinence phase (Volkow et al., 2001).

Further evidence for the catecholamine hypothesis came with the discovery of the tricyclic antidepressants. Many studies noted that the primary biochemical action of these drugs was inhibition of the reuptake of catecholamines back into the axon terminal, thus allowing extracellular levels to accumulate and to have greater access to their receptors. Similar actions occur with later-developed nontricyclic antidepressants. However, it was with these observations that the catecholamine hypothesis began to show signs of strain, because the reuptake-blocking action of tricyclics was observed to occur within minutes of exposure, but their mood-elevating effects generally take several days or weeks of chronic exposure. Furthermore, nondepressed humans evidence no signs of mood elevation when these drugs are administered.

Direct evidence for NE dysfunction in depressed patients is weak. The results of studies attempting to correlate levels of MHPG, the major NE metabolite, in urine or blood with depressive symptoms have been inconsistent (Delgado, 2000). Few studies have been conducted on the potential association between depressive symptoms and MHPG levels in the CSF, which is more likely to represent noradrenergic activity in the CNS. However, a study has shown a substantial correlation between CSF MHPG concentrations and self-rated depression in abstinent alcoholics (Heinz et al., 1999). Several studies have suggested that depressed patients have higher densities or greater sensitivities of presynaptic alpha-2-adrenoceptors (autoreceptors), which could result in lower NE availability, and antidepressant response has been shown to be associated with decreases in the density or activity of these receptors (Delgado, 2000; Gurguis et al., 1999).

It is unlikely that a single neurotransmitter is responsible for both mood and mood disorders. Dysfunction in serotonergic systems was proposed as a factor in affective disorders in the 1960s, but until the mid-1980s most attention was focused on noradrenergic systems in these disorders. However, later there was refocus on 5-HT with the recognition that some very effective tricyclic antidepressants potently block 5-HT reuptake—actually having a greater affinity for the 5-HT uptake transport pump than for the NE pump. Furthermore, several studies have found that people who commit suicide are likely to have low levels of a 5-HT metabolite, 5-HIAA, in their CSF as well as more 5-HT_2 receptors in their prefrontal cortex—both of which are consistent with diminished serotonergic transmission (Arango et al., 1990). Thus, the monoamine 5-HT is also viewed as being important in certain cases of depression. In fact, it was the belief that 5-HT plays a role in depression that led to the development of the SSRIs as a potential treatment. That the symptoms of depression may be the result of either insufficient noradrenergic or serotonergic activity would not be surprising, considering the fact that in the CNS both systems greatly overlap in terms of distribution and physiological activity (see, for example, Figure 5.11).

It would seem that the most direct way of determining whether insufficient levels of catecholamines or 5-HT in the CNS are direct causes of depression would be to deplete the brain of one or the other of these monoamines in normal, healthy humans and see if they develop the symptoms of depression. Acute depletion of catecholamines can easily be accomplished by treatment with the drug alpha-methyl-p-tyrosine (AMPT), which prevents the conversion of the amino acid tyrosine into the catecholamines, or with the administration of an amino acid mixture that is deficient in the catecholamine precursors phenylalanine and tyrosine. Similarly, acute depletion of 5-HT can easily be accomplished with the administration of an amino acid mixture that is deficient in tryptophan (the amino acid precursor for 5-HT). (See Chapter 5 for an explanation for why this procedure affects CNS monoamine levels.) Although numerous studies of this nature have been conducted since the 1960s, no clear picture has emerged from their findings. Although both catecholamine and 5-HT depletion have been shown to lower mood in many individuals without a history of depression, the effects are inconsistent and the mood-lowering effect is not as great as that seen in depressed patients (Delgado 2000; Leyton et al., 1999: Smith et al., 1987; Young et al., 1985). The effect of these treatments on mood may depend on whether the individual has a genetic susceptibility for major affective disorders (Benkelfat et al., 1994; Ellenbogen et al., 1996), or is exposed to aversive psychological conditions (Leyton et al., 2000). Similar studies conducted with unmedicated, depressed patients have not found that depletion of either catecholamines or 5-HT reliably worsens their depression (although this may be due to the patients already being close to "basement" levels). On the other hand, a consistent pattern of results has been found with depressed patients who differentially respond to either noradrenergic- or serotonergic-specific antidepressants. That is, patients who responded well to serotonergic-specific antidepressants were much more likely to show relapse with 5-HT depletion than with catecholamine depletion, and patients who responded well to noradrenergic-specific antidepressants were much more likely to show relapse with catecholamine depletion than with 5-HT depletion (Delgado & Moreno, 2000).

Although these studies with monoamine depletion based upon drug or nutritional manipulations do not provide a clear link between brain monoamine levels and depression, they do appear to provide useful information about the vulnerability to depression and about the neurochemical basis of the therapeutic effects of antidepressant drugs (Ruhe et al., 2007). One clear-cut conclusion from these studies is that the availability of NE appears to be essential for maintaining an antidepressant response to noradrenergic-enhancing drugs and that the availability of 5-HT appears to be essential for maintaining an antidepressant response to serotonergic-enhancing drugs (Delgado, 2000; Miller et al., 1996; Ruhe et al., 2007). Thus, it appears that there is no single mechanism of antidepressant drug action; the therapeutic effects of noradrenergic uptake blockers depend upon catecholamine synthesis, whereas the actions of serotonergic uptake blockers depend upon 5-HT synthesis. In addition, although normal control subjects as a group tend to show no alteration of mood as a result of monoamine depletion, there is evidence that normal control subjects with a history of major depression in their family do show alterations in mood with monoamine depletion (Ruhe et al., 2007). These findings serve to underscore the complex nature of the interactions between a number of factors that jointly influence the likelihood of a person becoming depressed.

In summary, although it is generally accepted that most antidepressant drugs, acutely administered, enhance monoaminergic neurotransmission, it is not clear how their actions are related to depression symptom remission. The NE or 5-HT uptake blockade by the tricyclics and the SSRIs and the inhibition of MAO by MAOIs are rapid, but the alleviation of symptoms is slow. This clearly indicates that these drugs' acute actions per se are not responsible for the antidepressant response to these drugs, but rather that it is the neuroadaptive changes in the nervous system that occur with chronic exposure that underlie the therapeutic response to them. Several lines of research suggest that these neuroadaptive changes include desensitization of the 5-HT reuptake process; desensitization of 5-HT autoreceptors (5-HT_{1A} and 5-HT_{1D} receptors) regulating serotonergic neuron firing and release of 5-HT; and desensitization of α-2-adrenoceptors that normally inhibit NE and/or 5-HT release. Most effective antidepressant treatments, including ECT, have been shown to have one or more of these properties, with the net effect of enhancing 5-HT neurotransmission (Blier & de Montigny, 1994; Cryan & Leonard, 2000; Stahl, 1998). However, there is an unresolved discrepancy between the effects of ECT, a very effective antidepressant treatment that seems to up-regulate 5-HT_2 receptors, and virtually all known antidepressant drugs, which are capable of down-regulating 5-HT_2 receptors with chronic exposure, a phenomenon that correlates well with the reduction in the symptoms of depression in depressed patients. Furthermore, up-regulation of beta-adrenoceptors has been suggested to occur in depressed patients, and the down-regulation of beta-adrenoceptors with chronic drug treatment is often regarded as a marker of antidepressant efficacy (Delgado, 2000).

The Neurotrophic Theory of Affective Disorders

Since the 1960s, the monoamine hypothesis of affective disorders has been a useful model for our understanding of mood disorders and for developing new pharmacological treatments for them. Over the past several years, another view of how affective disorders come about and how antidepressants and mood stabilizers work has developed. This view proposes that the symptoms of affective disorders come about because of subtle brain damage induced by exposure to chronic stress, perhaps in combination with individual genetic predispositions, and that antidepressants work not by enhancing neurotransmission between neurons but by enhancing factors that allow CNS neurons to grow and develop (Coyle & Duman, 2003; Holden, 2003).

The general premise of this model is that exposure to chronic early life stress (e.g., abuse, neglect, and parental loss) induces the hypersecretion of corticotropin-releasing hormone (CRH) from the hypothalamus, which stimulates the pituitary gland to release glucocorticoids (stress hormones) from the adrenal glands. These then decrease the levels of chemicals (e.g., brain-derived neurotrophic factor [BDNF]) necessary for neurogenesis and neuronal growth and development. Eventually, this leads to the neuronal atrophy and cell loss in the prefrontal cortex, hippocampus, and other limbic structures, which then result in the symptoms of depression. This model explains the natural course of untreated depression whereby continued exposures to stressors over time, even though less severe than earlier ones, may result in depressive episodes. Similarly, it explains how more frequent, more severe, and more treatment-resistant depression may occur over time with shorter intervals between depressive episodes.

Several lines of research indicate that in addition to their serving as neurotransmitters and neuromodulators that produce relatively short-lived changes in the membrane potentials of neurons, 5-HT and NE play pivotal roles in the homeostasis of neural tissue and protection or promotion of recovery from neural damage (Azmitia, 1999; Marien et al., 2004). Thus antidepressants, by increasing monoaminergic activity, are proposed to enhance neurogenesis and neuronal growth, for example, through stimulation of BDNF (Coyle & Duman, 2003). This would explain their delayed therapeutic effects because it typically takes days to weeks to create fully functional neurons and/or their connections with other neurons. This may also explain why treatments that induce relatively brief reductions in monoaminergic activity in the brain rarely induce the classic symptoms of depression in normal, nondepressed individuals. As indicated later in this chapter, mood stabilizers and ECT may also have properties that enhance neurogenesis and synaptic plasticity. Various forms of psychotherapy, which typically also take several treatment sessions before symptoms are reduced, may work in a similar fashion because they result in patients making cognitive and behavioral changes that allow them to reduce or avoid stressors, or they alter their belief systems that contribute to their stress response.

Several lines of evidence support this neurotrophic theory (Coyle & Duman, 2003). For example, studies with animals have found that chronic stress can induce atrophy and reduced neurogenesis of hippocampal neurons and decreased volume in the hippocampus. Studies with rodents indicate that there is an increase in brain-cell growth in response to antidepressant drugs, whereas treatments that block antidepressant-induced neurogenesis in the hippocampus also prevent the behavioral response that occurs with chronic exposure to antidepressants (Santarelli et al., 2003). Postmortem studies of depressed patients have demonstrated a reduction in the size of their neurons and the number of glia in their prefrontal cortex. In a study utilizing magnetic resonance imaging, it was determined that depressed women whose symptoms were in remission averaged approximately 10% less hippocampal gray-matter volumes than matched control subjects and that the longer the duration during which depressive episodes went untreated with antidepressants, the greater the reductions in hippocampal volume (Sheline et al., 2003). Finally, elevated levels of BDNF have been found in postmortem tissue of patients receiving antidepressant treatment at the time of death (Chen et al., 2001).

The neurotrophic theory has its own problems in explaining the cause of mood disorders and mechanisms through which antidepressants and mood stabilizers alleviate the symptoms. For example, it is not clear how stress-induced damage may be reflected in unipolar symptoms in some individuals and bipolar symptoms in others. Also, if both antidepressants and mood stabilizers have neurotrophic properties, why does one class work better with unipolar depression and another class work better with bipolar disorders? It is also not clear how the theory can explain why treatments that acutely deplete 5-HT or NE in the brain induce a rapid onset of depression symptoms in medicated patients whose symptoms are in remission. However, if this model does have some degree of validity, it suggests that more direct means of alleviating the symptoms of mood disorders, or preventing them from occurring in the first place, may be developed in the near future. These include drugs that inhibit CRH or block cortisol, that block receptors for the glucocorticoids produced by the adrenal glands, or that reduce activity at NMDA receptors, which when stimulated excessively can result in neurotoxicity (Holden, 2003).

Other Potential Neurotransmitters Involved in Mood Disorders

Acetylcholine (ACh) has also been implicated in affective disorders. It has been suggested that an overactive ACh system or an imbalance between ACh and NE is a causative factor in depression (Janowsky, 2007). This hypothesis is supported by the clinical finding that physostigmine, an inhibitor of the enzyme that normally inactivates acetylcholine, may aggravate depression and reduce mania. However, because later-developed antidepressants (e.g., SSRIs) are essentially void of anticholinergic properties, it is unlikely that excessive cholinergic activity plays much of a role in depression. Decreased GABAergic function may play a role in various forms of endogenous depressions, because GABA-mimetic drugs have been found to be effective antidepressants. Consistent with this hypothesis are studies noting that the CSF of severely depressed patients contains significantly higher concentrations of endogenous inhibitors of benzodiazepine agonists than found in age- and sex-matched normal volunteers (Barbaccia et al., 1988). Finally, endorphins have also been implicated in some cases of depression. They are found in relatively high concentrations in the limbic system and appear to modulate many of its activities. Also, narcotics have long been recognized for their euphoric and antidepressant properties. There has been speculation that many narcotic addicts comprise a subclass of depressed individuals who take narcotics to feel "normal" (Khantzian, 1985). Unfortunately, should this hypothesis prove to be valid, it would make drug treatment difficult because all known substitutes for endorphins—both exogenous and endogenous—have the strong potential for inducing tolerance and physical dependence with chronic use.

NONDRUG TREATMENTS FOR DEPRESSION

Clearly, not all grief, misery, and general disappointments associated with life in human society call for drug intervention. Most episodes of these types, even severe cases, evidence a very high rate of spontaneous remission with sufficient time passage. Psychological intervention that changes the person's interpersonal relationships or belief structures may be beneficial in these cases. Several studies that have compared the effectiveness of interpersonal psychotherapy or cognitive therapy with that of pharmacotherapy (mostly tricyclics) have not found any notable differences between these two forms of psychotherapy and antidepressant medication (Frank & Thase, 1999). There is also growing evidence that combining pharmacotherapy and psychological treatment of depression is more effective than drug treatment alone, especially in more severe cases (Glick, 2004; Pampallona et al., 2004). Some severe depressions may not respond to drug therapy, or a patient may be so suicidal that waiting for a drug to take effect would be inadvisable (Feighner et al., 1985). In such cases, ECT may be considered, because it remains the most rapid and effective treatment for severe acute depression and is potentially lifesaving for the suicidal patient (Fink, 1994).

Although physicians play the most direct role in pharmacotherapy for depression, those of you who will work or are now working in the mental health field outside of medicine may also serve important functions. Because you are the ones most likely to deal initially with a depressed client, or to have the most contact with such an individual during his or her treatment, you may serve as information gatherers to determine whether drug therapy may be a useful adjunct to traditional psychotherapies. You may also oversee the progress of a client who is under drug treatment. Your interaction with the patient during the evaluation and your reassurances may in themselves prove therapeutic. You can determine whether there are precipitating events underlying the clients' symptoms, assess how chronic the problem is and whether there is a cyclical nature to it, determine whether the client is suicidal, gather family history, and so on. This is valuable information in establishing whether or not a person may be a good candidate for drug intervention. Mere inquiry into the nature of your clients' dysphoria can challenge them to confront their lives and their inability to respond appropriately to these events. If your clients are taking medication for their disorders, you can look for side effects of the drugs and signs of drug toxicity. Your optimism over the likely benefits of a prescribed medication may have tremendous value in alleviating distress, guilt, and hopelessness in the patients and may be the difference between their compliance and noncompliance in sticking with a drug regimen that may take 2 to 4 weeks before any benefits are realized. Those of you who practice psychotherapy may find that antidepressants make your clients more amenable to your particular therapeutic techniques.

PLACEBO EFFECTS AND ANTIDEPRESSANT ACTIONS

Some researchers have argued that the difference in efficacy rate between antidepressant therapy and placebo may be largely an illusion (Ioannidis, 2008; Kirsch, 2000; Kirsch & Sapirstein, 1998), perhaps resulting from clinician bias (e.g., because clues from side effects of the active drug may be distinguished from inactive placebo), or expectancies that are generated by receiving some type of treatment. Moreover, there is evidence that an experiment in which the participant is supposed to be blind may not turn out that way; subjects may identify that they are receiving some type of drug treatment because some identifiable effects are produced, and thus the "blind" condition of the experiment may be broken, because the person realizes he or she is not receiving an inert control. For that reason, it is advisable to use active placebos (drugs that are meant to be placebos, but produce an identifiable effect, so that the patient remains blind to the particular treatment group he or she is in) in research. In fact, there are reports that some drugs labeled as active placebos can produce similar effects to those produced by antidepressant drugs (Kirsch, 2000; Kirsch & Sapirstein, 1998). Furthermore, in a recent meta-analysis (Kirsch et al., 2008), it was observed that the overall differences between antidepressants and placebos were very small, and that the severity of depression was an important factor (e.g., the antidepressant difference from placebo was clinically relevant only in more severely depressed patients).

In contrast, others who have reanalyzed many of the original sources that led to these claims have failed to provide support for these arguments. For example, Quitkin et al. (2000) has demonstrated that antidepressant and placebo responses show different time courses; as discussed earlier, the placebo response tends to occur relatively early in treatment compared to the antidepressant drug response. In addition, one needs to be careful when selecting drugs to use as active placebos, because some of the drugs that have been used actually turn out to be agents such as thyroid hormone, lithium, anticholinergics, and adenazolam, all of which have been employed either to treat depression or as augmentation agents (Salamone, 2002). Furthermore, the effect of psychotherapy versus placebo behavioral treatments (e.g., organized activities) also has been shown to be negligible (Salamone, 2002). Yet despite these concerns, there are some important points to emphasize from this research on placebos. First of all, it should be stressed that the effect size of antidepressant treatment can be relatively small. In addition, there appear to be many activities that depressed people can be exposed to (e.g., exercise, joining a book discussion group, psychotherapy, receiving a control treatment in a clinical trial, and antidepressant drugs) that produce at least some degree of improvement in symptoms. This could be because depression is fundamentally an impairment in the interaction of the person with his or her environment, and activities that promote interaction with the environment can produce some improvement (Salamone, 2002). Finally, it is useful that Kirsch and colleagues are challenging the conventional wisdom in this area, because scientific hypotheses should constantly be challenged and scrutinized. Thus, more controlled studies should be performed with carefully selected active placebos. Furthermore, the results from successive trials should be examined for more accuracy; for example, Quitkin et al. (2005) reported results from a succession of three clinical trials, and observed that efficacy rates were relatively high when one looked at the cumulative rate of remission of symptoms across all trials. All of this could be more costly (in terms of drug development costs), but this would be worth the benefit in terms of the severity and frequency of depression, and its impact on society.

PHARMACOTHERAPY IN MANIA AND BIPOLAR ILLNESSES

The symptoms of mania and bipolar disorders greatly impact afflicted individuals' health-related quality of life, physical and social functioning, employment, and work productivity. Bipolar disorder patients have been found to utilize health-care services more than those patients with depression or chronic medical conditions. However, available treatments have been shown to improve health-related quality of life and physical and social functioning in patients with bipolar disorder and reduce their utilization of health-care services and cost, and there are some data to indicate that the available treatments may improve self-reported work impairment and absenteeism (Dean et al., 2004). The effectiveness of a particular drug treatment for mania may depend on whether the patient experiences only manic symptoms, which occur intermittently between episodes of normal mood, or experiences cycles of mania and depression, that is, bipolar disorders. Treatment efficacy may also depend on whether episodes of mania and depression occur infrequently and separately (typical bipolar disorder), or involve rapid cycling (i.e., patients experience four or more episodes per year in which there is either a period of full remission between episodes [either manic or depressive] or there is a switch to an episode of the opposite polarity), or involve dysphoric (mixed) mania, in which manic and depressive symptoms occur together. Drugs that generally decrease the intensity or duration of both manic and depressive episodes, or prevent them from occurring, are commonly referred to as **mood stabilizers.** Of these, lithium (Eskalith) is generally the first-line drug used in the treatment of all bipolar disorders, but its effectiveness is most apparent in cases of typical bipolar disorder (Calabrese & Woyshville, 1995). Antidepressants are commonly used in combination with lithium if the patient does not respond to lithium after several weeks or is experiencing a severe depressive episode. Some anticonvulsant drugs, either alone or in combination with lithium, may be somewhat more effective than lithium in the treatment of rapid-cycling or mixed bipolar patients. A number of other drug treatments (i.e., calcium blockers, cholinergic agents, and adrenergic blockers) and nondrug treatments (e.g., ECT, phototherapy, and psychosurgery) have been explored as alternatives to these, but research supporting their efficacy is very limited, and none have gained widespread acceptance (Prien & Potter, 1990). Studies with the atypical antipsychotic drugs suggest that they may be useful alternatives or adjunctive treatments for bipolar disorders.

Lithium

The properties of lithium are unique, such that it stands alone among all the psychotherapeutic drugs (Baldessarini & Tarazi, 2001). Although the first report of its antimanic effects by Australian psychiatrist John Cade in 1949 would seem to put it at the forefront of the psychopharmacological revolution begun in the 1950s, it had little impact in the United States until 20 years later. One reason was its high toxicity, particularly when combined with low sodium intake. Several months prior to Cade's report, a number of deaths were reported in patients with kidney and heart problems who were given lithium salt as a substitute for ordinary table salt (sodium chloride). Thus, despite its remarkable antimanic properties, physicians were reluctant to use such a toxic drug. Furthermore, a few years later, chlorpromazine was noted to possess antimanic effects as well as considerably lower toxicity. A rapid succession of similar compounds, as well as antidepressants, new stimulants, sedatives, and hypnotics, came into being, each requiring considerable study with respect to its safety and efficacy. Another factor in the lack of enthusiasm for lithium was its minimal marketability because, as an element of nature, it was unpatentable. Eventually, however, lithium's remarkable properties became well recognized, and its use has become commonplace.

Lithium is unique for several reasons (Baldessarini & Tarazi, 2001). First, it is a light metal ion (positively charged) that exists in nature as a salt (lithium carbonate and lithium chloride). Although the ion is found in trace amounts in animal tissues, it plays no known physiological role. Second, therapeutic levels of lithium have almost negligible psychotropic effects in normal individuals—that is, there are no sedative, depressant, stimulant, or euphoriant effects. Third, and most important, it is highly specific in relieving manic symptoms without oversedating the person (a common problem with antipsychotics) or inducing depression (as was the case with reserpine). Furthermore, continued treatment with lithium salt can prevent or decrease the severity of future episodes of mania and depression in most bipolar patients (this is what experts mean when they say lithium has prophylactic properties).

Efficacy of Lithium in Mood Disturbances

The efficacy of lithium in treating acute mania and preventing subsequent episodes of both mania and depression in bipolar disorder is unquestioned, with approximately 60% to 80% of such cases displaying partial to complete symptom remission (Prien & Potter, 1990). Studies have suggested that persons with a strong genetic link to manic depression—for example, patients in whose families the disorder has occurred—may show the most favorable response to lithium (Campbell et al., 1984). Although many bipolar patients relapse, even with lithium maintenance treatment, whether there is a loss of prophylactic efficacy of lithium is controversial. Some authors have questioned its long-term effectiveness in general, and others have argued that loss of efficacy may be due to factors such as underdosing and noncompliance, or due to the fact that the natural course of affective disorders is capricious and tends to become more severe over time (Kleindienst et al., 1999). The general conclusion at this time is that although affective recurrences do occur in some bipolar patients after apparently successful treatment with lithium, there is no clear evidence that these are the result of a loss of lithium efficacy. However, there is a general consensus among experts that abrupt discontinuation of lithium, especially after acute treatment, may make patients' symptoms worse than if they had no treatment at all (Calabrese et al., 2004). In some individuals maintained on lithium, there is an unusual mood stability, which might be viewed unfavorably by these patients (Johnson, 1979). Most bipolar patients probably do not want to experience the uncontrolled onset of depressive or manic moods, but would like to experience normal emotions. However, lithium patients often report being emotionless in situations where mood shifts are expected, or at least appropriate.

Although lithium appears to have little antidepressant activity in persons experiencing a depressive episode, it can prevent depressive episodes in some patients with recurrent unipolar depression. Several studies have reported impressive results indicating that patients who are refractory to traditional antidepressants (including lithium) may respond favorably to lithium in combination with traditional antidepressants (Goodnick & Schorr-Cain, 1991).

Side effects are not generally a factor in lithium's efficacy. Although a majority of patients experience some adverse consequences—such as tremor, thirst, fluid retention, weight gain, and frequent need to urinate—these are relatively minor problems. Lithium's potential interactions with other drugs that patients may also likely be taking (antipsychotics, diuretics, and nonsteroidal antiinflammatory drugs) may limit its efficacy (Tollefson, 1991).

Lithium salts have also been used with varying degrees of success in other disorders with an affective component that have a cyclical nature to them, such as recurrent hyperactivity in children (however, not in the attention deficit hyperactivity disorder described in Chapter 11; Campbell et al., 1984), the premenstrual syndrome, and episodic anger or aggression. There is considerable evidence that lithium is effective in reducing aggressiveness with an affective component (explosiveness) in children aged 5 to 12 years with conduct disorder (Campbell et al., 1995). The benefits of lithium in these cases have been attributed to lithium's ability to reduce impulsiveness or explosiveness—as if a delay mechanism or filter device were inserted between stimulus analysis and decision mechanisms in patients who previously went automatically from stimulus to response (Johnson, 1979).

Pharmacokinetics of Lithium

Although lithium's therapeutic index can be as low as 2 or 3, it is important to monitor its concentrations in the body on a regular basis, at least until stable levels can be assured (Baldessarini & Tarazi, 2001). Lithium is usually administered orally in a salt form, most commonly lithium carbonate (the particular salt used is not important in the therapeutic action because the anionic partner serves only as an inert vehicle for transport). It is readily absorbed from the gastrointestinal tract, with almost complete absorption occurring within 8 hours. Passage through the blood–brain barrier is slow, but once plasma levels have stabilized, CSF levels stabilize at approximately half that of plasma concentrations. Because of its very low therapeutic index, lithium dosages are based on plasma concentration of lithium ion, generally determined in milliequivalent units per liter of blood (mEq/L; *milliequivalent* refers to the number of grams of solute dissolved in 1 milliliter of a normal solution). Therapeutic doses are achieved when plasma levels of lithium reach 0.6 to 1.5 mEq/L (generally achievable with two to three 300-mg tablets of lithium carbonate per day).

Above these levels, toxic signs of diarrhea, vomiting, drowsiness, confusion, and muscular weakness may occur (Annitto, 1979). At levels above 2.0 mEq/L, ataxia, tinnitus, and interference with kidney function can occur, and levels above 3.0 mEq/L may result in coma, respiratory depression, and death. Even at therapeutic levels, side effects of fine hand tremors, nausea, thirst, and excessive sweating may occur. In comparison to most other drugs requiring chronic exposure, the side effects of therapeutic levels of lithium are rather mild or uncommon. Nevertheless, idiosyncratic reactions can occur; for instance, its use has been associated with diabetes, seizure activity, and neurological disturbances, particularly when combined with other drugs.

The pharmacokinetics of lithium may vary considerably among individuals, but they are relatively stable over time within individuals. Although lithium has a relatively long plasma half-life (about 20 to 24 hours), it is generally given in divided doses because of its low therapeutic index. Slow-release preparations have been developed that produce smoother lithium plasma level curves, allow administration once a day or every other day, and may have fewer side effects (Goodnick & Schorr-Cain, 1991). Concentration levels of lithium are heavily dependent on sodium intake. Lithium is generally excreted more readily with high sodium intake, and high, toxic concentrations of lithium may occur with low sodium intake or drug-induced sodium depletion (as might occur with diuretics) as a result of enhanced retention. Also, lithium's urinary retention and elimination half-life may double during mania (Goodnick & Schorr-Cain, 1991).

Alternatives to Lithium in the Treatment of Bipolar Disorders

Despite the evidence of lithium efficacy in the treatment of bipolar disorders, a number of naturalistic studies have found that bipolar patients exhibit frequent relapses, even with maintenance drug treatment (Gitlin et al., 1995; Goldberg et al., 1996). These studies have observed that 68% to 89% of bipolar patients relapse within 4 to 5 years, with the majority of them exhibiting multiple relapses during this time. As one might expect, bipolar patients with more previous episodes of mood dysfunction tend to relapse earlier than patients with fewer previous episodes. Poor psychosocial functioning—particularly, poor job functioning—is also associated with a shorter time to relapse, with depressive episodes most strongly related to social and family dysfunction. Thus, not surprisingly, concomitant psychotherapy and social support have been suggested to greatly improve the outcome of prophylactic drug therapy (Miklowitz et al., 1996; Werder, 1995). Nevertheless, alternatives to lithium clearly are needed because a substantial number of bipolar patients fail lithium prophylaxis, including those with a high frequency of prior episodes, mixed (dysphoric) mania, comorbid personality disturbances, and rapid cycling (Solomon et al., 1995).

Antipsychotic drugs have been used for almost 5 decades in the treatment of bipolar disorders, particularly for the acute emergency management of mania. In many cases, attempting to manage a manic patient with lithium alone is not practical during the first week of the illness, so antipsychotics or benzodiazepines, which suppress manic symptoms more quickly than lithium, are often combined with lithium (Werder, 1995). Alternatively, ECT may be used. In fact, in a series of studies conducted over a period of several years, ECT with sparing use of antipsychotics followed by lithium was found to be the most effective short-term intervention for acute mania in bipolar patients (Small et al., 1996).

Because the efficacy of atypical antipsychotics is comparable to that of conventional antipsychotics in the treatment of psychotic mood disorders but exhibit less problematic side effects (described in Chapter 12), these should be the preferred treatment when used for patients with bipolar disorders (Keck et al., 2000). Once the manic symptoms have subsided, these drugs may be withdrawn, although as noted later they may be useful in cases in which mania reemerges. A number of the atypical antipsychotics (quetiapine [Seroquel] and olanzapine [Zyprexa]) have been approved for use either as monotherapy in the treatment of acute manic episodes associated with bipolar I disorder or as adjunctive therapy with lithium and other mood stabilizers in the treatment of acute manic episodes associated with bipolar I disorder.

Research with the oldest atypical antipsychotic clozapine (Clozaril) indicates that it is effective and well tolerated in the short-term and maintenance treatment of severe or psychotic mood disorders, particularly in the manic-excited phases of bipolar disorders (about 75% response rate), even in patients who have not responded well to conventional pharmacotherapies (Ciapparelli et al., 2000; Zarate et al., 1995). Clozapine may also have sustained mood-stabilizing activity, or at least a prophylactic antimanic effect. Acutely manic patients who respond to clozapine appear to do so within 2 weeks. Like most mood-stabilizing agents, clozapine may be more effective for mania than for unipolar or bipolar depression. Finally, clozapine may usefully and safely be combined with lithium or valproate in the long-term maintenance treatment of bipolar disorders. As discussed earlier, clozapine's tendency to induce agranulocytosis is a limiting factor in its use.

For a number of years the primary pharmacologic alternatives to lithium for long-term bipolar treatment have been the anticonvulsants lamotrigine (Lamictal), carbamazepine (Tegretol), and valproate (various forms; for example, valproic acid, sodium valproate, divalproex, Depakote, Depakene; Bowden, 1995; Guay, 1995; Solomon et al., 1995). These drugs have been used for a number of years in the treatment of epilepsy. Of these, lamotrigine appears to have the most empirical support as a first-line treatment for bipolar I disorder (Calabrese et al., 2004). It has been found to be superior to placebo for the outcomes of improvement on several depression scales, the proportion of bipolar patients who do not require other interventions (including use of antidepressants and ECT) for depressive episodes, and the time before an intervention for a depressive episode is needed. In comparisons between lamotrigine and lithium in bipolar I patients, lamotrigine was found to be more effective at delaying depressive episodes whereas lithium was more effective at delaying manic episodes. In nonrapid cycling bipolar I patients who do not respond to monotherapy with either of these two first-line treatments, it may be useful to combine them. Other options are to add valproate or the atypical antipsychotics olanzapine or risperidone (Risperdal). Limited evidence suggests that other atypical antipsychotics (aripiprazole [Abilify], ziprasidone [Geodon], or quetiapine [Seroquel]) may also be useful in augmentation to the first-line treatments.

For acute treatment of bipolar I depression, it is recommended that the first-line treatment should be lithium or lamotrigine (Calabrese et al., 2004). An alternative is to use the atypical antipsychotic olanzapine as monotherapy or in combination with the SSRI fluoxetine. Symbyax (a combination of olanzapine and fluoxetine) is also used for this purpose. A third option would be to add an antidepressant to the first-line treatments, although the use of tricyclics or MAOIs is not recommended, as there is evidence that these classes of antidepressants are the most likely to induce mania. This is also the reason that antidepressants by themselves are not recommended for use in bipolar patients. Although all classes of antidepressants may induce a conversion to mania, an analysis involving a large number of patients prescribed antidepressants for an anxiety or a nonbipolar mood disorder indicated that the risk of a conversion to mania in those patients treated with SSRIs was significantly greater than patients with no antidepressant exposure but was approximately half that associated with tricyclic or other antidepressants (Martin et al., 2004). Interestingly, this study also indicated that conversion to mania may be an age-dependent phenomenon, as it was found that treatment with antidepressants was associated with highest conversion hazards among children aged 10 to 14 years. In addition, another study has shown that antidepressant monotherapy is significantly less effective at preventing depressive relapse in bipolar patients than an antidepressant–mood stabilizer combination (Ghaemi et al., 2003). Unfortunately, many patients with bipolar disorder prefer antidepressant monotherapy, particularly if they enjoy their hypomanic periods, and they may try to exert pressure on their physicians to follow this course of action rather than prescribe a mood stabilizer.

A number of clinical trials have verified that two other anticonvulsants, carbamazepine and valproate, are also efficacious in the short-term management of bipolar manic symptoms, and the response may be maintained for extended periods of time. As yet, there is little evidence from rigorous clinical trials to support the widespread use of these anticonvulsants in maintenance therapy for bipolar disorders (Dardennes et al., 1995; Solomon et al., 1995). There is limited evidence that these anticonvulsants may be more effective in bipolar patients who respond poorly to lithium, for example, those exhibiting mixed mania, rapid cycling, or comorbid substance abuse (Bowden, 1995; Calabrese & Woyshville, 1995; Guay, 1995). Unfortunately, these drugs are capable of inducing severe toxic side effects—for example, fatal hepatic failure with valproate, and agranulocytosis and aplastic anemia (white and red blood cell deficiency) with carbamazepine. Although these side effects are rare, their seriousness may limit these drugs' usefulness.

There is a general consensus among experts that bipolar disorder is a chronic condition requiring lifelong management with first-line and combination treatments that include pharmacotherapy and psychological interventions. There is considerable evidence of the safety and efficacy in the use of lithium, lamotrigine, olanzapine, and olanzapine–fluoxetine combination therapy in bipolar disorders, and there are suitable alternatives to these if patients are not responsive.

Neurochemical Effects of Mood Stabilizers

Lithium and the anticonvulsant mood stabilizers have virtually nothing in common with respect to their neurochemical properties, and few of the properties appear on the surface to be compatible with the monoamine hypothesis of mood disorders. As a small ion, lithium has the potential for altering the distribution and exchange of ions involved in the process of neural excitability (see Chapter 4). Therefore, there has been some speculation that such interactions may account for lithium's mood-stabilizing properties, although it is uncertain whether important interactions with these ions occur at therapeutic concentrations of lithium (Tosteson, 1981). In brain tissue at therapeutic concentrations, lithium reduces the stimulation-produced and calcium-dependent release of catecholamines (but not 5-HT) from nerve endings (Baldessarini & Tarazi, 2001). It may also enhance the reuptake of catecholamines. These actions are consistent with the catecholamine hypothesis of mania but do not really fit the opposite side of the hypothesis regarding catecholamines and depression. Lithium appears to have no direct influence on postsynaptic catecholamine receptors, nor does it affect the binding of ligands to catecholamine receptors.

In studies attempting to determine whether lithium is able to reduce the effects of amphetamine (which, you should recall, initially amplifies catecholamine release and reduces their reuptake), there have been a variety of outcomes. Although studies have found that lithium attenuates several of amphetamine's behavioral effects, in other tests it has either produced no change or has intensified amphetamine's effects (Cox et al., 1971; Flemenbaum, 1974; Furukawa et al., 1975; Matussek & Linsmayer, 1968). However, the problem with many of these studies, in terms of trying to understand the relationship between lithium's actions and its ability to lessen manic symptoms, is that they are all acute studies. It is well established that a minimum of 7 to 10 days of chronic lithium administration is usually required before therapeutic benefits are observed.

Additional evidence points to lithium's actions on at least two independent signaling systems in the CNS that could be involved in its mood-stabilizing effects (Jope, 1999). In both cases, lithium is proposed to increase basal neuronal activity but attenuate stimulus-induced (e.g., neurotransmitter-activated) increases in neuronal activity. For example, receptor-mediated production of cyclic AMP (one of the most prevalent second messengers in the brain) is controlled by a stimulatory g-protein (Gs) and a counterbalancing inhibitory g-protein (Gi), with the Gi influence predominating under basal conditions. Lithium appears to inhibit both g-protein-mediated processes, which would allow increases in basal cyclic AMP levels but reduce the stimulus-induced increases in cyclic AMP production. Thus, the ability for lithium to stabilize fluctuations in neuronal responses—a property shared with other mood stabilizers (discussed later)—could be the foundation for its mood-stabilizing effects. Another potential target for lithium is an enzyme called glycogen synthase kinase 3 (GSK-3), which is involved in regulating several functions in neurons. Studies show that lithium reduces GSK-3 activity in two ways—one direct and the other indirect. These dual effects can act in concert to magnify the influence of lithium on crucial GSK-3-regulated functions, such as cyclic AMP stabilization, gene expression, cell structure, and survival (Jope, 2003). These in turn may be factors in lithium's putative role in promoting neurogenesis, as suggested by the neurotrophic theory described earlier. Lithium's actions on this enzyme may also be a factor in the changes in Gi and Gs attributed to lithium that stabilize cyclic AMP signaling. More recent studies indicate that chronic administration of lithium can down-regulate both alpha and beta adrenergic receptors, and can affect production of the second messengers c-AMP and IP3 (Devaki et al., 2006).

The mechanism of action that is responsible for the mood-stabilizing effects of anticonvulsants is equally unclear, but these drugs have all been shown to limit the sustained repetitive firing of action potentials evoked by a sustained depolarization of mouse cortical neurons at therapeutically relevant concentrations. This action is mediated by prolonging the inactivation of voltage-activated Na^+ channels that occurs after depolarization of the neuron (Baldessarini, 2001). However, lamotrigine may have an additional mechanism, for example, possibly the inhibition of the release of the excitatory neurotransmitter glutamate, that may account for its efficacy.

Mood-stabilizing anticonvulsants also have properties that are consistent with the neurotrophic model of mood enhancement. Evidence indicates that the mood stabilizer valproate promotes an extracellular signal-regulated kinase pathway in rats that is used by neurotrophic factors to regulate neurogenesis, axon and dendrite outgrowth, and neuronal survival (Hao et al., 2004). Thus both lithium and anticonvulsant mood stabilizers, as well as antidepressants and ECT, apparently through very different mechanisms, appear to activate interconnected extracellular and intracellular signaling pathways that promote neurogenesis and synaptic plasticity (Coyle & Duman, 2003). These provocative findings support recent proposals that drugs that are effective in reducing the symptoms of mood disorders do so not because they enhance monoaminergic neurotransmission but because they promote neurogenesis and reestablish functional connections between neurons that have been damaged through a sequence of biochemical events that are initiated by exposure to chronic stress.

Websites for Further Information

Sites providing general information on mood/affective disorders and pharmacotherapy:

http://www.depression.com

Information on FDA-approved medications for depression:

http://www.healthyplace.com/communities/depression/treatment/antidepressants/index.asp

Sedative–Hypnotics, Anxiolytics, and Anticonvulsants

Drugs with sedative–hypnotic properties are perhaps the most commonly used and abused drugs in U.S. society, with alcohol topping the list. Despite the fact that they possess all the qualities that society deems unacceptable with respect to drugs (namely, toxicity, lethality, social disruptiveness, and dependence), and despite the fact that they are more destructive to individuals and society than all other drugs combined, they are readily accepted in both recreational and medicinal contexts. It has been estimated that alcoholics alone represent approximately 20% of the patients seen in psychiatric facilities (Guze et al., 1986), and according to the most recent World Health Organization (WHO) reports, 4% of all deaths are related to alcohol, with this value reaching 9% in the group of age between 15 and 29.

The term **sedative–hypnotic** is used because, in most individuals, the lower doses of these drugs have a psychological calming effect, and somewhat higher doses have a hypnotic, or sleep-inducing, effect. As discussed in Chapter 2, these drugs at lower doses can also induce activating effects. The term *hypnotic* in this context should not be confused with the state induced by hypnosis, which is a state in which the individual is actually very much awake.

Alcohol (technically ethyl alcohol or ethanol) is the most used and abused recreational sedative–hypnotic drug in the world, and barbiturates and benzodiazepines are among the most frequently abused prescription sedative–hypnotics. In addition, there are many drugs with very similar properties, including hydroxyzine (Vistaril), zolpidem (Ambien), chloral hydrate, ethchlorvynol (Placidyl), glutethimide (Doriden), and methaqualone (Quaalude), most of which are no longer marketed (legitimately) because of their abuse potential. For the most part, all of these drugs differ primarily in their quantitative aspects—that is, the latency of onset, the intensity of effect, and the duration of action—without having any distinct qualitative differences. Their qualitative effects are directly dose related: At very low doses most of them induce a mild activational effect; moderate doses induce sedation and sleep; high doses induce anesthesia; and successively higher doses can cause coma, respiratory arrest, and death.

To some extent, there is overlap between drugs that act as sedative–hypnotics, anxiolytics ("minor tranquilizers" or antianxiety drugs), and anticonvulsants, as some drugs (e.g., benzodiazepines and barbiturates) belong to all three categories, and some drugs (e.g., barbiturates) tend to produce all three effects at roughly the same dose range. Nevertheless, these three classes of action are dissociable because depending upon the drug, these effects can be evident at different doses and also because some drugs are highly selective for one of these actions.

ALCOHOL (ETHANOL)

Alcohol is the most widely consumed sedative–hypnotic drug. According to recent data from the WHO, almost half of all men and one-third of women in the world consume alcohol. Worldwide consumption in 2005 was equal to 6.13 liters of pure alcohol consumed per person aged 15 years or older. The alcohol in wine, hard cider, and beer is derived through the interaction of yeast and sugar (fermentation) in fruits or grains, thus it cannot reach alcohol concentrations higher than 12–20% of total volume before the yeast is inactivated. Spirits are produced from concentration (distillation) of fermented solutions, and therefore have a higher alcohol content (more than 20%). The alcohol content of these beverages is generally specified in terms of **proof,** which is exactly double the actual percentage of ethanol they contain. For example, 90-proof whiskey is 45% ethanol.

Alcohol has a number of characteristics that make it somewhat unique in comparison to most other drugs (Fleming et al., 2001). First, it is not a very potent drug, requiring several grams to exert noticeable effects on behavior, rather than the milligram amounts needed with other drugs. It takes somewhere between 25 mg and 50 mg of ethanol per 100 milliliters of blood (**a blood alcohol content, or BAC,** of 0.025% to 0.05%) to exert measurable effects in most individuals. For that reason, in most countries legal BAC limits for driving are set between 0.0% and 0.05%. In the United States, a limit of 0.08% BAC for determination of legal intoxication in terms of driving was established by federal legislation in 2000, which requires states to impose this standard or lose federal funds for highway improvement. A person can achieve this level by consuming one drink (0.6 ounce ethanol) for every 50 pounds of body weight in 1 hour. (In this context, a drink equals 1.5 ounces of 80-proof liquor, 6 ounces of wine, or 12 ounces of beer.)

Alcohol also has somewhat different pharmacokinetic properties than most other drugs. Unlike many drug molecules, the ethanol molecule is a relatively small, neutrally charged particle. These characteristics make it readily absorbed from all compartments of the gastrointestinal (GI) tract. In contrast to many psychoactive drugs, it is highly water-soluble. Its oil/water partition coefficient is just high enough for it to readily pass the blood–brain barrier, and the placenta, but low enough so that it is not fat-soluble. Therefore, its onset of action is rather quick and its duration of action rather short. Its low fat solubility also generally results in females achieving somewhat higher plasma concentrations than males, even when the same amount of alcohol is ingested and they weigh the same, because females have more body fat proportionally than males. This also can be applied to older men. Unlike most other drugs, whose rate of metabolism is proportional to their concentration, alcohol is metabolized (by the enzyme alcohol dehydrogenase [ADH]) at a fairly constant rate (i.e., it exhibits zero-order kinetics). Furthermore, with most drugs where there is considerable first-pass metabolism, the liver is responsible. With alcohol, it also occurs at an upper GI tract site (DiPadova et al., 1987). Women have only about half the ADH in their stomachs as men, which (in addition to possessing a higher body fat to water ratio) explains their relatively higher levels of intoxication when consuming similar amounts of alcohol as men. There are also differences among people of different ethnic backgrounds; for instance East Asians have a lower level of ADH in the stomach than Caucasians. Finally, alcohol is a high-calorie liquid that is almost always ingested orally as a beverage (though in Scandinavian countries it is inhaled in saunas). Thus, it provides the body with a ready source of calories.

To some extent, these characteristics contribute to some of the unique problems associated with alcohol. For example, chronic users of alcohol often suffer from liver damage, partially because the liver spends a lot of time and energy trying to metabolize alcohol, and brain damage, partially because the individuals are consuming a large portion of their calories in alcohol and neglecting to eat proper amounts of other foods containing proteins, vitamins, and minerals essential for neuron maintenance.

Considering its widespread use, one would hope that the relative margin of safety of alcohol would be high. Unfortunately, it is not. The BAC of persons who have died of acute alcohol exposure is typically around 0.5% (a level achieved in a 165-pound male drinking 23 drinks in 4 hours). Because responsible social drinking generally results in BACs of around 0.05% (achieved in the same man drinking four drinks in 4 hours), the therapeutic index of alcohol is around 10—not very high. Fortunately, there are two built-in mechanisms that generally prevent lethal levels from being reached. If one approaches a BAC of around 0.12% rapidly enough, vomiting may occur, because of local irritation of the GI tract or disturbances in vestibular functioning. Past this point, most persons become stuporous or pass out when a BAC of around 0.35% is reached. Therefore, the lethal limit would be achieved only by those who consume alcohol rapidly enough to achieve higher concentrations before they pass out.

Ethanol Pharmacokinetics

It takes approximately 1 hour for 90% of the alcohol in a drink to get into the bloodstream. However, because alcohol is rapidly and readily absorbed from the stomach (in 1 to 2 minutes), its accumulation in the brain is rapid enough to exert noticeable effects within minutes. Whereas solid food in the stomach increases the absorption time, carbonated alcoholic beverages tend to enhance the absorption of alcohol because the carbonation forces the alcohol into the small intestine, where there is greater surface area for the absorption to take place and, thus, more rapid accumulation of alcohol in the brain. Although there is some relationship between plasma level of alcohol and its behavioral effects, there is a considerable lack of correspondence between the peak plasma levels of alcohol in the blood and the peak behavioral and subjective effects induced (Figure 10.1). That is, it has long been recognized that the behavioral effects of

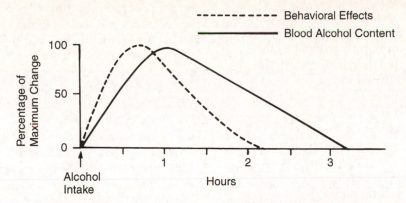

FIGURE 10.1 Percentage change in BAC levels and behavioral variables as a function of time since alcohol is administered. Note that the peak behavioral effects of alcohol occur prior to attaining peak BAC levels and that the behavioral effects dissipate considerably before all the alcohol has left the body.

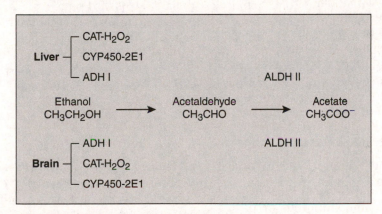

FIGURE 10.2 Metabolism of ethanol in liver and brain.

alcohol are far greater when plasma levels are on the rise than when they are falling (Fleming et al., 2001). The fact that the same brain concentrations of ethanol during the rising and falling portions of the time-concentration function (a matter of an hour or two) induce substantially different effects suggests the development of acute tolerance (tachyphylaxis).

Alcohol is metabolized at a rate of approximately 12 to 18 ml/hour, or 1.0 to 1.5 ounces of 80-proof vodka per hour (Fleming et al., 2001). The oxidative metabolism of ethanol (Figure 10.2) into its first metabolite, acetaldehyde, can involve several organs and multiple enzymes, including ADH I (around 90% is carried by this enzyme), cytochrome $P_{450}2E1$ (CYP2E1), and catalase-H_2O_2 (Deng & Deitrich, 2008). The liver accounts for approximately 90% of the alcohol metabolized. Acetaldehyde is very efficiently metabolized in the liver into acetic acid (acetate), primarily by NAD-linked aldehyde dehydrogenase (ALDH; Deng & Deitrich, 2008), which is further metabolized into carbon dioxide and water and then excreted. Approximately 5% of the alcohol is excreted by way of the lungs, and a minimal amount of alcohol is directly eliminated in the urine. It has been shown that acetaldehyde can be formed locally in the brain from the ethanol that escapes liver metabolism. ADH I, the main enzyme that metabolizes ethanol in the liver, is not widely present in the brain; thus the local formation of acetaldehyde in this organ after alcohol ingestion is done by the other two enzymatic systems: CYP2E1 and catalase (Arizzi-LaFrance et al., 2006; Correa et al., 2009). It has been calculated that approximately 60% of brain ethanol metabolism is accounted for by catalase, whereas 20% is mediated by CYP2E1 (Zimatkin et al., 2006).

In 40% of East Asian and Native American people and less than 10% of Caucasians, the ALDH2*2 allele, which encodes for an inactive ALDH II form, appears to protect against alcoholism (Mulligan et al., 2003; Peng et al., 2007). In agreement with the human data, ALDH2 KO mice that accumulate higher levels of acetaldehyde show a reduction in their preference for ethanol (Isse et al., 2002). Acetaldehyde has been considered as a highly toxic substance when accumulated in significant amounts in the periphery, because it induces nausea, headache, and high blood pressure ("flushing response"; Chao, 1995), as well as causing cellular damage. However, acetaldehyde, in very small amounts in the brain, has been demonstrated to be a psychoactive substance capable of regulating neuronal activity (Segovia et al., 2009; Spina et al., 2010; Vinci et al., 2010) and behavioral processes, including self-administration by animals (Arizzi-LaFrance et al., 2006; Rodd et al., 2005; Spina et al., 2010). Thus acetaldehyde can have different effects depending upon its concentration. This is an important factor that can explain some of the failures that can occur after the implementation of pharmacological treatments for alcoholism based on the aversive reaction induced by acetaldehyde accumulation.

Neurochemical Effects of Ethanol

Acute ethanol administration induces marked changes in the patterns of regional brain metabolism (e.g., glucose metabolism or cerebral blood flow; Pawlosky et al., 2010; Wang et al., 2000) with relative increases in some areas and decreases in others, which may be correlated with the different behavioral effects of alcohol (Zhu et al., 2004). This effect is also mimicked by its second metabolite, acetate (Pawlosky et al., 2010).

At the neuropharmacological level, alcohol at high doses is believed to act directly on neuronal membranes by altering their basic structure and making them more "fluid" (Goldstein, 1989). This fluidizing action may inhibit the movements of the Na^+ and K^+ ions across the membranes and interfere with the ability of the neuron to generate and conduct action potentials. At lower doses that lead to intoxication, ethanol directly or indirectly affects the function of a wide variety of neurotransmitter systems in the brain. This makes it particularly difficult to determine which ones are most relevant to intoxication, tolerance, dependence, and withdrawal, as well as which ones might be targets for drug therapy in dealing with alcoholism. As is the case with most other drugs of abuse, acute exposure to ethanol dose-dependently increases the release of dopamine (DA) in the nucleus accumbens, thus promoting behavioral activation (Salamone & Correa, 2002). Rats will press levers that lead to delivery of microinjections of ethanol in the ventral tegmental area (VTA), which provides dopaminergic input into the nucleus accumbens (Weiss & Porrino, 2002). It has also been demonstrated that an oral dose of ethanol promotes DA release in the human nucleus accumbens (Boileau et al., 2003).

Ethanol also appears to enhance activity of opioid receptors (Krystal et al., 2003). Acetaldehyde was demonstrated to produce very similar pattern of effects on the dopaminergic and opioid systems (Hipólito et al., 2009; Melis et al., 2007).

However, two key receptors that appear to be particularly relevant to ethanol's subjective effects and the development of tolerance and dependence with chronic use are the $GABA_A$ and the NMDA (N-Methyl-D-aspartic acid) receptors (Krystal et al., 2003; Weiss & Porrino, 2002). Activation of $GABA_A$ receptors allows Cl^- to flow into neurons and hyperpolarizes them, whereas activation of NMDA receptors allows Ca^{++} to flow into neurons and depolarizes neurons. Ethanol enhances the activity of GABA (gamma-aminobutyric acid) at $GABA_A$ receptors (i.e., enhances inhibition) and inhibits NMDA receptors (i.e., reduces excitation). Ethanol's ability to enhance Cl^- conductance via $GABA_A$ receptors may be due to its ability to elevate levels of a neuroactive steroid (allopregnanolone) that is a potent modulator of this receptor subtype (VanDoren et al., 2000). A number of other receptors (e.g., neuropeptide Y, $5-HT_3$, cannabinoid, and nicotinic) also have been implicated in the reactions to low doses of ethanol.

As discussed shortly, several drugs affecting these receptors have been tested as potential treatments for alcohol abuse/dependence—with limited success. For example, a benzodiazepine derivative, Ro15-4513, which is an inverse agonist at $GABA_A$ receptors, can block ethanol's intoxicating properties. However, because it does not reduce the lethal effects of high doses of ethanol, the drug is unlikely to come into clinical use because if people drink to get drunk and they take the drug beforehand, they could end up drinking so much ethanol in order to override the drug's effects that they could die (Britton et al., 1988).

Alcohol's ability to potentiate the action of GABA at $GABA_A$ receptors appears to mediate its anxiolytic and sedative–hypnotic effects, an action shared by other sedative–hypnotic drugs. Its ability to inhibit the action of glutamate (GLU) at NMDA receptors appears to mediate some other primary reinforcing properties—possibly by reducing these receptors' tonic control over dopaminergic neurons in the VTA and increasing the release of DA in the nucleus accumbens (Tabakoff & Hoffman, 1996).

Psychological Effects of Ethanol

Alcohol has been used for centuries, and by many cultures, for a variety of effects. It is well established in humans that alcohol has both positive (e.g., mood enhancement and increased social integration) and negative (e.g., aggression and hostility) social consequences that are highly dependent on the context the person is in (Graham, 2003) and on individual physiological factors (e.g., metabolizing enzyme polymorphisms, tolerance) that determine what primary effects the drug has on the person. Thus, across the different psychological effects of alcohol, some are due to primary pharmacological action of the drug acting on some brain circuits, and others are conditioned effects due to previous learning.

It has been demonstrated that the primary activational effect of alcohol is important for predicting if a person is going to be a heavy drinker. Thus, about half of the people who consume a high dose of alcohol experience stimulant effects, and individuals who experience greater stimulant-like effects during the ascending limb and lesser sedative-like effects on the descending limb of the BAC curve may be at greater risk for developing ethanol- use disorders. The neurobiological basis for individual differences in sensitivity to the stimulant and sedative effects of alcohol is related to the activity of the dopaminergic and GABAergic neurotransmitters, respectively (Holdstock et al., 2000).

On the other hand, the expectancies can be powerful predictors of both adolescent drinking status and adult alcoholism. Heavy drinkers generally expect more positive and fewer negative consequences than do light drinkers. People who consumed alcohol in the presence of others reported increased ratings of drug liking and were more likely to perceive increased feelings related to sociability (e.g., friendliness, euphoria), and to exhibit objective indicators of sociability (e.g., smiling, laughing) compared with those who consumed a placebo beverage in that setting. However, those who consumed the same amount of alcohol in a solitary setting reported significantly more sedative effects (e.g., sleepier, dizzier, less able to think clearly) and increased ratings of dysphoria and demonstrated few effects related to sociability compared with those consuming the placebo (Holdstock et al., 2000; Pliner & Cappell, 1974).

Thus alcohol induces a pattern of behavioral disinhibition that allows for a greater interaction with the environment. This can be seen in anxious individuals who drink to be able to socialize, but also can be a part of the induction of aggressive behavior in other people (Pihl & Zacchia, 1986). It has been proposed that the disinhibitory effect of alcohol is due to the loss of inhibitory control by the prefrontal cortex (Hobbs et al., 1996). Statistically, alcohol consumption is the single-most common denominator to criminal activity and family violence (Cychosz, 1996; Guze et al., 1986).

Alcohol tends to disrupt ongoing psychological processes in a dose-dependent manner. In general, the types of faculties affected by increasingly larger doses of alcohol are affected in the reverse order in which they were ontogenetically developed (i.e., developed in early life): first, complex cognitive skills (e.g., planning and problem solving); then fine-learned motor skills (golfing); then gross-learned motor skills (walking); and finally, visual accommodation and unconditioned reflexes (hand jerk upon touching a hot surface, breathing). Although alcohol induces sleep, it is not a normal pattern of sleep, because REM (the sleep stage in which rapid eye movements and vivid dreams are most pronounced) is considerably reduced (Ritchie, 1985).

A substantial proportion of deaths from unintentional injury also involve alcohol. Over 20% of work-related accidents are likely to involve alcohol use (Hingson & Howland, 1993). About 40% of all fatal traffic accidents in North America and Europe are alcohol related, and the risk of a fatal car accident increases exponentially with a driver's BAC. In the early 1990s, following the recommendations of many experts that the legal BAC limit for driving and piloting aircraft be lowered, many states did so, apparently with beneficial consequences. According to a 1999 review by the federal government's General Accounting Office, studies assessing the consequences of decreasing the legal limit have generally found decreases (somewhere around 12–16%) in alcohol-related collisions, injuries, and/or fatalities in most jurisdictions that lowered the legal limit to 0.08% BAC.

Various processes involved with learning and memory are also disrupted by alcohol (Mello, 1978; Nelson et al., 1986; see Figure 11.1 for a summary of the various stages involved in learning and memory). Attention to relevant stimuli, ability to encode new information, and short-term memory (ability to maintain new information in storage for several seconds) all decrease. In the most extreme case, these processes may be so affected that the person may experience *blackouts*—that is, complete amnesia regarding events that took place over much of the period of intoxication. These dose-related black-outs occur in approximately a quarter of social drinkers and may occur in up to 90% of problem drinkers and alcoholics (Anthenelli et al., 1994; Campbell & Hodgins, 1993). This phenomenon may be related to the ability of ethanol to inhibit NMDA receptor activity and enhance GABA$_A$ receptor activity, and completely block long-term potentiation and memory formation (Schummers & Browning, 2001). More often, long-term memory is affected, primarily with respect to a person's ability to retrieve information from storage, possibly because of state-dependency.

Chronic Effects of Alcohol Use

Alcohol has numerous effects on tissues other than the brain. It increases blood circulation to the skin, causing a warm, flushing sensation. However, this change increases the rate of loss of body heat when exposed to the cold. The galvanic skin response, or GSR (actually a measure of sweat gland activity), is suppressed, and heart rate decreases, although in some individuals the initial effect of alcohol is to increase blood pressure, heart rate, and blood sugar level. These increases are probably related to an elevation in catecholamine blood levels stemming from a decrease in their clearance from the blood, possibly due to alcohol's disruption of norepinephrine (NE) neuronal reuptake (Ritchie, 1985). After an hour or so, these activities often decline below normal. Alcohol stimulates production of acid and pepsin in the stomach (potentially contributing to ulcers), and this effect could explain why some people's appetites are enhanced by alcohol. Alcohol inhibits the release of antidiuretic hormone from the hypothalamus, causing water to be eliminated at a high rate. Thus drinking alcoholic beverages to relieve thirst is counterproductive.

The liver is one of the organs most likely to be affected by chronic alcohol consumption. Alcohol reduces the rate at which the liver forms glucose, oxidizes fats, and releases complex fats. As a result, when there is extensive exposure to alcohol, the liver accumulates fat, and blood sugar levels are depressed. Free fatty acids are not broken down and are deposited in the liver cells themselves. Thus, early stages of chronic alcohol consumption are characterized by fatty livers. Eventually, the cells may rupture or become isolated and die. Cell death is followed by the formation of fibrous connective tissue (fibrosis), which is nonfunctional, at least with respect to what the liver is supposed to do. Some individuals eventually develop *cirrhosis* (severe hardening and contraction of the liver; Schanne et al., 1981). Although liver damage associated with alcohol consumption was once believed to be primarily due to malnutrition, research has shown that excellent nutrition does not prevent the development of alcoholic hepatitis or its progression to cirrhosis (Hobbs et al., 1996).

Alcohol also interferes with the normal metabolic activities of the liver because of its own metabolism. Chronic exposure to ethanol can significantly change its rate of metabolism and alter its BAC levels. Initially, ethanol induces greater synthesis of the enzymes responsible for its metabolism, thus enhancing the rate at which ethanol is metabolized. Therefore, CYP2E1 increases and its role in peripheral alcohol metabolism goes from 7% in occasional consumers up to 22% in chronic consumers (Song & Cederbaum, 1996). However, in those individuals who use large doses of alcohol chronically and develop liver damage, the rate at which alcohol is metabolized can be dramatically reduced, which increases ethanol levels and prolongs its stay in the body.

Among long-term alcoholics, 40% show reduction in brain volume along with increases in the ventricular volume, and 70% manifest some type of neurological effects, even after detoxification. Some of these effects are primarily due to the alcohol molecule, and others are secondary due to malnutrition, such as deficiencies in thiamine that lead to the Wernicke-Korsakoff syndrome. A wide variety of studies have indicated that, as a group, chronic alcoholics develop a relatively enduring pattern of cognitive and motor deficits (McEntee & Mair, 1978; Oscar-Berman, 1980; Svanum & Schladenhauffen, 1986). Alcoholics show ataxia (incoordination) of gait and balance, which is likely due to reduction of pontocerebellar volume (Sullivan et al., 2010). The hippocampus and the cortex (especially the frontal lobe) are very sensitive to alcohol (Volkow et al., 1994). Thus, other impairments are often displayed in abstract reasoning ability, new learning and memory consolidation, problem solving, and perceptual motor functions. Inability to shift cognitive and attentional sets may also occur (e.g., a person who has developed one strategy for a task or who attends to one type of stimulus may continue using that strategy when it is no longer appropriate or may not perceive a new type of stimulus if one is suddenly presented). A considerable body of evidence suggests that right-hemisphere functions (e.g., visual-spatial skills and visual-perceptual analysis) are more impaired in alcoholics than left-hemisphere functions (e.g., verbal-linguistic abilities). Because this pattern of cognitive decline in chronic heavy drinkers is similar to that observed in aged individuals, some have suggested that alcoholism is associated with "premature aging" of cognitive capabilities (Ryan, 1982).

Much of the alcohol-associated brain damage (Wernicke's disease) and the resulting impairment in learning and memory (Korsakoff's syndrome) have traditionally been attributed to malnutrition, especially thiamine deficiency, rather than to the direct neurotoxic effect of ethanol (Fleming et al., 2001). These problems come about because a large portion of the alcoholic's diet is derived from alcohol, which happens to be very high in calories but contains no other essential nutrients, and the consumption of proper amounts of proteins, vitamins, and essential nutrients is low. Poor diet associated with chronic alcohol intake can also depress appetite and prevent proper absorption of nutrients from the GI tract (Pezzarossa et al., 1986). Therefore, treatment of these neurological disorders with thiamine and glucose is generally helpful (Gold, 1995; Zubaran et al., 1997), although it will not reverse symptoms that are the result of neuronal loss.

Chronic alcohol consumption has also been associated with brain shrinkage and a number of functional deficits in cerebral and cerebellar functions (Carlen et al., 1978; Golden et al., 1981; Sullivan & Marsh, 2003). Alcoholics suffering from these conditions can show some recovery when abstinence is maintained over periods of weeks to many months (Carlen et al., 1978; Volkow et al., 1994), with similar improvements occurring regardless of gender or family history of alcoholism (Drake et al., 1995; Mann et al., 1992). Rapid recovery may be attributed to the resolution of the alcohol withdrawal syndrome, whereas gradual functional improvement may have a structural basis, a reversible atrophy indicative of the plasticity in the central nervous system (CNS; Mann et al., 1993), and a subsequent improvement in glucose utilization in some areas of the brain (Volkow et al., 1994). Thus, although the frontal lobe is one of the structures that is most affected by alcoholism, it also recovers quite rapidly after abstinence, and its functional recovery is associated with protracted abstinence success (Volkow et al., 1994).

Studies with rodents maintained on nutritional diets and given large quantities of alcohol have revealed a wide variety of brain damage that occurs with chronic exposure, binge exposure, and withdrawal—each with different likely mechanisms for inducing damage, with genetics and age as contributing factors (Crews et al., 2004). These animal models suggest that binge drinking may be most damaging, with *oxidative stress* (damage caused by free radicals, which are highly reactive chemicals that capture electrons and modify chemical structures) and factors resulting in brain inflammation as potential causes. Ethanol withdrawal can induce brain damage because chronic ethanol exposure results in NDMA receptor supersensitivity, which then results in excitotoxic effects on neurons when these receptors are no longer suppressed with ethanol (you might recall from Chapters 4 and 5 that GLU exerts excitatory influences on neurons via activation of NMDA receptors; this can lead to toxic levels of calcium ions accumulating in neurons). The newly recognized ability of the adult brain to regenerate neurons in certain areas of the brain has also led to research indicating that both chronic and binge ethanol exposure can retard cell proliferation and increase cell death, thus preventing neuroregeneration that normally occurs. The good news is that studies with humans indicate that neurodegeneration associated with alcoholism begins to reverse over several years of sobriety (Pfefferbaum et al., 1998). In any case, it is likely that the pathophysiology of alcoholic brain damage is due to a variety of factors—for example, synergistic effects of alcohol, acetaldehyde, thiamine deficiency, liver disease, and excessive NMDA receptor activity during ethanol withdrawal (Butterworth, 1995; Hunt, 1993; Kril, 1995; Lancaster, 1995).

Chronic alcohol consumption can also severely affect numerous sexual functions. Male alcoholics, with or without overt liver disease, exhibit certain underactive gonadal functions, including testicular atrophy, impaired sperm production, impotence, and decreased libido, as well as abnormalities in the metabolism of sex hormones. Much of the evidence suggests that these deficits are due to increased activities of the drug-metabolizing enzymes in the liver resulting from chronic alcohol exposure, which, in turn, severely reduces testosterone levels (Van Thiel et al., 1974).

Fetal alcohol syndrome (FAS) is the leading cause of mental retardation in the United States and is completely preventable because it is caused by prenatal exposure to alcohol (Williams et al., 1994). First described in 1968, FAS is commonly characterized by mild to moderate mental retardation, absence of the groove between the nose and upper lip, inordinate profusion of hair on the face at birth, folds on eyelids, underdeveloped jaw area, cleft palate, joint anomalies, and cardiac irregularities. FAS children show smaller head circumference, smaller brain size, and proportionally smaller basal ganglia, diencephalon, and corpus callosum areas than do normal children (Mattson et al., 1994; Riley et al., 1995). Behavioral characteristics are reported in more than 50% of the cases. Compared with normal children, FAS children generally have poor attention spans; exhibit a lack of guilt after misbehaving; are impulsive, poorly coordinated, hyperactive, and irritable; and exhibit speech problems (Janzen et al., 1995; Wekselman et al., 1995). Many of their behavioral symptoms are very similar to those of children with attention deficit hyperactivity disorder (ADHD; discussed in Chapter 11). It is generally accepted that alcohol-related birth defects exist along a continuum, with complete FAS at one end of the spectrum and incomplete features of FAS, termed **fetal alcohol effects** (FAE), which include more subtle cognitive-behavioral deficits at the other.

Many of the symptoms and some of the facial features of FAS may diminish over time, but in most cases, the low IQ, attention deficits, poor scholastic achievement, and behavioral and social problems observed in FAS individuals persist into their adult years (Eustace et al., 2003). For example, one study found that IQ in FAS patients remained stable from a mean age of 8 years, 4 months (mean IQ of 66) to a mean age of 16 years, 7 months (mean IQ of 67; Streissguth et al., 1991). Follow-up studies of FAS children have found that short stature persists into adolescence and adulthood, although weight may catch up to normal or above-normal levels (Wekselman et al., 1995). Behaviorally, their hyperactivity is replaced by inattentiveness, distractibility, restlessness, and agitation. Adults with FAS tend to use poor judgment, make poor decisions, lack self-direction, and demonstrate difficulty in recognizing social cues. In adulthood, prenatal alcohol exposure has been found to be associated with high rates of trouble with the law, inappropriate sexual behavior, depression, suicide, and failure to care for children (Kelly et al., 2000).

The incidence of FAS and the severity of the symptoms are directly related to the amount of alcohol consumed by the mother during the first trimester. Numerous mechanisms have been proposed for the production of FAS. Some studies have pointed to ethanol's ability to disrupt the synthesis of retinoic acid, a metabolite of vitamin A, as a mechanism for inducing FAS, because an optimal level of retinoic acid is needed for normal development of the limbs and CNS (Shean & Duester, 1993). Others have suggested that the teratogenic effects of alcohol are due to altered umbilical–placental blood flow (Randall & Saulnier, 1995) or to the formation of free radicals that have cytotoxic effects (Guerri et al., 1994). Another possibility stems from some of the pharmacodynamic properties of ethanol discussed earlier: that ethanol reduces NMDA receptor activity (i.e., reduces neuronal excitation) and enhances GABA$_A$ receptor activity (i.e., enhances neuronal inhibition). Several lines of animal research suggest that when neuronal activity is abnormally suppressed during the developmental period of synaptogenesis, the timing and sequence of synaptic connections are disrupted. This causes nerve cells to receive an internal signal to commit suicide, a form of programmed cell death known as *apoptosis* (Ikonomidou et al., 2000; Olney et al., 2004). Thus there is the likelihood that by suppressing neuronal activity, alcohol causes millions of nerve cells in the developing brain to commit suicide. The window of vulnerability for this abnormal apoptosis in humans would include the entire third trimester of pregnancy, because expression of NMDA receptors peaks during this period.

To account for why most women who drink during pregnancy do not give birth to children with FAS/FAE, it has been argued that specific sociobehavioral risk factors—for example, those associated with low socioeconomic status, such as excessive pollutant exposure and poor nutrition—provide the context for biological factors—for example, maternal/fetal hypoxia and free radical formation—to provoke FAS/FAE in vulnerable fetuses (Abel & Hannigan, 1995). The risk of FAS has been reported to be seven-fold higher in Blacks than in Whites, even after adjustment for the frequency of maternal alcohol intake, occurrence of chronic alcohol problems, and number of children borne (Sokol et al., 1986), raising the question of some kind of genetic susceptibility to FAS.

More than a third of the neonates of mothers who drank heavily throughout pregnancy exhibited growth retardation. The minimal amount of alcohol necessary for inducing FAS has not been determined, but most of the evidence suggests that it can occur when more than 1 ounce of ethanol is consumed per day. One cannot assume, however, that smaller amounts do not have any adverse effect on fetal brain growth and differentiation. Nor can one assume that such effects will not occur during the last trimester of pregnancy, when the fetus is generally considered to be least susceptible to environmental influence.

Beneficial Effects of Alcohol

Despite all the maladaptive consequences of high levels of alcohol consumption, chronic exposure to less than 1.75 ounces of ethanol per day (approximately 2 drinks), often described as moderate drinking, may have some health benefits. Relative to abstainers, moderate drinkers (i.e., those who drink one to two drinks per day) have the lowest mortality rate, and heavy drinkers (i.e., those who drink over three drinks per day) have the highest mortality rate, with the mortality rate increasing monotonically with higher alcohol intake (Britton & Marmot, 2004; Dawson, 2000; Gaziano et al., 2000; Liao et al., 2000). The lower mortality rate among moderate drinkers has been attributed to a decreased risk of cardiovascular and cerebrovascular disease, possibly due to alcohol's ability to stimulate production of an enzyme, t-PA, that helps break down blood clots (Ridker et al., 1994) or to raise the body's levels of HDL cholesterol—the type of cholesterol that keeps the arteries free of dangerous buildups (Gaziano & Hennekens, 1995). Enhanced quality of life and decreased arousal from stress may also be a factor in this phenomenon. However, former drinkers exhibit risk characteristics that could enhance their mortality, and, compared with light or occasional drinkers or lifelong teetotalers, these individuals may have the highest risk of mortality from all causes (Fillmore et al., 1998; Shaper & Wannamethee, 2000).

Alcoholism: Tolerance, Abstinence, and Withdrawal

There are several approaches to understand alcoholism. Some experts describe alcoholism in terms of the amount of alcohol consumed, whereas others feel the consequences of alcohol and the attendant behaviors associated with it, whatever the amount ingested, should be emphasized. The idea that alcoholism is a disease dominates U.S. treatment programs, with advocates of such a model hypothesizing an underlying process based on physical dependency, genetic disposition, and the assumption that it is progressive (Marlatt et al., 1988). In 1988 the U.S. Supreme Court ruled that the government may continue viewing alcoholism as "willful misconduct" rather than as a disease when awarding veterans education benefits. However, the disease designation— adopted by the American Medical Association in 1957—is commonly accepted (Guze et al., 1986).

More recently, alcoholism has been considered as a compulsive drug-use disorder (Chapter 6). Addictions (even the ones that do not involve substance use, such as compulsive gambling) share common neurobiological mechanisms, although there are factors that are unique to each specific substance. Thus, alcohol dependence and alcoholism are defined by the International Classification of Diseases, 10th edition (ICD-10), as "a cluster of behavioural, cognitive, and physiological phenomena that develop after repeated alcohol use and that typically include a strong desire to consume, difficulties in controlling its use, persisting in its use despite harmful consequences, a higher priority given to alcohol use than to other activities and obligations, increased tolerance, and sometimes a physical withdrawal state." For example, there may be one or more unsuccessful efforts to cut down on or control alcohol use, or the person may continue to use alcohol despite knowledge of having persistent or recurrent social, psychological, or physical problems that are caused by his or her alcohol use. Alcoholics may have numerous driving accidents under the influence of alcohol, physically abuse their spouses or children, spend a great deal of money on alcohol, miss work because of drinking alcohol or recovering from its effects, or experience ulcers or high blood pressure. Alcoholics may also display a marked tolerance to alcohol and a characteristic withdrawal syndrome when alcohol use ceases. It should be emphasized that physical dependence is not a necessity in order for a person to be diagnosed as an alcoholic; many individuals who are not physically dependent on alcohol are still considered alcoholic if the other characteristics are evidenced. However, if a person is physically dependent on alcohol, then he or she is definitely an alcoholic. The prevailing view is that even after such persons stop drinking for some length of time, they are still considered to be alcoholic because, should they return to drinking alcohol, the likelihood of the noted characteristics being evidenced is quite high.

Loss of control over one's consumption of alcohol is one factor that is highly debated (Fingarette, 1988). Some experts in the area of alcoholism view alcoholics as being qualitatively different from nonalcoholics in this dimension, as if alcohol acts like an "on-off" switch for them. Others view loss of control along a continuum of degrees of control. This is not a subtle distinction, as it has important bearing on the type of treatment prescribed for alcoholism. For those who believe that alcohol acts like an "on" switch, the primary treatment goal is complete abstinence from alcohol (Mello, 1978). For those who believe that there is a continuum of control, drinking in moderation is not only feasible but is perhaps a more appropriate goal in many individuals with an alcohol problem (Robertson et al., 1986). The reasoning here is that some individuals will avoid all treatment modalities that emphasize complete abstinence, because they cannot see themselves going through life without ever taking another drink.

As is the case with most drugs, **tolerance** to the various effects of ethanol develops at different rates, and there are different underlying mechanisms responsible (Suwaki et al., 2001). Just about all of the mechanisms described in Chapter 6 for the development of tolerance seem to operate with alcohol. There is some pharmacokinetic tolerance in that the ethanol-metabolizing enzymes of the liver may be increased by approximately 15% to 30% with chronic use (Fleming et al., 2001). There is evidence that pharmacodynamic tolerance occurs with respect to ethanol's actions at $GABA_A$ and NMDA receptors (recall that acutely ethanol facilitates activity at the former and inhibits activity at the latter). Several lines of evidence suggest that chronic ethanol exposure in animals induces down-regulation of certain subunits of the $GABA_A$ receptor and up-regulation of brain NMDA receptors (Davidson et al., 1995; Krystal et al., 2003; Mhatre & Ticku, 1993; Tabakoff & Hoffman, 1996). The adaptive changes in the $GABA_A$ receptor system may have a more significant relationship to the development of ethanol tolerance than to withdrawal, whereas the change in NMDA receptors appears to play a significant role in both tolerance development as well as many of the symptoms associated with hyperexcitability during ethanol withdrawal (e.g., seizures; Tabakoff & Hoffman, 1996).

Thus, in addition to the acute tolerance phenomenon described earlier, a low to moderate degree of tolerance develops to most of the behavioral and mood-altering effects of alcohol, such that the chronic user must take larger and larger amounts in order to obtain the desired effects. There is also cross-tolerance among alcohol and all the sedative–hypnotic drugs. Studies with animals indicate that some tolerance may be due to the development of Pavlovian conditioned compensatory responses, which may counter the direct actions of alcohol (Crowell et al., 1981; O'Brien, 2001). This implies that the degree of intoxication with alcohol can be very situationally dependent; that is, the effects of alcohol are most pronounced in novel situations or tasks.

Abstinence symptoms following chronic use of greater than moderate doses of alcohol (say, a pint of whiskey per day for several weeks) may be limited to prolonged disturbances in the EEG during sleep. After cessation of larger doses, the symptoms may be evidenced as a high degree of arousal associated with weakness, tremor, anxiety, and elevated blood pressure, pulse rate, and respiratory rate. In severe reactions, 12 to 48 hours after the person stops drinking, convulsions may occur, and a toxic psychosis may appear with symptoms such as irritability, headaches, fever, nausea, agitation, confusion, and visual hallucinations. This latter syndrome is referred to as **delirium tremens** or the DTs, which typically appear 2 to 4 days after drinking stops (Romach & Sellers, 1991). Withdrawal-related symptoms have been noted in numerous clinical studies to become increasingly more severe after repeated episodes of alcohol intoxication and withdrawal, perhaps through a "kindling" process, in which each episode of withdrawal sensitizes the brain toward progressively more intense withdrawal responses (Booth & Blow, 1993). A study using a positron emission tomography (PET) scan technique has suggested that reduced blood flow to certain areas of the brain following withdrawal periods may be a factor in this phenomenon (George et al., 1999). Because of the convulsions and the associated respiratory arrest, withdrawal from alcohol and other short-duration sedative–hypnotics can be lethal. Therefore, medical treatment is strongly advised.

Although physical dependence on alcohol generally requires several months or years of exposure to alcohol to develop, a single day's exposure to a large quantity of alcohol can induce an acute abstinence syndrome, which is commonly experienced as a hangover (Gauvin et al., 1993). The fact that re-exposure to alcohol can "cure" a hangover ("the hair of the dog that bit you") supports this idea. Some of the symptoms of a hangover may be related to depletion of NE, lack of sleep, dehydration, and low blood sugar. In addition, by-products of fermentation in alcoholic beverages called *congeners*—many of which are toxic to the body—may enhance a hangover. This is probably why some alcoholic beverages induce greater hangovers than others (generally the darker the beverage, the more congeners it has).

Etiology of Alcoholism

Alcoholism is found in all spheres of society, but not everyone who consumes alcohol becomes an alcoholic. WHO estimates that among alcohol consumers, about 11.5% have heavy episodic drinking (Global Status Report on Alcohol and Health, WHO, 2011). National surveys in the United States estimated that there are 17.1 million heavy drinkers out of 130.6 million Americans aged 12 and older who reported current use of alcohol in 2009 (National Survey on Drug Use and Health, 2009). Thus, around 1 out of 10 drinkers could be considered an alcoholic. The incidence of alcoholism is disproportionately much higher in men than in women. Worldwide, for every 4 men there is 1 woman who has weekly episodes of heavy drinking, and men also have much lower rates of abstinence compared to women (Global Status Report on Alcohol and Health, WHO, 2011). In the United States approximately 13% more men than women are current drinkers; the incidence of alcohol dependence is approximately three times higher in men than women (Grant et al., 2004; National Survey on Drug Use and Health, 2009).

There is no consistent evidence to indicate that a particular personality type develops the disorder; however, individuals high in antisocial characteristics, as measured by a variety of personality tests, have been consistently shown to be prone to alcoholism (Cadoret et al., 1987; Cloninger, 1987). Such individuals are generally males with an early onset of alcoholism and whose pattern of drinking is fairly continuous. They often engage in thrill-seeking behavior, fights, and criminal activities; rarely indulge in binge drinking; display little guilt or anxiety over their drinking; and are low in the need for social rewards. Individuals with these characteristics are sometimes designated as type 2 alcoholics (Cloninger, 1987). Conversely, type 1 alcoholics develop symptoms later in adulthood and are much more likely to abstain from drinking for periods of time and then binge once they start drinking. They tend not to engage in thrill-seeking and anti-social activities, they have high social reward dependence, and they often feel guilty or fearful about their alcohol dependence. Female alcoholics are more likely to display type 1 characteristics, but many male alcoholics also share these characteristics.

Many studies have indicated that there are specific genetic bases for many forms of this disorder (Cadoret et al., 1987; Cloninger, 1987; Plomin et al., 1994; Vanyukov & Tarter, 2000). First of all, numerous studies assessing the acute responses of normal humans to alcohol have shown some degree of genetic control in a wide variety of responses (Kreek et al., 2004). For example, many Asians possess a type of gene that results in an inactive form of an enzyme that normally metabolizes acetaldehyde, which allows for acetaldehyde levels to build up. As a result, these individuals experience a more intense reaction to alcohol, with some reactions being pleasant (i.e., "high") and others being aversive (i.e., facial flushing, nausea), which may contribute to their lower tendency to drink excessively.

Second, with respect to alcoholism per se, several studies have noted that the *concordance rate** for alcoholism in identical twins is double that obtained in fraternal twins (approximately 55% vs. 28%; Kendler et al., 2003). People whose biological parents (one or both) display alcoholism and who were adopted as children by nonalcoholic parents have an almost four times higher incidence of alcoholism than adoptees whose biological parents were not alcoholics (Cloninger, 1987; Vaillant & Milofsky, 1982). This finding appears to be particularly true for the type 2 pattern of alcoholism discussed earlier. In general, most of the evidence suggests that genetic factors account for about half of the variance in liability to alcoholism and that they are of similar etiologic importance for alcoholism in women and men (Kendler et al., 2003). However, other analyses suggest that type 2 alcoholism (more common in men) has a very high genetic influence (estimated heritability of 90%), whereas type 1 alcoholism (more common in women) is only moderately influenced by genetic factors (estimated heritability of less than 40%; McGue, 1999; Sigvardsson et al., 1996). Also, there appear to be differences in the development of alcoholism in men and women (e.g., a history of child

---

*Concordance rate refers to the percentage of pairs of individuals who share some trait or characteristic. Say, for example, you locate 70 pairs of twins and you observe that in 5 pairs both members share the trait, but only one member in each of 5 other pairs displays the trait. In this case the concordance rate for that trait is 50% ([5/10] × 100 = 50%). (Note that in 60 pairs, neither individual displays the trait, but these pairs do not figure into the determination of concordance rate.) If the concordance rate for alcoholism was 1% in pairs of genetically unrelated people raised apart, and was 100% in pairs of identical twins raised apart (i.e., in every case either both members of a pair were alcoholic or neither member was alcoholic), then there would be overwhelming evidence that genetics was the sole determinant of alcoholism. Conversely, if the concordance rates were 1% in both unrelated and genetically identical sets, the evidence would be overwhelmingly in favor of environmental factors.

abuse is predictive of women but not men and age of onset of alcoholism is typically later in women than in men; McGue, 1999). Interestingly, there is evidence that genetics may have a stronger influence on the amount of alcohol consumed than on the likelihood of alcoholism (Plomin et al., 1994).

For several years, researchers have been trying to identify biological characteristics or even actual genes that are associated with a predisposition to alcoholism—so far without much success. Although there is general agreement that many genes are involved in the disorder and that they are different for different groups of individuals, many scientists suspect that there are no specific genes for alcoholism per se. More likely there are a variety of genes that lead to a susceptibility to a number of compulsive behaviors—for example, alcohol or other drug addictions, gambling, or eating disorders—in which the type of disorder is shaped by environmental and temperamental factors (Vanyukov et al., 2003). This suggestion is supported by the fact that there is a tremendous variability among alcoholics. Also, alcoholism can set in early and fast or gradually develop over decades; some are binge drinkers whereas others are chronic maintenance drinkers. Thus, it is likely to be some time before we can fit all the disparate pieces of the puzzle together so that the predisposing factors behind this disorder are established with some certainty.

Over the years several studies have suggested that there are a number of biological and behavioral characteristics or markers of alcoholics. Most studies looking for biological differences between alcoholics and nonalcoholics have been retrospective; that is, these characteristics were noted after alcoholism was evidenced. Thus, it is not clear whether these characteristics preceded heavy alcohol use or were caused by it. To circumvent the problem, researchers have attempted to determine whether non-alcohol-abusing young adults with a family history of alcoholism (FH$^+$) differ, in terms of their reactions to alcohol, from those without a family history of alcoholism (FH$^-$). The general findings in these studies are that young adult FH$^+$ males, when given alcohol, are more sensitive to alcohol's effects during the rising arm of the BAC curve (see Figure 10.1) and exhibit reduced effects (i.e., they exhibit acute tolerance) as the BAC level falls, compared with FH– males, despite the fact that the groups do not differ in their BAC curves (Newlin & Thomson, 1990; Schuckit, 1994a). This suggests that males at risk for alcoholism find alcohol more rewarding because the pleasurable, excitatory aspects at the early stage of intoxication are accentuated and the dysphoric feelings—that is, anxiety and depression—that predominate as BAC levels drop are attenuated. In fact, the differential reactions to alcohol in these males have been found to be a potent predictor of their becoming alcoholic 8 to 12 years later (Schuckit, 1994b). (Note that very few studies of this nature from which one can draw general conclusions have been conducted with females, due primarily to the much lower incidence of alcoholism in females; thus, there are fewer subjects of this type for researchers to study—a considerable problem for this particular methodological approach. Also, there was a common belief that there was much less of a genetic basis for alcoholism in females.) On the other hand, there is evidence that individuals at risk for alcoholism experience more frequent and intense hangover effects than do low-risk individuals, which may be a factor in their initiating further drinking to relieve these aversive symptoms (Earleywine, 1993; Newlin & Pretorius, 1990).

Other studies have noted that brain wave deficits that are often seen in alcoholics also appear in the sons of alcoholics before the individuals have ever used alcohol

(Porjesz & Begleiter, 2003). These results, in addition to supporting the view that some of the variation in the propensity for alcoholism is biologically based, suggest that it may be possible to determine which individuals are prone to alcoholism prior to their becoming heavy users of alcohol and to warn such individuals about their predisposition to developing the disorder.

Environmental factors also are implicated in the vulnerability to alcoholism (Zucker & Gomberg, 1986). As noted earlier, even in identical twins the concordance rates are nowhere close to 100%. Furthermore, one-third of alcoholics have no family history of alcoholism, and only 17% to 25% of sons of alcoholics become alcoholics (Vanyukov & Tarter, 2000). Not surprisingly, exposure to stressors and trauma has commonly been linked to alcoholism, and stress-relief drinking has been suggested to be one of several prominent factors in the etiology of alcohol abuse and dependency (Powers & Kutash, 1985). Although many early studies investigating this hypothesis did find support for it, many did not. In some studies alcohol use intensified the tension or anxiety of the individuals tested. In many cases, it was the subjects' expectations as to whether alcohol would reduce or increase tension, which was a critical element in their response to alcohol. Alcoholics typically report more acute and chronic stressors and fewer social resources than do nonalcoholics (Moos et al., 1988). Perhaps as many as a third of alcoholics are raised in homes with an alcoholic parent. Numerous studies have indicated that having an alcoholic parent greatly increases the likelihood of experiencing a wide range of childhood stressors (e.g., embarrassment, verbal, emotional, physical, and sexual abuse; Sher et al., 1997).

Numerous studies have also identified a strong association between posttraumatic stress disorder (PTSD) and alcohol and other substance abuse (Brady et al., 2004; Kessler et al., 1997). For example, in a sample of Vietnam combat veterans with PTSD, more than half subsequently showed signs of alcoholism (Bremner et al., 1996). The onset of alcohol and substance abuse typically was associated with the onset of symptoms of PTSD, and the increase in use paralleled the increase of symptoms. Similarly, alcohol abuse symptoms have been found to be double in women exposed to childhood rape, who often report turning to alcohol to reduce symptoms of PTSD (Epstein et al., 1998). Of several explanations for the linkage between PTSD and alcohol abuse, most of the evidence supports the self-medication hypothesis (Brady et al., 2004).

Although it is clear that there is a relationship between exposure to stressors and the incidence of alcoholism, in many cases it is difficult to disentangle all the confounding variables that may contribute to the association. For example, alcoholic parents not only provide a highly stressful environment for their children but also contribute their genes. Also, dependency on alcohol typically leads to negative consequences for the individual that are stressful, and with retrospective studies it is often difficult to determine which came first. There is a very high (approximately 80%) comorbidity between the lifetime incidence of alcoholism and other psychiatric disorders (Kessler et al., 1997), which commonly contribute to the individual's exposure to stressors. In general, adoption studies indicate that exposure to chronic stress, for example, being raised in an alcoholic home, does not put one at risk for alcoholism unless the individual has a genetic liability for alcoholism (McGue, 1999). Furthermore, the effects of stress may depend on which heritable form of alcoholism is involved. In the adoption studies conducted (Cloninger et al., 1981; Sigvardsson et al., 1996), it was determined that the lifetime risk of severe alcoholism was increased four-fold in adopted men with both genetic and environmental risk factors characteristic of type 1 alcoholism, but that neither genetic nor environmental risk factors by themselves were sufficient to cause alcoholism. In contrast, the risk of type 2 alcoholism was increased six-fold in adopted sons whose biological fathers were type 2 alcoholics, regardless of their postnatal environment.

Treatment of Alcoholism

There are a multitude of ways of treating alcoholism, none of which has had universal success with all individuals (Miller et al., 1995). Because withdrawal from alcohol can be lethal, medical intervention is advisable. This generally entails substituting a long-acting anxiolytic—for example, diazepam (Valium)—and then gradually reducing the dose over several days (Romach & Sellers, 1991). However, anxiolytics that remain in the body for a shorter period of time, such as oxazepam (Serax), may be preferable because they allow physicians to more easily adjust dosages as needed. Carbamazepine (Tegretol), an anticonvulsant and mood stabilizer with no abuse potential, has been shown to be effective in the treatment of acute alcohol withdrawal and may also have efficacy in the long-term treatment of alcohol dependence (Mueller et al., 1997). Once the physical dependence phase is over with, other interventions can be applied (chemical, psychological, or both).

Chemical treatments for maintaining abstinence have ranged from drugs that induce nausea when accompanied by alcohol to drugs that attempt to promote insight into the causes of one's drinking. One of the most common chemical interventions is disulfiram, which has been used for several decades. This drug blocks ALDH II activity, the same enzyme that normally metabolizes the alcohol metabolite acetaldehyde into acetate. Thus, with the intake of alcohol, there is a build-up of acetaldehyde in the body, and a toxic reaction occurs ("flushing response"), consisting of nausea and headache among other aversive symptoms. The patient is either told of these unpleasant reactions or is given small test amounts of alcohol to precipitate the reaction, so that he or she will know what to expect. ALDH inhibitors such as disulfiram (Antabuse) and calcium carbimide (Abstem, Temposil) have been used with mixed success to stop consumption and to prevent relapse in alcoholics. Support for the general use of disulfiram is equivocal, mostly being found in the form of reduced quantity of alcohol consumed and a reduced number of drinking days. Evidence for an effect on increasing the proportion of patients who achieve abstinence is not clear (Hughes & Cook, 1997). One of the basic problems with disulfiram is that its effectiveness as a drinking deterrent depends entirely on the person's willingness to comply with the treatment regimen or even accept it in the first place—both of which are rare (Brubaker et al., 1987). For example, in a special group of patients selected for being highly motivated to stop drinking, the success in being abstinent after Antabuse was around 40% (Sereny et al., 1986). In animal studies it has been demonstrated that its main effect of reducing ethanol consumption occurs when the rats did not have a lot of experience consuming alcohol, but its therapeutic properties are not manifested if the animal has been consuming ethanol voluntarily for a long time (Tampier et al., 2008). Thus, the aversive properties can deter ethanol consumption, especially in individuals with little experience with alcohol or in individuals more sensitive to punishment, like people with PTSD in which disulfiram seems to be a good therapeutic agent (Barth & Malcolm, 2010; Kozarić-Kovacić, 2009). In other subjects the aversive effects can be partly responsible for the lack of compliance with the treatment. Another problem is that disulfiram may not even work (i.e., produce a disulfiram-alcohol reaction) in patients with significant liver disease, because of insufficient build-up of acetaldehyde levels (Wicht et al., 1995).

Antabuse was introduced as a treatment for alcoholism in 1948. It took almost 50 years for the Food and Drug Administration (FDA) to approve for use (in 1995) the next drug for this purpose. It is naltrexone (ReVia), which was originally approved for the treatment of opiate addiction in 1984 (and marketed as Trexan). Several studies have now demonstrated that naltrexone is effective in the rehabilitation of alcoholics, presumably because of its ability to reduce alcohol-induced euphoria and to dampen the craving for another drink (O'Malley et al., 1996a, 1996b; Volpicelli et al., 1995a, 1995b). For example, in one study the relapse rate in naltrexone-treated alcoholics was half that of placebo-treated alcoholics (23% vs. 54%) over a 3-month period, and among patients who did revert to drinking, those given naltrexone were much less likely to drink heavily. Naltrexone works by blocking the receptors for endorphins, which in alcoholics may be unusually elevated when they drink (possibly as a result of alcohol-induced physical stress, which animal research indicates can trigger the release of endorphins). However, the efficacy of naltrexone in the treatment of alcoholism may depend on its severity. The only study that has not found naltrexone to produce benefits significantly better than placebo was conducted with men with chronic, severe alcohol dependence (Krystal et al., 2001). Thus severely dependent individuals may not benefit because they can override naltrexone's effects by drinking large amounts of ethanol. Compliance to the treatment regimen has also been a problem. Thus a depot-injection form of naltrexone that can be administered on a once-a-month basis has been developed and shown to be effective for treating alcohol dependence (Kranzler et al., 2004). Depot drug preparations can be useful because they can enhance compliance to the treatment regimen. This preparation also has the advantages over oral administration of naltrexone by producing less variability in plasma concentrations of both the active drug and the major metabolite, involving less first-pass metabolism (which results in a greater ratio of the metabolite to the parent compound), and potentially exhibiting greater efficacy and fewer adverse effects.

Nalmefene (Revex), an opioid antagonist that is structurally similar to naltrexone, also has been found to be effective in preventing relapse to heavy drinking relative to placebo in alcohol-dependent outpatients (Mason et al., 1999). A study assessing the impact of nalmefene or naltrexone on alcohol consumption among nontreatment-seeking alcoholics and social drinkers found that relative to placebo both opiate antagonists were comparable in reducing drinking amounts and frequency in the alcoholics—but not the social drinkers—during natural environment and bar-lab alcohol consumption evaluations (Drobes et al., 2003). Nalmefene may have a number of potential pharmacological advantages over naltrexone for the treatment of alcohol dependence, including no dose-dependent association with toxic effects to the liver, greater oral bioavailability, longer duration of antagonist action, and more competitive binding with opioid receptor subtypes that are thought to reinforce drinking.

Acamprosate (Campral) is another drug approved by the FDA (in 2004) for use in the maintenance of abstinence in alcoholic patients who are abstinent at treatment initiation. This approval came as a result of multiple clinical studies showing that acamprosate was more effective than placebo in maintaining abstinence in detoxified patients. As is the case with other drugs used in the treatment of alcoholism, acamprosate is intended for use as part of a comprehensive management program that includes psychological support. Several studies have indicated that acamprosate does not imitate the subjective or reinforcing effects of alcohol, does not have any reinforcing or aversive effects on its own, and does not block the subjective qualities of alcohol (Zornoza et al., 2003). However, it has anticraving properties (Littleton, 1995). Several mechanisms have been proposed to explain acamprosate's efficacy in alcoholism treatment, with most of the evidence supporting its being a functional antagonist at NMDA receptors (Zornoza et al., 2003).

At this point, the efficacy of acamprosate appears to be comparable to that of the opiate antagonists in the treatment of alcoholism. As is the case with the opiate antagonists, the practical value of acamprosate treatment in alcoholism is questionable, particularly if not used in combination with other psychosocial therapies. For example, in a 6-month randomized controlled study of acamprosate versus placebo in preventing relapse in detoxified alcoholic patients, only 57% of the patients were judged to be taking at least 90% of their tablets after 2 weeks, and only 35% of the patients completed the study (Chick et al., 2000). Not surprisingly, there was no significant difference between the two groups in the total days of abstinence and the percentage of complete abstainers at the end of the study. In contrast, in a similarly designed study, but in which the patients also participated in an outpatient program that included medical counseling, psychotherapy, and self-help groups, only 25% of the patients dropped out after 6 months, and the abstinence rate and cumulative days of abstinence were significantly better in the acamprosate-treated group (Tempesta et al., 2000). Based on the findings that naltrexone and acamprosate are fairly comparable in efficacy and work via different pharmacological mechanisms, a double-blind study was conducted to determine if a combination of both drugs would enhance the efficacy of reducing relapse in alcoholic patients (Kiefer et al., 2003). Compared with placebo, naltrexone and acamprosate alone were somewhat better in reducing the time to first drink and the time to relapse, and as predicted, the combination of the two drugs was the most effective treatment.

Because several lines of evidence suggest that serotonergic dysfunction may be a factor in alcoholism, the efficacy of serotonergic agents, including serotonin (5-HT) uptake inhibitors (discussed later in this chapter and in Chapter 9), has been assessed in numerous clinical trials. The evidence from these trials is not very promising, although most studies of this nature have been confounded by high rates of comorbid mood disorders in the patients (Garbutt et al., 1999). In patients with comorbid major depressive disorder and alcohol dependence, long-term treatment with the 5-HT uptake inhibitors fluoxetine has been shown to produce substantial reductions in depressive symptoms and drinking behaviors relative to placebo treatment, although none of the subjects in either treatment group was completely abstinent from alcohol throughout the entire period (Cornelius et al., 2000). Evidence suggests that alcohol enhances the activity of 5-HT_3 receptors, which are ionotrophic receptors that promote DA release in mesocorticolimbic regions of the brain. Blocking 5-HT_3 receptors has been shown to reduce alcohol consumption in several animal species (McBride et al., 2004). On the basis of evidence that early-onset alcoholism differs from late-onset alcoholism by its association with greater serotonergic abnormality and antisocial behaviors, treatment with ondansetron, a selective 5-HT$_3$ receptor antagonist, was assessed in early- and late-onset alcoholics. As predicted, low doses of ondansetron were found to be superior to placebo in increasing percentage of days abstinent and total days abstinent per study week in the patients with early-onset alcoholism (Johnson et al., 2000). A subsequent study found that an intermediate dosage of ondansetron reduced alcohol craving in early-onset alcoholics and that decreased overall craving was positively correlated with reduced drinking and negatively correlated with increased abstinence. In contrast, a lower dosage of ondansetron significantly increased craving in late-onset alcoholics (Johnson et al., 2002). These results indicate that ondansetron (at a specific dosage) may be an effective treatment for patients with early-onset alcoholism; they also suggest that the efficacy of pharmacological treatments may depend on the specific type of alcoholism.

Lithium, commonly used in the treatment of manic depression, has been periodically touted as an effective treatment for alcoholism since the 1970s, but an exhaustive study of this treatment failed to support its efficacy in this regard (Dorus et al., 1989). However, because manic depression has been found to be one of the most likely of major mental disorders to co-occur with alcohol or other drug abuse (Brady & Sonne, 1995), there may be a specific subgroup of alcoholics who may profit from treatment with lithium or some other type of mood stabilizer.

A number of other drug therapies for alcoholism have been tried—most of which failed or remain unproven for effectiveness. For example, anthropological reports have suggested that Native Americans belonging to the Native American Church, who use the mescaline-containing peyote plant in their religious ceremonies, have a lower incidence of alcohol problems than other Indian groups. In the early 1960s, a few pilot studies with LSD (lysergic diethylamide) were conducted with alcoholics to see if the supposedly insight-promoting properties of this drug would be useful in reducing their alcohol problem (Brecher, 1972). These generally involved one or two exposures to LSD under medical supervision. Although there was some indication of an initial reduction in alcohol consumption, 6-month follow-ups showed no greater improvement with LSD than with a placebo. However, before more extensive research could be conducted with LSD, governmental restrictions became so difficult for researchers that no further studies were attempted.

Among the psychologically based treatments, a number of behavior modification techniques and group therapies have been applied in the treatment of alcoholism. Strategies that empirical research has suggested may be helpful in the treatment of alcoholism include self-help groups (i.e., Alcoholics Anonymous (AA), Narcotics Anonymous; McCrady & Delaney, 1995), marital and family therapy (O'Farrell, 1995), coping and social skills training (Monti et al., 1995), anxiety and stress management (Stockwell, 1995), and behavior modification utilizing social, recreational, familial, and vocational reinforcers (Smith & Meyers, 1995). Cue exposure therapy, in which patients are exposed to potential conditioned stimuli (e.g., the sight and smell of alcohol) associated with alcohol's reinforcing effects in order to extinguish alcoholics' conditioned craving for alcohol, has produced some promising results in terms of reducing alcoholics' responsivity to alcohol cues (Staiger et al., 1999). However, its long-term efficacy for achieving and maintaining abstinence remains to be established. Strategies that empirical research has uniformly found to be ineffective include relaxation training, confrontational counseling, videotape self-confrontation, individual psychotherapy, general alcoholism counseling, and educational lectures/films (Miller et al., 1995).

Perhaps one of the most well-known approaches to dealing with alcoholism is the one taken by AA. This organization, founded by a group of alcoholics in 1935, believes that alcoholism is a disease and that abstinence is required to deal with the disease. Unfortunately, there is considerable difficulty in determining the actual effectiveness of AA, because the group is reluctant to give researchers access to their records or members. Furthermore, participation in AA is almost always voluntary, raising questions of how self-selection might be a factor in the efficacy of AA. In one study, it was found that those who chose to participate in AA were less pathological in their personality profile than those who did not voluntarily participate (Thurstin et al., 1986). Research suggests that problem drinkers who choose to participate actively in AA experience more favorable outcomes than those who just attend meetings—that is, those who are mandated or coerced to attend meetings by the courts or by employers—for whom controlled studies have found no unique efficacy of AA (Montgomery et al., 1995).

Alcoholics who respond well, regardless of treatment, are those with jobs, stable family relationships, minimal psychopathology, no history of past treatment failures, and minimal involvement with other drugs. Unfortunately, however, most alcoholics do not fall into this favored category. Furthermore, alcohol abusers whose history suggests a primary diagnosis of depression have been found to respond to treatment better than substance abusers with a diagnosis of antisocial personality. In short, it is important to take with a grain of salt any claim of effective alcoholism treatment unless the characteristics of the clients are indicated. The fact is, on the basis of reviews of controlled comparisons among treatment settings (where different types of patients have been clumped together), there is little evidence that there is an overall advantage for residential over nonresidential settings, for longer over shorter inpatient programs, for more cost-intensive over less cost-intensive programs, or for inpatient over outpatient programs (Agosti, 1994; Miller & Hester, 1986, 1989).

Virtually all strategies involved in the treatment of alcoholism in the United States and Canada focus on abstinence as the goal—primarily due to the belief that once an individual becomes an alcoholic, it is not possible for that individual to return to moderate drinking. However, in long-term follow-up studies of alcoholic patients treated in abstinence-oriented programs, controlled drinkers constitute 10% to 30% of the treated sample, and abstainers constitute an additional 10% to 30%, with relapsers often comprising the largest outcome group (Booth et al., 1992; Miller et al., 1992). There are a number of authorities who have suggested that controlled drinking training may still be a viable alternative for those individuals exhibiting less severe forms of alcoholism— that is, problem drinkers who have not developed a heavy physical dependence on alcohol (Elal-Lawrence et al., 1987; Marlatt et al., 1993; Robertson et al., 1986). Controlled drinking training is widely accepted in the United Kingdom as a viable treatment for alcoholism (Rosenberg et al., 1992; Rosenberg & Davis, 1994). As mentioned earlier, there is a concern that many problem drinkers will simply not seek treatment if abstinence is the only option. The fact is, many individuals who receive extensive treatment for their alcoholism return to what can be considered controlled drinking (defined as less than 2.5 and 2.0 ounces of ethanol per day for men and women, respectively) following the period of abstinence required while they are in treatment. The success of controlled drinking programs is still unclear, with some studies finding uncontrolled drinking frequently following a period of moderate drinking (Finney & Moos, 1991), and others finding that moderate drinking was sustained for follow-up periods of a year or longer

(Booth et al., 1992; Miller et al., 1992). Those who return to moderate drinking are more likely to have received some type of training in controlled drinking, such as self-recording of drinking and blood alcohol levels; setting daily and weekly consumption limits; pacing drinking by sipping, diluting, and alternating alcoholic and nonalcoholic beverages; learning about the antecedents of drinking; learning how to refuse drinks; changing drinking environments and companions; and learning alternatives to drinking (Alden, 1988; Booth et al., 1992). It is important to note that the distribution of approximately equal abstinent and nonabstinent successful outcomes is similar to that found following treatment programs that promote a single goal of abstinence (Booth et al., 1992; Miller et al., 1992).

As a summary, only about 15% of alcoholics ever receive formal treatment. Depending on the criteria used for assessing treatment outcomes, somewhere between one-third and two-thirds of the alcoholics who are treated can be viewed as successes; that is, the person becomes abstinent or engages in nonproblem drinking (Marlatt et al., 1988). Interestingly, numerous studies have indicated that many alcohol abusers are able to positively change their use patterns without the assistance of formal treatment. Factors associated with successful self-change include a high level of motivation and commitment to change, public announcements, social support, alterations in one's social and leisure-time activities, general lifestyle changes that decrease exposure to conditioned craving cues, development of stress-coping strategies, and the generation of negative expectations over continued use and positive expectations concerning continued abstinence (Marlatt et al., 1988).

BARBITURATES AND OTHER SEDATIVE–HYPNOTICS

Barbiturates have become the dinosaurs of drugs; they enjoyed a century of use as sedative and hypnotic agents, but have only a few specialized uses today. Furthermore, these and other drugs in the sedative–hypnotic class have effects so similar to alcohol's effects (Harvey, 1985) that little further discussion of them is needed, except to note that long-term alcohol exposure probably has more toxic physiological consequences (see earlier discussion on alcohol's unique characteristics and chronic effects of alcoholism). Sedative–hypnotic compounds without the barbiturate structure, such as methaqualone and glutethimide, have been synthesized, but their actions are essentially indistinguishable from those of the barbiturates (Harvey, 1985).

Barbiturates differ from each other primarily in terms of pharmacokinetics, which determines how quickly the drugs act, their intensity of action, and their duration of action. All three of these properties are tied together. The differences in these properties are a major factor in determining what these drugs are used for. Representative barbiturates are thiopental, a fast-acting, ultrashort-duration (approximately 15 minutes) drug used primarily as an anesthetic; secobarbital, a short-duration (approximately 1.5 hours) drug used as a sleep inducer; pentobarbital and amobarbital, short- to intermediate-duration (approximately 4 hours) drugs used for either their sedative or sleep-inducing qualities; and phenobarbital, a relatively long-acting (approximately 6 hours) drug used as a sedative or an anticonvulsant.

The medical uses for these drugs have declined considerably over the past 3 decades, primarily because of the development of compounds with less toxicity or dependence liability (such as the benzodiazepines, which will be discussed shortly;

Harvey, 1985). The primary advantage of the barbiturates at present is their cost. They are no longer under patent, and thus they are very inexpensive.

The general tendency of these drugs is to decrease the excitability of neurons throughout the nervous system (Harvey, 1985). The inhibitory influence of barbiturates has been postulated to be due to their ability to enhance GABA's activity at the $GABA_A$-type receptor, which results in the opening of Cl^- channels, allowing Cl^- to flow into neurons and hyperpolarizing them. The primary action of barbiturates appears to be one of prolonging the duration that these channels remain open. The inhibitory effects of barbiturates may also be due to increases in potassium (K^+) conductance (i.e., the flow of K^+ from the inside neurons to the outside; O'Beirne et al., 1986). Accompanying these activities is an increase in the levels of most neurotransmitters, in all likelihood because of their decreased utilization. The rate of oxygen consumption and cerebral glucose metabolism in all areas of the brain is reduced with these drugs (Hibbard et al., 1987).

A wide variety of behaviors, perceptual processes, and mental activities are affected by these drugs that are used for their calming and sedating effects, even at low doses. A consistent feature of barbiturates (and the nonbarbiturate alternatives) in humans is to increase EEG slow wave activity (theta and delta waves) and reduce alpha wave and fast beta wave activity (Patat, 2000). (Alpha activity predominates when a person is in a relaxed awake state with his or her eyes closed; beta activity is more frequent when a person concentrates on a task with his or her eyes open, and is associated with alertness; theta activity often occurs when a person has the eyes closed under resting conditions, and is linked to sleepiness; and delta waves, when they predominate, correspond to sleep.) Although they are all used for enhancing or inducing sleep, the pattern of sleep induced is not really what one would consider normal. In general, during an 8-hour night of sleep, we go through several stages of sleep. These stages differ with respect to how easy it is to wake the person, how physiologically aroused the body is, the mental content, the types of EEG waves produced, and the person's eye movements. All stages have been presumed to have some functional significance, but there is no consensus as to what specific functions they have. Most nonbenzodiazepine sedative–hypnotics tend to prolong the deeper stages of sleep and reduce the stage known as REM (Harvey, 1985). REM is the stage in which vivid dreams are most common. However, the ability to suppress REM sleep is not restricted to the sedative–hypnotics. This characteristic has been noted to occur with many other types of drugs as well, including psychostimulants and marijuana.

The mechanisms for inducing tolerance to alcohol apply to the barbiturates, although the latter appear to have a greater effect than alcohol on the drug-metabolizing enzymes of the liver (increasing their levels up to five times their normal level; Harvey, 1985). As indicated earlier, cross-tolerance occurs with all of these substances, and the psychological and physical dependence associated with them is quite similar. The faster-acting compounds, which also have more intense effects and shorter durations, are more likely to be abused, and the abstinence syndrome associated with them is likely to be more intense, but less protracted, than that associated with the longer-acting compounds.

INHALANTS: ANESTHETIC GASES AND SOLVENTS

Inhalants consist of a wide variety of gases (ether, halothane, nitrous oxide, chloroform) and industrial solvents (e.g., toluene, a component of some glues) that have sedative–hypnotic properties. Some of these are used as general anesthetics to put patients to sleep before surgery. Others are used for their intoxicating and euphoric properties. Inhalants, although not necessarily illicit drugs, are often used illicitly to get "high," particularly by very young individuals; for example, approximately 16% of eighth graders in 2003 reported having used these at least once. Inhalants comprise one of the "gateway" drugs to further illicit drug use, but unlike almost all other substances that are used to get high, use of inhalants actually declines from the eighth grade to the end of high school (Monitoring the Future Survey, 2003).

Although these substances comprise a rather heterogeneous group of drugs, most of them are believed to work indiscriminately by dissolving in neuronal membranes to somehow modify neuronal ion channel activity, because their potency is highly correlated with their lipid-solubility. However, some anesthetic gases, such as isoflurane, appear to act by binding directly to specific proteins in the CNS, because different isomers exert stereospecific effects on neuronal ion channels (Franks & Lieb, 1991). Whatever the mechanism of action, high doses of most of these substances decrease neuronal activities; at low doses they may increase some types of neuronal activity, most likely as a result of disinhibition (Jaffe, 1990).

Typically, after several minutes of inhalation, dizziness and intoxication occur. The characteristics of this high commonly include euphoria, visual and auditory hallucinations, a sense of empowerment, loss of motor coordination, nausea, and decreased heart and respiratory rates. Following the high, a period of drowsiness and stupor may persist for several hours (Miller & Gold, 1991).

Because of the heterogeneity of actions and because few of the many compounds of this nature have been systematically studied, little is known about their intoxicating properties. Some of them have been shown to have addictive qualities; for example, animals will self-administer nitrous oxide, chloroform, and toluene (Jaffe, 1990). Tolerance occurs with those substances that have been tested, but cross-tolerance may occur between some of these but not others.

Clinical problems associated with chronic use of many of the inhalants—for example, hexane and toluene—include cardiac arrhythmias, bone marrow depression, cerebral degeneration, and damage to the liver, kidney, and peripheral nerves (Jaffe, 1990; O'Brien, 2001). Deaths have occasionally been attributed to inhalant abuse; most of these are associated with heart failure, suffocation, or accidents (Johns, 1991).

ANXIOLYTICS

At their core, anxiety disorders involve unrealistic, irrational fears or anxiety of disabling intensity. There are several primary types of anxiety disorders. Collectively, these disorders are the most frequently observed type of mental disorders in adults. For centuries, alcohol and to some extent opiate-type drugs were commonly used to reduce the symptoms of anxiety disorders; the barbiturates (and drugs with similar properties) were subsequently used in their treatment. However, because of the high abuse potential and toxicity of these drugs, along with the development of drugs with more selective actions, the use of the former drugs in treating anxiety disorders has virtually ceased, with perhaps the exception involving those individuals who use them for "self-medication" purposes. Anxiety disorders are now treated with drugs that are collectively referred to as **anxiolytics,** because they induce a "dissolution" or "loosening" of anxiety. A number of these drugs have pharmacological and behavioral properties similar to alcohol and barbiturates—differing only in a matter of degree. Others in this class have very different pharmacological and behavioral properties. In many cases the latter drugs have a higher efficacy rate, are less prone to abuse, and generally have minimal potential for inducing death through overdose.

Anxiety Disorders Treated with Anxiolytics

Phobias are characterized by persistent and disproportionate fear of some specific object or situation that presents little or no actual danger to the person. When persons with a phobia encounter a feared object or situation, they often experience the flight-or-fight response, which prepares them for escaping from the situation. *Specific phobias* generally involve fears of other species (e.g., snakes, spiders) or fears of specific features of the environment (e.g., large bodies of water, heights). *Social phobias* involve fears of social situations in which the individual feels exposed to the scrutiny of other people (such as during public speaking) and is afraid of acting in a humiliating or embarrassing way.

Panic disorder is related to phobias but is much less common. It is characterized by recurrent panic attacks, which are accompanied by heart palpitations or chest pain, a choking or smothering feeling, dizziness, numbness and tingling in the hands or feet, sweating, and trembling. The symptoms come on quite suddenly and unpredictably. The individual is persistently worried over experiencing a panic attack and "going crazy" or losing control. Long-term sufferers may begin to feel anxious in anticipation of an attack.

Agoraphobia is a common complication of panic disorder (although it can occur without experiencing prior panic attacks), in which the individual fears being in places or situations from which escape would be difficult or embarrassing should they experience a panic attack or something bad happen to them. In extreme cases, agoraphobics don't even venture outside their homes.

Generalized anxiety disorder (GAD) is characterized by chronic excessive worry over just about everything (i.e., family, finances, work, or personal illness). Not only do individuals with this disorder exhibit much higher levels of worry over these than normal, but they also can't control or prevent their worrying. Other symptoms of this disorder include muscle tension, insomnia, attention and concentration problems, and social withdrawal.

Posttraumatic stress disorder (PTSD) is characterized by a pathological reexperiencing of prior traumatic events in the form of intrusive thoughts, flashbacks, and dreams; avoidance of situations reminiscent of the trauma; and numbed responsiveness to the environment, manifested as diminished interest in significant activities, detachment from others, and restricted affect as well as symptoms of hyperarousal, including hypervigilance, exaggerated startle response, sleep disturbances, and impairment of concentration.

Obsessive–compulsive disorder (OCD) is characterized by the occurrence of unwanted and intrusive obsessive thoughts or distressing images; these are usually accompanied by compulsive behaviors that may temporarily neutralize the obsessive thoughts or images or prevent some anticipated dreaded event or situation. Both obsessions and compulsions may occur in the disorder, or they may occur separately. Individuals diagnosed with OCD typically recognize that these symptoms are excessive and unreasonable. This syndrome is considered to be in the spectrum of the anxiety disorders in the *DSM-IV-R;* however its core symptoms are not anxiety related.

Behavioral Tests Used to Assess Anxiolytic Actions

As described in several other chapters in this book, some behavioral tests in animals are particularly useful for identifying patterns of effects that allow one to predict a particular therapeutic action, or identify a drug as belonging to a specific class. This has been particularly true of anxiolytic drugs (File et al., 2004). In Chapter 2, we discussed the *elevated plus maze* (Pellow & File, 1986), which is a widely used test in rodents that is sensitive to the anxiolytic and anxiogenic (i.e., anxiety-inducing) effects of drugs (Figure 2.1). The natural tendency of rodents is to avoid open spaces, such as the open arms in the elevated plus maze, which are exposed to the ambient lighting conditions and have no walls. Instead, they prefer to be in the closed spaces, such as the closed arms, which have solid walls and are shaded. Thus, increases in the number of times a rat or mouse enters into the open arms, or the amount of time it spends in the open arms, as opposed to the closed arms, can be used as a preclinical marker of potential anxiolytic effects in humans. The idea is that avoidance of the open space is a marker of anxiety in the animal, and the anxiolytic drug is alleviating this effect, which results in the animal spending more time in the open arms. Several common anxiolytic drugs produce this effect. In contrast, *anxiogenic* drugs produce the opposite effect; in other words, they increase time spent in the closed arms. Another behavioral test that is sometimes used to assess this type of function is the *open field*, which is a large open arena. Again, rodents will tend to stay in the outer portions of the arena, near the walls, and avoid the center; increased movement into the center can be used as a measure of anxiolytic activity, whereas the opposite effect can be used to assess potential anxiogenic effects. Although seemingly similar, these tests do not always yield the same effects (Sink et al., 2010). Other behavioral tests related to anxiety include the *Geller-Seifter* conflict test (which is done in an operant chamber), *punished drinking*, the *social interaction* test, *light/dark exploration*, and *defensive burying* (File et al., 2004; Treit et al., 2010). There is some variability of drug action across these different tests, and it appears that some tests are differentially sensitive to drugs with different pharmacological actions (Treit et al., 2010). Nevertheless, these behavioral models in animals have been particularly useful for identifying novel drugs, and characterizing the brain mechanisms involved in the effects of anxiolytic drugs (particularly the benzodiazepines).

Benzodiazepines

Over the years, a number of drugs have come into clinical use with claims of being highly selective in their ability to reduce anxiety symptoms without inducing other undesirable effects. In the 1950s meprobamate (Miltown) was highly touted as one of these. However, it did not quite live up to its reputation in subsequent clinical tests and was not found to be significantly different from earlier sedative–hypnotic compounds. The introduction of chlordiazepoxide (Librium) into clinical use in 1961 ushered in the era of a new class of drugs called the benzodiazepines, and they essentially took over as the prototypic anxiolytic, primarily for safety reasons (Hobbs et al., 1996). These drugs are also sometimes referred to as "minor tranquilizers," because they are used predominantly in minor or less severe cases of pathology. Of the over 3,000 benzodiazepines synthesized, about three dozen are in clinical use in various parts of the world. In the United States the most commonly prescribed benzodiazepines for anxiety are chlordiazepoxide

(Librium), diazepam (Valium), oxazepam (Serax), clorazepate (Tranxene), lorazepam (Ativan), and alprazolam (Xanax). For many years the Valium brand of diazepam was the most popular drug of this group, but Xanax has replaced it as the most commonly prescribed anxiolytic, probably because of growing fears of dependence with Valium, competition from generic forms of diazepam, and limited evidence that Xanax may possess somewhat better antidepressant, antipanic, and antiphobic effects (DeVane et al., 1991).

The properties of benzodiazepines are very similar to those just described for the sedative–hypnotics. For example, they are effective anticonvulsants and muscle relaxants, they reduce a variety of aggressive tendencies, and they decrease anxiety. However, the actions of these drugs are hypothesized to be more specific than barbiturates and similar compounds in affecting the limbic system (which modulates emotionality, fear, aggression, sexuality, and motivation in general) at doses that do not affect the cerebral cortex (involved in higher mental processes like thinking and problem solving). In contrast to barbiturates, the benzodiazepines are not effective as general anesthetics.

There are a number of differences between the benzodiazepine anxiolytics and earlier compounds (including meprobamate) used in the treatment of anxiety-related disorders. The most striking difference is their high therapeutic index (Hobbs et al., 1996). Very few deaths are attributable to overdoses of benzodiazepines by themselves, although they have been involved in a number of deaths when combined with other sedative-like drugs, because of their additive effects. Their high therapeutic index is probably due to their specific ability to enhance the activity of GABA (a normally endogenous inhibitory neurotransmitter), as opposed to the more generalized neuronal suppressive effects of other sedative–hypnotic drugs. This may also account for why benzodiazepines have minimal general anesthetic effects except at very high doses. Another advantage is that they have minimal effects on the drug-metabolizing enzymes of the liver and therefore do not enhance the hepatic metabolism of themselves or other drugs.

Part of the more selective action of the benzodiazepines is due to the fact that there are binding sites for them on $GABA_A$ receptors that mediate their action in the CNS. These benzodiazepine receptor sites are highly specific for benzodiazepine receptor ligands (including competitive antagonists and inverse agonists). The highest concentrations of these sites are found in the cerebral cortex, limbic structures such as the amygdala, and the cerebellum. Thus, benzodiazepines are not technically GABA agonists, as they do not bind directly to GABA binding sites, but instead occupy another binding site on the $GABA_A$ receptor complex, and their binding results in an enhancement in the affinity of the GABA binding site to bind to and activate $GABA_A$ receptors (Figure 10.3). Thus, the benzodiazepines are referred to as *allosteric modulators* of GABA (the term *allosteric* refers to the fact that the benzodiazepine recognition site is physically distinct from the GABA recognition site; see Chapter 5). As a result, the degree of effect of benzodiazepines depends on the concentration of GABA; that is, they produce marked effects at low GABA concentrations and minimal effects when high GABA concentrations are present. The lack of effect on maximal GABA responses may, in part, account for the lower toxicity of benzodiazepines compared with barbiturates in cases of overdose, because at high doses a number of barbiturates increase Cl^- flow into neurons in the absence of GABA—that is, barbiturates act more like GABA agonists (Hobbs et al., 1996). The rodent behavioral tests of anxiety described earlier are highly sensitive

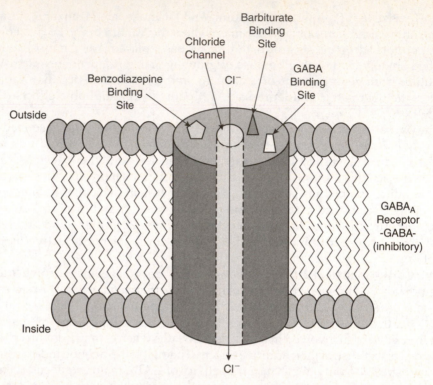

FIGURE 10.3 Schematic drawing of the GABA$_A$ receptor complex, showing binding sites for GABA, benzodiazepines, and barbiturates. Benzodiazepine agonists, antagonists, and inverse agonists all bind to the benzodiazepine binding site. This inhibitory receptor is ionotropic and is linked to a Cl$^-$ channel. The actual receptor protein complex has several different components. The outer ring protein complex that contains the GABA, barbiturate, and benzodiazepine binding sites is pentameric (with five different proteins), with several possible protein subunits that can be present (e.g., alpha, beta, gamma, delta with multiple subunit variations of each). This organization allows for a large number of specific variations of this receptor. Some drugs interact with the GABA$_A$ receptor differentially, depending upon which specific protein subunits are present. (See Nutt, 2006, and Iversen et al., 2009, for more details.)

to the effects of benzodiazepines (File et al., 2004; Pellow & File, 1986; Treit et al., 2010). Moreover, they have been used to identify potential brain mechanisms for the anxiolytic effects of benzodiazepines. In particular, studies with animals have revealed that the amygdala is the brain area most closely associated with the anxiolytic effects of benzodiazepines (Jiménez-Velázquez et al., 2010; Shibata et al., 1989; Thomas et al., 1985).

Some of the endogenous ligands for these "benzodiazepine" sites, termed *DBIs* for diazepam-binding inhibitors, have been identified (Barbaccia et al., 1988). Some of these may function to exert a natural anxiolytic action, whereas others have been shown to induce anxiety reactions (i.e., *anxiogenic* effects). Some drugs (such as Ro15–4513, beta-carbolines such as FG-7142 and beta-CCE) have been found to induce anxiogenic effects; because these drugs produce actions opposite of the benzodiazepines and their actions can be blocked with benzodiazepine antagonists (e.g., flumazenil), they have been termed *inverse agonists* (see Chapter 5). The action and thus the effects of benzodiazepines can be blocked completely with flumazenil (Romazicon). Flumazenil acts by competitively displacing benzodiazepines from their specific binding sites. In addition to its valuable use in locating and identifying specific benzodiazepine receptor sites, flumazenil has been used to rapidly reverse the effects of benzodiazepines used in surgical procedures, as an antidote in cases of benzodiazepine poisoning, and to reverse benzodiazepine comas (Hoffman & Warren, 1993).

The benzodiazepines are effective in reducing anxiety-related symptoms in approximately 70% to 80% of the persons with these symptoms. Their clinical efficacy must be evaluated against the fact that these symptoms vary considerably across time, and remission of symptoms with a placebo occurs in approximately 25% to 30% of patients. Perhaps for this reason, physicians who believe in the efficacy of these drugs seem to have greater success with their patients than do physicians who do not believe in their efficacy (Leavitt, 1982). The drug's effectiveness may also depend upon its effects on the patients' other defenses for combating anxiety or behaviors, which they typically find useful. For instance, a professional golfer who takes a benzodiazepine to deal with tournament anxiety may actually play worse, and subsequently feel worse, because the drug disrupts his or her motor abilities. Persons who are least likely to benefit from anxiolytic therapy are those with chronic dissatisfaction or insecurity, and those with character disorders, such as an antisocial personality. Such individuals are more likely to escalate their dosage, engage in impulsive overdosing, and succumb to physical dependence.

Many of the benzodiazepines are good anxiolytics because they are absorbed relatively slowly when given orally, with peak plasma levels occurring after several hours. This allows them to be taken only once or twice a day and induces a smooth, long-lasting effect. Diazepam is rapidly absorbed and reaches peak plasma levels in about an hour, which may account for its popularity both in clinical practice and on the streets. Most of the benzodiazepines are converted into active metabolites, which may partially account for the long duration of their action (Harvey, 1985). Their duration of action may be up to three or four times longer in premature neonates and the elderly than in young adults and children (Kerns, 1986).

As a family, benzodiazepines differ primarily in terms of their pharmacokinetic properties, which in turn are a factor in their therapeutic uses, as well as their liability for abuse and dependence. Basically, there are four categories: (1) ultrashort-acting; (2) short-acting; (3) intermediate-acting; and (4) long-acting (Charney et al., 2001). Ultrashort-acting benzodiazepines are typically used as preanesthetic and intraoperative medications and for treatment of *status epilepticus* (a constant or near-constant state of having seizures, most commonly associated with epilepsy, but also potentially induced by alcohol withdrawal). Short-acting benzodiazepines are commonly used for the treatment of insomnia and status epilepticus; these have a high abuse liability, and if used frequently and chronically, they could trigger severe withdrawal symptoms upon abrupt cessation of use. Intermediate-acting benzodiazepines are commonly used in treating anxiety-related symptoms and for alcohol detoxification; although less likely to be abused, they can trigger protracted withdrawal following chronic use. Long-acting benzodiazepines are used primarily for the treatment of seizure disorders and have limited abuse liability and withdrawal effects. However, the long-acting benzodiazepines can lead to drug accumulation and neuropsychological deficits during the day, for example, attention problems and drowsiness.

One benzodiazepine that has gained considerable notoriety for its uses is Rohypnol (flunitrazepam). Although not marketed in the United States, there has been an increase in the illicit use and abuse of this drug, which is used clinically primarily as a sleeping aid (Rickert et al., 1999). The fact that it is quite potent—5 to 10 times more potent than Valium—thus requiring very small amounts to be effective, coupled with its propensity to impair judgment and motor skills and to induce amnesia—particularly when combined with alcohol—has led to its use as a "date rape" drug. Several reports have appeared around the country in which women have awakened in unfamiliar surroundings with no clothes on or have been sexually assaulted after unknowingly (or knowingly) consuming Rohypnol. Its amnesia-inducing effects may prevent users from remembering how or why they took the drug or even having taken it, making investigation of sexually related offenses associated with its use very difficult. Because of its reputation for abuse, the Drug Enforcement Administration has classified flunitrazepam as a Schedule I drug—the first benzodiazepine to be so classified. Severe felony penalties have also been enacted for possession of Rohypnol and other similar drugs with the intent to commit a violent crime, including sexual assault.

As is the case with other drugs with sedative–hypnotic properties, tolerance develops to some of the pharmacological actions of benzodiazepines (File, 1985), and cross-tolerance may occur. However, the rate of tolerance may be slow (e.g., to the anxiolytic effects), fast (e.g., to sedative and anticonvulsant actions), or nonexistent (as in stimulant-type actions). The tolerance to benzodiazepines does not appear to be critically dependent upon altered metabolism or Pavlovian conditioning processes (Griffiths & Goudie, 1987). As discussed shortly, alterations in the GABA receptor complex may be responsible for some degree of tolerance.

As discussed earlier, there is a potential for abuse and development of dependence with chronic use of benzodiazepines, but not to the extent observed with barbiturates and related drugs, alcohol, or other typical drugs of abuse. In most cases of abuse, benzodiazepines are used in individuals with a pattern of multiple drug abuse, in which benzodiazepines are commonly combined with other drugs to intensify their effects (e.g., alcohol, opiates) or reduce their side-effects (e.g., cocaine; Charney et al., 2001). Their abuse liability can be lessened considerably by formulating them in extended-release preparations, which slow their absorption rate without reducing their overall anxiolytic efficacy (Mumford et al., 1995).

Following chronic usage of moderate dosages of benzodiazepines, abrupt discontinuation of use induces withdrawal symptoms consisting of anxiety and agitation (which could be confused with the symptoms for which the drugs were initially prescribed), increased sensitivity to light and sound, strange sensations, muscle cramps and twitches, sleep disturbance, and dizziness (Hobbs et al., 1996). Following high-dose usage, panic, depression, seizures, and delirium can develop. The severity of withdrawal is inversely related to the plasma half-life of the benzodiazepine (DeVane et al., 1991). However, because many benzodiazepines, and their active metabolites, accumulate and persist in the body for several days, withdrawal symptoms after chronic use may not appear for a week or so after abrupt discontinuation of these drugs, and the withdrawal symptoms are generally less intense than those occurring with other sedative–hypnotics. Furthermore, high doses must be given for a considerable length of time before marked withdrawal symptoms develop. Withdrawal following chronic benzodiazepine exposure can also be triggered by the administration of the benzodiazepine antagonist flumazenil. As might be expected, chronic exposure to benzodiazepines is associated with progressive development of GABA$_A$ receptor desensitization, which is concomitant with the development of tolerance as well as withdrawal symptoms upon discontinuation of these drugs (Lader, 1994).

The toxic reactions and side effects of benzodiazepines are similar to those of the barbiturates. In some cases, a paradoxical increase in hostility and irritability, and even anxiety, as well as vivid or disturbing dreams, may accompany benzodiazepine use (Hobbs et al., 1996). Confusional states in the elderly are commonly induced with these and other sedative compounds, and these states may be incorrectly attributed to senility. Other potential side effects of benzodiazepines include amnesia, hallucinations, skin rashes, nausea, headaches, vertigo, light-headedness, sexual impotence, lowered white cell counts, and menstrual irregularities.

Buspirone

For centuries, people have used alcohol and opium or its derivatives to reduce the consequences of stress and relieve the symptoms of anxiety. Then from the mid-1800s through the mid-1900s, thousands of barbiturates and similar drugs were synthesized and used for the same purposes. Then the benzodiazepines took over in the 1960s. All of these drugs had anxiolytic qualities, but they were accompanied by side effects of impaired motor coordination and disruptions in working memory and alertness, and had the potential for abuse and dependence. That all changed with the development of buspirone (BuSpar) in the early 1980s. After several decades and multiple variations on the basic benzodiazepine molecule (resulting in numerous patented drugs with the same properties), pharmacologists finally synthesized this novel anxiolytic agent, which was unrelated to the benzodiazepines and other sedative–hypnotics in structure and pharmacological profile. As is typical in this field, the drug was originally developed for something other than what it may actually be most useful for. Initially, it looked like it might have antipsychotic properties. However, extensive clinical studies have shown buspirone to be comparable to the benzodiazepines diazepam and clorazepate in the treatment of anxiety (Gorman, 2003). It is also effective in patients with mixed anxiety and depression (Gammans et al., 1992). However, buspirone may be more effective in reducing the emotional problems of anxiety (i.e., anger, hostility, worry, concentration difficulty) than the somatic symptoms (i.e., muscle tension, insomnia). This may account for its lack of efficacy in treating panic disorder (Sheehan et al., 1993)—a more physical/somatic manifestation of anxiety—although it may enhance the effects of cognitive behavior therapy in the treatment of patients with panic disorder with agoraphobia (Cottraux et al., 1995).

For several reasons, buspirone is often referred to as an "atypical" anxiolytic. Unlike the benzodiazepines, buspirone (1) lacks hypnotic, anticonvulsant, and muscle-relaxant properties; (2) takes 1 or 2 weeks of daily treatment before the onset of its anxiolytic effects is noted; (3) is much less likely to induce drowsiness and fatigue; (4) does not impair psychomotor or cognitive function; (5) has no potential for abuse and dependence (in fact, it may have dysphoric properties in moderate doses); (6) has no synergistic effect with alcohol; and (7) is not cross-tolerant with benzodiazepines and does not help reduce benzodiazepine withdrawal (Lader & Olajide, 1987). Pharmacokinetic interactions of buspirone with other coadministered drugs seem to be minimal

(Chouinard et al., 1999). The most frequently reported adverse effects with buspirone treatment are dizziness, headache, and nausea, although adverse effects are typically mild and do not generally lead to treatment discontinuation (Sramek et al., 1999).

Buspirone lacks affinity for the benzodiazepine binding site and does not act via GABA mechanisms. The mechanism of action of the drug is thought to be due to its ability to act as a 5-HT$_{1A}$ partial agonist (Davidson, 2009; Leslie, 2001). Because 5-HT$_{1A}$ receptors serve as both postsynaptic receptors and somatodendritic 5-HT autoreceptors, buspirone can have multiple effects on serotonergic activity with acute exposure, and it is not clear which action is responsible for the therapeutic action of the drug (Leslie, 2001). A proposed mechanism of action regarding its anxiolytic properties is one of down-regulating 5-HT$_{1A}$ and 5-HT$_2$ receptors, which may explain why chronic exposure is needed before its benefits are evidenced (Charney et al., 1990). Buspirone's unique properties have led to its being labeled as "anxioselective." Buspirone belongs to a class of compounds known as *azapirones* (including gepirone [Ariza, Variza]), several of which have been shown to be effective for the treatment of GAD compared to placebo (Chessick et al., 2006). It appears that buspirone will be most useful in anxious patients, for whom daytime alertness is particularly important, and in the elderly, in whom the benzodiazepines may exacerbate cognitive impairment and cause adverse psychomotor effects (Steinberg, 1994). However, for patients who would benefit from a fast onset of action, or sedative and muscle-relaxant effects, the benzodiazepines would be preferred. Also, because there is no cross-tolerance with benzodiazepines, patients who are switched immediately from a benzodiazepine to buspirone may perceive the drug as ineffective. In fact, in patients who have been on a benzodiazepine for a long time and are then switched to buspirone, withdrawal symptoms may occur. These may be misinterpreted by the patients as an indication of the drug's ineffectiveness or as side effects. For patients with GAD, the more recent their prior exposure to benzodiazepines, the less effective buspirone appears to be (DeMartinis et al., 2000). However, if anxious patients are first stabilized on benzodiazepines and then shifted to buspirone while the benzodiazepine is gradually tapered off, the anxiolytic efficacy can be retained without the patient experiencing rebound anxiety or benzodiazepine withdrawal (Delle Chiaie et al., 1995).

Since its approval for use for GAD by the FDA in 1986, numerous studies have examined the efficacy and safety of buspirone for patients with other symptoms and disorders. Although relatively few placebo-controlled trials have been conducted on patients with problems other than GAD, an ever-growing body of research suggests that buspirone may be beneficial in the treatment of a variety of disorders. These include panic disorder, major depressive disorder, obsessive–compulsive disorder, body dysmorphic disorder, social phobia, PTSD, dementia, behavioral disturbances, ADHD, and tobacco dependency (Apter & Allen, 1999). Research also indicates that buspirone can be effective in attenuating the objective and subjective withdrawal symptoms that follow opiate use cessation (Rose et al., 2003).

Additional Treatments for Anxiety

Anxiety disorders share a common affective state characterized by high psychological arousal, ranging from excessive worry to anxiety to extreme fear. Thus, it would seem that these disorders would be most amenable to treatment with the types of drugs described in this chapter up to this point. Curiously, however, other drugs not commonly viewed as anxiolytics have been shown to be equally or more effective in the treatment of these disorders (Gorman, 2003). In clinical settings, anxiety and depression symptoms frequently coexist. Thus, a variety of antidepressants have been used in the treatment of patients with anxiety with some degree of success. Several of the long-acknowledged antidepressant drugs described in Chapter 9, for example, tricyclics, have been shown to be effective treatments for panic and phobic disorders, with an efficacy rate comparable to benzodiazepines such as alprazolam (Xanax; Mattick et al., 1990). The monoamine oxidase inhibitors (MAOIs) have also been recommended for treatment of these disorders (Den Boer et al., 1995). Curiously, the efficacy of these antidepressants in the treatment of anxiety-related symptoms did not appear to be related to whether or not the patient was depressed.

Since 1987 another class of antidepressants, collectively called "selective serotonin reuptake inhibitors," or SSRIs, have come into clinical use. Their clinical use has broadened dramatically, and they are being used in the treatment of a wide variety of disorders, including several in the anxiety category. The first of these was OCD, for which it was found that a variety of SSRIs were superior to placebo (Greist et al., 1995; Piccinelli et al., 1995), with approximately 60% to 70% of patients exhibiting at least moderate relief from their OCD symptoms. The SSRIs were shown to be more effective in the treatment of OCD than antidepressant drugs that did not have selective serotonergic properties. In good responders, maintenance therapy with SSRIs for up to 2.5 years has been shown to provide substantial protection against OCD symptom worsening, compared to patients not receiving active medication, even when the maintenance SSRI dose is half that of the acute treatment dose (Ravizza et al., 1996). These findings eventually led to several pharmaceutical companies applying for, and being granted, FDA approval for their SSRI drugs (e.g., Prozac, Paxil, Zoloft) for the treatment of OCD.

The SSRIs also have demonstrated clinical efficacy in the treatment of panic disorder (with or without agoraphobia; Bakish et al., 1996), GAD and social phobia (Jefferson, 1995; Roy-Byrne et al., 1993), and PTSD (van der Kolk et al., 1994). In most of these disorders, the efficacy of SSRIs is comparable to, or in some cases better than, the efficacy of more established anxiolytics. For example, a meta-analysis revealed that the SSRIs are superior to imipramine and alprazolam in alleviating panic attacks (Boyer, 1995). Furthermore, the SSRIs are effective even in patients without symptoms of depression. Compared to tricyclics and MAOIs, the SSRIs exhibit a better side-effect profile and possess greater safety in overdose. In addition, SSRIs do not pose the risk of addiction and withdrawal that may occur with the benzodiazepines. Thus, it is not surprising that this class of drugs is more popular in the treatment of a variety of anxiety-related disorders.

The use of herbal preparations as alternative medical treatments has increased dramatically over the past several years in the United States and other parts of the world. Kava, a beverage prepared from the oceanic kava plant (*Piper methysticum*) and used extensively throughout the South Pacific for recreational and medicinal purposes, is one plant-based therapeutic option for treating anxiety. In 1998 it was among the top-selling herbs in the United States (Brevoort, 1998). Based on anecdotal reports of its calming influence, several double-blind, randomized, placebo-controlled trials of its efficacy have been conducted. Virtually all of these trials suggested that, relative to placebo, kava extract can significantly reduce anxiety (Pittler & Ernst, 2000). Based on in vitro studies of kavapyrones, the pharmacologically active components of kava extracts, the effects are probably due to actions in the CNS, with the possibility of actions mediated through $GABA_A$ receptors (Davies et al., 1992; Jussofie et al., 1994). CNS effects of kava derivative have also been demonstrated by using EEG measurements in humans (Saletu et al., 1989).

Unfortunately, since 1999, health-care professionals in a number of countries have reported the occurrence of severe hepatic toxicity possibly associated with the consumption of products containing kava, with some individuals who used kava products experiencing liver failure and requiring subsequent liver transplantation (Russmann et al., 2001). Although liver damage appears to be rare, in response to five such case reports, in 2002 the FDA issued a consumer advisory that advised consumers and health-care providers about the potential risk for hepatic toxicity associated with the use of kava-containing products. Several countries have also restricted the sale of kava-containing products based on the occurrence of hepatic adverse effects associated with kava-containing products.

Because many of the anxiety disorders present very specific behavioral symptoms, behavior therapy techniques such as biofeedback, systematic desensitization, and progressive relaxation may be useful in their treatment. Considerable research suggests this to be the case. Therefore, behavior therapy programs should definitely be involved in the treatment of these disorders, either in lieu of or in conjunction with drug therapy (Davis & Gelder, 1991). It is difficult to compare efficacy rates between pharmacotherapy and psychotherapy, because there are so many factors determining the efficacy of drugs by themselves and so many different types of psychotherapy. Both seem to be in the same efficacy range in comparison to a placebo; that is, the average treated person is better off than 75% of placebo-treated patients (Smith & Glass, 1977). There is no consensus about combining anxiolytics with psychotherapy. Many clinicians feel that it is impossible to do successful psychotherapy (i.e., behavioral, cognitive, or interpersonal therapy) in the presence of drug therapy. They believe the presence of discomfort is a motivating force for psychotherapy and that if the drug lessens the discomfort, patients will avoid dealing with the forces that are making them uncomfortable in the first place. Other clinicians feel that anxiolytics may be useful adjuncts to psychotherapy—if for no other reason than that if one treatment does not work, the other might.

SEDATIVE–HYPNOTICS AND INSOMNIA

Insomnia is a sleep disorder that involves (1) the real or perceived inability to get to sleep or to stay asleep at night, resulting in subjective feelings of fatigue; (2) the chronic inability to maintain the amount and quality of sleep necessary for efficient daytime functioning; and (3) complaints of poor sleep, unrefreshing sleep, and sleep punctuated by abnormal restlessness. Chronic insomniacs not only report higher rates of difficulty with concentration, memory, and ability to cope with minor irritations, but also have two-and-a-half times more fatigue-related automobile accidents than do good sleepers (Mendelson & Jain, 1995).

In doses somewhat higher than those needed to sedate, the sedative–hypnotics induce sleep, and for many years barbiturates were the most common treatment for insomnia. However, the use of barbiturates for this purpose has virtually ceased, primarily because they have been supplanted by somewhat safer drugs. It has long been recognized that the barbiturate sedative–hypnotics have numerous liabilities. Among these are their relatively low therapeutic index, their strong tendency to suppress REM sleep, their high psychological dependence potential, and their potentially lethal withdrawal effects when physical dependence develops. Furthermore, there is a relatively fast tolerance development to their sleep-inducing effects. Although the functions of REM sleep and the consequences of suppressing it are still being debated, it is clear that, once the suppressing factors have been removed, REM activity increases dramatically for a few days and the dream content tends to be very bizarre and emotionally upsetting.

Because of these properties, drugs in the benzodiazepine class, such as flurazepam (Dalmane), became a popular treatment for insomnia. These drugs have considerably higher therapeutic indexes, have minimal effects on REM sleep, have less psychological dependence potential, and are less likely to induce severe physical dependence and withdrawal effects. However, benzodiazepines do have characteristics that make them less than ideal treatments for insomnia. They can raise the arousal threshold to such an extent that outside noises that should awaken the person, such as a smoke alarm, do not do so (Johnson et al., 1987). Also, there is evidence that benzodiazepines disrupt the deeper stages of sleep (stages 3 and 4; Harvey, 1985), an effect that may prove to be just as significant as REM inhibition. On the other hand, this may be a factor in the efficacy of benzodiazepines in the treatment of sleepwalking and night terrors (the latter involving a sudden and intense arousal from slow-wave, deep sleep, accompanied by sharp body movements, a rise in heart rate and respiration, mental confusion, and extreme fright), which are most commonly observed to occur during the deeper stages of sleep (Rall, 1990).

Flurazepam and its several active metabolites tend to accumulate in the body over several days of use. This accumulation can produce daytime aftereffects such as lethargy and decreased coordination (also possible with the sedative–hypnotics). Another benzodiazepine, temazepam (Restoril), does not appear to have detrimental effects on next-day performance in psychomotor activities. This advantage is primarily due to its having no active metabolites. On the other hand, shorter-acting drugs, like temazepam and triazolam (Halcion), are more likely to induce early-morning insomnia (an increase in wakefulness during the final hours of drug nights), similar to rebound insomnia that occurs after withdrawal from the drug (Kales et al., 1983).

All of the benzodiazepines used in the treatment of insomnia have a number of problems in common. They are all synergistic with alcohol and other CNS depressants; their combination with alcohol or other CNS depressants is one of the major causes of "overdose" deaths. In the elderly, who traditionally complain and suffer from insomnia, the diminished alertness that can come about with the use of these drugs can be confused with senility or dementia. The fact that these drugs do effectively induce sleep may prevent a patient from dealing with the problems causing insomnia.

Zolpidem (Ambien) is a nonbenzodiazepine that was approved for treatment of insomnia in the United States in 1992 and is now the most commonly prescribed hypnotic (Rush, 1998). It has demonstrated efficacy equal to that of benzodiazepines, in terms of shortening sleep latency and prolonging total sleep time in insomniacs, and has actions resembling the latter class of drugs, but its advantages are that it appears to have low potential for inducing rebound insomnia or tolerance and withdrawal effects with chronic use (Hoehns & Perry, 1993). Furthermore, unlike the benzodiazepines, zolpidem has little effect on the stages of sleep in normal human subjects. At therapeutic doses, zolpidem infrequently produces residual daytime sedation or amnesia, and the incidence of other adverse effects (such as gastrointestinal complaints, dizziness) is also low. As is the case with benzodiazepines, zolpidem does not produce severe respiratory depression with large doses, unless other sedative–hypnotic type agents are also ingested. Although the available data indicate that under most of these circumstances the risk of abuse or dependence with zolpidem is minimal, there are several case reports of zolpidem abuse and dependence (Courtet et al., 1999). Furthermore, studies conducted with humans suggest that, on the basis of its reinforcing and pharmacokinetic properties, zolpidem's abuse potential is comparable to that of the hypnotic benzodiazepines (e.g., triazolam; Rush, 1998).

Zolpidem's mechanism of action is essentially the same as that of the benzodiazepines; that is, it binds to a site on the $GABA_A$ class of receptor that enhances the action of GABA, which prolongs Cl^- flow into postsynaptic neurons and increases neuronal inhibition. However, the $GABA_A$ receptor is a very heterogenous type of receptor made up of five subunits that can combine in a wide variety of configurations. The affinity for zolpidem at approximately 35% of the $GABA_A$ receptor subtypes in the CNS is lower than that of benzodiazepines; thus it exerts somewhat more selective actions than benzodiazepines (Möhler et al., 2002). It has been suggested that the $GABA_A$ receptor subtype for which zolpidem has the highest affinity is associated with sleep-inducing activity but not motor incoordination, and agonists at these receptors appear to produce little or no tolerance and dependence (Sanger et al., 1994).

Although this nonbenzodiazepine hypnotic seems to be equally efficacious as the short-acting benzodiazepines in the treatment of insomnia and has a better adverse-effect profile, neither it nor any other drug treatment for insomnia should be used as the sole treatment, but should be used in conjunction with nonpharmacological techniques, such as adherence to good sleep hygiene, sleep restriction, stimulus control, and biofeedback (Mendelson & Jain, 1995).

DRUG TREATMENT OF EPILEPSY: ANTICONVULSANT DRUGS

Epilepsy is a term used to categorize a number of diverse chronic disorders characterized by sudden attacks of brain dysfunction (seizures) that are usually associated with some alteration of consciousness. The seizures are almost always correlated with abnormal and excessive discharges in the EEG and are often accompanied by violent muscle spasms (convulsions). (By now you are probably aware that essentially the same symptoms may accompany withdrawal from sedative–hypnotics after chronic exposure.) In the past, people with epilepsy were considered demonically possessed, keepers of mystical powers, or mentally ill. We now know the symptoms of epilepsy are the result of a sudden change in behavior and mental activity caused by abnormal neuronal discharge in the brain. The epilepsies—there are over 40 distinct forms—are common and frequently devastating disorders, affecting approximately 2.5 million people in the United States alone (McNamara, 2001).

Several lines of evidence suggest that in most of these disorders the seizure begins with and is sustained by the synchronous firing at high frequency of a relatively localized group of neurons, which then spreads to adjacent neurons. A reduction in inhibitory components of neuronal circuits (such as GABA activity) is a likely mechanism for this action (Dichter & Ayala, 1987). For example, a reduction in GABA levels because of a diet deficient in pyridoxine (vitamin B6), which is required for GABA synthesis, can result in seizures; the problem can be successfully reversed by adding pyridoxine to the diet (Iversen et al., 2009). Modulatory substances such as NE and opioid peptides may also play a role.

Because there are a variety of disorders involved, the etiology varies considerably, with suspected causes ranging from hereditary factors to head injuries, infectious diseases, allergies, and nutritional abnormalities, among others. As is the case with numerous brain disorders, neurotoxicity resulting from overactivity of the excitatory amino acid neurotransmitters at NMDA receptors has been proposed as a mechanism for promoting seizure activity (Olney, 1990). However, in many cases, no cause for the seizures can be identified (idiopathic epilepsy). In approximately three-fourths of the cases, the symptoms are evidenced prior to adulthood.

Because seizures appear to involve a hyperexcitability of neuronal tissue, it is not surprising that most sedative–hypnotic drugs are anticonvulsants and that most anticonvulsants have sedative–hypnotic properties. However, because the sedative–hypnotic properties are not necessary for antiseizure efficacy and are viewed as undesirable, drugs that are most effective in the treatment of epilepsy are those that can reduce or eliminate seizure activity without inducing sedation or sleep (McNamara, 2001).

For most of the 20th century, the primary drugs available for treating seizure disorders consisted of the barbiturate phenobarbital, phenytoin (or diphenylhydantoin [Dilantin]) and primidone (Mysoline), which are structurally related to the barbiturates, carbamazepine (Tegretol), related chemically to the tricyclic antidepressants, valproic acid (Depakene) and ethosuximide (Zarontin). However, beginning in the 1990s, a number of antiepileptic medications have been approved that may be useful as monotherapy or add-on treatments to the established drugs. The newer drugs may be better tolerated, have fewer interactions with other drugs, and may be less disruptive to cognitive functions than the older medications (Beghi, 2004). These drugs include felbamate (Felbatol), gabapentin (Neurontin), topiramate (Topamax), oxcarbazepine (Trileptal), zonisamide (Zonegran), tiagabine (Gabitril), levetiracetam (Keppra), and lamotrigine (Lamictal). Although studies indicate that most of these drugs may be effective in a wide range of seizure disorders and may be used in monotherapy for patients who don't respond adequately to older anticonvulsant drugs, it is likely that most of these drugs will be used initially as add-ons to conventional drugs in a polydrug regimen (Beghi, 2004; Gatti et al., 2000). Because these drugs can interact with established antiepileptic drugs, they may need more frequent monitoring during polydrug therapy.

Several mechanisms have been suggested that contribute to the ability of anticonvulsants to either enhance inhibitory or reduce excitatory control over neuronal firing, which is believed to be responsible for seizure activity. Drugs effective against the most common forms of seizures, partial and secondarily generalized tonic–clonic seizures, appear to work by way of a number of mechanisms that limit the sustained repetitive firing of a neuron (McNamara, 2001). Following depolarization-triggered opening of sodium ion (Na^+) channels during the action potential, the Na^+ channels spontaneously close; this process is termed *inactivation*. Drugs that reduce the recovery rate of Na^+ channels from inactivation would limit the ability of a neuron to fire at high frequencies. Another mechanism would be to reduce neuronal excitability by enhancing GABA-mediated inhibition either postsynaptically at $GABA_A$ receptors (e.g., with benzodiazepines or barbiturates) or presynaptically by reducing the metabolism of GABA (e.g., valproate, vigabatrin), enhancing the amount of GABA released (e.g., gabapentin), or inhibiting its reuptake (e.g., tiagabine). Reducing the excitability of neurons by inhibiting the excitatory actions of GLU at some of its receptors (e.g., α-amino-3-hydroxy-5-methyl-4-isoxazolepropionic acid and kainate receptors) may also be involved in the actions of some antiepileptic drugs (e.g., topiramate; Skradski & White, 2000). Felbamate exhibits dual actions of both inhibiting NMDA-evoked (excitatory) responses and potentiating GABA-evoked (inhibitory) responses (McNamara, 2001). Levetiracetam, which has been shown to be highly effective as an add-on treatment in refractory partial-onset and generalized epilepsies and may be used as monotherapy (Kumar & Smith, 2004), appears to possess a mechanism of action distinct from that of other antiseizure medications. It acts by binding to and modulating the function of a synaptic vesicle protein that is involved in vesicle exocytosis (Lynch et al., 2004).

Overall, the drugs we have discussed abolish seizure activity in approximately half of the cases, and significantly reduce seizure frequency in another quarter of patients. It is important to realize that seizure disorders are due to a variety of mechanisms and thus are effectively treated by different groups of anticonvulsant drugs (McNamara, 2001). For example, most drugs that are effective in the treatment of partial seizure disorders and tonic–clonic seizures are not effective in absence seizures. Conversely, most drugs effective in reducing absence seizures are not effective in the treatment of partial and tonic–clonic seizures. However, valproate appears to be effective in virtually all types of epilepsy. Although there is no clear difference among drugs within a group in terms of overall efficacy, some patients refractory to one compound within a group may respond to another in that group. Each anticonvulsant has its own spectrum of side effects—which range from minimal CNS disturbances to death from aplastic anemia (blood cell suppression) or liver failure—and these must be considered in selecting an appropriate drug or a combination of drugs. Lower-than-effective dosages of drugs within a group may be combined to decrease the relative incidence or degree of side effects induced by larger doses of the individual drugs. Multiple drug therapy may also be required in cases in which more than one type of seizure activity occurs in the same patient.

Although epilepsy is viewed as a chronic disorder requiring continuous drug treatment, it may be desirable at some point to withdraw medication (very gradually over a period of months, because the risk of status epilepticus is great with abrupt cessation). Medication may be withdrawn because of evidence of unacceptable side effects or to prevent potential side effects from occurring or if the patient has been seizure-free for a considerable length of time. Studies have indicated that the majority of patients who have been free of seizures for several years with medication will not show a recurrence of symptoms when the medications are gradually withdrawn over a period of months (McNamara, 2001). However, because a history of a single recent seizure may be detrimental to one's employment or access to a driver's license, the decision to withdraw medication must be made with some deliberation.

Websites for Further Information

World Health Organization:

> http://www.who.int/topics/
> alcohol_drinking/en/

For information on the National Survey on Drug Use and Health:

> http://oas.samhsa.gov/nsduh/2k9nsduh/
> 2k9resultsp.pdf

The National Institute on Alcohol Abuse and Alcoholism home page:

> http://www.niaaa.nih.gov

Facts on alcohol from Rutgers University's Center of Alcohol Studies:

> http://www.rci.rutgers.edu/~cas2/
> online.shtml

Sites related to Fetal Alcohol Syndrome (FAS):

> http://www.nofas.org (home page for the National Organization on Fetal Alcohol Syndrome)
> http://w3.ouhsc.edu/fas (information on FAS and photographs of common FAS facial abnormalities)

Home pages for several alcoholism-related support groups:

> http://www.alcoholics-anonymous.org (Alcoholics Anonymous)
> http://www.adultchildren.org (Adult Children of Alcoholics)
> http://www.nacoa.org (National Association for Children of Alcoholics)
> http://www.al-anon-alateen.org (Al-Anon and Alateen)

Sites related to the temperance movement and prohibition:

> http://www.prohibition.osu.edu
> http://www.druglibrary.org/schaffer/
> alcohol/alcohol.htm

Information on barbiturates and benzodiazepines:

> http://faculty.washington.edu/chudler/
> sleep.html
> http://www.benzodiazepines.net
> http://www.benzodiazepine.org

Drug Treatment of Cognitive Dysfunction

It is becoming increasingly common to use drugs to treat various types of cognitive dysfunction (Floresco and Jentsch, 2011). Several conditions that are generally classed as movement disorders or psychoses also can have cognitive manifestations. For example, the cognitive symptoms of Parkinson's disease and schizophrenia are receiving increasing attention in the literature (see Chapters 7 and 8). In this chapter, the focus will be upon drug treatments for attention deficit hyperactivity disorder, as well as Alzheimer's disease and related dementias. In addition, the effects of stimulants on learning and memory processes will be reviewed.

ATTENTION DEFICIT HYPERACTIVITY DISORDER

The most common childhood disorder for which medication is most likely to be used is called *attention deficit hyperactivity disorder (ADHD)* because excessive motor activity is one of the more common characteristics of children with the disorder. Over the years it has been known as *hyperactivity,* the *hyperkinetic syndrome,* and *minimal brain dysfunction,* among other terms. ADHD may be evidenced in 1.7% to 17.8% of the school-age population (the wide range is indicative of the difficulties in diagnosis and the differences in criteria used in diagnosis of the disorder), with boy-to-girl estimates ranging from 2:1 in community surveys of school-age children to 3:1 to 9:1 in children referred to child psychiatrists or psychologists (Elia et al., 1999). In addition, it is becoming more common to consider ADHD as a disorder that carries on into adulthood as well (Barkley & Fisher, 2011).

The primary symptoms are lack of investment, organization, and maintenance of attention and effort in completing tasks, working memory, and executive planning; inability to delay gratification; and disinhibited or impulsive responding without attention to relevant stimuli in the environment (Chamberlain et al., 2010). Excessive levels of motor activity and fidgetiness are common but not always present in ADHD. Neurological signs are sometimes evidenced along with these behavioral symptoms. These may include abnormal EEG patterns; mild visual or auditory impairments; crossed eyes; fine, jerky, lateral eye movements; poor visuomotor coordination; or handedness confusion (Dulcan, 1986).

Because ADHD symptoms present a number of difficulties in learning situations, the disorder is of considerable concern in classroom settings. Other characteristics that may be evidenced are extreme aggressiveness and rapid mood swings. These are most often seen in times of stress or in groups, but they may be absent in some calm situations. The children generally show little evidence of fear, and their behavior is refractory to punishment involving aversive stimulation (i.e., pain). Many symptoms of ADHD tend to induce dominating and negative controlling responses on the part of teachers, parents, and peers (i.e., they yell and scold a lot). These in turn may compound the ADHD child's difficulties (Cunningham et al., 1985).

The etiology of the disorder (if indeed it is one disorder) is unclear, although there is sometimes evidence of notable birth trauma or abnormalities during pregnancy. Research utilizing magnetic resonance imaging techniques has indicated that children and adolescents diagnosed with ADHD have somewhat smaller cerebral and cerebellar volumes (around 3%–4%) compared with sex- and age-matched controls, and the results were comparable for male and female patients (Castellanos et al., 2002). The brain volumes in previously unmedicated children with ADHD were slightly smaller than those in medicated ADHD children (although not significantly so), which indicates that the smaller brain volumes were not attributable to medication. Genetic factors have been implicated in ADHD, and there is often a family history of the disorder (Biederman et al., 1995). One study indicated that the concordance rate for ADHD in identical twin pairs was 60% (Sharp et al., 2003). Longtime speculations that there is insufficient catecholamine activity in the brains of individuals with ADHD have been supported with the observation that adults diagnosed with ADHD have a higher density of dopamine (DA) transporters (the proteins responsible for DA reuptake; Dougherty et al., 1999; Krause et al., 2000). Theoretically, higher DA transporter availability would result in insufficient levels of DA to act on receptors. Not surprisingly, DA release through reverse transport and reuptake inhibition is a prominent pharmacodynamic property of the medications shown to have the highest efficacy in the treatment of ADHD, and treatment with one of these drugs (methylphenidate) was shown to decrease DA transporter availability in adults diagnosed with ADHD (Krause et al., 2000). Associations of both the DA D4 receptor gene and the DA transporter gene with ADHD have also been reported (Cook et al., 1995; Faraone et al., 1999).

Before drug intervention is resorted to, a complete physical and neurological examination of the child should be conducted to establish that he or she is not suffering from hypoxia (insufficient blood supply to the brain), low calcium levels, low blood sugar levels, or hyperthyroidism, all of which can result in hyperactive symptoms. It is also important to determine whether or not the child is actually hyperactive. Surprisingly, this is not always easy because the term *hyperactivity* is broadly defined, and no norms for child activity levels exist. For example, in a 1958 report based on questionnaires submitted to parents, approximately half of the children were noted to be overactive. A similar rate of distractibility and hyperactive symptoms in children was noted in a 1971 report based on questionnaires submitted to teachers. These reports suggest that parents and teachers may have unrealistic views as to what normal behavior in children is (Weiss & Hechtman, 1979).

The most common drugs used in the treatment of ADHD are the psychostimulants methylphenidate (e.g., Ritalin [a mixture of *d*- and *l*-enantiomers] and Focalin [the *d*-isomer]), amphetamine (Adderall), dextroamphetamine (Dexedrine), and pemoline (Cylert); as discussed later, several of these are available in extended release form. Of these, methylphenidate is by far the most often prescribed. As discussed in Chapter 7, methylphenidate and dextroamphetamine have similar pharmacodynamic properties—that is, both act by enhancing the release of norepinephrine (NE) and DA and inhibiting their reuptake. Although there hasn't been much research on the pharmacodynamic properties of pemoline, there is some evidence that it acts primarily by enhancing DA release and inhibiting its reuptake (Sallee et al., 1992). Atomoxetine (Strattera), a nonstimulant that selectively inhibits NE reuptake, has been approved by the Food and Drug Administration (FDA) for the treatment of ADHD in children, adolescents, and adults. As discussed shortly, it differs from the psychostimulants in several potentially important areas. Interestingly, caffeine, which has minor psychostimulant qualities and is sometimes preferred by laypersons who do not believe in giving a "drug" to children, has virtually no efficacy in reducing ADHD symptoms but does have side effects. Sedative–hypnotics such as barbiturates also induce no beneficial effects with respect to any of the target symptoms of ADHD and oftentimes prove to be worse than placebo.

Methylphenidate, amphetamine, and pemoline are virtually indistinguishable from each other in terms of efficacy in reducing ADHD symptoms and side-effect profile (Elia et al., 1999). However, because pemoline is more slowly absorbed and exerts effects a few hours longer, it has the least abuse liability (it is a Schedule IV controlled substance as opposed to the Schedule II designation for the other two drugs). This decreases the likelihood of its being diverted to illicit use, as is sometimes the case with the other two drugs. Unfortunately, pemoline has been linked to increased risk of liver toxicity, which is usually mild and reversible, and acute liver failure, which, although extremely rare, can be lethal (Shevell & Schreiber, 1997). Thus, pemoline is likely to be considered an alternative treatment for ADHD only if other drugs fail to produce satisfactory results, and its use would require vigilant monitoring of liver function.

A number of extended release preparations of amphetamine and methylphenidate have been developed that only require once-daily dosing (e.g., Adderall XR, Concerta, Metadate CD, Ritalin LA, Ritalin SR). These vary somewhat in their pharmacokinetic profiles, which could be important in terms of efficacy (Markowitz et al., 2003). For example, Metadate CD allows for an initial rapid increase in methylphenidate plasma concentrations, which are maintained for several hours before concentrations gradually decrease. Concerta allows for rapid increases in plasma concentrations that are maintained at a lower plateau for 3–4 hours, which is followed by another rapid increase in plasma concentration before concentrations gradually decrease. Ritalin LA allows for rapid initial increase in plasma concentrations that then decrease over the next 3–4 hours, which is followed by another rapid increase in plasma concentrations to even greater levels before concentrations gradually decrease again. There are few head-to-head comparisons among these formulations that allow one to make general conclusions regarding their relative efficacy. However, because there is little evidence of chronic tolerance to methylphenidate and virtually all of the drug is eliminated from the body prior to the next day's dose, every morning represents an opportunity for the evaluation of a different formulation that can be ideally tailored to the patient's specific needs (Markowitz et al., 2003).

Although there is no compelling empirical evidence to support the wide disparity in the use of methylphenidate and amphetamine in the treatment of ADHD, some studies have indicated that perhaps as many as 20% of ADHD children who do not respond to one type of psychostimulant may respond to another (Dulcan, 1986). This may be due to their differences in their pharmacodynamic properties. Amphetamine primarily promotes the release of DA from neurons, whereas methylphenidate primarily inhibits the reuptake of DA. Thus the degree to which they increase extracellular levels of DA may depend upon differences among individuals with respect to DA neuron activity (Volkow et al., 2002). In individuals with low DA neuron activity, that is, the rate of DA release, the blockade of DA reuptake by methylphenidate may induce minimal accumulations of extracellular DA. In these individuals, amphetamine, which directly promotes the release of DA, may be beneficial. These drugs also differ somewhat with respect to their actions on other monoamines, for example, NE, which may also be involved in reducing the symptoms of ADHD.

For nonresponders to psychostimulants, a number of alternative drugs are sometimes beneficial in the treatment of ADHD. A number of the older antidepressants, for example, tricyclics and monoamine oxidase (MAO) inhibitors, have been shown to possess efficacy comparable to methylphenidate and amphetamine. However, because of their potential toxicity and their spectrum of undesirable side effects, described in Chapter 9, these are likely to be used as last resorts when other drugs are ineffective.

Atomoxetine (Strattera), which is presently considered an appropriate second-line therapy for patients who fail to respond to stimulant therapy or who desire an alternative to stimulants, may soon gain credibility as a first-line treatment for ADHD. Unlike psychostimulants, which appear to work primarily by enhancing dopaminergic and noradrenergic activity, atomoxetine's primary pharmacodynamic property is to selectively inhibit the reuptake of NE. Several double-blind, placebo trials have shown atomoxetine to be significantly more effective than placebo in reducing the symptoms of this disorder in children and adults, and it has been shown to be comparable to methylphenidate in efficacy (Caballero & Nahata, 2003; Eiland & Guest, 2004). However, the onset of the benefit with atomoxetine may not be as immediately evident or as pronounced as it is with methylphenidate. Common adverse effects of atomoxetine include headache, decreased appetite, vomiting, somnolence, and dizziness. Adults may experience decreased libido and other sexual disturbances. As is the case with psychostimulants, atomoxetine may induce slight transient weight losses; thus growth should be monitored in children taking atomoxetine. However, the adverse effects and discontinuation rates observed with atomoxetine and methylphenidate appear to be comparable.

One concern over atomoxetine is due to the fact that it is metabolized primarily by a cytochrome P450 enzyme (CYP2D6) that varies considerably among individuals. A small percentage of individuals, primarily Whites, have a deficiency of this enzyme; thus they metabolize atomoxetine very slowly, which may result in substantially higher plasma concentrations of atomoxetine and slower elimination than individuals who have normal CYP2D6 activity. Thus dosage adjustments may be required for poor metabolizers who may be at an increased risk of adverse events. Similar dosage adjustments may be required with individuals with normal CYP2D6 activity, who concomitantly take other drugs that are strong CYP2D6 inhibitors, for example, the selective serotonin reuptake inhibitors, paroxetine and fluoxetine.

Unlike psychostimulants, atomoxetine is not a controlled substance as it has none of the euphoric properties associated with the former drugs and has no abuse potential—most likely due to the fact that it does not elevate extracellular DA levels in the nucleus accumbens. Thus atomoxetine is an alternative for parents seeking nonstimulants for their children with ADHD and for patients who are unable to tolerate psychostimulants or whose previous treatment with these drugs has failed. Of course as a proprietary drug, its prescription costs are considerably higher than that of the nonproprietary psychostimulants.

Clonidine (Catapres), an α-2-adrenergic receptor agonist, has been shown in several studies to be effective in reducing the symptoms of ADHD, particularly in children with comorbid tic disorders such as Tourette's syndrome (Hunt et al., 1986; Steingard et al., 1993). Similar improvements have been found with guanfacine (Tenex), also an α-2-adrenergic receptor agonist, but without clonidine's sedative effects (Chappell et al., 1995; Hunt et al., 1995). (Both Catapres and Tenex are FDA approved for treatment of hypertension.) Clonidine has also been shown to induce clinical improvement in children with comorbid ADHD and conduct disorder who failed trials of conventional psychostimulant drug therapy (Schvehla et al., 1994). These findings add considerable confusion to the pursuit of understanding the pathophysiology of ADHD. Whereas psychostimulants predominantly amplify noradrenergic activity (by enhancing NE release and blocking its reuptake), α-2-adrenergic receptor agonists (which supposedly activate noradrenergic autoreceptors) reduce the release of NE. Thus, we have a most curious paradox: Drugs that amplify and drugs that reduce noradrenergic functioning have both been shown to be beneficial in reducing ADHD symptoms.

Approximately 60% to 80% of the children diagnosed with ADHD respond favorably to psychostimulants—in some cases dramatically—with significant increases in attention span and significant decreases in motor activity and restlessness. However, if one tries both methylphenidate and dextroamphetamine and uses a wide range of doses, some degree of behavioral improvement almost always occurs in ADHD children (Elia et al., 1999; Rapport et al., 1994). This is reflected in better learning of rote material and improved performance of fine motor tasks like handwriting. Also, aggression and impulsivity are decreased. The amount and quality of the child's interpersonal relationships with both peers and teachers are generally improved, thus increasing the child's self-esteem and normalizing student–teacher interactions (Cunningham et al., 1985).

It should be pointed out that few children with ADHD respond favorably to psychostimulants across all behavioral dimensions. Thus, depending on the parameters of the study and the characteristics of the children involved, the efficacy rate reported in studies of psychostimulant treatment of ADHD has varied widely—anywhere from 33% to 100% (Swanson et al., 1991). For example, if one is using multiple measures of response, multiple psychostimulant drugs, and different doses of the drugs, the favorable response rate on at least one measure approaches 100%; in contrast, if the requirement is a favorable response on all measures, almost all individuals would be identified as nonresponders. ADHD children most likely to respond favorably to methylphenidate are those with high IQ, considerable inattentiveness, young age, low severity of disorder, low rates of anxiety, and a positive response to their first dose of methylphenidate (Buitelaar et al., 1995; Tannock et al., 1995).

Psychostimulant intervention should be accompanied by elimination of disturbing influences in the family or classroom through counseling and psychotherapy, implementation of behavior modification and cognitive training programs, and possibly enrollment of the child in learning disabilities classrooms (to help restore the confidence of the child, whose experiences are typically failures). In some cases these interventions alone may be sufficient to ameliorate the condition, or they may interact synergistically with psychostimulant treatment (Ajibola & Clement, 1995). However, in general, the benefits of nondrug interventions have been less substantial than those of drug treatment (Brown et al., 1985; Pelham et al., 1993). There is also evidence that the positive reinforcers used in behavior modification programs may actually take the ADHD child's attention away from the task at hand and direct it toward the reinforcing agent. Finally, there are economic factors that must be considered. Unfortunately, most psychological treatments are rather arduous and costly to implement, particularly in comparison to the few cents a day it costs for *d*-amphetamine.

If improvement with psychostimulants is going to occur, it will be apparent immediately. If these drugs produce only doubtful benefits in a few days (or, at most, a couple of weeks), their use should be terminated. Unfortunately, determining whether benefits occur may sometimes be difficult, because not all ADHD children respond to the same dose and not all of the different target symptoms may respond equally to the same doses of these drugs. In fact, the effects of methylphenidate (the most commonly studied psychostimulant) on cognitive function in ADHD children interact with and are interdependent on a host of variables—for example, dose, time course following administration, child characteristics, type of information processing required, task factors, and prevailing social and environmental conditions (Rapport & Kelly, 1991). In general, children's performance on tasks requiring primarily vigilance appears most benefited with low (0.1–0.4 mg/kg) doses (or shortly after the drug is administered). For highly effortful tasks that require greater behavioral inhibition, optimal benefits are most likely with high (0.6–0.9 mg/kg) doses (or 3 to 4 hours after the drug is administered). For tasks requiring nearly equal degrees of vigilance and inhibition, such as learning tasks, optimal performance is most likely with intermediate (0.3–0.7 mg/kg) doses (or 2 to 4 hours after drug administration). Thus, whether one observes benefits or not may depend on what the observer is looking for, what dose has been given, and the time after the drug is given.

Perhaps for these reasons, there has been no resolution to the long-standing debate over whether higher doses of methylphenidate (those in the 1.0 mg/kg range) induce cognitive toxicity—that is, detrimental effects on high-level cognitive processes necessary for learning. See, for example, Sprague and Sleator (1977), who reported an inverted U-shaped dose–response function on learning with disruption of learning occurring at a 1.0 mg/kg dose; Swanson et al. (1991), who reviewed the literature on this issue up to 1990; and Douglas et al. (1995), who found linear improvement on measures of mental flexibility (e.g., divergent thinking and ability to shift mental set) and other cognitive processes in ADHD children with doses of methylphenidate up to 0.9 mg/kg.

It has long been believed that the response to psychostimulants of ADHD children with hyperactivity is different from that of "normal" children and adults, or that it is "paradoxical" because hyperactive children appear to be calmer, rather than more excited, under their influence. However, studies have found that normal children and hyperactive children respond in a qualitatively similar way to psychostimulants; the effect is just more apparent in hyperactive children (Rapoport et al., 1980). In a variety of measures, both types of children respond to psychostimulants as adults do, with the exception of mood. Adults tend to report mood elevation or euphoria with psychostimulants, whereas children tend to say that these drugs make them feel "funny" or "strange." Finally, ADHD children without hyperactivity benefit as much with psychostimulant treatment as those children with hyperactivity, although the latter children may require somewhat higher doses because they have greater difficulty in the area of behavioral inhibition (Barkley et al., 1991).

The paradoxical reduction in motor activity with psychostimulants may be resolved by noting that sustained attention and high motor activity are incompatible; when attention increases, activity is most likely going to decrease. (Have you ever noticed how "zombie-like" children appear when they are watching their favorite Saturday morning cartoon?) Another possibility is that hyperactive children may actually be physiologically underaroused, and that psychostimulants bring arousal up to normal, whereas sedative–hypnotics decrease arousal even further and worsen the symptoms. (You may notice that many of the characteristics of the hyperactive child are analogous to those of a moderately drunken adult—that is, inattentiveness, belligerence, and unresponsiveness to normal social controls.)

Studies attempting to determine whether activity in the brains of ADHD children differs from that of normal children have not yielded definitive answers. For example, the results of studies examining cerebral glucose metabolism (a measure of the level of brain activity) with positron emission tomography (PET) scan techniques have been inconclusive; low cerebral glucose metabolism has been found in adolescent girls and adults with ADHD but not in adolescent boys with ADHD (Ernst et al., 1994; Zametkin et al., 1990, 1993). Also, no robust effects of psychostimulants on cerebral glucose metabolism have been demonstrated, although they may produce differential patterns of increases and decreases in metabolism in certain regions of the brain (Matochik et al., 1993, 1994). Other studies have found that the amplitudes of a particular type of brain wave pattern (called the P3 wave of event-related potentials), which tends to reflect the impact of information processing such as attention and decision making, are abnormally small in ADHD children, but can be normalized by psychostimulants (Verbaten et al., 1994).

Despite the consistent improvement in the symptoms of the disorder, which should theoretically allow the children to learn more efficiently, there is little empirical evidence that long-term learning and academic achievement are benefited by psychostimulants (Dulcan, 1986). However, a modest improvement in IQ was found after 15 months of amphetamine treatment (a mean of 4.5 IQ points versus 0.7 IQ points with placebo) in ADHD children in a randomized, double-blind, placebo-controlled study (Gillberg et al., 1997). This paradox has not been resolved, but it may be due in part to the practice of using doses that most facilitate classroom behavior but have the least effectiveness with respect to learning. It is also possible, because of the long duration of exposure to these drugs, that much of the learning accomplished under the drug was state-dependent (Swanson & Kinsbourne, 1976). If such is the case, then it is not surprising that individuals who were treated with drugs do not show any long-term gains from the treatment when they are later tested as adolescents or adults without the drugs. Although there has been no definitive study of this possibility, as discussed later, adults who were diagnosed with ADHD as children (and treated with psychostimulants) do perform better in some psychomotor tasks when treated with psychostimulants.

Some long-term benefits of psychostimulant treatment in ADHD have been suggested. One study compared young adults who had been treated for hyperactivity with psychostimulants during childhood with a similar group of unmedicated individuals and a control group (Hechtman et al., 1984). They found that the adults who had been hyperactive as youths differed greatly from the control group, regardless of their therapy as children. However, the adults who had been treated with psychostimulants as youths differed from the untreated adults on only a few variables. It seemed that the treated young adults had fewer car accidents, viewed their childhood more positively, stole less in elementary school, and generally had better social skills and self-esteem. The authors suggested that the medicated individuals may have suffered less from early social ostracism and subsequently developed better feelings toward themselves and others.

It is generally believed that ADHD is eventually outgrown in puberty and that the effectiveness of psychostimulant medication ceases at this time. Therefore, some experts suggest that these medications should be withdrawn at puberty. However, neither belief is supported by empirical evidence (Faraone et al., 2000). Although the symptoms do tend to dissipate at puberty, many ADHD symptoms, such as impulsivity, poor social skills, learning disabilities, and lower educational achievement, often continue into adulthood in 30% to 70% of childhood-onset cases. Furthermore, several studies have indicated that adolescents and adults diagnosed with ADHD can benefit markedly from psychostimulant drug therapy. It is possible that the decreased positive response to psychostimulants over time in some individuals is due to tolerance.

The most common side effects associated with psychostimulant treatment of ADHD are decreased appetite, which may result in small, temporary effects on normal weight gain, and insomnia (Fine & Johnston, 1993). However, some studies have questioned whether insomnia or related sleep disturbances are a direct result of psychostimulant treatment or are a result of the disorder itself, as they found essentially the same degree of sleep disturbances with placebo as with methylphenidate in ADHD children (Fine & Johnston, 1993; Kent et al., 1995). Less common, but more problematic, side effects are symptoms of social withdrawal (as noted, interpersonal relationships are generally improved with psychostimulant treatment) or acute psychotic reactions.

There have also been concerns that psychostimulants may exacerbate or induce motor and phonic tics in individuals predisposed to multiple tics or Tourette's syndrome (to be described shortly), and some clinicians have advised against their use in individuals who exhibit comorbidity between ADHD and Tourette's syndrome. There is conflicting evidence in this issue, with some research indicating that many Tourette's patients do not experience tic worsening with psychostimulant treatment or in some cases show evidence of a reduction in tics. Other studies suggest that the benefits in reducing the symptoms of ADHD outweigh the potential for tic worsening. A randomized controlled trial comparing clonidine, methylphenidate, clonidine combined with methylphenidate, and placebo in children diagnosed with ADHD and a chronic tic disorder has provided further evidence that these concerns are unwarranted (Tourette's Syndrome Study Group, 2002). Compared with placebo, there were significant improvements with respect to ADHD symptomatology in both the clonidine and methylphenidate groups, and the greatest improvements occurred in the clonidine plus methylphenidate group. Clonidine appeared most beneficial in reducing impulsivity and hyperactivity, and methylphenidate appeared most beneficial in improving attention. Importantly, the incidence of tic worsening was no higher with methylphenidate than with clonidine or placebo.

For a number of years there have been concerns expressed over the potential for psychostimulant treatment for ADHD increasing the individual's risk for subsequent drug use, abuse, and dependence. Numerous studies have attempted to determine if such an association exists (see Barkley et al., 2003, and references cited therein). However, the majority of these studies have found no compelling evidence that stimulant treatment of children with ADHD leads to an increased risk for substance experimentation, use, dependence, or abuse by adulthood. In fact, although it has long been recognized that individuals with ADHD have a significantly higher risk for substance abuse (Clure et al., 1999; Milberger et al., 1997), research suggests that pharmacotherapy of ADHD dramatically reduces the risk for substance abuse disorders (Biederman et al., 1999).

These findings may be due to the fact that ADHD children do not experience any pleasurable effects from these drugs and are quite willing to terminate this therapy when the suggestion to do so is made. The fact that ADHD children dislike taking these medications can lead to noncompliance, which some authorities have suggested may be partially responsible for the variable and conflicting results from drug studies and the lack of long-term efficacy of psychostimulants in this disorder. Therefore, children should not be given sole responsibility for taking their medication and should not be allowed to take it to school with them, because they may "forget" to take it or succumb to pressure from peers to "share" their medication. In a survey of ADHD children being treated with Ritalin, 16% of the children reported that they had been approached to sell, give, or trade their medication (Musser et al., 1998). The use of extended-release formulations of psychostimulants should minimize both the concerns of noncompliance with treatment and the diversion of medications to others.

Over the past 3 decades there has been considerable discussion about the benefits of nutritional interventions for the treatment of hyperactivity, such as elimination of foods containing artificial colors and flavors, natural and artificial salicylates (aspirin-like substances), preservatives, and sugar. This is sometimes referred to as the Feingold diet, named after Ben Feingold, the allergist who initially proposed the association between these substances and contended that as many as 50% of hyperactive children may benefit from such dietary restrictions. However, a number of studies have either found no empirical evidence to substantiate this claim or have shown only a small effect (see Bateman et al., 2004, and studies cited therein). The most recent of these (Bateman et al., 2004) assessed preschool children during alternating periods of exposure to food additives (artificial food coloring and the food preservative sodium benzoate) and placebo. Prior to treatment, the children were differentiated as to whether or not they exhibited hyperactive symptoms and whether or not they tested positive for atopy (the genetic tendency to develop classic allergic diseases). The investigators found no difference between the treatments utilizing objective clinical tests. However, the parents of the children detected significantly greater increases in hyperactivity in their children during food additive phases than the placebo phases, but these effects did not depend on whether or not the children were hyperactive or tested positive for atopy prior to the treatments. In general, the evidence suggests that perhaps between 5% and 10% of hyperactive children may show behavioral improvements after the removal of food additives from their diet (Kolata, 1982); as suggested by Bateman et al., some benefit may occur for most children if artificial food colors and preservatives are removed from their diet. Finally, despite the common popular belief that sugar worsens hyperactive behavior in children, the majority of well-controlled experimental studies have failed to provide any support for this belief (Spring et al., 1987). A largely carbohydrate meal does tend to disrupt children's concentration, but that effect is common with just about everybody.

PSYCHOMOTOR STIMULANTS, LEARNING, AND MEMORY

In view of the beneficial effects of stimulants on attentional processes in people with ADHD, it is reasonable to discuss how these drugs might affect memory processes. The evidence on the issue is equivocal, primarily because learning is never observed directly and involves a variety of complex processes for it to take place. Therefore, before beginning a discussion of this issue, one must be familiar with the basic phases of learning and memory. These consist of an acquisition phase, a consolidation phase, a retention phase, and a retrieval phase (Heise, 1981).

Acquisition is the phase in which the behavior or information is initially practiced and encoded. *Retention* is the preservation of this behavior or information between the end of the training period and the period during which it is utilized. *Retrieval* is the phase during which the organism attempts to utilize the behavior or information acquired earlier. Note that the acquisition phase corresponds to what we commonly refer to as *learning*, and the retention and retrieval phases correspond to what we refer to as *memory*. Memory is commonly viewed as consisting of two different storage systems. The first is short-term memory, lasting a few seconds or minutes; in humans this is commonly referred to as *working memory*, which is a larger, more elaborate system that not only maintains limited amounts of information temporarily but also involves conscious processes that regulate attention, retrieval, and symbolic encoding of information. The second is long-term memory, which is relatively permanent. During the time that it takes to create the long-term changes (perhaps resulting from the creation of new proteins that modify the permanent responsiveness of neurons), the information is maintained in short-term memory. There is a time period during which only temporary (short-term) memory exists and the permanent memory has not yet been established. The establishment of permanent traces from temporary ones is called *consolidation*, and the time it takes to form the permanent traces is called the *consolidation phase*.

A schematic representation of these four phases is shown in Figure 11.1. In the figure, times A, B, C, and D indicate where a drug would be administered in order to assess its effects on different components of learning and memory. Differences in performance between drug-treated and nontreated animals are assessed during retest procedures. Any differences would be due to the drug's effects on acquisition processes (e.g., attention, motivation, and general arousal) if the drug were administered at time A, consolidation if administered at time B (or if the duration of action of the drug given at A was such that it was also present during time B), retention if administered at time C, and retrieval if administered at time D (modified from Heise, 1981). From this discussion, we

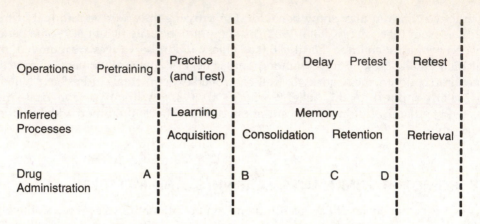

FIGURE 11.1 Schematic representation of operations over time and phases of inferred processes in the study of effects of drugs on learning and memory (modified from Heise, 1981)

can see that when we ask the question of whether a particular drug affects learning or memory, we must first clarify during which phase(s) the drug is present.

Under conditions in which the person is fatigued or has ADHD, there do seem to be some beneficial effects of low doses of amphetamine in the acquisition of new information, presumably because of increased attention to the material. Under conditions in which the person is already alert and rested, or with higher doses of amphetamine, the evidence is not as clear. In some cases, it facilitates and in some cases it interferes with acquisition. Perhaps these contradictory results occur because, although amphetamine may enhance attentional processes, it may also increase one's attention to irrelevant details or tangential material. Thus, relevant information may not be acquired. Regardless of whether there are benefits to the acquisition process or not, there are questions as to whether the information will be efficiently retrieved at appropriate times later on. This issue will be dealt with shortly.

If exposure to adrenaline-stimulating drugs, like amphetamine, occurs immediately following a novel experience (i.e., during consolidation), there is some evidence that this can affect the experience's subsequent retention—with retention being enhanced by low doses and impaired by high doses (McGaugh, 1990). These influences appear to be mediated by activation of noradrenergic receptors, particularly β-adrenergic receptors, within the part of the limbic system called the amygdala (McGaugh et al., 1993). Most of the evidence for these phenomena comes from studies with nonhumans learning a very particular type of behavior referred to as "passive avoidance." Briefly, the task involves placing a rat or a mouse in an area that it generally will move away from, such as on a platform raised an inch or so off the ground. Normally, the animal will step down off the platform after a few seconds. It is then subjected to a brief aversive shock, and then transferred back to its home cage. Later, after about 24 hours, the animal is placed on the platform again, to see how long it takes to step down. Animals that were not shocked earlier will generally step down very quickly, whereas animals that had been shocked will generally stay on the platform for a considerably longer period of time, presumably because they remember what happened the last time they stepped down. If the animal is administered an appropriate dose of amphetamine just after the initial shock, it generally will stay on the platform the next time even longer than saline-treated (undrugged) animals, presumably because it remembers even better what had happened to it the first time it stepped down.

Similar enhancements of retention in nonhumans with adrenaline-stimulating drugs have been obtained using positively motivated discrimination tasks (McGaugh, 1990). However, the tasks used to assess the effects of drugs on the consolidation phase of learning involve very special situations that may have no counterpart in the every-day learning experiences of humans. Thus we cannot really say that information ac-quired by humans will be similarly enhanced if it is immediately followed by amphetamine exposure, although there is evidence that enhanced memory associated with emotional events in humans does involve activation of the β-adrenergic system (Cahill et al., 1994).

Once information has been acquired and consolidated, there is little likelihood that amphetamine and similar-acting drugs will facilitate retrieval at a later time, unless the person is particularly fatigued to begin with. In fact, there is evidence of state-dependent learning with amphetamine. This means that if learning occurred without the drug, its presence during retention may actually interfere with the retrieval of the previously learned material. For example, in one study, hyperactive and normal children engaged in a paired-associate learning task (one in which the subjects are required to learn a set of stimulus–response pairs, such that when a stimulus item is presented, the subjects are supposed to produce the appropriate response) after being administered a placebo or Ritalin. They were then tested at a later time for their retention of the material, again after being given Ritalin or a placebo. Both groups showed greater retention when the drug state during retesting was the same as that during learning, as opposed to when the drug state was changed between the learning and testing phases (Swanson & Kinsbourne, 1976).

TREATMENT OF ALZHEIMER'S DISEASE AND SENILE DEMENTIA

Although we would like to emphasize that growing old is not considered a disease in and of itself, the fact remains that as we grow older a number of drugs are often used to treat cognitive, emotional, or behavioral deficits that are alleged to be caused by the normal aging process. Also, drugs may be used to treat a disease or condition that is found solely, or at least more frequently, among the elderly. Although most persons over the age of 65 are in good mental health, close to a quarter of this population suffer from disorders ranging from depression (which is reflected in a high suicide rate within this group) to *dementia*, that is, central nervous system (CNS) changes that lead to mem-ory deficits, confusion, irritability, apathy, or disturbed behavior (Domino et al., 1978; Finch, 1982).

Reduction in blood flow to the brain as a result of cerebral arteriosclerosis may cause progressive mental impairment. Specific neurological lesions in the brain can cause such disorders as Parkinson's disease and Alzheimer's disease. The latter condi-tion is characterized by loss of intellectual abilities, including memory, judgment, ab-stract thought, and higher cortical functions, as well as changes in personality and behavior. Although senile onset occurs after age 65 and presenile onset usually occurs between the ages of 50 and 65, these two conditions are indistinguishable forms of dementia with respect to cellular pathology. Mental depression is also common among the elderly (Ban, 1984). Some of the symptoms of these disorders respond well to drug therapy, but in many cases drugs do little good and may even make psychogeriatric illnesses worse.

There are special problems in treating the elderly with drugs. The first of these centers on diagnoses (Ban, 1984). For example, the treatment of dementia is likely to include psychotropic medication. However, dementia is defined by changes in behavior, not by laboratory tests or CT (computerized axial tomography) or PET scans. Because mental capacities tend to decline with age, it is difficult to decide when normal aging ends and dementia begins. Furthermore, many different types of conditions can induce symptoms of dementia: antihypertensive and antiulcer drugs, depression, altered thyroid function and kidney failure, isolation, vascular disease, AIDS and other viral infections, brain tumors, vitamin deficiencies, alcoholism, and other drug abuse—the list is endless (Kolata, 1987). Diagnosing other behaviors or emotional problems amenable to psychotropic drug treatment is equally difficult. To compound this problem, because of numerous health problems, geriatric patients often take many drugs (prescription, over-the-counter, and social), a practice that not only makes diagnosis difficult but also puts the elderly at a much higher risk for complex and harmful drug interactions than younger patients.

Another problem, or set of problems, is related to the alteration of pharmacokinetics that occurs with aging (Friedel, 1978). The increase in percentage of body fat means that psychotropic drugs, which for the most part are lipid-soluble, may accumulate in adipose tissue in older persons, which could result in a longer duration of action and an increased sensitivity to the drugs. Decreased plasma proteins may lead to less drug binding and an increased accumulation in the organs, which could increase the possibility of toxicity. The potential for reaching toxicity is further enhanced by the decreased efficiency of metabolism of drugs in the liver and reduced filtration of drugs by the kidneys. Thus, higher levels of a drug may be present in the body for a longer period of time than would be the case in younger subjects. For these reasons, it is generally recommended that pharmacological treatment should commence with one-third to one-half the recommended young adult dosage with most drugs, and the dosage should be increased only very gradually (Ban, 1984)—start low and go slow.

A classic example of these difficulties can be seen in the treatment of depression—the most commonly diagnosed psychological disorder in the elderly (Ban, 1984). The anticholinergic side effects of many antidepressants, which may be merely troublesome to most younger individuals, can be very annoying and possibly life-endangering in the elderly. Examples would be aggravation of prostate hypertrophy, precipitation of glaucoma, or bowel impaction. Antidepressants may cause delirium or confusional states in geriatric patients whose symptoms are misdiagnosed (and dismissed) as symptoms of dementia. Reduced cardiovascular functioning of the elderly person, in combination with antidepressant medication, can lead to bradycardia (abnormally low heart rate), orthostatic hypotension, severe cardiac arrhythmias, or complete disruption of cardiac conduction. The coexistence of chronic medical illness with depression or mental disturbances in many geriatric persons makes psychotropic treatment particularly complex.

Fortunately, and in spite of the potential hazards and discomforts of using antidepressants in elderly patients, they can be just as effective in elderly patients as in nonelderly patients (Ban, 1984; Volz et al., 1995). If the drug is cautiously selected and the initial dosage is one-third to one-half the amount given to younger patients, and plasma levels are carefully monitored, then antidepressant treatment can be safe and effective. Antidepressants may also reduce symptoms similar to those of early senile dementia, which occur secondary to depression (e.g., pseudodementia). At this point, the serotonin (5-HT) uptake blockers, because of their low toxicity, absence of anticholinergic side effects, and lack of detrimental effects on cognitive functioning, appear to be the best antidepressants for the elderly (Knegtering et al., 1994). If they become approved for use, the reversible inhibitors of MAO-A (RIMAs) appear to be a good second choice. They have minimal influence on cognitive performance, are void of hypotensive effects, including orthostatic hypotension, and do not interact with foods to induce a hypertensive crisis (Norman & Burrows, 1995). This class of antidepressant also appears to be effective in the treatment of depression that accompanies dementia, and may improve cognitive ability as well (Priest et al., 1995).

For those psychiatric or psychological dysfunctions common to both younger and older individuals (such as anxiety, sleep disturbances, psychotic reactions, and manic depression), as long as the pharmacokinetic considerations that we have noted are taken into account, pharmacological interventions are essentially the same for both groups (Ban, 1984). For example, benzodiazepines are recommended for anxiety-related symptoms, but the shorter-acting benzodiazepines, such as oxazepam, should be used to prevent excessive accumulation of these compounds. Buspirone and the 5-HT uptake blockers would also be appropriate for many of these symptoms.

Drug intervention for sleep disturbances in the elderly should take into consideration the fact that the need for sleep normally decreases with age. Hypnotic doses of chloral hydrate are less likely to cause persistent effects in the elderly than other hypnotic agents, and drug "hangover" may be less common with chloral hydrate than with most barbiturates and some benzodiazepines. However, chloral hydrate may exert both peripheral side effects (gastric distress, vomiting, and flatulence) and undesirable CNS effects (malaise, light-headedness, ataxia, and nightmares). It should definitely be avoided in patients with marked liver or kidney impairment and should probably be avoided in patients with severe cardiac disease.

Antipsychotics are legitimately used in cases in which there is a recurrence of a psychotic episode or in patients with dementia who are extremely agitated to the point of hurting themselves or others (Katz et al., 1999; Salzman, 1988). Because of potential rapid onset of tardive dyskinesia with the use of conventional antipsychotics in older patients, atypical antipsychotics should be used in such patients if necessary. However, unless there is evidence of symptoms specific to psychosis, antipsychotics are likely to overly sedate the patients. Unfortunately, antipsychotics tend to be overused in most nursing homes and institutions, and they are more likely given for the benefit of the staff than of the patients. Lithium treatment for manic depression symptoms is just as effective in elderly patients as it is in younger patients, although with considerably lower doses (approximately 15% to 20% of normal).

With respect to the primary sources of the cognitive and memory dysfunctions common to the geriatric population, most drug interventions have yet to produce clear successes in clinical trials. Psychostimulants such as amphetamines, methylphenidate, pemoline, and pipradol have not been found to benefit cognitive functioning in geriatric patients (Galizia, 1984). Furthermore, although psychostimulants may be useful in the treatment of apathetic, withdrawn, disheartened, or demoralized older people (Salzman, 1985), these drugs may produce an increase in agitation and psychotic thinking and behavior when the demented states are severe (Salzman, 1988). At one time it was believed that cerebrovasodilators might be beneficial by increasing blood flow; however, such interventions have not produced reliable results (Ban, 1978). For example, a popular drug of this type, Hydergine (ergoloid mesylates), has been touted as having vasodilating and cerebral metabolic activity with concomitant cognitive improvement, but several studies have found contrary results. A review of the clinical trials assessing Hydergine's efficacy in dementia indicated that it may produce significant benefits as assessed by either global ratings or comprehensive rating scales (Olin et al., 2001). However, due to a number of concerns over methodological problems, there is still uncertainty regarding Hydergine's efficacy in dementia. There is also a question regarding the mechanism behind these benefits; for example, Hydergine acts as a mood elevator, such that improvement in cognitive function may be secondary to the antidepressant effects.

Neuropeptides have been investigated but are generally ineffective in reducing mild cognitive impairment resulting from age, dementia, or other trauma (Galizia, 1984). ACTH 4-10 (a fragment of adrenocorticotropic hormone) may increase arousal and improve cognitive functioning in some areas in the elderly (Koob, 1987). Vasopressin (a peptide found in the pituitary gland) has resulted in improvement in tests of concentration, attention, and memory, including storage and retrieval of information in humans (Crook, 1988). However, it is not clear whether these effects are directly linked to memory or are simply due to improvements in mood, attentiveness, or some other aspect of performance. For example, vasopressin causes hypertension via its action at peripheral blood vessel receptors; thus, the apparent CNS effect of vasopressin may be indirectly mediated by an arousal secondary to the inappropriate hypertension induced by peripheral receptor activation.

Piracetam, a GABA (gamma-aminobutyric acid) derivative that was one of the first drugs to be referred to as a **nootropic** (a term coined to describe drugs that specifically enhance cognitive functioning), has a considerable popular lore regarding its ability to enhance cognitive functions such as memory and learning, without having any sedative, analgesic, stimulant, neuroleptic, or autonomic effects. Despite over 100 studies conducted around the world over the past 3 decades, many of which report positive results with piracetam (or its analogues), its efficacy in enhancing cognitive functions in a variety of subjects, including the elderly, is still elusive.

In summary, a wide variety of different classes of drugs have been tested for the treatment of dementia, specifically Alzheimer's disease, including psychostimulants, anticoagulants, vasodilators, hyperbaric oxygen, hormones, nootropics, monoaminergics, and neuropeptides, without conclusive evidence of any of these being beneficial for the treatment of this condition (Soares & Gershon, 1994). Based on the consistent finding that there is a deterioration in cholinergic neurotransmitter systems in Alzheimer's patients (although there are a number of other systems that deteriorate as well), clinical trials attempted to compensate pharmacologically for the cholinergic disturbance by increasing the availability of acetylcholine precursors (i.e., by administering choline or lecithin), reducing acetylcholine metabolic degradation with drugs that inhibit the enzyme cholinesterase, or administering nicotine or muscarinic agonists (Evans et al., 2004).

Of these treatments, the cholinesterase inhibitor tacrine (Cognex) emerged with the most empirical support, and it was the first drug to be approved (in 1993) specifically for the treatment of Alzheimer's disease. Research indicated that a definite subpopulation of patients benefited from therapy with tacrine, in terms of enhancing cognitive functioning and adaptive living skills (Madden et al., 1995). Unfortunately, the benefits of tacrine were most apparent at doses that induced significant adverse reactions in two-thirds of the patients, with most problematic being the induction of high levels of enzymes that can lead to liver damage (Soares & Gershon, 1994). The primary benefit of tacrine over physostigmine, a widely used cholinesterase inhibitor with a long history, appeared to be primarily pharmacokinetic. Physostigmine has an extremely short half-life (approximately 30 minutes), whereas tacrine's duration of action is five to six times longer.

Shortly after the establishment of tacrine's efficacy, a number of other **cholinesterase inhibitors** with better safety and pharmacokinetic profiles were developed (Birks, 2006; van Marum, 2008). These include donepezil (Aricept), rivastigmine (Exelon), and galantamine (Reminyl), which have been approved for the treatment of mild to moderately severe cases of Alzheimer's. These drugs have greater specificity than tacrine in augmenting cholinergic functioning in the brain, as opposed to affecting cholinergic activity in other parts of the body. Galantamine also interacts with nicotinic ACh receptors to stimulate these receptors; as indicated in Chapter 7, nicotine may enhance certain cognitive functions even in healthy individuals. These drugs do not appear to induce serious liver abnormalities, although they may cause diarrhea and nausea. Another advantage is that they only need to be taken once a day—in contrast to tacrine, which needs to be taken four times a day to be effective.

The benefits of cholinesterase inhibitors in reducing the symptoms of Alzheimer's disease or preventing further deterioration are modest at best. The percentage of patients obtaining a clinically relevant benefit from treatment with these drugs ranges from 25% to 54% versus 7% to 27% with placebo for cognitive improvement, and ranges from 25% to 32% versus 11% to 19% with placebo for improvement in global measures of functioning (Wettstein, 2000; Wilcock, 2000). A meta-analysis of clinical trials with donepezil, galantamine, and rivastigmine concluded that all three drugs had similar cognitive benefits, although both galantamine and rivastigmine treatments were associated with a greater likelihood of trial dropout than with placebo, especially with higher dosages (Ritchie et al., 2004). The major side effects of anticholinesterases include parasympathetic effects, but also CNS effects including the induction of parkinsonian motor symptoms such as slowness of movement and tremor (Gurevich et al. 2006; Litvinenko et al. 2008; Ott & Lannon, 1992; Song et al. 2008).

Interestingly, in a review comparing the cholinesterase inhibitors donepezil and rivastigmine and gingko extracts (Gingko special extract EGb 761) in placebo-controlled studies of at least 6 months' duration, it was determined that there were no major differences in efficacy (expressed as the delay in symptom progression or the difference in response rate between active substance and placebo) between the cholinesterase inhibitors and the gingko extracts in the treatment of mild to moderate Alzheimer's dementia (Wettstein, 2000). Only tacrine exhibited a high dropout rate due to adverse drug reactions. However, another review concluded that there is insufficient evidence regarding the efficacy of gingko biloba in the treatment of Alzheimer's disease (Evans et al., 2004).

Studies suggest that the benefits from treatment with the FDA-approved cholinesterase inhibitors in patients diagnosed with Alzheimer's disease may last for up to 4 years (Winblad & Jelic, 2004). Generally, there is an initial improvement in cognition for up to 1 year, which is then followed by a decline in function to below baseline levels. However, the cognitive functioning with treatment tends to remain above those levels that would be predicted in individuals who are not treated. These studies also indicate that early diagnosis and continuous treatment with cholinesterase inhibitors produce better long-term outcomes.

The reason for the failure of most drug treatments to reverse Alzheimer's disease symptoms may be that neuronal death is so severe that the affected systems are incapable of responding to pharmacologic manipulation. As a result, it has been suggested that pharmacological strategies designed to slow neuronal death rate may have therapeutic value. Estrogen, the predominantly female hormone widely used for the treatment of a variety of disorders, has been suggested in a number of studies to have protective effects against Alzheimer's disease and to enhance mood and specific aspects of cognitive functioning in postmenopausal women. Unfortunately, a randomized, double-blind, placebo-controlled clinical trial found that estrogen replacement therapy for 1 year did not slow progression of the disease, nor did it improve global, cognitive, or functional outcomes in women with mild to moderate Alzheimer's disease (Mulnard et al., 2000). Thus, the potential efficacy of estrogen in the prevention of Alzheimer's disease remains unclear.

Although neuronal cell death may occur because of a wide variety of pathological and toxicological processes (e.g., insufficient oxygen or low blood glucose levels), as well as normal gene-programmed processes, in most of them the final common pathway for the activation involves a sustained elevation of free intracellular Ca^{++} concentration (Branconnier et al., 1992). Thus, chronic treatment with calcium-channel blockers or antagonists of NMDA (N-Methyl-D-aspartic acid) receptors (which mediate Ca^{++} flow into cells) may have therapeutic value in preventing or delaying the onset of the disease. (This is a tricky procedure because NMDA receptor activity plays a vital role in a variety of CNS functions [e.g., memory formation], so blocking NMDA receptor activity with phencyclidine [PCP] would not be useful for this purpose because it has psychotomimetic effects.)

One drug with these properties is memantine (Namenda), a low- to moderate-affinity, noncompetitive NMDA receptor antagonist (Farlow, 2004). Because of its low affinity for the NMDA receptor, it may only have an effect when the glutamate system is hyperactive and potentially neurotoxic, which would decrease the progression of cell death in Alzheimer's disease. However, it allows for the normal physiological activation of NMDA channels, for example, during memory formation. For a number of years, it has been approved in Germany for the treatment of dementias, and it was approved by the FDA (in 2003) for the treatment of moderate to severe Alzheimer's disease—the first drug approved for the treatment of patients with this severity of disease. In a double-blind, placebo-controlled trial in care-dependent patients with severe dementia, memantine was shown to reduce care dependence and produce global behavioral improvements, relative to placebo controls, after 4 weeks of treatment, and the improvements became even greater after 12 weeks of treatment (73% improved with memantine vs. 45% with placebo; Winblad & Poritis, 1999). In a clinical trial with patients diagnosed with moderate to severe Alzheimer's disease who were already receiving stable dosages of donepezil, it was determined that memantine produced significantly better outcomes than placebo on measures of cognitive functioning, activities of daily living, behavior, and clinical global status (Tariot et al., 2004). Consistent with previous studies, there were minimal adverse reactions with memantine treatment.

Other approaches in preclinical and clinical phases involve decreasing the neurodegeneration processes believed to underlie the development of Alzheimer's disease. These involve the use of drugs that mimic nerve growth factor (which is heavily involved in the maintenance of function of the cholinergic forebrain system), anti-inflammatory drugs (based on reports that individuals using nonsteroidal anti-inflammatory drugs are less likely to develop Alzheimer's disease), drugs that reduce cholesterol levels (based on evidence that cholesterol may foster ß amyloid production), and drugs that reduce oxidative stress (e.g., vitamins C and E, estrogen; Helmuth, 2002). Vaccines that help clear ß amyloid from the brain are also being explored. Perhaps the greatest focus is in developing inhibitors of the enzymes that are believed to be responsible for the formation of ß amyloid and its plaques, which are the hallmarks of Alzheimer's disease and the primary causes of the neurodegeneration.

Websites for Further Information

Website of Children and Adults with Attention Deficit Hyperactivity Disorder:

> http://www.chadd.org

Current, comprehensive Alzheimer's disease information and resources:

http://www.alz.org
http://www.alzheimers.org

Naturally Occurring and Synthetic Opiates and Their Antagonists

Some of the oldest psychotropic drugs used by humans are morphine and codeine; their use may go back 7,000 years. Originally these drugs were used in the form of extracts from the poppy plant, which contains opium, and in purified form they are still used extensively. They belong to a class of drugs that includes the most effective pain relievers available, so they are the most commonly used analgesic treatments for moderate to severe pain. Because users often experience euphoria, drowsiness, and mental clouding—perhaps resulting in the feeling that all their problems are trivial—these drugs are also used recreationally and are highly subject to abuse.

The most common term for morphine and similar-acting drugs is *narcotic*, which is a derivation of the Greek word for stupor (narkē). Unfortunately, the term *narcotic* has taken on many unwarranted connotations. It has been used primarily to refer to a class of drugs that promote sleep and induce analgesia, but many laypersons often think of narcotics as any highly abusable or addicting drug. From this perspective, drugs that bear little similarity to morphine in terms of their neurochemical actions or their psychological effects (like cocaine and marijuana) have been designated as narcotics for legal purposes. However, pharmacologically, only a drug with the following qualities can be appropriately classified as a narcotic: (1) It generally has sedative–hypnotic and analgesic properties; (2) it acts stereospecifically on endorphin/enkephalin receptors; and (3) its actions are antagonized by naloxone (Narcan). In essence, narcotics are restricted to extracts of opium (*opiates*), opiate derivatives, and synthetic drugs with opiate properties. Perhaps because of the confusion surrounding the term *narcotic*, many authorities now refer to these substances as *opioids*. Routinely throughout this chapter, we will refer to these substances as *narcotics, opiates,* and *opioids* interchangeably. In this way, we will become familiar with all three terms.

ENDOGENOUS OPIOID PEPTIDES AND THEIR RECEPTORS

The definition of a narcotic has become more confusing and complex since the discovery of a multitude of substances, endogenous to the brain and body, with opiate properties (researchers often refer to these as *endogenous opioid peptides*). Three distinct families have been identified thus far: the *enkephalins,* the *endorphins,* and the *dynorphins* (Gutstein & Akil, 2001). However, as mentioned previously, these are often categorized in a general sense as endorphins. Each family is derived from different precursor polypeptides, more than 200 amino acids long, with different anatomical distributions. Each precursor contains a number of biologically active opioid and nonopioid peptides, which are cleaved (split) at specific sites by specific enzymes (called *proteases*) to produce the active agents. For example, the precursor pro-opiomelanocortin contains three separate hormones, one of which contains the opioid peptide β-endorphin, which in turn contains the opioid peptide met-enkephalin (a peptide of five amino acids with methionine at one end). The precursor proenkephalin contains several met-enkephalin segments and a leu-enkephalin segment (the same amino acid sequence as met-enkephalin except that leucine is substituted for methionine). The precursor prodynorphin contains two endorphin segments, three leu-enkephalin segments, and two types of the opioid peptide dynorphin.

Pro-opiomelanocortin peptides are found in the pituitary gland (indicating that they play a role in a variety of neuroendocrine functions) and in relatively limited areas of the central nervous system (CNS). Peptides from the other two precursors are distributed widely throughout the CNS, particularly on those regions related to the modulation of pain perception (e.g., the spinal cord and midbrain), affective states (e.g., amygdala, hippocampus, locus coeruleus, and cerebral cortex), and the autonomic nervous system (e.g., medulla). They are also found in other parts of the body, such as the stomach and intestines.

Though the endogenous opioid peptides are believed to function as neurotransmitters, neurohormones, or neuromodulators, their physiological role is not well understood. Furthermore, they frequently coexist with other hormones or neurotransmitters within a given neuron. As discussed in Chapter 5, endogenous opioid peptides have been implicated in a myriad of psychological processes and activities, for example, acute stress responses, pain perception, social attachment in primates, and placebo responses in humans.

All opioid receptors identified so far are g-protein–coupled (metabotropic) receptors. Three major classes of opioid receptors have been recognized since the 1970s (called mu, delta, and kappa). A fourth class, called nociceptin/orphanin FQ (N/OFQ) receptors, was identified in the early 1990s. A number of subtypes have been proposed for each of these classes (Gutstein & Akil, 2001), which may account for why opiates that appear to act selectively on one class of opioid receptor don't always induce the same effects. The actions and selectivities of representative ligands and drugs for these various opioid receptors are shown in Table 12.1 (based on Ferrante [1996], Gutstein & Akil [2001]). Those designated as *mu* receptors are morphine- and naloxone-selective (i.e., morphine and naloxone bind to these receptors more readily than enkephalins do) and probably mediate the euphoria-inducing

TABLE 12.1 Opioid Receptors and Their Ligands

Opioid/Ligand	mu (μ)	delta (δ)	kappa (κ)
Endogenous agonists			
Met-enkephalin	++	+++	
Leu-enkephalin	++	+++	
β-endorphin	+++	+++	
Dynorphin A	++		+++
Dynorphin B	+	+	+++
α-neoendorphin	+	+	+++
Exogenous agonists			
Morphine	+++		+
Methadone	+++		
Fentanyl	+++		
Meperidine	+++		
Hydromorphone	+++		
Etorphine	+++	+++	+++
Butorphanol	Partial agonist		+++
Mixed agonist–antagonists			
Buprenorphine	Partial agonist		
Nalorphine	− − −		+
Pentazocine	Partial agonist		++
Cyclazocine	− − −		++
Antagonists			++
Naloxone	− − −	−	− −
Naltrexone	− − −	−	− −
Nalmefene	− − −		
Diprenorphine	− − −	− −	− − −

Note: Activities of drugs are given at the receptors for which the agent has documented affinity in nonhumans. Agonists are indicated by + and antagonists are indicated by − with the degree of potency indicated by the number of symbols.

properties of typical opiates (e.g., morphine, methadone). Other prominent effects of mu receptor agonists include supraspinal and spinal analgesia, respiratory depression, cardiovascular effects, slowing of gastrointestinal (GI) motility, and sedation. *Delta* receptors are more enkephalin-selective and induce spinal analgesia. *Kappa* receptors have a high affinity for dynorphin and may mediate spinal analgesia as well as sedation. Kappa receptors also probably mediate aversive, psychosis-mimicking opiate effects, and this fact may explain why some narcotics that are primarily kappa agonists (e.g., cyclazocine) do not produce drug-seeking behavior (Slifer & Dykstra, 1987). N/OFQ receptors have been proposed to be involved in a bewildering array of psychological processes, and the pharmacological profile of N/OFQ (the neuropeptide agonist at these receptors) is different from, and in many cases opposite to, that of the classical opiates; for example, in some rodent assays it induces hyperalgesia, decreases the analgesic actions of opiates, and blocks the rewarding effects of morphine. These receptors could account for why buprenorphine, an agonist at both mu and

N/OFQ receptors, induces analgesia at low doses but often exhibits diminished analgesic qualities with higher doses (Lutfy et al., 2003).

TYPICAL OPIATES

Considering the various types and subtypes of opioid receptors, it should not come as any surprise that not all drugs classified as narcotics have identical effects. In some cases, drugs with narcotic-like effects by themselves may actually block the effects of other narcotics.

In addition to the natural opiates (morphine and codeine), derivatives or semisynthetic opiates, like heroin, nalorphine, and hydromorphone (Dilaudid), have resulted from minor modifications in structure. A number of other drugs with very similar properties, but very dissimilar molecular structures, have been synthesized, including meperidine (Demerol), fentanyl (Sublimaze), propoxyphene (Darvon), and methadone (Dolophine).

In addition to having somewhat different pharmacological effects, these drugs differ with respect to potency, intensity, duration of action, and oral effectiveness, in many cases because of differences in pharmacokinetics (Oldendorf et al., 1972). For example, heroin is considered to be one of the most potent of the nonendogenous types of opiates. It is approximately two to four times more potent than morphine when injected (i.e., one-third as much is needed to achieve the same degree of analgesia as morphine). Because of this difference in potency, many individuals have campaigned to make heroin, which is presently a Schedule I drug, a legally available medication in the United States for the treatment of severe pain for use in terminally ill patients (Holden, 1977). However, what most people do not realize is that the differential potency is due to pharmacokinetics and not to efficacy at receptors. First, the potency of heroin and morphine is equivalent when taken orally. Second, the heroin molecule is simply a slight modification of morphine. This modification allows heroin to penetrate the blood–brain barrier (BBB) much more rapidly than morphine does. This characteristic allows it to accumulate in the brain much more quickly. Once in the brain, heroin is metabolized into morphine, but because it gets there so much more quickly, it exerts effects that are much more rapid and intense.

Administered subcutaneously in humans, methadone has approximately the same potency as morphine and approximately half the potency of heroin for inducing comparable analgesia (Gutstein & Akil, 2001). With respect to its ability to suppress opiate withdrawal symptoms, methadone is about twice as potent as heroin and four times as potent as morphine. At the same doses administered orally, methadone is much more effective than either heroin or morphine and has an action approximately three to four times longer than that of heroin or morphine. Codeine is approximately 12 times less potent than morphine when injected, primarily due to the fact that codeine needs to be metabolically converted into morphine to become effective. However, it is more readily absorbed through oral administration than morphine. Because they are weak alkaloids that become ionized in acidic media, neither heroin nor morphine is readily absorbed orally; for example, heroin administered orally is about 100 times less potent than when it is administered intravenously. The endogenous opioid peptides are far more potent than heroin (Smith & Griffin, 1978), but they are rapidly inactivated by enzymes throughout the body (Schulties et al., 1989). Fentanyl is one of the most potent of the

TABLE 12.2   Effects of Opiate Administration and Opiate Withdrawal

Opiate Administration	Opiate Withdrawal
Hypothermia	Hyperthermia
Decrease in blood pressure	Increase in blood pressure
Peripheral vasodilation, skin flushed and warm	Piloerection (gooseflesh), chilliness
Miosis (pupillary constriction)	Mydriasis (pupillary dilation)
Drying of secretions	Lacrimation, rhinorrhea
Constipation	Diarrhea
Respiratory depression	Yawning, panting
Decreased urinary 17-ketosteroid levels	Increased urinary 17-ketosteroid levels
Antitussive	Sneezing
Decreased sex drive	Spontaneous ejaculations and orgasms
Relaxation	Restlessness, insomnia
Analgesia	Pain and irritability
Euphoria	Depression

Source: From Jaffe (1985) and Jaffe and Martin (1985).

nonendogenous opiates (approximately 50 times more potent than heroin when injected intramuscularly). Its short duration of action makes it useful as an adjunctive treatment during surgical procedures, but its potency can lead to lethal overdoses in individuals who believe they are injecting heroin.

Behavioral and Physiological Effects of Opiates

Some of the more notable effects of narcotics are shown in Table 12.2. Although some of the more prominent behavioral effects of narcotics resemble those effects induced by sedative–hypnotics, there may be a brief stimulant-like effect immediately after administration, particularly if administered intravenously. Some species, such as cats, and some people show only the stimulant type of effect (Jaffe & Martin, 1985). The most prominent clinically useful effect of opiates is to reduce pain—a complex perceptual and emotional phenomenon dependent on several neurotransmitter systems located in the spinal cord and supraspinal structures (i.e., areas above the spinal cord such as the locus coeruleus and medulla). Opiates have relatively little influence on the sharp pain initially induced by a noxious (harmful, injurious) stimulus; their major effectiveness is in reducing moderate to severe dull pain that persists after a noxious stimulus. This is why opiates are typically used in chronic pain conditions and in treatment of postoperative pain but are not by themselves effective during surgery.

The use of narcotics in medicine to control chronic pain is a particularly contentious issue due to the conflict between physicians' desire to ease pain and their concern over causing addiction. Thus for several decades many chronic pain patients have suffered needlessly, even those with intractable pain at the end of life. Later, however, most physicians acknowledge opioid therapy to be an invaluable and accepted treatment for acute cancer-related pain and pain caused by a terminal disease (Ballantyne & Mao, 2003). The traditional approach in the treatment of chronic pain patients has been to administer morphine or other opiates at fixed intervals, with the expectation that the analgesia will last 4 to 6 hours. The general approach now takes into account that pain in these patients is typically not constant across the day but ebbs and flows with occasional breakthrough pain that if not controlled fairly quickly may be difficult to manage without administering very high doses of an opiate, which then increases the likelihood of side effects, such as mental clouding and nausea.

Fortunately, there are a variety of choices of opiates that come in immediate, controlled, or rapid-release formulations. Thus the general approach now is to: (1) use the lowest effective dose of a controlled-release formulation that satisfies the patients' baseline pain management needs; (2) determine the frequency, intensity, and timing of their breakthrough pain; and (3) use a rapid-acting opiate to cover breakthrough pain. Furthermore, because each opiate has a unique pharmacokinetic and pharmacodynamic profile, for example, compounds with a higher affinity for mu receptors than for delta receptors and vice versa, there is growing recognition that rotation among different opiate medications is beneficial for reducing adverse side effects resulting from chronic use.

Better methods of administering opiates have also been developed to improve their efficacy, reduce their side effects, or lower the cost of treatment—for example, transdermally administered opioid analgesics and patient-controlled opiate analgesia, in which the patient is allowed to self-administer opiates (with some constraints to protect against inadvertent overdose), either orally or by pushing a button on an electronically controlled pump that delivers small doses of morphine through an intravenous (IV) tube (Bloor et al., 1994). The highly potent opiate fentanyl has been formulated for transdermal delivery via a subcutaneous patch (Duragesic) that provides extended pain relief. It has also been formulated into a flavored lozenge on a handle (Actiq) for oral transmucosal administration, which allows it to be rapidly absorbed and provides better pain control for cancer patients. The handle allows the lozenge to be removed from the mouth if excessive opioid effects appear during administration. A patient-controlled system has been developed for the rapid transdermal delivery of fentanyl, which eliminates the need for venous access and complicated programming of pumps. It has been found to provide postsurgical pain relief equivalent to that of a standard IV morphine regimen delivered by a pump (Viscusi et al., 2004).

Contrary to popular belief, patients taking opiates solely to control pain generally do not become addicted, that is, develop an uncontrollable compulsion to use opiates. As noted earlier, this common misconception often results in the patients being undertreated and having to experience unnecessary agony. A more enlightened approach that has come into use involves the patient-controlled approach described earlier. Numerous studies have shown that patients generally maintain their doses at a reasonable level, often using lower amounts of morphine than when it is administered in the traditional fashion, experience more effective pain relief, and decrease their dosage when pain diminishes. Rarely do such patients develop rapid and marked tolerance to, and dependence on, the narcotic; those who do usually are patients who have a history of psychological disturbance or substance abuse (Ferrante, 1996; Melzack, 1990).

In addition to their analgesic properties, opiates, presumably because of activity in the limbic system, also relieve what some call psychological pain—that is, anxieties, feelings of inadequacy, and hostile or aggressive drives—as well as induce extremely pleasant mood states or euphoria in the majority of users. IV administration, or so-called *mainlining*, results in what is subjectively referred to as a "whole-body orgasm" or "rush." Imaging studies in human males indicate that the areas of the brain most active during ejaculation (e.g., the ventral tegmental area [VTA], which is involved in various aspects of reinforcement and motivation) include those most active following heroin injection (Holstege et al., 2003). However, in general, chronic narcotic use severely reduces the user's sex drive and leads to impotence.

Many people who take opiates experience a subjective sense of mental dullness and often report feeling "fuzzy," "confused," "dreamy," or "spacey." They may also assert that they are forgetful, have difficulties attending to an activity or with problem solving, lack concentration, are unable to think, and make mistakes and get into accidents (McCracken & Iverson, 2001). For the recreational user, many of these subjective qualities may be viewed as pleasurable or inconsequential, but for the chronic pain patient, they can be distressing and lead to discontinuation of opiate treatment. More dramatic changes in cognitive functioning, such as delirium, have been observed in opiate-treated patients. Despite the subjective experience of impaired cognition, the existing empirical literature does not indicate that opiates necessarily cause marked deficits in objective measures of cognition (Ersek et al., 2004). Administration of opiates via injection, particularly in patients who have not been exposed to opiates before, likely causes dose-dependent impaired memory, reasoning, and reaction time. However, chronic oral opiate therapy for patients in pain is rarely associated with significant decreases in cognitive functioning—quite likely because the patients develop tolerance to these effects. In some patients, chronic pain itself can cause cognitive disturbances; in these patients, opiate treatment may actually enhance their cognitive functioning.

Actions in the medulla decrease the rate and depth of breathing (respiratory depression—a primary cause of death associated with narcotic use), suppress the cough reflex, and induce vomiting (emesis) and nausea. This last effect generally occurs with the first administration, unless the person is in pain or is lying down, but shows relatively rapid tolerance.

Narcotics have a number of peripheral actions. Most notably, they induce a marked constriction of the pupil, called "pinpoint pupil" or miosis (primarily found with morphine, heroin, and hydromorphone, but not with meperidine), and they slow the movement of the contents of the GI tract, resulting in constipation.

Some drugs that are classified as narcotics have unusual properties that distinguish them from the prototype narcotics like morphine and heroin. Some, like nalorphine and cyclazocine, have an analgesic effect, but they may induce a dysphoric reaction, cause anxiety, or have psychotomimetic effects. These are also capable of blocking the effects of the prototype narcotics. Because these drugs have agonist as well as antagonist properties—depending on the type of opioid receptor—they are often referred to as **mixed agonist–antagonists.** Although these drugs have no psychological dependence liability (e.g., there is an absence of craving for them), if taken chronically, discontinuing their use can precipitate an abstinence syndrome similar to that of other narcotics, indicating that they can induce physical dependence. However, as indicated in Chapter 6, because physical dependence plays a minimal role in motivating drug-seeking behavior, these drugs are viewed as having little or no potential for abuse. Other mixed agonist–antagonist drugs that have the more typical narcotic effects that make them prone to abuse have been synthesized. Pentazocine (Talwin) is such a drug. Nevertheless, they are capable of blocking the effects of prototypic (mu type) narcotics, and in fact, may provoke withdrawal if taken by someone physically dependent on morphine or heroin.

Although the chronic use of narcotics might be expected to lead to significant deterioration in the body, many studies have found no major damage to any organ of the body that is solely due to the presence of a narcotic—even heroin (Brecher, 1972). Most of the damage that is found is due to the poor nutritional practices of addicts, the use of adulterated drugs under nonsterile conditions, the concomitant use of other drugs, and the general lifestyle of the addicts. Also their narcotic use decreases their ability to recognize pain that normally is present when something is pathologically wrong with them, and thus they fail to seek treatment. Their recognition that medical treatment may also reveal their addiction and lead to termination of their drug use may also be a factor in failing to seek treatment. If pure narcotics are taken under sterile conditions and proper nutritional practices are followed, there is little damage to the body. It is possible for chronic exposure to narcotics to permanently alter the body's synthesis or regulation of endorphins and their receptors so that normal psychological processes that are believed to be associated with them, like pain perception, mood, and pleasure, may be affected for the remainder of the person's lifetime.

It has long been observed that opiate addicts have increased susceptibility to infections. Whether this is a result of the addict's lifestyle or a direct result of opioid exposure is not clear, because opiates have been shown to exert detrimental effects on immune functions of the body (Carballo-Dieguez et al., 1994; Weber & Pert, 1989). For example, opiate agonists tend to suppress antibody production, alter the ability of white blood cells to respond to substances that stimulate white blood cell transformation, and decrease the toxicity of other types of natural killer cells. Many of these effects are mediated through opiate receptors in the midbrain. Research with animals has indicated that chronic opiate exposure may also disrupt immune responsiveness indirectly through the increased production of adrenal corticosteroids (by opiate activation of what is called the "hypothalamic–pituitary–adrenal axis"; Freier & Fuchs, 1994). It has been well established that chronic exposure to corticosteroids can have a variety of toxic consequences, one of which is an increase in a person's susceptibility to infection from a variety of bacterial and fungal pathogens (Schimmer & Parker, 1996).

There may be significant damage to a fetus and neonate if a woman is chronically exposed to narcotics during pregnancy (Bauman & Levine, 1986). Newborns of narcotic-dependent women tend to have lower birth weights and be more excitable and irritable than normal babies. Some of these symptoms are probably due to their experiencing narcotic withdrawal at birth. Symptoms that persist for several weeks or months, or longer, may be due to any number of factors. Prior to birth, the developing nervous system of the fetus may be particularly sensitive to the periodic withdrawal that the mother (and the fetus) probably undergoes (Kuwahara & Sparber, 1981). Or there may be alterations in the endorphin systems of the fetus during development. After birth, the mother–infant bonding may be disrupted, inadequate maternal care or nutrition may be provided, and dependent mothers may perform less adaptively in areas of intelligence, personality, and parenting behaviors. For example, a study assessing 2-year-old children born to methadone-using women determined that mother–infant interactions following birth were a factor in their children's developmental outcome, but that methadone exposure alone did not have a negative impact on the developmental measures studied (Bernstein & Hans, 1994).

Opioid Pharmacodynamics

Opiates depress the rate of neuronal firing in most areas of the brain, but some groups of neurons increase their rate of firing, possibly because they are released from the inhibitory control by other neurons whose rate of firing has been directly depressed by opiates (Iversen et al., 2009). Opioid receptors act through g-protein secondary messenger systems to inhibit adenylate cyclase and cyclic AMP (adenosine monophosphate). Activation of opiate receptors on presynaptic axon terminals inhibits the Ca^{++} influx that underlies release of neurotransmitters. At the postsynaptic membrane, their activation hyperpolarizes the membrane by enhancing K^+ flow out of neurons. In some cases these two processes appear to operate independently, and in others they appear to work synergistically to reduce transmission in neuronal pathways, for instance, those underlying pain transmission (Taddese et al., 1995). The euphoria, tranquility, and other mood changes induced by mu and delta opioid agonists have been linked to their ability to indirectly activate dopaminergic systems via stimulation of opioid receptors. Because opioid receptor stimulation generally inhibits neuronal excitability and the release of neurotransmitters, it is unlikely that opiates directly induce the release of dopamine (DA). Rather it appears to be a classic case of activation by way of inhibition. That is, a variety of studies with animals suggest that opioids inhibit gamma-aminobutyric acid (GABA) releasing neurons that normally tonically inhibit the dopaminergic neurons in the VTA, which leads to a surge of DA in the nucleus accumbens and other mesolimbic–mesocortical brain regions (van den Brink & van Ree, 2003). However, the finding that DA antagonists do not consistently prevent the reinforcing effects of opiates in animals suggests that some nondopaminergic mechanism may also play a role in these effects (Reisine & Pasternak, 1996). Kappa receptor agonists exert aversive qualities in animal tests, possibly due to their ability to decrease mesolimbic release of DA in the nucleus accumbens (Mansour et al., 1995).

Tolerance and Dependence on Opiates

After continued use of an opiate, especially if it is taken often and in fairly high doses, the user becomes very tolerant to many of its effects, and cross-tolerance occurs to all of the narcotics, including the endorphins. After several months of heavy use, some users can administer 40 to 50 times the dose that would kill the nontolerant individual. In a study in which rats were trained to self-administer heroin via IV infusions and allowed to administer it 24 hours a day, they increased their heroin intake from under 2 mg/kg/day up to 336 mg/kg/day (a dose that was lethal in drug-naïve rats) within a 29- to 39-day period (Sim-Selley et al., 2000). Tolerance occurs to some but not all effects of narcotics. The rush and euphoria probably show the fastest tolerance, whereas there is little or no tolerance developed to the constipation and pupil constriction.

Many of the mechanisms for inducing tolerance discussed in Chapter 6 have been suggested to be involved in tolerance development to narcotics with chronic exposure (Reisine & Pasternak, 1996; Williams et al., 2001). These include associative, context-dependent processes (instrumental conditioning, Pavlovian conditioning, habituation) and nonassociative processes. Although pharmacokinetic changes have been shown (e.g., a slight elevation in the drug metabolizing enzymes in the liver that could lead to faster metabolic inactivation of opiates), these probably play a minor role in tolerance and none in withdrawal and craving. On the other hand, a wide variety of nonassociative, pharmacodynamic changes in neuronal systems are believed to be responsible for the neuroadaptations that take place with acute and chronic opiate exposure. These can account for both tolerance development as well as withdrawal effects and long-term drug craving.

Some short-term changes that develop during and abate shortly (minutes to hours) after exposure to agonists can be accounted for by opiate receptor internalization (i.e., where the receptors move from the neuronal membrane into the cytoplasm of the neuron and are no longer accessible to agonist binding) or to opioid receptor g-proteins becoming uncoupled from their effectors. Recovery from these can occur quickly by the receptors being reinserted into neuronal membranes or being recoupled with their effectors. Changes that develop slowly and then persist for many hours to days after removal of agonists include down-regulation of opioid receptors, long-term desensitization of receptor to effector coupling, and counter adaptations that take place either within opioid-sensitive neurons or between opioid and nonopioid systems. Each of these in turn has been suggested to be mediated by a number of processes, which differ to some degree depending on the specific opiate agonist.

Brain structures responsible for adaptations in response to chronic opioids may also exhibit forms of synaptic plasticity that are remarkably similar to those observed in areas primarily involved in learning and memory formation, for example, the hippocampus (Williams et al., 2001). Thus it appears that synaptic plasticity initiated by opioids and processes involved in learning and memory (e.g., long-term potentiation and long-term depression) may be linked by common mechanisms. Unfortunately, due to the complex nature of opioid actions, both direct and indirect, as well as the fact that virtually all research in this area is done with nonhumans or with isolated tissues, it is impossible at this time to determine which of these is most relevant for explaining tolerance, withdrawal, and craving that develops in humans with chronic opiate exposure.

For example, although in vitro studies have been fairly consistent in demonstrating opiate receptor down-regulation with chronic opiate exposure, this phenomenon has been more difficult to demonstrate in animals, with up-regulation, down-regulation, or no change in receptor number being observed (Harrison et al., 1998). Furthermore, when down-regulation does occur, the time course does not correspond to the time course of tolerance development.

Opioid receptors belong to the family of inhibitory g-protein–coupled receptors. Both in vitro and in vivo studies have suggested that many of the cellular adaptations underlying tolerance and physical dependence to opiates occur at the level of the signal-transducing g-protein—that is, a desensitization of opiate receptors and a corresponding up-regulation or loss of inhibition of the adenylate cyclase cyclic AMP system (Sim-Selley et al., 2000; Wang & Gintzler, 1995). These phenomena appear to occur at least in part at the level of gene expression (Maldonado et al., 1996). This mechanism may also explain why nonopioid agonists—for example, the α-2-adrenergic agonist clonidine—that also inhibit this secondary messenger system may be effective in reducing the symptoms of opiate withdrawal.

Because opiates inhibit the release of several types of neurotransmitters, the receptors for these neurotransmitters may exhibit adaptation in terms of up-regulation or sensitization, which could also account for some of the physical withdrawal symptoms that occur with opiate use. Research has suggested that continual stimulation of opiate receptors may gradually increase the activity of anti-opioid peptide (e.g., cholecystokinin) systems that counteract opiate effects. These systems could also account for some tolerance and dependence phenomena associated with opiate use (Stinus et al., 1995). Several studies have also demonstrated that a variety of treatments that suppress the immune system significantly reduce the severity of withdrawal signs in morphine-dependent animals (Dougherty et al., 1990). Thus, at least with opiates, it appears that the immune system may play a role in abstinence symptoms.

N-Methyl-D-aspartic acid (NMDA) receptors may also be a factor in the development of opiate tolerance and dependence because antagonists (e.g., MK-801, phencyclidine) at this type of receptor have been shown to reduce morphine analgesia tolerance and withdrawal symptoms but do not affect morphine-induced analgesia (Trujillo & Akil, 1994). Although NMDA receptors are a subtype of glutamate receptor important in mediating several forms of neural and behavioral modifiability—for instance, learning—it appears that pharmacodynamic rather than learning mechanisms are involved in these phenomena.

In addition to these pharmacodynamic processes, learning processes can account for some tolerance and dependence phenomena associated with chronic opiate use (see the discussion in Chapter 6). Due to the disruptive effects of opiates on task-related performance, it is not surprising that individuals may learn compensatory behaviors to these disruptive effects via instrumental conditioning. Learned tolerance may also occur by way of the Pavlovian model, which hypothesizes that environmental cues associated with the drug elicit compensatory conditioned responses (CRs; i.e., CRs that oppose the drug-induced unconditioned responses [URs]; Siegel et al., 2000). However, although some studies indicate that environmental cues associated with the drug effects can be a factor in tolerance to some opiate-induced effects, others suggest that environmental cues can have an additive effect (Eikelboom & Stewart, 1982). Other researchers suggest that the context-specific tolerance attributed to Pavlovian compensatory CRs may be due to simple stimulus habituation, because most attempts to demonstrate specifically the presence of a compensatory response with opiates have generally failed (Tiffany et al., 1983).

As noted in Table 12.1, the symptoms of withdrawal from opiates are essentially opposite of the direct effects of these drugs. The intensity and duration of the abstinence syndrome are directly correlated with the intensity and duration of the particular drug's effects (Figure 12.1). For example, the withdrawal from heroin, which induces rapid and intense effects of short duration, is relatively intense but dissipates within a few days. On the other hand, withdrawal from methadone, which induces gradual and mild effects of long duration, is relatively mild, but the syndrome takes several days to weeks to subside (O'Brien, 2001). For this reason, many opiate addicts find methadone withdrawal to be more disruptive and disturbing than heroin withdrawal.

The opioid withdrawal syndrome can be very unpleasant, consisting of symptoms much like those experienced during a bad case of the flu. It begins 6 to 12 hours after the last dose of a short-acting opiate like heroin and may be delayed up to 72 to 84 hours after a long-lasting opiate (O'Brien, 1996). Several investigators have suggested that many of the physical complaints are really of psychological rather than physical origin, in which case they would be very context-specific (Childress et al., 1986a, 1986b). In fact, in one study the psychological factors of neuroticism and the expected degree of distress were more related to the severity of withdrawal symptoms during methadone detoxification than either the methadone dose or the length of opiate use prior to

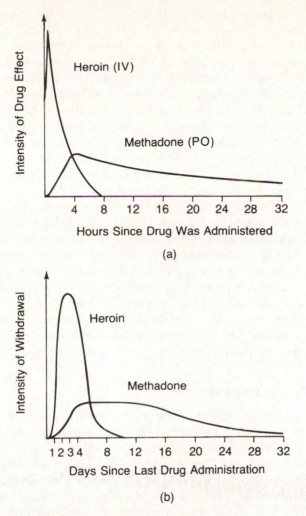

FIGURE 12.1 Intensity–duration relationships for the direct effects *(a)* and abstinence symptoms *(b)* of the narcotics heroin and methadone.

methadone treatment (Phillips et al., 1986). Unlike the withdrawal associated with the sedative–hypnotics and alcohol, opiate withdrawal is rarely life-threatening, unless there are preexisting cardiovascular problems that could result in stroke or heart failure during the heightened sympathetic nervous system activity.

For a number of years, many experts believed that the physical dependence on opiates was the primary motivating factor in continued drug taking. However, study after study has noted that even after the abstinence syndrome has long since dissipated, the vast majority of addicts, if left without further treatment, eventually start taking opiates again. Addicts often report that the craving for opiates may be present even after several months of abstinence. This craving has been attributed to the development of a Pavlovian conditioned drive state, which is triggered any time the person is in a context previously associated with the drug experience. This type of CR is different from the compensatory CR discussed earlier, but functionally it does the same thing; that is, it creates an unpleasant state that can be effectively eliminated by administering a narcotic. Studies demonstrating how the context (e.g., seeing a bag of drugs or a syringe inserted into someone's vein) can trigger conditioned reactions that could subserve the craving subsequently supported these reports (Childress et al., 1986a, 1986b). Also, as noted in Chapter 6, conditioned abstinence symptoms have been shown to develop when organisms undergo physical withdrawal when opiate actions are terminated rapidly in specific contexts (which would occur with a short-acting opiate such as heroin, or if an opiate antagonist were administered). Thus, the prevailing view now is that the psychological dependence on opiates is the far more powerful factor, in the long run, in maintaining opiate drug-taking behavior.

All forms of dependence—primary and secondary psychological, as well as physiological—have been documented to occur with narcotics. Other than these effects, heroin and other narcotics are not particularly damaging as far as the body is concerned. However, they have such primary reinforcing value that people will engage in some maladaptive behaviors (e.g., using dirty syringes and dirty water, exposing themselves to unknown adulterants, or engaging in criminal activities) to obtain them and experience their effects (O'Brien, 1996). (As will be discussed shortly, many of these maladaptive behaviors are due to American culture's legal system regarding access to narcotics.) The high incentive value of narcotics may also decrease the person's desire for engaging in more socially acceptable activities.

Treatment for Opiate Dependence

Although some chronic compulsive opiate users eventually stop of their own accord, for the most part dependence on opiates is so strong that some type of intervention is required in order to overcome it. Most of the psychosocial approaches for dealing with alcoholism have been employed in the treatment of narcotic addiction, such as residential inpatient and outpatient treatment, self-help groups (e.g., Narcotics Anonymous), and therapeutic communities. Their efficacy in achieving abstinence for some period of time is dependent on a multitude of factors such as age, length of opiate use, educational and occupational level, use of alcohol or other drugs of abuse, comorbidity with other mental disorders, and so on (Llorente del Pozo et al., 1998). However, regardless of their success in achieving abstinence, narcotic addicts inevitably experience cravings for narcotics that are a major factor in relapse. Thus approaches for dealing with these cravings have been extensively explored.

The finding that abstinent opiate abusers (who completed a 30-day treatment program in a therapeutic community setting) experienced intense drug craving and withdrawal symptoms when exposed to drug-related stimuli has led to attempts to eliminate these responses through the process of extinction. This process basically involves exposing the person to the conditioned stimuli that provoke the craving without allowing the person to experience the drug (i.e., the unconditioned stimulus). This has been found to virtually eliminate the conditioned craving and withdrawal symptoms within 20-hour-long treatment sessions (Childress et al., 1986a). How long these reductions last and how well they generalize to other drug-related stimuli after the patients' discharge remain to be determined.

Some of the more common treatments for narcotic addicts involve the use of drugs that either block narcotic effects or are substitute narcotics with less disruptive effects than those on which the person is dependent (van den Brink & van Ree, 2003). One of the first drug treatments for narcotic dependence involved the administration of narcotic antagonists, thereby theoretically breaking up the relationship between the drug-taking behavior and the reinforcing effects of these drugs. Initially, nalorphine and cyclazocine were used. Although these drugs did block the effects of heroin and morphine, they had a number of properties that prevented them from being practical tools in the treatment of narcotic dependence. These drugs sometimes induced dysphoric side effects, and taken chronically, they were capable of inducing a mild physical dependence. The introduction of the pure narcotic antagonist naloxone (Narcan) eliminated these problems because it induced neither dysphoria nor physical dependence. The disadvantages of naloxone were its short duration and its ineffectiveness when taken orally. These problems were surmounted with the subsequent development of naltrexone (Trexan, now marketed as ReVia), which is not only more effective when taken orally but also has opiate-blocking actions for up to 3 days, thus eliminating the need for several daily administrations.

Although the use of pure opiate antagonists like naltrexone in the treatment of opiate abuse and dependence sounds great in theory, it is not an approach that is likely to be very effective in the treatment of most compulsive opiate users because these drugs do not deal with the major motivating factor behind the narcotic use; that is, they do not eliminate the psychological craving for narcotics (van den Brink & van Ree, 2003). Therefore, without any further intervention, these individuals will probably stop taking the antagonist and go back to taking narcotics. In addition, unlike the opiate agonist methadone, which can be administered at any stage of addiction, treatment with opiate antagonists such as naltrexone typically would not begin until after the addict has been detoxified and all signs of abstinence have dissipated because these drugs would induce a rapid onset of abstinence symptoms that could be quite severe. (However, see the discussion of ultrarapid opioid detoxification on p. 316.) It is argued that these drugs would be useful only in highly motivated individuals. These concerns have been supported by a study indicating that only 27% of naltrexone-maintained narcotic addicts remained in treatment for the 12-week observation period, whereas 87% of methadone-maintained addicts remained in treatment (Osborn et al., 1986). However, opiate-addicted professionals who routinely have ready access to opiates (e.g., doctors, nurses, pharmacists) make excellent candidates for this treatment approach (O'Brien, 2001). A depot form of naltrexone may also be used in the treatment of opiate dependence to enhance compliance to the treatment regimen, because it needs to be administered only once a month.

Perhaps one of the most successful drug treatments for narcotic dependence is not really a treatment at all, in that it involves substituting one narcotic for another, with the substitute narcotic having more socially acceptable qualities and fewer disruptive effects on the individual. The first of these narcotics to be employed was methadone (Dolophine), a synthetic narcotic developed in Nazi Germany during World War II. Although it is a very effective analgesic, it did not come into use in the United States until the late 1960s.

The way in which methadone came into use for the treatment of narcotic dependence is an interesting story (Dole & Nyswander, 1976). It came about somewhat by accident through the combined efforts of Vincent Dole, a specialist in metabolic disorders, and Marie Nyswander, a psychiatrist who specialized in the treatment of narcotic addicts. Dole was interested in establishing whether narcotic addicts had a metabolic disorder that resulted in their craving for narcotics, and Nyswander was interested in pursuing alternatives to the multiple approaches to the treatment of addiction that were being used in the 1960s, and that almost always failed.

To pursue the metabolism research, a few heroin addicts were first maintained on morphine. This required several injections per day to keep the patients in a generally lethargic and inactive state. For detoxification purposes, the patients were given methadone, which was known to produce a more protracted, but less intense, withdrawal. However, rather than immediately beginning to decrease the dose of methadone, the patients were maintained on rather high doses so that the metabolic studies could be repeated with methadone. Although the metabolic research did not turn up anything notable, the researchers noticed a number of other developments in their patients. First, the patients' craving for narcotics was eliminated, and second, they began to engage in socially relevant activities. Follow-ups with more patients revealed other developments. There was a dramatic decrease in their heroin use and drug-related crimes, and an increase in their ability to function in the community. Patients began attending school, receiving passing grades, maintaining a family, and working at a job.

In summary, Dole and Nyswander concluded that, despite most of their patients' preexisting disadvantages of low socioeconomic levels, poor education, prison records, and years of addiction, the majority of those individuals maintained on methadone became self-supporting, law-abiding citizens. Furthermore, the longer they were maintained on methadone, the more probable this scenario became. Since that report, a large number of studies have led to essentially the same conclusion—that is, of all treatments for heroin dependence, methadone maintenance treatment has the most evidence of benefit in terms of reducing heroin use, as well as other illicit drug use, mortality, criminal activity, and risk of HIV infection, and of improving social rehabilitation (Bertschy, 1995; Fairbank et al., 1993; Taj et al., 1995; Wodak, 1994).

The primary advantages of methadone over other narcotics are that it is readily and reliably absorbed orally and has a relatively long duration of action—approximately 24 hours. These characteristics eliminate the hazards of the injection method, and although it has some mood-elevating effects, methadone induces a more gradual and stable effect on the individual than heroin or morphine does. Tolerance develops to methadone, and through cross-tolerance, methadone blocks the effects of other narcotics unless they are taken in very high (and expensive) amounts. Because it is active at opiate receptors, it greatly reduces the craving for narcotics generally experienced by addicts and reduces their motivation for returning to their original drug-taking behavior (van den Brink & van Ree, 2003). The side effects of methadone—namely, constipation and impotence—are qualitatively the same as those of other narcotics.

Using sufficiently high daily doses of methadone (optimally using plasma methadone concentrations as a guide) is a critical factor in its efficacy (Banys et al., 1994; Caplehorn et al., 1993; Hartel et al., 1995; Kell, 1995). Higher methadone dosages may be necessary in individuals with higher degrees of psychopathological symptoms, regardless of their heroin-use history (Maremmani et al., 1993). Also, exposure to high-quality medical and psychosocial services, clear orientation toward social rehabilitation and treatment retention (to allow a sufficient duration of treatment), and a slow detoxification regimen of well-stabilized patients are all factors contributing to better efficacy with methadone treatment (Bertschy, 1995; Wodak, 1994).

Methadone is used either as a maintenance drug, much as insulin is used by diabetics, or as a drug that can be administered in smaller and smaller doses to gradually reduce the addict's physical dependence on narcotics. Most studies indicate that the former approach is more satisfactory in decreasing illicit narcotic use. Further decreases in illicit drug use can be obtained if the dose of methadone is made contingent on drug-free urinalysis; for example, when the urine is drug-free, the client receives a higher dose of methadone (Stitzer et al., 1986; Taj et al., 1995).

Although methadone does decrease the use of illicit narcotics, it does not eliminate their use in a large portion of addicts. They often get into methadone treatment, gradually reducing the dose until their tolerance to narcotics decreases, and then return to their original drug-taking activities. Addicts under methadone are also more likely to have higher employment rates than nontreated addicts and are less likely to engage in criminal activities. However, access to methadone does not eliminate criminal behavior entirely, because most addicts in the United States eventually develop a number of skills, such as selling drugs and stealing, that may still be useful to them, even though those skills may no longer be needed for obtaining narcotics.

The scientific data are substantial in showing that methadone therapy helps control illicit drug use and prevent associated diseases such as AIDS. In France, where methadone and buprenorphine (discussed later) became widely used in the maintenance treatment of heroin addicts in the mid-1990s, the incidence of fatal heroin overdoses decreased 75% in a 4-year period (Lepere et al., 2001). Unfortunately, in the United States methadone has been available only under strict federal and state laws and licensing procedures that control dosage. In 1997, an expert panel organized by the National Institutes of Health recommended that officials relax these controls and encourage more physicians to become more involved in treating the nation's estimated 600,000 opiate addicts (NIH, 1999). It is still not clear whether public officials have paid much attention to this recommendation.

The success of methadone has led to the development and evaluation of other opiate drugs in narcotic addiction with even more favorable qualities. These drugs include LAAM (levo-α-acetyl-methadol; Orlamm) and buprenorphine (Suboxone, Subutex). LAAM is a narcotic agonist similar to methadone, and buprenorphine is a mixed opiate agonist–antagonist (van den Brink & van Ree, 2003). Both of these have even longer durations of action than methadone. Thus, they induce a much more stable effect on mood and psychological processes and induce a very mild withdrawal when drug administration is terminated. The efficacy of both of these drugs has been shown to be comparable to that of methadone in terms of suppressing addicts' use of heroin, effectiveness in withdrawal detoxification, blocking the effects of other opiates, and satisfying the addicts' craving for opiates (Fischer et al., 1999; Prendergast et al., 1995; Schottenfeld et al., 1997). They have advantages over methadone specifically with regard to requiring only one to three doses weekly, possible cost savings, and possible improved clinic–community relations.

LAAM was approved for the management of opiate dependence in 1995, but its manufacturer discontinued its sale and distribution in 2003 due to increasing reports of severe cardiac-related adverse events associated with its use and the availability of less toxic treatment alternatives that have been approved for the same purpose, such as Subutex and Suboxone. Subutex contains only buprenorphine and is recommended for use during the first few days of treatment, whereas Suboxone also contains naloxone to guard against misuse and is recommended for use during the maintenance phase of treatment. Subutex and Suboxone are the first narcotic drugs available for the treatment of opiate dependence that can be prescribed in a physician's office, which will allow more patients the opportunity to access treatment. Methadone can be dispensed only in clinics that specialize in addiction treatment. Also, as patients progress in therapy, their doctors may write a prescription for a take-home supply of the medication. Only qualified physicians with an identification number required by the Drug Enforcement Administration (DEA) will be able to start in-office treatment and provide prescriptions for ongoing medication.

One of the advantages of buprenorphine over other opiates is the absence of dangerous respiratory depression—even at doses 100 times those necessary for inducing analgesia. Preliminary studies have found buprenorphine to be acceptable to heroin addicts who will not accept methadone maintenance treatment, either because they view methadone as "just another addicting drug" with less desirable effects than heroin or have experienced methadone effects as aversive (Resnick et al., 1992). Buprenorphine maintenance treatment in opiate-dependent pregnant women has also shown to be well accepted by them, and is associated with a low incidence of neonatal abstinence syndrome (Fischer et al., 2000). Because of preclinical studies finding that buprenorphine reduced cocaine self-administration in non–opiate-dependent animals, researchers have suggested that buprenorphine might have some specific additional value in reducing cocaine use in opiate addicts. However, studies with humans have not shown buprenorphine to be particularly effective—that is, compared with methadone—in this regard (Compton et al., 1995; Schottenfeld et al., 1997).

One potential problem with the use of long-acting narcotics is that, after a history of taking other narcotics daily or several times daily, addicts may not feel subjectively that the longer-acting substance is actually working. Therefore, they may feel some psychological discomfort with a compound that needs to be taken only once or twice a week. On the other hand, research with LAAM indicated that many opiate addicts preferred LAAM over methadone because they needed to attend a clinic less frequently, experienced fewer side effects, and felt that LAAM had a better maintenance effect (Tennant et al., 1986).

With the discovery of the endogenous opioid peptides, there was hope that one or more of these might be usefully employed as a nonaddicting substitute for opiates. Unfortunately, the duration of effect of these peptides proved to be short because they are rapidly inactivated in the body by enzymes. Furthermore, tolerance occurs with chronic endorphin or enkephalin exposure, and withdrawal may occur when administration ceases (Iversen et al., 2009).

Nonopiate α-2-adrenoceptor agonists, for example, clonidine, have been found to significantly alleviate opiate withdrawal without inducing euphoria (Amato et al., 2004). Detoxification with clonidine is generally faster but less effective than methadone in terms of retention in treatment, relapse rate, and side effects. Its efficacy appears to be due to its ability to reduce noradrenergic activity within the locus coeruleus, a part of the reticular activating system. It projects extensively to limbic regions and autonomic centers. Firing rates and norepinephrine release from locus coeruleus neurons tend to be inhibited by opiates initially, but these effects show tolerance with repeated opiate use. When opiate use ceases, locus coeruleus cells become hyperactive. Clonidine significantly reduces this hyperactivity via its actions at these cells' autoreceptors; that is, it activates the inhibitory feedback system regulating norepinephrine synthesis and release. Although facilitating opiate detoxification, clonidine is not a drug likely to be beneficial in reducing the psychological cravings for opiates, perhaps because these feelings are more directly tied to opiate receptor activity. Furthermore, clonidine is only effective in suppressing withdrawal symptoms specifically associated with heightened activity in the locus coeruleus of the CNS and the sympathetic nervous system (both are heavily noradrenergic). Anxiety, restlessness, insomnia, and muscular aches are suppressed only minimally.

As discussed in previous chapters, the hallucinogenic alkaloid ibogaine has been claimed to possess broad-spectrum antiaddictive properties. In some, but not all, studies with nonhumans it has been shown to reduce self-administration of morphine, to inhibit morphine-induced locomotor activity, and to inhibit at least some components of the morphine withdrawal syndrome (Popik et al., 1995). Anecdotal and case reports with humans have also suggested that ibogaine can decrease the intensity and duration of withdrawal in opiate addicts and reduce opiate craving (Sheppard, 1994). In several instances, the effects appeared to last several days or even weeks. However, as indicated in Chapters 7 and 13, ibogaine has a number of undesirable qualities that make it unlikely to be accepted by authorities for use in opiate dependence, and some of its derivatives are being explored for this purpose.

Many users of narcotics never seek treatment. Those who do not are less likely to have severe non–drug-related problems (e.g., employment, legal, or psychiatric problems) than those who do (Corty & Ball, 1986). Many of those who do not seek treatment may eventually become abstinent on their own—a process called "maturing out." Although maturing out tends to be a time-related phenomenon, it is less likely to occur in addicts who are deeply involved in crime and drug dealing (Brecht et al., 1987).

THE "OVERDOSE" PHENOMENON

Perhaps one of the more notable properties of narcotics in the eyes of the general public is their lethality. Reports occur periodically in the mass media describing what appears to be a death induced by an overdose of a narcotic. However, there is little scientific evidence that the vast majority of these deaths are actually due to narcotic overdose. An excellent discussion of this phenomenon was presented in 1972 (Brecher, 1972), but remarkably little has been done to advance our knowledge of it since then. First of all, although respiratory depression and death do occur at high doses of narcotics, such doses are much higher than those that addicts are likely to use. We don't know what the minimum lethal dose of pure heroin is in humans, but in normal, pain-free adults, there is no serious toxicity with less than 30 mg of morphine administered via injection (O'Brien, 2001), and it takes approximately 7 mg/kg of morphine to kill nontolerant baboons (Brecher, 1972). Assuming that humans are physiologically similar to baboons and that heroin is three times more potent than morphine, it would take somewhere between 10 and 160 mg of heroin administered intravenously to kill the average nontolerant human. To the vast majority of addicts, that is a lot of heroin to be administered at one time. However, because of the tremendous variation in actual concentration of heroin in illicit samples, it is possible for one to overdose if one were "unlucky" enough to administer a particularly pure amount—or to administer what one thinks is heroin but is instead some much more potent opiate like fentanyl. Furthermore, addicts generally have developed tolerance to narcotics. Second, there is little evidence from autopsies of addicts who supposedly have died from narcotics that an excessive amount of narcotic was in the body. Nor is there clear evidence that the concentration of heroin found in the syringe or supplies used by the person was particularly high. Third, addicts often share a supply of heroin, but only one may die from the injection. Finally, in some cases, death is so rapid that the needle is still in the arm of the deceased, whereas sufficient respiratory depression to cause death with narcotics generally occurs after several minutes or hours.

If the majority of deaths associated with illicit narcotics are not due to excessive amounts of narcotics, then to what can these deaths be attributed? One possibility is that they are due to an interaction between an opiate and another drug (a phenomenon common to a wide variety of drug-related deaths). The fact is, it is a rare narcotic user who uses only narcotics. Alcohol use is quite abundant. Mixing a narcotic with cocaine (commonly called a "speedball") or with a drug that has sedative–hypnotic properties (like Valium) is also common. Such drug mixtures can have synergistic effects or interact in ways still not understood. The deaths of Janis Joplin, Jimi Hendrix, and Elvis Presley, as well as many other well-known celebrity narcotic-related deaths, probably occurred in this fashion. Although Elvis's autopsy did not reveal large concentrations of any particular drug, traces of a dozen or so psychoactive substances, including opiates, were found in his body. John Belushi died following an injection of heroin and cocaine, administered after a night of heavy drinking.

The adulterants mixed with illicit narcotics may also be a factor. There is an interesting direct correlation between death rates associated with heroin use and the percentage of quinine mixed with heroin. Adding quinine to heroin was first done in the 1930s as a way of preventing malaria, but it was soon discovered to be an effective way of disguising the actual purity of heroin because of its taste and because it acted synergistically with heroin. Since the 1930s, as adding quinine to heroin became more common, the death rates associated with heroin use increased dramatically. It is also possible that many narcotic-related deaths are due to *anaphylactic shock*—an immediate, transient kind of extreme allergic reaction characterized by contraction of smooth muscle and dilation of capillaries resulting from the release of histamine and other pharmacologically active substances (Gutstein & Akil, 2001). Such a reaction could result in rapid pulmonary edema (a filling of the lungs with fluid) and asphyxiation, which are not uncommon among narcotic-related deaths. The Pavlovian conditioning model of tolerance has even been proposed as a factor (Siegel et al., 2000). That is, an addict may inject a narcotic—perhaps one that is purer than usual—in a novel environment. In such an environment, compensatory CRs normally elicited by the environment associated with the drug would not be present to counteract the drug's URs. In effect, much of the tolerance to the drug would be lost, and the person could die.

Whatever the case, there are a multitude of factors, other than simply an overdose of narcotics, that may contribute to deaths associated with their use. For example, of the almost 2,000 narcotic-related deaths in New York City in 1986, approximately 12% were regarded as general overdose deaths. The remainder were attributed to AIDS (45%) and other diseases resulting from the addicts' lifestyles (e.g., pneumonia, liver damage, cardiovascular complications, tuberculosis; Stoneburner et al., 1988).

In cases of true pure opiate overdoses, which would be evidenced by the triad of coma, pinpoint pupils, and depressed respiration, an injection of naloxone rapidly reverses these symptoms—although too high a dose of naloxone can precipitate severe withdrawal and induce cardiac arrhythmias and pulmonary edema (Reisine & Pasternak, 1996). Based on evidence that patients with severe pain may tolerate larger doses of morphine, it is likely that exposure to a painful stimulus may have a stimulatory effect and temporarily reverse the respiratory depression induced by opiate overdose.

LEGAL FACTORS IN THE NARCOTICS PROBLEM

It seems appropriate at this point to discuss briefly the legal system's contribution to the present problem with narcotics in the United States. Up until the early 1900s, it was possible to obtain any drug available over the counter for a relatively small price. A wide variety of tonics and medicines contained unknown mixtures of alcohol, opium, cocaine, and other psychoactive substances. We can assume that, with such easy access to these mixtures, dependence was widespread. However, we can also assume that the dependence was rather mild, because the common route of administration was oral. With the recognition of increasing dependence associated with these drugs, a number of governments around the world became concerned about the ramifications of this problem. In 1914, the United States legislated the Harrison Narcotics Tax Act to deal with it. In essence, it classified a number of drugs as narcotics (curiously, cocaine was among these) and made it illegal for them to be sold except by prescription obtained from a physician, who could only prescribe them during the course of professional practice. Initially, this restriction presented no problem to those dependent on opium or heroin, because they simply went to their local doctor for a prescription. However, before long, some law officials began prosecuting physicians for prescribing narcotics to dependent persons, because addiction was not viewed as a disease, and therefore, prescribing narcotics solely to alleviate the symptoms of withdrawal was not an acceptable medical practice. Physicians soon stopped prescribing narcotics to their addicted patients.

Immediately, some enterprising individuals, recognizing the ready market for narcotics, set up shop and started dispensing narcotic drugs—at somewhat inflated prices. The law's attempts to prosecute these individuals, as well as to legislate more severe penalties for the sale and possession of narcotics, started a vicious cycle that escalated for more than a half century.

With higher and higher prices for narcotics, individuals turned to crime to support their habits. Little money went for proper nutrients, and the physical health of the average addict began to decline. More and more misrepresentation of drugs, in terms of quantity, quality, and type of drug, and the addition of adulterants led to increased toxicity and lethality in the addicted population.

The danger of adulteration was well illustrated in the 1980s by the discovery that the sloppy laboratory practices of a man attempting to synthesize analogues of the narcotic meperidine for street sale in northern California resulted in the chemical 1-methyl-4-phenyl-1,2,5,6-tetrahydro-pyridine (MPTP; Lewin, 1984). The substance has been found to metabolize in the brain into a compound that kills midbrain dopaminergic cells whose axons project to neurons in the basal ganglia. This effect produces clinical symptoms essentially identical to those of Parkinson's disease. This phenomenon was first described in 1979 in the case of a 23-year-old graduate student who had developed a parkinsonian-like condition after injecting a meperidine-like drug that he had synthesized in his own laboratory. In taking shortcuts in his manufacturing process, the student contaminated his chosen product with MPTP. Unfortunately, the student was not the only one who used the adulterated substance, and several dozen young users of this synthetic opiate succumbed to a similar fate—a lifetime (which could be quite short) of tremors, partial or complete paralysis, and abnormal posture. Unfortunately, these symptoms can only be temporarily reversed with the drug most commonly used in the treatment of Parkinson's disease (L-DOPA [L-dihydroxyphenylalanine]), and they get worse with time.

Low availability of narcotics also eventually led to the more dangerous IV method of administration. Problems with the injection procedure were compounded by the failure to protect against infectious diseases, in part because of lack of education. Finally, vigorous enforcement of narcotics laws in the United States allowed organized crime to strengthen itself with the immense profits associated with narcotic sales. That is, the greater the penalties for sale, the higher the price and the greater the profit from selling. This phenomenon persists to this day. The basic problem is that the majority of the money spent to buy illicit drugs like heroin or cocaine goes to the bottom level of the market—to the street and near-street sellers. Only a small portion of the final price goes to the production and smuggling sector. As a result, seizures of big drug shipments, which may cost the government on the order of $1 million per drug seizure, have almost no impact on buyers and thus no impact on demand or on the huge profits to be made (Marshall, 1988).

In essence, what started out as an effort to protect consumers from becoming mildly dependent on relatively nontoxic substances resulted in their becoming strongly dependent on very toxic and lethal substances. The question many of us ask is: Would we have been better off to have left well enough alone? Although there is no way of knowing the answer to this question as far as the United States is concerned, another "experiment," conducted in Great Britain at about the same time, leads many to answer yes to the question, or at least suggests that an alternative route might have been more productive.

Around the time the United States legislated the Harrison Act, Great Britain was instituting its own similar legislation. However, it viewed dependence from a less moralistic perspective, as something to be treated. Thus, narcotic addicts in Great Britain were able to obtain heroin and other narcotics by prescription from their family physicians, while the law attempted to keep illicit narcotics out of the hands of nonaddicts. Thus, illicit trade in narcotics was minimized and the population of addicts was maintained at a fairly constant level until the 1960s. Unfortunately, some physicians were rather lackadaisical in their prescription practices, and more narcotics were being prescribed than was necessary to maintain just the addicted population (Spear, 1994). This excessive prescribing led to a change in policy in 1968, whereby only specifically licensed physicians are allowed to prescribe heroin, some other abused opiates, and cocaine to addicts on a maintenance basis (Power, 1994). In addition, until 1996 addicts treated by these physicians had to be reported to what is called the Home Office (Hall et al., 2000). Most of these physicians are affiliated with special drug treatment centers (called Drug Dependence Units), although any physician can apply for a license to write prescriptions for these drugs for their addicted patients (Connell & Strang, 1994). Over the past 3 decades, there has been a trend in Great Britain to emphasize (push?) oral methadone as the most appropriate drug treatment for heroin addiction, and any medical physician in the United Kingdom is permitted to prescribe methadone for the purpose of treating opiate dependence. Due to a variety of reasons (e.g., hassles with bureaucracy, not wanting to be identified by the government, insufficient amounts of opiates prescribed), the true addict population is approximately 2 to 10 times the actual number reported.

Great Britain's policy with respect to narcotic addiction is not a panacea. Addicts still die of narcotic-related causes and suffer infectious diseases because of nonsterile injection procedures (Hall et al., 2000). There is still a black market trade in narcotics, and the rate of addiction in Great Britain is still growing (Fountain et al., 2000). In any event, the problems with narcotics in Great Britain appear to be of a lower magnitude than those in the United States, and the lower incidence of criminal activities by addicts who do not need much money to obtain clean supplies of narcotics definitely benefits the general population.

OPIATE ANTAGONISTS: POTENTIAL USES

For over 2 decades, the relatively pure opioid receptor antagonists naloxone and naltrexone have been the mainstays of research and treatments associated with the opioids and their receptors. Naloxone is fast acting, with a short duration of action (less than 4 hours), and is poorly absorbed when taken orally. Naltrexone is more potent than naloxone and is quite effective when taken orally, and its duration of opiate-blocking action is between 24 and 48 hours. Nalmefene (Revex) is a pure opiate antagonist that is structurally similar to naloxone and naltrexone. Compared with naloxone, nalmefene is more potent in blocking opiate receptors, more readily absorbed when taken orally, acts as quickly, and lasts somewhat longer. However, it is not clear whether it has any other particular properties that distinguish it from naloxone and naltrexone.

These opioid antagonists have a variety of clinical uses, and numerous other uses have been suggested for them. Naloxone and nalmefene are used primarily for their ability to reverse the effects of narcotics in acute overdose cases. From a harm-reduction perspective, one area in which naloxone would be particularly useful is in preventing overdoses associated with illicit narcotic use. A typical opiate-related overdose fatality occurs in a longtime heroin user who uses heroin after a period of abstinence and also uses alcohol or other drugs. Most overdoses occur with other people around, but because of fear of police, they fail to call for help. Unfortunately a survey conducted in Great Britain found that although the majority of injecting drug abusers had experienced or witnessed at least one drug overdose (mostly involving opiates), with perhaps a third witnessing a fatal overdose, only 35% were aware of the existence and effects of naloxone (Strang et al., 1999). The results suggested that at least two-thirds of witnessed overdose fatalities could be prevented by administration of home-based supplies of naloxone. Naloxone may also be used as a diagnostic tool for assessing the actual degree of physical dependence in opiate-abusing individuals (e.g., by administering a low, fixed dose of naloxone that induces withdrawal symptoms), to determine the appropriate dose of methadone for detoxification or maintenance purposes. Naltrexone and nalmefene are being used as a prophylactic measure in opiate addicts who have terminated their opiate use but who are concerned that they may relapse. Should they do so and administer a narcotic such as heroin, they are aware that they would not experience any of the effects and that it would be a waste of money.

Naloxone may also be used to reduce the illicit use of prescription opiates. Some opiates that are normally taken orally for their analgesic effects often are converted for illicit use into injectable form for IV administration. This enhances the opiate's euphoric properties as well as its dependence liability. However, if naloxone is added to the tablet, injecting the combination is ineffective. That is, naloxone, which in small amounts is ineffective orally, does not reduce an opiate's effectiveness if taken orally. But when the combination is injected, sufficient amounts of naloxone get into the brain to effectively block the opiate's action. This significantly reduces its likelihood of being channeled into illicit use. Such an approach has been taken with the opiate analgesic pentazocine (Talwin Nx) and buprenorphine (Suboxone) used in the treatment of opiate addiction. A derivative of naltrexone, methylnaltrexone, was assessed in clinical trials in patients undergoing opioid treatment for postoperative or chronic pain to evaluate its effectiveness in reducing the peripheral side effects of opiates, for example, constipation, which are associated with activation of mu opioid receptors outside the CNS (Kurz & Sessler, 2003). Methylnaltrexone blocks these receptors but is unable to cross the BBB and interfere with the analgesic effects of opioids or precipitate withdrawal in nonsurgical patients receiving opioids for chronic pain. Moreover, a slow-release naltrexone preparation (Vivitrol) was approved by the Food and Drug Administration in 2010.

Naltrexone is a key ingredient in a technique that has gained considerable popularity—called ultrarapid opioid detoxification—in which opiate-dependent patients are anaesthetized or heavily sedated and exposed to high, repetitive doses of nalmefene, naloxone, or naltrexone for 24 to 48 hours (Gowing et al., 2002). The patients undergo physiological withdrawal but are not consciously aware of it. Maintenance treatment with naltrexone is provided following this rapid detoxification. Proponents claim that a significant proportion of these patients remain abstinent after completion of the treatment. However, there have been some drawbacks to this approach. The treatment is more expensive than conventional procedures because of the additional procedures involved; carries more risks, such as pulmonary and renal failure and cardiovascular complications; and increases the risk of overdose should the patient return to opiate use (Pfab et al., 1999). Finally, several deaths have been attributed to this procedure. Whether relapse rates are significantly different with this technique than with more traditional approaches remains to be determined, for although the physical withdrawal from opiates is a factor in maintaining opiate dependence, it is the psychological components to dependence that are the key factors in relapse.

Because opiates have some neuropharmacological actions that are shared with several other drugs of abuse (e.g., cocaine, amphetamine, alcohol, nicotine), a number of studies have attempted to determine whether opiate antagonists may be useful in the treatment of other drug addictions. As discussed in Chapter 10, the most promising results have been in the area of alcoholism treatment.

Opioid antagonists may have a variety of other potential uses outside the scope of drug dependence. With the discovery of a variety of endogenous opioid peptides in the body, there has been much speculation as to their function. Obviously, one of these is in the area of pain regulation, but there are many other areas. It has been speculated that endogenous opioids are involved in a variety of psychopathological conditions, including autism, self-injurious behavior, schizophrenia, obsessive–compulsive disorders, eating disorders such as bulimia, sleep apnea syndrome (disruptions in breathing possibly associated with sudden infant death syndrome), and attention deficit disorders.

As discussed in this book, numerous studies have explored the potential involvement of opioids in these disorders and the use of opioid antagonists in reducing the symptoms of these disorders, unfortunately with very limited success. Although positive reports have frequently been made, failures to replicate are quite common. In many cases, this may be due to initial investigations being done without appropriate controls (e.g., use of the double-blind procedure in which neither the person receiving the drug nor the person measuring the effects is aware of the actual drug given), or small sample sizes. In some studies noting positive effects, the test procedures themselves may have been stressful. It has now been established that acute stressors may activate endorphin systems. If the test procedures were sufficiently stressful to activate endorphin activity and exacerbate the pathological symptoms being measured, then it would appear that the symptoms would be reduced if an opiate antagonist were administered. In other cases, the heterogeneity of the factors causing similar symptoms may lead to discrepant findings. Finally, the degree to which opioid antagonists have therapeutic effects may depend on whether endogenous opioids are active all the time in a particular disorder or only under specific conditions, if indeed they are involved at all. Clearly, much work remains to be done in this area before we will have any definitive answers regarding the efficacy of opiate antagonists in these disorders.

Websites for Further Information

Sites providing information on the social ramifications of opium use:

> http://www.gober.net/victorian/reports/opium.html (in nineteenth-century England)
>
> http://www.druglibrary.org/schaffer/heroin/opichin1.html (in China, 1700–1860)

Site covering many aspects of heroin, along with a number of links (images, chemistry, law):

> http://www.erowid.org/chemicals/heroin/heroin.shtml

Information on methadone and the treatment of opiate dependence, along with a number of links:

> http://www.erowid.org/chemicals/methadone/methadone.shtml

Site providing a brief, but fascinating, history of opiates:

> http://www.opioids.com/timeline

CHAPTER

13

Dissociative Anesthetics, Psychedelics, and Hallucinogens

What does one call a class of drugs taken primarily because of their ability to elicit in normal individuals such alterations as visual or auditory hallucinations, depersonalization, perceptual disturbances, and disturbances of thought processes at doses that exert minimal changes in other bodily functions? Before we answer this question, note that both the quantitative and the qualitative effects of these drugs are heavily dependent on the dose. Lower doses may alter mood and thought content with minimal sensory disturbances; somewhat higher doses may induce clear perceptual distortions without inducing true hallucinations (strongly experienced false perceptions that have a compulsive sense of the reality of the object but that have no relevant or adequate stimuli for their induction); and higher doses may actually induce true hallucinations. Common examples of such drugs with which you may be familiar are LSD (lysergic acid diethylamide), mescaline, and marijuana.

Because hallucinations are one of the more striking symptoms associated with such drugs, many authors commonly refer to this class of drugs as **hallucinogens.** Others prefer to use the term **psychotomimetic** (literally psychosis-mimicking) or **psychotogenic** (for psychosis-generating) because these drugs induce actual hallucinations only at the higher doses, whereas with the lower doses some of the fundamental characteristics of psychosis are still evidenced (such as gross distortion or disorganization of a person's mental capacity, affective response, and capacity to recognize reality, communicate, and relate to others). However, these two terms are also somewhat inappropriate. First, numerous drugs referred to in this fashion rarely induce a condition that mimics the types of psychoses naturally found in humans—namely, schizophrenia and mania. Second, doses of some drugs that do mimic natural psychotic states, such as large doses of cocaine and amphetamine, are not voluntarily taken for this expressed purpose. The term **psychedelic** (for mind-expanding, -manifesting, -clarifying, or -revealing) has also been applied to these drugs, but the functional meaning of this term is also unclear. Philosophers and psychologists have grappled for years with the question of what the mind is or what it means. So what do we mean when we say it is expanded? Perhaps a new term should be coined for these drugs, but I will not be coining a new one here. For the purposes of this chapter, I will refer to them as psychotomimetic/psychedelic/hallucinogenic substances, or simply P/P/Hs. (See Jaffe, 1985, for further discussion of this issue.)

Many have been intrigued by the P/P/Hs for a variety of reasons. For centuries, a variety of aboriginal groups have used P/P/H-containing plants in their rituals and ceremonies for healing and sacramental purposes and to promote group cohesiveness, spirituality, and mystical experiences—for example, the peyote (mescaline) sessions of the Native American Church, yage or hoasca (harmine) ceremonies of South American Amazon Indians, ingestion of sacred mushrooms (psilocybin) by a number of Indian tribes in Mexico, or the iboga (ibogaine) rites of some tribes in Central-West Africa (Dobkin de Rios, 1996; Grof, 1980). In many cases, these practices are still conducted today, with evidence that they may contribute to reduction in psychopathological characteristics of the participants (Grob et al., 1996). Over the past 50 years, a number of conventional psychotherapists have proposed the use of P/P/Hs as adjuncts in the treatment of a variety of mental disorders. Many scientists have utilized a variety of P/P/Hs as potential tools for understanding the biochemical bases of psychoses. And, of course, our society in general is so deeply concerned over their recreational use, abuse, and potential toxicity that we have raised most of them to our highest official status of controlled substance—Schedule I.

SOME GENERAL CHARACTERISTICS OF P/P/Hs

Although P/P/Hs are used occasionally in a clinical context, the preponderant use of these substances is recreational. There are four major classes of P/P/Hs:

1. The **monoamine-related substances,** whose molecular structures and biochemical activity suggest that their effects are mediated by alterations in the activity of serotonin (5-HT), dopamine (DA), and norepinephrine (NE) in the central nervous system (CNS).
2. The **cannabinoids,** derivatives of the *Cannabis sativa* (marijuana) plant or synthetic analogues.
3. **Anticholinergics,** which block acetylcholine activity in the brain.
4. **Dissociative anesthetics,** which are analgesic–anesthetic drugs with P/P/H effects.

Another P/P/H drug that will be discussed in this chapter is **ibogaine**—a drug with pharmacological properties so unique that it doesn't fit into any of the four classes but shares some properties with at least two of them.

Many of these drugs gain their reinforcing value for humans because of their ability to alter consciousness and perceptual processes, rather than because they exert their effects on the primary reward centers of the brain, as do some of the drugs described earlier. I say this for several reasons. First, the subjective reports of humans consistently contain references to the perceptual and cognitive aspects of the drug-induced experience, whereas comments on the mood and emotions evoked appear secondary to these (Feeney, 1976; Wallace & Fisher, 1999). Second, although euphoria is commonly expressed as an effect of these drugs, it is highly context-specific. In some cases, an extreme dysphoric reaction, described as a panic or paranoid feeling, may occur without warning and may persist for several minutes to hours (Jaffe, 1985).

A third line of evidence that the reward value of some P/P/Hs is not directly related to their effects on the primary reward centers of the brain comes from research with nonhumans. Nonhumans will not self-administer many of the P/P/Hs in their pure form (Jaffe, 1985), whereas they will do so with psychostimulants, sedative–hypnotics, and narcotics. There are reports of animals ingesting plants that contain P/P/H substances, but because they have nutritional value, it is not clear whether they are eating them for their P/P/H properties or for the nutrients (Siegel, 1979).

When pure LSD or mescaline is used with the catheter infusion method, animals avoid administering them. There are exceptions to this general rule, though. For example, in one report of monkeys self-administering a P/P/H substance under experimental conditions, the monkeys were completely isolated from all visual and auditory stimulation (Siegel & Jarvik, 1980). They were then allowed to self-administer the very short-acting P/P/H dimethyltryptamine (DMT) by way of smoking (the monkeys were trained to do this via a special device). Under these conditions, two of the three monkeys did so. Unfortunately, the interpretation of these observations is unclear because of the well-documented stress that occurs with isolation. Under such conditions, any perceptual experience, drug-induced or not, can have reinforcing properties. Furthermore, when the monkeys were returned to their normal test environment with visual and auditory stimulation, they refused to administer the DMT, even when the monkeys were water-deprived and water reward was made contingent on DMT smoking. Three types of P/P/Hs that are readily administered by nonhumans are delta-9-tetrahydrocannabinol (the major psychoactive ingredient in marijuana), phencyclidine (PCP), and derivatives of amphetamine with P/P/H properties (such as 3,4-methylenedioxymethamphetamine [MDMA]). However, this finding is still not unambiguous evidence that nonhumans will administer P/P/Hs for their consciousness-altering or perceptual effects, because these drugs have a variety of properties that could account for their reinforcing effects.

Before beginning a discussion on P/P/Hs, it should be pointed out that research on most P/P/Hs over the last three decades, particularly with humans, has been very limited, primarily because of governmental restraints and a lack of funding for this type of research. Furthermore, because many of these substances are classified as Schedule I drugs, researchers have to apply for a special DEA (Drug Enforcement Administration) license to conduct research with them. Some of the restraints have come about because of public wariness over the potent consciousness-altering properties of these drugs (Holden, 1980). In some cases the early research was conducted without proper controls, with subjects who were not sufficiently informed of the type of research being conducted (or were not informed at all that they were involved in a drug experiment). Some subjects experienced very dysphoric, and occasionally long-lasting, reactions. During the 1960s, literally thousands of people experienced the effects of P/P/Hs, either in clinical settings as a potential therapeutic tool or in recreational settings (Novak, 1998). Unfortunately, information from these individuals consists mostly of self-reports of a highly variable nature.

Because present ethical concerns limit the type of research conducted with P/P/Hs in humans, much of the research with these substances is done with animals. Many of the questions we would like to address concerning P/P/Hs are somewhat limited by the nature of the primary properties of P/P/Hs. That is, animals cannot communicate about the highly subjective drug-induced experience, so their role is primarily one of determining what the neuropharmacological and biochemical actions of these drugs are. Unfortunately, trying to relate these actions to the cognitive and perceptual effects of P/P/Hs in humans is exceedingly difficult.

One very powerful tool for assessing subjective effects of P/P/H drugs (or any other psychoactive drugs) in animals is a technique known as the **drug discrimination paradigm** (Appel et al., 1982). Essentially, animals are trained to tell the difference (discriminate) between the effects of a placebo injection (saline) and those produced by a particular drug. For example, a hungry rat may be rewarded with food occasionally for pressing a left lever if it was injected with saline a few minutes earlier and rewarded for pressing a right lever if injected with a small dose of LSD. Rats can learn to make the appropriate choice fairly quickly. After the rat learns to respond on the appropriate lever more than 90% of the time, it is injected with a test compound. If the test compound induces subjective effects similar to LSD, the rat will press the lever previously associated with the LSD cue; if the effects are not LSD-like, the lever previously associated with saline will be pressed. This procedure can also be used to see which neurotransmitter systems are involved in a particular drug's subjective effects. After an animal has learned to discriminate between the presence and absence of a particular drug, the animal can be injected with a drug whose properties at specific receptors are known, prior to being injected with the placebo or the particular drug being tested. If, for example, we want to know if a particular drug works by activating 5-HT receptors, we could inject the drug after injecting a known 5-HT antagonist and test the animal to see whether it will press the lever that has been associated with the placebo. Thus, the drug discrimination paradigm is a useful way in which to use animals to compare and contrast drugs with unknown CNS effects with those whose CNS effects have been established with humans, as well as to determine the specific sites at which a drug acts.

MONOAMINE-RELATED P/P/Hs

Monoamine-related drugs are so named because they share a basic similarity with the molecular structures of the monoamine neurotransmitters 5-HT, DA, and NE (see Figure 13.1 for representative P/P/Hs of this type; Glennon & Rosecrans, 1982). Examples of the 5-HT-type (indoleamine) P/P/H are LSD, psilocybin and psilocin (found in the *Psilocybe* genus of mushroom), bufotenine (found in glands of certain toads, e.g., *Bufo alvarius*), DMT, and diethyltryptamine (DET). Examples of the catecholamine-type P/P/H are mescaline (found in the peyote cactus); dimethoxymethylamphetamine (DOM or DMMA, the main ingredient in the street drug known as STP); 3,4-methylenedioxyamphetamine (MDA); and methoxymethylenedioxyamphetamine (MMDA). Most of the discussion of this group of drugs will center on LSD, because the majority of work has been done with this compound.

The subjective effects of the monoamine-related P/P/Hs in the dose ranges that are effective are quite similar and often indistinguishable in both humans and animals.

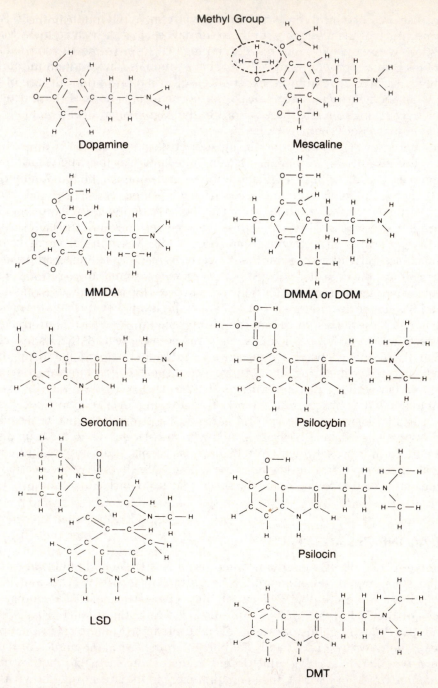

FIGURE 13.1 Examples of molecular structures of some drugs with psychotomimetic properties and two of the monoamine neurotransmitters in the brain. Note that all the psychotomimetic molecules have a number of methyl (CH$_3$) groups attached to them.

For example, in animal drug discrimination procedures, the indoleamine-and cate-cholamine-type P/P/Hs generalize to each other (Appel et al., 1982). However, their potency may vary tremendously; for example, LSD is approximately 100 times more potent than psilocybin and approximately 4,000 times more potent than mescaline in humans (Jaffe, 1985). They may also differ in terms of their durations of action; for instance, the effects of LSD may last for several hours, whereas the effects of DMT may dissipate within 1 hour. The durations of action of mescaline, psilocin, and psilocybin are in between these two.

The effects of monoamine P/P/Hs range from those very similar to amphetamine (strongly psychostimulant-like and weakly hallucinogenic, such as MDA) to those very similar to LSD (weakly psychostimulant-like and strongly hallucinogenic, such as mescaline and psilocybin; Jaffe, 1985; Nichols, 1986). In some cases, the type of effect is largely dependent on which isomer of the compound is administered. For example, the dextro isomer of MDA induces amphetamine-like effects, whereas the levo isomer induces LSD-like effects (Nichols, 1986).

Most drugs in this category induce fairly rapid tolerance to both their mental and sympathomimetic effects; tolerance appears to be complete after three or four daily exposures (Freedman & Halaris, 1978). They are also cross-tolerant with each other but do not appear to exhibit cross-tolerance with drugs in the other three P/P/H classes. The one exception seems to be DMT, in which tolerance (in humans) has not been shown to develop (Strassman, 1996) nor does tolerance development to LSD transfer to DMT (Jaffe, 1985). However, the lack of tolerance to DMT may be due to the fact that DMT has a very short duration of action of less than 30 minutes (perhaps tolerance would develop if an organism were exposed to DMT on an hourly basis for several days). In most cases, tolerance is lost after a few days of no drug exposure. As far as we know, there are no signs of an abstinence syndrome following chronic exposure to any of the monoamine-related P/P/Hs.

In addition to the similarity of the subjective effects of the monoamine-related P/P/Hs, as one might expect of drugs with some of the properties of the psychostimulants, they share the tendency to produce bodily effects largely sympathomimetic in nature. These may consist of pupillary dilation, increases in blood pressure and heart rate, exaggeration of deep tendon reflexes, tremor, nausea, piloerection (hair erection), and increased body temperature. As will be discussed later in this chapter, the other classes of P/P/Hs share these characteristics in some respects but differ greatly in other respects. For example, anticholinergics may increase heart rate and blood pressure and produce pupillary dilation, but unlike the monoamine-related P/P/Hs, the pupillary dilation is not responsive to light. Whereas the monoamine-related P/P/Hs induce signs of heightened arousal, anticholinergics and cannabinoids tend to induce sedative-like effects, drowsiness, and fatigue. You should note other fundamental differences in the effects of the other P/P/Hs discussed in this chapter as we go along.

LSD's Historical Significance

LSD is a derivative of ergot, which is present in bread blighted by ergot-producing fungi and produces a wide variety of neuropsychiatric and vascular symptoms. There have been speculations that ergot may have contributed to historical accounts of the emergence of Jewish mystical movements in Europe and the bizarre behaviors of the young adolescent girls who the townsfolk accused of witchcraft during the Salem witchcraft trials in 1692 (Packer, 1998; Woolf, 2000). We do know that in 1938 a pharmacologist, Albert Hofmann, synthesized LSD while working with several derivatives of ergot. Five years later, Hofmann was the first to describe its profound effects on consciousness, after he accidentally ingested the compound while working on it in the laboratory. As Hofmann also found out rather quickly (after purposely taking what he considered to be a trivial amount—one-quarter of a milligram—and experiencing a psychotic reaction), it is one of the most potent pharmacological agents known. It can exert subjectively detectable effects in most people with doses as low as 50 micrograms (about the weight of a grain of table salt). It is up to 10 times more potent than our own hormones at its sites of action.

Following Hofmann's discovery of LSD, interest in it went through three distinct phases (Neill, 1987). The first was an interest in LSD's potential use for revealing the biochemical basis of psychosis, a phase that began to wane in the mid-1950s—primarily because it was determined that its effects did not mimic the symptoms of any natural psychosis. The second phase began in 1953 when it was proposed to be a potentially useful adjunct to various psychotherapeutic techniques, principally Freudian and Jungian psychoanalysis. Therapists, who often took LSD themselves so that they could better understand the therapeutic process in their clients, felt the drug could facilitate regression to obtain early childhood memories, shorten therapy, and, in particular, open up heretofore difficult patients, such as obsessive–compulsives (who curiously turned out to be very resistant to LSD's effects [Grof, 1980]). LSD was also used to treat other disorders, such as alcoholism, drug addiction, and the emotional distress and physical pain of terminally ill patients. For example, in the 1960s one study of over 100 alcoholics found that half of the high-dose LSD treatment participants reported abstinence 6 months after treatment, in comparison with one-third of those in a low-dose LSD group and only 12% in a conventionally treated group. Other research in the 1960s indicated that a majority of cancer patients suffering from anxiety, depression, and uncontrollable pain showed improvement in their physical and emotional status after LSD treatment. The researchers also observed that many of these LSD-treated patients reported that their desire for addictive pain medicines, such as morphine, diminished or vanished, along with the pain. In fact, at that time the National Institute of Mental Health recognized that the use of LSD in these types of patients was legitimate.

This LSD therapy phase began to wane in the mid-1960s for two primary reasons. First, the psychiatric community was unable to decide how LSD should be used in the therapeutic process or to document its efficacy scientifically. Second, by the mid-1960s, nonmedical use of LSD, especially by young people comprising a counterculture that was opposed to traditional values ("hippies"), led to the belief that LSD had become a public health problem. As a result the U.S. government passed a law that banned the use and sale of LSD, as well as peyote, mescaline, and several similar drugs, by the public. At that point, legitimate research on its effects on humans and on its potential therapeutic uses declined precipitously—not only because of the legal difficulties and maze of bureaucratic procedures required, but also because psychedelic research with humans was not viewed as reputable by the vast majority of those in the scientific community.

In this third phase, LSD and similar drugs became just another class of abusable drugs that mainstream culture attempted to suppress. Psychedelic drug therapy still goes on unofficially—practitioners would not continue using it under difficult conditions unless they believed that they were accomplishing something. Whether it will ever return to mainstream use remains to be seen. However, in the 1990s the Food and Drug Administration (FDA) has sought ways to allow human studies to test LSD and other Schedule I psychedelic drugs to assess their potential medical usefulness and has granted IND status to several psychedelic drugs (Kurtzweil, 1995). (The IND status means that the drugs have been studied in the laboratory for their major physical and chemical properties and tested in laboratory animals for their pharmacological and toxic effects.) The National Institute on Drug Abuse funds some of these studies. It is still difficult for researchers to conduct human research with psychedelic drugs, but at least this type of research has returned to some degree of respectability.

Neurochemical Effects of LSD and Related Compounds

LSD is absorbed within 30 to 60 minutes after oral administration, and its high lipid-solubility allows it to rapidly penetrate the blood–brain barrier (BBB) and stay in the body for up to 15 hours. The potency of LSD is even more emphasized by the fact that there is general distribution of the drug throughout the body, with relatively low levels found in the brain, where there is widespread regional distribution of LSD binding sites (Freedman & Halaris, 1978). Thus, its mechanism and precise sites of action are difficult to determine because of the very small doses needed to induce its effects. Despite its potency with respect to perceptual, emotional, and cognitive alterations, there are only few documented cases of fatal poisoning by LSD in the literature (Fysh et al., 1985).

LSD and several other monoamine P/P/Hs appear to induce their subjective effects via a variety of mechanisms, but many of their effects are most likely linked to serotonergic systems in the brain. Because of structural similarities between the LSD and the 5-HT molecule and because LSD was observed to inhibit the spontaneous firing of serotonergic neurons of the reticular activating system, in the early 1970s it was proposed that LSD acted on serotonergic somatodendritic receptors (later identified as 5-HT autoreceptors; Aghajanian & Marek, 1999). This hypothesis also fit nicely with the observation that during normal REM (rapid eye movement) sleep, when dreams are most vivid, these neurons also cease firing. Thus, LSD was hypothesized to induce the intense emotions and vivid imagery of the dream state although the person was awake (Jacobs, 1976). However, several subsequent lines of evidence were incompatible with this theory—the most important being that tolerance to its psychotomimetic effects occurred with chronic LSD exposure, but tolerance to its inhibitory actions on serotonergic neuron firing did not. These phenomena led to the theory that LSD and other P/P/Hs with its subjective effects acted as agonists postsynaptically—specifically via postsynaptic 5-HT$_2$ receptors (Jacobs, 1987). This theory was supported by two major observations. First, the affinity of LSD-like P/P/Hs for 5-HT$_2$ receptors correlated highly with their potencies for causing hallucinations in humans. Second, 5-HT$_2$ antagonists were found to block the discriminative cue properties of LSD-like P/P/Hs in animals (Cunningham & Appel, 1987). But, again, subsequent research failed to support the theory—the most notable observation being that some highly specific 5-HT$_2$ antagonists did not block the discriminative cue properties of LSD (Pierce & Peroutka, 1990).

Research on this issue still points to alterations in serotonergic functions, but the picture is much more complicated than previous theories assumed. By 1990, it was apparent that (1) LSD-like P/P/Hs bind to a variety of 5-HT receptors; (2) the hallucinogenic potencies of LSD-like P/P/Hs correlate well with their binding affinity at many of these receptors; (3) some of these 5-HT receptors are autoreceptors and some are postsynaptic receptors; and (4) depending on the type of receptor, LSD-like P/P/Hs may act as agonists, partial agonists, or antagonists (Frazer et al., 1990; Pierce & Peroutka, 1990; Sanders-Bush & Breeding, 1991).

By the mid-1990s, with further refinement in subcategorizing 5-HT receptors, research findings suggested that the $5-HT_{1A}$, $5-HT_{2A}$, and $5-HT_{2C}$ receptor subtypes, for which LSD is an agonist, were the major receptors responsible for the stimulus effects of monoamine-related hallucinogens—at least in nonhumans (Fiorella et al., 1995; Krebs & Geyer, 1994; Penington & Fox, 1994). Unfortunately, we have not narrowed down their location and function to the point at which we can conclusively determine the primary mechanisms through which these drugs act to induce the complete hallucinogenic experience.

As the foregoing discussion should indicate, LSD-like drugs would be expected to exert a mixture of excitatory and inhibitory actions on serotonergic functioning. For example, inhibition of 5-HT release by somatodendritic $5-HT_{1A}$ receptor activation could reduce competition between 5-HT and LSD-like drugs for agonistic activity at postsynaptic $5-HT_{2A}$ and $5-HT_{2C}$ receptors—thus altering the mixture of intrinsic activity at these receptors. However, questions remain as to which neuronal systems and areas of the brain are mostly affected by the serotonergic receptors acted on by the monoamine P/P/Hs.

Research with animals suggests that two brain regions, the locus coeruleus (the point of origin for the dorsal noradrenergic bundle, see Chapter 5) and the cerebral cortex, are where the actions of both LSD and many of the other monoamine hallucinogens are mediated primarily by $5-HT_{2A}$ receptors (Aghajanian & Marek, 1999). Locus coeruleus neurons are primarily noradrenergic, and their axon terminals make connections with many areas of the brain including the cerebral cortex (Figure 5.11). These neurons in turn receive an extraordinary convergence of somatic, visceral, and other sensory inputs from all regions of the body. As noted earlier in Chapter 5, noradrenaline released from locus coeruleus neurons plays a modulatory role on target neurons, in which it induces primarily inhibitory actions if the organism is in a vegetative state; however, noradrenergic input may enhance the activity of target neurons with sudden changes in the organism's environment (e.g., the introduction of a novel stimulus or a predator). Research with rats suggests that LSD and other monoamine-related P/P/Hs, via activation of $5-HT_{2A}$ receptors, may indirectly decrease the spontaneous activity of locus coeruleus neurons but facilitate the activation of locus coeruleus neurons by sensory stimuli. The decrease in spontaneous firing of locus coeruleus neurons appears to be the result of activation of inhibitory inputs mediated by $GABA_A$ receptors, whereas the enhancement of phasic sensory responses appears to be the result of activation of excitatory glutamatergic inputs mediated by NMDA (N-Methyl-D-aspartic acid) receptors. Thus the disruptions in this area vital to the modulation of global brain functions such as emotion and vigilance may contribute to the subjective experience induced by monoamine-related P/P/Hs.

Evidence also indicates that alterations in the cerebral cortex by these drugs may be due to their ability to prolong the Ca^{++}-dependent release of glutamate (GLU) onto cortical cells through a presynaptic mechanism involving the activation of 5-HT$_{2A}$ receptors. As described in Chapter 5, under normal conditions, neurotransmitter release is closely and rapidly coupled to the action potential invasion of nerve terminals with a subsequent flooding of Ca^{++} into the terminal through voltage-gated Ca^{++} channels. This form of neurotransmitter release is termed *synchronous release* (Goda & Stevens, 1994). However, following the evoked synchronous phase, there is also a slow, *asynchronous* phase of transmitter release with a slightly longer latency (approximately 50 ms) that can persist for approximately 0.5–1.0 seconds. This is due to low levels of residual Ca^{++} remaining within the terminal following the initial wave of Ca^{++} influx. Studies have found that LSD and other hallucinogenic drugs, acting as partial agonists at 5-HT$_{2A}$ receptors, enhance this asynchronous-evoked release of GLU (Aghajanian & Marek, 1999), which would provide a possible synaptic mechanism for the hallucinogenic effects of these drugs. That is, rather than the normal fast on–off signals that occur at glutamatergic synapses, with these drugs there could be an overlapping or blending of synaptic signals in the cortex, which results in the blending and accentuation of images and sounds and creates the distortions in perception and hallucinatory experiences. Clearly, much remains to be done to determine the mechanisms of these drugs regarding their effects on the human experience.

Psychological Effects of Monoamine P/P/Hs

The psychological effects of LSD and other P/P/Hs are very difficult to describe because they are almost entirely subjective and depend on self-reports. Furthermore, the effects are very dependent on the context and on the expectations of the person. The person may express deep religious feelings one moment, sexual feelings another, and extreme sadness, anxiety, and paranoia at another (Novak, 1998). Bizarre thoughts and feelings may represent a major break with reality and may lead the person to believe that he or she can fly, stop automobiles by stepping in front of them, or perform some other amazing feat. Occasionally, these feelings can lead to self-destructive behavior, such as attempting suicide or jumping out of windows.

The most prominent physiological symptoms of monoamine-related P/P/Hs are indicative of slightly heightened arousal, for example, slightly elevated blood pressure and increased heart rate, although the individuals often experience states of inactivation, tiredness, and drowsiness. Increases in introversion and dreaminess are commonly reported by subjects under their influence. Not surprisingly individuals under the influence of these drugs display impairments in alertness and cognitive performance. However, the latter is confounded by the individual's lack of motivation to perform well in tasks requiring attention and cognitive effort. Individuals administered LSD or psilocybin under controlled conditions have reported predominantly positive emotional states ranging from heightened mood to euphoria associated with derealization and depersonalization phenomena (Hasler et al., 2004; Novak, 1998). Typically there is a loosening of the demarcation between self and environment, which is generally accompanied by insight and experienced as "touching" or "unifying with a higher reality."

In many instances, users report that they develop insights that never occurred to them before or that they see things regarding themselves or others that they have never seen before—much like looking into a mirror that strips away all preconceived notions about how they look, who they are, and the meaning of their existence. In some cases, this transcendental experience can leave them feeling quite at peace with themselves and their world; in others, it can be very disturbing.

LSD and similarly acting P/P/Hs induce dose-dependent alterations in sensory perception (including colorful visual illusions, complex scenic hallucinations, and synesthesias), as well as alterations in perception of time, space, and self (Hasler et al., 2004; Novak, 1998; Strassman et al., 1994). Perceptual alterations are usually visual, auditory, or tactile and may involve extreme distortions of the physical environment or, with higher doses, actual hallucinations. With the eyes closed, the person experiences a virtual kaleidoscope of changing patterns and intense colors. Synesthesia, the transposition of sensations such as sounds into visual images, may occur. In a study with humans administered DMT, many subjects remarked on the strong degree of similarity between their dreams and their subjective experiences following the higher doses of DMT (Strassman et al., 1994). As one of the participants commented, "This was a dream, not a hallucination. Dreams have story lines as I experienced today; hallucinations do not."

Dysphoric reactions, often referred to as bad trips, generally occur if users take a larger-than-usual dose of these substances and suddenly get the feeling that they are completely losing control over the experience and that they may never return to normal. People and objects in the environment, as well as the person's own body image, may become so distorted that they are grotesque and threatening. Anxiety, panic, and paranoia (the belief that people are out to get you) are very common. Although these feelings may lead to assaultive behavior, the person is generally so paralyzed with fear that this is unlikely.

Although these acute effects dissipate rapidly (within 6 to 12 hours after ingesting LSD), a very small minority of individuals continue to experience psychotic-like effects, such as mental confusion, perceptual distortions, and poor concentration beyond this time—in some cases for days or weeks (Abraham & Aldridge, 1993). In very rare cases, individuals have complained about mental and emotional disturbances several years after being exposed to LSD. The incidence of prolonged psychosis (i.e., lasting more than 48 hours) following LSD in research or clinical settings falls in the range of 0.08% to 4.6%, with the lower estimates derived from experimental subjects and the higher estimates derived from clinical populations (Abraham & Aldridge, 1993).

Incidentally, several individuals have tried to sue the U.S. government because of mental or emotional problems they allegedly suffered from involuntarily being administered LSD in experimental projects funded by or carried out by governmental agencies between 1953 and 1973. Although governmental officials have generally conceded that these projects were unethical, because of complicated circumstances these suits have not been successful. In one case—*U.S. v. Stanley*, 107 S. Ct. 3054 (1987)—the Supreme Court held that a former army serviceman who was secretly administered LSD four times as part of an army experiment could not seek redress through a suit for violations of his constitutional rights on the ground that the suit was barred by a doctrine that precludes governmental liability for injuries to servicemen resulting from activity incident to service. In another suit—*Orlikow v. U.S.*, 682 F. Supp. 77 (D.D.C. 1988)—nine individuals claimed that they suffered mental or emotional problems resulting from their psychiatric treatment in a CIA-subsidized experimental program that included being administered LSD without their knowledge. The case dragged through the courts for a number of years until an out-of-court settlement was reached in October 1988.

One of the key questions is whether the occasional prolonged psychotic-like reaction to LSD-like P/P/Hs constitutes a distinct syndrome or is a nonspecific reaction in personalities vulnerable to stress. Although this issue has not been resolved, most of the findings support the position that it is a drug-induced schizophrenia-like reaction in persons vulnerable to both substance abuse and psychosis (Vardy & Kay, 1983).

Antipsychotic drugs like chlorpromazine and haloperidol can reduce most of the effects of LSD-like P/P/Hs, but these treatments are generally not needed in cases of dysphoric reactions. Furthermore, antipsychotics may intensify the experience if the LSD-like drug has been adulterated with another type of P/P/H (e.g., PCP, scopolamine). In most cases, placing the person in a quiet environment and talking him or her "down"—that is, talking to the person and offering continual reassurances that the effects will dissipate soon—are sufficient to calm the person (Jaffe, 1985). However, in cases in which this process is difficult to accomplish—for instance, in the emergency room—administering a benzodiazepine has been shown to induce rapid and effective relief from LSD toxicity (Abraham & Aldridge, 1993).

In a review of studies in which neuropsychological tests were administered to users of LSD or other hallucinogens to assess whether there was evidence of residual toxicity, it was concluded that there are few, if any, long-term neuropsychological deficits attributable to hallucinogen use (Halpern & Pope, 1999). Unfortunately, all of the studies had methodological problems that limit interpretation of the findings; for example, most studies failed to control for premorbid attributes of the hallucinogen users versus controls, and virtually all failed to control for the subjects' use of other illicit drugs and alcohol. However, there is considerable evidence for neurotoxicity associated with the chronic use of the mildly hallucinogenic MDMA, which will be discussed shortly.

Some users of LSD (and other P/P/Hs) may experience what they report as brief episodes similar to the LSD-induced state—commonly termed **flashbacks**—several weeks or months after they have ingested LSD. These are often, but not always, in the form of altered visual perceptions: geometric pseudohallucinations (patterns or figures that are clearly recognized by the observer as not being real), illusionary movements in the peripheral visual field, images that trail moving objects, flashes of color, intensified color for brief periods of time, and prolonged afterimages. Emergence into a dark environment is one of the most common precipitants of the disturbances (Abraham, 1983). Flashbacks may be upsetting to some individuals, or they may be viewed as novel, curious phenomena by others. In cases in which the flashback experience is disturbing and long lasting, the diagnosis of *posthallucinogen perceptual disorder* may be made.

Explanations for these phenomena are hard to come by because of confounding factors in the individuals who experience them (e.g., multiple drug use or the presence of eccentric personality characteristics). Also, there is no way of determining when they might occur or of experimentally validating them. A pharmacological mechanism is an exceedingly remote possibility; these drugs simply do not stay in the body long enough (Cohen, 1981). Furthermore, the tendency to experience LSD flashbacks does not appear to be related to the time since the drug was last used, and most studies have not observed a clear relationship between the percentage of users who experience flashbacks and the number of times they have used LSD (Abraham, 1983). However, the incidence of LSD-induced flashbacks may be related to the abuse of other drugs. For example, a study found that there was a significant positive relationship between the number of LSD exposures and the incidence of flashbacks in alcoholic inpatients in an alcoholism treatment facility (Batzer et al., 1999). Also, as noted previously, because the incidence of psychotic episodes (schizophrenia type) in the general population is not uncommon (approximately 1%), it is possible that the prolonged reactions to LSD occur in those individuals predisposed to psychosis and that the intense psychological disturbances of the LSD state then trigger the endogenous psychosis-like symptoms.

It has been suggested that flashbacks represent some type of learning phenomenon that occurs in predisposed individuals during acute stress (Cohen, 1981). Studies of individuals who have experienced flashbacks suggest that these individuals had strong tendencies to fantasize and were highly suggestible prior to their LSD use (Silling, 1980). Therefore, it is possible that after an LSD experience they may encounter a situation that reminds them of the experience (e.g., a stressful situation that induces sympathetic arousal) and elicits a small conditioned response that they are able to elaborate on and interpret as a drug-like experience. Others have hypothesized that some flashbacks represent episodes of visual seizures (Abraham, 1983). This theory would be consistent with reports that antipsychotics, which may reduce the seizure threshold (see Chapter 8), may actually enhance flashback episodes in some individuals.

Ever since the effects of LSD were first expressed, there has been much speculation about the similarity between these effects and those that occur during endogenous psychoses like schizophrenia. A number of authors have noted that there is a considerable difference between the two conditions (Jacobsen, 1968). With LSD, the hallucinations are mostly visual, generally consist of extreme distortions of the existing environment, and are viewed predominantly as pleasant or neutral in content. The LSD-induced psychotic state is highly responsive to suggestions from others, and persons under the influence of LSD tend to be greatly concerned about their interpersonal relations. With schizophrenia, the hallucinations are almost entirely auditory, are generally superimposed on the environment, and are almost universally viewed as threatening and unpleasant. Schizophrenics are exceedingly resistant to suggestion (which makes psychotherapy difficult), and there is an almost total lack of concern over interpersonal relations. Finally, reports from schizophrenics in remission who have taken LSD indicate that they can distinguish between the two kinds of psychotic states.

Although the preceding accounts of both LSD and schizophrenia are highly simplified, they do suggest that different mechanisms are involved in the two conditions. However, it is important to point out that to some extent we may be comparing apples with oranges; with LSD and related monoamine hallucinogens, the psychosis is generally known by the person to be drug-induced and is short-lived, whereas, with schizophrenia, the psychotic episodes have no explainable cause and may be chronic or recurrent. For example, imaging studies have indicated that psilocybin results in an elevated metabolic pattern in the frontal regions of the brain that is similar to metabolic patterns associated with acute psychotic episodes in schizophrenic patients, but which contrasts with the abnormally low levels of metabolic activity typically observed in chronic schizophrenic patients (Vollenweider et al., 1997). These factors may contribute to some of the differences between the two kinds of psychoses. For example, if one's ability to communicate effectively with others is severely disrupted for a length of time, one might very well withdraw from contact with others and avoid any attempt to have normal interpersonal relations.

MDMA ("Ecstasy")

The latest controversy over monoamine-related P/P/Hs is centered on a chemical relative of methamphetamine known as "Ecstasy" or MDMA. Although commonly referred to as a *designer drug,* it was synthesized by a legitimate pharmaceutical company over 90 years ago as a potential appetite suppressant—long before the concept of designer drugs came into being. Subjectively MDMA induces both amphetamine-like and LSD-like effects (Tancer & Johanson, 2003), although it is relatively free of the hallucinations produced by the LSD-related compounds (Greer & Tolbert, 1986; Nichols, 1986). Users claim that it leaves them feeling more empathetic, insightful, and aware. Some psychotherapists who have used MDMA in their practice have claimed that it is useful in facilitating more direct communication between people involved in a significant emotional relationship. Others claim that it induces a state of reduced anxiety and lowered defensiveness, which makes it attractive to therapists wishing to speed up the therapeutic process (Greer & Tolbert, 1986).

A reported use pattern for MDMA has been in the context of large, organized social settings known as "raves," which are typically held in large warehouses or dance halls and involve all-night dancing to techno music, computer-generated video, and laser light shows (Hegadoren et al., 1999). Partygoers, who may number in the thousands, typically use MDMA and often drink beverages with amino acids (so-called smart drugs) added to them (perhaps they think this will prevent the neurotoxicity, discussed later, that has been associated with MDMA).

MDMA is one of three analogues of amphetamine with very similar subjective effects. The other two are MDA (a P/P/H of the 1960s that had a reputation as a "love drug") and MDE (3,4-methylendioxy-*N*-ethylamphetamine, popularly known as "Eve"; Hegadoren et al., 1999). As is the case with other monoamine-related P/P/Hs, MDMA exerts many of its effects through its actions on serotonergic systems. However, their mechanisms of action are very different. In contrast to exerting direct actions on subtypes of 5-HT receptors, MDMA is a potent releaser and/or reuptake inhibitor of monoamines, boosting extracellular levels of 5-HT, as well as DA, noradrenaline, and acetylcholine (ACh; Cole & Sumnall, 2003). Because low doses appear to produce experiences characterized by consciousness-altering effects unaccompanied by intense hallucinations, users have often argued that MDMA is a unique drug that is distinctively different from mescaline and LSD. Tests with animals, using the drug-discrimination procedure, support these assertions. MDA, but not MDMA, has been found to induce LSD-like stimulus properties, whereas MDMA has been found to induce amphetamine-like stimulus properties (Steele et al., 1994). With higher doses, the perceptual effects of MDMA intoxication are typical of those induced by the classic monoamine-type P/P/Hs (Siegel, 1986). Users commonly report an orderly progression of visual imagery from simple geometric forms to complex scenes, a characteristic of these and other P/P/Hs. Auditory and body-image changes are also frequently reported.

As with other P/P/H drugs, MDMA intoxication is neither uniformly predictable nor uniformly controllable. Most users view the MDMA experience as positive and pleasant. The most common subjective positive effects include, in declining order of incidence, changes in feelings and emotions; enhanced communication, empathy, and understanding; cognitive insight or mental association changes; euphoria; perceptual distortions or hallucinations; and transcendental or religious experiences. Common negative effects are mostly of physiological origin and include, in declining order of incidence, elevation of blood pressure and pulse; muscle tension and jaw clenching; fatigue; insomnia; sweating; blurred vision; loss of motor coordination; and anxiety (Siegel, 1986).

The pattern of MDMA use is also typical of other P/P/H use, in that it is primarily social and experimental. Adverse reactions depend on the set and setting of the user or occur when higher than usual doses are taken. Most users adopt patterns of use and take doses that generally do not lead to dependence or significant psychopathology, although use of high doses can lead to prolonged physical and psychological reactions, such as anxiety. It does not appear that MDMA is conducive to regular and frequent use because tolerance is commonly reported to develop to the positive effects of MDMA, whereas negative effects increase with use (Solowij et al., 1992). In one study a substantial percentage of Ecstasy users (around 80%) reported experiencing low mood and impaired concentration between Ecstasy-taking sessions. The long-term effects most frequently reported included the development of tolerance to MDMA (59%), impaired ability to concentrate (38%), depression (37%) and "feeling more open toward people" (31%; Verheyden et al., 2003). As is the case with other P/P/Hs, MDMA may predispose people to a recurrence of previous psychological disturbance (Steele et al., 1994).

Present concerns over MDMA are related to its involvement in fatalities and potential neurotoxic effects. Although Ecstasy-related deaths are relatively uncommon, acute MDMA exposure can be lethal, frequently as the result of the development of a 5-HT syndrome and/or of sympathomimetic overstimulation, which are exacerbated by dehydration and overheating (Schifano, 2004). Numerous studies with a variety of animal species have indicated that even short-term exposure to doses of MDMA that closely approximate those used by humans can cause long-lasting, possibly irreversible, neurotoxic effects on serotonergic systems of the brain, particularly with respect to 5-HT axons (Green et al., 2003). Studies with animals have shown that following MDMA's 5-HT-releasing action there is an acute depletion of cortical 5-HT between 3 and 6 hours after administration, with recovery of normal 5-HT levels within 24 hours. However, cerebral 5-HT concentrations then decline due to specific neurotoxic damage to 5-HT nerve endings in the forebrain. In general, other neurotransmitter systems appear unaffected. This neurodegeneration, observed in both biochemical and histological assays, can last for months in rats and years in primates. Research has indicated that MDMA polydrug users have decreased gray matter concentration in several brain regions (Cowan et al., 2003), and positron emission tomography (PET) scans have revealed that 5-HT transporter availability in current MDMA users may be significantly reduced in a variety of brain areas compared with former MDMA users and drug-naïve and polydrug comparison subjects (Buchert et al., 2004; Thomasius et al., 2003).

In agreement with these findings, many adverse neurological and neuropsychiatric consequences suggestive of serotonergic dysfunction have been noted in human

MDMA users (McCann et al., 1994, 1998). A few days after MDMA exposure, users may report feeling more depressed, abnormal, unsociable, unpleasant, and ill-tempered than control subjects. Long-lasting (up to 12 months following abstinence) adverse effects of recreational MDMA exposure in humans consistent with serotonergic dysfunction have been found with respect to sleep, mood, neuroendocrine function, impulsivity, and other dimensions of personality (Allen et al., 1993; Gerra et al., 2000; Parrott, 2000). One study found that although MDMA use was not associated with mood disorders, heavy MDMA users exhibited higher levels of depressed mood, which was correlated with the total number of Ecstasy tablets used but was not associated with decreases in 5-HT transporter density (de Win et al., 2004). Numerous studies with humans have indicated that MDMA users do more poorly than nonusers in tests of verbal short-term memory, verbal long-term memory, processing speed, and attention (Bolla et al., 1998; Gouzoulis-Mayfrank et al., 2000; McCardle et al., 2004; Morgan, 1999; Verbaten, 2003). In addition, deficits in memory performance and visuospatial working memory span have been observed in abstinent MDMA users relative to nonusers (Gouzoulis-Mayfrank et al., 2003; Hanson & Luciana, 2004; Wareing et al., 2004).

Thus there is a considerable body of research that indicates that MDMA use may induce long-lasting neurological deficits in humans. Several key questions remain unresolved. First, is MDMA exposure the causal agent? All studies involving the regular recreational use of MDMA by humans are necessarily retrospective. Thus these studies cannot rule out the possibility that any dysfunctional characteristics observed may have existed prior to the users' exposure to MDMA. Also, because regular MDMA users are typically polydrug users, it is possible that the disturbances associated with MDMA use may be due to the use of these other drugs. Some studies have found that when the confounding use of other drugs is controlled for, the differences between MDMA users and nonusers are diminished or nonsignificant (Dafters et al., 2004; Roiser & Sahakian, 2004). Somewhat related to this issue is the fact that Ecstasy used recreationally is not always pure and may contain other drugs. However, it appears that since the late 1990s, non-MDMA tablets are found very infrequently, with purity levels between 90% and 100%, although the dose of MDMA has tended to be higher (Parrott, 2004). Second, if MDMA causes neurological damage in humans, is the damage reversible and, if so, how long does it take? Later PET scan studies have suggested that the decreases in 5-HT transporter density associated with MDMA use may be reversible (Buchert et al., 2004; Thomasius et al., 2003).

Because of factors discussed earlier, MDMA's potential dependence liability is relatively low compared with other drugs of abuse. However, early studies showing that animals will self-administer MDMA by way of the catheter method, which suggested it had abuse liability (Lamb & Griffiths, 1987), was a factor leading to the DEA's original classification of MDMA as a Schedule I drug in the mid-1980s. Interestingly, several psychiatrists contested this classification in court, saying that they should be allowed to explore the use of mind-altering drugs in psychotherapy, and the DEA was forced to remove the Schedule I classification. Six months later, the DEA reclassified MDMA as a Schedule I compound on the basis that it had no proven medical value. Later, the FDA has approved limited human MDMA studies to assess MDMA's potential medical uses. The Multidisciplinary Association for Psychedelic Studies (www.maps.org) has long advocated for a trial employing MDMA in the treatment of posttraumatic stress disorder, and other psychiatrists have proposed its use to help rape or cancer victims (Green, 2004).

CANNABINOIDS

The leaves and buds of the *Cannabis sativa* plant have been used as an intoxicant and as a medicinal herb for centuries, perhaps as far back as 2737 B.C. Only for the last 100 years or so have the recreational uses of this plant been emphasized. Its medicinal use gradually declined, partially because other drugs for which it was used came into being, with more selective action, and partially because the shelf-life of the active ingredients was short. About the same time, its recreational use began to increase gradually. Perhaps reflecting this shift in use, the term *marijuana* (also spelled "marihuana") was coined after the Mexican–Spanish word *mariguana,* which means "intoxicant."

Because its use changed from a medicinal one to a recreational one, certain public officials, particularly a zealous commissioner of the Federal Bureau of Narcotics by the name of Harry Anslinger, became concerned about its use (Carroll, 1991). In the 1930s, Anslinger and other officials began to circulate stories about marijuana causing permanent brain damage and insanity, enhancing criminal and aggressive tendencies, and inducing sexual perversion. (These effects were duly noted in a 1936 film called *Reefer Madness,* a completely serious movie that became a cult movie in the 1970s, when it came to be viewed by the audience as outrageously humorous. Although the movie depicted all the hazards of marijuana that Anslinger attributed to it, he did not like the film because he believed that just seeing drugs being used could provoke people to use them.) In reaction to these allegations, Congress enacted the Marijuana Tax Act of 1937, which made possession of marijuana without having paid a special tax on it a federal crime. (The catch-22 was that one had to be in possession of the marijuana before one could obtain the tax stamp for it, and possession of marijuana without the stamp was illegal. Needless to say, nobody ever applied for the tax stamp, nor did the federal government ever grant one.)

A number of people were still skeptical of the potential damaging effects of marijuana. One of them was New York City's Mayor Fiorello La Guardia. In the early 1940s, he set up a special commission of experts to determine the actual consequences of marijuana use on people. The final report of La Guardia's panel suggested that marijuana was a fairly mild intoxicant with few side effects, even when used to excess. The panel's findings essentially concurred with those noted in the 1890s by the Indian Hemp Commission. Despite the findings of these presumably objective and unbiased observers, the report had little impact on the opinions of the majority of people in the United States. In most cases the report was ridiculed and criticized for its lack of rigor and its methodology—particularly by Anslinger who effectively undermined the results of the report well before its publication (Brecher, 1972; Carroll, 1991).

In the 1950s the beliefs about marijuana's effects changed somewhat. Its use supposedly resulted in a strong psychological dependence, led users to escalate their use to more potent and dangerous drugs (such as the dreaded heroin), induced a so-called *amotivational syndrome*, and was a cause of permanent brain damage. A plethora of empirical research on the effects of marijuana in the late 1960s and early 1970s dispelled some of these beliefs but led to speculation over some new, potentially detrimental effects (Harris, 1978; Hollister, 1986). There was a report that substantiated the view that irreversible brain damage was associated with its use—a report that was quickly and severely criticized for its methodological deficiencies. Other researchers suggested that heavy marijuana use was the cause of severe personality changes. The amotivational syndrome was still being discussed. However, contrary to the notions that marijuana caused one to become a sex maniac, studies suggested that marijuana might actually cause sexual impotence and sterility in males due to reductions in the male sex hormone testosterone. Chromosomal aberrations, decreases in certain kinds of white blood cells and immunity, and alterations in DNA potentially leading to cancer were suggested by studies to be associated with cannabis use. The reliability and potential ramifications of these findings are still being debated.

Marijuana is not a drug itself; the word actually refers to the plant material, which contains over 400 different chemicals, more than 60 of which are specific to cannabis. These chemicals are referred to as *cannabinoids*. Most of these are probably not psychoactive even in high doses (Dewey, 1986; Hollister, 1986). The molecular structures of cannabinoids, which have no nitrogen atom and are not alkaloids, are very different from those of other classes of P/P/Hs. It appears that cannabinoids possess complex and particularly unique properties, even though they induce effects similar to numerous other drugs.

The major psychoactive chemical in marijuana is delta-9-tetrahydrocannabinol, or THC for short. (Due to differences in numbering systems in describing chemical structures, the molecule may also be referred to as delta-1-THC.) Two other cannabinoids, cannabinol and cannabidiol, may be active at high doses. Although these two drugs may have minimal effects in the amounts found in street marijuana, research has indicated that they interact with THC to modify its effects (Karniol & Carlini, 1972). This finding is consistent with the common belief that varieties of marijuana grown in different localities have different effects not wholly related to their THC content.

Although numerous "authorities" have claimed that the "potency" of marijuana (technically, the concentration of THC in the plant material) has increased dramatically since the early 1970s, with the implication that it presents greater hazards now than then, this claim is difficult to substantiate. For example, in a study that assessed changes in confiscated cannabis products from 1980 to 1997, it was determined that the average THC content in marijuana increased from 1.2% to 4.1% (ElSohly et al., 2000). However, these investigators also determined that the proportion of cannabis samples that contained high levels of THC (e.g., sinsemilla, hashish, hash oil) declined dramatically during this time frame from around 36% to 6%. Also, there is much published evidence about the availability of highly potent varieties of cannabis from the 19th century through the present day (Mikuriya & Aldrich, 1988). Second, an important consideration in regard to the potency issue is *autotitration*, the adjustment of dose by the individual user to obtain optimal effects and avoid unpleasant ones. Smoking marijuana, the customary practice in present social use of the drug, gives the user rapid feedback with regard to levels of effect, because the drug goes directly to the brain from the lungs, unimpeded by the gut or the liver, and whatever the potency of the drug used, individuals tend to smoke only the amount necessary to achieve the desired effect.

Psychological Effects of Marijuana

Interpreting the effects of marijuana on behavioral variables is complicated by the fact that set and setting variables—for example, context, the user's personality, previous marijuana experiences, and expectations—have been shown to play a critical role in changes in mood and behavior that occur following marijuana use (Ferraro, 1980), and may even influence the rate of THC metabolism (Cami et al., 1991). Thus, all the effects noted in this discussion of marijuana are likely to be due to the interaction between these factors and the actions of the drug on the nervous system.

The acute effects of marijuana (i.e., being "stoned") generally consist of an increasingly dose-dependent impairment of memory and cognitive functions, such as attending, speaking, problem solving, and concept formation (Azorlosa et al., 1992; Dewey, 1986; Ferraro, 1980). The person's speech is fragmented, suggestive of disjointed thought patterns, and the speaker often forgets what (s)he or others have recently said. Ideas extraneous to the focus of an individual's attention appear to enter consciousness, producing a loosening of associations. Phenomena that are not usually associated with each other in normal waking life tend to appear connected under the influence of marijuana, and phenomena or ideas that are commonly associated in normal waking life may seem irrelevant or unconnected. Sometimes the person under the influence of marijuana gains insights of great importance. Unfortunately, when under the influence, the person's ability to reflect on or analyze the quality of these insights is greatly impaired, and when the intoxication phase is over, the great insights often turn out to be mundane or unworkable ideas.

A multitude of studies using a wide variety of cognitive tasks strongly suggest that many of the cognitive deficits produced by marijuana can be attributed to alterations in memory functions (Hooker & Jones, 1987). There is a great deal of variability in the degree to which marijuana disrupts cognitive functions, some of which is dependent upon differences in the drug dose used and the specific task (Azorlosa et al., 1992). It is also well established that the level of motivation to perform well may affect the degree to which marijuana impairs performance (Cami et al., 1991). Cognitive and behavioral tolerance to marijuana's effects can also occur, such that cognitive deficits noted in infrequent users may not be observed in individuals who use it frequently. Although the subjective effects of marijuana and alcohol can be easily distinguished by experienced users of marijuana and alcohol, a number of the cognitive deficits and subjective ratings of impairment induced by recreational doses of marijuana have been found to be comparable to those induced by recreational doses (e.g., blood alcohol content between .035 and .09) of alcohol (Heishman et al., 1997).

One of the primary effects of marijuana is interference with short-term memory (the ability to maintain access to newly acquired information for several seconds or minutes). This is found to occur with both verbal and graphic material. Marijuana also disrupts long-term memory retrieval (the ability to gain access to information acquired several hours, or longer, prior to marijuana intoxication). This effect is more predominant with recall (the ability to reproduce the previously learned material) than with recognition (the ability to choose from a number of items which of those the person has previously learned). Much of the memory disruption appears to be due to increased imagery and thought flow coming out of the intrusion of irrelevant associations (Hooker & Jones, 1987). However, there is little evidence that, once the person returns from the intoxicated state, retrieval of information learned prior to the intoxicated state is affected.

There is also evidence for weak state-dependent retrieval effects with marijuana, in which information acquired under the influence of marijuana is retrieved better under marijuana than under nondrug conditions. But these effects are more likely to occur under recall conditions that provide minimal external cues to the person (Eich et al., 1975).

The detrimental effects of marijuana on complex psychomotor skills in the laboratory have also been observed in real-life situations of driving and flying (Hollister, 1986). Although marijuana may be less detrimental to driving performance than alcohol is, it nevertheless is a potential causal factor in accidents that occur when driving or engaging in similar activities. Some of the detrimental effects on performance may persist for some time, possibly up to 24 hours, beyond the period of subjective intoxication (Pope et al., 1995; Pope & Yurgelun-Todd, 1996). One factor that contributes to alcohol's detrimental effects on driving is its tendency to provoke risk taking, whereas in simulated and actual driving tests, marijuana typically makes drivers more cautious, and drivers under the influence of marijuana consciously attempt to compensate for its detrimental effects (Zimmer & Morgan, 1997).

Psychoactive cannabinoids have a sedative-like action in most people, as opposed to the sympathomimetic-like effects of the monoamine-related compounds. There is no cross-tolerance between these two classes, and the monoamine-related compounds are more potent in their perceptual and hallucinatory actions (Jaffe, 1985). Although many people find the marijuana experience pleasurable, others do not. Those who do experience pleasurable effects may find them to wax and wane during the period of intoxication, and in some cases they may develop a dysphoric reaction. This generally occurs if the person ingests an amount that is considerably higher than he or she is used to. Such cases are more common with oral administration, because the absorption of THC from the gastrointestinal (GI) tract is considerably slower than absorption through smoking, and also because the person has difficulty in regulating the amount of marijuana ingested.

Another effect of marijuana that may be viewed positively by the user is its effects on appetite (Foltin et al., 1986; Williams & Kirkham, 1999). (Sometimes this effect is referred to as the "munchies.") For example, North Americans commonly report and, in some cases, exhibit increases in appetite (particularly sweets) and weight gain (Foltin et al., 1986). Furthermore, cannabinoid CB1 receptor agonists have been investigated for their potential utility as treatments for anorexia and wasting syndrome associated with cancer chemotherapy and AIDS. Interestingly, a number of cannabinoid antagonists and inverse agonists have been developed in the last few years, including rimonabant, AM251, and AM4113. Preclinical studies showed that these drugs reduce food intake and body weight (Arnone et al., 1997; Colombo et al., 1998; McLaughlin et al., 2003, 2006; Sink et al., 2008), and after the initial preclinical and clinical research, rimonabant (Acomplia) was released in Europe as an appetite suppressant. However, clinical research revealed that Acomplia, which is an inverse agonist at CB1 receptors, produced several side effects including nausea, anxiety, and depression. For these reasons, it was not approved for use by the FDA, and it was later removed from the European market. Currently, research is focusing on drugs that act as CB1 receptor neutral antagonists (i.e., drugs that are competitive antagonists, so they have no intrinsic activity) as alternatives to the inverse agonists, because they may produce fewer side effects (Le Foll et al., 2009; Sink et al., 2008, 2010).

Some studies also report that subjects experience enhanced sexual stimulation under the influence of marijuana (Meyer, 1978). In other countries, cannabis is used as a sexual depressant (in India, for example) or to suppress feelings of hunger (in Jamaica). Although acute use of marijuana in low doses may enhance the sexual experience, high doses or prolonged use may lead to a depression of sexual desire and even impotence (Hollister, 1986).

Numerous studies indicate that cannabinoid agonists exert a profound decrease in the reaction of animals to painful stimuli (Ameri, 1999). These findings suggest that cannabinoid systems are involved in pain perception and that cannabinoids may be therapeutically useful as analgesics. However, studies with humans administered THC and other cannabinoid agonists have not found them to be particularly effective analgesics, and doses that do induce analgesia also produce a number of side effects, such as blurred vision, drowsiness, and mental clouding (Greenwald & Stitzer, 2000; Holdcroft et al., 1997; Jain et al., 1981; Jochimsen et al., 1978; Martin & Lichtman, 1998; Noyes et al., 1975). Selective mu opiate antagonists typically do not block the analgesic effects of cannabinoid agonists in either animals or humans (Ameri, 1999; Greenwald & Stitzer, 2000; Hamann & DiVadi, 1999), which is consistent with evidence that although the analgesic effects of cannabinoids and opiates may involve similar brain-stem circuitry, they are mediated by different receptor mechanisms (Meng et al., 1998).

What makes the marijuana experience rewarding? We really do not know. The ability of THC to enhance the release of DA in reward-relevant areas of the brain (discussed shortly) may be one factor. The transient cognitive and memory disruptions associated with marijuana may account for its popularity in some, but by no means all, humans (Feeney, 1976). That is, the new and unrelated intrusions into thought, the loosening of traditional or learned associations among stimuli and responses, the encoding of new information subject to associative links that normally would be inhibited, the ambiguity and variability in the perceptual experience, and so forth result in novel experiences, feelings of creativity, and insightfulness (Feeney, 1976; Hooker & Jones, 1987). Those individuals who are not particularly anxious about the unfamiliar or the unconventional or about loss of control and the unpredictability of their world may find such effects pleasurable, as long as they can retain control over the time and degree of these effects. Those who are anxious about these may find such effects unpleasurable. Other drugs described in this chapter may have similar qualities, but marijuana's effects are relatively short-lasting and are easier to control, tolerance to them develops relatively slowly, and the immediate side effects associated with marijuana are less troublesome.

Cannabinoid Pharmacokinetics

Marijuana is most commonly administered by smoking a "joint" (an average joint contains approximately 10 to 20 mg of THC). However, most cannabinoids are highly lipid-soluble and are also readily absorbed orally (Agurell et al., 1986). Because of stomach acid degradation, enzyme alterations, and slow absorption, oral THC is about one-third as potent as THC that is smoked. Because, at most, only half of the original THC in the smoked cannabis is actually delivered and absorbed, inhalation may be 5 to 10 times as effective a mode of administration. However, if one takes sufficient amounts of THC orally in order to achieve the same peak intensity effects of smoked THC, because of the slower accumulation of the drug in the blood, the effects last considerably longer than when the THC is smoked.

Initial metabolism of cannabinoids in marijuana smoke occurs in the lungs, whereas orally administered cannabinoids are metabolized in the GI tract and by the liver. There are more than 30 metabolites of THC, and over 20 each of cannabinol and cannabidiol. Many of these metabolites are also psychoactive. One of the principal psychoactive metabolites of THC is 11-hydroxy-delta-9-THC, which crosses the BBB more readily than THC, and therefore may be more active than THC. However, because of the multitude of biotransformation pathways and metabolites and the complex interaction of the cannabinoids, no practical method has been developed for determining levels of intoxication based on detectable cannabinoids and metabolites.

What is quite apparent about cannabinoids is that their extremely high lipid-solubility results in their persisting in the body for long periods of time. Studies have shown that after a single administration of THC, detectable levels of THC are found in the body for weeks or longer, depending on how much was administered and the sensitivity of the assessment method. A number of investigators have suggested that this is an important factor in marijuana's effects, perhaps because cannabinoids may accumulate in the body, particularly in the lipid membranes of neurons. However, it is most likely that the major site of accumulation is adipose tissue (comprising some 10% to 20% of the human body), which would mean that these drugs would have no significant psychological consequences (Hollister, 1986).

Neurochemical Effects of Delta-9-THC

For many years, little was known about the mechanisms of action of THC at the neuronal level due to some unique characteristics of THC (Martin, 1986). First, THC has such high lipid-solubility that it is absorbed in high concentrations in practically all tissues. Second, THC alters just about every biological system in which it is examined. It has been recognized for some years that THC exerts nonspecific "fluidizing" effects on lipid membranes—similar to those of general anesthetics and alcohol, but to a much lesser extent (Martin, 1986). This fluidizing could partially explain why THC has sedative-like effects without having anesthetic properties, but evidence for this possibility is still weak. Most of the evidence indicates that THC works through specific receptors because modest structural modifications of the THC molecule can result in profound changes in its behavioral effects, and there is a definite stereospecificity of the THC molecule, with the levo isomer being from 6 to 100 times more active than the dextro isomer, depending on the species and the behavioral tests used.

Researchers have confirmed that THC exerts its most prominent effects via its actions on two types of cannabinoid receptors, CB1 and CB2, which are g-protein–coupled receptors. The CB1 receptor is found primarily in the brain as well as in some peripheral tissues, and the CB2 receptor is found exclusively in peripheral tissues (Wilson & Nicoll, 2002). THC appears to alter mood and cognition through its agonist actions on CB1 receptors, which inhibit a secondary messenger system (adenylate cyclase) in a dose-dependent manner. These actions can be blocked by the selective CB1 receptor antagonist SR141716A (rimonabant), which interestingly has been shown in clinical trials to be an effective treatment for smoking cessation, weight loss, and as a means of controlling or reducing metabolic syndrome risk factors (Fernandez & Allison, 2004).

Two endogenous ligands for cannabinoid receptors, that is, endocannabinoids, have been isolated from brain tissue (Mechoulam & Lichtman, 2003). Like THC, these ligands are fat-soluble but are simpler molecules that are derived from arachidonic acid, a fatty acid common to cell membranes. The first of these ligands to be identified was christened *anandamide*, from a Sanskrit word meaning "internal bliss." The second to be identified is 2-arachidonoylglycerol (2-AG).

Some physiological, pharmacological, and high-resolution anatomical studies indicate that endocannabinoids serve as retrograde neurotransmitters. That is, following the release of classical neurotransmitters from a presynaptic terminal and the activation of receptors on a postsynaptic neuron, the postsynaptic neuron releases endocannabinoids from its membranes. These endocannabinoids then travel "backward" across the synaptic cleft, where 1 or 2 seconds later they activate CB1 receptors on the presynaptic terminal, which reduces Ca^{++} influx into presynaptic terminals and inhibits the release of neurotransmitters from the presynaptic terminal for up to several seconds (Brown et al., 2004; Kushmerick et al., 2004). However, sites other than presynaptic terminals may also be affected in a similar fashion. Endocannabinoids then undergo reuptake into neurons and glial cells and are degraded by intracellular enzymes (Wilson & Nicoll, 2002). Numerous neurotransmitters are affected by this process, including the inhibitory transmitter GABA (gamma-aminobutyric acid) and the excitatory transmitter GLU. Thus, endocannabinoids induce a mixture of excitatory and inhibitory effects on neurons (i.e., they inhibit the release of both excitatory and inhibitory neurotransmitters).

THC appears to work in the same fashion, except that THC exerts longer actions and suppresses neurotransmitter release without the first step, that is, postsynaptic receptor activation. In other words, rather than postsynaptic neurons signaling the presynaptic neurons that a message has been received, indicating that no further neurotransmitter needs to be released for a while, THC signals the presynaptic neurons that they have sent a message when they have not. For example, THC may induce some of its disruptions in human cognition and memory through its inhibition of ACh release in the hippocampus (Davies et al., 2002), a major area involved in memory formation and retrieval.

The fact that THC exerts both excitatory and inhibitory effects (by reducing GABA and GLU release) in different areas of the brain could account for its ability to induce a variety of excitatory and depressant psychological effects (e.g., sedation, euphoria). This could also account for why THC has been demonstrated to protect neurons against excitotoxic damage in some studies whereas augmenting excitotoxicity in others, depending on the dose, animal species, its age, the severity of trauma, and the type of injury (Mechoulam & Lichtman, 2003). THC also inhibits the release of the neuropeptide cholecystokinin, which generally antagonizes the neuronal and behavioral effects of opioids. This could account for THC-induced analgesia and its synergistic effects when combined with opiates. However, although some effects of THC in nonhumans can be antagonized with the opiate receptor antagonists, naloxone and naltrexone, these drugs have not been shown to block or attenuate the subjective, physiological, and behavioral effects of THC in humans (Greenwald & Stitzer, 2000; Hamann & DiVadi, 1999; Wachtel & de Wit, 2000).

Cannabinoid receptors are widely distributed in the brain, but the pattern is uneven. The highest levels are found in the cerebral cortex, hippocampus, hypothalamus, and amygdala. These areas are critically important for higher mental processes, memory formation, primary drive regulation, and emotional expression—all of which are altered to some degree by cannabinoids. High cannabinoid receptor densities have also been observed in the basal ganglia and cerebellum of the rodent brain, consistent with the marked effects of cannabinoids on spontaneous locomotory activity in rodents. In contrast, there is a low abundance of cannabinoid receptors in the human cerebellum, which is in line with the absence of gross motor disturbances in humans who use marijuana (Ameri, 1999).

Reliable self-administration of THC via the intravenous catheter method has been demonstrated in squirrel monkeys (Justinova et al., 2003; Tanda et al., 2000). That the effect was due to the THC was supported by the finding that self-administration ceased when the CB1 receptor antagonist SR141716A was administered prior to the test sessions. Previous attempts may have failed due to the use of too-high doses of THC (possibly in combination with an inappropriate vehicle—typically a fluid in which the drug is suspended or dissolved that doesn't have psychoactive properties itself). For humans, there is a range of doses of THC delivered by smoking that produces pleasurable effects; doses below this range are ineffective and doses above this range produce dysphoric effects. When the doses of THC delivered intravenously by the monkeys approximated the doses obtained by humans smoking a typical joint, they self-administered the THC. When they were higher than these doses, the animals did not. Thus, THC joins the list of drugs, such as cocaine, heroin, nicotine, and alcohol, that are self-administered by nonhumans and abused by humans.

Psychopathological Effects of Marijuana

The acute panic anxiety reaction, noted particularly when unexpectedly strong marijuana is used, is the most common adverse psychological effect induced by cannabis use. As is commonly found with other drugs of abuse, the extensive use of cannabis has been found to be associated with an increased incidence of psychological disturbances and psychiatric symptoms. For example, several studies have found significant associations between the use of cannabis and symptoms of depression and anxiety (Bovasso, 2001; Patton et al., 2002; Rey et al., 2002). As discussed later, there are also data to suggest that the development or recurrence of acute psychosis in the context of marijuana use may be associated with a genetic predisposition to schizophrenia (McGuire et al., 1995). However, in many cases, individuals diagnosed with cannabis-induced psychosis may actually be individuals with paranoid schizophrenia who have used marijuana (Mathers & Ghodse, 1992). Interestingly, out of the hundreds of studies investigating the effects of acute exposure to marijuana or THC in thousands of human subjects, not one has reported a single case of a long-lasting psychotic reaction in the subjects—perhaps because individuals with a history of psychological problems were excluded from participating in the research.

It has been known for a number of years that there is a relationship between cannabis use and schizophrenia, but numerous confounding factors, selection bias, and the effects of other drug use have made interpretation of this relationship difficult. Several large-scale longitudinal studies conducted in a number of countries (Sweden, New Zealand, Israel, and the Netherlands) have attempted to resolve these problems (Arseneault et al., 2004; Fergusson et al., 2005; Smit et al., 2004). The general approach taken in these studies was to evaluate adolescents for symptoms of psychopathology and to obtain self-reports regarding their drug-taking practices. Then several years later, these individuals were again evaluated in terms of having been diagnosed with schizophrenia or exhibiting some psychotic-like symptoms. After attempting to statistically adjust for other confounding factors, for example, the individuals' other drug use, social, family, personality characteristics, the general conclusions that were derived from these studies were that cannabis users had roughly double the risk of developing schizophrenia than nonusers, that the risk increased as cannabis use increased, and that the risk of developing the disorder is greater in "vulnerable" people. These results suggest that, although numerically the risk of developing schizophrenia or related symptoms in cannabis users may be small, in clinical terms it could be a serious problem.

The key question that is impossible to resolve from these studies is whether these associations involve a causal linkage between cannabis use and the development of pathological symptoms. Studies investigating the link between cannabis use and schizophrenia have generally ruled out alternative explanations involving the use of cannabis as a form of self-medication, other drug use by the individuals, and effects of some other known confounding variables. However, there may be underlying confounding factors that may have not been recognized in these studies that result in the association. For example, people with poor judgment and low self-control, who exhibit dissocial behaviors and are preoccupied with magical ideas, may be drawn to cannabis use. These may also be precursors to the development of schizophrenia and may not be easily detected in general clinical interviews or tests. As discussed in Chapter 8, the symptoms of schizophrenia are variable and not always present in individuals actually diagnosed with the disease. A plausible neurological explanation for why cannabis use might lead to the symptoms, for example, damage to the hippocampus, prefrontal cortex, thalamus, or up-regulation of DA receptors, would be helpful in determining whether cannabis use actually causes the disorder.

Most studies that have investigated the effects of prolonged and heavy use of cannabinoids have not shown any systematic long-lasting decrements in mental activities suggestive of impairments of brain or cerebral function and cognition (Gonzalez et al., 2002). For example, in one study of long-term cannabis use in 10 subjects born, raised, and educated in the United States, no cognitive deficits could be determined in any of the subjects, most of whom had engaged in extremely heavy use for over 7 years (the subjects used a cannabis-tobacco mixture daily as a sacrament of communion in the context of their particular religion; Schaeffer et al., 1981). In fact, the intellectual functioning among the adults tested was above average, and in two of the subjects where similar tests had been conducted 15 and 20 years previously, the IQ scores were virtually unchanged. It should be stressed that these adults were well educated prior to their cannabis use; did not use other psychoactive substances; observed a good diet, consisting of vegetables, fruit, and small amounts of meat; and adhered to a strict religious doctrine. Obviously, such individuals are not particularly representative of a very broad spectrum of people.

Several studies conducted in the 1970s in Jamaica, Greece, and Costa Rica did not find any notable cognitive or physical differences between heavy users of cannabis (who had smoked approximately 10 joints a day for several years) and suitably matched nonusers (Hollister, 1986). Follow-up studies conducted on similar samples in Costa Rica and India also found few significant differences between users and nonusers on most tests of a variety of intellectual functions (Fletcher et al., 1996; Page et al., 1988; Varma et al., 1988). These later studies did find that some cannabis users, particularly older individuals, evidenced small, but reliable, deficits in some perceptual-motor tasks and sustained-attention and short-term memory tests requiring considerable mental effort. Further studies, which assessed brain wave patterns during a complex auditory selective-attention task, have indicated that some chronic marijuana users had more difficulty than nonusers in setting up an accurate focus of attention and in filtering out irrelevant information, even after cessation of their cannabis use for several months (Hall & Solowij, 1998). Unfortunately, from a methodological standpoint, the users in some of these studies were asked to abstain from cannabis use for only 12 to 24 hours prior to testing; considering the amount of cannabis normally consumed by many of the users in these studies, it is quite possible they were still somewhat "stoned" during these tests. This factor may account for the differences among the studies investigating the potential effects of long-term heavy cannabis use on cognitive functioning. One study employed heavy cannabis users who were seeking treatment for their cannabis dependence and assessed their cognitive functioning with a battery of neuropsychological tests after a period of abstinence, which ranged from 7 hours to 10 days (median = 17 hours). The results indicated that the users showed impairments in memory and attention, with the degree of impairment increasing with years of regular cannabis use (Solowij et al., 2002). Two other studies recruited current heavy cannabis users who had reported smoking cannabis at least 5,000 times and also utilized a battery of neuropsychological tests (Harrison et al., 2002; Pope et al., 2001). These studies found that the heavy users showed deficits on memory on days 0, 1, and 7 of a supervised abstinence period, but by day 28 there were virtually no significant differences between the cannabis users and controls on any of the tests, and there were no significant associations between cumulative lifetime cannabis use and test performance. And, of course, in none of these studies were there pre-cannabis use measures on these individuals to assure that these deficits were not present prior to their cannabis use—deficits that could potentially be related to their use of cannabis in the first place.

In summary, in assessing residual neuropsychological effects of marijuana use, one must first differentiate among those effects that are direct effects of the drug or those that are symptoms of actual psychiatric disorders that are caused or exacerbated by marijuana from those that are simply attributes of heavy marijuana users. Then one must determine whether the drug residue effects are short-lived, due to the persistence of cannabinoids in the body, or are long lasting, due to toxic effects on the CNS that persist even after all cannabinoids have been eliminated from the body following prolonged abstinence. The data support a residual effect of marijuana on attention, psychomotor tasks, and short-term memory during the 12- to 24-hour period immediately after use, but evidence for a more prolonged residual drug effect or a toxic effect on the CNS that persists even after cannabinoids have left the body is weak. Furthermore, these impairments are so subtle that it remains unclear how important they are for everyday functioning and whether they are reversed after an extended period of abstinence. It is clear that the long-term heavy use of cannabis does not produce the severe or grossly debilitating impairment of memory, attention, and cognitive function that is found with chronic heavy alcohol use (Hall & Solowij, 1998).

Some of the variability in studies in this area no doubt can be attributed to the variability in the users' personalities and emotional dispositions, so that marijuana use may have positive, negative, or benign effects on mental health and adjustment depending on the user's disposition (Zablocki et al., 1991). Also, it is difficult to distinguish between drug-induced psychological problems and preexisting determinants. It is often the case that extensive drug users are those who have had emotional problems prior to use (Hollister, 1986). Whatever the case, most clinicians caution against the use of marijuana by persons with a history of serious psychological problems. This caution also applies to adolescents, who are generally going through a lot of turmoil regarding the psychosocial development of their identity, their role in the adult world ahead, and their cognitive and interpersonal skills.

Although violence and aggression have sometimes been suggested to be associated with marijuana use, there is little evidence to support such an association (Dewey, 1986; Hollister, 1986). In fact, the predominant finding is that low doses of marijuana have little effect on aggression, and moderate to high doses tend to inhibit aggression in humans. There may be some individuals with poor impulse control or a proneness to violence, or who are under stress, for whom marijuana use may trigger an aggressive episode.

Rarely, the flashback phenomenon may also occur with cannabis use (Fischer & Taschner, 1991). However, there does not appear to be a correlation between the amount of cannabis consumed and the occurrence of a flashback. On the other hand, the probability of the occurrence of a flashback in a cannabis user seems to increase with the amount of LSD-like P/P/Hs the person has used (Abraham, 1983). Therefore, these individuals' cannabis use may simply be coincidental with their experiencing flashbacks, or it may be a precipitating factor in inducing LSD flashbacks. Although a flashback may range from a mild to a quite vivid recreation of the drug-induced experience, most clinicians feel that it requires little or no treatment.

Although concerns over the possibility that cannabis use may induce brain damage have been expressed for over a century, there is little evidence that doses typically used by humans are neurotoxic (Zimmer & Morgan, 1997). Several studies using echoencephalography and computerized transaxial tomography with heavy cannabis users failed to find any evidence of cerebral atrophy. (However, one's interpretation of these findings must be tempered by the fact that many individuals diagnosed with endogenous psychosis have no gross brain abnormalities that can be detected with present neuroassessment techniques—for example, a PET, magnetic resonance imaging, or computerized axial tomography scan.) Several laboratories have reported that chronic exposure to THC or marijuana extracts persistently alter the structure and function of the rat hippocampus (Scallet, 1991). However, the relevance of these studies is questionable because the studies employed massive doses of THC, which humans would never self-administer. Studies of monkeys after up to 12 months of daily exposure have not consistently reported neurotoxicity, and the results of longer exposures have not yet been studied. Interestingly, although some in vitro studies with cultured cortical neurons have indicated that cannabinoid agonists may exert neurotoxic effects on cortical neurons (1998), others (both in vitro and in vivo) have indicated that cannabinoids may protect cortical neurons from excitotoxicity associated with various types of brain insults and slow the progression of neurodegenerative diseases (Hampson et al., 2000; Nagayama et al., 1999; Shen & Thayer, 1998). The differences in these studies may depend on such factors as the specific procedures used, the source of the cells, the dosage and type of cannabinoid agonist, and so on, but at this point we still have not resolved the debate.

Tolerance and Dependence on Cannabis

Many users of marijuana report that continued use of it results in their becoming more sensitive to its effects (sensitization or reverse tolerance). As suggested in Chapter 6, this phenomenon may be due to the novice user—exposed to low doses of THC—learning to be more aware of marijuana's subjective effects, or to drug accumulation, because cannabinoids are stored in fat. However, the vast majority of studies indicate that tolerance can develop to most of the psychological effects (Dewey, 1986), but as is the case with most drugs, tolerance development to THC is dose dependent. Apparently, the usual patterns of marijuana smoking by North Americans—on the order of a joint or less a day (about 10 mg THC)—is such that tolerance to marijuana's effects does not develop (Perez-Reyes et al., 1991). However, with sufficiently high dosages, tolerance to most of THC's effects is likely to occur. Considerable evidence suggests that much of the tolerance phenomena observed in humans is due to learned adaptations to marijuana's disruptive effects on behavioral and perceptual processes. Pharmacodynamic processes could account for some tolerance phenomena, because chronic treatment with THC in rats has been shown to produce down-regulation of cannabinoid receptors in some areas of the brain (Oviedo et al., 1993; Rodriguez de Fonseca et al., 1994). However, increased density of cannabinoid receptors in some areas of the rat brain have also been observed with chronic THC exposure (Romero et al., 1995). Rats treated chronically with THC have been shown to develop differential tolerance to the neurophysiological effects of THC on different dopaminergic systems in the brain, which could account for differential degrees of tolerance to marijuana's behavioral, physiological, and subjective effects (Wu & French, 2000). The relevance of these findings to humans is unknown, because the doses of THC used in these animal studies were extremely high.

Dependence on marijuana is primarily psychological—that is, it is due to its mood- and cognitive-altering properties. Although in some ways it is like comparing apples with oranges, most experts would probably agree that psychological dependence associated with cannabinoids (i.e., the compulsive need to experience the effects) is of a considerably lower degree than that associated with alcohol and other sedative–hypnotics, opiates, or the psychostimulants (Dewey, 1986; Hollister, 1986; Jaffe, 1985; Zimmer & Morgan, 1997). Physical dependence as a result of social use of marijuana is even more atypical; until the mid-1970s most experts even denied its existence. However, studies conducted in the late 1970s and early 1980s demonstrated that cessation of extremely high dosage (e.g., 210 mg THC per day—equivalent to 10 to 20 average joints) chronic marijuana use by humans can precipitate an abstinence syndrome that may include one or more of the following: irritability, restlessness, decreased appetite, sleep disturbance, sweating, tremor, nausea, vomiting, and diarrhea. Later, signs of withdrawal were shown in humans following 4 days of smoking four marijuana cigarettes (with 3.1% THC content—an amount typically found in illegal joints) a day (Haney et al., 1999). Interestingly, none of the participants in this study requested to be terminated from the study during the abstinence periods, suggesting that the withdrawal symptoms were not particularly uncomfortable. This is consistent with reports by heavy marijuana users that when withdrawal symptoms do occur, they tend to be mild (compared with those associated with other drugs like alcohol or opiates) and transitory. Although there has been an increase in the number of people entering treatment programs with a primary diagnosis of marijuana dependence, most of these are polydrug abusers who also report problems with alcohol, cocaine, amphetamine, tranquilizers, or heroin (Zimmer & Morgan, 1997).

Non-CNS-Related Effects of Marijuana

Although they are outside the scope of the present text, there are a number of other potential consequences of marijuana use that the reader should be aware of, so these will briefly be discussed (see Dewey, 1986, and Hollister, 1986, for a more complete description). The peripheral manifestations of acute marijuana intoxication are minimal and consist predominantly of tachycardia (rapid heart rate) and conjunctival reddening of the eyes. There may be a slight increase in blood pressure with low doses and a slight decrease with high doses. Some individuals may experience blurred vision or headaches. Following acute intoxication, there are generally no residual physiological effects analogous to the alcohol hangover, unless particularly large quantities are used. As an illustration of how high the dosage of THC must be to induce such effects, some of the studies cited earlier in this chapter reported no discomfort in the marijuana users who had smoked 10 to 15 joints a day for years (on the order of 150 mg THC a day) when they were asked to abstain from smoking for 12 to 24 hours.

Numerous studies have indicated that marijuana smoking produces inflammation, edema, and cell injury in lung tissues of smokers and may be a risk factor for lung cancer, although there is no empirical evidence for lung cancer related solely to marijuana smoking (Zimmer & Morgan, 1997). Studies in humans who smoked cigarettes containing THC indicate that marijuana smoke may be a source of cellular oxidative stress that could contribute significantly to cell injury and dysfunction in the lungs of smokers (Sarafian et al., 1999). As one might expect, because human marijuana smokers generally autotitrate to a desired level of intoxication, smoking higher potency (i.e., higher THC content) marijuana relative to lower potency marijuana has been shown to reduce pulmonary exposure to noxious smoke components due to a reduced intake of smoke and/or a reduced tar yield from the stronger marijuana preparations (Matthias et al., 1997). Comparisons of heavy, habitual smokers of marijuana alone, smokers of marijuana plus tobacco, regular smokers of tobacco alone, and nonsmokers of either substance have indicated that regular tobacco, but not marijuana, smoking is associated with greater annual rates of decline in lung function than is nonsmoking (Tashkin et al., 1997).

Some studies have suggested that reproductive functioning may be impaired with marijuana, which may be reflected in lower testosterone levels (although generally within normal levels), reduced sex drive, and less vigorous sperm motility in males and interference with fertility in females. Most studies, however, have failed to show any significant effects of chronic marijuana use on the reproductive hormones of either men or women (Block et al., 19911). Given the potential alterations in hormonal functions, and the importance of these in the developing fetus, marijuana use (or any other drug use) during pregnancy is strongly discouraged. Although some studies have suggested that marijuana may interfere with the immune response and affect chromosomes, the clinical significance of those studies is questionable. Furthermore, many other studies have found no effects of marijuana in these areas (Zimmer & Morgan, 1997).

On the other side of the coin, there is considerable evidence that cannabinoids have some therapeutic value (Hall & Degenhardt, 2003; Hollister, 2000). THC (dronabinol; Marinol) is available for medical use in oral form in the United States (it is presently a Schedule III controlled substance). Smoked marijuana does not share this legal position, although several states have passed initiatives that would allow, contrary to federal regulations, the sale and use of smoked marijuana for a variety of medical indications. In 2001, Canada became the first country in the world to allow individuals with chronic illnesses (at least those whose physicians write a certificate saying they need it for medical purposes) to legally grow and use marijuana. The primary advantages of smoked marijuana come from the ability to achieve a rapid onset of effect and of users to autotitrate the THC concentrations needed to produce the maximal benefits, whereas oral THC produces a slower onset of effect, with greater variability in degree of effect. Advocates cite anecdotal and clinical evidence that cannabinoids can reduce nausea and vomiting associated with chemotherapy for cancer, reverse the wasting syndrome associated with AIDS, ease muscle spasms in the paralyzed, reduce arthritis pain, reduce the tics and obsessive–compulsive behavior of individuals with Tourette's syndrome, and significantly reduce the pressure in the eye associated with glaucoma.

Although cannabinoids generally are not superior to other medications used for these problems, they may prove useful in certain patients for whom these drugs are ineffective. Some doctors and federal health officials, however, say there is insufficient evidence to prove that marijuana is beneficial; some suggest that smoking it could be harmful, particularly for AIDS patients vulnerable to lung ailments. Because of the development of synthetic cannabinoid compounds with fewer intoxicating qualities and concerns over the potential harmfulness of marijuana, in 1992 the U.S. government stopped accepting new participants in its medicinal marijuana program, which, for some 15 years, had been supplying government-grown marijuana to patients suffering from cancer, glaucoma, and AIDS (Bowersox, 1992).

DISSOCIATIVE ANESTHETICS: PHENCYCLIDINE AND KETAMINE

One of the most predominant effects of phencyclidine (or PCP, which stands for its chemical name phencyclohexyl piperidine) and its analogue ketamine is profound anesthesia. Because patients anesthetized with these drugs are awake but appear disconnected from their environment, perhaps the simplest term to be used to describe these drugs is **dissociative anesthetic** (Jaffe, 1985). As is almost universally the case, PCP was discovered serendipitously. In the 1950s, while searching for new psychoactive drugs with therapeutic properties, chemists synthesized the drug, which psychopharmacologists immediately recognized as having some very unique effects in animals (Domino, 1980). In rats it had an amphetamine-like action, but, as with sedative–hypnotics, it disrupted muscular coordination. In dogs it induced convulsions, and in monkeys low doses had a calming effect (the monkeys appeared so serene that the drug was later marketed as Sernylyn), whereas higher doses eliminated sensitivity to touch or pain. It was this anesthetic action that was most promising for therapeutics, because most drugs with general anesthetic activity also have a strong lethal potential— due to the depression of the body's vital functions—at doses approximately double the anesthetic dose. With PCP the lethal dose was approximately 10 times the anesthetic dose. At appropriate doses, PCP induced insensitivity to pain while increasing blood pressure and heart rate. Also unlike any other general anesthetic, the organism remained awake with the eyes open.

When PCP was tested in human volunteers, it soon became apparent that it had profound psychotomimetic properties. PCP prompted distortions in body image, feelings of depersonalization, and a sense of timelessness—a transient feeling of being in outer space or dead or not having any arms or legs. In approximately a third of the individuals, the drug also prompted symptoms that mimicked very closely those of schizophrenia (apathy, ambivalence, autism, and an inability to associate thoughts or ideas), which, in some cases, persisted for several days or weeks. For this reason, the pharmaceutical company that developed Sernylyn withdrew it from the market, except for veterinary purposes. Until it was totally withdrawn from the market, Sernylyn was used primarily as an anesthetic in primates and not, as it is commonly assumed, as an animal tranquilizer.

For some of the same reasons that clinical use of PCP with humans was discontinued, illicit drug manufacturers in the 1960s started synthesizing the drug (a relatively easy process) and selling it as a substitute for LSD, THC, mescaline, and amphetamine. Until the 1970s it was rarely purchased intentionally as PCP (in which case, it was most commonly referred to as "angel dust"). Although still used by a very small minority of illicit drug users, PCP presents a severe drug abuse problem in that it has been reliably linked to suicides (as a result of severe depression) and drownings, self-inflicted wounds, and violence (as a result of the dissociation from reality, incoordination, and hallucinations).

Neurochemical and Psychological Effects of PCP

The CNS actions of PCP are quite complex and probably involve a wide variety of neurotransmitter systems. Stereospecific binding sites for PCP have been noted. Almost all of these sites appear to be located deep within an ion channel regulated by the NMDA receptor for the excitatory amino acids GLU and aspartate; by binding to this site, PCP prevents Ca^{++} and Na^+ flow through the channel and into the neuron (Johnson & Jones, 1990). PCP's ability to antagonize NMDA-type GLU receptor activity also appears to be a major factor in its ability to increase extracellular DA concentrations in the nucleus accumbens, prefrontal cortex, and basal ganglia (Hanson et al., 1995; Hondo et al., 1994; Yonezawa et al., 1995). Although these DA-enhancing effects may be responsible for some of PCP's rewarding properties and its psychotomimetic effects, there is evidence that PCP's blockade of NMDA receptor function is sufficient to explain both (Carlezon & Wise, 1996; Halberstadt, 1995). As is the case with most drugs of abuse, PCP has been shown to potentiate the effects of electrical stimulation of the brain (Carlezon & Wise, 1993).

Studies have also suggested that some of the properties of PCP are similar to those of the mixed agonist–antagonist narcotics like cyclazocine, which are generally viewed as kappa opioid receptor agonists (Pfeiffer et al., 1986). Adenosine receptors may be involved, because agonists at these receptors block the CNS properties of PCP (Browne & Welch, 1982). Finally, behavioral and pharmacodynamic measures in rats indicate that high doses of PCP can enhance serotonergic activity by binding to 5-HT transporters and inhibiting 5-HT reuptake (Hori et al., 2000).

Although PCP is often misrepresented as LSD, mescaline, or THC, the CNS effects of PCP are distinct from those of most other drugs, including amphetamine, THC, LSD, methaqualone, scopolamine, and morphine (Jaffe, 1985). PCP's CNS effects are also clearly different from those of the monoamine-related P/P/Hs. In the drug discrimination procedure, animals show no generalization between PCP and any monoamine

P/P/H (Appel et al., 1982) or, for that matter, between PCP and any cholinergic, dopaminergic, serotonergic, GABAergic, or opioid drugs (Johnson & Jones, 1990). PCP is one of the P/P/Hs that animals have been shown (using catheter/infusion method) to self-administer (Balster & Chait, 1976). Finally, whereas chlorpromazine (the antipsychotic) blocks the effects of LSD, it tends to potentiate PCP's depressant actions (Balster & Chait, 1976).

Electrophysiologically, sensory impulses to the cortex appear to be grossly distorted by PCP, particularly those involved in proprioception (the perceptual processing of stimuli originating in muscles, tendons, and other internal tissues; Domino, 1980). Peripherally, PCP has the sympathomimetic effects of increasing heart rate and blood pressure. The persistence of the PCP-induced effects can be traced to the fact that PCP has a relatively long plasma half-life, in some cases as long as 3 days (Jaffe, 1985). In addition to the confusing array of effects possessed by PCP, there are dozens of its metabolites, with potential psychoactive properties, that also persist in the body for several days.

Behaviorally in humans, low doses of PCP (1–5 mg) produce a drunken state, or "floaty" euphoria, with numbness in the hands and feet. Persons often describe their experience as involving grotesquely distorted body shape, unreal size of body parts, a sensation of floating or hovering in a weightless condition in space, or a sensation of leaving the body. Radiantly colorful visions that include images of moving from one room to another and moving, glowing geometrical patterns and figures are also reported, and the user may experience a complete absence of time sense (Domino, 1980). Intriguingly, the verbal reports of subjective experiences induced by PCP and ketamine are very similar to the reports of individuals claiming to have had a "near-death experience" resulting from various types of brain trauma (Jansen, 1990), which suggests that the latter experiences have a neurobiological explanation. Thus it would be quite interesting to assess the effects of these drugs in individuals who claim to have had a near-death experience to determine how similar the two types of experiences actually are. To my knowledge, no such study has been conducted.

Moderate doses (5–15 mg) induce analgesia and anesthesia, and an excited, confused intoxication can develop. Communication is definitely impaired. A body position may be rigidly maintained over extended periods of time (catalepsy). Larger doses of PCP induce a very definite psychosis and, in rare cases, convulsions (although low doses of PCP generally have anticonvulsant properties due to NMDA-mediated response blockade). Death is rarely directly caused by PCP because of its moderately high therapeutic index. There are distinct species differences in terms of reaction to PCP; some animals become very excited, and others become very sedated. The anesthetic dose is dependent on the complexity of the organism; as one progresses up the phylogenetic scale, lower doses are needed to induce anesthesia (Domino, 1980).

Tolerance develops to many of the effects of PCP, but much of it appears to be due to behavioral adaptations. For example, monkeys administered PCP (1.0 mg/kg) daily for 4 months were less affected by 1.0 mg/kg PCP than nondrug-treated monkeys in terms of their ability to stand on their hind limbs to reach for a food pellet, their ability to track a food pellet moved laterally across the field of vision, and their ability to reach out and take an offered pellet. However, in terms of nystagmus (rhythmical oscillation of the eyeballs), both groups of monkeys were affected to the same degree (Balster & Chait, 1976).

Notice that the dependent variables to which tolerance developed were the ones in which you would expect behavioral adjustments to occur. Other studies with animals have confirmed these findings. For example, studies have demonstrated that tolerance occurs to some behavioral effects with both PCP and ketamine, although the anticonvulsant action (with low doses) of these drugs remains unaffected after chronic drug exposure (Leccese et al., 1986).

PCP may also produce mild physical dependence, because abrupt withdrawal from PCP after chronic use may be followed by fearfulness, tremors, and facial twitches (Jaffe, 1985). Alterations in PCP receptors with chronic PCP exposure do not appear to play a major role in the production of PCP dependence (Burke et al., 1995). Some craving after stopping PCP use may also be experienced by chronic users.

With such a confusing array of pharmacological actions, it is not clear what accounts for PCP's popularity. The majority of PCP users report that they enjoy the intoxication state, viewing it as a novel experience that provides an escape from anxieties, depression, and other external pressures (Domino, 1980). To this outside observer, these effects seem a little like the effects from a combination of a sedative–hypnotic, a monoamine-related P/P/H, and an opiate.

PCP-Induced Psychosis

Although it has euphoriant effects in the majority of users, PCP can induce a distinct psychotic reaction in a significant minority of people (Erard et al., 1980). These people can generally be placed in one of three categories: (1) normal individuals who experience a schizophrenic-like syndrome lasting for several hours; (2) individuals with no previous history of psychotic episodes or other psychiatric problems, whose PCP-induced psychosis lasts an average of 2 weeks; and (3) those previously diagnosed with schizophrenia, in whom PCP triggers or exacerbates their original psychosis, a condition that may last for several weeks. Whether these three types of reactions are qualitatively different or are simply variations along a continuum involving persons with varying degrees of predisposition toward the development of schizophrenic symptoms is unclear.

The symptoms of PCP psychosis are indistinguishable from the core symptoms of schizophrenia (Ellison, 1995). Most patients treated for it present global paranoia, persecutory and grandiose delusions, and auditory hallucinations, with periods of suspiciousness alternating with extreme anger or terror. As is common with schizophrenia, affect is blunted, and patients are ambivalent toward close friends and relatives. In some cases, they profess superhuman strength and invulnerability, and they may become violent without provocation (it should be mentioned that this is rarely the case with schizophrenia). Other clinical signs are negativism, hostility, disorientation, repetitive motor behavior, and rigidity. In very rare cases, the psychosis is more similar to mania, with symptoms including elation, grandiose and paranoid delusions, and widely fluctuating affect, but no thought disorder or disorientation. Generally, the patients are amnesic about the events occurring during the PCP-induced state.

Schizophrenics are particularly sensitive to PCP and show profound disorganization in reaction to it (Erard et al., 1980). This is considerably different from their reaction to other P/P/Hs such as LSD or mescaline. Intelligent schizophrenics can distinguish the effects of these latter drugs from their psychosis, and, as with normal individuals, they experience the kaleidoscopic visual effects (Jacobsen, 1968).

Although acute exposure to PCP can produce many of the symptoms characteristic of schizophrenia, the most complete spectrum of schizophrenic symptoms occurs with repeated exposures to PCP. First, although both acute and long-term exposure to PCP produces intense psychosis, hallucinations, delusions, thought disorder, and impaired cognition, these effects are considerably longer lasting with long-term than with acute exposure (e.g., days to weeks rather than a few hours). Second, whereas acute PCP exposure produces visual illusions, euphoric to catatonic affect, and increased frontal lobe blood flow, long-term PCP exposure is more likely to produce anxious, labile, or paranoid affect; auditory and paranoid hallucinations; delusions that are frequently religious; and decreased frontal lobe blood flow (Jentsch & Roth, 1999). The latter symptoms more completely model the behavioral and metabolic dysfunctions of schizophrenia.

Treatment for PCP Psychosis

The treatment of PCP toxic reactions is somewhat different from treatments for other P/P/Hs (Aronow et al., 1980), which for the most part simply require time passage and reassurance. Some of the psychotomimetic effects of PCP can be antagonized by the nonsedating antipsychotics like haloperidol (Haldol), although some clinicians feel that these drugs may exacerbate the behavioral dyscontrol of PCP. Diazepam may be used to help control muscle spasms and restlessness, and the anticonvulsant Dilantin may be used prophylactically against convulsions. Nondrug treatment generally involves lavage (washing out the GI tract with large amounts of fluid) or gastric suctioning if the psychosis is treated shortly after the drug has been administered. Because PCP is a weak alkaloid administered as a salt (phencyclidine hydrochloride), a technique called *ion trapping*, in which the urine is acidified to ensure ionization of the PCP base, is used to facilitate PCP's removal from the body. Unlike the "talking down" strategy suggested for dealing with LSD-like or cannabinoid psychoses, it is suggested that the person experiencing a PCP psychosis be placed in as quiet and nonstimulating an environment as possible, because he or she may exhibit unexpected violence or aggression.

Ketamine

After noting the many side effects of PCP, chemists synthesized a number of analogues of PCP. Ketamine (Ketalar) was found to have the most therapeutic value as an anesthetic. Although possessing the desirable characteristics of PCP (i.e., high therapeutic index, minimal effect on respiration, and elevation of blood pressure and cardiac output), it did not induce convulsions and was short-acting than PCP (recovery occurs in less than 2 hours; Domino, 1980). Ketamine's pharmacodynamic actions are similar to those of PCP; that is, it antagonizes NMDA receptor-sensitive glutamatergic neurotransmission in the brain. Like PCP, ketamine also induces memory impairments in humans and animals (Chrobak et al., 2008).

Except for their duration, the psychological effects of ketamine are very similar to those of PCP. In healthy volunteers, ketamine has been shown to produce dose-dependent impairments in episodic, recognition, and working memory and procedural learning, as well as a slowing of semantic processing (Morgan et al., 2004). Essentially the same perceptual distortions in vision, audition, body image, sense of time, and the like noted with PCP can occur during the recovery period following ketamine anesthesia, but to a lesser degree (Hansen et al., 1988). Furthermore, like PCP, ketamine has been shown to induce positive and negative symptoms of schizophrenia (see Chapter 8) in both healthy subjects and schizophrenic patients (Krystal et al., 1999; Lahti et al., 1995). The symptoms in these schizophrenic patients were strikingly similar to those exhibited by the patients during active episodes of their illness. However, in neither group were the psychotic symptoms reduced with the typical antipsychotic haloperidol, although some of the disruptive effects of ketamine on cognitive functions of the healthy subjects were lessened. Interestingly, the atypical antipsychotic clozapine was found to significantly blunt the increase in positive symptoms induced by ketamine in antipsychotic drug-free schizophrenics (Malhotra et al., 1997). As discussed in Chapter 8, clozapine is one of several atypical antipsychotics with a different spectrum of actions and effects than those displayed with conventional antipsychotics (e.g., haloperidol).

Unfortunately, since the 1980s, ketamine has gained popularity for its dissociative, sedative, and hallucinatory effects by recreational drug users, and it has joined the list of popular club drugs (e.g., MDMA, gamma hydroxybutyrate [GHB]), with which ketamine is often combined (Smith et al., 2002). Ketamine is used recreationally in a variety of settings apart from the club or rave environments, where it is usually administered intranasally. However, it is not uncommon for it to be injected, which produces more reliable and intense dissociative effects than when taken orally or intranasally (Lankenau & Clatts, 2002). Ketamine is also considered one of the "date-rape" drugs due to its colorless, odorless, tasteless nature, and its ability to immobilize individuals, disorientate them, and induce amnesia. Concerns over its abuse led to its being classified as a Schedule III drug by the DEA in 1999.

Anticholinergics

One of the oldest known groups of P/P/Hs is called the **anticholinergics** because these drugs are pharmacological, competitive antagonists of the subclass of ACh receptors called muscarinic receptors (Chapter 5). Thus they are often, and more appropriately, termed *antimuscarinics*. Their blocking action at ACh receptors activated by nicotine (nicotinic receptors) is very weak. The early writings of Homer describe potent agents with properties similar to those of the anticholinergics. These drugs are often called belladonna alkaloids because at one time women used one of these compounds (*Atropa belladonna*) to dilate their pupils and enhance their beauty (*belladonna* means "beautiful lady"). Throughout the Middle Ages, many witchcraft potions contained mushrooms and herbs with anticholinergic properties. The four deadly nightshades—*Atropa belladonna* (death's herb), *Datura stramonium* (Jamestown weed, jimson weed, thornapple, stinkweed), *Hyoscyamus niger* (henbane), and *Mandragora officinarum* (mandrake)—were also well known to oracles, assassins, seducers, and physicians. Jamestown weed was commonly used as an intoxicant by the early settlers of Jamestown, Virginia (circa 1676).

At the present time, anticholinergics are not schedule-controlled substances, even though they can only be purchased through prescription, nor is there any law preventing the cultivation of plants containing these alkaloids, primarily because the recreational use and the abuse potential for these drugs is currently very minimal. They have a number of side effects that reduce their reward value, and there are other drugs available with similar euphoriant properties that do not have these side effects.

The three most common anticholinergics are atropine, scopolamine, and *l*-hyoscyamine. These drugs are discussed in this chapter because of their ability to induce hallucinatory experiences at sufficiently high doses, but they have myriad effects that are heavily dose-dependent (Weiner, 1985). In small doses, scopolamine induces quiet sedation, with euphoria, amnesia, and dreamless sleep (probably associated with reduced REM activity). Sometimes, however, especially when the person is in pain, scopolamine causes excitement, hallucinations, or delirium in small doses. In general, the effects of anticholinergics resulting from their CNS activity include the following: (1) confusion, slurred speech, disorientation similar to alcohol intoxication; (2) psychotic behavior similar to hebephrenia (a state in which the person acts very childish and silly); (3) hallucinations, primarily consisting of brightly colored objects and pleasant sounds; (4) drowsiness and fatigue; and (5) amnesia, whereby the person may forget the entire episode of intoxication. (At one time anticholinergics, in combination with morphine, were given to women in labor to induce a "twilight sleep" so that they would forget the pain of childbirth.) At extremely high doses, coma can result. Although these drugs can be lethal and have been used as poisons in the past, their margin of safety is actually rather large. Deaths attributed to them nowadays generally involve abusers who might wander off into heavy traffic or fall into swimming pools, and children who ingest berries or seeds containing belladonna alkaloids. The most commonly used antidote to anticholinergic poisoning is to administer physostigmine, a drug that inhibits the action of acetylcholinesterase (the enzyme that metabolizes ACh in the synaptic cleft) and increases extracellular levels of acetylcholine.

Tolerance to the belladonna alkaloids occurs in humans to a limited extent. Psychological dependence at the present time is extremely rare. Physical dependence is minimal, although vomiting, malaise, excessive sweating, and salivation have been recorded upon sudden withdrawal in parkinsonism patients treated with large doses (required for therapeutic benefit) of these compounds.

Ibogaine

Ibogaine is one of several psychoactive indole alkaloids found in a shrub, *Tabernanthe iboga*, indigenous to Central-West Africa. Peoples of this region have used the shrub for many years for a variety of purposes—for instance, in initiation rite ceremonies (in which members ingesting the iboga root believe it allows them to make contact with ancestors in the spirit world), for the enhancement of endurance and strength of warriors, and as an aphrodisiac (Popik et al., 1995b). The plant was introduced to Western medicine over a century ago, and ibogaine was isolated from the plant in 1901. At that time, a number of potential medical uses were suggested for ibogaine, but interest in its therapeutic properties didn't gain momentum until the 1930s and 1940s, when it was promoted primarily as a tonic or stimulant in the treatment of fatigue, sleeping sickness (trypanosomiasis), and depression. In the 1960s, the use of ibogaine for its purported performance-enhancing effects in athletes and for its hallucinogenic effects among members of the counterculture ("hippies") led to its being prohibited in many countries, including the United States which in 1970 classified ibogaine as a Schedule I controlled substance. Interest in ibogaine resurfaced in the 1980s when Howard S. Lotsof acquired a series of patents for the use of ibogaine (called Endabuse) as a rapid and easy means of treating addiction to opiates, psychostimulants, alcohol, and nicotine. At the present time, a number of clinical trials are being conducted with ibogaine to evaluate its safety and efficacy in the treatment of a variety of drug addictions. For example, in one study of heroin addicts undergoing detoxification, the signs of opioid withdrawal were eliminated in 25 of 33 patients within 24 hours after ibogaine administration without further drug-seeking behavior—an effect that was sustained throughout the 72-hour period of posttreatment observation (Alper et al., 2000).

Although stimulant-like effects predominate with lower doses of the crude extract of iboga, when taken in sufficiently high doses (which are sometimes fatal), iboga is reported by users to result in fantastic visions, feelings of excitement, drunkenness, mental confusion, and hallucinations. The verbal reports of users of ibogaine or the total iboga extract suggest that the subjective experience, which lasts about 6 hours, is very similar to that of the more potent monoamine-related P/P/Hs. This is consistent with the fact that ibogaine has a 5-HT-like (indoleamine) molecular structure and the finding that animals trained to discriminate between saline and the monoamine P/P/Hs LSD or DMMA in the two-choice drug discrimination paradigm respond to ibogaine as if it were the LSD or DMMA cue (Palumbo & Winter, 1992). On the other hand, in studies with humans, the drug has been reported to elicit a state of drowsiness in which the subjects did not want to move, open their eyes, or attend to the environment. Many subjects were light-sensitive and covered their eyes or asked that lights be turned off. Sounds or noises were disturbing. These are characteristics commonly observed with PCP. As is the case with many P/P/Hs, severe anxiety and apprehension can accompany the hallucinations. Some reports indicate that the psychic state produced by ibogaine is similar to a dream state without the loss of consciousness, which some psychoanalytic therapists suggested might be useful as a psychological catalyst that could compress a long psychotherapeutic process into a shorter time period (Naranjo, 1969). Similar dreamlike experiences have been reported to occur with the indoleamine–related P/P/H DMT (Strassman et al., 1994). Ibogaine is also reported to be a highly valued aphrodisiac in Africa. Whether this is due to a direct effect on sexual function or is due to an expectancy effect, an increase in self-confidence, or a decrease in fatigue is unknown.

What ibogaine's abuse potential is in humans is not clear at this point. There are no reports of animals self-administering pure ibogaine (although in Africa wild animals have been observed by local inhabitants to dig up and eat the root of the iboga plant and then enter into a wild frenzy—which may have been how humans learned about the properties of the plant [Pope, 1969]). Furthermore, as noted in earlier chapters, ibogaine has been shown to inhibit the self-administration of drugs of abuse in animals.

Some effects of ibogaine have been observed up to 1 week after administration in both humans and animals. Because detectable levels of ibogaine are no longer present within about 12 hours after administration, it has been hypothesized that ibogaine may be metabolized into a long-lasting psychoactive compound. Although an active metabolite of ibogaine has been found (12-hydroxyibogamine), it is not clear that it accounts for ibogaine's long-term effects (Mash et al., 1995).

Ibogaine's pharmacodynamic properties are even more complex and varied, with potent actions on dopaminergic, opioid, and serotonergic systems, and NMDA and calcium channels, among others (Popik et al., 1995b), suggesting that multiple mechanisms of action are responsible for ibogaine's effects. One of its most prominent actions is to block NMDA receptor–activated ion channels by binding to a site within the channel (Popik et al., 1995a). This is also a property of PCP, which, as described earlier, has psychotomimetic and subjective effects similar to ibogaine. Ibogaine and one of its metabolites also block 5-HT reuptake sites and elevate extracellular 5-HT levels. In addition to actions on several neurotransmitter systems, high doses of ibogaine in rats have been reported to cause the degeneration of a subset of neurons in the cerebellum (O'Hearn et al., 1995; O'Hearn & Molliver, 1993), which could account for some of ibogaine's long-lasting effects. Unfortunately, if neurotoxicity occurs with lower doses, or is the major factor in ibogaine's "antiaddiction" properties (should they be verified), justification of its therapeutic use will be difficult.

DISSOCIATIVE ANESTHETICS, PSYCHEDELICS, AND HALLUCINOGENS: THE HUMAN EXPERIENCE

We are built to process stimuli, and an important aspect of our living is the seeking out of stimuli to process. The popularity of P/P/Hs is a function of this general characteristic of stimulus seeking. The central property of any of the P/P/Hs is the enhancement of experience (Aaronson & Osmond, 1970). They seem to increase the capacity of the human brain to respond to fine gradations of stimulus input, to enhance our responses to stimulation at both the upper and lower levels of perceptual processing, and to remove the constraints imposed by the different sensory pathways through which stimulation is received. They produce new perceptions, alter our ways of looking at the world, and in some cases induce hallucinations. The experience can be very exhilarating or very frightening. In contrast, the sedative–hypnotics and narcotics reduce our attention to sensory input, although these substances may induce hypnagogic and dreamlike states. Psychostimulants may enhance endurance, improve mood, and increase alertness, but they do not alter our attention to the fine nuances of sensory experience to the degree that P/P/Hs do.

However, in order for the enhanced capacity for experience to occur with P/P/Hs, an adequate range of stimuli must be available, because exposure to them under conditions of sensory deprivation seems to reduce their effects considerably (Aaronson & Osmond, 1970). On the other hand, as the complexity of the stimulus situation increases, the variability of the experiences and perceptual reactions increases. Furthermore, in addition to the setting, the person's attitudes, motivations, cognitive set, and expectations play such a large role in the experience that it is impossible to predict in advance the type of experience one may have with these substances. This unpredictability may, in fact, be another reason why humans use them.

Websites for Further Information

Site providing information on a wide variety of hallucinogens (e.g., psilocybin, cannabis, mescaline, LSD, PCP), along with a number of links:

> http://www.erowid.org/general/big_chart.shtml

The Albert Hofmann Foundation website (the use of LSD to explore the unconscious):

> http://www.hofmann.org

Sites concerned with the history of legal restrictions on marijuana:

> http://www.forces.org/articles/files/whiteb/white.htm ("The History of the Non-Medical Use of Drugs in the United States," by Charles Whitebread, USC Law School, 1995)

> http://www.druglibrary.org/schaffer/hemp/taxact/taxact.htm (testimony and documentation concerned with the Marijuana Tax Act of 1937)

> http://www.druglibrary.org/schaffer/library/studies/nc/ncmenu.htm (The Report of the National Commission on Marihuana and Drug Abuse commissioned by Richard M. Nixon, 1972)

The National Organization for the Reform of Marijuana Laws' (NORML) home page:

> http://www.norml.org

Information on the nature and extent of marijuana use in the United States:

> http://www.cedro-uva.org/lib/harrison.cannabis.03.html

Site providing news about marijuana:

> http://www.marijuananews.com

Site providing information on making marijuana legal for medical use:

> http://www.mpp.org

APPENDIX

Drug Name Index

Brand Name	Generic Name	Brand Name	Generic Name
Abilify	aripiprazole	Dolophine	methadone
Abstem, Temposil	calcium carbimide	Doriden	glutethimide
Acomplia	rimonabant	Duragesic	fentanyl
Actiq	fentanyl	Edronax	reboxetine
Adderall	amphetamine	Effexor	venlafaxine
Akeniton	biperiden	Elavil	amitriptyline
Ambien	zolpidem	Eldepryl	selegiline
Anafranil	clomipramine	Endabuse	ibogaine
Antabuse	disulfiram	Eskalith	lithium
Aricept	donepezil	Exelon	rivastigmine
Ariza, Variza	gepirone	Felbatol	felbamate
Artane	trihexyphenidyl	Focalin	dexmethylphenidate
Asendin	amoxapine	Gabitril	tiagabine
Ativan	lorazepam	Geodon	ziprasidone
Benadryl	diphenhydramine	Halcion	triazolam
Benzedrine	amphetamine	Haldol	haloperidol
Buprenex	buprenorphine	Hydergine	ergoloid mesylates
BuSpar	buspirone	Inderal	propranolol
Campral	acamprosate	Ionamin	phentermine
Catapres	clonidine	Keppra	levetiracetam
Celexa	citalopram	Ketalar	ketamine
Chantix	varenicline	Klonopin	clonazepam
Clozaril	clozapine	Lamictal	lamotrigine
Cogentin	benztropine	Lexapro	escitalopram
Cognex	tacrine	Librium	chlordiazepoxide
Comtan	entacapone	Loxitane	loxapine
Concerta	methylphenidate	Ludiomil	maprotiline
Cylert	pemoline	Luvox	fluvoxamine
Cymbalta	duloxetine	Marinol	dronabinol
Dalmane	flurazepam	Marplan	isocarboxazid
Darvon	propoxyphene	Mellaril	thioridazine
Decanoate	decanoate	Meratran	pipradol
Demerol	meperidine	Merital	nomifensine
Depakene	valproic acid	Metadate CD	methylphenidate
Depakote	valproic acid	Miltown	meprobamate
Desoxyn	methamphetamine	Mirapex	pramipexole
Desoxyn, Methedrine	methamphetamine	Moban	molindone
Desyrel	trazodone	Moclobamine	moclobemide
Dexedrine	d-amphetamine	Mysoline	primidone
Dilantin	phenytoin	Namenda	memantine
Dilaudid	hydromorphone	Narcan	naloxone

(Continued)

Brand Name	Generic Name	Brand Name	Generic Name
Nardil	phenelzine	Serax	oxazepam
Navane	thiothixene	Serentil	mesoridazine
Neurontin	gabapentin	Seroquel	quetiapine
Norflex	orphenadrine	Sinemet	l-dopa
Norpramin	desipramine	Sinequan	doxepin
Novocain	procaine	Stalevo	entacapone + carbidopa + L-dopa
Orap	pimozide		
Orlamm	levo-alpha-acetyl-methadol	Stelazine	trifluoperazine
		Strattera	atomoxetine
Pamelor	nortriptyline	Sublimaze	fentanyl
Parlodel	bromocriptine	Suboxone	buprenorphine + naloxone
Parnate	tranylcypromine	Subutex	buprenorphine
Paxil	paroxetine	Surmontil	trimipramine
Paxipam	halazepam	Symbyax	olanzapine + fluoxetine
Permax	pergolide	Symmetrel	amantadine
Placidyl	ethchlorvynol	Talwin	pentazocine
Pondimin	fenfluramine	Tegretol	carbamazepine
Preludin	phenmetrazine	Tenex	guanfacine
Prolixin	fluphenazine	Thorazine	chlorpromazine
Provigil	modafinil	Tofranil	imipramine
Prozac	fluoxetine	Topamax	topiramate
Quaalude	methaqualone	Tranxene	clorazepate
Redux	dexfenfluramine	Trilafon	perphenazine
Remeron	mirtazapine	Trileptal	oxcarbazepine
Reminyl	galantamine	Valium	diazepam
Requip	ropinirole	Vistaril	hydroxyzine
Restoril	temazepam	Vivactil	protriptyline
Revex	nalmefene	Vivitrol	naltrexone time release
ReVia	naltrexone	Wellbutrin	bupropion
Risperdal	risperidone	Xanax	alprazolam
Ritalin	methylphenidate	Zarontin	ethosuximide
Rohypnol	flunitrazepam	Zoloft	sertraline
Romazicon	flumazenil	Zonegran	zonisamide
Selegiline	deprenyl	Zyban	bupropion
Serafem	fluoxetine	Zyprexa	olanzapine

Note: Most of the drugs in this list are those cited in this book and have been approved (or were approved at one time) by the Food and Drug Administration (FDA) for marketing in the United States. Some of these drugs are only marketed outside the United States. Other drugs that have been cited in this text, but for which a brand name has not been provided, are under investigation or have not been approved by the FDA.

BIBLIOGRAPHY

Aaronson, B., & Osmond, H. (1970). Introduction: Psychedelics, technology, psychedelics. In B. Aaronson & H. Osmond (Eds.), *Psychedelics* (pp. 3–18). Garden City, NY: Anchor Books.

Abel, E. L., & Hannigan, J. H. (1995). Maternal risk factors in fetal alcohol syndrome: Provocative and permissive influences. *Neurotoxicology & Teratology, 17,* 445–462.

Aberman, J. E., & Salamone, J. D. (1999). Nucleus accumbens dopamine depletions make rats more sensitive to high ratio requirements but do not impair primary food reinforcement. *Neuroscience, 92,* 545–552.

Abraham, H. D. (1983). Visual phenomenology of the LSD flashback. *Archives of General Psychiatry, 40,* 884–889.

Abraham, H. D., & Aldridge, A. M. (1993). Adverse consequences of lysergic acid diethylamide. *Addiction, 88,* 1327–1334.

Acevedo, B. P., Aron, A., Fisher, H. E., & Brown, L. L. (2011). Neural correlates of long-term intense romantic love. *Social Cognitive and Affective Neuroscience* [Epub ahead of print].

Acquas, E., Carboni, E., Leone, P., & Di Chiara, G. (1989). SCH 23390 blocks drug-conditioned place-preference and place-aversion: Anhedonia (lack of reward) or apathy (lack of motivation) after dopamine-receptor blockade? *Psychopharmacology, 99,* 151–155.

Advokat, C., Dixon, D., Schneider, J., & Comaty, J. E. J. (2004). Comparison of risperidone and olanzapine as used under "real-world" conditions in a state psychiatric hospital. *Progress in Neuro-Psychopharmacology and Biological Psychiatry, 28,* 487–495.

Aghajanian, G. K., & Marek, J. (1999). Serotonin and hallucinogens. *Neuropsychopharmacology, 21*(Suppl. 2), 16S–23S.

Agnati, L. F., Zoll, M., Stromberg, I., & Fuxe, K. (1995). Intercellular communication in the brain: Wiring versus volume transmission. *Neuroscience, 69,* 711–726.

Agosti, V. (1994). The efficacy of controlled trials of alcohol misuse treatments in maintaining abstinence: A meta-analysis. *International Journal of the Addictions, 29,* 759–769.

Agurell, S., Halldin, M., Lindgren, J.-E., et al. (1986). Pharmacokinetics and metabolism of delta-1-tetrahydro-cannabinol and other cannabinoids with emphasis on man. *Pharmacological Reviews, 38,* 21–43.

Aigner, T. G., & Balster, R. L. (1978). Choice behavior in rhesus monkeys: Cocaine versus food. *Science, 201,* 534–535.

Ajibola, O., & Clement, P. W. (1995). Differential effects of methylphenidate and self-reinforcement on attention-deficit hyperactivity disorder. *Behavior Modification, 19,* 211–233.

Akam, E., & Strange, G. (2004). Inverse agonist properties of atypical antipsychotic drugs. *Biochemical Pharmacology, 67,* 2039–2045.

Alden, L. E. (1988). Behavioral self-management controlled-drinking strategies in a context of secondary prevention. *Journal of Consulting and Clinical Psychology, 56,* 280–286.

Alexander, K. S., Brooks, J. M., Sarter, M., & Bruno, J. P. (2009). Disruption of mesolimbic regulation of prefrontal cholinergic transmission in an animal model of schizophrenia and normalization by chronic clozapine treatment. *Neuropsychopharmacology, 34,* 2710–2720.

Alger, B. E. (2002). Retrograde signaling in the regulation of synaptic transmission: Focus on endocannabinoids. *Progress in Neurobiology, 68,* 247–286.

Allen, R. P., McCann, U. D., & Ricaurte, G. A. (1993). Persistent effects of (+/−) 3,4-methyl-enedioxymethamphetamine (MDMA, "ecstasy") on human sleep. *Sleep, 16,* 560–564.

Allison, D., Mentore, J., Heo, M., et al. (1999). Antipsychotic-induced weight gain: A comprehensive research synthesis. *American Journal of Psychiatry, 156,* 1686–1696.

Alper, K. R., Lotsof, H. S., Frenken, G. M., et al. (2000). Ibogaine in acute opioid withdrawal. An open label case series. *Annals of the New York Academy of Sciences, 909,* 257–259.

Alsene, K., Deckert, J., Sand, P., & de Wit, H. (2003). Association between A_{2a} receptor gene polymorphisms and caffeine-induced anxiety. *Neuropsychopharmacology, 28,* 1694–1702.

Altman, S. E., Shankman, S. A., & Spring, B. (2010). Effect of acute tryptophan depletion on emotions in individuals with personal and family history of depression following a mood induction. *Neuropsychobiology, 62,* 171–176.

Amato, L., Davoli, M., Ferri, M., et al. (2004). Effectiveness of interventions on opiate withdrawal treatment: An overview of systematic reviews. *Drug and Alcohol Dependence, 73,* 219–226.

Ambre, J. J. (1993). Acute tolerance to pressor effects of cocaine in humans. *Therapeutic Drug Monitoring, 15,* 537–540.

Ameri, A. (1999). The effects of cannabinoids on the brain. *Progress in Neurobiology, 58,* 315–348.

American Psychiatric Association. (2000). *Diagnostic and statistical manual of mental disorders (DSM-IV)* (textual revisions, 4th ed.). Washington, DC: Author.

American Society for Pharmacology and Experimental Therapeutics and Committee on Problems of Drug Dependence. (1987). Scientific perspectives on cocaine abuse. *Pharmacologist, 29,* 20–27.

Ames, D., Wirshing, W. C., & Marder, S. R. (1996). Advances in antipsychotic pharmacotherapy: Clozapine, risperidone, and beyond. *Essential Psychopharmacology, 1,* 5–26.

Amtage, J., & Schmidt, W. J. (2009). Context-dependent catalepsy intensification is due

to classical conditioning and sensitization. *Behavioural Pharmacology, 14,* 563–567.

Anderson, I. M. (2000). Selective serotonin reuptake inhibitors versus tricyclic antidepressants: A meta-analysis of efficacy and tolerability. *Journal of Affective Disorders, 58,* 19–36.

Anderson, K. J., & Revelle, W. (1983). The interactive effects of caffeine, impulsivity and task demands on a visual search task. *Personality and Individual Differences, 4,* 127–134.

Anderson, L. T., Campbell, M., Grega, D. M., Perry, R., Small, A. M., & Green, W. H. (1984). Haloperidol in the treatment of infantile autism: Effects on learning and behavioral symptoms. *American Journal of Psychiatry, 141,* 1195–1202.

Andreasen, N. C., Arndt, S., Swayze, V., et al. (1994). Thalamic abnormalities in schizophrenia visualized through magnetic resonance image averaging. *Science, 266,* 294–298.

Annitto, W. J. (1979, March). Recognizing lithium-associated neurotoxicity. *Drug Therapy,* 45–51.

Annoni, J., Ptak, R., Caldara-Schnetzer, A., Khateb, A., & Pollermann, B. Z. (2003). Decoupling of autonomic and cognitive emotional reactions after cerebellar stroke. *Annals of Neurology, 53,* 654–658.

Annual smoking-attributable mortality, years of potential life lost, and economic costs—United States, 1995–1999. (2002). *MMWR Morbidity and Mortality Weekly Report, 51*(14), pp. 300–303.

Anstrom, K. K., & Woodward, D. J. (2005). Restraint increases dopaminergic burst firing in awake rats. *Neuropsychopharmacology, 30,* 1832–1840.

Antelman, S. M., Eichler, A. J., Black, C. A., & Kocan, D. (1980). Interchangeability of stress and amphetamine in sensitization. *Science, 207,* 329–331.

Anthenelli, R. M., Klein, J. L., Tsuang, J. W., et al. (1994). The prognostic importance of blackouts in young men. *Journal of Studies on Alcohol, 55,* 290–295.

Appel, J. B., White, F. J., & Holohean, A. M. (1982). Analyzing mechanisms of hallucinogenic drug action with drug discrimination procedures. *Neuroscience and Biobehavioral Reviews, 6,* 529–536.

Apter, J. T., & Allen, L. A. (1999). Buspirone: Future directions. *Journal of Clinical Psychopharmacology, 19,* 86–93.

Arango, V., Ernsberger, P., Marzuk, P. M., et al. (1990). Autoradiographic demonstration of increased serotonin 5-HT2 and beta-adrenergic receptor binding sites in the brain of suicide victims. *Archives of General Psychiatry, 47,* 1038–1047.

Argo, T. R., Carnahan, R. M., & Perry, P. J. (2004). Aripiprazole, a novel atypical antipsychotic drug. *Pharmacotherapy, 24,* 212–228.

Arizzi-LaFrance, M. N., Correa, M., Aragon, C. M., & Salamone, J. D. (2006). Motor stimulant effects of ethanol injected into the substantia nigra pars reticulata: Importance of catalase-mediated metabolism and the role of acetaldehyde. *Neuropsychpharmacology, 31,* 997–1008.

Arnold, L. E. (1993). A comparative overview of treatment research methodology: Adult vs. child and adolescent, psychopharmacological vs. psychosocial treatments. *Psychopharmacology Bulletin, 29,* 5–18.

Arnone, M., Maruani, J., Chaperon, F., Thiebot, M. H., Poncelet, M., Soubrie, P., et al. (1997). Selective inhibition of sucrose and ethanol intake by SR141716, an antagonist of central cannabinoid (CB1) receptors. *Psychopharmacology, 132,* 104–106.

Arnt, J., & Skarsfeldt, T. (1998). Do novel antipsychotics have similar pharmacological characteristics? A review of the evidence. *Neuropsychopharmacology, 18,* 63–101.

Aronow, R., Miceli, J. N., & Done, A. K. (1980). A therapeutic approach to the acutely overdosed PCP patient. *Journal of Psychedelic Drugs, 12,* 259–266.

Aronson, T. A., & Craig, T. J. (1986). Cocaine precipitation of panic disorder. *American Journal of Psychiatry, 143,* 643–645.

Arseneault, L., Cannon, M., Witton, J., & Murray, R. M. (2004). Causal association between cannabis and psychosis: Examination of the evidence. *British Journal of Psychiatry, 184,* 110–117.

Azcona, O., Barbanoj, M. J., Torrent, J., & Jane, F. (1995). Evaluation of the central effects of alcohol and caffeine interaction. *British Journal of Clinical Pharmacology, 40,* 393–400.

Azmitia, E. C. (1999). Serotonin neurons, neuroplasticity, and homeostasis of neural tissue. *Neuropsychopharmacology, 21*(Suppl. 2), 33S–45S.

Azorlosa, J. L., Heishman, S. J., Stitzer, M. L., & Mahaffey, J. M. (1992). Marijuana smoking: Effect of varying delta-9-tetrahydrocannabinol content and number of puffs. *Journal of Pharmacology and Experimental Therapeutics, 261,* 114–122.

Bach-y-Rita, P. (1994). Psychopharmacologic drugs: Mechanisms of action. *Science, 264,* 640–641.

Bachtell, R. K., Choi, K. H., Simmons, D. L., Falcon, E., Monteggia, L. M., Neve, R. L., et al. (2008). Role of GluR1 expression in nucleus accumbens neurons in cocaine sensitization and cocaine-seeking behavior. *European Journal of Neuroscience, 27,* 2229–2240.

Baker, T. B., & Tiffany, S. T. (1985). Morphine tolerance as habituation. *Psychological Review, 92,* 78–108.

Bakish, D., Hooper, C. L., Filteau, M. J., et al. (1996). A double-blind placebo-controlled trial comparing fluvoxamine and imipramine in the treatment of panic disorder with or without agoraphobia. *Psychopharmacology Bulletin, 32,* 135–142.

Bakshi, V. P., & Kelley, A. E. (1991). Dopaminergic regulation of feeding behavior: I. Differential effects of haloperidol microinjection in three striatal subregions. *Psychobiology, 19,* 223–232.

Baldessarini, R. J. (2001). Drugs and the treatment of psychiatric disorders: Depression and anxiety disorders. In J. G. Hardman & L. E. Limbird (Eds.), *Goodman & Gilman's The pharmacological basis of therapeutics* (10th ed., pp. 447–483). New York: McGraw-Hill.

Baldessarini, R. J., & Frankenburg, F. R. (1991). Clozapine: A novel antipsychotic agent. *New England Journal of Medicine, 324,* 746–754.

Baldessarini, R. J., & Tarazi, F. I. (2001). Drugs and the treatment of psychiatric disorders: Psychosis and mania. In J. G. Hardman & L. E. Limbird (Eds.), *Goodman & Gilman's The pharmacological basis of therapeutics* (10th ed., pp. 485–519). New York: McGraw-Hill.

Baldo, B. A., & Kelley, A. E. (2007). Discrete neurochemical coding of distinguishable motivational processes: Insights from nucleus accumbens control of feeding. *Psychopharmacology, 191,* 439–459.

Baldo, B. A., Sadeghian, K., Basso, A. M., & Kelley, A. E. (2002). Effects of selective dopamine D1 or D2 receptor blockade within nucleus accumbens subregions on ingestive behavior and associated motor activity. *Behavioural Brain Research, 137,* 165–177.

Ballantyne, J. C., & Mao, J. (2003). Opioid therapy for chronic pain. *New England Journal of Medicine, 349,* 1943–1953.

Balster, R. L., & Chait, L. D. (1976). The biobehavioral pharmacology of phencyclidine. *Clinical Toxicology, 9,* 513–529.

Ban, T. (1984). Chronic disease and depression in the geriatric population. *Journal of Clinical Psychiatry, 45,* 18–23.

Ban, T. A. (1975). Nicotinic acid in the treatment of schizophrenias. *Neuropsychobiology, 1,* 133–145.

Ban, T. A. (1978). Vasodilators, stimulants and anabolic agents in the treatment of geropsychiatric patients. In M. A. Lipton, A. DiMascio, & K. F. Killman (Eds.), *Psychopharmacology* (pp. 1525–1534). New York: Raven Press.

Banys, P., Tusel, D. J., Sees, K. L., & Reilly, P. M. (1994). Low (40 mg) versus high (80 mg) dose methadone in a 180-day heroin detoxification program. *Journal of Substance Abuse Treatment, 11,* 225–232.

Barak, Y., Ring, A., Levy, D., et al. (1995). Disabling compulsion in 11 mentally retarded adults: An open trial of clomipramine SR. *Journal of Clinical Psychiatry, 56,* 459–461.

Barbaccia, M. L., Costa, E., & Guidotti, A. (1988). Endogenous ligands for high-affinity recognition sites of psychotropic drugs. *Annual Review of Pharmacology and Toxicology, 28,* 451–476.

Barch, D. M. (2010). Pharmacological strategies for enhancing cognition in schizophrenia. *Current Topics in Behavioral Neuroscience, 4,* 43–96.

Barden, J. A., & Mason, P. (1977). Conformation of (leu5)enkephalin from x-ray diffraction: Features important for recognition at opiate receptor. *Science, 199,* 1214–1215.

Barinaga, M. (1990). The high culture of neuroscience. *Science, 250,* 206–207.

Barkley, R. A., DuPaul, G. J., & McMurray, M. B. (1991). Attention deficit disorder with and without hyperactivity: Clinical response to three dose levels of methylphenidate. *Pediatrics, 87,* 519–531.

Barkley, R. A., & Fischer, M. (2011). Predicting impairment in major life activities and occupational functioning in hyperactive children as adults: Self-reported executive function (EF) deficits versus EF tests. *Developmental Neuropsycholology, 36,* 137–161.

Barkley, R., Fischer, M., Smallish, L., & Fletcher, K. (2003). Does the treatment of attention-deficit/hyperactivity disorder with stimulants contribute to drug use/abuse? A 13-year prospective study. *Pediatrics, 111,* 97–109.

Barondes, S. H. (1994). Thinking about prozac. *Science, 263,* 1102–1104.

Barone, J. J., & Roberts, H. R. (1996). Caffeine consumption. *Food and Chemical Toxicology, 34,* 119–129.

Bartfai, T., Iverfeldt, K., & Fisone, G. (1988). Regulation of the release of coexisting neurotransmitters. *Annual Review of Pharmacology and Toxicology, 28,* 285–310.

Barth, K. S., & Malcolm, R. J. (2010). Disulfiram: An old therapeutic with new applications. *CNS Neurological Disorders Drug Targets, 9,* 5–12.

Bartlett, E., Hallin, A., Chapman, B., & Angrist, B. (1997). Selective sensitization to the psychosis-inducing effects of cocaine: A possible marker for addiction relapse vulnerability. *Neuropsychopharmacology, 16,* 77–82.

Bateman, B., Warner, J., Hutchinson, E., et al. (2004). The effects of a double blind, placebo controlled, artificial food colourings and benzoate preservative challenge on hyperactivity in a general population sample of preschool children. *Archives of Disease in Childhood, 89,* 506–511.

Batzer, W., Ditzler, T., & Brown, C. (1999). LSD use and flashbacks in alcoholic patients. *Journal of Addictive Diseases, 18,* 57–63.

Bauman, P. S., & Levine, S. A. (1986). The development of children of drug addicts. *International Journal of the Addictions, 21,* 849–863.

Beasley, C. M., Dornseif, B. E., Bosomworth, J. C., et al. (1991). Fluoxetine and suicide: A meta-analysis of controlled trials of treatment for depression. *British Medical Journal, 303,* 685–692.

Beghi, E. (2004). Efficacy and tolerability of the new antiepileptic drugs: Comparison of two recent guidelines. *The Lancet Neurology, 3,* 618–621.

Bekris, L. M., Mata, I. F., & Zabetian, C. P. (2010). The genetics of Parkinson disease. *Journal of Geriatric Psychiatry and Neurology, 23,* 228–242.

Belin, D., Jonkman, S., Dickinson, A., Robbins, T. W., & Everitt, B. J. (2009). Parallel and interactive learning processes within the basal ganglia: Relevance for the understanding of addiction. *Behavioural Brain Research, 199,* 89–102.

Belmaker, R. H., & Agam, G. (2008). Major depressive disorder. *New England Journal of Medicine, 358,* 55–68.

Benedetti, F., Arduino, C., & Amanzio, M. (1999). Somatotopic activation of opioid systems by target-directed expectations of analgesia. *Journal of Neuroscience, 19,* 3639–3648.

Benkelfat, C., Ellenbogen, M. A., Dean, P., et al. (1994). Mood-lowering effect of tryptophan depletion: Enhanced susceptibility in young men at genetic risk for major affective disorders. *Archives of General Psychiatry, 51,* 687–697.

Benowitz, N., Hall, S., & Modin, G. (1989). Persistent increase in caffeine concentrations in people who stop smoking. *BMJ (Clinical Research Ed.), 298,* 1075–1076.

Berigan, T. (2004). Modafinil treatment of excessive sedation associated with divalproex sodium. *Canadian Journal of Psychiatry, 49,* 72–73.

Bernstein, V. J., & Hans, S. L. (1994). Predicting the developmental outcome of two-year-old children born exposed to methadone: Impact of social-environmental risk factors. Special issue: Impact of poverty of children, youth, and families. *Journal of Clinical Child Psychology, 23,* 349–359.

Berridge, K. C. (2007). The debate over dopamine's role in reward: the case for incentive salience. *Psychopharmacology, 191,* 391–431.

Berridge, K. C., & Kringlebach, M. L. (2008). Affective neuroscience of pleasure: Reward in humans and animals. *Psychopharmacology, 199,* 457–480.

Bertschy, G. (1995). Methadone maintenance treatment: An update. *European Archives of Psychiatry and Clinical Neuroscience, 245,* 114–124.

Betz, A., Ishiwari, K., Wisniecki, A., Huyn, N., & Salamone, J. D. (2005). Quetiapine

(Seroquel) shows a pattern of behavioral effects similar to the atypical antipsychotics clozapine and olanzapine: Studies with tremulous jaw movements in rats. *Psychopharmacology, 179,* 383–392.

Betz, A. J., McLaughlin, P. J., Burgos, M., Weber, S. M., & Salamone, J. D. (2007). The muscarinic receptor antagonist tropicamide suppresses tremulous jaw movements in a rodent model of parkinsonian tremor: Possible role of M4 receptors. *Psychopharmacology, 194,* 347–359.

Betz, A. J., Vontell, R., Valenta, J., Worden, L., Sink, K. S., Font, L., et al. (2009). Effects of the adenosine A_{2A} antagonist KW-6002 (istradefylline) on pimozide-induced oral tremor and striatal c-Fos expression: Comparisons with the muscarinic antagonist tropicamide. *Neuroscience, 163,* 97–108.

Biederman, J., Faraone, S. V., Mick, E., et al. (1995). High risk for attention-deficit hyperactivity disorder among children of parents with childhood onset of the disorder: A pilot study. *American Journal of Psychiatry, 152,* 431–435.

Biederman, J., Wilens, T., Mick, E., et al. (1999). Pharmacotherapy of attention-deficit/hyperactivity disorder reduces risk for substance use disorder. *Pediatrics, 104,* e20.

Biel, J. H. (1970). Structure-activity relationships of amphetamine and derivatives. In E. Costa & S. Garattini (Eds.), *International symposium on amphetamines and related compounds* (pp. 3–19). New York: Raven Press.

Biel, J. H., Bopp, B., & Mitchell, B. D. (1978). Chemistry and structure-activity relationships of psychotropic drugs: Part 2. In W. G. Clark & J. del Guidice (Eds.), *Principles of psychopharmacology* (pp. 140–168). New York: Academic Press.

Bien, T. H., & Burge, R. (1990). Smoking and drinking: A review of the literature. *International Journal of the Addictions, 25,* 1429–1454.

Bilder, R., Goldman, R., Volavka, J., et al. (2002). Neurocognitive effects of clozapine, olanzapine, risperidone, and haloperidol in patients with chronic schizophrenia or schizoaffective disorder. *American Journal of Psychiatry, 159,* 1018–1028.

Birks, J. (2006). Cholinesterase inhibitors for Azheimer's disease. *Cochrane Database System Reviews,* no. 1, CD005593.

Bisaga, A., & Popik, P. (2000). In search of a new pharmacological treatment for drug and alcohol addiction: N-methyl-D-aspartate (NMDA) antagonists. *Drug and Alcohol Dependence, 59,* 1–15.

Blair-West, G. W., Cantor, C. H., Mellsop, G. W., & Eyeson-Annan, M. L. (1999). Lifetime suicide risk in major depression: Sex and age determinants. *Journal of Affective Disorders, 55,* 171–178.

Blass, E. M. (1992). The ontogeny of motivation: Opioid bases of energy conservation and lasting affective change in rat and human infants. *Current Directions in Psychological Science, 1,* 116–120.

Blaze-Temple, D., & Lo, S. K. (1992). Stages of drug use: A community survey of Perth teenagers. *British Journal of Addiction, 87,* 215–225.

Blier, P., & de Montigny, C. (1994). Current advances and trends in the treatment of depression. *Trends in the Pharmacological Sciences, 15,* 220–226.

Block, R. I., Farinpour, R., & Schlechte, J. A. (1991). Effects of chronic marijuana use on testosterone, luteinizing hormone, follicle stimulating hormone, prolactin and cortisol in men and women. *Drug and Alcohol Dependence, 28,* 121–128.

Bloom, F. E. (2001). Neurotransmission and the central nervous system. In J. G. Hardman & L. E. Limbird (Eds.), *Goodman & Gilman's The pharmacological basis of therapeutics* (10th ed., pp. 293–319). New York: McGraw-Hill.

Bloor, L. B., Leese, B., & Maynard, A. (1994). The cost of managing severe cancer pain and potential savings from transdermal administration. *European Journal of Cancer, 30A,* 463–468.

Boehm, S., & Kubista, H. (2002). Fine tuning of sympathetic transmitter release via ionotropic and metabotropic presynaptic receptors. *Pharmacological Reviews, 54*(1), 43–99.

Boettiger, C. A., Mitchell, J. M., Tavares, V. C., Robertson, M., Joslyn, G., D'Esposito, M., Fields, H. L. (2007). Immediate reward bias in humans: fronto-parietal networks and a role for the catechol-O-methyltransferase 158 (Val/Val) genotype. *Journal of Neuroscience, 27,* 14383–14391.

Boileau, I., Assaad, J., Pihl, R., et al. (2003). Alcohol promotes dopamine release in the human nucleus accumbens. *Synapse, 49,* 226–231.

Bolla, K., Eldreth, D., London, E., et al. (2003). Orbitofrontal cortex dysfunction in abstinent cocaine abusers performing a decision-making task. *NeuroImage, 19,* 1085–1094.

Bolla, K. I., McCann, U. D., & Ricaurte, G. A. (1998). Memory impairment in abstinent MDMA ("Ecstasy") users. *Neurology, 51,* 1532–1537.

Booth, B. M., & Blow, F. C. (1993). The kindling hypothesis: Further evidence from a U.S. national study of alcoholic men. *Alcohol and Alcoholism, 28,* 593–598.

Booth, P. G., Dale, B., Slade, P. D., & Dewey, M. E. (1992). A follow-up study of problem drinkers offered a goal choice option. *Journal of Studies of Alcohol, 53,* 594–600.

Bossert, J. M., & Shaham, Y. (2004). Drug onset cues, conditioned withdrawal, and drug relapse: Comment on McDonald and Siegel. *Experimental and Clinical Psychopharmacology, 12,* 15–17.

Bouvard, M. P., Leboyer, M., Launay, J. M., et al. (1995). Low-dose naltrexone effects on plasma chemistries and clinical symptoms in autism: A double-blind, placebo-controlled study. *Psychiatry Research, 58,* 191–201.

Bovasso, G. B. (2001). Cannabis abuse as a risk factor for depressive symptoms. *American Journal of Psychiatry, 158,* 2033–2037.

Bowden, C. L. (1995). Predictors of response to divalproex and lithium. *Journal of Clinical Psychiatry, 56,* 25–30.

Bowers, M. B., Swigar, M. E., Jatlow, P. I., et al. (1987). Early neuroleptic response: Clinical profiles and plasma catecholamine metabolites. *Journal of Clinical Psychopharmacology, 7,* 83–86.

Bowersox, J. (1992). PHS cancels availability of medicinal marijuana. *Journal of the National Cancer Institute, 84,* 475–476.

Bowles, T. M., & Levin, M. (2003). Aripiprazole: A new atypical antipsychotic drug. *Annals of Pharmacotherapy, 37,* 687–694.

Boye, S. M., & Rompre, P. (2000). Behavioral evidence of depolarization block of dopamine neurons after chronic treatment with haloperidol and clozapine. *Journal of Neuroscience, 20,* 1229–1239.

Boyer, W. (1995). Serotonin uptake inhibitors are superior to imipramine and alprazolam in alleviating panic attacks: A meta-analysis. *International Clinical Psychopharmacology, 10,* 45–49.

Bradberry, C. W. (2007). Cocaine sensitization and dopamine mediation of cue effects in rodents, monkeys, and humans: Areas of agreement, disagreement, and implications for addiction. *Psychopharmacology, 191,* 705–717.

Bradizza, C. M., Gulliver, S. B., Stasiewicz, P. R., et al. (1999). Alcohol cue reactivity and private self-consciousness among male alcoholics. *Addictive Behaviors, 24,* 543–549.

Brady, J. V., & Griffiths, R. R. (1977). Drug-maintained performance and the analysis of stimulant reinforcement effects. In E. E. Ellinwood & M. M. Kilbey (Eds.), *Cocaine and other stimulants* (pp. 599–614). New York: Plenum Press.

Brady, K. T., Back, S. E., & Coffey, S. F. (2004). Substance abuse and posttraumatic stress disorder. *Current Directions in Psychological Science, 13,* 206–209.

Brady, K. T., Lydiard, R. B., Malcolm, R., & Ballenger, J. C. (1991). Cocaine-induced psychosis. *Journal of Clinical Psychiatry, 52,* 509–512.

Brady, K. T., & Sonne, S. C. (1995). The relationship between substance abuse and bipolar disorder. *Journal of Clinical Psychiatry, 56*(Suppl. 3), 19–24.

Branconnier, R. J., Branconnier, M. E., Walshe, T. M., et al. (1992). Blocking the Ca^{2+}-activated cytotoxic mechanisms of cholinergic neuronal death: A novel treatment strategy for Alzheimer's disease. *Psychopharmacology Bulletin, 28,* 175–182.

Brandon, T. H. (1994). Negative affect as motivation to smoke. *Journal of the American Psychological Society, 3,* 33–37.

Brannan, T., & Yahr, M. D. (1995). Comparative study of selegiline plus L-dopa-carbidopa versus L-dopa-carbidopa alone in the treatment of Parkinson's disease. *Annals of Neurology, 37,* 95–98.

Brauer, L. H., & de Wit, H. (1997). High dose pimozide does not block amphetamine-induced euphoria in normal volunteers. *Pharmacology, Biochemisry, and Behavior, 56,* 265–272.

Brecher, E. M. (Ed.). (1972). *Licit and illicit drugs.* Boston, MA: Little, Brown.

Brecht, M. L., Anglin, M. D., Woodward, J. A., & Bonett, D. G. (1987). Conditional factors of maturing out: Personal resources and preaddiction sociopathy. *International Journal of the Addictions, 22,* 55–69.

Bremner, J., Southwick, S., Darnell, A., & Charney, D. S. (1996). Chronic PTSD in Vietnam combat veterans: Course of illness and substance abuse. *American Journal of Psychiatry, 153,* 369–375.

Breslau, N., & Chilcoat, H. D. (2000). Psychiatric sequelae of low birth weight at 11 years of age. *Biological Psychiatry, 47,* 1005–1011.

Breslau, N., Kilbey, M. M., & Andreski, P. (1992). Nicotine withdrawal symptoms and psychiatric disorders: Findings from an epidemiologic study of young adults. *American Journal of Psychiatry, 149,* 464–469.

Brevoort, P. (1998). The booming US botanical market: A new overview. *Herbalgram, 44,* 36–46.

van den Brink, W., & van Ree, M. (2003). Pharmacological treatments for heroin and cocaine addiction. *European Neuropsychopharmacology, 13,* 476–487.

Brischoux, F., Chakraborty, S., Brierley, D. I., & Ungless, M. A. (2009). Phasic excitation of dopamine neurons in ventral VTA by noxious stimuli. *Proceedings of the National Academy of Sciences, 106,* 4894–4899.

Britton, A., & Marmot, M. (2004). Different measures of alcohol consumption and risk of coronary heart disease and all-cause mortality: 11-year follow-up of the Whitehall II Cohort Study. *Addiction, 99,* 109–116.

Britton, K. T., Ehlers, C. L., & Koob, G. F. (1988). Is ethanol antagonist Ro15-4513 selective for ethanol? *Science, 239,* 648–649.

Broom, S. L., & Yamamoto, B. K. (2005). Effects of subchronic methamphetamine exposure on basal dopamine and stress-induced dopamine release in the nucleus accumbens shell of rats. *Psychopharmacology, 181,* 467–476.

Brown, A. S., & Gershon, S. (1993). Dopamine and depression. *Journal of Neural Transmission General Section, 91,* 75–109.

Brown, E. S., Nejtek, V., Perantie, D., et al. (2003). Lamotrigine in patients with bipolar disorder and cocaine dependence. *Journal of Clinical Psychiatry, 64,* 197–201.

Brown, R. T., Borden, K. A., & Clingerman, S. R. (1985). Pharmacotherapy in ADD adolescents with special attention to multimodality treatments. *Psychopharmacology Bulletin, 21,* 192–211.

Brown, S. P., Safo, P. K., & Regehr, W. G. (2004). Endocannabinoids inhibit transmission at granule cell to Purkinje cell synapses by modulating three types of presynaptic calcium channels. *Journal of Neuroscience, 24,* 5623–5631.

Brown, W. A. (1988). Predictors of placebo response in depression. *Psychopharmacology Bulletin, 24,* 14–17.

Browne, R. G., & Welch, W. M. (1982). Stereoselective antagonism of phencyclidine's discriminative properties by adenosine receptor agonists. *Science, 217*, 1157–1159.

Brownell, K. D., Marlatt, G. A., Lichtenstein, E., & Wilson, G. T. (1986). Understanding and preventing relapse. *American Psychologist, 41*, 765–781.

Brubaker, R. G., Prue, D. M., & Rychtarik, R. G. (1987). Determinants of disulfiram acceptance among alcohol patients: A test of the theory of reasoned action. *Addictive Behaviors, 12*, 43–51.

Buchert, R., Thomasius, R., Wilke, F., et al. (2004). A voxel-based PET investigation of the long-term effects of "Ecstasy" consumption on brain serotonin transporters. *American Journal of Psychiatry, 161*, 1181–1189.

Buchsbaum, M. S., Wu, J. C., DeLisi, L. E., et al. (1987). Positron emission tomography studies of basal ganglia and somatosensory cortex neuroleptic drug effects: Differences between normal controls and schizophrenic patients. *Biological Psychiatry, 22*, 479–494.

Buigues, J., & Vallejo, J. (1987). Therapeutic response to phenelzine in patients with panic disorder and agoraphobia with panic attacks. *Journal of Clinical Psychiatry, 48*, 55–59.

Buisson, B., & Bertrand, D. (2002). Nicotine addiction: The possible role of functional upregulation. *Trends in Pharmacological Sciences, 23*, 130–136.

Buitelaar, J. K., Van der Gaag, R. J., Swaab-Barneveld, H., & Kuiper, M. (1995). Prediction of clinical response to methylphenidate in children with attention-deficit hyperactivity disorder. *Journal of the American Academy of Child and Adolescent Psychiatry, 34*, 1025–1032.

Burke, T. F., Buzzard, S., & Wessinger, W. D. (1995). [3H]MK-801 binding to well-washed rat brain membranes following cessation of chronic phencyclidine treatment. *Pharmacology, Biochemistry, and Behavior, 51*, 435–438.

Burnstock, G. (2004). Cotransmission. *Current Opinion in Pharmacology, 4*, 47–52.

Butterworth, R. F. (1995). Pathophysiology of alcoholic brain damage: Synergistic effects of ethanol, thiamine deficiency and alcoholic liver disease. *Metabolic Brain Disease, 10*, 1–8.

Butzlaff, R. L., & Hooley, J. M. (1998). Expressed emotion and psychiatric relapse. *Archives of General Psychiatry, 55*, 547–552.

Caballero, J., & Nahata, M. C. (2003). Atomoxetine hydrochloride for the treatment of attention-deficit/hyperactivity disorder. *Clinical Therapeutics, 25*, 3065–3083.

Cadet, J. L., & Kahler, L. A. (1994). Free radical mechanisms in schizophrenia and tardive dyskinesia. *Neuroscience and Biobehavioral Reviews, 18*, 457–467.

Cadoret, R. J., Troughton, E., & O'Gorman, T. W. (1987). Genetic and environmental factors in alcohol abuse and antisocial personality. *Journal of Studies on Alcohol, 48*, 1–8.

Cagniard, B., Balsam, P. D., Brunner, D., & Zhuang, X. (2006). Mice with chronically elevated dopamine exhibit enhanced motivation, but not learning, for a food reward. *Neuropsychopharmacology, 31*, 1362–1370.

Cahill, L., Prins, B., Weber, M., & McGaugh, J. L. (1994). Beta-adrenergic activation and memory for emotional events. *Nature, 371*, 702–704.

Calabrese, J., Kasper, S., Johnson, G., et al. (2004). International Consensus Group on Bipolar I depression treatment guidelines. *Journal of Clinical Psychiatry, 65*, 571–579.

Calabrese, J. R., & Woyshville, M. J. (1995). Lithium therapy: Limitations and alternatives in the treatment of bipolar disorders. *Annals of Clinical Psychiatry, 7*, 103–112.

Caldwell, A. E. (1978). History of psychopharmacology. In W. G. Clark & J. Del Giudice

(Eds.), *Principles of psychopharmacology* (pp. 9–40). New York: Academic Press.

Cami, J., Guerra, D., Ugena, B., et al. (1991). Effect of subject expectancy on the THC intoxication and disposition from smoked hashish cigarettes. *Pharmacology, Biochemistry, and Behavior, 40,* 115–119.

Campbell, M. (1978). Use of drug treatment in infantile autism and childhood schizophrenia: A review. In M. A. Lipton, A. DiMascio, & K. F. Killman (Eds.), *Psychopharmacology* (pp. 1451–1462). New York: Raven Press.

Campbell, M., & Cueva, J. E. (1995). Psychopharmacology in child and adolescent psychiatry: A review of the past seven years. Part II. *Journal of the American Academy of Child and Adolescent Psychiatry, 34,* 1262–1272.

Campbell, M., Kafantaris, V., & Cueva, J. E. (1995). An update on the use of lithium carbonate in aggressive children and adolescents with conduct disorder. *Psychopharmacology Bulletin, 31,* 93–102.

Campbell, M., Perry, R., & Green, W. H. (1984). Use of lithium in children and adolescents. *Psychosomatics, 25,* 95–106.

Campbell, M., Schopler, E., Cueva, J. E., & Hallin, A. (1996). Treatment of autistic disorder. *Journal of the American Academy of Child and Adolescent Psychiatry, 35,* 134–143.

Campbell, W. G., & Hodgins, D. C. (1993). Alcohol-related blackouts in a medical practice. *American Journal of Drug and Alcohol Abuse, 19,* 369–376.

Cannon, C. M., & Bseikri, M. R. (2004). Is dopamine required for natural reward? *Physiology and Behavior, 81,* 741–748.

Cannon, C. M., & Palmiter, D. (2003). Reward without dopamine. *Journal of Neuroscience, 23,* 10827–10831.

Cannon, C. M., Scannell, C. A., & Palmiter, R. D. (2005). Mice lacking dopamine D1 receptors express normal lithium chloride-induced conditioned taste aversion for salt but not sucrose. *European Journal of Neuroscience, 21,* 2600–2604.

Cantin, L., Lenoir, M., Augier, E., Vanhille, N., Dubreucq, S., Serre, F., et al. (2010). Cocaine is low on the value ladder of rats: Possible evidence for resilience to addiction. *PLoS One, 5,* e11592.

Caplehorn, J. R., Bell, J., Kleinbaum, D. G., & Gebski, V. J. (1993). Methadone dose and heroin use during maintenance treatment. *Addiction, 88,* 119–124.

Carballo-Dieguez, A., Sahs, J., Goetz, R., & El Sadr, W. (1994). The effect of methadone on immunological parameters among HIV-positive and HIV-negative drug users. *American Journal of Drug & Alcohol Abuse, 20,* 317–329.

Carelli, R. M., & Wondolowski, J. (2003). Selective encoding of cocaine versus natural rewards by nucleus accumbens neurons is not related to chronic drug exposure. *Journal of Neuroscience, 23,* 11214–11223.

Carlen, P. L., Holgate, R. C., Wortzman, G., & Wilkinson, D. A. (1978). Reversible cerebral atrophy in recently abstinent chronic alcoholics measured by computed tomography scans. *Science, 200,* 1076–1078.

Carlezon, W. A., Jr., Thome, J., Olson, V. G., et al. (1998). Regulation of cocaine reward by CREB. *Science, 282,* 2272–2275.

Carlezon, W. A., Jr., & Wise, R. A. (1993). Phencyclidine-induced potentiation of brain stimulation reward: Acute effects are not altered by repeated administration. *Psychopharmacology, 111,* 402–408.

Carlezon, W. A., Jr., & Wise, R. A. (1996). Rewarding reactions of phencyclidine and related drugs in nucleus accumbens shell and frontal cortex. *Journal of Neuroscience, 16,* 3112–3122.

Carlson, N. R. (1988). *Foundations of physiological psychology.* Boston, MA: Allyn & Bacon.

Carlson, N. R. (2004). *Physiology of behavior* (8th ed.). Boston, MA: Allyn & Bacon.

Carlsson, A. (1978). Mechanism of action of neuroleptic drugs. In M. A. Lipton, A. DiMascio, & K. F. Killam (Eds.),

Psychopharmacology (pp. 1057–1070). New York: Raven Press.

Carlsson, A. (1987). Perspectives on the discovery of central monoaminergic neurotransmission. *Annual Review of Neuroscience, 10,* 19–40.

Carman, J., Peuskens, J., & Vangeneugden, A. (1995). Risperidone in the treatment of negative symptoms of schizophrenia: A meta-analysis. *International Clinical Psychopharmacology, 10,* 207–213.

Caroff, S. N., Hurford, I., Lybrand, J., & Campbell, E. C. (2011). Movement disorders induced by antipsychotic drugs: Implications of the CATIE schizophrenia trial. *Neurologic Clinics, 29,* 127–148.

Caroff, S. N., & Mann, S. C. (1993). Neuroleptic malignant syndrome. *Medical Clinics of North America, 77,* 185–202.

Carr, G. D., & White, N. M. (1983). Conditioned place preference from intra-accumbens but not intra-caudate amphetamine injections. *Life Sciences, 33,* 2551–2557.

Carroll, K. M., Fenton, L. R., Ball, S. A., et al. (2004). Efficacy of disulfiram and cognitive behavior therapy in cocaine-dependent outpatients: A randomized placebo-controlled trial. *Archives of General Psychiatry, 61,* 264–272.

Carroll, R. (1991). A rhetorical biography of Harry J. Anslinger, Commissioner of the Federal Bureau of Narcotics, 1930–1962 (Doctoral dissertation, University of Pittsburgh, 1991). *Dissertation Abstracts International, 52,* 1569.

Cases, O., Seif, I., Grimsby, J., Gaspar, P., Chen, K., Pournin, S., et al. (1995). Aggressive behavior and altered amounts of brain serotonin and norepinephrine in mice lacking MAOA. *Science, 268,* 1763–1766.

Caspi, A., Sugden, K., Moffitt, T., et al. (2003). Influence of life stress on depression: Moderation by a polymorphism in the 5-HTT gene. *Science, 301,* 386–389.

Castañeda, E., Fleming, S., Paquette, M. A., Boat, K., Moffett, J., Stachowiak, E. K., et al.

(2005). Assessment of recovery in the hemiparkinson rat: Drug-induced rotation is inadequate. *Physiology and Behavior, 84,* 525–535.

Castellanos, F. X., Lee, P., Sharp, W., et al. (2002). Developmental trajectories of brain volume abnormalities in children and adolescents with attention-deficit/hyperactivity disorder. *The Journal of the American Medical Association, 288,* 1740–1748.

Cazzullo, A. G., Musetti, M. C., Musetti, L., et al. (1999). β-Endorphin levels in peripheral blood mononuclear cells and long-term naltrexone treatment in autistic children. *European Neuropsychopharmacology, 9,* 361–366.

Chadwick, M. J., Gregory, D. L., & Wendling, G. (1990). A double-blind amino acids, L-tryptophan and L-tyrosine, and placebo study with cocaine-dependent subjects in an inpatient chemical dependence treatment center. *American Journal of Drug and Alcohol Abuse, 16,* 275–286.

Chakko, S., & Myerberg, R. J. (1995). Cardiac complications of cocaine abuse. *Clinical Cardiology, 18,* 67–72.

Chakos, M. H., Alvir, J. M., Woerner, M. G., et al. (1996). Incidence and correlates of tardive dyskinesia in first episode of schizophrenia. *Archives of General Psychiatry, 53,* 313–319.

Chaloupka, F. J., & Grossman, M. (1996). *Price, tobacco control policies and youth smoking* (Working Paper 5740). Cambridge, MA: National Bureau of Economic Research.

Chamberlain, S. R., Robbins, T. W., Winder-Rhodes, S., Müller, U., Sahakian, B. J., Blackwell, A. D., et al. (2011). Translational approaches to frontostriatal dysfunction in attention-deficit/hyperactivity disorder using a computerized neuropsychological battery. *Biological Psychiatry* [Epub ahead of print].

Chan, G. C., Hinds, T. R., Impey, S., et al. (1998). Hippocampal neurotoxicity of delta 9-tetrahydrocannabinol. *Journal of Neuroscience, 18,* 5322–5332.

Chang, J. (2000). Medicinal herbs: Drugs or dietary supplements? *Biochemical Pharmacology, 59,* 211–219.

Chao, H. M. (1995). Alcohol and the mystique of flushing. *Alcohol Clinical and Experimental Research, 19,* 104–109.

Chappell, P. B., Riddle, M. A., Scahill, L., et al. (1995). Guanfacine treatment of comorbid attention-deficit hyperactivity disorder and Tourette's syndrome: Preliminary clinical experience. *Journal of the American Academy of Child and Adolescent Psychiatry, 34,* 1140–1146.

Charney, D. S., Heninger, G. R., & Jatlow, P. I. (1985). Increased anxiogenic effects of caffeine in panic disorders. *Archives of General Psychiatry, 42,* 233–243.

Charney, D. S., Krystal, J. H., Delgado, P. L., & Heninger, G. R. (1990). Serotonin-specific drugs for anxiety and depressive disorders. *Annual Review of Medicine, 41,* 437–446.

Charney, D. S., Mihic, S. J., & Harris, R. A. (2001). Hypnotics and sedatives. In J. G. Hardman & L. E. Limbird (Eds.), *Goodman & Gilman's The pharmacological basis of therapeutics* (10th ed., pp. 399–427). New York: McGraw-Hill.

Chaudhuri, A., & Behan, P. O. (2004). Fatigue in neurological disorders. *Lancet, 363,* 978–988.

Chen, B., Dowlatshahi, D., MacQueen, G., et al. (2001). Increased hippocampal BDNF immunoreactivity in subjects treated with antidepressant medication. *Biological Psychiatry, 50,* 260–265.

Chen, C., Rainnie, D. G., Greene, R. W., & Tonegawa, S. (1994). Abnormal fear response and aggressive behavior in mutant mice deficient for alpha-calcium-calmodulin kinase II. *Science, 266,* 291–294.

Chen, Y. C., Peng, G. S., Tsao, T. P., Wang, M. F., Lu, R. B., & Yin, S. J. (2009). Pharmacokinetic and pharmacodynamic basis for overcoming acetaldehyde-induced adverse reaction in Asian alcoholics, heterozygous for the variant ALDH2*2 gene allele. *Pharmacogenetics and Genomics, 19,* 588–599.

Chessick, C. A., Allen, M. H., Thase, M., Batista Miralha da Cunha, A. B., Kapczinski, F. F., de Lima, M. S., et al. (2006, July 19). Azapirones for generalized anxiety disorder. *Cochrane Database System Reviews,* no. 3, CD006115.

Chick, J., Howlett, H., Morgan, M. Y., et al. (2000). United Kingdom multicentre acamprostate study (UKMAS): A 6-month prospective study of acamprostate versus placebo in preventing relapse after withdrawal from alcohol. *Alcohol and Alcoholism, 35,* 176–187.

Childress, A. R., Ehrman, R., McLellan, A. T., et al. (1994). Can induced moods trigger drug-related responses in opiate abuse patients? *Journal of Substance Abuse Treatment, 11,* 17–23.

Childress, A. R., McLellan, A. T., & O'Brien, C. P. (1986a). Abstinent opiate abusers exhibit conditioned craving, conditioned withdrawal and reductions in both through extinction. *British Journal of Addiction, 81,* 655–660.

Childress, A. R., McLellan, A. T., & O'Brien, C. P. (1986b). Conditioned responses in a methadone population. *Journal of Substance Abuse Treatment, 3,* 173–179.

Childress, A. R., Mozley, D., McElgin, W., et al. (1999). Limbic activation during cue-induced cocaine craving. *American Journal of Psychiatry, 156,* 11–18.

Cho, A. K. (1993). Ice: D-methamphetamine hydrochloride. In S. G. Korenman & J. D. Barchas (Eds.), *Biological basis of substance abuse* (pp. 119–142). New York: Oxford University Press.

Chouinard, G., Lefko-Singh, K., & Teboul, E. (1999). Metabolism of anxiolytics and hypnotics: Benzodiazepines, buspirone, zopiclone, and zolpidem. *Cellular and Molecular Neurobiology, 19,* 533–552.

Chrobak, J. J., Hinman, J. R., Sabolek, H. R. (2008). Revealing past memories: Proactive interference and ketamine-induced memory deficits. *Journal of Neuroscience, 28,* 4512–4520.

Chuhma, N., Choi, W. Y., Mingote, S., & Rayport, S. (2009). Dopamine neuron glutamate cotransmission: Frequency-dependent modulation in the mesoventromedial projection. *Neuroscience, 16,* 1068–1083.

Ciapparelli, A., Dell'Osso, L., Pini, S., et al. (2000). Clozapine for treatment-refractory schizophrenia, schizoaffective disorder, and psychotic bipolar disorder: A 24-month naturalistic study. *Journal of Clinical Psychiatry, 61,* 329–334.

Clayton, R. R., & Voss, H. L. (1981). *Young men and drugs in Manhattan: A causal analysis* (NIDA Research Monograph No. 39). Rockville, MD: National Institute on Drug Abuse, Department of Health and Human Services.

Cloninger, C. R. (1987). Neurogenetic adaptive mechanisms in alcoholism. *Science, 236,* 410–416.

Cloninger, C. R., Bohman, M., & Sigvardsson, S. (1981). Inheritance of alcohol abuse: Cross-fostering analysis of adopted men. *Archives of General Psychiatry, 38,* 861–868.

Clure, C., Brady, K. T., Saladin, M. E., et al. (1999). Attention-deficit/hyperactivity disorder and substance use: Symptom pattern and drug choice. *American Journal of Drug and Alcohol Abuse, 25,* 441–448.

Coffey, S. F., Dansky, B. S., Carrigan, M. H., & Brady, K. T. (2000). Acute and protracted cocaine abstinence in an outpatient population: A prospective study of mood, sleep and withdrawal symptoms. *Drug and Alcohol Dependence, 59,* 277–286.

Cohen, D. J., Riddle, M. A., & Leckman, J. F. (1992). Pharmacotherapy of Tourette's syndrome and associated disorders. *Psychiatric Clinics of North America, 15,* 109–129.

Cohen, H., Gibson, G., & Alderman, M. H. (2000). Excess risk of myocardial infarction in patients treated with antidepressant medication: Association with use of

tricyclic agents. *American Journal of Medicine, 108,* 2–8.

Cohen, S. (1981). *The substance abuse problems.* New York: Haworth Press.

Cohen, S., Fitzgerald, B., Khan, S. R., & Khan, A. (2004). The effect of a switch to ziprasidone in an adult population with autistic disorder: Chart review of naturalistic, open-label treatment. *Journal of Clinical Psychiatry, 65,* 110–113.

Cohen-Cory, S. (2002). The developing synapse: Construction and modulation of synaptic structures and circuits. *Science, 298,* 770–776.

Cole, J. C., & Sumnall, R. (2003). The preclinical behavioural pharmacology of 3,4-methylenedioxymethamphetamine (MDMA). *Neuroscience and Biobehavioral Reviews, 27,* 199–217.

Collins, E., Ward, A., McDowell, D., et al. (1998). The effects of memantine on the subjective, reinforcing and cardiovascular effects of cocaine in humans. *Behavioural Pharmacology, 9,* 587–598.

Collins, L. E., Galtieri, D. J., Brennum, L. T., Sager, T. N., Hockemeyer, J., Muller, C. E., et al. (2010a). Oral tremor induced by the muscarinic agonist pilocarpine is suppressed by the adenosine A2A antagonists MSX-3 and SCH58261, but not the adenosine A1 antagonist DPCPX. *Pharmacology, Biochemistry and Behavior, 94,* 561–569.

Collins, L. E., Galtieri, D. J., Collins, P., Jones, S. K., Port, R. G., Paul, N. E., et al. (2010b). Interactions between adenosine and dopamine receptor antagonists with different selectivity profiles: Effects on locomotor activity. *Behavioral Brain Research, 211,* 148–155.

Colombo, G., Agabio, R., Diaz, G., Lobina, C., Reali, R., & Gessa, G. L. (1998). Appetite suppression and weight loss after the cannabinoid antagonist SR141716. *Life Sciences, 63,* PL113–PL117.

Compton, P. A., Ling, W., Charuvastra, V. C., & Wesson, D. R. (1995). Buprenorphine as a pharmacotherapy for cocaine abuse: A review of the evidence. *Journal of Addictive Diseases, 14,* 97–114.

Connell, P., & Strang, J. (1994). The creation of the clinics: Clinical demand and the formation of policy. In J. Strang & M. Gossop (Eds.), *Heroin addiction and drug policy: The British system* (pp. 167–177). Oxford, OH: Oxford University Press.

Conrad, A. J., & Scheibel, A. B. (1987). Schizophrenia and the hippocampus: The embryological hypothesis extended. *Schizophrenia Bulletin, 13,* 577–587.

Cook, E. H., Jr., Rowlett, R., Jaselskis, C., et al. (1992). Fluoxetine treatment of children and adults with autistic disorder and mental retardation. *Journal of American Academy of Child and Adolescent Psychiatry, 31,* 739–745.

Cook, E. H., Jr., Stein, M. A., Krasowski, M. D., et al. (1995). Association of attention-deficit disorder and the dopamine transporter gene. *American Journal of Human Genetics, 56,* 993–998.

Coombs, R. H., Fawzy, F. I., & Gerber, B. I. (1986). Patterns of cigarette, alcohol, and other drug use among children and adolescents: A longitudinal study. *International Journal of the Addictions, 21,* 897–913.

Cooper, M. L. (1994). Motivations for alcohol use among adolescents: Development and validation of a four-factor model. *Psychological Assessment, 6,* 117–128.

Coplan, J., Souders, M., Mulberg, A., et al. (2003). Children with autistic spectrum disorders. II: Parents are unable to distinguish secretin from placebo under double-blind conditions. *Archives of Disease in Childhood, 88,* 737–739.

Cornelius, J. R., Salloum, I. M., Haskett, R. F., et al. (2000). Fluoxetine versus placebo in depressed alcoholics: A 1-year follow-up study. *Addictive Behaviors, 25,* 307–310.

Cornish, J. L., Duffy, P., & Kalivas, P. W. (1999). A role for nucleus accumbens glutamate transmission in the relapse to cocaine-seeking behavior. *Neuroscience, 93,* 1359–1367.

Correa, M., Sanchis-Segura, C., Pastor, R., & Aragon, C. M. (2004). Ethanol intake and motor sensitization: The role of brain catalase activity in mice with different genotypes. *Physiology and Behavior, 82,* 231–240.

Correa, M., Viaggi, C., Escrig, M. A., Pascual, M., Guerri, C., Vaglini, F., et al. (2009). Ethanol intake and ethanol-induced locomotion and locomotor sensitization in CYPyp2e1 knockout mice. *Pharmacogenetics and Genomics, 19,* 217–225.

Correa, M., Wisniecki, A., Betz, A., Dobson, D. R., O'Neill, M. F., O'Neill, M. J., et al. (2004). The adenosine A_{2A} antagonist KF 17837 reverses the locomotor suppression and tremulous jaw movements induced by haloperidol in rats: Possible relevance to parkinsonism. *Behavioural Brain Research, 148,* 47–54.

Corty, E., & Ball, J. C. (1986). What can we know about addiction from the addicts we treat? *International Journal of the Addictions, 21,* 1139–1144.

Corty, E., O'Brien, C. P., & Mann, S. (1988). Reactivity to alcohol stimuli in alcoholics: Is there a role for temptation? *Drug and Alcohol Dependence, 21,* 29–36.

Cottraux, J., Note, I. D., Cungi, C., et al. (1995). A controlled study of cognitive behaviour therapy with buspirone or placebo in panic disorder with agoraphobia. *British Journal of Psychiatry, 167,* 635–641.

Courtet, P., Pignay, V., Castelnau, D., et al. (1999). Abuse of and dependence on zolpidem: A report of seven cases. *Encephale, 25,* 652–657.

Couzin, J. (2004). Volatile chemistry: Children and antidepressants. *Science, 305,* 468–470.

Cowan, R., Lyoo, I. K., Sung, S. M., et al. (2003). Reduced cortical gray matter density in human MDMA (Ecstasy) users: A voxel-based morphometry study. *Drug and Alcohol Dependence, 72,* 225–235.

Cox, C., Harrison-Read, P. E., Steinberg, H., & Tomkiewicz, M. (1971). Lithium attenuates drug-induced hyperactivity in rats. *Nature, 232,* 336–338.

Coyle, J. T., & Duman, S. (2003). Finding the intracellular signaling pathways affected by mood disorder treatments. *Neuron, 38,* 157–160.

Crabbe, J. C., Belknap, J. K., & Buck, K. J. (1994). Genetic animal models of alcohol and drug abuse. *Science, 264,* 1715–1723.

Creese, I., & Iversen, S. D. (1975). The pharmacological and anatomical substrates of the amphetamine response in the rat. *Brain Research, 83,* 419–436.

Crews, F., Collins, M., Dlugos, C., et al. (2004). Alcohol-induced neurodegeneration: When, where and why? *Alcoholism, Clinical and Experimental Research, 28,* 350–364.

Crook, T. (1988). Pharmacotherapy of cognitive deficits in Alzheimer's disease and age-associated memory impairment. *Psychopharmacology Bulletin, 24,* 31–38.

Crosby, R. D., Pearson, V. L., Eller, C., et al. (1996). Phenytoin in the treatment of cocaine abuse: A double-blind study. *Clinical Pharmacology & Therapeutics, 59,* 458–468.

Crowell, C. R., Hinson, R. E., & Siegel, S. (1981). The role of conditional drug responses in tolerance to hypothermic effects of ethanol. *Psychopharmacology, 73,* 51–54.

Cryan, J. F., & Leonard, B. E. (2000). 5-HT1A and beyond: The role of serotonin and its receptors in depression and the antidepressant response. *Human Psychopharmacology: Clinical and Experimental, 15,* 113–135.

Cubells, J. F., Rayport, S., Rajendran, G., & Sulzer, D. (1994). Methamphetamine neurotoxicity involves vacuolation of endocytic organelles and dopamine-dependent intracellular oxidative stress. *Journal of Neuroscience, 14,* 2260–2271.

Cummings, N. (1979). Turning bread into stones. *American Psychologist, 34,* 1119–1129.

Cunningham, C. E., Siegel, L. S., & Offord, D. R. (1985). A developmental dose-response analysis of the effects of methylphenidate on the peer interactions of attention deficit disordered boys. *Journal of Child Psychology and Psychiatry, 26,* 955–971.

Cunningham, C. L., Gremel, C. M., & Groblewski, P. A. (2006). Drug-induced conditioned place preference and aversion in mice. *Nature Protocols, 1,* 1662–1670.

Cunningham, K. A., & Appel, J. B. (1987). Neuropharmacological reassessment of the discriminative stimulus properties of d-lysergic acid diethylamide (LSD). *Psychopharmacology, 91,* 67–73.

Cychosz, C. M. (1996). Alcohol and interpersonal violence: Implications for educators. *Journal of Health Education, 27,* 73–77.

Dackis, C. A., & Gold, M. S. (1985). New concepts in cocaine addiction: The dopamine depletion hypothesis. *Neuroscience and Biobehavioral Reviews, 9,* 469–477.

Dackis, C. A., & O'Brien, C. (2003). Glutamatergic agents for cocaine dependence. *Annals of the New York Academy of Sciences, 1003,* 328–345.

Dafters, R. I., Hoshi, R., & Talbot, A. C. (2004). Contribution of cannabis and MDMA ("ecstasy") to cognitive changes in long-term polydrug users. *Psychopharmacology, 173,* 405–410.

Dahchour, A., & De Witte, P. (2000). Ethanol and amino acids in the central nervous system: Assessment of the pharmacological actions of acamprosate. *Progress in Neurobiology, 60,* 343–362.

Dakof, G. A., & Mendelsohn, G. A. (1986). Parkinson's disease: The psychological aspects of a chronic illness. *Psychological Bulletin, 99,* 375–387.

Dardennes, R., Even, C., Bange, F., & Heim, A. (1995). Comparison of carbamazepine and lithium in the prophylaxis of bipolar disorders. A meta-analysis. *British Journal of Psychiatry, 166,* 378–381.

Davidson, J. R. (2009). First-line pharmacotherapy approaches for generalized anxiety disorder. *Journal of Clinical Psychiatry, 70*(Suppl. 2), 25–31.

Davidson, M., Shanley, B., & Wilce, P. (1995). Increased NMDA-induced excitability during ethanol withdrawal: A behavioural and histological study. *Brain Research, 674,* 91–96.

Davidson, R. A., & Smith, B. D. (1991). Caffeine and novelty: Effects on electrodermal activity and performance. *Physiology, Biochemistry and Behavior, 49,* 1169–1175.

Davies, L. P., Drew, C. A., Duffield, P., et al. (1992). Kava pyrones and resin: Studies on GABAA, GABAB, and benzodiazepine binding sites in rodent brain. *Pharmacology and Toxicology, 71,* 120–126.

Davies, S., Pertwee, R., & Riedel, G. (2002). Functions of cannabinoid receptors in the hippocampus. *Neuropharmacology, 42,* 993–1007.

Davis, J. D., & Gelder, M. (1991). Long-term management of anxiety states. *International Review of Psychiatry, 3,* 5–17.

Davis, J. M., Wang, Z., & Janicak, P. G. (1993). A quantitative analysis of clinical drug trials for the treatment of affective disorders. *Psychopharmacology Bulletin, 29,* 175–182.

Davis, W. (1985). *The serpent and the rainbow* (pp. 92–95). New York: Simon & Schuster.

Dawkins, K., & Potter, W. Z. (1991). Gender differences in pharmacokinetics and pharmacodynamics of psychotropics: Focus on women. *Psychopharmacology Bulletin, 27,* 417–426.

DAWN Survey. (2002). Retrieved January 4, 2005, from http://dawninfo.samhsa.gov/old_dawn/pubs_94_02/edpubs/2002final

Dawson, D. A. (2000). Alcohol consumption, alcohol dependence, and all-cause mortality. *Alcoholism, Clinical and Experimental Research, 24,* 72–81.

Dean, B. B., Deborah Gerner, D., & Gerner, R. H. (2004). A systematic review evaluating health-related quality of life, work impairment, and healthcare costs and utilization in bipolar disorder. *Current Medical Research Opinion, 20,* 139–154.

DeBattista, C., Lembke, A., Solvason, H. B., et al. (2004). A prospective trial of modafinil as an adjunctive treatment of major depression. *Journal of Clinical Psychopharmacology, 24,* 87–90.

Delay, J., & Deniker, P. (1956). Chlorpromazine and neuroleptic treatments in psychiatry. *Journal of Clinical and Experimental Psychopatholpgy, 17,* 19–24.

Delgado, M. R., Li, J., Schiller, D., Phelps, E. A. (2008). The role of the striatum in aversive learning and aversive prediction errors. *Philosophical Transactions of the Royal Society, 363,* 3787–3800.

Delgado, M. R., Jou, R. L., Phelps, E. A. (2011). Neural systems underlying aversive conditioning in humans with primary and secondary reinforcers. *Frontiers in Neuroscience, 5,* 71.

Delgado, P. L. (2000). Depression: The case for a monoamine deficiency. *Journal of Clinical Psychiatry, 61,* 7–11.

Delgado, P. L., & Moreno, F. A. (2000). Role of norepinephrine in depression. *Journal of Clinical Psychiatry, 61,* 5–12.

Delle Chiaie, R., Pancheri, P., Casacchia, M., et al. (1995). Assessment of the efficacy of buspirone in patients affected by generalized anxiety disorder, shifting to buspirone from prior treatment with lorazepam: A placebo-controlled, double-blind study. *Journal of Clinical Psychopharmacology, 15,* 12–19.

DeLong, G. R., Teague, L. A., & McSwain, K. M. (1998). Effects of fluoxetine treatment in young children with idiopathic autism. *Developmental Medicine and Child Neurology, 40,* 551–562.

DeMartinis, N., Rynn, M., Rickels, K., et al. (2000). Prior benzodiazepine use and buspirone response in the treatment of generalized anxiety disorder. *Journal of Clinical Psychiatry, 61,* 91–94.

Demyttenaere, K., De Fruyt, J., & Stahl, S. M. (2005). The many faces of fatigue in major depressive disorder. *International Journal of Neuropsychopharmacology, 8,* 93–105.

Den Boer, J. A., Van Vliet, I. M., & Westenberg, H. G. (1995). Recent developments in the psychopharmacology of social phobia. *European Archives of Psychiatry & Clinical Neuroscience, 244,* 309–316.

Deng, X. S., & Deitrich, R. A. (2008). Putative role of brain acetaldehyde in ethanol addiction. *Current Drug Abuse Reviews, 1,* 3–8.

Derivan, A. T. (1995). Antidepressants: Can we determine how quickly they work? Issues from the literature. *Psychopharmacology Bulletin, 31,* 23–28.

Deroche-Gamonet, V., Belin, D., & Piazza, P. V. (2004). Evidence for addiction-like behavior in the rat. *Science, 305,* 1014–1017.

Devaki, R., Shankar Rao, S., & Nadgir, S. M. (2006). The effect of lithium on the adreno-ceptor-mediated second messenger system in the rat brain. *Journal of Psychiatry and Neuroscience, 31,* 246–252.

DeVane, C. L. (1994). Pharmacokinetics of the newer antidepressants: Clinical relevance. *American Journal of Medicine, 97,* 13S–23S.

DeVane, C. L., Rudorfer, M. V., & Potter, W. Z. (1991). Dosage regimen for cyclic antide-pressants: A review of pharmacokinetic methods. *Psychopharmacology Bulletin, 27,* 619–632.

DeVane, C. L., & Sallee, F. R. (1996). Serotonin selective reuptake inhibitors in child and adolescent psychopharmacology: A review of published experience. *Journal of Clinical Psychiatry, 57,* 55–66.

DeVane, C. L., Ware, M. R., & Lydiard, R. B. (1991). Pharmacokinetics, pharmacody-namics, and treatment issues of benzodi-azepines: Alprazolam, adinazolam, and clonazepam. *Psychopharmacology Bulletin, 27,* 463–473.

Dewey, W. L. (1986). Cannabinoid pharmacol-ogy. *Pharmacological Reviews, 38,* 151–178.

Dews, P. B. (1958). Studies on behavior. IV. Stimulant actions of methamphetamine. *Journal of Pharmacology and Experimental Therapeutics, 122,* 137–147.

Dial, J. (1992). The interaction of alcohol and cocaine: A review. *Psychobiology, 20,* 179–184.

Diaz, E., Levine, H., Sullivan, M., et al. (2001). Use of the Medication Event Monitoring System to estimate medication compliance in patients with schizophrenia. *Journal of Psychiatry and Neuroscience, 26,* 325–329.

Dichter, M. A., & Ayala, G. F. (1987). Cellular mechanisms of epilepsy: A status report. *Science, 237,* 157–164.

DiMascio, A., Lipton, M. A., & Killman, K. F. (Eds.). (1978). *Psychopharmacology: A genera-tion of progress* (pp. 1499–1506). New York: Raven Press.

Dimeff, L. A., & Marlatt, G. A. (1995). Relapse prevention. In R. K. Hester & W. R. Miller (Eds.), *Handbook of alcoholism treatment ap-proaches* (pp. 176–194). Boston, MA: Allyn and Bacon.

DiPadova, C., Worner, T. M., Julkunen, R. J. K., & Lieber, C. S. (1987). Effects of fasting and chronic alcohol consumption on the first-pass metabolism of ethanol. *Gastroenterol-ogy, 92,* 1169–1173.

Dobkin de Rios, M. (1996). On "Human phar-macology of hoasca": A medical anthropol-ogy perspective. *Journal of Nervous and Mental Disease, 184,* 95–98.

Dohan, F. C., Harper, E. H., Clark, M. H., et al. (1984). Is schizophrenia rare if grain is rare? *Biological Psychiatry, 19,* 385–399.

Dolan, R. J., Fletcher, P., Frith, C. D., et al. (1995). Dopaminergic modulation of im-paired cognitive activation in the anterior cingulate cortex in schizophrenia. *Nature, 378,* 180–182.

Dolder, C. R., & Jeste, V. (2003). Incidence of tardive dyskinesia with typical versus atypical antipsychotics in very high risk patients. *Biological Psychiatry, 53,* 1142–1145.

Dole, V. P., & Nyswander, M. E. (1976). Methadone maintenance treatment. *The Journal of the American Medical Association, 235,* 2117–2119.

Domino, E. F. (1980). History and pharmacol-ogy of PCP and PCP-related analogs. *Journal of Psychedelic Drugs, 12,* 223–227.

Domino, E. F., Dren, A. T., & Giardina, W. J. (1978). Biochemical and neurotransmitter changes in the aging brain. In M. A. Lipton, A. DiMascio, & K. F. Killman (Eds.), *Psychopharmacology* (pp. 1507–1516). New York: Raven Press.

Donny, E. C., Caggiula, A. R., Mielke, M. M., et al. (1999). Nicotine self-administration in rats on a progressive ratio schedule of reinforcement. *Psychopharmacology, 147,* 135–142.

Dorus, W., Ostrow, D. G., Anton, R., et al. (1989). Lithium treatment of depressed and nondepressed alcoholics. *The Journal of the American Medical Association, 262,* 1646–1652.

Dougherty, D. D., Bonab, A. A., Spencer, T. J., et al. (1999). Dopamine transporter density in patients with attention deficit hyperactivity disorder. *Lancet, 354,* 2132–2133.

Dougherty, P. M., Pellis, N. R., & Dafny, N. (1990). The brain and the immune system: An intact immune system is essential for the manifestation of withdrawal in opiate addicted rats. *Neuroscience, 36,* 285–289.

Douglas, V. I., Barr, R. G., Desilets, J., & Sherman, E. (1995). Do high doses of stimulants impair flexible thinking in attention-deficit hyperactivity disorder? *Journal of the American Academy of Child and Adolescent Psychiatry, 34,* 877–885.

Drake, A. I., Butters, N., Shear, P. K., et al. (1995). Cognitive recovery with abstinence and its relationship to family history for alcoholism. *Journal of Studies on Alcohol, 56,* 104–109.

Drevets, W. C. (1999). Prefrontal cortical-amygdalar metabolism in major depression. *Annals of the New York Academy of Sciences, 877,* 614–637.

Drewes, L. R. (1999). What is the blood-brain barrier? A molecular perspective. Cerebral vascular biology. *Advances in Experimental Medicine and Biology, 474,* 111–122.

Drobes, D., Anton, R., Thomas, S., & Voronin, K. (2003). A clinical laboratory paradigm for evaluating medication effects on alcohol consumption: Naltrexone and nalmefene. *Neuropsychopharmacology, 28,* 755–764.

Dubini, A., Bosc, M., & Polin, V. (1997a). Do noradrenaline and serotonin differentially affect social motivation and behaviour? *European Neuropsychopharmacology, 7,* S49–S55.

Dubini, A., Bosc, M., & Polin, V. (1997b). Noradrenaline-selective versus serotonin-selective antidepressant therapy: Differential effects on social functioning. *Journal of Psychopharmacology, 11,* S17–S23.

Dukes, R. L., Stein, J. A., & Ullman, J. B. (1997). Long-term impact of Drug Abuse Resistance Education (D.A.R.E.): Results of a 6-year follow-up. *Evaluation Review, 21,* 483–500.

Dulcan, M. K. (1986). Comprehensive treatment of children and adolescents with attention deficit disorders: The state of the art. *Clinical Psychology Review, 6,* 539–569.

Dunner, D., Goldstein, D., Mallinckrodt, C., et al. (2003). Duloxetine in treatment of anxiety symptoms associated with depression. *Depression and Anxiety, 18,* 53–61.

Durante, A. J., Hart, G. J., Brady, A. R., et al. (1995). The Health of the Nation target on syringe sharing: A role for routine surveillance in assessing progress and targeting interventions. *Addiction, 90,* 1389–1396.

Dustin, M. L., & Colman, R. (2002). Neural and immunological synaptic relations. *Science, 298,* 785–789.

Dutta, A., Zhang, S., Kolhatkar, R., & Reith, M. E. A. (2003). Dopamine transporter as target for drug development of cocaine dependence medications. *European Journal of Pharmacology, 479,* 93–106.

Duvoisin, R. C. (1986). Etiology of Parkinson's disease: Current concepts. *Clinical Neuropharmacology, 9,* S3–S11.

Earleywine, M. (1993). Personality risk for alcoholism covaries with hangover symptoms. *Addictive Behavior, 18,* 415–420.

Edwards, S., & Glover, E. (1986). Snuff and neuromuscular performance. *American Journal of Public Health, 76,* 45.

Edwards, S., Glover, E., & Schroeder, K. (1987). The effects of smokeless tobacco on heart rate and neuromuscular reactivity in athletes and nonathletes. *Physician and Sportsmedicine, 15,* 141–147.

Ehlers, C. L., Havstad, J., Prichard, D., et al. (1998). Low doses of ethanol reduce evidence for nonlinear structure in brain activity. *Journal of Neuroscience, 18,* 7474–7486.

Ehrman, R. N., Robbins, S. J., Childress, A. R., & O'Brien, C. P. (1992). Conditioned responses to cocaine-related stimuli in cocaine abuse patients. *Psychopharmacology, 107,* 523–529.

Eich, J. E., Weingartner, H., Stillman, R. C., & Gillin, J. C. (1975). State-dependent accessibility of retrieval cues in the retention of a categorized list. *Journal of Verbal Learning and Verbal Behavior, 14,* 408–417.

Eikelboom, R., & Stewart, J. (1982). Conditioning of drug-induced physiological responses. *Psychological Review, 89,* 507–528.

Eiland, L. S., & Guest, L. (2004). Atomoxetine treatment of attention-deficit/hyperactivity disorder. *Annals of Pharmacotherapy, 38,* 86–90.

Eissenberg, T., & Balster, R. L. (2000). Initial tobacco use episodes in children and adolescents: Current knowledge, future directions. *Drug and Alcohol Dependence, 59,* S41–S60.

Elal-Lawrence, G., Slade, P. D., & Dewey, M. E. (1987). Treatment and follow-up variables, discriminating abstainers, controlled drinkers and relapsers. *Journal of Studies on Alcohol, 48,* 39–46.

Elia, J., Ambrosini, P. J., & Rapoport, J. L. (1999). Treatment of attention-deficit-hyperactivity disorder. *New England Journal of Medicine, 340,* 780–788.

Elia, J., Katz, I. R., & Simpson, G. (1987). Teratogenicity of psychotherapeutic medications. *Psychopharmacology Bulletin, 23,* 531–586.

Ellenbogen, M. A., Young, S. N., Dean, P., et al. (1996). Mood response to acute tryptophan depletion in healthy volunteers: Sex differences and temporal stability. *Neuropsychopharmacology, 15,* 465–474.

Ellickson, P. L., & Bell, R. M. (1990). Drug prevention in junior high: A multi-site longitudinal test. *Science, 247,* 1299–1305.

Ellingrod, V. L., & Perry, P. J. (1994). Venlafaxine: A heterocyclic antidepressant. *American Journal of Hospital Pharmacy, 51,* 3033–3046.

Ellinwood, E. H., Kilbey, M. M., Castellani, S., & Khoury, C. (1977). Amygdala hyperspindling and seizures induced by cocaine. In E. H. Ellinwood & M. M. Kilbey (Eds.), *Cocaine and other stimulants* (pp. 303–326). New York: Plenum Press.

Elliott, R., Newman, J., Longe, O., & Deakin, J. F. W. (2003). Differential response patterns in the striatum and orbitofrontal cortex to financial reward in humans: A parametric functional magnetic resonance imaging study. *Journal of Neuroscience, 23,* 303–307.

Ellison, G. (1995). The N-methyl-D-aspartate antagonists phencyclidine, ketamine and dizocilpine as both behavioral and anatomical models of the dementias. *Brain Research-Brain Research Reviews, 20,* 250–267.

Ellison, G. D. (1993). Paranoid psychosis following continuous amphetamine or cocaine: Relationship to selective neurotoxicity. In S. G. Korenman & J. D. Barchas (Eds.), *Biological basis of substance abuse* (pp. 355–372). New York: Oxford University Press.

ElSohly, M., Ross, S., Mehmedic, Z., et al. (2000). Potency trends of delta9-THC and other cannabinoids in confiscated marijuana from 1980–1997. *Journal of Forensic Sciences, 45,* 24–30.

Emerson, T. S., & Cisek, J. E. (1993). Methcathinone: A Russian designer amphetamine infiltrates the rural midwest. *Annals of Emergency Medicine, 22,* 1897–1903.

Emmett-Oglesby, M. W., Peltier, R. L., Depoortere, R. Y., et al. (1993). Tolerance to self-administration of cocaine in rats: Time course and dose-response determination using a multi-dose method. *Drug and Alcohol Dependence, 32,* 247–256.

Emslie, G., Heiligenstein, J., Wagner, K. D., et al. (2002). Fluoxetine for acute treatment of depression in children and adolescents: A placebo-controlled, randomized clinical trial. *Journal of the American Academy of Child and Adolescent Psychiatry, 41,* 1205–1215.

Engelhardt, D. M., & Polizos, P. (1978). Adverse effects of pharmacotherapy in childhood psychosis. In M. A. Lipton, A. DiMascio, & K. F. Killman (Eds.), *Psychopharmacology* (pp. 1463–1471). New York: Raven Press.

Engelman, H. S., & MacDermott, B. (2004). Presynaptic ionotropic receptors and control of transmitter release. *Nature Reviews Neuroscience, 5,* 135–145.

Epstein, J., Saunders, B., Kilpatrick, D., & Resnick, H. S. (1998). PTSD as a mediator between childhood rape and alcohol use in adult women. *Child Abuse and Neglect, 22,* 223–234.

Erard, R., Luisada, P. V., & Peele, R. (1980). The PCP psychosis: Prolonged intoxication or drug-precipitated functional illness? *Journal of Psychedelic Drugs, 12,* 235–245.

Erikson, G. C., Hager, L. B., Houseworth, C., et al. (1985). The effects of caffeine on memory for word lists. *Physiology and Behavior, 35,* 47–51.

Ernst, E. (1999). Second thoughts about safety of St. John's wort. *Lancet, 354,* 2014–2016.

Ernst, M., Liebernauer, L. L., King, A. C., et al. (1994). Reduced brain metabolism in hyperactive girls. *Journal of the American Academy of Child and Adolescent Psychiatry, 33,* 858–868.

Ersek, M., Cherrier, M., Overman, S., & Irving, G. A. (2004). The cognitive effects of opioids. *Pain Management Nursing, 5,* 75–93.

Esposito, R. U., Perry, W., & Kornetsky, C. (1980). Effects of d-amphetamine and naloxone on brain stimulation reward. *Psychopharmacology, 69,* 187–191.

Eustace, L., Kang, D., & Coombs, D. (2003). Fetal alcohol syndrome: A growing concern for health care professionals. *Journal of Obstetric Gynecologic and Neonatal Nursing, 32,* 215–221.

Evans, D. A., McLeod, H. L., Pritchard, S., et al. (2001). Interethnic variability in human drug responses. *Drug Metabolism and Disposition: The Bioligical Fate of Chemicals, 29,* 606–610.

Evans, J. G., Wilcock, G., & Birks, J. (2004). Evidence-based pharmacotherapy of Alzheimer's disease. *International Journal of Neuropsychopharmacology, 7,* 351–369.

Everitt, B. J., & Robbins, T. W. (2005). Neural systems of reinforcement for drug addiction: From actions to habits to compulsion. *Nature Neuroscience, 8,* 1481–1489.

Everitt, B. J., & Wolf, E. (2002). Psychomotor stimulant addiction: A neural systems perspective. *Journal of Neuroscience, 22,* 3312–3320.

Eysenck, H. J. (1967). *Biological basis of personality.* Springfield, IL: Thomas Charles.

Fairbank, J. A., Dunteman, G. H., & Condelli, W. S. (1993). Do methadone patients substitute other drugs for heroin? Predicting substance use at 1-year follow-up. *American Journal of Drug and Alcohol Abuse, 19,* 465–474.

Falkenburger, B. H., Barstow, K. L., & Mintz, I. M. (2001). Dendrodendritic inhibition through reversal of dopamine transport. *Science, 293,* 2465–2470.

Faraone, S. V., Biederman, J., Chen, W. J., et al. (1995). Genetic heterogeneity in attention-deficit hyperactivity disorder (ADHD): Gender, psychiatric comorbidity, and maternal ADHD. *Journal of Abnormal Psychology, 104,* 334–345.

Faraone, S. V., Biederman, J., Spencer, T., et al. (2000). Attention-deficit/hyperactivity disorder in adults: An overview. *Biological Psychiatry, 48,* 9–20.

Faraone, S. V., Biederman, J., Weiffenbach, B., et al. (1999). Dopamine D4 gene 7-repeat allele and attention deficit hyperactivity disorder. *American Journal of Psychiatry, 156,* 768–770.

Faraone, S. V., Curran, J. P., Laughren, T., et al. (1986). Neuroleptic bioavailability, psychosocial factors, and clinical status: A 1-year study of schizophrenic outpatients after dose reduction. *Psychiatry Research, 19,* 311–322.

Farlow, M. R. (2004). NMDA receptor antagonists. A new therapeutic approach for Alzheimer's disease. *Geriatrics, 59,* 22–27.

Farrar, A. M., Segovia, K. N., Randall, P. A., Nunes, E. J., Collins, L. E., Stopper, C. M., et al. (2010). Nucleus accumbens and effort-related functions: Behavioral and neural markers of the interactions between adenosine A_{2A} and dopamine D2 receptors. *Neuroscience, 166,* 1056–1067.

Farre, M., de la Torre, R., Llorente, M., et al. (1993). Alcohol and cocaine interactions in humans. *Journal of Pharmacology & Experimental Therapeutics, 266,* 1364–1373.

Fasano, A., & Petrovic, I. (2010). Insights into pathophysiology of punding reveal possible treatment strategies. *Molecular Psychiatry, 15,* 560–573.

Fatemi, S. H., Realmuto, G. M., Khan, L., et al. (1998). Fluoxetine in treatment of adolescent patients with autism: A longitudinal open trial. *Journal of Autism and Developmental Disorders, 28,* 303–307.

Faure, A., Reynolds, S. M., Richard, J. M., & Berridge, K. C. (2008). Mesolimbic dopamine in desire and dread: Enabling motivation to be generated by localized glutamate disruptions in nucleus accumbens. *Journal of Neuroscience, 28,* 7184–7192.

Fava, M. (2000). New approaches to the treatment of refractory depression. *Journal of Clinical Psychiatry, 61,* 26–32.

Fava, M., & Rosenbaum, J. F. (1991). Suicidality and fluoxetine: Is there a relationship? *Journal of Clinical Psychiatry, 52,* 108–111.

Feeney, D. M. (1976). The marijuana window: A theory of cannabis use. *Biobehavioral Biology, 18,* 455–471.

Feighner, J. P., Herbstein, J., & Damlouji, N. (1985). Combined MAOI, TCA, and direct stimulant therapy of treatment-resistant depression. *Journal of Clinical Psychiatry, 46,* 206–209.

Feingold, A., & Rounsaville, B. (1995). Construct validity of the abuse-dependence distinction as measured by DSM-IV criteria for different psychoactive substances. *Drug & Alcohol Dependence, 39,* 99–109.

Feldman, H. M., Kolmen, B. K., & Gonzaga, A. M. (1999). Naltrexone and communication skills in young children with autism. *Journal of the American Academy of Child and Adolescent Psychiatry, 38,* 587–593.

Fennig, S., Fennig, S. N., Pato, M., & Weitzman, A. (1994). Emergence of symptoms of Tourette's syndrome during fluvoxamine treatment of obsessive-compulsive disorder. *British Journal of Psychiatry, 164,* 839–841.

Fenton, W. S. (2000). Prevalence of spontaneous dyskinesia in schizophrenia. *Journal of Clinical Psychiatry, 61,* 10–14.

Ferdinand, K. C., & Saunders, E. (2006). Hypertension-related morbidity and mortality in African Americans—why we need to do better. *Journal of Clinical Hypertension, 8,* 21–30.

Fergusson, D. M., Horwood, L. J., & Ridder, E. M. (2005). Tests of causal linkages between cannabis use and psychotic symptoms. *Addiction, 100,* 354–366.

Fergusson, D. M., Lynskey, M. T., & Horwood, L. J. (1996). Comorbidity between depressive disorders and nicotine dependence in a cohort of 16-year-olds. *Archives of General Psychiatry, 53,* 1043–1047.

Fernandez, J. R., & Allison, B. (2004). Rimonabant Sanofi-Synthelabo. *Current Opinion in Investigational Drugs, 5,* 430–435.

Fernstrom, J. D. (1994). Dietary amino acids and brain function. *Journal of the American Dietetic Association, 94,* 71–77.

Fernstrom, M. H., & Fernstrom, J. D. (1995). Brain tryptophan concentrations and serotonin synthesis remain responsive to food consumption after the ingestion of sequential meals. *American Journal of Clinical Nutrition, 61,* 312–319.

Ferrante, F. M. (1996). Principles of opioid pharmacotherapy: Practical implications of basic mechanisms. *Journal of Pain and Symptom Management, 11,* 265–273.

Ferraro, D. P. (1980). Acute effects of marijuana on human memory and cognition. In *NIDA Research Monograph Series 31* (pp. 98–119). Rockville, MD: National Institute on Drug Abuse, Department of Health and Human Services.

Ferré, S. (2008). An update on the mechanisms of the psychostimulant effects of caffeine. *Journal of Neurochemistry, 105,* 1067–1079.

Ferré, S. (2010). Role of the central ascending neurotransmitter systems in the psychostimulant effects of caffeine. *Journal of Alzheimer's Disease, 20*(Suppl. 1), S35–S49.

Ferré, S., Ciruela, F., Canals, M., Marcellino, D., Burgueno, J., Casadó, V., et al. (2004). Adenosine A_{2A}-dopamine D2 receptor-receptor heteromers. Targets for neuropsychiatric disorders. *Parkinsonism & Related Disorders, 10,* 265–271.

Ferré, S., Quiroz, C., Woods, A. S., Cunha, R., Popoli, P., Ciruela, F., et al. (2008). An update on adenosine A_{2A}-dopamine D2 receptor interactions: Implications for the function of G protein-coupled receptors. *Current Pharmacology Design, 14,* 1468–1474.

Fields, R. D., & Stevens-Graham, B. (2002). New insights into neuron-glia communication. *Science, 298,* 556–562.

File, S. E. (1985). Tolerance to the behavioural actions of benzodiazepines. *Neuroscience and Biobehavioral Reviews, 9,* 113–121.

File, S. E., Lippa, A. S., Beer, B., & Lippa, M. T. (2004). Animal tests of anxiety. *Current Protocols in Neuroscience* [Chapter 8: Unit 8.3].

Fillmore, K. M., Golding, J. M., Graves, K. L., et al. (1998). Alcohol consumption and mortality. *Addiction, 93,* 183–203.

Finch, C. E. (1982). The neurobiology of aging. *Science, 216,* 49–50.

Findling, R., Aman, M., Eerdekens, M., et al. (2004). Long-term, open-label study of risperidone in children with severe disruptive behaviors and below-average IQ. *American Journal of Psychiatry, 161,* 677–684.

Findling, R. L., & McNamara, K. (2004). Atypical antipsychotics in the treatment of children and adolescents: Clinical applications. *Journal of Clinical Psychiatry, 65*(Suppl. 6), 30–44.

Fine, S., & Johnston, C. (1993). Drug and placebo side effects in methylphenidate-placebo trial for attention-deficit hyperactivity disorder. *Child Psychiatry & Human Development, 24,* 25–30.

Fingarette, H. (1988). *Heavy drinking: The myth of alcoholism as a disease.* Berkeley, CA: University of California Press.

Fingerhut, L. A., & Cox, C. S. (1998). Poisoning mortality, 1985–1995. *Public Health Reports, 113,* 218–233.

Fink, M. (1994). Indications for the use of ECT. *Psychopharmacology Bulletin, 30,* 269–275.

Finkle, B. S., & McCloskey, K. L. (1977). The forensic toxicology of cocaine. In R. C. Peterson & R. C. Stillman (Eds.), *Cocaine: 1977.* National Institute of Drug Abuse-Research Monograph Series, *13,* pp. 153–179.

Finney, J. W., & Moos, R. H. (1991). The long-term course of treated alcoholism: I. Mortality, relapse and remission rates and comparisons with community controls. *Journal of Studies on Alcohol, 52,* 44–54.

Fiorella, D., Rabin, R. A., & Winter, J. C. (1995). The role of the 5-HT2A and 5-HT2C receptors in the stimulus effects of hallucinogenic drugs. I: Antagonist correlation analysis. *Psychopharmacology, 121,* 347–356.

Fiorillo, C., Tobler, P., & Schultz, W. (2003). Discrete coding of reward probability and uncertainty by dopamine neurons. *Science, 299,* 1898–1902.

Fischer, G., Gombas, W., Eder, H., et al. (1999). Buprenorphine versus methadone maintenance for the treatment of opioid dependence. *Addiction, 94,* 1337–1347.

Fischer, G., Johnson, R. E., Eder, H., et al. (2000). Treatment of opioid-dependent pregnant women with buprenorphine. *Addiction, 95,* 239–244.

Fischer, J., & Taschner, K. L. (1991). Flashback following use of cannabis: A review. *Fortschritte der Neurologie, Psychiatrie, und Ihrer Grenzgebiete, 59,* 437–446.

Fischman, M. W., Schuster, C. R., Javaid, J., et al. (1985). Acute tolerance development to the cardiovascular and subjective effects of cocaine. *Journal of Pharmacology and Experimental Therapeutics, 235,* 677–682.

Fish, E. W., Riday, T. T., McGuigan, M. M., Faccidomo, S., Hodge, C. W., & Malanga, C. J. (2010). Alcohol, cocaine, and brain stimulation-reward in C57Bl6/J and DBA2/J mice. *Alcohol Clinical and Experimental Research, 34,* 81–89.

Fitzgerald, L. W., Ortiz, J., Hamedani, A. G., & Nestler, E. J. (1996). Drugs of abuse and stress increase the expression of GluR1 and NMDAR1 glumate receptor subunits in the rat ventral tegmental area: Common adaptations among cross-sensitizing agents. *Journal of Neuroscience, 16,* 274–282.

Flagel, S. B., Watson, S. J., Akil, H., & Robinson, T. E. (2008). Individual differences in the attribution of incentive salience to a reward-related cue: Influence on cocaine sensitization. *Behavioural Brain Research, 186,* 48–56.

Flemenbaum, A. (1974). Does lithium block the effects of amphetamine? *American Journal of Psychiatry, 131,* 820–821.

Fleming, M. F., Mihic, S. J., & Harris, R. A. (2001). Ethanol. In J. G. Hardman & L. E. Limbird (Eds.), *Goodman & Gilman's The pharmacological basis of therapeutics* (10th ed., pp. 429–445). New York: McGraw-Hill.

Fleming, R., Leventhal, H., Glynn, K., & Ershler, J. (1989). The role of cigarettes in the initiation and progression of early substance use. *Addictive Behaviors, 14,* 261–272.

Fletcher, J., Page, J., Francis, D., et al. (1996). Cognitive correlates of long-term cannabis use in Costa Rican men. *Archives of General Psychiatry, 53,* 1051–1057.

Floresco, S. B. & Jentsch, J. D. (2011). Pharmacological enhancement of memory and executive functioning in laboratory animals. *Neuropsychopharmacology, 36,* 227–250.

Floresco, S. B., Zhang, Y., Enomoto, T. (2009). Neural circuits subserving behavioral flexibility and their relevance to schizophrenia. *Behavioural Brain Research, 204,* 396–409.

Flynn, P., Joe, G., Broome, K., et al. (2003). Looking back on cocaine dependence: Reasons for recovery. *American Journal on Addictions, 12,* 398–411.

Foltin, R., Ward, A., Haney, M., et al. (2003). The effects of escalating doses of smoked cocaine in humans. *Drug and Alcohol Dependence, 70,* 149–157.

Foltin, R. W., Brady, J. V., & Fischman, M. W. (1986). Behavioral analysis of marijuana effects on food intake in humans. *Pharmacology, Biochemistry and Behavior, 25,* 577–582.

Foltin, R. W., & Fischman, M. W. (1991). Smoked and intravenous cocaine in humans: Acute tolerance, cardiovascular and subjective effects. *Journal of Pharmacology and Experimental Therapeutics, 157,* 247–261.

Foltin, R. W., Fischman, M. W., & Levin, F. R. (1995). Cardiovascular effects of cocaine in humans: Laboratory studies. *Drug and Alcohol Dependence, 37,* 193–210.

Fountain, J., Strang, J., Gossop, M., et al. (2000). Diversion of prescribed drugs by drug users in treatment: Analysis of the UK market and new data from London. *Addiction, 95,* 393–406.

Fowler, J. S., Volkow, N. D., Wang, G. J., et al. (1996). Inhibition of monoamine oxidase B in the brains of smokers. *Nature, 379,* 733–736.

Frank, E., Karp, J. F., & Rush, A. J. (1993). Efficacy of treatments for major depression. *Psychopharmacology Bulletin, 29,* 457–476.

Frank, E., & Thase, M. E. (1999). Natural history and preventative treatment of recurrent mood disorders. *Annual Review of Medicine, 50,* 453–468.

Franken, I. H., De Haan, H. A., Haffmans, P. M., et al. (1999). Cue reactivity and effects of cue exposure in abstinent posttreatment drug users. *Journal of Substance Abuse Treatment, 16,* 81–85.

Franks, N. P., & Lieb, W. R. (1991). Stereospecific effects of inhalational general anesthetic optical isomers on nerve ion channels. *Science, 254,* 427–430.

Franks, N. P., & Lieb, W. R. (1994). Molecular and cellular mechanisms of general anaesthesia. *Nature, 367,* 607–614.

Frazer, A., Maayani, S., & Wolfe, B. B. (1990). Subtypes of receptors for serotonin. *Annual Review of Pharmacology and Toxicology, 30,* 307–348.

Freed, H. (1955). Chlorpromazine and reserpine; new era in psychiatry? *American Practitioner and Digest of Treament, 6,* 706–708.

Freedman, D. X., & Halaris, A. E. (1978). Monoamines and the biochemical mode of action of LSD at synapses. In M. A. Lipton, A. DiMascio, & K. F. Killam (Eds.), *Psychopharmacology* (pp. 347–360). New York: Raven Press.

Freier, D. O., & Fuchs, B. A. (1994). A mechanism of action for morphine-induced immunosuppression: Corticosterone mediates morphine-induced suppression of natural killer cell activity. *Journal of Pharmacology and Experimental Therapeutics, 270,* 1127–1133.

Frezza, M., Di Padova, C., Pozzato, G., et al. (1990). High blood alcohol levels in women. *New England Journal of Medicine, 322,* 95–99.

Friedel, R. O. (1978). Pharmacokinetics in the geropsychiatric patient. In M. A. Lipton, A. DiMascio, & K. F. Killman (Eds.), *Psychopharmacology* (pp. 1499–1506). New York: Raven Press.

Friedman, J. H., Brown, R. G., Comella, C., Garber, C. E., et al. (2007). Fatigue in Parkinson's disease: A review. *Movement Disorders, 22,* 297–308.

Fry, J. M. (1998). Treatment for narcolepsy. *Neurology, 50,* S43–S48.

Fuchs, R. A., Evans, K. A., Parker, M. P., & See, R. E. (2004). Differential involvement of orbitofrontal cortex subregions in conditioned cue-induced and cocaine-primed reinstatement of cocaine seeking in rats. *Journal of Neuroscience, 24,* 6600–6610.

Fudin, R., & Nicastro, R. (1988). Can caffeine antagonize alcohol-induced performance decrements in humans? *Perceptual and Motor Skills, 67,* 375–391.

Fugh-Berman, A. (2000). Herb-drug interactions. *Lancet, 355,* 134–138.

Fuller, R. C. (1992). Biographical origins of psychological ideas: Freud's cocaine studies. *Journal of Humanistic Psychology, 32,* 67–86.

Furukawa, T., Ushizima, I., & Ono, N. (1975). Modifications by lithium of behavioral responses to methamphetamine and tetrabenazine. *Psychopharmacologia, 42,* 243–248.

Fuxe, K., Agnati, L.F., Jacobsen, K., Hillion, J., Canals, M., Torvinen, M., et al. (2003). Receptor heteromerization in adenosine A_{2A} receptor signaling: relevance for striatal function and Parkinson's disease. *Neurology, 61*(11 Suppl. 6), S19–S23.

Fuxe, K., Dahlström, A. B., Jonsson, G., Marcellino, D., Guescini, M., Dam, M., et al. (2010). The discovery of central monoamine neurons gave volume transmission to the wired brain. *Progress in Neurobiology, 90,* 82–100.

Fysh, R. R., Oon, M. C. H., Robinson, K. N., et al. (1985). A fatal poisoning with LSD. *Forensic Science International, 28,* 108–114.

Gadow, K. D. (1992). Pediatric psychopharmacotherapy: A review of recent research. *Journal of Child Psychology and Psychiatry, 33,* 153–195.

Gage, F. H. (2000). Mammalian neural stem cells. *Science, 287,* 1433–1438.

Gagliano, A., Germano, E., Pustorino, G., et al. (2004). Risperidone treatment of children with autistic disorder: Effectiveness, tolerability, and pharmacokinetic implications. *Journal of Child and Adolescent Psychopharmacology, 14,* 39–47.

Galizia, V. J. (1984). Pharmacotherapy of memory loss in the geriatric patient. *Drug Intelligence and Clinical Pharmacy, 18,* 784–791.

Gammans, R. E., Stringfellow, J. C., Hvizdos, A. J., Seidhamel, R. J., Cohn, J. B., Wilcox, C. S., et al. (1992). Use of buspirone in patients with generalized anxiety disorder and coexisting depressive symptoms: A meta-analysis of eight randomized, controlled studies. *Neuropsychobiology, 25,* 193–201.

Garbutt, J. C., West, S. L., Carey, T. S., et al. (1999). Pharmacological treatment of alcohol dependence: A review of the evidence. *The Journal of the American Medical Association, 281,* 1318–1325.

Gardner, E. L., & Lowinson, J. H. (1991). Marijuana's interaction with brain reward systems: Update 1991. *Pharmacology, Biochemistry and Behavior, 40,* 571–580.

Garriock, H. A., Tanowitz, M., Kraft, J. B., Dang, V. C., Peters, E. J., Jenkins, G. D., et al. (2010). Association of mu-opioid receptor variants and response to citalopram treatment in major depressive disorder. *American Journal of Psychiatry, 167,* 565–573.

Gatti, G., Bonomi, I., Jannuzzi, G., & Perucca, E. (2000). The new antiepileptic drugs: Pharmacological and clinical aspects. *Current Pharmaceutical Design, 6,* 839–860.

Gauvin, D. V., Cheng, E. Y., & Holloway, F. A. (1993). Recent developments in alcoholism: Biobehavioral correlates. *Recent Developments in Alcoholism, 11,* 281–304.

Gawin, F. H. (1986). Neuroleptic reduction of cocaine-induced paranoia but not euphoria? *Psychopharmacology, 90,* 142–143.

Gawin, F. H. (1993). Cocaine addiction: Psychology, neurophysiology, and treatment. In S. G. Korenman & J. D. Barchas (Eds.), *Biological basis of substance abuse* (pp. 425–442). New York: Oxford University Press.

Gaziano, J. M., Gaziano, T. A., Glynn, R. J., et al. (2000). Light-to-moderate alcohol consumption and mortality in the Physicians' Health Study enrollment cohort. *Journal of the American College of Cardiology, 35,* 96–105.

Gaziano, J. M., & Hennekens, C. (1995). Royal colleges' advice on alcohol consumption. *British Medical Journal, 311,* 3–4.

Geller, B. (1991). Psychopharmacology of children and adolescents: Pharmacokinetics and relationships of plasma/serum levels to response. *Psychopharmacology Bulletin, 27,* 401–410.

Gentry, M. V., Hammersley, J. J., Hale, C. R., et al. (2000). Nicotine patches improve mood and response speed in a lexical decision task. *Addictive Behaviors, 25,* 549–557.

George, M. S., Teneback, C. C., Malcolm, R. J., et al. (1999). Multiple previous alcohol detoxifications are associated with decreased medial temporal and paralimbic function in the postwithdrawal period. *Alcoholism, Clinical and Experimental Research, 23,* 1077–1084.

Georgotas, A., McCue, R. E., Friedman, E., & Cooper, T. (1987). Prediction of response to nortriptyline and phenelzine by platelet MAO activity. *American Journal of Psychiatry, 144,* 338–340.

Gerdeman, G., Partridge, J., Lupica, C., & Lovinger, D. M. (2003). It could be habit forming: Drugs of abuse and striatal synaptic plasticity. *Trends in Neurosciences, 26,* 184–192.

Gerlach, J., & Peacock, L. (1995). New antipsychotics: The present status. *International Clinical Psychopharmacology, 10*(Suppl. 3), 39–48.

Gerra, G., Zaimovic, A., Ferri, M., et al. (2000). Long-lasting effects of (+) 3,4-methylene-dioxymethamphetamine (ecstasy) on serotonin system function in humans. *Biological Psychiatry, 47,* 127–136.

Gerstein, D. R., Johnson, R. A., Harwood, H., et al. (1994). *Evaluating recovery services, the california drug and alcohol treatment assessment (CALDATA).* Sacramento, CA: State of California Department of Drug and Alcohol Programs.

Ghaemi, S. N., Hsu, D., Soldani, F., & Goodwin, F. K. (2003). Antidepressants in bipolar disorder: The case for caution. *Bipolar Disorders, 5,* 421–433.

Ghods-Sharifi, S. & Floresco, S. B. (2010) Differential effects on effort discounting induced by inactivations of the nucleus accumbens core or shell. *Behavioral Neuroscience, 124,* 179–191.

Ghosh, A., & Greenberg, M. E. (1995). Calcium signaling in neurons: Molecular mechanisms and cellular consequences. *Science, 268,* 239–246.

Giardino, W. J., Pastor, R., Anacker, A. M., Spangler, E., Cote, D. M., Li, J., et al. (2011). Dissection of corticotropin-releasing factor system involvement in locomotor sensitivity to methamphetamine. *Genes, Brain, and Behavior, 10,* 78–89.

Gilbert, P. L., Harris, M. J., McAdams, L. A., & Jeste, D. V. (1995). Neuroleptic withdrawal in schizophrenic patients. *Archives of General Psychiatry, 52,* 173–188.

Gillberg, C. (1995). Endogenous opioids and opiate antagonists in autism: Brief review of empirical findings and implications for clinicians. *Developmental Medicine & Child Neurology, 37,* 239–245.

Gillberg, C., Melander, H., von Knorring, A. L., et al. (1997). Long-term stimulant treatment of children with attention-deficit hyperactivity disorder symptoms. A randomized, double-blind, placebo-controlled trial. *Archives of General Psychiatry, 54,* 857–864.

Gillette, J., Weisburger, E. K., Kraybill, H., & Kelsey, M. (1985). Strategies for determining the mechanisms of toxicity. *Clinical Toxicology, 23,* 1–78.

Gillin, J. C., Stoff, D. M., & Wyatt, R. J. (1978). Transmethylation hypothesis: A review of progress. In M. A. Lipton, A. DiMascio, & K. F. Killam (Eds.), *Psychopharmacology* (pp. 1097–1112). New York: Raven Press.

Giovino, G. A., Henningfield, J. E., Tomar, S. L., & Escobedo, L. G. (1995). Epidemiology of tobacco use and dependence. *Epidemiologic Reviews, 17,* 48–65.

Gitlin, M. J., Swendsen, J., Heller, T. L., & Hammen, C. (1995). Relapse and impairment in bipolar disorder. *American Journal of Psychiatry, 152,* 1635–1640.

Gitlin, T. (1990). On drugs and mass media in America's consumer society. In H. Resnick (Ed.), *Youth and drugs: Society's mixed messages* (pp. 31–52). Rockville, MD: U.S. Department of Health and Human Services.

Gjedde, A., Reith, J., & Wong, D. (1995). Dopamine receptors in schizophrenia. *Lancet, 346,* 1302–1303.

Glassman, A. H., Helzer, J. E., Covey, L. S., et al. (1990). Smoking, smoking cessation, and major depression. *The Journal of the American Medical Association, 264,* 1546–1549.

Glazer, W. M. (2000a). Expected incidence of tardive dykinesia associated with atypical antipsychotics. *Journal of Clinical Psychiatry, 61,* 21–26.

Glazer, W. M. (2000b). Extrapyramidal side effects, tardive dyskinesia, and the concept of atypicality. *Journal of Clinical Psychiatry, 61,* 16–21.

Glazer, W. M. (2000c). Review of incidence studies of tardive dyskinesia associated with typical antipsychotics. *Journal of Clinical Psychiatry, 61,* 15–20.

Glazer, W. M., Pino, C. D., & Quinlan, D. (1987). The reassessment of chronic patients previously diagnosed as schizophrenic. *Journal of Clinical Psychiatry, 48,* 430–433.

Glennon, R. A., & Rosecrans, J. A. (1982). Indolealkylamine and phenalkylamine hallucinogens: A brief overview. *Neuroscience and Biobehavioral Reviews, 6,* 489–498.

Glennon, R. A., Young, R., Martin, B. R., & Dal Cason, T. A. (1995). Methcathione ("cat"): An enantiomeric potency comparison. *Pharmacology, Biochemistry and Behavior, 50,* 601–606.

Glick, I. D. (2004). Adding psychotherapy to pharmacotherapy: Data, benefits, and guidelines for integration. *American Journal of Psychotherapy, 58,* 186–208.

Global status report on alcohol and health. (2011). World Health Organization.

Goda, Y., & Stevens, F. (1994). Two components of transmitter release at a central synapse. *Proceedings of the National Academy of Sciences of the United States of America, 91,* 12942–12946.

Gold, M. S., & Dackis, C. A. (1984). New insights and treatments: Opiate withdrawal and cocaine addiction. *Clinical Therapeutics, 7,* 6–21.

Gold, P. E. (1995). Role of glucose in regulating the brain and cognition. *American Journal of Clinical Nutrition, 61*(Suppl. 4), 987S–995S.

Gold, R., & Lenox, R. H. (1995). Is there a rationale for iron supplementation in the treatment of akathisia? A review of the evidence. *Journal of Clinical Psychiatry, 56,* 476–483.

Goldberg, J. F., Harrow, M., & Leon, A. C. (1996). Lithium treatment of bipolar affective disorders under naturalistic followup conditions. *Psychopharmacology Bulletin, 32,* 47–54.

Goldberg, J. R. (1987). Healthy addiction. *Health, 19,* 18.

Goldberg, S. R., Spealman, R. D., & Goldberg, D. M. (1981). Persistent behavior at high rates maintained by intravenous self-administration of nicotine. *Science, 214,* 573–575.

Golden, C. J., Graber, B., Blose, I., Berg, R., Coffman, J., & Bloch, S. (1981). Difference in brain densities between chronic alcoholic and normal control patients. *Science, 211,* 508–510.

Goldstein, A., & Kalant, H. (1990). Drug policy: Striking the right balance. *Science, 249,* 1513–1521.

Goldstein, D. B. (1989). Alcohol and biological membranes. In H. W. Goedde & D. P. Agarwal (Eds.), *Alcoholism* (pp. 87–98). New York: Pergamon Press.

Goldstein, D., Lu, Y., Detke, M., et al. (2004). Duloxetine in the treatment of depression: A double-blind placebo-controlled comparison with paroxetine. *Journal of Clinical Psychopharmacology, 24,* 389–399.

Goldstein, G. W., & Betz, A. L. (1986). The blood-brain barrier. *Scientific American, 255,* 74–83.

Gonzalez, N. M., & Campbell, M. (1994). Cocaine babies: Does prenatal exposure to cocaine affect development? *Journal of the American Academy of Child and Adolescent Psychiatry, 33,* 16–19.

Gonzalez, N. M., Campbell, M., Small, A. M., et al. (1994). Naltrexone plasma levels, clinical response and effect on weight in autistic children. *Psychopharmacology Bulletin, 30,* 203–208.

Gonzalez, R., Carey, C., & Grant, I. (2002). Nonacute (residual) neuropsychological effects of cannabis use: A qualitative analysis and systematic review. *Journal of Clinical Pharmacology, 42*(Suppl. 11), 48S–57S.

Goodman, A. B., & Pardee, A. B. (2000). Meeting report; "Molecular neurobiological mechanisms in schizophrenia: Seeking a synthesis," April 11–14, 1999. *Biological Psychiatry, 48,* 173–183.

Goodman, E., & Capitman, J. (2000). Depressive symptoms and cigarette smoking among teens. *Pediatrics, 106,* 748–755.

Goodnick, P. J. (1991a). Pharmacokinetics of second generation antidepressants: Fluoxetine. *Psychopharmacology Bulletin, 27,* 503–512.

Goodnick, P. J. (1991b). Pharmacokinetics of second generation antidepressants: Bupropion. *Psychopharmacology Bulletin, 27,* 513–520.

Goodnick, P. J., & Schorr-Cain, C. B. (1991). Lithium pharmacokinetics. *Psychopharmacology Bulletin, 27,* 475–492.

Gordon, C. T., Frazier, J. A., McKenna, K., et al. (1994). Childhood-onset schizophrenia: An NIMH study in progress. *Schizophrenia Bulletin, 20,* 697–712.

Gorman, J. M. (2003). Treating generalized anxiety disorder. *Journal of Clinical Psychiatry, 64*(Suppl. 2), 24–29.

Gossop, M., Griffiths, P., Powis, B., & Strang, J. (1992). Severity of dependence and route of administration of heroin, cocaine and amphetamines. *British Journal of Addiction, 87,* 1527–1536.

Gossop, M., Marsden, J., & Stewart, D. (2000). Treatment outcomes of stimulant misusers: One-year follow-up results from the national treatment outcome research study (NTORS). *Addictive Behaviors, 25,* 509–522.

Gottleib, A. M., Killen, J. D., Marlatt, G. A., & Taylor, C. B. (1987). Psychological and pharmacological influences in cigarette smoking withdrawal: Effects of nicotine gum and expectancy on smoking withdrawal symptoms and relapse. *Journal of Counseling and Clinical Psychology, 55,* 606–608.

Gouzoulis-Mayfrank, E., Daumann, J., Tuchtenhagen, F., et al. (2000). Impaired cognitive performance in drug free users of recreational ecstasy (MDMA). *Journal of Neurology, Neurosurgery, and Psychiatry, 68,* 719–725.

Gouzoulis-Mayfrank, E., Thimm, B., Rezk, M., et al. (2003). Memory impairment suggests hippocampal dysfunction in abstinent ecstasy users. *Progress in Neuro-Psychopharmacology and Biological Psychiatry, 27,* 819–827.

Gowing, L., Ali, R., & White, J. (2002). Opioid antagonists under heavy sedation or anaesthesia for opioid withdrawal. *Cochrane Database of Systematic Reviews (Online: Update Software),* no. 2, CD002022.

Grabowski, J., & Dworkin, S. E. (1985). Cocaine: An overview of current issues. *International Journal of the Addictions, 20,* 1065–1088.

Grabowski, J., Rhoades, H., Elk, R., et al. (1995). Fluoxetine is ineffective for treatment of cocaine dependence or concurrent opiate and cocaine dependence: Two placebo-controlled, double-blind trials. *Journal of Clinical Psychopharmacology, 15,* 163–174.

Grabowski, J., Rhoades, H., Schmitz, J., et al. (2001). Dextroamphetamine for cocaine-dependence treatment: A double-blind randomized clinical trial. *Journal of Clinical Psychopharmacology, 21,* 522–526.

Grabowski, J., Rhoades, H., Stotts, A., et al. (2004). Agonist-like or antagonist-like treatment for cocaine dependence with methadone for heroin dependence: Two double-blind randomized clinical trials. *Neuropsychopharmacology, 29,* 969–981.

Grace, A. A. (1991). Phasic versus tonic dopamine release and the modulation of dopamine system responsivity: A hypothesis for the etiology of schizophrenia. *Neuroscience, 41,* 1–24.

Grace, A. A., Bunney, B. S., Moore, H., et al. (1997). Dopamine-cell depolarization block as a model for the therapeutic actions of antipsychotic drugs. *Trends in Neurosciences, 20,* 31–37.

Graham, K. (2003). The yin and yang of alcohol intoxication: Implications for research on the social consequences of drinking. *Addiction, 98,* 1021–1023.

Graham, T. E., Rush, J. W., & Van Soeren, M. H. (1994). Caffeine and exercise: Metabolism and performance. *Canadian Journal of Applied Physiology, 19,* 111–138.

Graham, T. E., & Spriet, L. L. (1995). Metabolic, catecholamine, and exercise performance responses to various doses of caffeine. *Journal of Applied Physiology, 78,* 867–874.

Grant, B., Dawson, D., Stinson, F., et al. (2004). The 12-month prevalence and trends in DSM-IV alcohol abuse and dependence: United States, 1991–1992 and 2001–2002. *Drug and Alcohol Dependence, 74,* 223–234.

Grant, S., London, E. D., Newlin, D. B., et al. (1996). Activation of memory circuits during cue-elicited cocaine craving. *Proceedings of the National Academy of Sciences of the United States, 93,* 12040–12045.

Graybiel, A. M., Aosaki, T., Flaherty, A. W., & Kimura, M. (1994). The basal ganglia and adaptive motor control. *Science, 265,* 1826–1831.

Green, A. R. (2004). MDMA: Fact and fallacy, and the need to increase knowledge in both the scientific and popular press. *Psychopharmacology, 173,* 231–233.

Green, A. R., Mechan, A., Elliott, J. M., et al. (2003). The pharmacology and clinical pharmacology of 3,4-methylene-dioxymethamphetamine (MDMA). *Pharmacological Reviews, 55,* 463–508.

Greengard, P. (2001). The neurobiology of slow synaptic transmission. *Science, 294,* 1024–1030.

Greenwald, M. K., & Stitzer, M. L. (2000). Antinociceptive, subjective and behavioral effects of smoked marijuana in humans. *Drug and Alcohol Dependence, 59,* 261–275.

Greer, G., & Tolbert, R. (1986). Subjective reports of the effects of MDMA in a clinical setting. *Journal of Psychoactive Drugs, 18,* 319–327.

Greist, J. H., Jefferson, J. W., Kobak, K. A., & Katzelnick, D. J. (1995). Efficacy and tolerability of serotonin transport inhibitors in obsessive-compulsive disorder. A meta-analysis. *Archives of General Psychiatry, 52,* 53–60.

Griffith, D. R., Azuma, S. D., & Chasnoff, I. J. (1994). Three-year outcome of children exposed prenatally to drugs. *Journal of the American Academy of Child and Adolescent Psychiatry, 33,* 20–27.

Griffith, J. D., Cavanaugh, J. H., Held, J., & Oates, J. A. (1970). Experimental psychosis induced by the administration of d-amphetamine. In E. Costa & S. Garattini (Eds.), *International symposium on amphetamines and related compounds* (pp. 897–904). New York: Raven Press.

Griffiths, J. W., & Goudie, A. J. (1987). Analysis of the role of behavioural factors in the development of tolerance to the benzodiazepine midazolam. *Neuropharmacology, 26,* 201–209.

Griffiths, R. R., Bigelow, G. E., & Liebson, I. A. (1986). Human coffee drinking: Reinforcing and physical dependence producing effects of caffeine. *Journal of Pharmacology and Experimental Therapeutics, 239,* 416–425.

Grilly, D. M. (1977). Rate dependent effects of amphetamine resulting from behavioral competition. *Biobehavioral Reviews, 1,* 87–93.

Grilly, D. M. (1980). Sherlock Holmes and cocaine: Fact and fiction. *Sherlock Holmes Journal, 15,* 11–13.

Grilly, D. M., & Gowans, G. C. (1986). Acute morphine dependence: Effects observed in shock and light discrimination tasks. *Psychopharmacology, 88,* 500–504.

Grilly, D. M., Gowans, G. C., McCann, D. S., & Grogan, T. W. (1989). Effects of cocaine and d-amphetamine on sustained and selective attention in rats. *Pharmacology, Biochemistry and Behavior, 33,* 733–739.

Grilly, D. M., & Grogan, T. W. (1990). Cocaine and level of arousal: Effects on vigilance task performance in rats. *Pharmacology, Biochemistry and Behavior, 35,* 269–271.

Grilly, D. M., & Loveland, A. (2001). What is a "low dose" of d-amphetamine for inducing behavioral effects in laboratory rats? *Psychopharmacology, 153,* 155–169.

Grimm, J., Lu, L., Hayashi, T., et al. (2003). Time-dependent increases in brain-derived neurotrophic factor protein levels within the mesolimbic dopamine system after withdrawal from cocaine: Implications for incubation of cocaine craving. *Journal of Neuroscience, 23,* 742–747.

Grob, C. S., McKenna, D. J., Callaway, J. C., et al. (1996). Human psychopharmacology of hoasca, a plant hallucinogen used in ritual context in Brazil. *Journal of Nervous and Mental Disease, 184,* 86–94.

Grof, S. (1980). *LSD psychotherapy.* Ponoma, CA: Hunter House Inc.

Guay, D. R. (1995). The emerging role of valproate in bipolar disorder and other psychiatric disorders. *Pharmacotherapy, 15,* 631–647.

Guengerich, F. P. (1993). Cytochrome P450 enzymes: They defend the body against environmental pollutants, detoxify drugs and synthesize several important signaling molecules. *American Scientist, 81,* 440–447.

Guerri, C., Montoliu, C., & Renau-Piqueras, J. (1994). Involvement of free radical mechanism in the toxic effects of alcohol: implications for fetal alcohol syndrome. *Advances in Experimental Medicine & Biology, 366,* 291–305.

Gupta, U., & Gupta, B. S. (1990). Caffeine differentially affects kinesthetic aftereffect in high and low impulsives. *Psychopharmacology, 102,* 102–105.

Gurevich, T. Y., Shabtai, H., Korczyn, A. D., Simon, E. S., & Giladi, N. (2006). Effect of rivastigmine on tremor in patients with Parkinson's disease and dementia. *Movement Disorders, 21,* 1663–1666.

Gurguis, G. N. M., Vo, S. P., & Griffith, J. (1999). Platelet alpha2A-adrenoceptor function in major depression. *Psychiatry Research, 89,* 73–95.

Gutstein, H. B., & Akil, H. (2001). Opioid analgesics. In J. G. Hardman & L. E. Limbird (Eds.), *Goodman & Gilman's The pharmacological basis of therapeutics* (10th ed., pp. 569–619). New York: McGraw-Hill.

Guyon, G. (1989). Pharmacokinetic considerations in neonatal drug therapy. *Neonatal Network, 7,* 9–12.

Guze, S. B., Cloninger, C. R., Martin, R., & Clayton, P. J. (1986). Alcoholism as a medical disorder. *Comprehensive Psychiatry, 27,* 501–510.

Hahn, J., Levitan, E. S., & Tse, T. E. (2003). Long-term K+ channel-mediated dampening of dopamine neuron excitability by the antipsychotic drug haloperidol. *Journal of Neuroscience, 23,* 10859–10866.

Halberstadt, A. L. (1995). The phencyclidine-glutamate model of schizophrenia. *Clinical Neuropharmacology, 18,* 237–249.

Hall, B., & Brown, M. (1999). NIH consensus panel recommends expanding access to and improving methadone treatment programs for heroin addiction. *European Addiction Research, 5,* 50–51.

Hall, W., & Degenhardt, L. (2003). Medical marijuana initiatives: Are they justified?

How successful are they likely to be? *CNS Drugs, 17,* 689–697.

Hall, W., Lynskey, M., & Degenhardt, L. (2000). Trends in opiate-related deaths in the United Kingdom and Australia, 1985–1995. *Drug and Alcohol Dependence, 57,* 247–254.

Hall, W., & Solowij, N. (1998). Adverse effects of cannabis. *Lancet, 352,* 1611–1616.

Halpern, J. H., & Pope, H. G., Jr. (1999). Do hallucinogens cause residual neuropsychological toxicity? *Drug and Alcohol Dependence, 53,* 247–256.

Hamann, W., & DiVadi, P. P. (1999). Analgesic effect of the cannabinoid analogue nabilone is not mediated by opioid receptors. *Lancet, 353,* 560.

Hamilton, S. H., Revicki, D. A., Genduso, L. A., et al. (1998). Olanzapine versus placebo and haloperidol: Quality of life and efficacy results of the North American double-blind trial. *Neuropsychopharmacology, 18,* 41–49.

Hampson, A. J., Grimaldi, M., Lolic, M., et al. (2000). Neuroprotective antioxidants from marijuana. *Annals of the New York Academy of Sciences, 899,* 274–282.

Haney, M., Ward, A. S., Comer, S. D., et al. (1999). Abstinence symptoms following smoked marijuana in humans. *Psychopharmacology, 141,* 395–404.

Haney, M., Ward, A. S., Foltin, R. W., & Fischman, M. W. (2001). Effects of ecopipam, a selective dopamine D1 antagonist, on smoked cocaine self-administration by humans. *Psychopharmacology, 155,* 330–337.

Hansen, G., Jensen, S. B., Chandresh, L., & Hilden, T. (1988). The psychotropic effect of ketamine. *Canadian Journal of Psychology, 36,* 527–531.

Hanson, G. R., Midgley, L. P., Bush, L. G., & Gibb, J. W. (1995). Response of extrapyramidal and limbic neurotensin systems to phencyclidine treatment. *European Journal of Pharmacology, 278,* 167–173.

Hanson, K. L., & Luciana, M. (2004). Neurocognitive function in users of MDMA: The importance of clinically significant patterns of use. *Psychological Medicine, 34,* 229–246.

Hao, Y., Creson, T., Zhang, L., et al. (2004). Mood stabilizer valproate promotes ERK pathway-dependent cortical neuronal growth and neurogenesis. *Journal of Neuroscience, 24,* 6590–6599.

Harris, J. E., & Chan, S. W. (1999). The continuum-of-addiction: Cigarette smoking in relation to price among Americans aged 15–29. *Health Economics, 8,* 81–86.

Harris, L. S. (1978). Cannabis: A review of progress. In M. A. Lipton, A. DiMascio, & K. F. Killam (Eds.), *Psychopharmacology* (pp. 1565–1574). New York: Raven Press.

Harris, L. S. (Ed.). (1980). *Problems of drug dependence.* Rockville, MD: National Institute on Drug Abuse.

Harris, L. S. (Ed.). (1981). *Problems of drug dependence.* Rockville, MD: National Institute on Drug Abuse.

Harrison, L. M., Kastine, A. J., & Zadina, J. E. (1998). Opiate tolerance and dependence: Receptors, G-proteins, and antiopiates. *Peptides, 19,* 1603–1630.

Harrison, W., Stewart, J. W., McGrath, P. J., et al. (1988). Is loss of antidepressant effect during continuation therapy related to a placebo effect? *Psychopharmacology Bulletin, 24,* 9–17.

Hartel, D. M., Schoenbaum, E. E., Selwyn, P. A., & Kline, J. (1995). Heroin use during methadone maintenance treatment: The importance of methadone dose and cocaine use. *American Journal of Public Health, 85,* 83–88.

Hartley, T., Lovallo, W., & Whitsett, T. L. (2004). Cardiovascular effects of caffeine in men and women. *American Journal of Cardiology, 93,* 1022–1026.

Harvey, P., Green, M., McGurk, S., & Meltzer, H. Y. (2003). Changes in cognitive functioning with risperidone and olanzapine treatment: A large scale, double-blind, randomized study. *Psychopharmacology, 169,* 404–411.

Harvey, P., Meltzer, H., Simpson, G., et al. (2004). Improvement in cognitive function following a switch to ziprasidone from conventional antipsychotics, olanzapine, or risperidone in outpatients with schizophrenia. *Schizophrenia Research, 66,* 101–113.

Harvey, P., Napolitano, J., Mao, L., & Gharabawi, G. (2003). Comparative effects of risperidone and olanzapine on cognition in elderly patients with schizophrenia or schizoaffective disorder. *International Journal of Geriatric Psychiatry, 18,* 820–829.

Harvey, P., Siu, C., & Romano, S. (2004). Randomized, controlled, double-blind, multicenter comparison of the cognitive effects of ziprasidone versus olanzapine in acutely ill inpatients with schizophrenia or schizoaffective disorder. *Psychopharmacology, 172,* 324–332.

Harvey, S. C. (1985). Hypnotics and sedatives. In A. G. Gilman, L. S. Goodman, T. W. Rall, & F. Murad (Eds.), *The pharmacological basis of therapeutics* (pp. 339–371). New York: Macmillan.

Hashino, Y., Yamamoto, T., Kaneko, M., et al. (1984). Blood serotonin and free tryptophan concentration in autistic children. *Neuropsychobiology, 11,* 22–27.

Hasler, F., Grimberg, U., Benz, M. A., et al. (2004). Acute psychological and physiological effects of psilocybin in healthy humans: A double-blind, placebo-controlled dose-effect study. *Psychopharmacology, 172,* 145–156.

Hatsukami, D. K., & Fischman, W. (1996). Crack cocaine and cocaine hydrochloride. Are the differences myth or reality? *The Journal of the American Medical Association, 276,* 1580–1588.

Hauser, R. A., & Zesiewicz, T. A. (1995). Sertraline-induced exacerbation of tics in Tourette's syndrome. *Movement Disorders, 10,* 682–684.

Hawkins, D. F. (1989). Drugs used to treat medical disorders in pregnancy and fetal abnormalities. In E. M. Scarpelli & E. V.

Cosmi (Eds.), *Reviews in perinatal medicine* (pp. 91–131). New York: Alan R. Liss.

Hayes, R. J., & Gardner, E. L. (2004). The basolateral complex of the amygdala mediates the modulation of intracranial self-stimulation threshold by drug-associated cues. *European Journal of Neuroscience, 20,* 273–280.

Hechtman, L., Weiss, G., & Perlman, T. (1984). Young adult outcome of hyperactive children who received long-term stimulant treatment. *Journal of the American Academy of Child Psychiatry, 23,* 261–269.

Hegadoren, K. M., Baker, G. B., & Bourin, M. (1999). 3,4-Methylenedioxy analogues of amphetamine: Defining the risks to humans. *Neuroscience and Biobehavioral Reviews, 23,* 539–553.

Heinz, A., Weingartner, H., George, D., et al. (1999). Severity of depression in abstinent alcoholics is associated with monoamine metabolites and dehydroepiandrosterone-sulfate concentrations. *Psychiatry Research, 89,* 97–106.

Heise, G. A. (1981, June). Learning and memory facilitators: Experimental definition and current status. *Trends in the Pharmacological Sciences, 2,* 158–160.

Heishman, S., Arasteh, K., & Stitzer, M. L. (1997). Comparative effects of alcohol and marijuana on mood, memory, and performance. *Pharmacology, Biochemistry & Behavior, 58,* 93–101.

Heishman, S. J. (1998). What aspects of human performance are truly enhanced by nicotine? *Addiction, 93,* 317–320.

Heishman, S. J., Taylor, R. C., & Henningfield, J. E. (1994). Nicotine and smoking: Review of effects on human performance. *Experimental and Clinical Psychopharmacology, 2,* 345–395.

Helmuth, L. (2002). New therapies. New Alzheimer's treatments that may ease the mind. *Science, 297,* 1260–1262.

Hendren, R. L. (1996). Management of psychosis in adolescents suffering from schizophrenia and bipolar disorder. *Essential Psychopharmacology, 1,* 38–53.

Henningfield, J. E., & Goldberg, S. R. (1988). Pharmacologic determinants of tobacco self-administration by humans. *Pharmacology, Biochemistry and Behavior, 30,* 221–226.

Heresco-Levy, U., Ermilov, M., Lichtenberg, P., et al. (2004). High-dose glycine added to olanzapine and risperidone for the treatment of schizophrenia. *Biological Psychiatry, 55,* 165–171.

Heresco-Levy, U., Silipo, G., & Javitt, D. C. (1996). Glycinergic augmentation of NMDA receptor-mediated neurotransmission in the treatment of schizophrenia. *Psychopharmacology Bulletin, 32,* 731–740.

Hernandez, G., Breton, Y. A., Conover, K., & Shizgal, P. (2010). At what stage of neural processing does cocaine act to boost pursuit of rewards? *PLoS One, 5*(11), e15081.

Hibbard, L. S., McGlone, J. S., Davis, D. W., & Hawkins, R. A. (1987). Three-dimensional representation and analysis of brain energy metabolism. *Science, 236,* 1641–1646.

Higgins, S. T., Budney, A. J., & Bickel, W. K. (1994a). Applying behavioral concepts and principles to the treatment of cocaine dependence. *Drug and Alcohol Dependence, 34,* 87–97.

Higgins, S. T., Budney, A. J., Bickel, W. K., & Badger, G. J. (1994b). Participation of significant others in outpatient behavioral treatment predicts greater cocaine abstinence. *American Journal of Drug and Alcohol Abuse, 20,* 47–56.

Higgins, S. T., Budney, A. J., Bickel, W. K., et al. (1994c). Alcohol dependence and simultaneous cocaine and alcohol use in cocaine-dependent patients. *Journal of Addictive Diseases, 13,* 177–189.

Hiller, S. (1991). A better way to make the medicine go down. *Science, 253,* 1095–1096.

Hines, T. (2008, May/June). Zombies and tetrodotoxin. *Skeptical Inquirer,* 60–62.

Hingson, R., & Howland, J. (1993). Alcohol and non-traffic unintended injuries. *Addiction, 88,* 877–883.

Hipólito, L., Sánchez-Catalán, M. J., Granero, L., & Polache, A. (2009). Locomotor stimulant effects of acute and repeated intrategmental injections of salsolinol in rats: Role of mu-opioid receptors. *Neurochemistry International, 55,* 187–192.

Hirschfeld, R. M. A. (2000). History and evolution of the monoamine hypothesis of depression. *Journal of Clinical Psychiatry, 61,* 4–6.

Hnasko, T. S., Sotak, B. N., & Palmiter, R. D. (2007). Cocaine-conditioned place preference by dopamine-deficient mice is mediated by serotonin. *Journal of Neuroscience, 27,* 12484–12488.

Hobbs, W. R., Rall, T. W., & Verdoorn, T. A. (1996). Hypnotics and sedatives: Ethanol. In A. G. Gilman, L. S. Goodman, J. G. Hardman, L. E. Limbard, P. B. Molinoff, & R. W. Ruddon (Eds.), *The pharmacological basis of therapeutics* (pp. 361–396). New York: McGraw-Hill.

Hoehns, J. D., & Perry, P. J. (1993). Zolpidem: A nonbenzodiazepine hypnotic for treatment of insomnia. *Clinical Pharmacy, 12,* 814–828.

Hoffman, E. J., & Warren, E. W. (1993). Flumazenil: A benzodiazepine antagonist. *Clinical Pharmacy, 12,* 641–656.

Holdcroft, A., Smith, M., Jacklin, A., et al. (1997). Pain relief with oral cannabinoids in familial Mediterranean fever. *Anaesthesia, 52,* 483–486.

Holden, C. (1977). New look at heroin could spur better medical use of narcotics. *Science, 198,* 807–809.

Holden, C. (1980). Arguments heard for psychedelics probe. *Science, 209,* 256–257.

Holden, C. (2001). "Behavioral addictions": Do they exist? *Science, 294,* 980–982.

Holden, C. (2003). Future brightening for depression treatments. *Science, 302,* 810–813.

Holdstock, L., King, A. C., & de Wit, H. (2000). Subjective and objective responses to ethanol in moderate/heavy and light social drinkers. *Alcohol Clinical and Experimental Research, 24,* 789–794.

Holland, P. C. (1984). Origins of behavior in Pavlovian conditioning. *The Psychology of Learning and Motivation, 18,* 129–173.

Hollis, K. L. (1984). The biological function of Pavlovian conditioning: The best defense is a good offense. *Journal of Experimental Psychology: Animal Behavior Processes, 10,* 413–425.

Hollister, L. E. (1986). Health aspects of cannabis. *Pharmacological Reviews, 38,* 1–20.

Hollister, L. E. (1987). Postmarketing surveillance of psychotherapeutic drugs: Concluding comments. *Psychopharmacology Bulletin, 23,* 405–406.

Hollister, L. E. (2000). An approach to the medical marijuana controversy. *Drug and Alcohol Dependence, 58,* 3–7.

Holmes, V. F. (1995). Medical use of psychostimulants: An overview. *International Journal of Psychiatry in Medicine, 25,* 1–19.

Holstege, G., Georgiadis, J., Paans, A. M., et al. (2003). Brain activation during human male ejaculation. *Journal of Neuroscience, 23,* 9185–9193.

Hondo, H., Yonezawa, Y., Nakahara, T., et al. (1994). Effect of phencyclidine on dopamine release in the rat prefrontal cortex: An in vivo microdialysis study. *Brain Research, 633,* 337–342.

Hooker, W. D., & Jones, R. T. (1987). Increased susceptibility to memory intrusions and the stroop interference effect during acute marijuana intoxication. *Psychopharmacology, 91,* 20–24.

Hooley, J. M. (2004). Do psychiatric patients do better clinically if they live with certain kinds of families? *Current Directions in Psychological Science, 13,* 202–205.

Hopson, J. L. (1988, July/August). A pleasurable chemistry. *Psychology Today,* 29–33.

Hori, T., Abe, S., Baba, A., et al. (2000). Effects of repeated phencyclidine treatment on serotonin transporter in rat brain. *Neuroscience Letters, 280,* 53–56.

Hornykiewicz, O. (1973). Dopamine in the basal ganglia. *British Medical Bulletin, 29,* 172–178.

Horst, W. D., & Preskorn, S. H. (1998). Mechanisms of action and clinical characteristics of three atypical antidepressants: Venlafaxine, nefazodone, bupropion. *Journal of Affective Disorders, 51,* 237–254.

Horton, D. L., & Mills, C. B. (1984). Human learning and memory. *Annual Review of Psychology, 35,* 361–394.

Horvath, K., Stefanatos, G., Sokolski, K. N., et al. (1998). Improved social and language skills after secretin administration in patients with autistic spectrum disorders. *Journal of the Association for Academic Minority Physicians, 9,* 9–15.

Horvitz, J. C. (2000). Mesolimbocortical and nigrostriatal dopamine responses to salient non-reward events. *Neuroscience, 96,* 651–656.

Howes, O. D., Kapur, S. (2009). The dopamine hypothesis of schizophrenia: version III— the final common pathway. *Schizophrenia Bulletin, 35,* 549–562.

Hoyer, D., Clarke, D. E., Fozard, J. R., et al. (1994). International union of pharmacology classification of receptors for 5-hydroxytryptamine (serotonin). *Pharmacological Reviews, 46,* 157–203.

Hoyumpa, A. M., & Schenker, S. (1982). Major drug interactions: Effect of liver disease, alcohol, and malnutrition. *Annual Review of Medicine, 33,* 113–149.

Hughes, J. C., & Cook, C. C. H. (1997). The efficacy of disulfiram: A review of outcome studies. *Addiction, 92,* 381–395.

Hughes, J. R., Gust, S. W., & Pechacek, T. F. (1987). Prevalence of tobacco dependence and withdrawal. *American Journal of Psychiatry, 144,* 205–208.

Hughes, J. R., Oliveto, A. H., Bickel, W. K., et al. (1993). Caffeine self-administration and withdrawal: Incidence, individual differences and interrelationships. *Drug and Alcohol Dependence, 32,* 239–246.

Hughes, J. R., Oliveto, A. H., Helzer, J. E., et al. (1992). Should caffeine abuse, dependence, or withdrawal be added to *DSM-IV* and *ICD-10*? *American Journal of Psychiatry, 149,* 33–40.

Human Rights Watch. (2000). *Punishment and prejudice: Racial disparities in the war on drugs.* Retrieved October 23, 2000, from http://www. Hrw.org/reports/2000/usa/

Hunsinger, D. M., Nguyen, T., Zebraski, S. E., & Raffa, R. B. (2000). Is there a basis for novel pharmacotherapy of autism? *Life Sciences, 67,* 1667–1682.

Hunt, R. D., Arnsten, A. F., & Asbell, M. D. (1995). An open trial of guanfacine in the treatment of attention-deficit hyperactivity disorder. *Journal of the American Academy of Child and Adolescent Psychiatry, 34,* 50–54.

Hunt, R. D., Minderaa, R. B., & Cohen, D. J. (1986). The therapeutic effect of clonidine in attention deficit disorder with hyperactivity: A comparison with placebo and methylphenidate. *Psychopharmacology Bulletin, 22,* 229–236.

Hunt, W. A. (1993). Are binge drinkers more at risk of developing brain damage? *Alcohol, 10,* 559–561.

Hyman, S. E. (1996). Addiction to cocaine and amphetamine. *Neuron, 16,* 901–904.

Hyman, S. E. (2000). The NIMH perspective: Next steps in schizophrenia research. *Society of Biological Psychiatry, 47,* 1–7.

Hyman, S. E., & Fenton, S. (2003). What are the right targets for psychopharmacology? *Science, 299,* 350–351.

Hypericum Depression Trial Study Group. (2002). Effect of hypericum perforatum (St John's wort) in major depressive disorder: A randomized controlled trial. *The Journal*

of the American Medical Association
1807–1814.

Ichikawa, J., Dai, J., O'Laughlin, I., et al.
(2002). Atypical, but not typical, antipsychotic drugs increase cortical acetylcholine
release without an effect in the nucleus accumbens or striatum. *Neuropsychopharmacology, 26,* 325–339.

Ikemoto, S. (2010). Brain reward circuitry beyond the mesolimbic dopamine system: A
neurobiological theory. *Neuroscience &
Biobehavioral Reviews, 35,* 129–150.

Ikonomidou, C., Bittigau, P., Ishimaru, M. J.,
et al. (2000). Ethanol-induced apoptotic
neurodegeneration and fetal alcohol
syndrome. *Science, 287,* 1056–1059.

Ioannidis, J. P. (2008). Effectiveness of antidepressants: An evidence myth constructed
from a thousand randomized trials?
*Philosophy, Ethics, and Humanities in
Medicine, 3,* 14.

Ishimaru, M., Kurumaji, A., & Toru, M. (1994).
Increases in strychnine-insensitive glycine
binding sites in cerebral cortex of chronic
schizophrenics: Evidence for glutamate hypothesis. *Biological Psychiatry, 35,* 84–95.

Ishiwari, K., Betz, A., Weber, S., Felsted, J., &
Salamone, J. D. (2005). Validation of the
tremulous jaw movement model for assessment of the motor effects of typical and
atypical antipychotics: Effects of pimozide
(Orap) in rats. *Pharmacology, Biochemistry
and Behavior, 80,* 351–362.

Ishiwari, K., Madson, L. J., Farrar, A. M.,
Mingote, S. M., Valenta, J. P., DiGianvittorio,
M. D., et al. (2007). Injections of the selective
adenosine A2A antagonist MSX-3 into the
nucleus accumbens core attenuate the locomotor suppression induced by haloperidol in
rats. *Behavioural Brain Research, 178,* 190–199.

Isner, J. M., & Chokshi, S. K. (1991). Cardiac
complications of cocaine abuse. *Annual
Review of Medicine, 42,* 133–138.

Isse, T., Oyama, T., Kitagawa, K., Matsuno, K.,
Matsumoto, A., Yoshida, A., et al. (2002).
Diminished alcohol preference in trans-

genic mice lacking aldehyde dehydrogenase activity. *Pharmacogenetics, 12,* 621–626.

Itoi, K., & Sugimoto, N. (2010). The brainstem
noradrenergic systems in stress,
anxiety and depression. *Journal of
Neuroendocrinology, 22,* 355–361.

Ivanenko, A., Tauman, R., & Gozal, D. (2003).
Modafinil in the treatment of excessive
daytime sleepiness in children. *Sleep
Medicine, 4,* 579–582.

Iversen, L. L., Iversen, S. D., Bloom, F. E., &
Roth, R. H. (2009) *Introduction to Neuropsy-
chopharmacology.* Oxford: Oxford University
Press.

Ives, N., Stowe, R., Marro, J., et al. (2004).
Monoamine oxidase type B inhibitors in
early Parkinson's disease: Meta-analysis of
17 randomised trials involving 3525 patients [Clinical research ed]. *British Medical
Journal, 329,* 593.

Iyer, R. N., Nobiletti, J. B., Jatlow, P. I., &
Bradberry, C. W. (1995). Cocaine and cocaethylene: Effects on extracellular
dopamine in the primate. *Psychopharmacology, 120,* 150–155.

Jacobs, B. L. (1976, March). Serotonin: The crucial substance that turns dreams on and off.
Psychology Today, 70–73.

Jacobs, B. L. (1987). How hallucinogenic drugs
work. *American Scientist, 75,* 386–392.

Jacobs, B. L. (1994). Serotonin, motor activity
and depression-related disorders. *American
Scientist, 82,* 456–463.

Jacobsen, E. (1968). The hallucinogens. In C. R.
B. Joyce (Ed.), *Psychopharmacology: Dimen-
sions and perspectives* (pp. 175–213).
Philadelphia, PA: J. B. Lippincott.

Jaffe, J. H. (1985). Drug addiction and drug
abuse. In A. G. Gilman, L. S. Goodman,
T. W. Rall, & F. Murad (Eds.), *The pharmacological basis of therapeutics* (pp. 532–581).
New York: Macmillan.

Jaffe, J. H. (1990). Drug addiction and drug
abuse. In A. G. Gilman, T. W. Rall, A. S.
Nies, & P. Taylor (Eds.), *The pharmacological*

basis of therapeutics (pp. 522–573). New York: Pergamon Press.

Jaffe, J. H., Cascella, N. G., Kumor, K. M., & Sherer, M. A. (1989). Cocaine-induced cocaine craving. *Psychopharmacology, 97,* 59–64.

Jaffe, J. H., & Martin, W. R. (1985). Opioid analgesics and antagonists. In A. G. Gilman, L. S. Goodman, T. W. Rall, & F. Murad (Eds.), *The pharmacological basis of therapeutics* (pp. 491–531). New York: Macmillan.

Jain, A. K., Ryan, J. R., & McMahon, F. G., et al. (1981). Evaluation of intramuscular levonantradol and placebo in acute postoperative pain. *Journal of Clinical Pharmacology, 21,* 320S–326S.

Janowsky, D. S. (2007). Scopolamine as an antidepressant agent: Theoretical and treatment considerations. *Current Psychiatry Reports, 9,* 447–448.

Jansen, K. L. (1990). Neuroscience and the near-death experience: Roles for the NMSA-PCP receptor, the sigma receptor and the endopsychosins. *Medical Hypotheses, 31,* 25–29.

Jansma, A., Breteler, M. H. M., Schippers, G. M., De Jong, C. A. J., & Van der Staak, C. P. F. (2000). No effect of negative mood on the alcohol cue reactivity on in-patient alcoholics. *Addictive Behaviors, 25,* 619–624.

Janssen, P. A., Niemegeers, C. J., & Schellekens, K. H. (1965). Is it possible to predict the clinical effects of neuroleptic drugs (major tranquillizers) from animal data? I. "Neuroleptic activity spectra" for rats. *Arzneimittelforschung, 15,* 104–117.

Janzen, L. A., Nanson, J. L., & Block, G. W. (1995). Neuropsychological evaluation of preschoolers with fetal alcohol syndrome. *Neurotoxicology & Teratology, 17,* 273–279.

Jarvik, M. E. (1990). The drug dilemma: Manipulating the demand. *Science, 250,* 387–392.

Jarvis, M. R. (1991). Clinical pharmacokinetics of tricyclic antidepressant overdose. *Psychopharmacology Bulletin, 27,* 541–550.

Jasinski, D. R. (2000). An evaluation of the abuse potential of modafinil using methylphenidate as a reference. *Journal of Psychopharmacology, 14,* 53–60.

Javitt, D. C., Zylberman, I., Zukin, S. R., et al. (1994). Amelioration of negative symptoms in schizophrenia by glycine. *American Journal of Psychiatry, 151,* 1234–1236.

Jefferson, J. W. (1995). Social phobia: A pharmacologic treatment overview. *Journal of Clinical Psychiatry, 56*(Suppl. 5), 18–24.

Jensen, J., McIntosh, A. R., Crawley, A. P., Mikulis, D. J., Remington, G., & Kapur, S. (2003). Direct activation of the ventral striatum in anticipation of aversive stimuli. *Neuron, 40,* 1251–1257.

Jentsch, J. D., & Roth, R. H. (1999). The neuropsychopharmacology of phencyclidine: From NMDA receptor hypofunction to the dopamine hypothesis of schizophrenia. *Neuropsychopharmacology, 20,* 202–225.

Jeste, D. V. (2000). Tardive dyskinesia in older patients. *Journal of Clinical Psychiatry, 61*(Suppl. 4), 27–32.

Jeste, D. V., Lindamer, L. A., Evans, J., & Lacro, J. P. (1996). Relationship of ethnicity to schizophrenia and pharmacology of neuroleptics. *Psychopharmacology Bulletin, 32,* 244–251.

Jibson, M. D., & Tandon, R. (1996). A summary of research findings on the new antipsychotic drugs. *Essential Psychopharmacology, 1,* 27–37.

Jibson, M. D., & Tandon, R. (1998). New atypical antipsychotic medications. *Journal of Psychiatric Research, 32,* 215–228.

Jick, H., & Kaye, J. A. (2003). Epidemiology and possible causes of autism. *Pharmacotherapy, 23,* 1524–1530.

Jick, H., Kaye, J., & Jick, S. S. (2004). Antidepressants and the risk of suicidal behaviors. *The Journal of the American Medical Association, 292,* 338–343.

Jiménez-Velázquez, G., López-Muñoz, F. J., & Fernández-Guasti, A. (2010). Parallel anxiolytic-like and antinociceptive actions of diazepam in the anterior basolateral amygdala and dorsal periaqueductal gray. *Brain Research, 1349,* 11–20.

Jochimsen, P. R., Lawton, R. L., VerSteeg, K., et al. (1978). Effect of benzopyranoperidine, a delta-9-THC congener, on pain. *Clinical Pharmacolgy and Therapeutics, 24,* 223–227.

Johns, A. (1991). Volatile solvent abuse and 963 deaths. *British Journal of Addiction, 86,* 1053–1056.

Johnson, B. A., Roache, J. D., Javors, M. A., et al. (2000). Ondansetron for reduction of drinking among biologically predisposed alcoholic patients: A randomized controlled trial. *The Journal of the American Medical Association, 284,* 963–971.

Johnson, B., Overton, D., Wells, L., et al. (1998). Effects of acute intravenous cocaine on cardiovascular function, human learning, and performance in cocaine addicts. *Psychiatry Research, 77,* 35–42.

Johnson, B., Roache, J., Ait-Daoud, N., et al. (2002). Ondansetron reduces the craving of biologically predisposed alcoholics. *Psychopharmacology, 160,* 408–413.

Johnson, B., Roache, J., Ait-Daoud, N., et al. (2004). Effects of isradipine on cocaine-induced subjective mood. *Journal of Clinical Psychopharmacology, 24,* 180–191.

Johnson, E. O., & Breslau, N. (2000). Increased risk of learning disabilities in low birth weight boys at age 11 years. *Biological Psychiatry, 47,* 490–500.

Johnson, F. N. (1979). The psychopharmacology of lithium. *Neuroscience and Biobehavioral Reviews, 3,* 15–30.

Johnson, K. M., & Jones, S. M. (1990). Neuropharmacology of phencyclidine: Basic mechanisms and therapeutic potential. *Annual Review of Pharmacology and Toxicology, 30,* 707–750.

Johnson, L. C., Spinweber, C. L., Webb, S. C., & Muzet, A. G. (1987). Dose level effects of

triazolam on sleep and response to a smoke detector alarm. *Psychopharmacology, 91,* 397–402.

Johnson, L. D., Spinweber, C. L., & Gomez, S. A. (1990). Benzodiazepines and caffeine: Effect on daytime sleepiness, performance, and mood. *Psychopharmacology, 101,* 160–167.

Johnston, L. D., O'Malley, P. M., & Bachman, J. G. (2003). *Demographic subgroup trends for various licit and illicit drugs, 1975–2002.* Monitoring the Future Occasional Paper No. 59, Institute for Social Research, Ann Arbor, MI.

Jonas, P., Bischofberger, J., & Sandkuhler, J. (1998). Corelease of two fast neurotransmitters at a central synapse. *Science, 281,* 419–424.

Jones, E. (1953). *Life and work of Sigmund Freud* (Vol. I., pp. 1856–1900). New York: Basic Books.

Jones, H. E., & Griffiths, R. (2003). Oral caffeine maintenance potentiates the reinforcing and stimulant subjective effects of intravenous nicotine in cigarette smokers. *Psychopharmacology, 165,* 280–290.

Jones, L. B., Stanwood, G. D., Reinoso, B. S., et al. (2000). In utero cocaine-induced dysfunction of dopamine D1 receptor signaling and abnormal differentiation of cerebral cortical neurons. *Journal of Neuroscience, 20,* 4606–4614.

Jonsson, L. E., & Gunne, L. M. (1970). Clinical studies of amphetamine psychosis. In E. Costa & S. Garattini (Eds.), *International symposium on amphetamines and related compounds* (pp. 929–936). New York: Raven Press.

Jope, R. S. (1999). A bimodal model of the mechanism of action of lithium. *Molecular Psychiatry, 4,* 21–25.

Jope, R. S. (2003). Lithium and GSK-3: One inhibitor, two inhibitory actions, multiple outcomes. *Trends in Pharmacological Sciences, 24,* 441–443.

Josiassen, R. C., Joseph, A., Kohegyi, E., et al. (2005). Clozapine augmented with risperidone in the treatment of schizophrenia. *American Journal of Psychiatry, 162,* 130–136.

Joy, C., Mumby-Croft, R., & Joy, L. A. (2003). Polyunsaturated fatty acid supplementation for schizophrenia. *Cochrane Database of Systematic Reviews (Online: Update Software),* no. 2, CD001257.

Jussofie, A., Schmiz, A., & Hiemke, C. (1994). Kavapyrone enriched extract from piper methysticum as modulator of the GABA binding site in different regions of rat brain. *Psychopharmacology, 116,* 469–474.

Justinova, Z., Tanda, G., Redhi, G., & Goldberg, S. R. (2003). Self-administration of delta9-tetrahydrocannabinol (THC) by drug naive squirrel monkeys. *Psychopharmacology, 169,* 135–140.

Kaakkola, S. (2000). Clinical pharmacology, therapeutic use and potential of COMT inhibitors in Parkinson's disease. *Drugs, 59,* 1233–1250.

Kales, A., Soldatos, C. R., Bixler, E. O., & Kales, J. D. (1983). Early morning insomnia with rapidly eliminated benzodiazepines. *Science, 220,* 95–97.

Kalivas, P. W. (2008). Addiction as a pathology in prefrontal cortical regulation of corticostriatal habit circuitry. *Neurotoxicology Research, 14,* 185–189.

Kalivas, P. W., & Stewart, J. (1991). Dopamine transmission in the initiation and expression of drug- and stress-induced sensitization of motor activity. *Brain Research Brain Research Reviews, 16,* 223–244.

Kaminski, R., Gasior, M., Carter, R., & Witkin, J. M. (2003). Protective efficacy of neuroactive steroids against cocaine kindled-seizures in mice. *European Journal of Pharmacology, 474,* 217–222.

Kampman, K., Pettinati, H., Lynch, K., et al. (2003). A pilot trial of olanzapine for the treatment of cocaine dependence. *Drug and Alcohol Dependence, 70,* 265–273.

Kanahara, N., Shimizu, E., Sekine, Y., Uchida, Y., Shibuya, T., Yamanaka, H., et al. (2009).

Does hypofrontality expand to global brain area in progression of schizophrenia? A cross-sectional study between first-episode and chronic schizophrenia. *Progress in Neuropsychopharmacology and Biological Psychiatry, 33,* 410–415.

Kandel, D. (1975). Stages in adolescent involvement in drug use. *Science, 190,* 912–914.

Kandel, E. R. (2001). The molecular biology of memory storage: A dialog between genes and synapses. *Bioscience Reports, 21,* 565–611.

Kando, J. C., Yonkers, K. A., & Cole, J. O. (1995). Gender as a risk factor for adverse events to medications. *Drugs, 50,* 1–6.

Kantak, K. M. (2003). Vaccines against drugs of abuse: A viable treatment option? *Drugs, 63,* 341–352.

Kapur, S., & Seeman, P. (2001). Does fast dissociation from the dopamine D(2) receptor explain the action of atypical antipsychotics? A new hypothesis. *American Journal of Psychiatry, 158,* 360–369.

Karlsson, P., Smith, L., Farde, L., et al. (1995). Lack of apparent antipsychotic effect of the D1-dopamine receptor antagonist SCH39166 in acutely ill schizophrenic patients. *Psychopharmacology, 121,* 309–316.

Karniol, J. G., & Carlini, E. A. (1972). The content of (–) delta-9-trans-tetrahydro-cannabinol (delta-9-THC) does not explain all biological activity of some Brazilian marihuana samples. *Journal of Pharmacy and Pharmacology, 24,* 833–835.

Kasai, H. (1999). Comparative biology of Ca^{2+} dependent exocytosis: Implications of kinetic diversity for secretory function. *Trends in Neurosciences, 22,* 88–93.

Katz, I. R., Jeste, D. V., Mintzer, J. E., et al. (1999). Comparison of risperidone and placebo for psychosis and behavioral disturbances associated with dementia: A randomized, double-blind trial. *Journal of Clinical Psychiatry, 60,* 107–115.

Katzenschlager, R., Sampaio, C., Costa, J., & Lees, A. (2003). Anticholinergics for symptomatic management of Parkinson's disease. *Cochrane Database System Reviews*, no. 2, CD003735.

Kauer, J. A., & Malenka, R. C. (2007). Synaptic plasticity and addiction. *Nature Reviews Neuroscience, 8*, 844–858.

Kaye, K., Elkind, L., Goldberg, D., & Tytun, A. (1989). Birth outcomes for infants of drug abusing mothers. *New York State Journal of Medicine, 89*, 256–261.

Kayser, A., Robinson, D. S., Nies, A., & Howard, D. (1985). Response to phenelzine among depressed patients with features of hysteroid dysphoria. *American Journal of Psychiatry, 142*, 486–488.

Keck, P. E., McElroy, S. L., Strakowski, S. M., et al. (2000). Antipsychotics in the treatment of mood disorders and risk of tardive dyskinesia. *Journal of Clinical Psychiatry, 61*, 33–38.

Keers, R., & Aitchison, K. J. (2011). Pharmacogenetics of antidepressant response. *Expert Review of Neurotherapeutics, 11*, 101–125.

Kegeles, L. S., Abi-Dargham, A., Frankle, W. G., Gil, R., Cooper, T. B., Slifstein, M., Hwang, D. R., Huang, Y., Haber, S. N., Laruelle, M. (2010). Increased synaptic dopamine function in associative regions of the striatum in schizophrenia. *Archives of General Psychiatry, 67*, 231–239.

Kegeles, L. S., Zea-Ponce, Y., Abi-Dargham, A., et al. (1999). Stability of [123I] IBZM SPECT measurement of amphetamine-induced striatal dopamine release in humans. *Synapse, 31*, 302–308.

Kell, M. J. (1995). Utilization of plasma and urine methadone concentration measurements to limit narcotics use in methadone maintenance patients: II. Generation of plasma concentration response curves. *Journal of Addictive Diseases, 14*, 85–108.

Keller, M. B., McCullough, J. P., Klein, D. N., et al. (2000). A comparison of nefazodone, the cognitive behavioral-analysis system of psychotherapy, and their combination for the treatment of chronic depression. *New England Journal of Medicine, 342*, 1462–1470.

Kelley, A. E., Baldo, B. A., Pratt, W. E., & Will, M. J. (2005). Corticostriatal-hypothalamic circuitry and food motivation: Integration of energy, action and reward. *Physiology and Behavior, 86*, 773–795.

Kelly, P. H., Seviour, P. W., & Iversen, S. D. (1975). Amphetamine and apomorphine responses in the rat following 6-OHDA lesions of the nucleus accumbens septi and corpus striatum. *Brain Research, 94*, 507–522.

Kelly, S. J., Day, N., & Streissguth, A. P. (2000). Effects of prenatal alcohol exposure on social behavior in humans and other species. *Neurotoxicology and Teratology, 22*, 143–149.

Kenakin, T. (1987). Agonists, partial agonists, antagonists, inverse agonists and agonist/antagonists? *Trends in the Pharmacological Sciences, 8*, 423–426.

Kendler, K., Prescott, C., Myers, J., & Neale, M. C. (2003). The structure of genetic and environmental risk factors for common psychiatric and substance use disorders in men and women. *Archives of General Psychiatry, 60*, 929–937.

Kennedy, M. B. (2000). Signal-processing machines at the postsynaptic density. *Science, 290*, 750–754.

Kent, J. D., Blader, J. C., Koplewicz, H. S., et al. (1995). Effects of late-afternoon methylphenidate administration on behavior and sleep in attention-deficit hyperactivity disorder. *Pediatrics, 96*, 320–325.

Kent, J. M. (2000). SNaRIs, NaSSAs, and NaRIs: New agents for the treatment of depression. *Lancet, 355*, 911–918.

Kerns, L. L. (1986). Treatment of mental disorders in pregnancy. *Journal of Nervous and Mental Disease, 174*, 652–659.

Kerr, J. S., Sherwood, N., & Hindmarch, I. (1991). Separate and combined effects of the social drugs on psychomotor performance. *Psychopharmacology, 104*, 113–119.

Kesner, R. P., & Cook, D. G. (1983). Role of habituation and classical conditioning in the development of morphine tolerance. *Behavioral Neuroscience, 97,* 4–12.

Kessler, D. A., & Feiden, K. L. (1995). Faster evaluation of vital drugs. *Scientific American, 272*(3), 48–54.

Kessler, D. A., Witt, A. M., Barnett, P. S., et al. (1996). The food and drug administration's regulation of tobacco products. *New England Journal of Medicine, 335,* 988–994.

Kessler, R., Crum, R., Warner, L., Nelson, C., Schulenberg, J., & Anthony, J. C. (1997). Lifetime co-occurrence of DSM-III-R alcohol abuse and dependence with other psychiatric disorders in the national comorbidity survey. *Archives of General Psychiatry, 54,* 313–321.

Keverne, E., Martensz, N., & Tuite, B. (1989). Beta-endorphin concentrations in cerebrospinal fluid of monkeys are influenced by grooming relationships. *Psychoneuroendocrinology, 14,* 155–161.

Khantzian, E. J. (1985). The self-medication hypothesis of addictive disorders: Focus on heroin and cocaine dependence. *American Journal of Psychiatry, 142,* 1259–1263.

Khantzian, E. J., & Treece, C. (1985). DSM-III psychiatric diagnosis of narcotic addicts. *Archives of General Psychiatry, 42,* 1067–1071.

Kiefer, F., Jahn, H., Tarnaske, T., et al. (2003). Comparing and combining naltrexone and acamprosate in relapse prevention of alcoholism: A double-blind, placebo-controlled study. *Archives of General Psychiatry, 60,* 92–99.

Kilbey, M. M., & Ellinwood, E. H. (1977). Reverse tolerance to stimulant-induced abnormal behavior. *Life Sciences, 20,* 1063–1076.

King, G. R., Joyner, C., Lee, T., et al. (1992). Intermittent and continuous cocaine administration: Residual behavioral states during withdrawal. *Pharmacology, Biochemistry and Behavior, 43,* 243–248.

Kirsch, I. (2000). Are drug and placebo effect in depression additive? *Biological Psychiatry, 47,* 733–735.

Kirsch, I., Deacon, B. J., Huedo-Medina, T. B., Scoboria, A., Moore, T. J., & Johnson, B. T. (2008). Initial severity and antidepressant benefits: A meta-analysis of data submitted to the food and drug administration. *PLoS Medicine, 5,* e45.

Kirsch, I., & Sapirstein, G. (1998). Listening to Prozac but hearing placebo: A meta-analysis of antidepressant medication. *Prevention and Treatment 1* Article 0002a.

Kleiman, M. A. R., & Satel, S. (1996, May 7). Speed is rushing back. *Plain Dealer,* B8.

Kleindienst, N., Greil, W., Ruger, B., & Moller, H.-J. (1999). The prophylactic efficacy of lithium-transient or persistent? *European Archives of Psychiatry and Clinical Neuroscience, 249,* 144–149.

Knegtering, H., Eijck, M., & Huijsman, A. (1994). Effects of antidepressants on cognitive functioning of elderly patients. A review. *Drugs and Aging, 5,* 192–199.

Knoll, J. (1995). Rationale for (-)deprenyl (selegiline) medication in Parkinson's disease and in prevention of age-related nigral changes. *Biomedicine and Pharmacotherapy, 49,* 187–195.

Kolata, G. (1982). Consensus on diets and hyperactivity. *Science, 215,* 958.

Kolata, G. (1986). Manic depression: Is it inherited? *Science, 232,* 575–576.

Kolata, G. (1987). Panel urges dementia be diagnosed with care. *Science, 237,* 725.

van der Kolk, B. A., Dreyfuss, D., Michaels, M., Shera, D., Berkowitz, R., Fisler, R., et al. (1994). Fluoxetine in posttraumatic stress disorder. *Journal of Clinical Psychiatry, 55,* 517–522.

Kolmen, B. K., Feldman, H. M., Handen, B. L., et al. (1997). Naltrexone in young autistic children: Replication study and learning measures. *Journal of the American Academy of Child and Adolescent Psychiatry, 36,* 1570–1578.

Koob, G. F. (1987). Neuropeptides and memory. In L. Iverson, S. Iverson, & S. Snyder

(Eds.), *New directions in behavioral pharmacology* (pp. 531–573). New York: Plenum Press.

Koob, G. F. (1996). Drug addiction: The yin and yang of hedonic homeostasis. *Neuron, 16,* 893–896.

Koob, G. F., Riley, S. J., Smith, S. C., & Robbins, T. W. (1978). Effects of 6-hydroxydopamine lesions of the nucleus accumbens septi and olfactory tubercle on feeding, locomotor activity, and amphetamine anorexia in the rat. *Journal of Comparative and Physiological Psychology, 92,* 917–927.

Koob, G., & Le Moal, M. (2005). Plasticity of reward neurocircuitry and the 'dark side' of drug addiction. *Nature Neuroscience, 8,* 1442–1444.

Koob, G., & Le Moal, M. (2008). Addiction and the brain antireward system. *Annual Review of Psychology, 59,* 29–53.

Kopin, I. J., & Markey, S. P. (1988). MPTP toxicity: Implications for research in Parkinson's disease. *Annual Review of Neuroscience, 11,* 81–96.

Korf, J., & van Praag, H. M. (1971). Retarded depression and the dopamine metabolism. *Psychopharmacologia, 19,* 199–203.

Koutouvidis, N., Pratikakis, M., & Fotiadou, A. (1999). The use of mirtazapine in a group of 11 patients following poor compliance to selective serotonin reuptake inhibitor treatment due to sexual dysfuntion. *International Clinical Psychopharmacology, 14,* 253–255.

Kozari-Kovaci, D. (2009). Pharmacotherapy treatment of PTSD and comorbid disorders. *Psychiatria Danubina, 21,* 411–414.

Kozel, N. J., & Adams, E. H. (1986). Epidemiology of drug abuse: An overview. *Science, 234,* 970–974.

Kranzler, H., Armeli, S., Feinn, R., & Tennen, H. (2004). Targeted naltrexone treatment moderates the relations between mood and drinking behavior among problem drinkers. *Journal of Consulting and Clinical Psychology, 72,* 317–327.

Kranzler, H., Wesson, D., & Billot, L. (2004). Naltrexone depot for treatment of alcohol dependence: A multicenter, randomized, placebo-controlled clinical trial. *Alcoholism, Clinical and Experimental Research, 28,* 1051–1059.

Krause, K.-H., Dresel, S. H., Krause, J., et al. (2000). Increased striatal dopamine transporter in adult patients with attention deficit hyperactivity disorder: Effects of methylphenidate as measured by single photon emission computed tomography. *Neuroscience Letters, 285,* 107–110.

Krebs, K. M., & Geyer, M. A. (1994). Cross-tolerance studies of serotonin receptors involved in behavioral effects of LSD in rats. *Psychopharmacology, 113,* 429–437.

Kreek, M. J., Nielsen, D., & LaForge, K. S. (2004). Genes associated with addiction: Alcoholism, opiate, and cocaine addiction. *Neuromolecular Medicine, 5,* 85–108.

Kril, J. J. (1995). The contribution of alcohol, thiamine deficiency and cirrhosis of the liver to cerebral cortical damage in alcoholics. *Metabolic Brain Disease, 10,* 9–16.

Krystal, J., Cramer, J., Krol, W., et al. (2001). Naltrexone in the treatment of alcohol dependence. *New England Journal of Medicine, 345,* 1734–1739.

Krystal, J. H., D'Souza, D. C., Karper, L. P., et al. (1999). Interactive effects of subanesthetic ketamine and haloperidol in healthy humans. *Psychopharmacology, 145,* 193–204.

Krystal, J. H., Petrakis, I. L., Mason, G., et al. (2003). N-methyl-D-aspartate glutamate receptors and alcoholism: Reward, dependence, treatment, and vulnerability. *Pharmacology and Therapeutics, 99,* 79–94.

Kuczewski, N., Porcher, C., Lessmann, V., Medina, I., & Gaiarsa, J. L. (2009). Activity-dependent dendritic release of BDNF and biological consequences. *Molecular Neurobiology, 39,* 37–49.

Kuhn, T. S. (1962). *The structure of scientific revolutions.* Chicago, IL: University of Chicago Press.

Kumar, S. P., & Smith, M. (2004). Levetiracetam as add-on therapy in generalised epilepsies. *Seizure, 13,* 475–477.

Kurtzweil, P. (1995). Medical possibilities for psychedelic drugs. *FDA Consumer, 29,* 1–5.

Kurz, A., & Sessler, I. (2003). Opioid-induced bowel dysfunction: Pathophysiology and potential new therapies. *Drugs, 63,* 649–671.

Kushmerick, C., Price, G. D., Taschenberger, H., et al. (2004). Retroinhibition of presynaptic Ca^{2+} currents by endocannabinoids released via postsynaptic mGluR activation at a calyx synapse. *Journal of Neuroscience, 24,* 5955–5965.

Kushnir, T. (1986). Smoking and drinking as psychological tools in stressful social situations: Assumptions of fiction writers. *International Journal of the Addictions, 21,* 1119–1123.

Kuwahara, M. D., & Sparber, S. B. (1981). Opiate withdrawal in utero increases neonatal morbidity in the rat. *Science, 212,* 943–947.

Lader, M. (1994). Biological processes in benzodiazepine dependence. *Addiction, 89,* 1413–1418.

Lader, M., & Olajide, D. (1987). A comparison of buspirone and placebo in relieving benzodiazepine withdrawal symptoms. *Journal of Clinical Psychopharmacology, 7,* 11–15.

Lahti, A. C., Koffel, B., LaPorte, D., & Tamminga, C. A. (1995). Subanesthetic doses of ketamine stimulate psychosis in schizophrenia. *Neuropsychopharmacology, 13,* 9–19.

Lamb, R. J., & Griffiths, R. R. (1987). Self-injection of d,1-3,4-methylenedioxymethamphetamine (MDMA) in the baboon. *Psychopharmacology, 91,* 268–272.

Lancaster, F. E. (1995). Alcohol and the brain: What's NO got to do with it? *Metabolic Brain Disease, 10,* 125–133.

Lane, R., & Baldwin, D. (1997). Selective serotonin reuptake inhibitor-induced serotonin syndrome: Review. *Journal of Clinical Psychopharmacology, 17,* 208–221.

Lane, R., & Blaha, C. D. (1987). Chronic haloperidol decreases dopamine release in striatum and nucleus accumbens in vivo: Depolarization block as a possible mechanism of action. *Brain Research Bulletin, 18,* 135–138.

Langer, D. H., Sweeney, K. P., Bartenbach, P. M., & Meander, D. K. B. (1986). Evidence of lack of abuse or dependence following pemoline treatment: Results of a retrospective survey. *Drug and Alcohol Dependence, 17,* 213–227.

Langer, R. (1990). New methods of drug delivery. *Science, 249,* 1527–1533.

Lankenau, S. E., & Clatts, C. (2002). Ketamine injection among high risk youth: Preliminary findings from New York City. *Journal of Drug Issues, 32,* 893–905.

Lapierre, Y., & Hum, S. (2007). Treating fatigue. *International Multiple Sclerosis Journal, 14,* 64–71.

Lapish, C. C., Kroener, S., Durstewitz, D., Lavin, A., & Seamans, J. K. (2007). The ability of themesocortical dopamine system to operate in distinct temporal modes. *Psychopharmacology, 191,* 609–625.

Larsen, J. P., Boas, J., & Erdal, J. E. (1999). Does selegiline modify the progression of early Parkinson's disease? Results from a five-year study. The Norwegian-Danish Study Group. *European Journal of Neurology, 6,* 539–547.

Latimer, P. R. (1995). Tardive dyskinesia: A review. *Canadian Journal of Psychiatry, 40,* S49–S54.

Laughlin, S. B., & Sejnowski, J. (2003). Communication in neuronal networks. *Science, 301,* 1870–1874.

Lavian, G., Finberg, J. P., & Youdim, M. B. (1993). The advent of a new generation of monoamine oxidase inhibitor antidepressants: Pharmacologic studies with moclobemide and brofaromine. *Clinical Neuropharmacology, 16,* S1–S6.

Lavin, A., Nogueira, L., Lapish, C. C., Wightman, R. M., Phillips, P. E., &

Seamans, J. K. (2005). Mesocortical dopamine neurons operate in distinct temporal domains using multimodal signaling. *Journal of Neuroscience, 25,* 5013–5023.

Le Foll, B., Gorelick, D. A., & Goldberg, S. R. (2009). The future of endocannabinoid-oriented clinical research after CB1 antagonists. *Psychopharmacology, 205,* 171–174.

Le Witt, P. A., Guttman, M., Tetrud, J. W., Tuite, P. J., Mori, A., Chaikin, P., & Sussman, N. M. (2008). 6002-US-005 Study Group. Adenosine A_{2A} receptor antagonist istradefylline (KW-6002) reduces "off" time in Parkinson's disease: a double-blind, randomized, multicenter clinical trial (6002-US-005). *Annals of Neurology, 63,* 295–302.

Leavitt, F. (1982). *Drugs and behavior* (2nd ed.). New York: John Wiley & Sons.

Leber, P. (2000). The use of placebo control groups in the assessment of psychiatric drugs: An historical context. *Biological Psychiatry, 47,* 699–706.

Lebrun-Frenay, C., & Borg, M. (2002). Choosing the right dopamine agonist for patients with Parkinson's disease. *Current Medical Research and Opinion, 18,* 209–214.

Leccese, A. P., Marquis, K. L., Mattia, A., & Moreton, J. E. (1986). The anticonvulsant and behavioral effects of phencyclidine and ketamine following chronic treatment in rats. *Behavioural Brain Research, 22,* 257–264.

Lecos, C. (1984). The latest caffeine scorecard. *Consumer's Research, 67,* 35–36.

Lees, A. J. (1995). Comparison of therapeutic effects and mortality data of levodopa and levodopa combined with selegiline in patients with early, mild Parkinson's disease. Parkinson's Disease Research Group of the United Kingdom. *BMJ, 311,* 1602–1607.

Lennartz, R. C., & Weinberger, N. M. (1992). Analysis of response systems in Pavlovian conditioning reveals rapidly versus slowly acquired conditioned responses: Support for two factors, implications for behavior and neurobiology. *Psychobiology, 20,* 93–119.

Lennie, P. (2003). The cost of cortical computation. *Current Biology, 13,* 493–497.

Leon, A. C., Shear, M. K., Portera, L., & Klerman, G. L. (1993). Effect size as a measure of symptom-specific drug change in clinical trials. *Psychopharmacology Bulletin, 29,* 163–168.

Leonard, B. E. (2001). Stress, norepinephrine and depression. *Journal of Psychiatry and Neuroscience, 26*(Suppl.), S11–S16.

Lepere, B., Gourarier, L., Sanchez, M., Adda, C., Peyret, E., Nordmann, F., et al. (2001). Reduction in the number of lethal heroin overdoses in France since 1994. Focus on substitution treatments. *Annales de Medecine Interne, 152*(Suppl. 3), IS5–IS12.

Lerner, S. (2000, May 17–23). Legal needles. *The Village Voice.* Retrieved October 23, 2000, from www.villagevoice.com/issues/0020/lerner.shtml

Leslie, R. A. (2001). Gepirone. Organon. *Current Opinion in Investigational Drugs, 2,* 1120–1127.

Lester, B. M., LaGasse, L. L., & Seifer, R. (1998). Cocaine exposure and children: The meaning of subtle effects. *Science, 282,* 633–634.

Letchworth, S., Nader, M., Smith, H., et al. (2001). Progression of changes in dopamine transporter binding site density as a result of cocaine self-administration in rhesus monkeys. *Journal of Neuroscience, 21,* 2799–2807.

Leucht, S., Wahlbeck, K., Hamann, J., & Kissling, W. (2003). New generation antipsychotics versus low-potency conventional antipsychotics: A systematic review and meta-analysis. *Lancet, 361,* 1581–1589.

Leventhal, B. L., Cook, E. H., Jr., Morford, M., et al. (1993). Clinical and neurochemical effects of fenfluramine in children with autism. *Journal of Neuropsychiatry and Clinical Neurosciences, 5,* 307–315.

Levin, E. D., & Simon, B. (1998). Nicotinic acetylcholine involvement in cognitive function in animals. *Psychopharmacology, 138*, 217–230.

Levin, E. D., Westman, E. C., Stein, R. M., et al. (1994). Nicotine skin patch treatment increases abstinence, decreases withdrawal symptoms, and attenuates rewarding effects of smoking. *Journal of Clinical Psychopharmacology, 14*, 41–49.

Levita, L., Hare, T. A., Voss, H. U., Glover, G., Ballon, D. J., & Casey, B. J. (2009). The bivalent side of the nucleus accumbens. *Neuroimage, 44*, 1178–1187.

Levy, W. B., & Baxter, A. (2002). Energy-efficient neuronal computation via quantal synaptic failures. *Journal of Neuroscience, 22*, 4746–4755.

Lewin, R. (1984). Trail of ironies to Parkinson's disease. *Science, 224*, 1083–1085.

Lewin, R. (1985). Parkinson's disease: An environmental cause. *Science, 228*, 257–258.

Lewin, R. (1987). More clues to the cause of Parkinson's disease. *Science, 237*, 978.

Lewis, D. F. V. (2000). On the recognition of mammalian microsomal cytochrome P450 substrates and their characteristics. *Biochemical Pharmacology, 60*, 293–306.

Lewis, M. H., Bodfish, J. W., Powell, S. B., & Golden, R. N. (1995). Clomipramine treatment for stereotype and related repetitive movement disorders associated with mental retardation. *American Journal of Mental Retardation, 100*, 299–312.

LeWitt, P. A. (1992). Clinical studies with and pharmacokinetic considerations of sustained-release levodopa. *Neurology, 42*(Suppl. 1), 29–32.

LeWitt, P. A. (1994). Clinical trials of neuroprotection in Parkinson's disease: Long-term selegiline and alpha-tocopherol treatment. *Journal of Neural Transmission, 43*, 171–181.

Leyton, M., Young, S. N., Pihl, R. O., et al. (1999). A comparison of the effects of acute tryptophan depletion and acute phenylalanine/tyrosine depletion in healthy women.

Advances in Experimental Medicine and Biology, 467, 67–71.

Leyton, M., Young, S. N., Pihl, R. O., et al. (2000). Effects on mood of acute phenylalanine/tyrosine depletion in healthy women. *Neuropsychopharmacology, 22*, 52–63.

Li, Y., Acerbo, M. J., & Robinson, T. E. (2004). The induction of behavioural sensitization is associated with cocaine-induced structural plasticity in the core (but not shell) of the nucleus accumbens. *European Journal of Neuroscience, 20*, 1647–1654.

Liao, Y., McGee, D. L., Cao, G., et al. (2000). Alcohol intake and mortality: Findings from the National Health Interview Surveys (1998 and 1990). *American Journal of Epidemiology, 151*, 651–659.

Liberzon, I., Taylor, S. F., Amdur, R., Jung, T. D., Chamberlain, K. R., Minoshima, S., et al. (1999). Brain activation in PTSD in response to trauma-related stimuli. *Biological Psychiatry, 45*, 817–826.

Lichtenfeld, P. J., Rubin, D. B., & Feldman, R. S. (1984). Subarachnoid hemorrhage precipitated by cocaine snorting. *Archives of Neurology, 41*, 223–224.

Lieberman, H. R., Wurtman, R. J., Emde, G. G., et al. (1987). The effects of low doses of caffeine on human performance and mood. *Psychopharmacology, 92*, 308–312.

Lieberman, J. A., Kane, J. M., & Alvir, J. (1987). Provocative tests with psychostimulant drugs in schizophrenia. *Psychopharmacology, 91*, 415–433.

Lima, M., Reisser, A., Soares, B., & Farrell, M. (2003). Antidepressants for cocaine dependence. *Cochrane Database of Systematic Reviews [Online: Update Software]*, no. 2, CD002950.

Lin, K., Poland, R. E., Wan, Y. Y., et al. (1996). The evolving science of pharmacogenetics: Clinical and ethnic perspectives. *Psychopharmacology Bulletin, 32*, 205–217.

Lindpaintner, K. (2003). Pharmacogenetics and the future of medical practice. *Journal of Molecular Medicine, 81*, 141–153.

Littleton, J. (1995). Acamprosate in alcohol dependence: How does it work? *Addiction, 90,* 1179–1188.

Litvinenko, I. V., Odinak, M. M., Mogil'naya, V. I., & Emelin, A. Y. (2008). Efficacy and safety of galantamine (reminyl) for demenia in patients with Parkinson's disease (an open controlled trial). *Neuroscience and Behavioral Physiology, 38,* 937–945.

Llorente del Pozo, J. M., Fernández Gómez, C., Gutiérrez Fraile, M., & Vielva Pérez, I. (1998). Psychological and behavioural factors associated with relapse among heroin abusers treated in therapeutic communities. *Addictive Behaviors, 23,* 155–169.

Lohr, J., Kuczenski, R., & Niculescu, A. B. (2003). Oxidative mechanisms and tardive dyskinesia. *CNS Drugs, 17,* 47–62.

Lombardo, J. A. (1986). Stimulants and athletic performance (part 1 of 2): Amphetamines and caffeine. *Physician and Sportsmedicine, 14,* 128–139.

London, E. D., Cascella, N. G., Wong, D. F., et al. (1990). Cocaine-induced reduction of glucose utilization in the human brain. *Archives of General Psychiatry, 47,* 567–574.

Lorist, M. M., & Tops, M. (2003). Caffeine, fatigue, and cognition. *Brain and Cognition, 53,* 82–94.

Lotufo-Neto, F., Trivedi, M., & Thase, M. E. (1999). Meta-analysis of the reversible inhibitors of monoamine oxidase type A moclobemide and brofaromine for the treatment of depression. *Neuropsychopharmacology, 20,* 226–247.

Love, R. C., & Conley, R. J. (2004). Long-acting risperidone injection. *American Journal of Health-System Pharmacy, 61,* 1792–1800.

Lu, L., Dempsey, J., Liu, S. Y., et al. (2004). A single infusion of brain-derived neurotrophic factor into the ventral tegmental area induces long-lasting potentiation of cocaine seeking after withdrawal. *Journal of Neuroscience, 24,* 1604–1611.

Luke, D. A., Stamatakis, K. A., & Brownson, R. C. (2000). State youth-access tobacco control policies and youth smoking behavior in the United States. *American Journal of Preventative Medicine, 19,* 180–187.

Lundahl, L. H., Henningfield, J. E., & Lukas, S. E. (2000). Mecamylamine blockade of both positive and negative effects of IV nicotine in human volunteers. *Pharmacology, Biochemistry and Behavior, 66,* 637–643.

Lutfy, K., Eitan, S., & Bryant, C. D., et al. (2003). Buprenorphine-induced antinociception is mediated by mu-opioid receptors and compromised by concomitant activation of opioid receptor-like receptors. *Journal of Neuroscience, 23,* 10331–10337.

Lynam, D. R., Milich, R., Zimmerman, R., et al. (1999). Project DARE: No effects at 10-year follow-up. *Journal of Consulting and Clinical Psychology, 67,* 590–593.

Lynch, B., Lambeng, N., Nocka, K., et al. (2004). The synaptic vesicle protein SV2A is the binding site for the antiepileptic drug levetiracetam. *Proceedings of the National Academy of Sciences of the United States of America, 101,* 9861–9866.

Lyon, M., & Robbins, T. W. (1975). The action of central nervous system drugs: A general theory concerning amphetamine effects. In W. Essman (Ed.), *Current developments in psychopharmacology* (Vol. 2, pp. 80–163). New York: Spectrum Publications.

Lyon, N., Mejsholm, B., & Lyon, M. (1986). Stereotyped responding by schizophrenic outpatients: Cross-cultural confirmation of perseverative switching on a two-choice task. *Journal of Psychiatric Research, 20,* 137–150.

Lyons, D., Friedman, D. P., Nader, M. A., & Porrino, L. J. (1996). Cocaine alters cerebral metabolism within the ventral striatum and limbic cortex of monkeys. *Journal of Neuroscience, 16,* 1230–1238.

Ma, G. X., & Shive, S. (2000). A comparative analysis of perceived risks and substance abuse among ethnic groups. *Addictive Behaviors, 25,* 361–371.

Macenski, M. J., & Meisch, R. A. (1994). Oral drug reinforcement studies with laboratory animals: Applications and implications for understanding drug-reinforced behavior. *Current Directions in Psychological Science, 1,* 22–27.

MacLennan, A. J., & Maier, S. F. (1983). Coping and the stress-induced potentiation of stimulant stereotypy in the rat. *Science, 219,* 1091–1092.

Madden, S., Spaldin, V., & Park, B. K. (1995). Clinical pharmacokinetics of tacrine. *Clinical Pharmacokinetics, 28,* 449–457.

Maehler, R., Dadmarz, M., & Vogel, W. H. (2000). Determinants of the voluntary consumption of nicotine in rats. *Neuropsychobiology, 41,* 200–204.

Maffei, A., Prestori, F., Shibuki, K., et al. (2003). NO enhances presynaptic currents during cerebellar mossy fiber-granule cell LTP. *Journal of Neurophysiology, 90,* 2478–2483.

Mahan, L. C., McKernan, R. M., & Insel, P. A. (1987). Metabolism of alpha- and beta-adrenergic receptors in vitro and in vivo. *Annual Review of Pharmacology and Toxicology, 27,* 215–235.

Maisonneuve, I. M., & Glick, D. (2003). Anti-addictive actions of an iboga alkaloid congener: A novel mechanism for a novel treatment. *Pharmacology, Biochemistry and Behavior, 75,* 607–618.

Maisonneuve, I. M., Ho, A., & Kreek, M. J. (1995). Chronic administration of a cocaine "binge" alters basal extracellular levels in male rats: An in vivo microdialysis study. *Journal of Pharmacology and Experimental Therapeutics, 272,* 652–657.

Maisonneuve, I. M., & Kreek, M. J. (1994). Acute tolerance to the dopamine response induced by a binge pattern of cocaine administration in male rats: An in vivo microdialysis study. *Journal of Pharmacology and Experimental Therapeutics, 268,* 916–921.

Makela, E., Miller, K., & Cutlip, W. D. (2003). Three case reports of modafinil use in treating sedation induced by antipsychotic medications. *Journal of Clinical Psychiatry, 64,* 485–486.

Maldonado, R., Blendy, J. A., Tzavara, E., et al. (1996). Reduction of morphine abstinence in mice with mutation in the gene encoding CREB. *Science, 273,* 657–659.

Malhotra, A. K., Adler, C. M., Kennison, S. D., et al. (1997). Clozapine blunts N-methyl-D-aspartate antagonist-induced psychosis: A study with ketamine. *Biological Psychiatry, 42,* 664–668.

Mann, K., Batra, A., Gunthner, A., & Schroth, G. (1992). Do women develop alcoholic brain damage more readily than men? *Alcoholism, Clinical and Experimental Research, 16,* 1052–1056.

Mann, K., Mundle, G., Langle, G., & Peterson, D. (1993). The reversibility of alcoholic brain damage is not due to rehydration: A CT study. *Addiction, 88,* 649–653.

Mansour, A., Fox, C. A., Akil, H., & Watson, S. J. (1995). Opioid-receptor mRNA expression in the rat CNS: Anatomical and functional implications. *Trends in Neuroscience, 18,* 22–29.

Maremmani, I., Zolesi, O., Agueci, T., & Castrogiovanni, P. (1993). Methadone doses and psychopathological symptoms during methadone maintenance. *Journal of Psychoactive Drugs, 25,* 253–256.

Marien, M., Colpaert, F., & Rosenquist, A. C. (2004). Noradrenergic mechanisms in neurodegenerative diseases: A theory. *Brain Research. Brain Research Reviews, 45,* 38–78.

Marinelli, P., Quirion, R., & Gianoulakis, C. (2004). An in vivo profile of beta-endorphin release in the arcuate nucleus and nucleus accumbens following exposure to stress or alcohol. *Neuroscience, 127,* 777–784.

Marinelli, S., Pascucci, T., Bernardi, G., Puglisi-Allegra, S., & Mercuri, N. B. (2005). Activation of TRPV1 in the VTA excites dopaminergic neurons and increases chemical- and noxious-induced dopamine release in the nucleus accumbens. *Neuropsychopharmacology, 30,* 864–875.

Markou, A., Kosten, T. R., & Koob, G. F. (1998). Neurobiological similarities in depression and drug dependence: A self-medication hypothesis. *Neuropsychopharmacology, 18,* 135–174.

Markov, D., Mosharov, E. V., Setlik, W., Gershon, M. D., & Sulzer, D. (2008). Secretory vesicle rebound hyperacidification and increased quantal size resulting from prolonged methamphetamine exposure. *Journal of Neurochemistry, 107,* 1709–1721.

Markowitz, J. S., Straughn, A. B., & Patrick, K. S. (2003). Advances in the pharmacotherapy of attention-deficit-hyperactivity disorder: Focus on methylphenidate formulations. *Pharmacotherapy, 23,* 1281–1299.

Markowitz, P. I. (1992). Effect of fluoxetine on self-injurious behavior in the developmentally disabled: A preliminary study. *Journal of Clinical Psychopharmacology, 12,* 27–31.

Marlatt, G. A., Baer, J. S., Donovan, D. M., & Kivlahan, D. R. (1988). Addictive behaviors: Etiology and treatment. *Annual Review of Psychology, 39,* 223–252.

Marlatt, G. A., Larimer, M. E., Baer, J. S., & Quigley, L. A. (1993). Harm reduction for alcohol problems: Moving beyond the controlled drinking controversy. *Behavior Therapy, 24,* 461–503.

Marsellis, M., Basile, V. S., Ozdemir, V., et al. (2000). Pharmacogenetics of antipsychotic treatment: Lessons learned from clozapine. *Biological Psychiatry, 47,* 252–266.

Marshall, E. (1988a). Flying blind in the war on drugs. *Science, 240,* 1605–1607.

Marshall, E. (1988b). A war on drugs with real troops? *Science, 241,* 13–15.

Martin, A., Young, C., Leckman, J. F., et al. (2004). Age effects on antidepressant-induced manic conversion. *Archives of Pediatrics and Adolescent Medicine, 158,* 773–780.

Martin, B. (1986). Cellular effects of cannabinoids. *Pharmacological Reviews, 38,* 45–74.

Martin, B. R., & Lichtman, A. H. (1998). Cannabinoid transmission and pain perception. *Neurobiology of Disease, 5,* 447–461.

Martin-Iverson, M. T., & Burger, L. Y. (1995). Behavioral sensitization and tolerance to cocaine and the occupation of dopamine receptors by dopamine. *Molecular Neurobiology, 11,* 31–46.

Maser, W. (1971). *Adolf Hitler: Legend, myth, and reality.* New York: Harper & Row.

Mash, D. C., Kovera, C. A., Buck, B. E., et al. (1998). Medication development of ibogaine as a pharmacotherapy for drug dependence. *Annals of the New York Academy of Sciences, 844,* 274–292.

Mash, D. C., Staley, J. K., Baumann, M. H., et al. (1995). Identification of a primary metabolite of ibogaine that targets serotonin transporters and elevates serotonin. *Life Sciences, 57,* 45–50.

Masino, S. A., Kawamura, M., Wasser, C. A., Pomeroy, L. T., & Ruskin, D. N. (2009). Adenosine, ketogenic diet and epilepsy: The emerging therapeutic relationship between metabolism and brain activity. *Current Neuropharmacology, 7,* 257–268.

Mason, B. J., Salvator, F. R., Williams, L. D., et al. (1999). A double-blind, placebo-controlled study of oral nalmefene for alcohol dependence. *Archives of General Psychiatry, 56,* 719–724.

Massana, J., Moller, H. J., Burrows, G. D., et al. (1999). Reboxetine: A double-blind comparison with fluoxetine in major depressive disorder. *International Clinical Psychopharmacology, 14,* 73–80.

Mathers, D. C., & Ghodse, A. H. (1992). Cannabis and psychotic illness. *British Journal of Psychiatry, 161,* 648–653.

Matheson, A. J., & Spencer, M. (2000). Ropinirole: A review of its use in the management of Parkinson's disease. *Drugs, 60,* 115–137.

Matochik, J. A., Liebenauer, L. L., King, A. C., et al. (1994). Cerebral glucose metabolism in adults with attention-deficit hyperactivity disorder after chronic stimulant treatment. *American Journal of Psychiatry, 151,* 658–664.

Matochik, J. A., Nordahl, T. E., Gross, M., et al. (1993). Effects of acute stimulant medication on cerebral metabolism in adults with hyperactivity. *Neuropsychopharmacology, 8,* 377–386.

Matsuda, K. T., Cho, M. C., Lin, K. M., et al. (1996). Clozapine dosage, serum levels, efficacy and side-effect profiles: A comparison of Korean-American and Caucasian patients. *Psychopharmacology Bulletin, 32,* 253–257.

Matthias, P., Tashkin, D. P., Marques-Magallanes, J. A., et al. (1997). Effects of varying marijuana potency on deposition of tar and delta-9-THC in the lung during smoking. *Pharmacology, Biochemistry and Behavior, 58,* 1145–1150.

Mattick, R. P., Andrews, G., Hadzi-Pavlovic, D., & Christensen, H. (1990). Treatment of panic and agoraphobia. An integrative review. *Journal of Nervous & Mental Disease, 178,* 567–576.

Mattson, S. N., Jernigan, T. L., & Riley, E. P. (1994). MRI and prenatal alcohol exposure: Images provide insight into FAS. *Alcohol Health and Research World, 18,* 49–52.

Matus, A. (2000). Actin-based plasticity in dendritic spines. *Science, 290,* 754–758.

Matussek, N., & Linsmayer, M. (1968). The effect of lithium and amphetamine or desmethylimipramine-RO 4-1284 induced motor hyperactivity. *Life Sciences, 7,* 371–375.

Mayersohn, M., & Guentert, T. W. (1995). Clinical pharmacokinetics of the monoamine oxidase-A inhibitor moclobemide. *Clinical Pharmacokinetics, 29,* 292–332.

Mayhew, K. P., Flay, B. R., & Mott, J. A. (2000). Stages in the development of adolescent smoking. *Drug and Alcohol Dependence, 59,* S61–S81.

McBride, W., Lovinger, D., Machu, T., Thielen, R., Rodd, Z., Murphy, J., et al. (2004). Serotonin-3 receptors in the actions of alcohol, alcohol reinforcement, and alcoholism. *Alcoholism, Clinical and Experimental Research, 28,* 257–267.

McBride, W. J., Murphy, J. M., & Ikemoto, S. (1999). Localization of brain reinforcement mechanisms: Intracranial self-administration and intracranial place-conditioning studies. *Behavioural Brain Research, 101,* 129–152.

McCance, E. F., Price, L. H., Kosten, T. R., & Jatlow, P. I. (1995). Cocaethylene: Pharmacology, physiology and behavioral effects in humans. *Journal of Pharmacology and Experimental Therapeutics, 274,* 215–223.

McCann, U. D., Ridenour, A., Shaham, Y., & Ricaurte, G. A. (1994). Serotonin neurotoxicity after (+/−) 3,4-methylenedioxymethamphetamine (MDMA; "Ecstasy"): A controlled study in humans. *Neuropsychopharmacology, 10,* 129–138.

McCann, U. D., Szabo, Z., Scheffel, U., et al. (1998). Positron emission tomographic evidence of toxic effect of MDMA ("ecstasy") on brain serotonin neurons in human beings. *Lancet, 352,* 1433–1437.

McCann, U. D., Wong, D. F., Yokoi, F., et al. (1998). Reduced striatal dopamine transporter density in abstinent methamphetamine and methcathinone users: Evidence from positron emission tomography studies with [11C] WIN-35,428. *Journal of Neuroscience, 18,* 8417–8422.

McCardle, K., Luebbers, S., Carter, J. D., et al. (2004). Chronic MDMA (ecstasy) use, cognition and mood. *Psychopharmacology, 173,* 434–439.

McCracken, L. M., & Iverson, L. (2001). Predicting complaints of impaired cognitive functioning in patients with chronic pain. *Journal of Pain and Symptom Management, 21,* 392–396.

McCrady, B. S., & Delaney, S. I. (1995). Self-help groups. In R. K. Hester & W. R. Miller (Eds.), *Handbook of alcoholism treatment approaches* (pp. 160–175). Boston, MA: Allyn & Bacon.

McCullough, L. D., & Salamone, J. D. (1992). Anxiogenic drugs beta-CCE and FG 7142 increase extracellular dopamine levels in nucleus accumbens. *Psychopharmacology, 109,* 379–382.

McCullough, L. D., Sokolowski, J. D., & Salamone, J. D. (1993). A neurochemical and behavioral investigation of the involvement of nucleus accumbens dopamine in instrumental avoidance. *Neuroscience, 52,* 919–925.

McCutcheon, J. E., Wang, X., Tseng, K. Y., Wolf, M. E., Marinelli, M. (2011). Calcium-permeable AMPA receptors are present in nucleus accumbens synapses after prolonged withdrawal from cocaine self-administration but not experimenter-administered cocaine. *Journal of Neuroscience, 31,* 5737–5743.

McEntee, W. M., & Mair, R. G. (1978). Memory impairment in Korsakoff's psychosis: A correlation with brain noradrenergic activity. *Science, 202,* 905–907.

McEvoy, J. P., Freudenreich, O., Levin, E. D., & Rose, J. E. (1995). Haloperidol increases smoking in patients with schizophrenia. *Psychopharmacology, 119,* 124–126.

McGaugh, J. L. (1990). Significance and re-membrance: The role of neuromodulatory systems. *Psychological Science, 1,* 15–25.

McGaugh, J. L., Introini-Collison, I. B., Cahill, L. F., Castellano, C., Dalmaz, C., Parent, M. B., et al. (1993). Neuromodulatory systems and memory storage: Role of the amygdala. *Behavioral Brain Research, 58,* 81–90.

McGinty, D., & Szymusiak, R. (1988). Neuronal unit activity patterns in behaving animals: Brainstem and limbic system. *Annual Review of Psychology, 39,* 135–168.

McGrath, P. J., Stewart, J. W., Nunes, E. V., et al. (1993). A double-blind crossover trial of imipramine and phenelzine for outpatients with treatment refractory depression. *American Journal of Psychiatry, 150,* 118–123.

McGue, M. (1999). The behavioral genetics of alcoholism. *Current Directions in Psychological Science, 8,* 109–115.

McGuire, P. K., Jones, P., Harvey, I., et al. (1995). Morbid risk of schizophrenia for rel-atives of patients with cannabis-associated psychosis. *Schizophrenia Research, 15,* 277–281.

McLaughlin, P. J., Qian, L., Wood, J. T., Wisniecki, A., Winston, K. M., Swezey, L. A., et al. (2006). Suppression of food intake and food-reinforced behavior produced by the novel CB1 receptor antagonist/inverse agonist AM1387. *Pharmacology, Biochemistry and Behavior, 83,* 396–402.

McLaughlin, P. J., Winston, K., Swezey, L., Wisniecki, A., Aberman, J., Tardif, D. J., et al. (2003). The cannabinoid CB1 antagonists SR141716A and AM251 suppress food intake and food-reinforced behavior in a variety of tasks in rats. *Behavioural Pharmacology, 14,* 583–588.

McLeman, E. R., Warsh, J. J., Ang, L., et al. (2000). The human nucleus accumbens is highly susceptible to G protein down-regulation by methamphetamine and heroin. *Journal of Neurochemistry, 74,* 2120–2126.

McNamara, J. O. (2001). Drugs effective in the treatment of the epilepsies. In J. G. Hardman & L. E. Limbird (Eds.), *Goodman & Gilman's The pharmacological basis of therapeutics* (10th ed., pp. 521–547). New York: McGraw-Hill.

McNeal, E. T., & Cimbolic, P. (1986). Antidepressants and biochemical theories of depression. *Psychological Bulletin, 99,* 361–374.

Mechoulam, R., & Lichtman, H. (2003). Stout guards of the central nervous system. *Science, 302,* 65–67.

Melega, W. P., Raleigh, M. J., Stout, D. B., et al. (1997). Recovery of striatal dopamine function after acute amphatamine- and methamphetamine-induced neurotoxicity in the vervet monkey. *Brain Research, 766,* 113–120.

Melis, M., Enrico, P., Peana, A. T., & Diana, M. (2007). Acetaldehyde mediates alcohol activation of the mesolimbic dopamine system. *European Journal of Neuroscience, 26,* 2824–2833.

Mello, R. E. (1978). Alcoholism and the behavioral pharmacology of alcohol, 1967–1977.

In M. A. Lipton, A. DiMascio, & K. F. Killman (Eds.), *Psychopharmacology* (pp. 1619–1638). New York: Raven Press.

Meyer-Lindenberg, A. (2010). Imaging genetics of schizophrenia. *Dialogues in Clinical Neuroscience, 12*, 449–456.

Meltzer, H. Y., Alphs, L., Green, A. I., Altamura, A. C., Anand, R., Bertoldi, A., et al. (2003). Clozapine treatment of suicidality in schizophrenia: International Suicide Prevention Trial (InterSePT). *Archives of General Psychiatry, 60*, 82–91.

Meltzer, H. Y. (1989). Clinical studies on the mechanism of action of clozapine: The dopamine-serotonin hypothesis of schizophrenia. *Psychopharmacology, 99*, s18–s27.

Meltzer, H. Y. (1991). The mechanism of action of novel antipsychotic drugs. *Schizophrenia Bulletin, 17*, 263–277.

Meltzer, H. Y. (2004). What's atypical about atypical antipsychotic drugs? *Current Opinion in Pharmacology, 4*, 53–57.

Melzack, R. (1990). The tragedy of needless pain. *Scientific American, 262*, 27–33.

Mendelson, J. H., & Mello, N. K. (1996). Management of cocaine abuse and dependence. *New England Journal of Medicine, 334*, 965–972.

Mendelson, J. H., Sholar, M., Mello, N. K., Teoh, S. K., & Sholar, J. W. (1998). Cocaine tolerance: Behavioral, cardiovascular, and neuroendocrine function in men. *Neuropsychopharmacology, 18*, 264–271.

Mendelson, W. B., & Jain, B. (1995). An assessment of short-acting hypnotics. *Drug Safety, 13*, 257–270.

Mendlewicz, J. (1995). Pharmacologic profile and efficacy of venlafaxine. *International Clinical Psychopharmacology, 10*, 5–13.

Meng, I. D., Manning, B. H., Martin, W. J., et al. (1998). An analgesia circuit activated by cannabinoids. *Nature, 395*, 381–383.

Mennella, J. A., & Beauchamp, G. K. (1998). Smoking and the flavor of breast milk. *New England Journal of Medicine, 339*, 1559–1560.

Meyer, R. E. (1978). Behavioral pharmacology of marijuana. In M. A. Lipton, A. DiMascio, & K. F. Killam (Eds.), *Psychopharmacology* (pp. 1639–1652). New York: Raven Press.

Mhatre, M. C., & Ticku, M. K. (1993). Alcohol: Effects on GABAA receptor function and gene expression. *Alcohol and Alcoholism, 2*(Suppl.), 331–335.

Michaelis, E. K. (1998). Molecular biology of glutamate receptors in the central nervous system and their role in excitotoxicity, oxidative stress and aging. *Progress in Neurobiology, 54*, 369–415.

Michelson, D., Fava, M., Amsterdam, J., et al. (2000). Interruption of selective serotonin reuptake inhibitor treatment. Double-blind, placebo-controlled trial. *British Journal of Psychiatry, 176*, 363–368.

Mihailescu, S., & Drucker-Colin, R. (2000). Nicotine, brain nicotinic receptors, and neuropsychiatric disorders. *Archives of Medical Research, 31*, 131–144.

Miklowitz, D. J., Frank, E., & George, E. L. (1996). New psychosocial treatments for the outpatient management of bipolar disorder. *Psychopharmacology Bulletin, 32*, 613–621.

Mikuriya, T. H., & Aldrich, M. R. (1988). *Cannabis 1988. Old drug, new dangers. The potency question*. Retrieved August 18, 2000, from http://www.druglibrary.org/schaffer/hemp/general/potency.htm

Milberger, S., Biederman, J., Faraone, S. V., et al. (1997). Associations between ADHD and psychoactive substance use disorders. Findings from a longitudinal study of high-risk siblings of ADHD children. *American Journal of Addictions, 6*, 318–329.

Miller, F. G. (2000). Placebo-controlled trials in psychiatric research: An ethical perspective. *Biological Psychiatry, 47*, 707–716.

Miller, H. L., Delgado, P. L., Salomon, R. M., Berman, R., Krystal, J. H., Heninger, G. R., et al. (1996). Clinical and biochemical effects of catecholamine depletion on antidepressant-induced remission of depression. *Archives of General Psychiatry, 53*, 117–128.

Miller, K. E. (2008). Energy drinks, race, and problem behaviors among college students. *Journal of Adolescent Health, 43,* 490–497.

Miller, N. S., & Flaherty, J. A. (2000). Effectiveness of coerced addiction treatment (alternative consequences). A review of the clinical research. *Journal of Substance Abuse Treatment, 18,* 9–16.

Miller, N. S., & Gold, M. S. (1991). Organic solvent and aerosol abuse. *American Family Physician, 44,* 183–189.

Miller, R. J., & Hiley, C. R. (1974). Antimuscarinic properties of neuroleptics and drug-induced parkinsonism. *Nature, 248,* 596–597.

Miller, W. R. (1995). Increasing motivation for change. In R. K. Hester & W. R. Miller (Eds.), *Handbook of alcoholism treatment approaches* (pp. 89–104). Boston, MA: Allyn & Bacon.

Miller, W. R., Brown, J. M., Simpson, T. L., et al. (1995). What works? A methodological analysis of the alcohol treatment outcome literature. In R. K. Hester & W. R. Miller (Eds.), *Handbook of alcoholism treatment approaches* (pp. 12–60). Boston, MA: Allyn & Bacon.

Miller, W. R., & Hester, R. K. (1986). Inpatient alcoholism treatment. *American Psychologist, 41,* 794–805.

Miller, W. R., & Hester, R. K. (1989). Inpatient alcoholism treatment: Rules of evidence and burden of proof. *American Psychologist, 44,* 1245–1246.

Miller, W. R., Leckman, A. L., Delaney, H. D., & Tinkcom, M. (1992). Long-term follow-up of behavioral self-control training. *Journal of Studies of Alcohol, 53,* 249–261.

Mingote, S., de Bruin, J. P., & Feenstra, M. G. P. (2004). Noradrenaline and dopamine efflux in the prefrontal cortex in relation to appetitive classical conditioning. *Journal of Neuroscience, 24,* 2475–2480.

Mingote, S., Weber, S. M., Ishiwari, K., Correa, M., & Salamone, J. D. (2005). Ratio and time requirements on operant schedules: Effort-related effects of nucleus accumbens dopamine depletions. *European Journal of Neuroscience, 21,* 1749–1757.

Mitchell, P. (1993). Chlorpromazine turns forty. *Psychopharmacology Bulletin, 29,* 341–344.

Möhler, H., Fritschy, J., & Rudolph, U. (2002). A new benzodiazepine pharmacology. *Journal of Pharmacology and Experimental Therapeutics, 300,* 2–8.

Mokdad, A., Marks, J., Stroup, D., & Gerberding, J. L. (2004). Actual causes of death in the United States, 2000. *The Journal of the American Medical Association, 291,* 1238–1245.

Moller, H. J. (2000). Are all antidepressants the same? *Journal of Clinical Psychiatry, 61,* 24–28.

Moncrieff, J. (2009). A critique of the dopamine hypothesis of schizophrenia and psychosis. *Harvard Review of Psychiatry, 17,* 214–225.

Monitoring the Future Survey. (2003). Retrieved January 4, 2005, from http://monitoringthefuture.org/pubs/monographs/overview2003.pdf

Montgomery, H. A., Miller, W. R., & Tonigan, J. S. (1995). Does Alcoholics Anonymous involvement predict treatment outcome? *Journal of Substance Abuse Treatment, 12,* 241–246.

Montgomery, S. A. (1995). Are 2-week trials sufficient to indicate efficacy? *Psychopharmacology Bulletin, 31,* 41–44.

Montgomery, S. A. (1999). Predicting response: Noradrenaline reuptake inhibition. *International Clinical Psychopharmacology, 14,* S21–S26.

Monti, P. M., Rohsenow, D. J., Colby, S. M., & Abrams, D. B. (1995). Coping and social skills training. In R. K. Hester & W. R. Miller (Eds.), *Handbook of alcoholism treatment approaches* (pp. 221–239). Boston, MA: Allyn & Bacon.

Moore, K. E., Chiueh, C. C., & Zeldes, G. (1977). Release of neurotransmitters from the brain in vivo by amphetamine, methylphenidate and cocaine. In

E. H. Ellinwood & M. M. Kilbey (Eds.), *Cocaine and other stimulants* (pp. 143–160). New York: Plenum Press.

Moos, R., Fenn, C., Billings, A., & Moos, B. S. (1988). Assessing life stressors and social resources: Applications to alcoholic patients. *Journal of Substance Abuse, 1,* 135–152.

Morgan, C. J., Mofeez, A., Brandner, B., et al. (2004). Acute effects of ketamine on memory systems and psychotic symptoms in healthy volunteers. *Neuropsychopharmacology, 29,* 208–218.

Morgan, M. J. (1999). Memory deficits associated with recreational use of "ecstasy" (MDMA). *Psychopharmacology, 141,* 30–36.

Morton, W. A., Sonne, S. C., & Verga, M. A. (1995). Venlafaxine: A structurally unique and novel antidepressant. *Annals of Pharmacotherapy, 29,* 387–395.

Mosher, J. F. (1990). Drug availability in a public health perspective. In H. Resnick (Ed.), *Youth and drugs: Society's mixed messages* (pp. 129–168). Rockville, MD: U.S. Department of Health and Human Services.

Moskovitz, C., Moses, H., & Klawans, H. L. (1978). Levodopa-induced psychosis: A kindling phenomenon. *American Journal of Psychiatry, 135,* 669–675.

Motzo, C., Porceddu, M. L., Dazzi, L., et al. (1997). Enhancement by flumazenil of dopamine release in the nucleus accumbens of rats repeatedly exposed to diazepam or imidazenil. *Psychopharmacology, 131,* 34–39.

Mozes, T., Greenberg, Y., Spivak, B., et al. (2003). Olanzapine treatment in chronic drug-resistant childhood-onset schizophrenia: An open-label study. *Journal of Child and Adolescent Psychopharmacology, 13,* 311–317.

Mueller, T. I., Stout, R. L., Rudden, S., et al. (1997). A double-blind, placebo-controlled pilot study of carbamazepine for the treatment of alcohol dependence. *Alcoholism, Clinical and Experimental Research, 21,* 86–92.

Müller, C. E. (2009). Prodrug approaches for enhancing the bioavailability of drugs with low solubility. *Chemical Biodiversity, 6,* 2071–2083.

Mulligan, C. J., Robin, R. W., Osier, M. V., Sambuughin, N., Goldfarb, L. G., Kittles, R. A., et al. (2003). Allelic variation at alcohol metabolism genes (ADH1B, ADH1C, ALDH2) and alcohol dependence in an American Indian population. *Human Genetics, 113,* 325–336.

Mulnard, R. A., Cotman, C. W., Kawas, C., et al. (2000). Estrogen replacement therapy for treatment of mild to moderate Alzheimer disease: A randomized controlled trial. *The Journal of the American Medical Association, 283,* 1007–1015.

Mulrow, C. D., Williams, J. W., Jr., Chiquette, E., et al. (2000). Efficacy of newer medications for treating depression in primary care patients. *American Journal of Medicine, 108,* 54–56.

Mumford, G. K., Evans, S. M., Fleishaker, J. C., & Griffiths, R. R. (1995). Alprazolam absorption kinetics affects abuse liability. *Clinical Pharmacology and Therapeutics, 57,* 356–365.

Murray, A. M., Hyde, T. M., Knable, M. B., et al. (1995). Distribution of putative D4 dopamine receptors in postmortem striatum from patients with schizophrenia. *Journal of Neuroscience, 15,* 2186–2191.

Murray, C. J., & Lopez, A. D. (1997). Mortality disability and contribution risk factors: Global burden disease study. *Lancet, 349,* 1436–1442.

Musser, C. J., Ahmann, P. A., Theye, F. W., et al. (1998). Stimulant use and the potential for abuse in Wisconsin as reported by school administrators and longitudinally followed children. *Journal of Developmental and Behavioral Pediatrics, 19,* 187–192.

Myllyla, V. V., Heinonen, E. H., Vuorinen, J. A., et al. (1995). Early selegiline therapy reduces levodopa dose requirement in Parkinson's disease. *Acta Neurologica Scandinavica, 91,* 177–182.

Nadelmann, E. A. (1995, July 10). Switzerland's heroin experiment. *National Review, 46–47.*

Nagayama, T., Sinor, A. D., Simon, R. P., et al. (1999). Cannabinoids and neuroprotection in global and focal cerebral ischemia and in neuronal cultures. *Journal of Neuroscience, 19,* 2987–2995.

Nann-Vernotica, E., Donny, E. C., Bigelow, G. E., & Walsh, S. L. (2001). Repeated administration of the D1/5 antagonist ecopipam fails to attenuate the subjective effects of cocaine. *Psychopharmacology, 155,* 338–347.

Naranjo, C. (1969). Psychotherapeutic possibilities of new fantasy-enhancing drugs. *Clinical Toxicology, 2,* 209–224.

Nathanson, N. M. (1987). Molecular properties of the muscarinic acetylcholine receptor. *Annual Review of Neuroscience, 10,* 195–236.

National Drug Monitor. (2000). *Drug policy.* Retrieved October 23, 2000, from http://www.trimbos.nl/indexuk.html

National Household Survey on Drug Abuse. (1999). *National estimates of drug abuse.* Retrieved October 23, 2000, from http://www.health.org.govstudy/bkd376/Chapter2.htm#

National survey on drug use and health. (2003). Retrieved January 4, 2005, from http://oas.samhsa.gov/nhsda.htm

Nedergaard, M. (1994). Direct signaling from astrocytes to neurons in cultures of mammalian brain cells. *Science, 263,* 1768–1772.

Neill, D. B., Fenton, H., & Justice, J. B., Jr. (2002). Increase in accumbal dopaminergic transmission correlates with response cost not reward of hypothalamic stimulation. *Behavioural Brain Research, 137,* 129–138.

Neill, J. R. (1987). "More than medical significance": LSD and American psychiatry. *Journal of Psychoactive Drugs, 19,* 39–45.

Nelson, T. O., McSpadden, M., Fromme, K., & Marlatt, G. A. (1986). Effects of alcohol intoxication on metamemory and on retrieval from long-term memory. *Journal of Experimental Psychology: General, 115,* 247–254.

Nestler, E. J. (1996). Under siege: The brain on opiates. *Neuron, 16,* 897–900.

Newcomb, M. D., & Bentler, P. M. (1989). Substance use and abuse among children and teenagers. *American Psychologist, 44,* 242–248.

Newlin, D. B., & Pretorius, M. B. (1990). Sons of alcoholics report greater hangover symptoms than sons of nonalcoholics: A pilot study. *Alcoholism, Clinical and Experimental Research, 14,* 713–716.

Newlin, D. B., & Thomson, J. B. (1990). Alcohol challenge with sons of alcoholics: A critical review and analysis. *Psychological Bulletin, 108,* 383–402.

Nichols, D. E. (1986). Differences between the mechanism of action of MDMA, MBDB, and the classic hallucinogens. Identification of a new therapeutic class: Entactogens. *Journal of Psychoactive Drugs, 18,* 305–313.

Nicola, S. M., Surmeier, D. J., & Malenka, R. C. (2000). Dopaminergic modulation of neuronal excitability in the striatum and nucleus accumbens. *Annual Review of Neuroscience, 23,* 185–215.

Nies, A. S. (2001). Principles of therapeutics. In J. G. Hardman & L. E. Limbird (Eds.), *Goodman & Gilman's The pharmacological basis of therapeutics* (10th ed., pp. 45–65). New York: McGraw-Hill.

Norman, T. R., & Burrows, G. D. (1995). A risk-benefit assessment of moclobemide in the treatment of depressive disorders. *Drug Safety, 12,* 46–54.

Novak, S. J. (1998). Second thoughts on psychedelic drugs. *Endeavour, 22,* 21–23.

Noyes, R., Jr., Brunk, S. F., Avery, D. A. H., et al. (1975). The analgesic properties of delta-9-tetrahydrocannabinol and codeine. *Clinical Pharmacology and Therapeutics, 18,* 84–89.

Nunes, E. J., Randall, P. A., Santerre, J. L., Given, A. B., Sager, T. N., Correa, M., et al.

(2010). Differential effects of selective adenosine antagonists on the effort-related impairments induced by dopamine D1 and D2 antagonism. *Neuroscience, 170,* 268–280.

Nunes, E. V., & Levin, R. (2004). Treatment of depression in patients with alcohol or other drug dependence: A meta-analysis. *The Journal of the American Medical Association, 291,* 1887–1896.

Nutt, D. (2006). GABAA receptors: Subtypes, regional distribution, and function. *Journal of Clinical Sleep Medicine, 2,* S7–S11.

O'Beirne, M., Gurevich, N., & Carlen, P. L. (1986). Pentobarbital inhibits hippocampal neurons by increasing potassium conductance. *Canadian Journal of Physiological Pharmacology, 65,* 36–41.

O'Brien, C. P. (2001). Drug addiction and drug abuse. In J. G. Hardman & L. E. Limbird (Eds.), *Goodman & Gilman's The pharmacological basis of therapeutics* (10th ed., pp. 31–43). New York: McGraw-Hill.

O'Brien, C. P., Childress, A. R., McLellan, A. T., & Ehrman, R. (1993). Developing treatments that address classical conditioning. *NIDA Research Monograph, 135,* 71–91.

O'Brien, C. P., Childress, A. R., McLellan, A. T., et al. (1992). Classical conditioning in drug-dependent humans. *Annals of the New York Academy of Sciences, 654,* 401–414.

O'Brien, C. P., McLellan, A. T., & Alterman, A. (1993). Effectiveness of treatment for substance abuse. In S. G. Korenman & J. D. Barchas (Eds.), *Biological basis of substance abuse* (pp. 487–510). New York: Oxford University Press.

O'Farrell, T. J. (1995). Marital and family therapy. In R. K. Hester & W. R. Miller (Eds.), *Handbook of alcoholism treatment approaches* (pp. 195–220). Boston, MA: Allyn & Bacon.

O'Hearn, E., & Molliver, M. E. (1993). Degeneration of the Purkinje cells in parasagittal zones of the cerebellar vermis after treatment with ibogaine or harmaline. *Neuroscience, 55,* 303–310.

O'Hearn, E., Zhang, P., & Molliver, M. E. (1995). Excitotoxic insult due to ibogaine leads to delayed induction of neuronal NOS in Purkinje cells. *Neuroreport, 6,* 1611–1616.

O'Malley, S. S., Jaffe, A. J., Chang, G., et al. (1996a). Six-month follow-up of naltrexone and psychotherapy for alcohol dependence. *Archives of General Psychiatry, 53,* 217–224.

O'Malley, S. S., Jaffe, A. J., Rode, S., & Rounsaville, B. J. (1996b). Experience of a "slip" among alcoholics treated with naltrexone or placebo. *American Journal of Psychiatry, 153,* 281–283.

O'Neill, M. J., Bleakman, D., Zimmerman, D. M., & Nisenbaum, E. S. (2004). AMPA receptor potentiators for the treatment of CNS disorders. *Current Drug Targets-CNS & Neurological Disorders, 3,* 181–194.

Okamoto, M., Rao, S., & Walewske, J. L. (1986). Effect of dosing frequency on the development of physical dependence and tolerance to pentobarbital. *Journal of Pharmacology and Experimental Therapeutics, 238,* 1004–1008.

Oldendorf, W. H., & Dewhurst, W. G. (1978). The blood-brain barrier and psychotropic drugs. In W. G. Clark & J. D. Giudice (Eds.), *Principles of psychopharmacology* (pp. 183–192). New York: Academic Press.

Oldendorf, W. H., Hyman, S., Braun, L., & Oldendorf, S. Z. (1972). Blood-brain barrier: Penetration of morphine, codeine, heroin and methadone after carotid injection. *Science, 178,* 984–986.

Olds, J., & Milner, P. (1954). Positive reinforcement produced by electrical stimulation of septal area and other regions of rat brain. *Journal of Comparative and Physiological Psychology, 47,* 419–427.

Olin, J., Schneider, L., Novit, A., & Luczak, S. (2001). Hydergine for dementia. *Cochrane Database of Systematic Reviews [Online: Update Software],* no. 2, CD000359.

Olney, J. W. (1990). Excitotoxic amino acids and neuropsychiatric disorders.

Annual Review of Pharmacology and Toxicology, 30, 47–71.

Olney, J. W., Young, C., Wozniak, D., et al. (2004). Do pediatric drugs cause developing neurons to commit suicide? *Trends in Pharmacological Sciences, 25,* 135–139.

Onaivi, E. S. (2009). Cannabinoid receptors in brain: Pharmacogenetics, neuropharmacology, neurotoxicology, and potential therapeutic applications. *International Review of Neurobiology, 88,* 335–369.

Osborn, E., Grey, C., & Reznikoff, M. (1986). Psychosocial adjustment, modality choice, and outcome in naltrexone versus methadone treatment. *American Journal of Drug and Alcohol Abuse, 12,* 383–388.

Oscar-Berman, M. (1980). Neuropsychological consequences of long-term chronic alcoholism. *American Scientist, 68,* 410–419.

Ott, B. R., & Lannon, M. C. (1992). Exacerbation of parkinsonism by tacrine. *Clinical Neuropharmacology, 15,* 322–325.

Oviedo, A., Glowa, J., & Herkenham, M. (1993). Chronic cannabinoid administration alters cannabinoid receptor binding in rat brain: A quantitative autoradiographic study. *Brain Research, 616,* 293–302.

Owen, M. J., O'Donovan, M. C., Thapar, A., & Craddock, N. (2011). Neurodevelopmental hypothesis of schizophrenia. *British Journal of Psychiatry, 198,* 173–175.

Packer, S. (1998). Jewish mystical movements and the European ergot epidemics. *Israel Journal of Psychiatry and Related Sciences, 35,* 227–239.

Pae, C. U., Lim, H. K., Han, C., Patkar, A. A., Steffens, D. C., Masand, P. S., et al. (2007). Fatigue as a core symptom in major depressive disorder: Overview and the role of bupropion. *Expert Reviews in Neurotherapeutics, 7,* 1251–1263.

Page, J. B., Fletcher, J., & True, W. R. (1988). Psychosociocultural perspectives on chronic cannabis use: The Costa Rican follow-up. *Journal of Psychoactive Drugs, 20,* 57–65.

Palumbo, P. A., & Winter, J. C. (1992). Stimulus effects of ibogaine in rats trained with yohimbine, DOM, or LSD. *Pharmacology, Biochemistry and Behavior, 43,* 1221–1226.

Pampallona, S., Bollini, P., Tibaldi, G., et al. (2004). Combined pharmacotherapy and psychological treatment for depression: A systematic review. *Archives of General Psychiatry, 61,* 714–719.

Panchagnula, R., & Thomas, N. S. (2000). Biopharmaceutics and pharmacokinetics in drug research. *International Journal of Pharmaceutics, 201,* 131–150.

Panksepp, J. (1986). The neurochemistry of behavior. *Annual Review of Psychology, 37,* 77–107.

Paone, D., Des Jarlais, D. C., Gangloff, R., & Milliken, J. (1995). Syringe exchange: HIV prevention, key findings, and future directions. *International Journal of the Addictions, 30,* 1647–1683.

Papakostas, G. I., Nutt, D. J., Hallett, L. A., Tucker, V. L., Krishen, A., & Fava, M. (2006). Resolution of sleepiness and fatigue in major depressive disorder: A comparison of bupropion and the selective serotonin reuptake inhibitors. *Biological Psychiatry, 60,* 1350–1355.

Papakostas, G., Petersen, T., Nierenberg, A., et al. (2004). Ziprasidone augmentation of selective serotonin reuptake inhibitors (SSRIs) for SSRI-resistant major depressive disorder. *Journal of Clinical Psychiatry, 65,* 217–221.

Pardridge, W. M. (1999). Blood-brain barrier biology and methodology. *Journal of NeuroVirology, 5,* 556–569.

Parent, M. B., Habib, M. K., & Baker, G. B. (2000). Time-dependent changes in brain monoamine oxidase activity and in brain levels of monoamines and amino acids following acute administration of the antidepressant/antipanic drug phenelzine. *Biochemical Pharmacology, 59,* 1253–1263.

Parkinson Study Group. (2004). Pramipexole vs levodopa as initial treatment for

Parkinson disease: A 4-year randomized controlled trial. *Archives of Neurology, 61,* 1044–1053.

Parnetti, L., Mignini, F., Tomassoni, D., Traini, E., & Amenta, F. (2007). Cholinergic precursors in the treatment of cognitive impairment of vascular origin: Ineffective approaches or need for re-evaluation? *Journal of Neurological Sciences, 257,* 264–269.

Parrott, A. C. (2000). Human research on MDMA (3,4-methylene-dioxymethamphetamine) neurotoxicity: Cognitive and behavioural indices of change. *Neuropsychobiology, 42,* 17–24.

Parrott, A. C. (2004). Is ecstasy MDMA? A review of the proportion of ecstasy tablets containing MDMA, their dosage levels, and the changing perceptions of purity. *Psychopharmacology, 173,* 234–241.

Patat, A. (2000). Clinical pharmacology of psychotropic drugs. *Human Psychopharmacology: Clinical and Experimental, 15,* 361–387.

Patat, A., Rosenzweig, P., Enslen, M., et al. (2000). Effects of a new slow release formulation of caffeine on EEG, psychomotor and cognitive functions in sleep-deprived subjects. *Human Psychopharmacology: Clinical and Experimental, 15,* 153–170.

Patel, N. C., Yeh, J. Y., Shepherd, M. D., et al. (2002). Secretin treatment for autistic disorder: A critical analysis. *Pharmacotherapy, 22,* 905–914.

Patton, G. C., Coffey, C., Carlin, J. B., et al. (2002). Cannabis use and mental health in young people: Cohort study. *BMJ, 325,* 1195–1198.

Paul, S. M. (1977). Movement and madness: Towards a biological model of schizophrenia. In J. D. Maser & M. E. P. Seligman (Eds.), *Psychopathology: Experimental models* (pp. 358–386). San Francisco, CA: W. H. Freeman.

Paulson, P. E., Camp, D. M., & Robinson, T. E. (1991). Time course of transient behavioral depression and persistent behavioral sensitization in relation to regional brain monoamine concentrations during amphetamine withdrawal in rats. *Psychopharmacology, 103,* 480–492.

Pavic, L. (2003). Alterations in brain activation in posttraumatic stress disorder patients with severe hyperarousal symptoms and impulsive aggressiveness. *European Archives of Psychiatry and Clinical Neuroscience, 253,* 80–83.

Pawlosky, R. J., Kashiwaya, Y., Srivastava, S., King, M. T., Crutchfield, C., Volkow, N., et al. (2010). Alterations in brain glucose utilization accompanying elevations in blood ethanol and acetate concentrations in the rat. *Alcohol Clinical and Experimental Research, 34,* 375–381.

Payne, J., Rivera, C., Voipio, J., & Kaila, K. (2003). Cation-chloride co-transporters in neuronal communication, development and trauma. *Trends in Neurosciences, 26,* 199–206.

Peciña, S., Cagniard, B., Berridge, K., Aldridge, J. W., & Zhuang, X. (2003). Hyperdopaminergic mutant mice have higher "wanting" but not "liking"for sweet rewards. *Journal of Neuroscience, 23,* 9395–9402.

Pei, L., Lee, F. J., Moszczynska, A., Vukusic, B., & Liu, F. (2004). Regulation of dopamine D1 receptor function by physical interaction with the NMDA receptors. *Journal of Neuroscience, 24,* 1149–1158.

Pelham, W. E., Jr., Carlson, C., Sams, S. E., et al. (1993). Separate and combined effects of methylphenidate and behavior modification on boys with attention-deficit hyperactivity disorder in the classroom. *Journal of Consulting and Clinical Psychology, 61,* 506–515.

Pellow, S., & File, S. E. (1986). Anxiolytic and anxiogenic drug effects on exploratory activity in an elevated plus-maze: A novel test of anxiety in the rat. *Pharmacology, Biochemistry and Behavior, 24,* 525–529.

Peng, G. S., Chen, Y. C., Tsao, T. P., Wang, M. F., & Yin, S. J. (2007). Pharmacokinetic and pharmacodynamic basis for partial protection against alcoholism in Asians, heterozygous for the variant ALDH2*2 gene allele. *Pharmacogenetics and Genomics, 17*, 845–855.

Penington, N. J., & Fox, A. P. (1994). Effects of LSD on CA^{++} currents in central 5-HT-containing neurons: 5-HT1A receptors may play a role in hallucinogenesis. *Journal of Pharmacology and Experimental Therapeutics, 269*, 1160–1165.

Penny, G. N., & Robinson, J. O. (1986). Psychological resources and cigarette smoking in adolescents. *British Journal of Psychology, 77*, 351–357.

Peral, M., Alcami, M., & Gilaberte, I. (1999). Fluoxetine in children with autism. *Journal of American Academy of Child and Adolescent Psychiatry, 38*, 1472–1473.

Perez-Reyes, M., White, W. R., McDonald, S. A., et al. (1991). The pharmacologic effects of daily marijuana smoking in humans. *Pharmacology, Biochemistry, and Behavior, 40*, 691–694.

Perez-Reyes, R. M., Jeffcoat, A. R., Myers, M., et al. (1994). Comparison in humans of the potency and pharmacokinetics of intravenously injected cocaethylene and cocaine. *Psychopharmacology, 116*, 428–432.

Peroutka, S. J. (1995). 5-HT receptors: Past, present and future. *Trends in Neuroscience, 18*, 68–69.

Petracek, F. J. (1978). Chemistry and structure-activity relationships of psychotropic drugs: Part 1. In W. G. Clark & J. del Guidice (Eds.), *Principles of psychopharmacology* (pp. 134–139). New York: Academic Press.

Pezzarossa, A., Cervigni, C., Ghinelli, F., et al. (1986). Glucose tolerance in chronic alcoholics after alcohol withdrawal: Effect of accompanying diet. *Metabolism, 35*, 984–988.

Pezze, M. A., & Feldon, J. (2004). Mesolimbic dopaminergic pathways in fear conditioning. *Progress in Neurobiology, 74*, 301–320.

Pfab, R., Hirtl, C., & Zilker, T. (1999). Opiate detoxification under anesthesia: No apparent benefit but suppression of thyroid hormones and risk of pulmonary and renal failure. *Journal of Toxicology. Clinical Toxicology, 37*, 43–50.

Pfefferbaum, A., Sullivan, E., Rosenbloom, M., Mathalon, D., & Lim, K. O. (1998). A controlled study of cortical gray matter and ventricular changes in alcoholic men over a 5-year interval. *Archives of General Psychiatry, 55*, 905–912.

Pfeiffer, A., Brantl, V., Herz, A., & Emrich, H. M. (1986). Psychotomimesis mediated by K opiate receptors. *Science, 233*, 774–775.

Pfeiffer, C., & Wagner, M. L. (1994). Clozapine therapy for Parkinson's disease and other movement disorders. *American Journal of Hospital Pharmacy, 51*, 3047–3053.

Pfeiffer, S. I., Norton, J., Nelson, L., & Shott, S. (1995). Efficacy of vitamin B6 and magnesium in the treatment of autism: A methodology review and summary of outcomes. *Journal of Autism & Developmental Disorders, 25*, 481–493.

Phan, K. L., Taylor, S. F., Welsh, R. C., Ho, S. H., Britton, J. C., & Liberzon, I. (2004). Neural correlates of individual ratings of emotional salience: A trial-related fMRI study. *Neuroimage, 21*, 768–780.

Phillips, G. T., Gossop, M., & Bradley, B. (1986). The influence of psychological factors on the opiate withdrawal syndrome. *British Journal of Psychiatry, 149*, 235–238.

Phillips, T. J., Kamens, H. M., & Wheeler, J. M. (2008). Behavioral genetic contributions to the study of addiction-related amphetamine effects. *Neuroscience and Biobehavioral Reviews, 32*, 707–759.

Piazza, P. V., Deminiere, J.-M., Le Moal, M., & Simon, H. (1989). Factors that predict individual vulnerability to amphetamine self-administration. *Science, 245*, 1511–1513.

Piccinelli, M., Pini, S., Bellantuono, C., & Wilkinson, G. (1995). Efficacy of drug treatment in obsessive-compulsive disorder. A meta-analytic review. *British Journal of Psychiatry, 166,* 424–443.

Pickworth, W. B., Herning, R. I., & Henningfield, J. E. (1986). Electroencephalographic effects of nicotine chewing gum in humans. *Pharmacology, Biochemistry and Behavior, 25,* 879–882.

Pierce, P. A., & Peroutka, S. J. (1990). Antagonist properties of d-LSD at 5-hydroxytryptamine2 receptors. *Neuropsychopharmacology, 3,* 503–508.

Pierce, R. C., & Vanderschuren, L. J. (2010). Kicking the habit: The neural basis of ingrained behaviors in cocaine addiction. *Neuroscience & Biobehavioral Reviews, 35,* 212–219.

Pihl, R. O., & Zacchia, C. (1986). Alcohol and aggression: A test of the affect-arousal hypothesis. *Aggressive Behavior, 12,* 367–375.

Pincus, J. H., & Kiss, A. (1986). Phenytoin reduces early acetylcholine release after depolarization. *Brain Research, 397,* 103–107.

Pinna, A., Schintu, N., Simola, N., Volpini, R., Pontis, S., Cristalli, G., et al. (2010). A new ethyladenine antagonist of adenosine A(2A) receptors: Behavioral and biochemical characterization as an antiparkinsonian drug. *Neuropharmacology, 58,* 613–623.

Piper, B., Briggs, M., Hufman, K., & Lubot-Conk, R. (2003). *State of the States: Drug Policy Reforms: 1996–2002. A report by the Drug Policy Alliance.* Retrieved January 17, 2005, from http://www.drugpolicy.org/docUploads/sos_report2003.pdf

Pittler, M. H., & Ernst, E. (2000). Efficacy of kava extract for treaty anxiety: Systematic review and meta-analysis. *Journal of Clinical Psychopharmacology, 20,* 84–89.

Pliner, P., & Cappell, H. (1974). Modification of affective consequences of alcohol: A comparison of social and solitary drinking. *Journal of Abnormal Psychology, 83,* 418–425.

Plomin, R., Owen, M. J., & McGuffin, P. (1994). The genetic basis of complex human behaviors. *Science, 264,* 1733–1739.

Polymeropoulos, M. H., Higgins, J. J., Golbe, L. I., et al. (1996). Mapping of a gene for Parkinson's disease to chromosome 4q21–q23. *Science, 274,* 1197–1199.

Pool, R. (1992). The third branch of science debuts. *Science, 265,* 44–47.

Pope, H. G. (1969). Tabernantha iboga: An African narcotic plant of social importance. *Economic Botany, 23,* 174–184.

Pope, H. G., Gruber, A. J., Hudson, J. I., et al. (2001). Neuropsychological performance in long-term cannabis users. *Archives of General Psychiatry, 58,* 909–915.

Pope, H. G., Jr. Gruber, A. J., Hudson, J. I., et al. (2002). Cognitive measures in long-term cannabis users. *Journal of Clinical Pharmacology, 42*(Suppl. 11), 41S–47S.

Pope, H. G., Gruber, A. J., & Yurgelun-Todd, D. (1995). The residual neuropsychological effects of cannabis: The current status of research. *Drug and Alcohol Dependence, 38,* 25–34.

Pope, H. G., & Yurgelun-Todd, D. (1996). The residual cognitive effects of heavy marijuana use in college students. *The Journal of the American Medical Association, 275,* 521–527.

Popik, P., Layer, R. T., Fossom, L. H., et al. (1995a). NMDA antagonist properties of the putative anti-addictive drug, ibogaine. *Journal of Pharmacology and Experimental Therapeutics, 275,* 753–760.

Popik, P., Layer, R. T., & Skolnick, P. (1995b). 100 years of ibogaine: Neurochemical and pharmacological actions of a putative anti-addictive drug. *Pharmacological Reviews, 47,* 235–253.

Porjesz, B., & Begleiter, H. (2003). Alcoholism and human electrophysiology. *Alcohol Research and Health, 27,* 153–160.

Porrino, L. J., Lyons, D., Miller, M. D., et al. (2002). Metabolic mapping of the effects of cocaine during the initial phases of self-administration in the nonhuman primate. *Journal of Neuroscience, 22,* 7687–7694.

Porrino, L. J., Lyons, D., Smith, H. R., et al. (2004). Cocaine self-administration produces a progressive involvement of limbic, association, and sensorimotor striatal domains. *Journal of Neuroscience, 24*, 3554–3562.

Post, R. M., & Contel, N. R. (1983). Human and animal studies of cocaine: Implications for development of behavioral pathology. In I. Creese (Ed.), *Stimulants: Neurochemical, behavioral, and clinical perspectives* (pp. 169–202). New York: Raven Press.

Post, R. M., Kotin, J., & Goodwin, F. K. (1974). The effects of cocaine on depressed patients. *American Journal of Psychiatry, 131*, 511–517.

Post, R. M., Weiss, S. R. B., & Pert, A. (1987). The role of context and conditioning in behavioral sensitization to cocaine. *Psychopharmacology Bulletin, 23*, 425–429.

Pothos, E. N., Przedborski, S., Davila, V., et al. (1998). D-like dopamine autoreceptor activation reduces quantal size in PC12 cells. *Journal of Neuroscience, 18*, 5575–5585.

Power, R. (1994). Drug trends since 1968. In J. Strang & M. Gossop (Eds.), *Heroin addiction and drug policy: The British system* (pp. 29–41). Oxford, OH: Oxford University Press.

Powers, R. J., & Kutash, L. (1985). Stress and alcohol. *International Journal of the Addictions, 20*, 461–482.

Prather, P. L. (2004). Inverse agonists: Tools to reveal ligand-specific conformations of G protein-coupled receptors. *Sciences STKE [electronic resource]: Signal transduction knowledge environment, 2004*(215), e1.

Prendergast, M. L., Grella, C., Perry, S. M., & Anglin, M. D. (1995). Levo-alpha-acetyl-methadol (LAAM): Clinical, research, and policy issues of a new pharmacotherapy for opioid addiction. *Journal of Psychoactive Drugs, 27*, 239–247.

Preskorn, S. H. (1991). Should bupropion dosage be adjusted based upon therapeutic drug monitoring? *Psychopharmacology Bulletin, 27*, 637–643.

Pruessner, J. C., Champagne, F., Meaney, M. J., & Dagher, A. (2004). Dopamine release in response to a psychological stress in humans and its relationship to early life maternal care: A positron emission tomography study using [11C]raclopride. *Journal of Neuroscience, 24*, 2825–2831.

Prien, R. F. (1988). Methods and models for placebo use in pharmacotherapeutic trials. *Psychopharmacology Bulletin, 24*, 4–8.

Prien, R. F., & Potter, W. Z. (1990). NIMH workshop report on treatment of bipolar disorder. *Psychopharmacology Bulletin, 26*, 409–428.

Priest, R. G., Gimbrett, R., Roberts, M., & Steinert, J. (1995). Reversible and selective inhibitors of monoamine oxidase A in mental and other disorders. *Acta Psychiatrica Scandinavica, 386*, 40–43.

Prochaska, J. O., DiClemente, C. C., & Norcross, J. C. (1992). In search of how people change. Applications to addictive behaviors. *American Psychologist, 47*, 1102–1114.

Przuntek, H., Conrad, B., Dichgans, J., et al. (1999). SELEDO: A 5-year long-term trial on the effect of selegiline in early parkinsonian patients treated with levodopa. *European Journal of Neurology, 6*, 141–150.

Pugh, M. C., & Pugh, C. B. (1987). Unlabeled uses for approved drugs. *American Druggist, 195*, 127–138.

Quinn, N. (1995). Drug treatment of Parkinson's disease. *BMJ, 310*, 575–579.

Quitkin, F. M., McGrath, P. J., Stewart, J. W., Deliyannides, D., Taylor, B. P., Davies, C. A., et al. (2005). Remission rates with 3 consecutive antidepressant trials: Effectiveness for depressed outpatients. *Journal of Clinical Psychiatry, 66*, 670–676.

Quitkin, F. M., Rabkin, J. G., Gerald, J., et al. (2000). Validity of clinical trials of antidepressants. *American Journal of Psychiatry, 157*, 327–337.

Quitkin, F. M., Stewart, J. W., McGrath, P. J., et al. (1993). Columbia atypical depression: A subgroup of depressives with better response to MAOI than to tricyclic antidepressants or placebo. *British Journal of Psychiatry Supplement, 21*, 30–34.

Raby, W. N., & Coomaraswamy, S. (2004). Gabapentin reduces cocaine use among addicts from a community clinic sample. *Journal of Clinical Psychiatry, 65,* 84–86.

Radulovacki, M. (1982). L-tryptophan's effects on brain chemistry and sleep in cats and rats: A review. *Neuroscience and Biobehavioral Reviews, 6,* 421–428.

Ragsdale, D. S., McPhee, J. C., Scheuer, T., & Catterall, W. A. (1994). Molecular determinants of state-dependent block of Na+ channels by local anesthetics. *Science, 265,* 1724–1728.

Rajkowska, G., Miguel-Hidalgo, J. J., Wei, J., et al. (1999). Morphometric evidence for neuronal and glial prefrontal cell pathology in major depression. *Biological Psychiatry, 45,* 1085–1098.

Rall, T. W. (1985). Central nervous stimulants (continued). In A. G. Gilman, L. S. Goodman, T. W. Rall, & F. Murad (Eds.), *The pharmacological basis of therapeutics* (pp. 589–603). New York: Macmillan.

Rall, T. W. (1990). Hypnotics and sedatives: Ethanol. In A. G. Gilman, T. W. Rall, A. S. Nies, & P. Taylor (Eds.), *The pharmacological basis of therapeutics* (pp. 345–382). New York: Pergamon Press.

Ramirez, A. (1989). The neonate's unique response to drugs: Unraveling the causes of drug iatrogenesis. *Neonatal Network, 7,* 45–49.

Rampello, L., Nicoletti, G., & Raffaele, R. (1991). Dopaminergic hypothesis for retarded depression: A symptom profile for predicting therapeutical responses. *Acta Psychiatrica Scandinavia, 84,* 552–554.

Randall, C. L., & Saulnier, J. L. (1995). Effect of ethanol on prostacyclin, thromboxane, and prostaglandin E production in human umbilical veins. *Alcoholism, Clinical and Experimental Research, 19,* 741–746.

Randall, P. A., Nunes, E. J., Janniere, S. L., Stopper, C. M., Farrar, A. M., Sager, T. N., et al. (2011). Stimulant effects of adenosine antagonists on operant behavior: Differential actions of selective A(2A) and A (1) antagonists. *Psychopharmacology* [Epub ahead of print].

Rao, G. A., Larkin, E. C., & Derr, R. F. (1986). Biologic effects of chronic ethanol consumption related to a deficient intake of carbohydrates. *Alcohol and Alcoholism, 21,* 369–373.

Rapoport, J. L., Buchsbaum, M. S., Weingartner, H., et al. (1980). Dextroamphetamine: Its cognitive and behavioral effects in normal and hyperactive boys and normal men. *Archives of General Psychiatry, 37,* 933–943.

Rapport, M. D., Denney, C., DuPaul, G. J., & Gardner, M. J. (1994). Attention-deficit disorder and methylphenidate: Normalization rates, clinical effectiveness, and response prediction in 76 children. *Journal of the American Academy of Child and Adolescent Psychiatry, 33,* 882–893.

Rapport, M. D., & Kelly, K. L. (1991). Psychostimulant effects on learning and cognitive function: Findings and implications for children with attention deficit hyperactivity disorder. *Clinical Psychology, 11,* 61–92.

Rascol, O., Brooks, D., Korczyn, A., et al. (2000). A five-year study of the incidence of dyskinesia in patients with early Parkinson's disease who were treated with ropinirole or levodopa. 056 Study Group. *New England Journal of Medicine, 342,* 1484–1491.

Raskin, J., Goldstein, D., Mallinckrodt, C., & Ferguson, M. B. (2003). Duloxetine in the long-term treatment of major depressive disorder. *Journal of Clinical Psychiatry, 64,* 1237–1244.

Rasmussen, K., & Aghajanian, G. K. (1986). Effect of hallucinogens on spontaneous and sensory-evoked locus coeruleus unit activity in the rat: Reversal by selective 5-HT2 antagonists. *Brain Research, 385,* 395–400.

Ratey, J. J., Mikkelsen, E., Sorgi, P., et al. (1987). Autism: The treatment of aggressive behaviors. *Journal of Clinical Psychopharmacology, 7,* 35–41.

Ravizza, L., Barzega, G., Bellino, S., et al. (1996). Drug treatment of obsessive-compulsive disorder (OCD): Long-term trial with clomipramine and selective serotonin reuptake inhibitors (SSRIs). *Psychopharmacology Bulletin, 32*, 167–173.

Ray, L. A., Chin, P. F., & Miotto, K. (2010). Naltrexone for the treatment of alcoholism: Clinical findings, mechanisms of action, and pharmacogenetics. *CNS & Neurological Disorders Drug Targets, 9*, 13–22.

Rech, R. H., & Rosecrans, J. A. (1982). Review of mechanisms of hallucinogenic drug action. *Neuroscience and Biobehavioral Reviews, 6*, 481–482.

Redgrave, P., Gurney, K., & Reynolds, J. (2008). What is reinforced by phasic dopamine signals? *Brain Research Reviews, 58*, 322–339.

Reed, T. E., & Hanna, J. M. (1986). Between- and within-race variation in acute cardiovascular responses to alcohol: Evidence for genetic determination in normal males in three races. *Behavioral Genetics, 16*, 585–598.

Reisine, T., & Pasternak, G. (1996). Opioid analgesics and antagonists. In A. G. Gilman, L. S. Goodman, J. G. Hardman, L. E. Limbard, P. B. Molinoff, & R. W. Ruddon (Eds.), *The pharmacological basis of therapeutics* (pp. 521–555). New York: McGraw-Hill.

Reissig, C. J., Strain, E. C., & Griffiths, R. R. (2009). Caffeinated energy drinks—a growing problem. *Drug and Alcohol Dependence, 99*, 1–10.

Remington, G., & Kapur, S. (2000). Atypical antipsychotics: Are some more atypical than others? *Psychopharmacology, 148*, 3–15.

Resnick, R. B., Galanter, M., Pycha, C., et al. (1992). Buprenorphine: An alternative to methadone for heroin dependence treatment. *Psychopharmacology Bulletin, 28*, 109–113.

Rettig, J., & Neher, E. (2002). Emerging roles of presynaptic proteins in Ca^{++}-triggered exocytosis. *Science, 298*, 781–785.

Revicki, D. A. (1999). Pharmacoeconomic studies of atypical antipsychotic drugs for the treatment of schizophrenia. *Schizophrenia Research, 35*, S101–S109.

Revicki, D. A., Genduso, L. A., Hamilton, S. H., et al. (1999). Olanzapine versus haloperidol in the treatment of schizophrenia and other psychotic disorders: Quality of life and clinical outcomes of a randomized clinical trial. *Quality of Life Research, 8*, 417–426.

Rey, J., Sawyer, M., Raphael, B., et al. (2002). Mental health of teenagers who use cannabis. Results of an Australian survey. *British Journal of Psychiatry, 180*, 216–221.

Reynaert, C., Parent, M., Mirel, J., et al. (1995). Moclobemide versus fluoxetine for a major depressive episode. *Psychopharmacology, 118*, 183–187.

Richelson, E., & Souder, T. (2000). Binding of antipsychotic drugs to human brain receptors focus on newer generation compounds. *Life Sciences, 68*, 29–39.

Richerson, G. B., & Wu, Y. (2003). Dynamic equilibrium of neurotransmitter transporters: Not just for reuptake anymore. *Journal of Neurophysiology, 90*, 1363–1374.

Richmond, B., Liu, Z., & Shidara, M. (2003). Predicting future rewards. *Science, 301*, 179–180.

Rickels, K., Amsterdam, J., Clary, C., et al. (1990). Buspirone in depressed outpatients: A controlled study. *Psychopharmacology Bulletin, 26*, 163–168.

Rickert, V. I., Wiemann, C. M., & Berenson, A. B. (1999). Prevalence, patterns, and correlates of voluntary flunitrazepam use. *Pediatrics, 103*, E6.

Ridker, P. M., Vaughan, D. E., Stampfer, M. J., et al. (1994). Association of moderate alcohol consumption and plasma concentration of endogenous tissue-type plasminogen activator. *The Journal of the American Medical Association, 272*, 929–933.

Riggs, J. E. (1992). Cigarette smoking and Parkinson disease: The illusion of a neuroprotective effect. *Clinical Neuropharmacology, 15*, 88–99.

Riley, E. P., Mattson, S. N., Sowell, E. R., et al. (1995). Abnormalities of the corpus callosum in children prenatally exposed to alcohol. *Alcoholism, Clinical and Experimental Research, 19,* 1198–1202.

Risby, E. D. (1996). Ethnic considerations in the pharmacotherapy of mood disorders. *Psychopharmacology Bulletin, 32,* 231–234.

Risby, E. D., Epstein, C. M., Jewart, R. D., Nguyen, B. V., Morgan, W. N., Risch, S. C., et al. (1995). Clozapine-induced EEG abnormalities and clinical response to clozapine. *Journal of Neuropsychiatry and Clinical Neurosciences, 7,* 466–470.

Ritchie, C., Ames, D., Clayton, T., & Lai, R. (2004). Metaanalysis of randomized trials of the efficacy and safety of donepezil, galantamine, and rivastigmine for the treatment of Alzheimer disease. *American Journal of Geriatric Psychiatry, 12,* 358–369.

Ritchie, J. M. (1985). The aliphatic alcohols. In A. G. Gilman, L. S. Goodman, T. W. Rall, & F. Murad (Eds.), *The pharmacological basis of therapeutics* (pp. 372–386). New York: Macmillan.

Ritvo, E. R., & Freeman, B. S. (1984). A medical model of autism: Etiology, pathology and treatment. *Pediatric Annals, 13,* 298–305.

Ritz, M. C., Lamb, R. J., Goldberg, S. R., & Kuhar, M. J. (1987). Cocaine receptors on dopamine transporters are related to self-administration of cocaine. *Science, 237,* 1219–1223.

Robbins, S. J., Ehrman, R. N., Childress, A. R., et al. (2000). Mood state and recent cocaine use are not associated with levels of cocaine cue reactivity. *Drug and Alcohol Dependence, 59,* 33–42.

Robbins, T. W., & Everitt, B. J. (2007). A role for mesencephalic dopamine in activation: Commentary on Berridge (2006). *Psychopharmacology, 191,* 433–437.

Roberts, B. M., Seymour, P. A., Schmidt, C. J., Williams, G. V., & Castner, S. A. (2010). Amelioration of ketamine-induced working memory deficits by dopamine D1 receptor agonists. *Psychopharmacology, 210,* 407–418.

Robertson, I., Heather, N., Dzialdowski, A., et al. (1986). A comparison of minimal versus intensive controlled drinking treatment interventions for problem drinkers. *British Journal of Clinical Psychology, 25,* 185–194.

Robinson, D., Woerner, M., Alvir, J., et al. (1999). Predictors of treatment response from a first episode of schizophrenia or schizoaffective disorder. *American Journal of Psychiatry, 156,* 544–549.

Robinson, D., Woerner, M., Alvir, J. M., et al. (2002). Predictors of medication discontinuation by patients with first-episode schizophrenia and schizoaffective disorder. *Schizophrenia Research, 57,* 209–219.

Robinson, D., Woerner, M., McMeniman, M., et al. (2004). Symptomatic and functional recovery from a first episode of schizophrenia or schizoaffective disorder. *American Journal of Psychiatry, 161,* 473–479.

Robinson, T. E., & Becker, J. B. (1986). Enduring changes in brain and behavior produced by chronic amphetamine administration: A review and evaluation of animal models of amphetamine psychosis. *Brain Research, 396,* 157–198.

Robinson, T. E., & Berridge, C. (2001). Incentive-sensitization and addiction. *Addiction, 96,* 103–114.

Robinson, T. E., & Berridge, C. (2003). Addiction. *Annual Review of Psychology, 54,* 25–53.

Rodd, Z. A., Bell, R. L., Zhang, Y., Murphy, J. M., Goldstein, A., Zaffaroni, A., et al. (2005). Regional heterogeneity for the intracranial self-administration of ethanol and acetaldehyde within the ventral tegmental area of alcohol-preferring (P) rats: Involvement of dopamine and serotonin. *Neuropsychopharmacology, 30,* 330–338.

Rodriguez De Fonseca, F., Gorriti, M. A., Fernandez-Ruiz, J. J., et al. (1994). Down-regulation of rat brain cannabinoid binding sites after chronic delta 9-tetrahydro-cannabinol treatment. *Pharmacology, Biochemistry and Behavior, 47*, 33–40.

Rogers, P. J., Martin, J., Smith, C., et al. (2003). Absence of reinforcing, mood and psychomotor performance effects of caffeine in habitual non-consumers of caffeine. *Psychopharmacology, 167*, 54–62.

Roiser, J. P., & Sahakian, J. (2004). Relationship between ecstasy use and depression: A study controlling for poly-drug use. *Psychopharmacology, 173*, 411–417.

Roitman, M., Stuber, G., Phillips, P. E., Wightman, R. M., & Carelli, R. M. (2004). Dopamine operates as a subsecond modulator of food seeking. *Journal of Neuroscience, 24*, 1265–1271.

Romach, M. K., & Sellers, E. M. (1991). Management of the alcohol withdrawal syndrome. *Annual Review of Medicine, 42*, 323–340.

Romero, J., Garcia, L., Fernandez-Ruiz, J. J., et al. (1995). Changes in rat brain cannabinoid binding sites after acute or chronic exposure to their endogenous agonist, anandamide, or to delta 9-tetrahydrocannabinol. *Pharmacology, Biochemistry and Behavior, 51*, 731–737.

Rose, J., Branchey, M., Wallach, L., & Buydens-Branchey, L. (2003). Effects of buspirone in withdrawal from opiates. *American Journal on Addictions, 12*, 253–259.

Rosen, O. M. (1987). After insulin binds. *Science, 237*, 1452–1458.

Rosenberg, H., & Davis, L. (1994). Acceptance of moderate drinking by alcohol treatment services in the United States. *Journal of Studies on Alcohol, 55*, 167–172.

Rosenberg, H., Melville, J., Levell, D., & Hodge, J. E. (1992). A 10-year follow-up survey of acceptability of controlled drinking in Britain. *Journal of Studies on Alcohol, 53*, 441–446.

Ross, E. M., & Kenakin, T. P. (2001). Pharmacodynamics: Mechanisms of drug action and the relationship between drug concentration and effect. In J. G. Hardman & L. E. Limbird (Eds.), *Goodman & Gilman's The pharmacological basis of therapeutics* (10th ed., pp. 31–43). New York: McGraw-Hill.

Ross, G. W., Abbott, R. D., Petrovitch, H., et al. (2000). Association of coffee and caffeine intake with the risk of Parkinson disease. *The Journal of the American Medical Association, 283*, 2674–2679.

Roth, B. L., Tandra, S., Burgess, L. H., Sibley, D. R., & Meltzer, H. Y. (1995). D4 dopamine receptor binding affinity does not distinguish between typical and atypical antipsychotic drugs. *Psychopharmacology, 120*, 365–368.

Rougé-Pont, F., Marinelli, M., & Le Moal, M. L. (1995). Stress-induced sensitization and glucocorticoids. II. Sensitization of the increase in extracellular dopamine induced by cocaine depends on stress-induced corticosterone secretion. *Journal of Neuroscience, 15*, 7189–7195.

Rowbotham, M. C., & Lowenstein, D. H. (1990). Neurologic consequences of cocaine use. *Annual Review of Medicine, 41*, 417–422.

Roy-Byrne, P., Wingerson, D., Cowley, D., & Dager, S. (1993). Psychopharmacologic treatment of panic, generalized anxiety disorder, and social phobia. *Psychiatric Clinics of North America, 16*, 719–735.

Rudolph, R. L., & Feiger, A. D. (1999). A double-blind, randomized, placebo-controlled trial of once-daily venlafaxine extended release (XR) and fluoxetine for the treatment of depression. *Journal of Affective Disorders, 56*, 171–181.

Rudolph, U., Crestani, F., & Mohler, H. (2001). GABA(A) receptor subtypes: Dissecting their pharmacological functions. *Trends in Pharmacological Sciences, 22*, 188–194.

Rudorfer, M. V. (1992). Monoamine oxidase inhibitors: Reversible and irreversible. *Psychopharmacology Bulletin, 28*, 45–57.

Rudorfer, M. V. (1993). Challenges in medication clinical trials. *Psychopharmacology Bulletin, 29*, 35–44.

Rugino, T. A., & Samsock, C. (2003). Modafinil in children with attention-deficit hyperactivity disorder. *Pediatric Neurology, 29,* 136–142.

Ruhe, H. G., Mason, N. S., & Schene, A. H. (2007). Mood is indirectly related to serotonin, norepinephrine, and dopamine levels in humans: A meta-analysis of monoamine depletion studies. *Molecular Psychiatry, 12,* 331–359.

Rush, C. R. (1998). Behavioral pharmacology of zolpidem relative to benzodiazepines: A review. *Pharmacology, Biochemistry and Behavior, 61,* 253–269.

Russmann, S., Lauterburg, B., & Helbling, A. (2001). Kava hepatotoxicity. *Annals of Internal Medicine, 135,* 68–69.

Ryan, C. (1982). Alcoholism and premature aging: A neuropsychological perspective. *Alcoholism, Clinical and Experimental Research, 6,* 79–96.

Safferman, A., Leiberman, J. A., Kane, J. M., et al. (1991). Update on the clinical efficacy and side effects of clozapine. *Schizophrenia Bulletin, 17,* 247–257.

Sahley, T. L., & Panksepp, J. (1987). Brain opioids and autism: An updated analysis of possible linkages. *Journal of Autism and Developmental Disorders, 17,* 201–216.

Salamone, J. D. (1994). The involvement of nucleus accumbens dopamine in appetitive and aversive motivation. *Behavioural Brain Research, 61,* 117–133.

Salamone, J. D. (2002). Antidepressants and placebos: Conceptual problems and research strategies. *Prevention & Treatment, 5,* Article 24.

Salamone, J. D. (2006). Will the last person who uses the term "reward" please turn out the lights? Comments on processes related to reinforcement, learning, motivation and effort. *Addiction Biology, 11,* 43–44.

Salamone, J. D. (2010a). Facing dyskinesia in Parkinson's disease: Nondopaminergic approches. *Drugs of the Future, 35,* 567–573.

Salamone, J. D. (2010b). Involvement of nucleus accumbens dopamine in behavioral activation and effort-related functions. In L. L. Iversen, S. D. Iversen, S. B. Dunnett, & A. Bjorklund (Eds.), *Dopamine handbook* (pp. 286–300). Oxford, OH: Oxford University Press.

Salamone, J. D. (2010c). Preladenant, a novel adenosine A(2A) receptor antagonist for the potential treatment of parkinsonism and other disorders. *IDrugs, 13,* 723–731.

Salamone, J. D., Betz, A. J., Ishiwari, K., Felsted, J., Madson, L., Mirante, B., et al. (2008). Tremorolytic effects of adenosine A2A antagonists: Implications for parkinsonism. *Frontiers in Bioscience, 13,* 3594–3605.

Salamone, J. D., Correa, M., Mingote, S. M., Weber, S. M., Farrar, A. M. (2006). Nucleus Accumbens Dopamine and the forebrain circuitry involved in behavioral activation and effort-related decision making: implications for understanding anergia and psychomotor slowing in depression. *Current Psychiatry Reviews, 2,* 267–280.

Salamone, J. D., & Correa, M. (2002). Motivational views of reinforcement: Implications for understanding the behavioral functions of nucleus accumbens dopamine. *Behavioural Brain Research, 137,* 3–25.

Salamone, J. D., Correa, M., Carlson, B. B., Wisniecki, A., Mayorga, A. J., Nisenbaum, E., et al. (2001). Neostriatal muscarinic receptor subtypes involved in the generation of tremulous jaw movements in rodents: Implications for cholinergic involvement in parkinsonism. *Life Sciences, 68,* 2579–2584.

Salamone, J. D., Correa, M., Farrar, A. M., Nunes, E. J., & Collins, L. E. (2010). Role of dopamine-adenosine interactions in the brain circuitry regulating effort-related decision making: Insights into pathological aspects of motivation. *Future Neurology, 5,* 377–392.

Salamone, J. D., Correa, M., Farrar, A. M., Nunes, E. J., & Pardo, M. (2009). Dopamine, behavioral economics, and effort. *Frontiers in Behavioral Neuroscience, 3,* 13.

Salamone, J. D., Correa, M., Mingote, S., & Weber, S. M. (2003). Nucleus accumbens dopamine and the regulation of effort in food-seeking behavior: Implications for studies of natural motivation, psychiatry, and drug abuse. *Journal of Neuroscience, 305*, 1–8.

Salamone, J. D., Correa, M., Mingote, S. M., & Weber, S. M. (2005). Beyond the reward hypothesis: Alternative functions of nucleus accumbens dopamine. *Current Opinion in Pharmacology, 5*, 34–41.

Salamone, J. D., Correa, M., Mingote, S. M., Weber, S. M., Farrar, A. M. (2006). Nucleus Accumbens Dopamine and the forebrain circuitry involved in behavioral activation and effort-related decision making: implications for understanding anergia and psychomotor slowing in depression. *Current Psychiatry Reviews, 2*, 267–280.

Salamone, J. D., Cousins, M. S., & Snyder, B. J. (1997). Behavioral functions of nucleus accumbens dopamine: Empirical and conceptual problems with the anhedonia hypothesis. *Neuroscience & Biobehavioral Reviews, 21*, 341–359.

Salamone, J. D., Farrar, A. M., Font, L., Patel, V., Schlar, D. E., Nunes, E. J., et al. (2009). Differential actions of adenosine A1 and A2A antagonists on the effort-related effects of dopamine D2 antagonism. *Behavioural Brain Research, 201*, 216–222.

Salamone, J. D., Ishiwari, K., Betz, A. J., Farrar, A. M., Mingote, S. M., Font, L., et al. (2008). Dopamine/adenosine interactions related to locomotion and tremor in animal models: Possible relevance to parkinsonism. *Parkinsonism and Related Disorders, 14*, S130–S134.

Salamone, J. D., Mahan, K., & Rogers, S. (1993). Ventrolateral striatal dopamine depletions impair feeding and food handling in rats. *Pharmacology Biochemistry & Behavior, 44*, 605–610.

Salamone, J. D., McLaughlin, P. J., Sink, K., Makriyannis, A., & Parker, L. A. (2007). Cannabinoid CB(1) receptor inverse agonists and neutral antagonists: Effects on food intake, food-reinforced behavior and food aversions. *Physiology and Behavior, 91*, 383–388.

Salamone, J. D., Steinpreis, R. E., McCullough, L. D., Smith, P., Grebel, D., Mahan, K. (1991). Haloperidol and nucleus accumbens dopamine depletion suppress lever pressing for food but increase free food consumption in a novel food choice procedure. *Psychopharmacology, 104*, 515–521.

Saletu, B., Gruenberger, J., Linzmayer, L., et al. (1989). EEG-brain mapping, psychometric and psychophysiological studies on central effects of kavain: A kava plant derivative. *Human Psychopharmacology Clinical and Experimental, 4*, 169–190.

Salimpoor, V. N., Benovoy, M., Larcher, K., Dagher, A., & Zatorre, R. J. (2011). Anatomically distinct dopamine release during anticipation and experience of peak emotion to music. *Nature Neuroscience, 14*, 257–262.

Sallee, F. R., Stiller, R. L., & Perel, J. M. (1992). Pharmacodynamics of pemoline in attention deficit disorder with hyperactivity. *Journal of the American Academy of Child and Adolescent Psychiatry, 31*, 244–251.

Salzman, C. (1985). Geriatric psychopharmacology. *Annual Review of Medicine, 36*, 217–228.

Salzman, C. (1988). Treatment of agitation, anxiety, and depression. *Psychopharmacology Bulletin, 24*, 39–42.

Samaha, A., Mallet, N., Ferguson, S., et al. (2004). The rate of cocaine administration alters gene regulation and behavioral plasticity: Implications for addiction. *Journal of Neuroscience, 24*, 6362–6370.

Samson, H. H., & Chappell, A. M. (2004). Effects of raclopride in the core of the nucleus accumbens on ethanol seeking and consumption: The use of extinction trials to measure seeking. *Alcohol Clinical and Experimental Research, 28*, 544–549.

Samson, H. H., & Czachowski, C. L. (2003). Behavioral measures of alcohol self-administration and intake control: Rodent models. *International Reviews of Neurobiology, 54*, 107–143.

Sanchis-Segura, C., Lopez-Atalaya, J. P., & Barco, A. (2009). Selective boosting of transcriptional and behavioral responses to drugs of abuse by histone deacetylase inhibition. *Neuropsychopharmacology, 34,* 2642–2654.

Sanders-Bush, E., & Breeding, M. (1991). Choroid plexus epithelial cells in primary cultures: A model of 5HT1C receptor activation by hallucinogenic drugs. *Psychopharmacology, 105,* 340–346.

Sandor, P. (2003). Pharmacological management of tics in patients with TS. *Journal of Psychosomatic Research, 55,* 41–48.

Sanger, D. J., Benavides, J., Perrault, G., et al. (1994). Recent developments in the behavioral pharmacology of benzodiazepine (omega) receptors: Evi-dence for the functional significance of receptor subtypes. *Neuroscience & Biobehavioral Reviews, 18,* 355–372.

Sanger, D. J., & Blackman, D. E. (1974). Rate-dependent effects of drugs: A review of the literature. *Pharmacology, Biochemistry and Behavior, 4,* 73–83.

Santarelli, L., Saxe, M., Gross, C., Surget, A., Battaglia, F., Dulawa, S., et al. (2003). Requirement of hippocampal neurogenesis for the behavioral effects of antidepressants. *Science, 301,* 805–809.

Sapolsky, R. M. (1996). Why stress is bad for your brain. *Science, 273,* 749–750.

Sarafian, T. A., Magallanes, J. A., Shau, H., et al. (1999). Oxidative stress produced by marijuana smoke: An adverse effect enhanced by cannabinoids. *American Journal of Respiratory Cell and Molecular Biology, 20,* 1286–1293.

Sarchiapone, M., Carli, V., Camardese, G., Cuomo, C., Di Guida, D., Calgagni, M. L., et al. (2006). Dopamine transporter binding in depressed patients with anhedonia. *Psychiatric Research: Neuroimaging, 147,* 243–248.

Sarter, M., Lustig, C., & Taylor, S. F. (2011). Cholinergic contributions to the cognitive symptoms of schizophrenia and the viability of cholinergic treatments. *Neuropharmacology* [Epub ahead of print].

Satel, S. L., Price, L. H., Palumbo, J. M., et al. (1991). Clinical phenomenology and neurobiology of cocaine abstinence: A prospective inpatient study. *American Journal of Psychiatry, 148,* 1712–1716.

Satel, S. L., Southwick, S. M., & Gawin, F. H. (1991). Clinical features of cocaine-induced paranoia. *American Journal of Psychiatry, 148,* 495–498.

Sato, M., Chen, C. C., Akiyama, K., et al. (1983). Acute exacerbation of paranoid psychotic state after long-term abstinence in patients with previous methamphetamine psychosis. *Biological Psychiatry, 18,* 429–440.

Saudou, F., & Hen, R. (1994). 5-Hydroxytryptamine receptor subtypes in vertebrates and invertebrates. *Neurochemistry International, 25,* 503–532.

Sawa, A., & Snyder, H. (2002). Schizophrenia: Diverse approaches to a complex disease. *Science, 296,* 692–695.

Sawyer, D. A., Julia, H. L., & Turin, A. C. (1982). Caffeine and human behavior: Arousal, anxiety, and performance effects. *Journal of Behavioral Medicine, 5,* 415–439.

Scallet, A. C. (1991). Neurotoxicology of cannabis and THC: A review of chronic exposure studies in animals. *Pharmacology, Biochemistry and Behavior, 40,* 671–676.

Schaeffer, J., Andrysiak, T., & Ungerleider, J. T. (1981). Cognition and long-term use of ganja (cannabis). *Science, 213,* 465–466.

Schanne, F. A. X., Zucker, A. H., & Farber, J. L. (1981). Alcohol-dependent liver cell necrosis in vitro: A new model. *Science, 212,* 338–340.

Schatzberg, A. F. (2003). Efficacy and tolerability of duloxetine, a novel dual reuptake inhibitor, in the treatment of major depressive disorder. *Journal of Clinical Psychiatry, 64*(Suppl. 13), 30–37.

Schelling, T. C. (1992). Addictive drugs: The cigarette experience. *Science, 255,* 430–433.

Schenker, S., & Speeg, K. V. (1990). The risk of alcohol intake in men and women. *New England Journal of Medicine, 322*, 127–129.

Schifano, F. (2004). A bitter pill. Overview of ecstasy (MDMA, MDA) related fatalities. *Psychopharmacology, 173,* 242–248.

Schimmer, B. P., & Parker, K. L. (1996). Adrenocorticotropic hormone; adrenocortical steroids and their synthetic analogs; inhibitors of the synthesis and actions of adrenocortical hormones. In A. G. Gilman, L. S. Goodman, J. G. Hardman, L. E. Limbard, P. B. Molinoff, & R. W. Ruddon (Eds.), *The pharmacological basis of therapeutics* (pp. 1459–1485). New York: McGraw-Hill.

Schinke, S. P., Tepavac, L., & Cole, K. C. (2000). Preventing substance use among Native American youth: Three-year results. *Addictive Behaviors, 25,* 387–397.

Schmidt, H. D., & Pierce, R. C. (2010). Cocaine-induced neuroadaptations in glutamate transmission: Potential therapeutic targets for craving and addiction. *Annals of the New York Acadami of Sciences, 1187,* 35–75.

Schotte, A., Janssen, P. F. M., Gommeren, W., Luyten, W. H. M. L., Van Gompel, P., Lesage, A. S., et al. (1996). Risperidone compared with new and reference antipsychotic drugs: In vitro and in vivo receptor binding. *Psychopharmacology, 124,* 57–73.

Schottenfeld, R. S., Pakes, J. R., Oliveto, A., et al. (1997). Buprenorphine vs methadone maintenance treatment for concurrent opioid dependence and cocaine abuse. *Archives of General Psychiatry, 54,* 713–720.

Schrader, E. (2000). Equivalence of St. John's wort extract (Ze 117) and fluoxetine: A randomized, controlled study in mild-moderate depression. *International Clinical Psychopharmacology, 15,* 61–68.

Schuckit, M. A. (1994a). A clinical model of genetic influences in alcohol dependence. *Journal of Studies on Alcohol, 55,* 5–17.

Schuckit, M. A. (1994b). Low level of response to alcohol as a predictor of future alcoholism. *American Journal of Psychiatry, 151,* 184–189.

Schulties, G., Weinberger, S. B., & Martinez, J. L., Jr. (1989). Plasma uptake and in vivo metabolism of (leu)enkephalin following its intraperitoneal administration to rats. *Peptides, 10,* 913–919.

Schultz, S. K., Miller, D. D., Arndt, S., et al. (1995). Withdrawal-emergent dyskinesia in patients with schizophrenia during antipsychotic discontinuation. *Biological Psychiatry, 38,* 713–719.

Schultz, W., & Dickinson, A. (2000). Neuronal coding of prediction errors. *Annual Review of Neuroscience, 23,* 473–500.

Schummers, J., & Browning, D. (2001). Evidence for a role for GABA(A) and NMDA receptors in ethanol inhibition of long-term potentiation. *Brain Research. Molecular Brain Research, 94,* 9–14.

Schuster, C. R., & Johanson, C. E. (1981). An analysis of drug-seeking behavior in animals. *Neuroscience and Biobehavioral Reviews, 5,* 315–324.

Schvehla, T. J., Mandoki, M. W., & Sumner, G. S. (1994). Clonidine therapy for comorbid attention deficit hyperactivity disorder and conduct disorder: Preliminary findings in a children's inpatient unit. *Southern Medical Journal, 87,* 692–695.

Schwartz, T. L., Nihalani, N., Jindal, S., et al. (2004). Psychiatric medication-induced obesity: A review. *Obesity Reviews, 5,* 115–121.

Schwarzschild, M. A., Schwid, S. R., Marek, K., Watts, A., Lang, A. E., Oakes, D., et al. (2008). Serum urate as a predictor of clinical and radiographic progression in Parkinson disease. *Archives of Neurology, 65,* 716–723.

Sdao-Jarvie, K., & Vogel-Sprott, M. (1986). Mental rehearsal of a task before or after ethanol: Tolerance facilitating effects. *Drug and Alcohol Dependence, 18,* 23–30.

Sedvall, G., & Farde, L. (1995). Chemical brain anatomy in schizophrenia. *Lancet, 346,* 743–749.

Sedvall, G., Farde, L., Hall, H., et al. (1995). Utilization of radioligands in schizophrenia research. *Clinical Neuroscience, 3,* 112–121.

Seeman, P. (1987). Dopamine receptors and the dopamine hypothesis of schizophrenia. *Synapse, 1,* 133–152.

Seeman, P., Guan, H. C., & Van Tol, H. H. (1995). Schizophrenia: Elevation of dopamine D4-like sites, using [3H]nemonapride and [125I]epidepride. *European Journal of Pharmacology, 286,* R3–R5.

Seeman, P., & Lee, T. (1975). Antipsychotic drugs: Direct correlation between clinical potency and presynaptic action on dopamine neurons. *Science, 188,* 1217–1219.

Seeman, P., Lee, T., Chau-Wong, M., & Wong, K. (1976). Antipsychotic drug doses and neuroleptic/dopamine receptors. *Nature, 261,* 717–719.

Segovia, K. N., Vontel, R., Sink, K., Salamone, J. D., & Correa, M. (2009). Cellular activation as measured by c-FOS immunoreactivity after central and peripheral administration of ethanol and acetaldehyde. *Behavioural Pharmacology, 20,* S25.

Segraves, R. T. (1998). Antidepressant-induced sexual dysfunction. *Journal of Clinical Psychiatry, 59,* 48–54.

Seiden, L. S., & Dykstra, L. A. (1977). *Psychopharmacology: A biochemical and behavioral approach.* New York: Van Nostrand Reinhold.

Self, D. W., Barnhart, W. J., Lehman, D. A., & Nestler, E. J. (1996). Opposite modulation of cocaine-seeking behavior by D1 and D2-like dopamine receptor agonists. *Science, 271,* 1586–1589.

Self, D. W., & Nestler, E. J. (1995). Molecular mechanisms of drug reinforcement and addiction. *Annual Review of Neuroscience, 18,* 463–495.

Sell, L., Morris, J., Bearn, J., et al. (1999). Activation of reward circuitry in human opiate addicts. *European Journal of Neuroscience, 11,* 1042–1048.

Sellers, E. M., & Tyndale, R. F. (2000). Mimicking gene defects to treat drug dependence. *Annals of the New York Academy of Sciences, 909,* 233–246.

Sellings, L. H., McQuade, L. E., & Clarke, P. B. (2006). Evidence for multiple sites within rat ventral striatum mediating cocaine-conditioned place preference and locomotor activation. *Journal of Pharmacology Experimental Therapeutics, 317,* 1178–1187.

Sereny, G., Sharma, V., Holt, J., & Gordis, E. (1986). Mandatory supervised antabuse therapy in an outpatient alcoholism program: A pilot study. *Alcohol Clinical and Experimental Research, 10,* 290–292.

Shadel, W. G., Shiffman, S., Niaura, R., et al. (2000). Current models of nicotine dependence: What is known and what is needed to advance understanding of tobacco etiology among youth. *Drug and Alcohol Dependence, 59,* S9–S21.

Shaper, A. G., & Wannamethee, S. G. (2000). Alcohol intake and mortality in middle aged men with diagnosed coronary heart disease. *Heart, 83,* 394–399.

Shapiro, A. K., & Shapiro, E. S. (1980). *Tics, Tourette syndrome and other movement disorders.* New York: Tourette Syndrome Association, Inc.

Sharp, W., Gottesman, R., Greenstein, D., et al. (2003). Monozygotic twins discordant for attention-deficit/hyperactivity disorder: Ascertainment and clinical characteristics. *Journal of the American Academy of Child and Adolescent Psychiatry, 42,* 93–97.

Shean, M. L., & Duester, G. (1993). The role of alcohol dehydrogenase in retinoic acid homeostasis and fetal alcohol syndrome. *Alcohol and Alcoholism, 2*(Suppl.), 51–56.

Shearer, J., Wodak, A., van Beek, I., et al. (2003). Pilot randomized double blind placebo-controlled study of dexamphetamine for cocaine dependence. *Addiction (Abingdon England), 98*(8), 1137–1141.

Sheehan, D. V., Raj, A. B., Harnett-Sheehan, K., Soto, S., & Knapp, E. (1993). The relative efficacy of high-dose buspirone and alprazolam in the treatment of panic disorder: A double-blind placebo-controlled study. *Acta Psychiatrica Scandinavica, 18,* 1–11.

Sheline, Y., Gado, M., & Kraemer, H. C. (2003). Untreated depression and hippocampal volume loss. *American Journal of Psychiatry, 160,* 1516–1518.

Shen, M., & Thayer, S. A. (1998). Cannabinoid receptor agonists protect cultured rat hippocampal neurons from excitoticity. *Molecular Pharmacology, 54,* 459–462.

Shen, W., Hamilton, S. E., Nathanson, N. M., & Surmeier, D. J. (2005). Cholinergic suppression of KCNQ channel currents enhances excitability of striatal medium spiny neurons. *Journal of Neuroscience, 25,* 7449–7458.

Sheng, M., & Kim, J. (2002). Postsynaptic signaling and plasticity mechanisms. *Science, 298,* 776–780.

Sheppard, S. G. (1994). A preliminary investigation of ibogaine: Case reports and recommendations for further study. *Journal of Substance Abuse Treatment, 11,* 379–385.

Sher, K., Gershuny, B., Peterson, L., & Raskin, G. (1997). The role of childhood stressors in the intergenerational transmission of alcohol use disorders. *Journal of Studies on Alcohol, 58,* 414–427.

Sherwood, N. (1993). Effects of nicotine on human psychomotor performance. *Human Psychopharmacology: Clinical and Experimental, 8,* 155–184.

Shevell, M., & Schreiber, R. (1997). Pemoline-associated hepatic failure: A critical analysis of the literature. *Pediatric Neurology, 16,* 14–16.

Shibata, S., Yamashita, K., Yamamoto, E., Ozaki, T., & Ueki, S. (1989). Effects of benzodiazepine and GABA antagonists on anticonflict effects of antianxiety drugs injected into the rat amygdala in a water-lick suppression test. *Psychopharmacology, 98,* 38–44.

Shizgal, P., & Arvanitogiannis, A. (2003). Gambling on dopamine. *Science, 299,* 1856–1858.

Shoaf, S. E., & Linnoila, M. (1991). Interaction of ethanol and smoking on the pharmacokinetics and pharmacodynamics of psychotropic medications. *Psychopharmacology Bulletin, 27,* 577–609.

Short, P. H., & Shuster, L. (1976). Changes in brain norepinephrine associated with sensitization to d-amphetamine. *Psychopharmacology, 48,* 59–67.

Siegel, R. K. (1979). Natural animal addictions: An ethological perspective. In J. D. Keehn (Ed.), *Psychopathology in animals.* New York: Academic Press.

Siegel, R. K. (1986). MDMA: Nonmedical use and intoxication. *Journal of Psychoactive Drugs, 18,* 349–354.

Siegel, R. K. (1989). *Intoxication.* New York: Pocket Books.

Siegel, R. K., & Jarvik, M. E. (1980). DMT self-administration by monkeys in isolation. *Bulletin of the Psychonomic Society, 16,* 117–120.

Siegel, S., Baptista, M., Kim, J., et al. (2000). Pavlovian psychopharmacology: The associative basis of tolerance. *Experimental and Clinical Psychopharmacology, 8,* 276–293.

Sigvardsson, S., Bohman, M., & Cloninger, C. R. (1996). Replication of the Stockholm Adoption Study of alcoholism. Confirmatory cross-fostering analysis. *Archives of General Psychiatry, 53,* 681–687.

Silbersweig, D. A., Stern, E., Frith, C., et al. (1995). A functional neuroanatomy of hallucinations in schizophrenia. *Nature, 378,* 176–179.

Silling, S. M. (1980, January). LSD flashbacks: An overview of the literature for counselors. *American Mental Health Counselors Association Journal, 2,* 39–45.

Silvestri, R., Raffaele, M., De Dominico, P., et al. (1994). Serotoninergic agents in the treatment of Gilles de la Tourette's syndrome. *Acta Neurologica, 16,* 58–63.

Sim-Selley, L. J., Selley, D. E., Vogt, L. J., et al. (2000). Chronic heroin self-administration desensitizes opioid receptor-activated G-proteins in specific regions of rat brain. *Journal of Neuroscience, 20,* 4555–4562.

Simola, N., Fenu, S., Baraldi, P. G., Tabrizi, M. A., & Morelli, M. (2004). Blockade of adenosine A2A receptors antagonizes parkinsonian tremor in the rat tacrine model by an action on specific striatal regions. Experimental Neurology, 189, 182–188.

Simon, G. E., VonKorff, M., Piccinelli, M., et al. (1999). An international study of the relation between somatic symptoms and depression. *New England Journal of Medicine, 341,* 1329–1335.

Simons, J., Correia, C. J., & Carey, K. B. (2000). A comparison of motives for marijuana and alcohol use among experienced users. *Addictive Behaviors, 25,* 153–160.

Simpson, D. D., Joe, G. W., Fletcher, B. W., et al. (1999). A national evaluation of treatment outcomes for cocaine dependence. *Archives of General Psychiatry, 56,* 507–514.

Simpson, G. M. (2000). The treatment of tardive dyskinesia and tardive dystonia. *Journal of Clinical Psychiatry, 61*(Suppl. 4), 39–44.

Singer, H. S., Brown, J., Quaskey, S., et al. (1995). The treatment of attention-deficit hyperactivity disorder in Tourette's syndrome: A double-blind placebo-controlled study with clonidine and desipramine. *Pediatrics, 95,* 74–81.

Singer, L., Minnes, S., Short, E., Arendt, R., Farkas, K., Lewis, B., et al. (2004). Cognitive outcomes of preschool children with prenatal cocaine exposure. *The Journal of the American Medical Association, 291,* 2448–2456.

Sink, K. S., McLaughlin, P. J., Wood, J. A., Brown, C., Fan, P., Vemuri, V. K., et al. (2008). The novel cannabinoid CB(1) receptor neutral antagonist AM4113 suppresses food intake and food-reinforced behavior but does not induce signs of nausea in rats. *Neuropsychopharmacology, 43,* 946–955.

Sink, K. S., Segovia, K. N., Sink, J., Randall, P. A., Collins, L. E., Correa, M., et al. (2010). Potential anxiogenic effects of cannabinoid CB1 receptor antagonists/inverse agonists in rats: Comparisons between AM4113, AM251, and the benzodiazepine inverse agonist FG-7142. *European Neuropsychopharmacology, 20,* 112–122.

Skradski, S., & White, S. (2000). Topiramate blocks kainate-evoked cobalt influx into cultured neurons. *Epilepsia, 41*(Suppl. 1), S45–S47.

Slifer, B. L., & Dykstra, L. A. (1987). Discriminative stimulus effects of N-Allylnormetazocine in rats trained to discriminate a kappa from a sigma agonist. *Life Sciences, 40,* 343–349.

Sloman, L. (1991). Use of medication in pervasive developmental disorders. *Psychiatric Clinics of North America, 14,* 165–182.

Slutsker, L. (1992). Risks associated with cocaine use during pregnancy. *Obstetrics and Gynecology, 79,* 778–789.

Small, J. G., Klapper, M. H., Milstein, V., et al. (1996). Comparison of therapeutic modalities for mania. *Psychopharmacology Bulletin, 32,* 623–627.

Smart, R. G., & Ogborne, A. C. (2000). Drug use and drinking among students in 36 countries. *Addictive Behaviors, 25,* 455–460.

Smit, F., Bolier, L., & Cuijpers, P. (2004). Cannabis use and the risk of later schizophrenia: A review. *Addiction, 99,* 425–430.

Smith, G. D., & Griffin, J. F. (1978). Conformation of (leu5) enkephalin from x-ray diffraction: Features important for recognition at opiate receptor. *Science, 199,* 1214–1216.

Smith, J. E., & Meyers, R. J. (1995). The community reinforcement approach. In R. K. Hester & W. R. Miller (Eds.), *Handbook of alcoholism treatment approaches* (pp. 263–266). Boston, MA: Allyn & Bacon.

Smith, K., Larive, L., & Romanelli, F. (2002). Club drugs: Methylenedioxymethamphetamine, flunitrazepam, ketamine hydrochloride, and gamma-hydroxybutyrate. *American Journal of Health-System Pharmacy, 59,* 1067–1076.

Smith, M. L., & Glass, G. V. (1977). Meta-analysis of psychotherapy outcome studies. *American Psychologist, 32,* 752–760.

Smith, S. E., Pihl, R. O., Young, S. N., et al. (1987). A test of possible cognitive and environmental influences on the mood lowering effect of tryptophan depletion in normal males. *Psychopharmacology, 91*, 451–457.

Snyder, S. H., Banerjee, S. P., Yamamura, H. I., & Greenberg, D. (1974). Drugs, neurotransmitters and schizophrenia. *Science, 184*, 1243–1253.

Soares, B. G., Lima, M., Reisser, A. A., & Farrell, M. (2003). Dopamine agonists for cocaine dependence. *Cochrane Database of Systematic Reviews (Online: Update Software)*, no. 2, CD003352.

Soares, J. C., & Gershon, S. (1994). Advances in the pharmacotherapy of Alzheimer's disease. *European Archives of Psychiatry & Clinical Neuroscience, 244*, 261–271.

Sobrero, A. P., & Bouton, M. E. (1989). Effects of stimuli present during oral morphine administration on withdrawal and subsequent consumption. *Psychobiology, 17*, 179–190.

Sokol, R. J., Ager, J., Martier, S., et al. (1986). Significant determinants of susceptibility to alcohol teratogenicity. *Annals of the New York Academy of Sciences, 477*, 87–102.

Solomon, D. A., Keitner, G. I., Miller, I. W., et al. (1995). Course of illness and maintenance treatments for patients with bipolar disorder. *Journal of Clinical Psychiatry, 56*, 5–13.

Solowij, N., Hall, W., & Lee, N. (1992). Recreational MDMA use in Sydney: A profile of "Ecstasy" users and their experiences with the drug. *British Journal of Addiction, 87*, 1161–1172.

Solowij, N., Stephens, R., Roffman, R., et al. (2002). Cognitive functioning of long-term heavy cannabis users seeking treatment. *The Journal of the American Medical Association, 287*, 1123–1131.

Sommese, T., & Patterson, J. C. (1995). Acute effects of cigarette smoking withdrawal: A review of the literature. *Aviation Space and Environmental Medicine, 66*, 164–167.

Somoza, E., Winhusen, T., Bridge, T. P., et al. (2004). An open-label pilot study of methylphenidate in the treatment of cocaine dependent patients with adult attention deficit/hyperactivity disorder. *Journal of Addictive Diseases, 23*, 77–92.

Song, B. J., & Cederbaum, A. I. (1996). Ethanol inducible cytochrome P450 (CYP2E1): Biochemistry, molecular biology and clinical relevance: 1996 update. *Alcohol Clinical and Experimental Research, 20*, 138A–146A.

Song, I. U., Kim, J. S., Ryu, S. Y., Lee, S. B., An, J. Y., & Lee, K. S. (2008). Donepezil-induced jaw tremor. *Parkinsoniam and Related Disorders, 14*, 584–585.

Sonsalla, P. K., Nicklas, W. J., & Heikkila, R. E. (1989). Role for excitatory amino acids in methamphetamine-induced nigrostriatal dopaminergic toxicity. *Science, 243*, 398–400.

Sovner, R., Fox, C. J., Lowry, M. J., & Lowry, M. A. (1993). Fluoxetine treatment of depression and associated self-injury in two adults with mental retardation. *Journal of Intellectual Disability Research, 37*, 301–311.

Spealman, R. D., Barrett-Larimore, R. L., Rowlett, J. K., et al. (1999). Pharmacological and environmental determinants of relapse to cocaine-seeking behavior. *Pharmacology, Biochemistry and Behavior, 64*, 327–336.

Spear, B. (1994). The early years of the "British System" in practice. In J. Strang & M. Gossop (Eds.), *Heroin addiction and drug policy: The British System* (pp. 3–28). Oxford, OH: Oxford University Press.

Spencer, T., Biederman, J., Coffey, B., et al. (2002). A double-blind comparison of desipramine and placebo in children and adolescents with chronic tic disorder and comorbid attention-deficit/hyperactivity disorder. *Archives of General Psychiatry, 59*, 649–656.

Spina, L., Longoni, R., Vinci, S., Ibba, F., Peana, A. T., Muggironi, G., et al. (2010). Role of dopamine D1 receptors and extracellular signal regulated kinase in the motivational properties of acetaldehyde as assessed by place preference conditioning. *Alcoholism: Clinical and Experimental Research, 34,* 607–616.

Sprague, R. L., & Sleator, E. K. (1977). Methylphenidate in hyperkinetic children: Differences in dose effects on learning and social behavior. *Science, 198,* 1274–1276.

Spring, B., Chiodo, J., & Bowen, D. J. (1987). Carbohydrates, tryptophan, and behavior: A methodological review. *Psychological Bulletin, 102,* 234–256.

Squires, R. F., Lajtha, A., Saederup, E., & Palkovits, M. (1993). Reduced [3H]fluni-trazepam binding in cingulate cortex and hippocampus of postmortem schizophrenic brains: Is selective loss of glutamatergic neurons associated with major psychoses? *Neurochemical Research, 18,* 219–223.

Sramek, J. J., Hong, W. W., Hamid, S., et al. (1999). Meta-analysis of the safety and tolerability of two dose regimens of buspirone in patients with persistent anxiety. *Depression and Anxiety, 9,* 131–134.

Stahl, S. M. (1998). Mechanism of action of serotonin selective reuptake inhibitors: Serotonin receptors and pathways mediate therapeutic effects and side effects. *Journal of Affective Disorders, 51,* 215–235.

Stahl, S. M. (2002). The psychopharmacology of energy and fatigue. *Journal of Clinical Psychiatry, 63,* 7–8.

Staiger, P. K., Greeley, J. D., & Wallace, S. D. (1999). Alcohol exposure therapy: Generalization and changes in responsivity. *Drug and Alcohol Dependence, 57,* 29–40.

Standaert, D. G., & Young, A. B. (2001). Treatment of central nervous system degenerative disorders. In J. G. Hardman & L. E. Limbird (Eds.), *Goodman & Gilman's The pharmacological basis of therapeutics* (10th ed., pp. 549–567). New York: McGraw-Hill.

Steele, T. D., McCann, U. D., & Ricaurte, G. A. (1994). 3,4-Methylenedioxymethamphetamine (MDMA, "Ec-stasy"): Pharmacology and toxicology in animals and humans. *Addiction, 89,* 539–551.

Stefanski, R., Ladenheim, B., Lee, S. H., et al. (1999). Neuroadaptations in the dopaminergic system after active self-administration but not after passive administration of methamphetamine. *European Journal of Pharmacology, 371,* 123–135.

Stefanski, R., Lee, S., Yasar, S., et al. (2002). Lack of persistent changes in the dopaminergic system of rats withdrawn from methamphetamine self-administration. *European Journal of Pharmacology, 439,* 59–68.

Steinberg, J. R. (1994). Anxiety in elderly patients. A comparison of azapirones and benzodiazepines. *Drugs and Aging, 5,* 335–345.

Steingard, R., Biederman, J., Spencer, T., et al. (1993). Comparison of clonidine in the treatment of attention-deficit hyperactivity disorder with and without comorbid tic disorders. *Journal of the American Academy of Child and Adolescent Psychiatry, 32,* 350–353.

Steingard, R., & Dillon-Stout, D. (1992). Tourette's syndrome and obsessive compulsive disorder. Clinical aspects. *Psychiatric Clinics of North America, 15,* 849–860.

Stephens, R. C. (1987). *Mind-altering drugs.* Newbury Park, CA: Sage.

Steriade, M. (1996). Arousal: Revisiting the reticular activating system. *Science, 272,* 225–226.

Stewart, J. (1984). Reinstatement of heroin and cocaine self-administration behavior in the rat by intracerebral application of morphine in the ventral tegmental area. *Pharmacology, Biochemistry and Behavior, 20,* 917–923.

Stewart, J., & Eikelboom, R. (1987). Conditioned drug effects. In L. L. Iversen, S. D. Iversen, & Snyder S. H (Eds.), *Handbook of psychopharmacology* (Vol. 19, pp. 1–57). New York: Plenum Press.

Stewart, J., & Vezina, P. (1988). A comparison of the effects of intra-accumbens injections of amphetamine and morphine on reinstatement of heroin intravenous self-administration behavior. *Brain Research, 457*, 287–294.

Stimmel, G. L. (1996). Benzodiazepines in schizophrenia. *Pharmacotherapy, 16*, 1485–1515.

Stine, S. M., & Kosten, T. R. (1994). Reduction of opiate withdrawal-like symptoms by cocaine abuse during methadone and buprenorphine maintenance. *American Journal of Drug & Alcohol Abuse, 20*, 445–458.

Stinus, L., Allard, M., Gold, L., & Simonnet, G. (1995). Changes in CNS neuropeptide FF-like material, pain sensitivity, and opiate dependence following chronic morphine treatment. *Peptides, 16*, 1235–1241.

Stitzer, M. L., Bickel, W. K., Bigelow, G. E., & Liebson, I. A. (1986). Effect of methadone dose contingencies on urinalysis test results of polydrug-abusing methadone-maintenance patients. *Drug and Alcohol Dependence, 18*, 341–348.

Stockwell, T. (1995). Anxiety and stress management. In R. K. Hester & W. R. Miller (Eds.), *Handbook of alcoholism treatment approaches* (pp. 242–250). Boston, MA: Allyn & Bacon.

Stolerman, I. P., & Jarvis, M. J. (1995). The scientific case that nicotine is addictive. *Psychopharmacology Bulletin, 117*, 2–10.

Stoneburner, R. L., Des Jarlais, D. C., Benezra, D., et al. (1988). A larger spectrum of severe HIV-1-related disease in intravenous drug users in New York City. *Science, 242*, 916–919.

Strakowski, S. M., & Sax, K. W. (1998). Progressive behavioral response to repeated d-amphetamine challenge: Further evidence for sensitization in humans. *Biological Psychiatry, 44*, 1171–1177.

Strakowski, S. M., Sax, K. W., Rosenberg, H., et al. (2001). Human response to repeated low-dose d-amphetamine: Evidence for behavioral enhancement and tolerance. *Neuropsychopharmacology, 25*, 548–554.

Strakowski, S. M., Sax, K. W., Setters, M. J., et al. (1996). Enhanced response to repeated d-amphetamine challenge: Evidence for behavioral sensitization in humans. *Biological Psychiatry, 40*, 872–880.

Strang, J., Powis, B., Best, D., et al. (1999). Preventing opiate overdose fatalities with take-home naloxone: Pre-launch study of possible impact and acceptability. *Addiction, 94*, 199–204.

Strassman, R. J. (1996). Human psychopharmacology of N, N-dimethyltryptamine. *Behavioral Brain Research, 73*, 121–124.

Strassman, R. J., Qualls, C. R., Uhlenhuth, E. H., & Kellner, R. (1994). Dose-response study of n,N-Dimethyltryptamine in humans. *Archives of General Psychiatry, 51*, 98–108.

Streissguth, A. P., Randels, S. P., & Smith, D. F. (1991). A test-retest study of intelligence in patients with fetal alcohol syndrome: Implications for care. *Journal of the American Academy of Child and Adolescent Psychiatry, 30*, 584–587.

Stripling, J. S., & Ellinwood, E. H. (1977). Sensitization to cocaine following chronic administration in the rat. In E. H. Ellinwood & M. M. Kilbey (Eds.), *Cocaine and other stimulants* (pp. 327–352). New York: Plenum Press.

Strous, R., Maayan, R., Lapidus, R., et al. (2003). Dehydroepiandrosterone augmentation in the management of negative, depressive, and anxiety symptoms in schizophrenia. *Archives of General Psychiatry, 60*, 133–141.

Sullivan, E. V., & Marsh, L. (2003). Hippocampal volume deficits in alcoholic Korsakoff's syndrome. *Neurology, 61*, 1716–1719.

Sullivan, E. V., Rohlfing, T., & Pfefferbaum, A. (2010). Pontocerebellar volume deficits and ataxia in alcoholic men and women: No evidence for "telescoping". *Psychopharmacology, 208*, 279–290.

Sulzer, D., Chen, T. K., Lau, Y. Y., et al. (1995). Amphetamine redistributes dopamine from synaptic vesicles to the cytosol and promotes reverse transport. *Journal of Neuroscience, 15*, 4102–4108.

Sulzer, D., Joyce, M. P., & Lin, L. (1998). Dopamine neurons make glutamatergic synapses in vitro. *Journal of Neuroscience, 18*, 4588–4602.

Suwaki, H., Kalant, H., Higuchi, S., et al. (2001). Recent research on alcohol tolerance and dependence. *Alcoholism, Clinical and Experimental Research, 25*, 189S–196S.

Svanum, S., & Schladenhauffen, J. (1986). Lifetime and recent alcohol consumption among male alcoholics. *Journal of Nervous and Mental Disease, 174*, 214–220.

Swanson, J. A., Lee, J. W., & Hopp, J. W. (1994). Caffeine and nicotine: A review of their joint use and possible interactive effects in tobacco withdrawal. *Addictive Behaviors, 19*, 229–256.

Swanson, J. M., Cantwell, D., Lerner, M., et al. (1991). Effects of stimulant medication on learning in children with ADHD. *Journal of Learning Disabilities, 24*, 219–230.

Swanson, J. M., & Kinsbourne, M. (1976). Stimulant-related state-dependent learning in hyperactive children. *Science, 192*, 1354–1356.

Swindle, R. W., Cronkite, R. C., & Moos, R. H. (1998). Risk factors for sustained nonremission of depressive symptoms: A 4-year follow-up. *Journal of Nervous and Mental Disorders, 186*, 462–469.

Szasz, T. (1974). *Ceremonial chemistry*. New York: Anchor Press/Doubleday.

Tabakoff, B., & Hoffman, P. L. (1996). Alcohol addiction: An enigma among us. *Neuron, 16*, 909–912.

Taddese, A., Seung-Yeol, N., & McCleskey, E. W. (1995). Selective opioid inhibition of small nociceptive neurons. *Science, 270*, 1366–1369.

Tadori, Y., Forbes, R. A., McQuade, R. D., & Kikuchi, T. (2008). Characterization of aripiprazole partial agonist activity at human dopamine D3 receptors. *European Journal of Pharmacology, 597*, 27–33.

Taj, R., Keenan, E., & O'Connor, J. J. (1995). A review of patients on methadone maintenance. *Irish Medical Journal, 88*, 218–219.

Tammiga, C. A., Schaffer, M. H., & Davis, J. M. (1978). Schizophrenic symptoms improve with apomorphine. *Science, 200*, 567–568.

Tampier, L., Quintanilla, M. E., & Israel, Y. (2008). Tolerance to disulfiram induced by chronic alcohol intake in the rat. *Alcohol Clinical and Experimental Research, 32*, 937–941.

Tancer, M., & Johanson, C.-E. (2003). Reinforcing, subjective, and physiological effects of MDMA in humans: A comparison with d-amphetamine and mCPP. *Drug and Alcohol Dependence, 72*, 33–44.

Tanda, G., Munzar, P., & Golderg, S. R. (2000). Self-administration behavior is maintained by the psychoactive ingredient of marijuana in squirrel monkeys. *Nature Neuroscience, 3*, 1073–1074.

Tannock, R., Ickowicz, A., & Schachar, R. (1995). Differential effects of methylphenidate on working memory in ADHD children with and without comorbid anxiety. *Journal of the American Academy of Child and Adolescent Psychiatry, 34*, 886–896.

Tariot, P., Farlow, M., Grossberg, G., et al. (2004). Memantine treatment in patients with moderate to severe Alzheimer disease already receiving donepezil: A randomized controlled trial. *The Journal of the American Medical Association, 291*, 317–324.

Tarsy, D. (1983). Neuroleptic-induced extrapyramidal reactions: Classification, description and diagnosis. *Clin Neuropsychopharmacology, 6*, s9–s26.

Tashkin, D. P., Simmons, M. S., Sherrill, D. L., et al. (1997). Heavy habitual marijuana smoking does not cause an accelerated decline in FEVI with age. *American Journal of Respiratory and Critical Care Medicine, 155*, 141–148.

Tauscher, J., Hussain, T., Agid, O., et al. (2004). Equivalent occupancy of dopamine D1 and

D2 receptors with clozapine: Differentiation from other atypical antipsychotics. *American Journal of Psychiatry, 161,* 1620–1625.

Taylor, P. (1985). Cholinergic agonists. In A. G. Gilman, L. S. Goodman, T. W. Rall, & F. Murad (Eds.), *The pharmacological basis of therapeutics* (pp. 100–109). New York: Macmillan.

Tecce, J. J., & Cole, J. O. (1974). Amphetamine effects in man: Paradoxical drowsiness and lowered electrical brain activity (CNV). *Science, 185,* 451–453.

Tempesta, E., Janiri, L., Bignamini, A., et al. (2000). Acamprosate and relapse prevention in the treatment of alcohol dependence: A placebo-controlled study. *Alcohol and Alcoholism, 35,* 202–209.

Tennant, F. S., Rawson, R. A., Pumphrey, E., & Seecof, R. (1986). Clinical experiences with 959 opioid-dependent patients treated with levo-alpha-acetylmethadol (LAAM). *Journal of Substance Abuse Treatment, 3,* 195–202.

Thase, M. E. (1999). How should efficacy be evaluated in randomized clinical trials of treatments for depression? *Journal of Clinical Psychiatry, 60,* 23–31.

Thomas, S. R., Lewis, M. E., & Iversen, S. D. (1985). Correlation of [3H]diazepam binding density with anxiolytic locus in the amygdaloid complex of the rat. *Brain Research, 342,* 85–90.

Thomasius, R., Petersen, K., Buchert, R., et al. (2003). Mood, cognition and serotonin transporter availability in current and former ecstasy (MDMA) users. *Psychopharmacology, 167,* 85–96.

Thompson, C. (1999). Mirtazapine versus selective serotonin reuptake inhibitors. *Journal of Clinical Psychiatry, 60,* 18–22.

Thompson, P. M., Hayashi, K. M., Simon, S. L., et al. (2004). Structural abnormalities in the brains of human subjects who use methamphetamine. *Journal of Neuroscience, 24,* 6028–6036.

Thompson, T., & Johanson, C. E. (Eds.). (1981). *Behavioral pharmacology of human drug dependence.* Rockville, MD: National Institute on Drug Abuse.

Thurstin, A. H., Alfano, A. M., & Sherer, M. (1986). Pretreatment MMPI profiles of A.A. Members and nonmembers. *Journal of Studies on Alcohol, 47,* 468–471.

Tiffany, S. T., Petrie, E. C., Baker, T. B., & Dahl, J. L. (1983). Conditioned morphine tolerance in the rat: Absence of a compensatory response and cross-tolerance with stress. *Behavioral Neuroscience, 97,* 335–353.

Tinley, E. M., Yeomans, M. R., & Durlach, P. J. (2003). Caffeine reinforces flavour preference in caffeine-dependent, but not long-term withdrawn, caffeine consumers. *Psychopharmacology, 166,* 416–423.

Tollefson, G. D. (1991). Antidepressant treatment and side effect consideration. *Journal of Clinical Psychiatry, 52*(Suppl.), 4–13.

Tosteson, D. C. (1981). Lithium and mania. *Scientific American, 244,* 164–174.

Tourette's Syndrome Study Group. (2002). Treatment of ADHD in children with tics: A randomized controlled trial. *Neurology, 58,* 527–536.

Treadway, M. T., & Zald, D. H. (2011). Reconsidering anhedonia in depression: Lessons from translational neuroscience. *Neuroscience and Biobehavioral Reviews, 35,* 537–555.

Treit, D., Engin, E., & McEown, K. (2010). Animal models of anxiety and anxiolytic drug action. *Current Topics in Behavioral Neuroscience, 2,* 121–160.

Trevitt, J. T., Atherton, A., Aberman, J., & Salamone, J. D. (1998). Effects of subchronic administration of clozapine, thioridazine and haloperidol on tests related to extrapyramidal motor function in the rat. *Psychopharmacology, 137,* 61–66.

Trevitt, J. T., Carlson, B. B., & Salamone, J. D. (1999). Behavioral assessment of atypical antipsychotics in rats: Studies of the effects of olanzapine (Zyprexa). *Psychopharmacology, 145,* 309–316.

Trevitt, J. T., Lyons, M., Aberman, J., Carriero, D., Finn, M., & Salamone, J. D. (1997) Effects of clozapine, thioridazine, risperidone, and haloperidol on behavioral tests related to extrapyramidal motor function. *Psychopharmacology, 132,* 74–81.

Troisi, A., Vicario, E., Nuccetelli, F., et al. (1995). Effects of fluoxetine on aggressive behavior of adult inpatients with mental retardation and epilepsy. *Pharmacopsychiatry, 28,* 73–76.

Trujillo, K. A., & Akil, H. (1994). Inhibition of opiate tolerance by non-competitive N-methyl-D-aspartate receptor antagonists. *Brain Research, 633,* 178–188.

Tsai, G., Crisostomo, G., Rosenblatt, M. L., & Stern, T. A. (1995). Neuroleptic malignant syndrome associated with clozapine treatment. *Annals of Clinical Psychiatry, 7,* 91–95.

Tsai, S. J., Hong, C. J., & Liou, Y. J. (2010). Effects of BDNF polymorphisms on antidepressant action. *Psychiatry Investigations, 7,* 236–242.

Tsuang, M. (2000). Schizophrenia: Genes and environment. *Biological Psychiatry, 47,* 210–220.

Tsuang, M. T., Stone, W. S., & Faraone, S. V. (2000). Towards the prevention of schizophrenia. *Biological Psychiatry, 48,* 349–356.

Tsuzuki, K., Xing, H., Ling, J., & Gu, J. G. (2004). Menthol-induced Ca^{2+} release from presynaptic Ca^{2+} stores potentiates sensory synaptic transmission. *Journal of Neuroscience, 24,* 762–771.

Turkington, D., Hedwat, D., Rider, I., & Young, A. H. (2004). Recovery from chronic fatigue syndrome with modafinil. *Human Psychopharmacology, 19,* 63–64.

Turner, D., Clark, L., Pomarol-Clotet, E., et al. (2004). Modafinil improves cognition and attentional set shifting in patients with chronic schizophrenia. *Neuropsychopharmacology, 29*(7), 1363–1373.

Turner, D., Robbins, T., Clark, L., et al. (2003). Cognitive enhancing effects of modafinil in healthy volunteers. *Psychopharmacology, 165,* 260–269.

Tylee, A., Gastpar, M., Lepine, J. P., & Mendlewicz, J. (1999). DEPRES II (Depression Research in European Society II): A patient survey of the symptoms, disability and current management of depression in the community. *International Clinical Psychopharmacology, 14,* 139–151.

U.S. Modafinil in Narcolepsy Multicenter Study Group. (2000). Randomized trial of modafinil as a treatment for the excessive daytime somnolence of narcolepsy. *Neurology, 54,* 1166–1175.

Ulus, I. H., Maher, T. J., & Wurtman, R. J. (2000). Characterization of phentermine and related compounds as monoamine oxidase (MAO) inhibitors. *Biochemical Pharmacology, 59,* 1611–1621.

Ungerstedt, U. (1971a). Adipsia and aphagia after 6-hydroxydopamine induced degeneration of the nigro-striatal dopamine system. *Acta Physiologica Scandinavia, 367*(Suppl.), 95–122.

Ungerstedt, U. (1971b). Postsynaptic supersensitivity after 6-hydroxy-dopamine induced degeneration of the nigro-striatal dopamine system. *Acta Physiologica Scandinavia, 367,* 69–93.

Unterwald, E. M., Ho, A., Rubenfeld, J. M., & Kreek, M. J. (1994a). Time course of the development of behavioral sensitization and dopamine receptor up-regulation during binge cocaine administration. *Journal of Pharmacology and Experimental Therapeutics, 270,* 1387–1396.

Unterwald, E. M., Rubenfeld, J. M., & Kreek, M. J. (1994b). Repeated cocaine administration upregulates kappa and mu, but not delta, opioid receptors. *Neuroreport, 5,* 1613–1616.

Urban, T. J. (2010). Race, ethnicity, ancestry, and pharmacogenetics. *Mount Sinai Journal of Medicine, 77,* 133–139.

Usdin, E. (1978). Classification of psychotropic drugs. In W. G. Clark & J. del Guidice (Eds.), *Principles of psychopharmacology* (pp. 193–246). New York: Academic Press.

Vaillant, G. E. (1988). What can long-term follow-up teach us about relapse and prevention of relapse in addiction? *British Journal of Addiction, 83,* 1147–1157.

Vaillant, G. E., & Milofsky, E. S. (1982). The etiology of alcoholism. *American Psychologist, 37,* 494–503.

Van Thiel, D. H., Gavaler, J., & Lester, R. (1974). Ethanol inhibition of vitamin a metabolism in the testes: Possible mechanism for sterility in alcoholics. *Science, 186,* 941–942.

Van Dyke, C., & Byck, R. (1982). Cocaine. *Scientific American, 246,* 128–141.

Vanderschuren, L. J. M. J., & Everitt, J. (2004). Drug seeking becomes compulsive after prolonged cocaine self-administration. *Science, 305,* 1017–1019.

Vanderschuren, L. J., & Pierce, R. C. (2010). Sensitization processes in drug addiction. *Current Topics in Behavioral Neuroscience, 3,* 179–195.

van den Hoogen, R. H. W. M., & Colpaert, F. C. (1987). Epidural and subcutaneous morphine, meperidine (pethidine), fentanyl and sufentanil in the rat: Analgesia and other in vivo pharmacologic effects. *Anesthesiology, 66,* 186–194.

VanDoren, M. J., Matthews, D. B., Janis, G. C., et al. (2000). Neuroactive steroid 3a-hydroxy-5a-pregnan-20-one modulates electrophysiological and behavioral actions of ethanol. *Journal of Neuroscience, 20,* 1982–1989.

VanDyke, C., & Byck, R. (1982). Cocaine. *Scientific American, 246,* 128–141.

Van Marum, R. J. (2008). Current and future therapy in Alzheimer's disease. *Fundamental and Clinical Pharmacology, 22,* 265–274.

Vanyukov, M. M., & Tarter, R. E. (2000). Genetic studies of substance abuse. *Drug and Alcohol Dependence, 59,* 101–123.

Vanyukov, M., Tarter, R., Kirisci, L., et al. (2003). Liability to substance use disorders: 1. Common mechanisms and manifestations. *Neuroscience and Biobehavioral Reviews, 27,* 507–515.

Vardy, M. M., & Kay, S. R. (1983). LSD psychosis or LSD-induced schizophrenia? *Archives of General Psychiatry, 40,* 877–883.

Varma, V. K., Malhotra, A. K., Dang, R., et al. (1988). Cannabis and cognitive functions: A perspective study. *Drug and Alcohol Dependence, 21,* 147–153.

Vega, W. A., Kolody, B., Hwang, J., & Noble, A. (1993). Prevalence and magnitude of perinatal substance exposures in California. *New England Journal of Medicine, 329,* 850–854.

Velders, F. P., Kuningas, M., Kumari, M., Dekker, M. J., Uitterlinden, A. G., Kirschbaum, C., et al. (2011). Genetics of cortisol secretion and depressive symptoms: A candidate gene and genome wide association approach. *Psychoneuroendocrinology* [Epub ahead of print].

Velicer, W. F., Hughes, S. L., Fava, J. L., et al. (1995). An empirical typology of subjects within stage of change. *Addictive Behaviors, 20,* 299–320.

Venugopalan, V. V., Casey, K. F., O'Hara, C., O'Loughlin, J., Benkelfat, C., Fellows, L. K., Leyton, M. (2011). Acute phenylalanine/tyrosine depletion reduces motivation to smoke cigarettes across stages of addiction. *Neuropsychopharmacology,* doi:10.1038/npp.2011.135. [Epub ahead of print]

Verbaten, M. N. (2003). Specific memory deficits in ecstasy users? The results of a meta-analysis. *Human Psychopharmacology, 18,* 281–290.

Verbaten, M. N., Overtoom, C. C., Koelega, H. S., et al. (1994). Methylphenidate influences on both early and late ERP waves of ADHD children in a continuous performance test. *Journal of Abnormal Child Psychology, 22,* 561–578.

Verghese, C., Kessel, J. B., & Simpson, G. M. (1991). Clinical pharmacokinetics of neuroleptics. *Psychopharmacology Bulletin, 27,* 541–564.

Verheyden, S., Henry, J., & Curran, H. V. (2003). Acute, sub-acute and long-term subjective consequences of "ecstasy" (MDMA) consumption in 430 regular users. *Human Psychopharmacology, 18,* 507–517.

Vezina, P. (2004). Sensitization of midbrain dopamine neuron reactivity and the self-administration of psychomotor stimulant drugs. *Neuroscience & Biobehavioral Reviews, 27,* 827–839.

Vezina, P., & Leyton, M. (2009). Conditioned cues and the expression of stimulant sensitization in animals and humans. *Neuropharmacology, 56*(Suppl. 1), 160–168.

Vezina, P., McGehee, D. S., & Green, W. N. (2007). Exposure to nicotine and sensitization of nicotine-induced behaviors. *Progress in Neuropsychopharmacology and Biological Psychiatry, 31,* 1625–1638.

Vigneswaran, N., Tilashalski, K., Rodu, B., & Cole, P. (1995). Tobacco use and cancer. A reappraisal. *Oral Surgery, Oral Medicine, Oral Pathology, Oral Radiology, and Endodontics, 80,* 178–182.

Vinci, S., Ibba, F., Longoni, R., Spina, L., Spiga, S., & Acquas, E. (2010). Acetaldehyde elicits ERK phosphorylation in the rat nucleus accumbens and extended amygdala. *Synapse, 64,* 916–927.

Viscusi, E., Reynolds, L., Chung, F., et al. (2004). Patient-controlled transdermal fentanyl hydrochloride vs intravenous morphine pump for postoperative pain: A randomized controlled trial. *The Journal of the American Medical Association, 291,* 1333–1341.

Volavka, J., & Cooper, T. B. (1987). Review of haloperidol blood level and clinical response: Looking through the window. *Journal of Clinical Psychopharmacology, 7,* 25–30.

Volavka, J., O'Donnell, J., Muragali, R., et al. (1986). Lithium and lecithin in tardive dyskinesia: An update. *Psychiatry Research, 19,* 101–104.

Volk, D. W., & Lewis, D. A. (2010). Prefrontal cortical circuits in schizophrenia. *Current Topics in Behavioral Neuroscience, 4,* 485–508.

Volkow, N. D., Chang, L., Wang, G. J., Fowler, J. S., Leonido-Yee, M., Franceschi, D., et al. (2001). Association of dopamine transporter reduction with psychomotor impairment in methamphetamine abusers. *American Journal of Psychiatry, 158,* 377–382.

Volkow, N. D., Ding, Y. S., Fowler, J. S., et al. (1995). Is methylphenidate like cocaine? Studies on their pharmacokinetics and distribution in the human brain. *Archives of General Psychiatry, 52,* 456–463.

Volkow, N. D., & Fowler, J. S. (2000). Addiction, a disease of compulsion and drive: Involvement of the orbitofrontal cortex. *Cerebral Cortex, 10,* 318–325.

Volkow, N. D., Fowler, J. S., Wang, G.-J., et al. (1993). Decreased dopamine D2 receptor availability is associated with reduced frontal metabolism in cocaine abusers. *Synapse, 14,* 169–177.

Volkow, N. D., Fowler, J. S., Wolf, A. P., et al. (1990). Effects of chronic cocaine abuse on postsynaptic dopamine receptors. *American Journal of Psychiatry, 147,* 719–724.

Volkow, N. D., Fowler, J. S., Wolf, A. P., et al. (1991). Changes in brain glucose metabolism in cocaine dependence and withdrawal. *American Journal of Psychiatry, 148,* 621–626.

Volkow, N. D., Wang, G. J., Fischman, M., et al. (2000). Effects of route of administration on cocaine induced dopamine transporter blockade in the human brain. *Life Sciences, 67,* 1507–1515.

Volkow, N. D., Wang, G. J., Fowler, J. S., et al. (2002). Relationship between blockade of dopamine transporters by oral methylphenidate and the increases in extracellular dopamine: Therapeutic implications. *Synapse, 43,* 181–187.

Volkow, N. D., Wang, G. J., Hitzemann, R., Fowler, J. S., Overall, J. E., Burr, G., et al. (1994). Recovery of brain glucose metabolism in detoxified alcoholics. *American Journal of Psychiatry, 151,* 178–183.

Vollenweider, F. X., Leenders, K., Scharfetter, C., et al. (1997). Positron emission tomography and fluorodeoxyglucose studies of metabolic hyperfrontality and psychopathology in the psilocybin model of psychosis. *Neuropsychopharmacology, 16,* 357–372.

Volpicelli, J. R., Clay, K. L., Watson, N. T., & O'Brien, C. P. (1995a). Naltrexone in the treatment of alcoholism: Predicting response to naltrexone. *Journal of Clinical Psychiatry, 57*(Suppl. 7), 39–44.

Volpicelli, J. R., Watson, N. T., King, A. C., et al. (1995b). Effect of naltrexone on alcohol "high" in alcoholics. *American Journal of Psychiatry, 152,* 613–615.

Volz, H. P., Heimann, H., Bellaire, J., et al. (1994). Brofaromine in non-endogenous major depressed inpatients-results of a preliminary dose-finding trial versus tranylcypromine. *Pharmacopsychiatry, 27,* 152–158.

Volz, H. P., & Laux, P. (2000). Potential treatment for subthreshold and mild depression: A comparison of St. John's wort extracts and fluoxetine. *Comprehensive Psychiatry, 41,* 133–137.

Volz, H. P., Muller, H., & Moller, H.-J. (1995). Are there any differences in the safety and efficacy of brofaromine and imipramine between non-elderly and elderly patients with major depression? *Neuropsychobiology, 32,* 23–30.

Vorel, S., Liu, X., Hayes, R., Spector, J., & Gardner, E. L. (2001). Relapse to cocaine-seeking after hippocampal theta burst stimulation. *Science, 292,* 1175–1178.

Wachtel, S. R., Ortengren, A., & de Wit, H. (2002). The effects of acute haloperidol or risperidone on subjective responses to methamphetamine in healthy volunteers. *Drug and Alcohol Dependence, 68,* 23–33.

Wachtel, S. R., & de Wit, H. (2000). Naltrexone does not block the subjective effects of oral d9-tetrahydrocannabinol in humans. *Drug and Alcohol Dependence, 59,* 251–260.

Wagner, F. A., & Anthony, C. (2002). From first drug use to drug dependence; developmental periods of risk for dependence upon marijuana, cocaine, and alcohol. *Neuropsychopharmacology, 26,* 479–488.

Wagner, G. C., Carelli, R. M., & Jarvis, M. F. (1985). Pretreatment with ascorbic acid attenuates the neurotoxic effects of methamphetamine in rats. *Research Communications in Chemical Pathology and Pharmacology, 47,* 221–228.

Wall, S., Gu, H., & Rudnick, G. (1995). Biogenic amine flux mediated by cloned transporters stably expressed in cultured cell lines: Amphetamine specificity for inhibition and efflux. *Molecular Pharmacology, 47,* 544–550.

Wallace, B., & Fisher, L. E. (1999). *Consciousness and behavior* (4th ed.). Boston, MA: Allyn & Bacon.

Wallack, L., & Corbett, K. (1990). Illicit drug, tobacco, and alcohol use among youth: Trends and promising approaches in prevention. In H. Resnick (Ed.), *Youth and drugs: Society's mixed messages* (pp. 5–30). Rockville, MD: U.S. Department of Health and Human Services.

Walsh, B. T., Stewart, J. W., Roose, S. P., et al. (1984). Treatment of bulimia with phenelzine. *Archives of General Psychiatry, 41,* 1105–1109.

Walsh, J., Randazzo, A., Stone, K., & Schweitzer, P. K. (2004). Modafinil improves alertness, vigilance, and executive function during simulated night shifts. *Sleep, 27,* 434–439.

Wang, G., Volkow, N., Franceschi, D., et al. (2000). Regional brain metabolism during alcohol intoxication. *Alcoholism Clinical and Experimental Research, 24,* 822–829.

Wang, L., & Gintzler, A. R. (1995). Morphine tolerance and physical dependence: Reversal of opioid inhibition to enhancement of cyclic AMP formation. *Journal of Neurochemistry, 64,* 1102–1106.

Wareing, M., Murphy, P., & Fisk, J. E. (2004). Visuospatial memory impairments in users of MDMA ("ecstasy"). *Psychopharmacology, 173,* 391–397.

Warshaw, M. G., & Keller, M. B. (1996). The relationship between fluoxetine use and suicidal behavior in 654 subjects with anxiety disorders. *Journal of Clinical Psychiatry, 57,* 158–166.

Waters, A. J., & Sutton, S. R. (2000). Direct and indirect effects of nicotine/smoking on cognition in humans. *Addictive Behaviors, 25,* 29–43.

Watts, S., Noble, S., Smith, P., & Disco, M. (2002). First-line pharmacotherapy for tobacco use and dependence. *Journal of the American Board of Family Practice, 15,* 489–497.

Weber, R. J., & Pert, A. (1989). The periaqueductal gray matter mediates opiate-induced immunosuppression. *Science, 245,* 188–190.

Weddington, W. W., Brown, B. S., Haertzen, C. A., et al. (1990). Changes in mood, craving, and sleep during short-term abstinence reported by male cocaine addicts. A controlled, residential study. *Archives of General Psychiatry, 47,* 861–868.

Weiden, P., Simpson, G., Potkin, S., & O'Sullivan, R. L. (2003). Effectiveness of switching to ziprasidone for stable but symptomatic outpatients with schizophrenia. *Journal of Clinical Psychiatry, 64,* 580–588.

Weinberger, D. R. (1987). Implications of normal brain development for the pathogenesis of schizophrenia. *Archives of General Psychiatry, 44,* 660–669.

Weinberger, D. R., & Berman, K. F. (1988). Speculation on the meaning of cerebral metabolic hypofrontality in schizophrenia. *Schizophrenia Bulletin, 14,* 157–168.

Weiner, N. (1985). Atropine, scopolamine, and related antimuscarinic drugs. In A. G. Gilman, L. S. Goodman, T. W. Rall, & F. Murad (Eds.), *The Pharmacological Basis of Therapeutics* (pp. 130–144). New York: Macmillan.

Weiss, F., & Porrino, J. (2002). Behavioral neurobiology of alcohol addiction: Recent advances and challenges. *Journal of Neuroscience, 22,* 3332–3337.

Weiss, G., & Hechtman, L. (1979). The hyperactive child syndrome. *Science, 205,* 1348–1354.

Weiss, R., Griffin, M., Mazurick, C., et al. (2003). The relationship between cocaine craving, psychosocial treatment, and subsequent cocaine use. *American Journal of Psychiatry, 160,* 1320–1325.

Weissman, A., & Milne, G. (1979). Cannabinoids: Definitional ambiguities and a proposal. *Neuroscience and Biobehavioral Reviews, 3,* 171–174.

Wekselman, K., Spiering, K., Hetteberg, C., et al. (1995). Fetal alcohol syndrome from infancy through childhood: A review of the literature. *Journal of Pediatric Nursing, 10,* 296–303.

Wender, P. H., Reimherr, F. W., & Wood, D. R. (1981). Attention deficit disorder ("minimal brain dysfunction") in adults. *Archives of General Psychiatry, 38,* 449–456.

Wenger, G. R., & Dews, P. B. (1976). The effects of phencyclidine, ketamine, delta-amphetamine and pentobarbital on schedule-controlled behavior in the mouse. *Journal of Pharmacology and Experimental Therapeutics, 196,* 616–624.

Werder, S. F. (1995). An update on the diagnosis and treatment of mania in bipolar disorder. *American Family Physician, 51,* 1126–1136.

Wesensten, N. J., Belenky, G., Kautz, M., et al. (2002). Maintaining alertness and performance during sleep deprivation: Modafinil versus caffeine. *Psychopharmacology, 159,* 238–247.

Wettstein, A. (2000). Cholinesterase inhibitors and Gingko extracts—are they comparable in the treatment of dementia? Comparison of published placebo-controlled efficacy studies of at least six months' duration. *Phytomedicine, 6,* 393–401.

Wheatley, D. P., VanMoffaert, M., Timmerman, L., et al. (1998). Mirtazapine: Efficacy and tolerability in comparison with fluoxetine in patients with moderate to severe major depressive disorder. *Journal of Clinical Psychiatry, 59,* 306–312.

White, F. J. (2002) A behavioral/systems approach to the neuroscience of drug addiction. *Journal of Neuroscience, 22,* 3303–3305.

Wicht, F., Fisch, H. U., Nelles, J., Raisin, J., et al. (1995). Divergence of ethanol and acetaldehyde kinetics and of the disulfiram-alcohol reaction between subjects with and without alcoholic liver disease. *Alcoholism, Clinical and Experimental Research, 19,* 356–361.

Wilcock, G. K. (2000). Treatment for Alzheimer's disease. *International Journal of Geriatric Psychiatry, 15,* 562–565.

Wilcox, C. S., Cohn, J. B., Linden, R. D., et al. (1992). Predictors of placebo response: A retrospective analysis. *Psychopharmacology Bulletin, 28,* 157–162.

Wilkinson, G. R. (2001). Pharmacokinetics: The dynamics of drug absorption, distribution, and elimination. In J. G. Hardman & L. E. Limbird (Eds.), *Goodman & Gilman's The pharmacological basis of therapeutics* (10th ed., pp. 3–29). New York: McGraw-Hill.

Willemsen-Swinkels, S. H., Buitelaar, J. K., Nijhof, G. J., & van Engeland, H. (1995a). Failure of naltrexone hydrochloride to reduce self-injurious and autistic behavior in mentally retarded adults. Double-blind placebo-controlled studies. *Archives of General Psychiatry, 52,* 766–773.

Willemsen-Swinkels, S. H., Buitelaar, J. K., Weijnen, F. G., & van Engeland, H. (1995b). Placebo-controlled acute dosage naltrexone study in young autistic children. *Psychiatry Research, 58,* 203–215.

Williams, B. F., Howard, V. F., & McLaughlin, T. F. (1994). Fetal alcohol syndrome: Developmental characteristics and directions for further research. *Education and Treatment of Children, 17,* 86–97.

Williams, C. M., & Kirkham, T. C. (1999). Anandamide induces overeating: Mediation by central cannabinoid (CB1) receptors. *Psychopharmacology, 143,* 315–317.

Williams, J., Christie, M., & Manzoni, O. (2001). Cellular and synaptic adaptations mediating opioid dependence. *Physiological Reviews, 81,* 299–343.

Williams, R. W., & Herrup, K. (1988). The control of neuron number. *Annual Review of Neuroscience, 11,* 423–453.

Willner, P. (1983). Dopamine and depression: A review of recent evidence. I. Empirical studies. *Brain Research, 287,* 211–224.

Wilson, J. M., Kalasinsky, K. S., Levey, A. I., et al. (1996). Striatal dopamine nerve terminal markers in human, chronic, methamphetamine users. *Nature Medicine, 2,* 699–703.

Wilson, J. S., Korsten, M. A., & Lieber, C. S. (1986). The combined effects of protein deficiency and chronic ethanol administration on rat ethanol metabolism. *Hepatology, 6,* 823–829.

Wilson, R. I., & Nicoll, A. (2002). Endocannabinoid signaling in the brain. *Science, 296,* 678–682.

de Win, M. M., Reneman, L., Reitsma, J., et al. (2004). Mood disorders and serotonin transporter density in ecstasy users—the influence of long-term abstention, dose, and gender. *Psychopharmacology, 173,* 376–382.

Winblad, B., & Jelic, V. (2004). Long-term treatment of Alzheimer disease: Efficacy and safety of acetylcholinesterase inhibitors. *Alzheimer Disease and Associated Disorders, 18*(Suppl. 1), S2–S8.

Winblad, B., & Poritis, N. (1999). Memantine in severe dementia: Results of the 9M-Best Study (benefit and efficacy in severely demented patients during treatment with memantine). *Journal of Geriatric Psychiatry, 14,* 135–146.

Winstanley, C. A., Green, T. A., Theobald, D. E., Renthal, W., LaPlant, Q., DiLeone, R. J., et al. (2009). DeltaFosB induction in orbitofrontal cortex potentiates locomotor sensitization despite attenuating the cognitive dysfunction caused by cocaine. *Pharmacology, Biochemistry and Behavior, 93,* 278–284.

Wise, R. A. (1995). D1 and D2-type contributions to psychomotor sensitization and reward: Implications for pharmacological treatment strategies. *Clinical Neuropharmacology, 18*, S74–S83.

Wise, R. A. (1998). Drug-activation of brain reward pathways. *Drug and Alcohol Dependence, 51*, 13–22.

Wise, R. A. (2008). Dopamine and reward: The anhedonia hypothesis 30 years on. *Neurotoxicology Research, 14*, 169–183.

Wodak, A. (1994). Managing illicit drug use. A practical guide. *Drugs, 47*, 446–457.

Wolf, M. E., & Ferrario, C. R. (2010). AMPA receptor plasticity in the nucleus accumbens after repeated exposure to cocaine. *Neuroscience & Biobehavioral Reviews, 35*, 185–211.

Wolf, S. S., Jones, D. W., Knable, M. B., et al. (1996). Tourette syndrome prediction of phenotypic variation in monozygotic twins by caudate nucleus D2 receptor binding. *Science, 273*, 1225–1227.

Wolfsohn, R., Sanfilipo, M., & Angrist, B. (1993). A placebo-controlled trial of L-dopa/carbidopa in early cocaine abstinence. *Neuropsychopharmacology, 9*, 49–53.

Wood, D. M., & Emmett-Oglesby, M. W. (1986). Characteristics of tolerance, recovery from tolerance and cross-tolerance for cocaine used as a discriminative stimulus. *Journal of Pharmacology and Experimental Therapeutics, 237*, 120–125.

Woods, J. H. (1978). Behavioral pharmacology of drug self-administration. In M. A. Lipton, A. DiMascio, & K. F. Killam (Eds.), *Psychopharmacology* (pp. 595–607). New York: Raven Press.

Woolf, A. (2000). Witchcraft or mycotoxin? The Salem witch trials. *Journal of Toxicology. Clinical Toxicology, 38*, 457–460.

Wu, L. G., & Saggau, P. (1997). Presynaptic inhibition of elicited neurotransmitter release. *Trends in the Neurosciences, 20*, 204–212.

Wu, X., & French, E. D. (2000). Effects of chronic delta-9-tetrahydrocannabinol on rat midbrain dopamine neurons: An electrophysiological assessment. *Neuropharmacology, 39*, 391–398.

Wu, Y., Le, W., & Jankovic, J. (2011). Preclinical biomarkers of Parkinson disease. *Archives of Neurology, 68*, 22–30.

Wurtman, R. J. (1982). Nutrients that modify brain function. *Scientific American, 246*, 50–59.

Yassa, R., Nair, V., & Schwartz, G. (1986). Early versus late onset psychosis and tardive dyskinesia. *Society of Biological Psychiatry, 21*, 1291–1297.

Yin, H. H., Ostlund, S. B., & Balleine, B. W. (2009). Reward-guided learning beyond dopamine in the nucleus accumbens: The integrative functions of cortico-basal ganglia networks. *European Journal of Neuroscience, 28*, 1437–1448.

Yin, S. J., & Peng, G. S. (2007). Acetaldehyde, polymorphisms and the cardiovascular system. *Novartis Foundation Symposium, 285*, 52–63.

Yonezawa, Y., Kuroki, T., Tashiro, N., et al. (1995). Potentiation of phencyclidine-induced dopamine release in the rat striatum by the blockade of dopamine D2 receptor. *European Journal of Pharmacology, 285*, 305–308.

Yong, V. W., & Perry, T. L. (1986). Monoamine oxidase B, smoking, and Parkinson's disease. *Journal of the Neurological Sciences, 72*, 265–272.

Young, K. A., Manaye, K. F., Liang, C., et al. (2000). Reduced number of mediodorsal and anterior thalamic neurons in schizophrenia. *Biological Psychiatry, 47*, 944–953.

Young, S. N., Smith, S. E., Pihl, R. O., et al. (1985). Tryptophan depletion causes a rapid lowering of mood in normal males. *Psychopharmacology, 87*, 173–177.

Yurgelun-Todd, D. A., Sava, S., & Dahlgren, M. K. (2007). Mood disorders. *Neuroimaging Clinics of North America, 17*, 511–521.

Zablocki, B., Aidala, A., Hansell, S., & White, H. R. (1991). Marijuana use, introspectiveness, and mental health. *Journal of Health and Social Behavior, 32,* 65–79.

Zahn, T. P., & Rapoport, J. L. (1987). Acute autonomic nervous system effects of caffeine in prepubertal boys. *Psychopharmacology, 91,* 40–44.

Zametkin, A. J., Liebenauer, L. L., Fitzgerald, G. A., et al. (1993). Brain metabolism in teenagers with attention-deficit hyperactivity disorder. *Archives of General Psychiatry, 50,* 333–340.

Zametkin, A. J., Nordahl, T. E., Gross, M., et al. (1990). Cerebral glucose metabolism in adults with hyperactivity of childhood onset. *New England Journal of Medicine, 323,* 1361–1366.

Zarate, C. A., Jr., Tohen, M., Banov, M. D., et al. (1995). Is clozapine a mood stabilizer? *Journal of Clinical Psychiatry, 56,* 108–112.

Zhang, L., Lou, D., Jiao, H., et al. (2004). Cocaine-induced intracellular signaling and gene expression are oppositely regulated by the dopamine D1 and D3 receptors. *Journal of Neuroscience, 24,* 3344–3354.

Zhu, W., Volkow, N., Ma, Y., et al. (2004). Relationship between ethanol-induced changes in brain regional metabolism and its motor, behavioural and cognitive effects. *Alcohol and Alcoholism, 39,* 53–58.

Zimatkin, S. M., Pronko, S. P., Vasiliou, V., Gonzalez, F. J., & Deitrich, R. A. (2006). Enzymatic mechanisms of ethanol oxidation in the brain. *Alcohol Clinical and Experimental Research, 30,* 1500–1505.

Zimmer, L., & Morgan, J. P. (1997). *Marijuana myths, marijuana facts.* New York: The Lindesmith Center.

Zink, C. F., Pagnoni, G., Martin, M. E., et al. (2003). Human striatal response to salient nonrewarding stimuli. *Journal of Neuroscience, 23,* 8092–8097.

Zisook, S., Shuchter, S. R., Gallagher, T., et al. (1993). Atypical depression in an outpatient psychiatric population. *Depression, 1,* 268–274.

Zito, J. M., Safer, D. J., DosReis, S., et al. (2000). Trends in the prescribing of psychotropic medications to preschoolers. *The Journal of the American Medical Association, 283,* 1025–1030.

Zito, J. M., Safer, D. J., DosReis, S., et al. (2003). Psychotropic practice patterns for youth: A 10-year perspective. *Archives of Pediatrics and Adolescent Medicine, 157,* 17–25.

Zornoza, T., Cano, M., Polache, A., & Granero, L. (2003). Pharmacology of acamprosate: An overview. *CNS Drug Reviews, 9,* 359–374.

Zubaran, C., Fernandes, J. G., & Rodnight, R. (1997). Wernicke-Korsakoff syndrome. *Postgraduate Medical Journal, 73,* 27–31.

Zucker, R. A., & Gomberg, E. S. L. (1986). Etiology of alcoholism reconsidered: The case for a biopsychosocial process. *American Psychologist, 41,* 783–792.

Zuckerman, B., Frank, D. A., Hingson, R., et al. (1989). Effects of maternal marijuana and cocaine use on fetal growth. *New England Journal of Medicine, 320,* 762–768.

Zuckerman, M. (1979). *Sensation seeking: Beyond the optimal level of arousal.* Hillsdale, NJ: Erlbaum.

Zwyghuizen-Doorenbos, A., Roehrs, T. A., Lipschutz, L., et al. (1990). Effects of caffeine on alertness. *Psychopharmacology, 100,* 36–39.

INDEX

Boldface page numbers indicate definition, *f* indicates figure, *t* indicates table.